D0051063

SECRETS OF THE SOUL

SECRETS OF THE SOUL

A Social and Cultural History
of Psychoanalysis

ELI ZARETSKY

Alfred A. Knopf
New York
2004

This Is a Borzoi Book
Published by Alfred A. Knopf

Library of Congress Cataloging-in-Publication Data
Zaretsky, Eli.
Secrets of the soul : a social and cultural history of
psychoanalysis / Eli Zaretsky.—1st ed.
p. cm.
Includes bibliographical references and index.
ISBN 0-679-44654-0 (alk. paper)
1. Psychoanalysis—History.   2. Psychoanalysis—Social aspects—History.
I.   Title.

BF173.Z37 2004
150.19'5'09—dc22   2003066125

For Nancy,
in whom grace,
beauty, and intellect
are deeply
entwined

Far removed from the immediate rationality of political discourse, the family appears to constitute the other pole of our societies, their darker side, an enigmatic figure to which oracles are drawn in order to peer into the depths where it moves and read the inflections of our collective unconscious, the encoded message of our civilization.

—Jacques Donzelot

Contents

Part Three

FROM THE PSYCHOLOGY OF AUTHORITY
TO THE POLITICS OF IDENTITY

Illustrations

Acknowledgments

The origins of this book lie in the great transformations of our society that began in the late 1960s. Among my generation—I was born in 1940—Freud had a grip on the imagination comparable to that exerted by the figures about whom he wrote: Leonardo, Goethe, Dostoyevsky. During the 1960s, my involvement in the New Left and my encounter with the women's liberation movement first led me to think about the relation of capitalism to the family. In the course of writing *Capitalism, the Family, and Personal Life,* I realized that it was impossible to pursue this subject at any depth without studying Freud. When the New Left disintegrated, I turned yet again to psychoanalysis, teaching in clinical training programs. As a historian and as a political person, I not only learned from psychoanalysis but wrestled with and against it. This book sums up a protracted, conflict-ridden but immensely productive encounter, one in which I accumulated more debts than I could possibly detail below.

The most important of these is to Nancy Fraser. Although I had been thinking about the problem of psychoanalysis since the sixties, it was only after meeting her that the project took shape. In the course of writing this book, she offered unstinting moral support, editorial advice, and intellectual guidance, sometimes neglecting her own work. Among other contributions, she coined the formulation "threefold promise of modernity," one of the many times she brought clarity to what had been merely intuition.

Many of those who read the manuscript are also close friends or family members. These include Richard Bernstein, Alexander Etkind, Martin Fleischer, Jim Gilbert, John Judis, Leonard Helfgott, Doreen Rappaport, Jonathan Wiesen, and Natasha Zaretsky (who also edited one full draft). My agent, Charlotte Sheedy, never lost her enthusiasm for the project. My experience with Knopf belies the cliché that today's publishers are interested only in profits. Victoria Wilson, my editor, patiently and incisively read and reread this book's many drafts.

No book of this scope can be based upon archival sources alone. I hope my debts to the many great scholars who preceded me in the history of psychoanalysis are sufficiently indicated in my notes. I am not sure, however, that my equally great debts to my fellow cultural historians, social historians, and historians of women and race are as manifest. This book owes a great deal to the revolution in historical thinking that has occurred over the course of my lifetime.

In the course of writing it, I made new friends and renewed older relationships. Stuart Hall first directed me to Antonio Gramsci's observations on psychoanalysis. Paul Roazen and Robert Wallerstein saved me from many errors, while bearing no responsibility for any that remain. Mari Jo Buhle, Barbara Epstein, Jeff Escoffier, Rainer Forst, Mary Gluck, Ted Koditschek, Laura Kipnis, Rebecca Plant, and Lynne Segal helped with individual chapters. Everywhere I traveled, I interviewed psychoanalysts, among them Werner Bohleber, Helmut Dahmer, and Lutz Rosenkutter in Germany; Ernst Federn in Vienna; Marcello Viñar in Montevideo; and Carlos Aslan, José Fischbein, and Susana Fischbein in Buenos Aires. Carmen Ilizarbe and Hanako Koyama provided excellent research assistance. Athena Angelos tracked down pictures. My father-in-law, Ed Shapiro, provided moral support, but in the end I decided not to use his suggested title: *Impact.*

Over the years, I received research support from the Newberry Library in Chicago, the American Council of Learned Societies, the University of Missouri at Columbia, and the Graduate Faculty of the New School in New York (from which I also received a blessed year off, and much inspiration). I benefited from the hospitality and excellent research facilities of the Institut für die Wissenschaften vom Menschen in Vienna, the Institut für Sozialforschung in Frankfurt, the Wellcome Library for the History and Understanding of Medicine in London, the Columbia University Oral History Collection, the Freud Collection at the Library of Congress, the New York Public Library, Bobst Library at New York University, the archives and libraries of the Psychoanalytic Societies of New York, Chicago, San Francisco, London, Berlin, Frankfurt, and Buenos Aires, the Freud Museums in London and Vienna, and the Wright Institute in Berkeley, California.

Finally, as one who is of an analytic turn of mind, I want to thank my parents, David Zaretsky and Pauline Silverman Zaretsky, undoubtedly the strongest influences on my thought. They would have been proud of this book, but then, they were proud of me without it. I also received much support from my brothers, Allen and Aaron Zaretsky, and their families. And while I cannot yet thank my grandson, Daniel Zaretsky Wiesen, he certainly brightened the book's completion.

SECRETS OF THE SOUL

THE AMBIGUOUS LEGACY
OF PSYCHOANALYSIS

Freud always stresses what great forces [are] in the mind, what strong prejudices work against the idea of psycho-analysis. But he never says what an enormous charm that idea has for people, just as it has for Freud himself.

—Ludwig Wittgenstein

One century after its founding, psychoanalysis presents us with a paradox. Almost instantly recognized as a great force for human emancipation, it played a central role in the modernism of the 1920s, the English and American welfare states of the 1940s and 50s, the radical upheavals of the 1960s, and the feminist and gay-liberation movements of the 1970s. Yet it simultaneously became a fount of antipolitical, antifeminist, and homophobic prejudice, a degraded profession, a pseudoscience whose survival is now very much in doubt. This book is an exploration of this paradox; it aims to identify and affirm the emancipatory dimension of analytic thought without denying the validity of the criticisms or the need to rethink its legacy.

The explanation offered here is social and historical. Psychoanalysis permanently transformed the ways in which ordinary men and women throughout the world understand themselves and one another. Yet in spite of uncounted studies, not to mention special pleadings and tendentious attacks, we have still not historicized psychoanalysis; we apparently still lack the large social, cultural, and intellectual frame necessary to understand a phenomenon so central to our *own* self-constitution. In order to situate psychoanalysis historically, it is not enough to know Freud's biography, or the history of psychiatry, or of Vienna, although these are certainly necessary. Any history will have to explain, above all, the intensity of its appeal and the breadth of its influence. But that very influence has made the task of achieving historical perspective difficult. Perspective requires distance. Lately, especially with the waning of the medical fortunes of psychoanalysis, this distance has begun to appear.

There has been one great attempt to grasp psychoanalysis historically: Carl Schorske's *Fin-de-siècle Vienna.*[1] Published in 1980, when the influence of analysis was beginning to recede, Schorske's book began by evoking the statue of Athena erected in front of Parliament in mid-nineteenth-century Vienna. For Schorske, the statue symbolized the Enlightenment, with its then-new middle-class ideals of rationality and autonomy and its focus on the courage and inner psychological structure (*Bildung*) that self-government required. From this heroic starting point, Schorske traced the breakdown of the Enlightenment ethos in mass politics, aestheticism, and a preoccupation with the irrational. Arguing that Freud responded to the rise of mass anti-Semitism in the 1890s by abandoning his earlier legal and political ambitions, Schorske concluded that psychoanalysis was a "counterpolitical" phenomenon: it reflected the fin de siècle withdrawal from reason and public life. While Schorske left open the implications of his interpretation, Philip Rieff, Christopher Lasch, representatives of the Frankfurt School, and others made related arguments about twentieth-century "psychological society," claiming that partly under the influence of psychoanalysis the Enlightenment ideal of autonomy had declined into a psychologistic "culture of narcissism."

Schorske's interpretation remains both indispensable and inadequate. On the one hand, Schorske rightly understood the extent to which psychoanalysis arose out of the late-nineteenth-century transformation of the bourgeois class, particularly (although he did not say this) out of the experiences of its younger members and its women. The decline of the family enterprise, the loosening of the structures of the bourgeois family, and a new emphasis on consumption as opposed to discipline, accumulation, and self-control created the climate for this new way of thinking. But Schorske failed to capture the dual character of psychoanalysis. By reducing Freudianism to a counterpolitical withdrawal from reason and public life, he failed to grasp the emancipatory aspects of its exploration of the human psyche, especially those of special relevance to marginal and exploited classes and to women.

Today, in contrast, it has become possible to see psychoanalysis whole, acknowledging both its repressive and its liberatory aspects. The key is to see it as the *first great theory and practice of "personal life."* By personal life, I mean the experience of having an identity distinct from one's place in the family, in society, and in the social division of labor. In one sense, the possibility of having a personal life is a universal aspect of being human, but that is not the sense I have in mind. Rather, I mean a historically specific experience of singularity and interiority, one that was sociologically grounded in modern processes of industrialization and urbanization, and in the history of the family.

Previously, the family was the primary locus of production and reproduction.[2] As a result, the individual's sense of identity was rooted in his or her place in the family. In the nineteenth century, however, the separation (both physical and emotional) of paid work from the household, which is to say the rise of industrial capitalism, gave rise to new forms of privacy, domesticity, and intimacy. At first these were experienced as the familial counterparts to the impersonal world of the market. Later they became associated with the possibility and goal of a personal life distinct from and even outside of the family. This goal found social expression in such phenomena as the "new" (or independent) woman, the emergence of public homosexual identities, and the turning of young people away from a preoccupation with business and toward sexual experimentation, bohemia, and artistic modernism. In the period that initiated what historians have called the "second industrial revolution," roughly from the 1880s to the 1920s, new urban spaces and media—popular theater, music halls, the kinetoscope—provided reference points from which individuals could imaginatively construct extrafamilial identities. As a result, personal identity became a problem and a project for individuals, as opposed to something given to them by their place in the family or the economy. Psychoanalysis was a theory and practice of this new aspiration for a personal life. Its original historical telos was *defamilialization,* the freeing of individuals from unconscious images of authority originally rooted in the family.

The founding idea of psychoanalysis, the idea of a dynamic or *personal unconscious,* reflected this new experience of personal life. According to that idea, stimuli that came to the individual from the society or culture were not directly registered but were first dissolved and internally reconstituted in such a way as to give them personal, even idiosyncratic, meanings. Thus, there was no direct or necessary connection between one's social condition and one's subjectivity. Equally important, Freud's idea of the unconscious signaled the absence, under modern conditions, of any pregiven fit or harmony between larger, public patterns of cultural symbolism and the private, inner symbolic worlds of individuals.[3] The idea of the unconscious marked a lived sense of disjuncture between the public and the private, the outer and the inner, the sociocultural and the personal. Of course, psychoanalysis also developed a general approach to culture, morality, and history. With such notions as the Oedipus complex, it suggested that there were universal patterns to which human life necessarily conformed. Nonetheless, it always returned to the contingent and particular ways in which individuals lived these patterns. Ultimately, then, the disjuncture between the individual and society was the terrain upon which psychoanalysis built its theories and practiced its therapy.

The idea of a *personal* unconscious was new. In traditional societies, healers were effective insofar as they mobilized symbols that were simultaneously internal *and* communal. When a priest performed a successful exorcism, it worked because he, the possessed person, and the surrounding community all believed in the devil.[4] Likewise, the French king cured scrofula by touch so long as his subjects believed he had the power to do so.[5] In contrast to such direct correspondences of inner and outer, public and private, early modern forms of self-consciousness stressed the privacy of the individual conscience.[6] But conscience was a restrictive, morality-centered notion of individuality, and the priority assigned to it generally rested on the assumption that there was a single right way of life. In contrast, the disjuncture between the individual psyche and the culture that became socially salient at the end of the nineteenth century fostered an unprecedented range of personal experience in such spheres as love, friendship, and daily life. It also carried a new sense of human depth that ultimately influenced art, philosophy, and politics.

Freud's key contribution lay in theorizing that disjuncture. Defining the subject matter of psychoanalysis as "what is most intimate in mental life, everything that a socially independent person must conceal," he implied that there was no necessary or direct connection between private and public.[7] His core insight, which differed fundamentally from romantic and Victorian notions of the self, was that the inner lives of modern men and women were organized through symbols and narratives that were idiosyncratic and apparently devoid of socially shared meaning. For that reason he insisted that, although the internal worlds of individuals could be interpreted and understood, they could not be reintegrated into any previously existing whole. Far from seeking to return a disturbed individual to a preexisting order, as the shaman, healer, or priest did, he formulated the analytic project as a personal and provisional hermeneutic of self-discovery, one that a psychoanalyst could facilitate but not control. In this way, he gave expression to possibilities of individuality, authenticity, and freedom that had only recently emerged, and opened the way to a new understanding of social life.

The result was two-sided. As Schorske argued, psychoanalysis could, indeed, undermine the emancipatory promise of the Enlightenment insofar as it served to mystify the basis for personal life, and thus to obscure the political, economic, and cultural preconditions necessary for its flourishing. But that tendency was contingent, not necessary. More important, the Enlightenment was not a high point to be emulated but an incomplete project to be developed. The statue of Athena evoked by Schorske symbolized the "Copernican revolution" of eighteenth-century modernity, which put a new principle of subjective freedom at the center of all modern pursuits such as art, morality, politics, and even science (which liberated the human subject at the same time as it objectified nature). But the larger implications of that principle remained to be unfolded in a "second modernity." Contrary to Schorske's narrative of decline, the fin de siècle era inaugurated that second modernity, which was associated with mass production, mass democracy, and the rise of women, homosexuals, and racial and national minorities. While the first modernity—the Enlightenment—viewed the subject as the locus of reason in the sense of universal and necessary truths, the second—call it "modernism"—viewed the subject as a concrete person, located in a particular time and place subject to historical contingency and possessing a unique individuality. Whereas philosophy was the hallmark of the first modernity, psychoanalysis, along with modernist art and literature, was the hallmark of the second.

Seen this way, the classical liberalism that Schorske extolled was based on three historically limited ideas. First, mid-nineteenth-century liberals equated autonomy with self-control. Second, despite feminist subcurrents, most believed that women's character and psychology differed fundamentally from men's. Third, liberals believed that even modern, democratic society required natural or social hierarchy to function. All three of these beliefs were challenged in the fin de siècle era. The emphasis on self-control was challenged by ideologies of "release" and "relaxation" that developed along with mass consumption. The belief in en bloc gender difference was challenged by the entry of women into public life and by a new openness concerning sexuality. Hierarchy was challenged by mass democracy, trade unionism, and socialism. These developments deepened and radicalized the ideals of the Enlightenment; they were not merely negations of it. As the first great theory and practice of modern personal life, psychoanalysis shared their potential for extending and deepening the emancipatory promise of modernity. As we shall see, it became caught up in the changed meanings of autonomy, women's equality, and democracy.

In general, then, psychoanalysis hovered between twin possibilities: mystification, on the one hand, and deepening the meaning of modernity, on the other. What determined the balance was the role psychoanalysis came to play in relation to larger historical forces. To put the matter in a nutshell: psychoanalysis served as the "Calvinism" of the second industrial revolution. It played a role analogous to that played by Calvinism in relation to early capitalism and by Methodism in relation to industrialization. Let me explain.

According to Max Weber, early Calvinism helped spark in its followers the personal transformations that made capitalism possible. Whereas Christianity began with Jesus urging his followers to leave their families for an authentic spiritual community, the Protestant "saints" of the seventeenth century redefined the family as a locus of charismatic meaning, sanctifying its everyday economic activities and giving them an ethical character, that of a "calling" or *Beruf.* Several centuries later, Methodism served related ends; embraced by the English and American industrial working classes, it became a vehicle of personal transformation, promoting abstinence, time discipline, and thrift. It thereby enabled the first industrial revolution. In both cases, a religious movement supplied the inner motivations for a socioeconomic transformation that could not have won committed followers on its own terms.[8] Psychoanalysis played a similar role for the *second* industrial revolution.

The first industrial revolution began in England and created the factory system. The second began in the United States and created the vertically integrated corporation, a corporation that organized not only raw materials and production but also advertising, marketing, and consumption. The first revolution extracted a surplus from manual labor; the second relied on higher education, science, and mental labor. In the first, work and life largely overlapped: factories were small and close to home, and agriculture was still the dominant way of life. In the second, work and life were sharply separated, as leisure and consumption took on a life of their own. During the first industrial revolution, individuals still tended to identify their fate with that of a community; the second, in contrast, was marked by the sense of a singular personal life and by revolutionary changes in the nature of the family.[9] The organization of this book mirrors the trajectory of the second industrial revolution: part one (1890–1914) evokes its origins, part two

(1919–1939) its Fordist heyday, and part three (1945–1976) its transformation into the Keynesian welfare state and its decline.

Just as men and women did not embark on the transition from agrarianism to industrial capitalism for merely instrumental or economic reasons, so in the twentieth century they did not become consumers in order to supply markets. Rather, they separated from traditional familial morality, gave up their obsession with self-control and thrift, and entered into the sexualized "dreamworlds" of mass consumption on behalf of a new orientation to personal life. Psychoanalysis was the Calvinism of this shift. In the early years of the twentieth century it authorized the extraordinary changes in personality and subjectivity that accompanied the second industrial revolution. Just as Jesus gathered the early Christians and Cromwell gathered the Protestant "Saints," Freud brought his followers together into a charismatic sect. Rather than sanctify the family, however, Freud urged them to leave behind their "families"—the archaic images of early childhood—not to preach but to develop more genuine, that is, more personal, relations. Over time, Freud's disciples went through the familiar Weberian cycle of idealization, rebellion, dissemination, institutionalization, and routinization. Ultimately, analytic charisma was adapted to a conformist culture, and to the mother-centered ideologies of the Keynesian welfare state. But in its heyday men and women used it to complicate, deepen, and radicalize the three emancipatory promises of modernity.

Some drew on psychoanalysis, first, to help recast the promise of individual autonomy. Autonomy encompassed the freedom to think one's own thoughts and to decide for oneself what to do with one's life, instead of following a path ordained by birth, custom, or economic status. Although prefigured in the great philosophical and religious traditions of every civilization, the project of individual autonomy was first articulated in a universalizable and secular way during the European and American Enlightenment, as Schorske rightly suggested. But the changes associated with the second industrial revolution expanded its meaning. No longer restricted to the sphere of morality, autonomy now applied as well to such extramoral experiences as creativity, love, and happiness. Psychoanalysis was associated with this new, modernist idea of personal—as distinguished from moral—autonomy. In their efforts to grasp why this autonomy was so difficult to achieve, analysts devised such concepts as ambivalence, resistance, and the defenses, and developed the theory of the ego. At the same time they risked sanctioning ideologies of "psychological man," which fostered the misleading idea that autonomy was simply an individual condition rather than a possibility grounded in a particular society and social relationships.

Similarly, psychoanalysis helped recast the second great Enlightenment promise: the emancipation of women. To eighteenth-century feminists, emancipation meant equal rights, which they defended on the grounds that men and women shared a common nature as rational beings. By the middle of the nineteenth century, however, most women's advocates stressed gender difference, invoking distinctive female virtues to support claims for social reform. By foregrounding individuality in the sphere of sexual love, the fin de siècle aspiration to a personal life exceeded both of those approaches. Psychoanalysis deepened and gave content to that aspiration. It dispelled the nineteenth-century idea of en bloc gender difference, redefined gender as sexual object-choice, and eventually helped uncover the psychological depths of human dependence, especially in regard to women's mothering. In this respect, as with autonomy, its legacy is ambivalent. Analysis advanced cultural understandings of female sexuality and homosexuality even as it became at times a vicious and effective enemy of feminists and homosexuals.

Finally, as an expression of personal life, psychoanalysis complicated and radicalized the third great promise of modernity: democracy. Traditional authority was paternal, centripetal, hierarchical, and family-centered. In its place, liberals sought to establish limited, accountable political authority by distinguishing between public and private spheres. Nineteenth-century liberals sharpened this distinction by extending it to the division between the family and the economy. The second industrial revolution, however, complicated the public/private division. With women's entry into public life and the rise of a sexualized mass culture, hitherto private matters began to become public. At the same time, familial authority, supposedly banished from the public sphere, persisted in the psychic worlds of individuals. These complications potentially deepened the idea of democracy, in part by suggesting the possibility of new, more reflective relations to authority. Psychoanalysis fostered the investigation of these relations. Its central object was "transference," which Freud conceived as the personal relation to authority, ultimately shaped by the infant's experience with its parents. The analysis of transference was at the center of every individual analysis. In the broader culture, too, Freudian thought helped lay bare the interplay between public and private by foregrounding the hidden transferences that cemented social movements and social groups. At the same time, as democratic society and the welfare state exerted new forms of constraint and control, psychoanalysis supplied much of their theory.

The same ironies played themselves out differtly in different contexts. In its central European birthplace, Freudian thought challenged an older, patriarchal order. Sometimes in uneasy alliance, sometimes in conflict with aesthetic modernism, surrealism, women's emancipation, and socialism, it accelerated the demise of already frayed Victorian ideologies of character, gender, and sex. In the conservative democracies of postwar England and the United States, in contrast, analysis played a quite different role, contributing to the medicalization of psychotherapy and the psychologization of authority. In the first case, it was a force for democratization; in the second, it tended to become an agent of social control.

In general, then, the second industrial revolution spawned new experiences of personal life that complicated and radicalized the emancipatory promises of modernity. But it also encouraged psychologization, an empty consumerism, and refamilialization. Psychoanalysis, as the Calvinism of the second industrial revolution, was at the heart of this ambivalence. On the one hand, it freed individuals to live more reflective, fuller lives, enriched the arts, humanities, and sciences, and deepened an understanding of the trust and solidarity on which political progress depends. On the other hand, it was absorbed, transfigured, and ultimately consumed by the sociology and culture of personal life to which it originally gave critical expression.

This book recounts that ambivalent trajectory. Situating the history of psychoanalysis in the context of the second industrial revolution, it covers what may be called the golden age of psychoanalysis, its classical epoch, and ends by explaining the decline of analysis that began in the 1960s. The 1960s and 1970s witnessed the transition from mass production to a globalized service- and information-based economy. Accompanied by far-reaching attempts to repudiate the Enlightenment *tout court*, this "third industrial revolution" changed the way in which personal life was understood. Its intrapsychic—private, internal, and idiosyncratic—character faded in importance as it became politicized and increasingly subject to cultural manipulation. New conceptions of the self emerged, alternatively more narrowly rational and more expressive. Much of the charisma of psychoanalysis entered into such new cultural formations as identity politics, Lacanian cultural criticism, and second-wave feminism. Psychoanalysis survived, but it was no longer a charismatic force. In its day it had held together at least three different projects: a quasi-therapeutic medical practice, a theory of cultural hermeneutics, and an ethic of personal self-exploration, one that was imbued with the devotion of a calling. These split apart. The age of Freud came to an end, but as with all great upheavals, it continued to shape everyday life as well as the landscape of intuitions, dreams, and shadowy memories that we all inhabit.

Part One

CHARISMATIC ORIGINS:
THE CRUMBLING OF
THE VICTORIAN FAMILY
SYSTEM

Chapter One

THE PERSONAL
UNCONSCIOUS

The dirty secret of analysis is that for the collaboration to succeed
the doctor has to be gifted. . . . What the analyst feels is as crucial as
the analysand's sorrows. Thus it follows that there is a fatal flaw in all
scientifically presented case histories because they are solely concerned with the patient's life and character. To understand why the
treatment proceeded the way it did one must also know about
the doctor—his brilliancies, his mistakes, and his own psychology.
The true story of a therapeutic exchange begins not with the
patient's present problem but with the healer's past.

—Rafael Yglesias, *Dr. Neruda's Cure for Evil*

In the modern West there have been two episodes of genuine, widespread
introspection: Calvinism and Freudianism. In both cases the turn inward
accompanied a great social revolution: the rise of capitalism in the first, and
its transformation into an engine of mass consumption in the second. In
both cases, too, the results were ironic. Calvinism urged people to look
inside themselves to determine whether they had been saved, but it wound
up contributing to a new discipline of work, savings, and family life.
Freudian introspection aimed to foster the individual's capacity to live an
authentically personal life, yet it wound up helping to consolidate consumer society. In both cases, finally, the turn toward self-examination generated a new language. In the case of Calvinism, the language centered on
the Protestant idea of the soul, an idea that helped shape such later concepts
as character, integrity, and autonomy. The new Freudian lexicon, by contrast, centered on the idea of the unconscious, the distinctive analytic contribution to twentieth-century personal life.

Of course, the idea of the unconscious was well known before Freud
published *The Interpretation of Dreams* in 1899. Medieval alchemists, German idealist philosophers, and romantic poets had all taught that the

ultimate reality was unconscious. The philosopher Schopenhauer, a profound influence on Freud's teacher Theodor Meynert, maintained that
human beings were the playthings of a blind, anonymous will. Toward the
end of the nineteenth century, the idea of the *sub*conscious was especially
widespread. Often termed a "secondary self," larger than the mere ego and
accessible through hypnosis or meditation, the subconscious implied the
ability to transcend everyday reality. Whether as cosmic force, impersonal
will, or subconscious, the unconscious was understood, before Freud, to be
anonymous and transpersonal. Frequently likened to the ocean, it aimed to
leave the "petty" concerns of the ego behind.

Freud, too, thought of the unconscious as impersonal, anonymous, and
radically other to the individual. But harbored within it, generally close to
consciousness, he discerned something new: an internal, idiosyncratic
source of motivations peculiar to the individual. In his conception, contingent circumstances, especially in childhood, forged links between desires
and impulses, on the one hand, and experiences and memories on the
other. The result was a *personal unconscious,* unique, idiosyncratic, and contingent. For Freud, moreover, there was no escaping into a "larger" or
transpersonal reality. The goal, rather, was to understand and accept one's
own idiosyncratic nature, a task that, in principle, could never be completed. While Freud went on to posit universal mental patterns, such as the
supposed stages of sexual development (oral, anal, genital) and the Oedipus
complex, his focus remained the concrete and particular ways that individuals lived out these patterns.

As Schorske suggested, Freud formulated the concept of the personal
unconscious in response to a crisis in the nineteenth-century liberal worldview. This crisis began with industrialization. Associated with the early factory system, the *first* industrial revolution seemed to reduce individuals to
mere cogs in a cruel and irresistible machine. The Victorians erected the
famous "haven in a heartless world"—the nineteenth-century middle-class
family—against what they viewed as "the petty spite and brutal tyranny" of
the workplace. Heavily gendered, the Victorian worldview was in one sense
proto-Freudian: it located the "true self" in a private or familial context.[1]
Nonetheless, it viewed that context as a counterpart to, or compensation
for, the economy—not as a discrete and genuinely personal sphere. The latter understanding emerged only with the crumbling of the Victorian family
ideal during the *second* industrial revolution, amid the beginnings of mass
production and mass consumption in the 1890s.

To be sure, mass production deepened the crisis in the liberal worldview,
for example, by introducing the assembly line. But it also revealed the

emancipatory potential of capitalism in mass culture, leisure, and personal life. By the mid-nineteenth century, cultural modernity, foretold by Baudelaire in Paris, Whitman in Brooklyn, and Dostoyevsky in St. Petersburg, had already weakened Victorianism's separate-spheres ideology and fostered an interest in hysteria, decadence, artistic modernism, the "new woman," and the homosexual. Fin de siècle culture exacerbated the crisis. As women entered public life, there emerged polyglot urban spaces and new forms of sensationalist, mass entertainment, such as amusement parks, dance halls, and film. The result was a conflict over the heritage of the Enlightenment. Suddenly, the liberal conception of the human subject seemed problematic to many, as did its highest value: individual autonomy.

For the Enlightenment, autonomy meant the ability to rise above the "merely" private, sensory, and passive or receptive propensities of the mind in order to reach universally valid rational conclusions. Convinced that fin de siècle culture undermined this ability, many observers lamented the new forces of "degeneration," "narcissism," and "decadence." Freud's fellow Viennese Otto Weininger, for example, warned of the threat to autonomy from what he called the "W" factor—passivity or dependency—which tended to be concentrated in women, homosexuals, and Jews. Thus, he joined an extensive chorus calling for a return to self-control, linked to hard work, abstinence, and savings. At the same time, the beginnings of mass consumption also gave rise to a party of "release." Especially among the middle classes, many people found that the conscious effort they had devoted to working hard and saving only made them (in William James's words) "twofold more the children of hell." Contending that modernity required "an anti-moralistic method," James and others commended "mind cure" and hypnosis as methods that allowed individuals to relax their efforts at self-control.[2]

It was in the context of this division that Freud developed his idea of the personal unconscious. In particular, he was responding to the alternation between "control" and "release" that characterized late-nineteenth-century psychiatry. On one side, the tradition of psychiatry that descended from the Enlightenment sought to restore control by strengthening the will and ordering the reasoning processes of "disordered" individuals. On the other side, a later generation of "dynamic" psychiatrists and neurologists sought to facilitate "release" through hypnotism and meditation. Freud's idea of the personal unconscious represented an alternative to both positions. Treating neither self-control nor release as a primary value, it encouraged a new, nonjudgmental or "analytic" attitude toward the self. The result was a major modification of the Enlightenment idea of the human subject. No longer the locus of universal reason and morality, the modern individual would henceforth be a contingent, idiosyncratic, and unique person, one whose highly charged and dynamic interiority would be the object of psychoanalytic thought and practice.

To appreciate Freud's innovation, we need to look briefly at the psychologies that preceded it. From the start, bourgeois society had generated a fresh emphasis on individual psychology. Earlier societies were premised on the model of a great chain of being: the important question was the individual's place in an objective hierarchy. With the rise of capitalism, however, lineage systems receded and ascribed identities ebbed. Increasingly, the important question became not where one stood but who one was. With the Enlightenment and the democratic revolutions that accompanied it, the conception of the human subject moved to the center of every pursuit, including government, education, and social reform.

Nevertheless, the Enlightenment idea of the subject had little to do with individuality in the twentieth-century sense of that word. Rather, it was linked to the Enlightenment project of a planned, orderly world, a world made up of rational individuals. The key discovery of the Enlightenment was that the manacles that enslaved humanity were, as William Blake wrote, "mind-forged." Progress was not simply a matter of facing up to external obstacles such as despots, priests, and outmoded institutions; it required overcoming internal obstacles as well. If a rational world was to be achieved, the ordering of the individual's internal or mental world would be necessary.

The Enlightenment psychology that described how rational order could prevail was associationism. Derived from John Locke's thought, and closely connected to the seventeenth-century revolution in physics, associationism assumed that the mind was composed of sensations or representations arising in the external environment and "associated" according to whether they were similar to one another, or whether they had entered the mind at the same time. In Britain, France, and the United States, associationism animated the entire Enlightenment project. For one thing, it explained the importance of infancy: in the early years the brain was soft, "almost liquid," so that tracks set down could last a lifetime.[3] Associationism also inspired the building of schools, prisons, and asylums. Modeled on the "well-run family," these new institutions manipulated architecture, schedules, and work regimes to reorder the mental associations of the students, criminals, and lunatics housed within them. Even professions that were aimed at everyday life, such as city building and public health, were based on associationist principles. So pervasive was its influence that one philosophe called associationism "the center whence the thinker goes outward to the circumference of human knowledge."[4]

Modern psychiatry, of which psychoanalysis was originally a part, was born out of Enlightenment associationism. Initially termed "moral" or psychological treatment, it was premised on the idea that reason was universal and therefore only a *part* of the mad person's mind was inaccessible. Accordingly, the advocates of moral treatment sought to reach the accessible part. Rejecting the isolation of the insane and the use of coercive techniques such as swaddling and chains, they championed psychological or "moral" methods, aimed at restoring the individual to his reason. Not surprisingly, the founders of modern psychiatry were all participants in the democratic revolutions. Thus, Philippe Pinel, the founder of French psychiatry, helped strike the chains off the mentally ill during the French Revolution, and Benjamin Rush, the founder of American psychiatry, signed the Declaration of Independence.[5]

The psychiatrists of the Enlightenment aimed to cure "folly" or madness, by which they meant a disruption in the reasoning process. Accordingly, they described the goal of psychiatry as the reordering of associations. At first they experimented with external regimes or asylums in the hope that an inner order would come to mimic an external one. Soon, however, they began to realize that there was more to the dynamics of control than could be accounted for by treating control as a function of an ordering environment. The great discovery made by nineteenth-century psychiatrists, one that began to undermine moral treatment, was that authority was personal—the primary instrument available to induce order in the disturbed individual's mind was the doctor's own person.[6] Thus, Benjamin Rush gave a series of rules to the physician entering the chamber of the "deranged": "catch his EYE, and look him out of countenance . . . there are keys in the eye . . . A second means of securing . . . obedience . . . should be by his VOICE. [Next,] the COUNTENANCE . . . should be accommodated to the state of the patient's mind and conduct."[7]

In spite of their discovery of the psychological character of authority, Enlightenment psychiatrists had no concept of the unconscious as a sphere of idiosyncratic individuality. Their single goal was to restore the individual to the "normal" reasoning processes common to all members of the human community. In the first half of the nineteenth century, however, two new developments began to transform Enlightenment associationism: romanticism and the "somatic model," or the emphasis on heredity. Both stressed the idea, lacking in associationism, that the mind itself was a shaping force and not merely a record of environmental influences.

The romantic idea of the imagination was the precursor to the late-nineteenth-century idea of the subconscious. It entered psychology as a kind of reproach or supplement to associationism, as the romantics despised Locke's "passive" conception of the mind. Drawing on the German tradition of *Naturphilosophie,* according to which the entire universe was a unitary, living organism, and on German idealism generally, romantics defined the imagination as an internal storehouse of images and creative drives. The artist, they insisted, was a "lamp" rather than a "mirror," an original source of values rather than a mere recorder of events.[8] With the romantic critique of associationism, Enlightenment psychology deepened. Still, the romantics viewed the imagination as transcendental and impersonal; likening it to the ocean or the sky, they considered it to be all that was not-self.

The romantic influence entered psychiatry especially through the discovery of "magnetism" (hypnotism) in 1775 and the rapid development of a popular tradition of magnetic healers. By appealing to what became known as the subconscious, these healers broke with associationism. Whereas associationism had been oriented toward the manipulation of ideas, magnetism was transmitted through feeling. Puysegur, an early systematizer of magnetic theory, advised that when the patient awakened from a trance, "one's first question must be: *How do you feel?* Then: *Do you feel that I am doing you good?*" In addition, the magnetists stressed the importance of the "rapport" between the *specific* magnetist and his patient.[9] Finally, magnetism made explicit the gendered overtones of self-control. During somnambulism, wrote E. T. A. Hoffman, the German romantic novelist, "the magnetized (the passive feminine part) is in sympathy with the magnetizer (the active masculine part)."[10]

The second development that transformed moral treatment was a new "somatic" model of the impact of heredity on the mind. Even before the publication of Charles Darwin's *Origin of Species* in 1859, most psychiatrists had concluded that heredity shaped the brain, which in turn shaped the mind. Just as magnetism was the point of entry for romantic ideas, so Franz-Joseph Gall's phrenology, influential from the 1820s through the 1850s, was the point of entry for biology. Maintaining that the brain was divided into regions, each of which corresponded to a particular mental faculty such as intelligence or "amativity," phrenologists initiated the attempt to ground psychology in a theory of the biological organism. Soon attention turned to the dissection of the brain and the nervous system. By

Freud's time the somatic model, in which lesions in the nervous system explained hysteria and other "neuroses," was the dominant theory among psychiatrists.

For all the impact of romanticism and phrenology, midcentury psychiatry retained the original Enlightenment goal of moral treatment: to adapt the individual to the universal laws governing the association of ideas. The particular qualities of an individual psyche were of little interest to psychiatrists, who followed Enlightenment precedent in valuing the universal over the particular, the rational over the emotional, the communal over the private, and the permanent over the transient. The momentary, transient, and fugitive experiences that Baudelaire defined in 1859 as being central to modernity had little or no place in the psychologies that developed in the wake of the Enlightenment. Even magnetism did not challenge this orientation. On the contrary, by reducing individuals to objects in order to make them subjects, it retained Enlightenment psychology's ideal of order, even as it revealed the tensions within it.

The origins of the second industrial revolution lay in the 1860s and '70s, the years of Freud's childhood and youth. These were the decades that saw the rise of its distinctive science and technology (the dynamo, steel, and chemicals), along with its distinctive forms of economic organization (large-scale banking, the corporation, international trade). Economic growth was accompanied by political reform, for example, in England, Austria, the United States, Germany, and Japan. England began its long decline and America its even longer ascent. An emerging worldwide network of railroads and steamships brought standardized weights, measures, time, and money. Literacy, schooling, and research institutions, especially universities, advanced dramatically, setting in motion the increased productivity that underlay the fin de siècle turn toward mass consumption.

From the beginning, the second industrial revolution witnessed a tremendous flourishing of psychological sciences and practices. Whereas the Enlightenment had known only psychiatry, the second half of the nineteenth century saw the rise of neurology (Freud's original profession), laboratory-based or academic psychology, and investigation into intelligence, psychopathology, and crime. Great research and teaching hospitals such as the Salpêtrière in Paris, Burghölzli in Zurich, and Bellevue in New York expanded, in part to deal with new "social problems" such as crime, alcoholism, and prostitution. Whereas Enlightenment psychiatry had been defined by the problem of "madness," the psychologists of the second industrial revolution invented the entire nomenclature of twentieth-century psychopathology, such as "neurosis," "obsession," "hysteria," and "abnormal." "Mental healing" directed at individuals in the home passed out of the hands of homeopaths, magnetists, and popular healers and into those of scientists, researchers, and professionals.

Charles Darwin's 1859 *Origin of Species,* followed twelve years later by his *Descent of Man,* was the major influence on the emerging scientific psychologies. In these works Darwin argued that such mental activities as thinking, emotion, and the moral sense arose out of the organism's struggle for survival. As a result of Darwin's influence, the passive sensationalism of associationism gave way to pragmatic psychologies that viewed thought as experimental and suspended action in specific environmental milieux. Comparative, developmental (infant and adolescent), and animal psychology all flourished. By the 1880s, such Darwinian-inflected concepts as reflex, instinct, and emotion spelled the end of associationism, turning psychology into a dynamic science, a science of motivation. In 1890, when William James wrote one of the first modern works on psychology, he likened the older psychology to *Hamlet* without the prince of Denmark.[11]

Under the impact of this revolution in psychological thinking, the idea of the subconscious entered medicine. There it came to refer to the "lower" or more primitive areas of the nervous system, those that had evolved earliest and were therefore closest to reflexes and furthest from consciousness. Crime, drunkenness, and impulsivity all supposedly arose from the subconscious, as did catalepsy, sleepwalking, hypnotic trances, automatic writing, and fugue states or absences. As a protopsychological effort to grasp "primitive" or nonlogical thinking, the medical idea was intrinsically connected to the popular notion of the subconscious as a transpersonal sphere to which the ego gained access through meditation or hypnosis, as well as to the somatic model, which by the 1860s had demonstrated that some psychical disturbances, notably aphasia, were the result of lesions localized in the brain or nervous system and caused either by heredity or by trauma.

The application of the somatic model to the neuroses, and to the closely related problem of "inversion" or homosexuality, was the seedbed within which psychoanalysis arose. Neurologists coined the term "neurosis" in the eighteenth century to signify an overly sensitive or irritable nervous system, but the term had been little used. Between 1869 and 1873, however, its usage exploded. Neurasthenia, anorexia nervosa, and agoraphobia were all named in those years, taking their place alongside even weirder maladies such as nostalgia, the "traveling neurosis" (inspired by the wandering Jew), Bovaryisme (dreaminess in women), and amok (in slaves "running amok").[12] Of all the "neuroses," hysteria was the most important, not only because of its prevalence but also because it manifested itself in physical symptoms such as paralyses or fainting spells that could not be correlated with any known anatomical or neurological lesion. Casting doubt on the somatic model, it seemed to compel a psychological explanation.[13]

The outbreak of the neuroses reflected the changes in the family that arose with the second industrial revolution. When, in the preceding period, the family had functioned as the unit of production, it had grounded identity in socially recognized and established roles, including men's and women's complementary labor. But the transfer of production from the household to the office and corporation psychologized and individualized family life. Childhood came to be understood as a fully separate stage of life at the same time that men and women were attempting to develop new forms of relationship, no longer mediated by family-based production. The emergence of the neuroses reflected these changes. The "neurotics," "hysterics," and "inverts" who appear in late-nineteenth-century case studies were all in flight from the sharp binary oppositions—male/female, active/passive, rational/irrational—that defined the Victorian family. But they lived at a time when there was scant language available to articulate this flight.

"Nervousness" was the primary rubric under which the flight proceeded. George Beard, who propounded the first medico-psychological theory of nervousness in 1869, explained it as a response to the overstimulation of modern life, as reflected in railroads, electricity, women's education, and the sensations of city streets. Paul Valéry explained it as a symptom of the growth of the "delirious professions," by which he meant those professions—such as teaching, law, or writing—in which one's principal resource was "the opinion that others have of one." Baudelaire extolled the "nervousness" of Poe's writing, and Josef Breuer, Freud's mentor, commented on "the overflowing productivity" of the hysterical mind.[14]

Hysteria, the most prevalent expression of nervousness, exemplified the contradictions in the Victorian understanding of autonomy or self-mastery. Far from enjoying the benefits of self-mastery, hysterics felt overwhelmed by their efforts at self-control. Alice James, for example, described her hysteria as a lifelong struggle to get five minutes' rest. Only through hypnosis had she learned to suspend, at least for brief intervals, "the individual watch dog, worn out with his ceaseless vigil to maintain the sanity of the modern complicated mechanism."[15] In its association with overexcitement and theatricality, on the one hand, and with passivity, on the other, hysteria converged with "femininity," which the Victorian age opposed to autonomy.

"Feminine" symptoms were also manifested in other nervous phenomena, such as anorexia (obsession with body image), agoraphobia (fear of going out alone), and neurasthenia (weakness). Then, too, the neuroses reflected the increasing significance of psychology to medicine. Thus, anorexia emerged when patients' complaints of stomach pain turned into an unwillingness to eat, and hypochondria, once a medically respectable disease, in the 1870s acquired the connotation of an imaginary one.[16]

Although hysteria was not the only "neurosis" that pointed toward psychology, it encapsulated the cultural tensions of the fin de siècle era. Those labeled hysterics tended to be prone to suggestion, and thus responsive to the preconscious and unconscious cultural currents that surrounded them. In their resort to gesture and unconscious communication, their theatricality, and their expression of the desire for love, they registered the core preoccupations of the newly emerging sphere of personal life, especially sexuality and "femininity." As a result, hysteria articulated the new possibilities of personal life, albeit in unconscious, distorted, and asocial forms.

The Salpêtrière in Paris was Europe's leading center for the study of hysteria. Vastly expanded to deal with the second industrial revolution's social problems, such as immigration, crime, and social policing, this vast psychiatric asylum was directed by Jean-Martin Charcot. In Freud's later recollection, "Charcot used to say that, broadly speaking, the work of anatomy was finished and that the theory of organic diseases of the nervous system might be said to be complete: what had next to be dealt with was the neuroses," above all, hysteria.[17] Charcot's goal was to explain hysteria in physiological or "dynamic-functional" rather than anatomical terms. In this he benefited from the French practice of observing living patients, in contrast to the approach of German and Austrian neurologists, who simply performed autopsies on the brain.[18]

Charcot was a direct descendant of the Enlightenment tradition; accordingly, his method for studying hysteria was to create a kind of grid. To begin with, he arranged the Salpêtrière's five thousand patients by classes of disease so as to constitute "an immense museum of living pathology." He revived hypnotism, which had been discredited, and used it to induce hysterical trances in order to compile a "cartography of the hysterogenic zones." He drew and photographed patients, publishing the results as *Iconographie photographique de la Salpêtrière* in order to show that hysterical postures paralleled those of the "possessed." In this way, he sought to bring Paris's asylums and hospitals under secular control, admonishing that "among the patients locked away today in the Salpêtrière there are many who would have been burned in former times."[19]

Jean-Martin Charcot studying the brain, not the mind

Charcot's conception of the nervous system was simultaneously spatial, visual, and hierarchical. The elementary or earliest levels of the psyche were reflexes; higher up were instincts, then sensations, perceptions, and finally, at the top, the conscious mind or ego. Hysteria was caused by an "unruly" piece of the "lower" mind that had not been brought into connection with the higher part of the mind or consciousness. The purpose of hypnotism, Charcot taught, was to access the "lower" or "feminine" parts of the mind, those that were outside consciousness and that became available when conscious control was relinquished. Charcot also followed the widely held view that the "weakness" of the "upper levels" of the mind was hereditary and linked to racial difference. B. H. Morel's 1857 *Traité des dégénérescences* had taught him that hysterics "were caught up in complex networks of pathological inheritance."[20] Following Morel, Charcot linked nervousness to other problems supposedly shaped by heredity, such as crime and suicide.

Charcot exemplified the neurological thinking that characterized the early years of the second industrial revolution. In his work the locus of psychological investigation had shifted from reason to the nervous system, and from madness to the subconscious. By using hypnosis, Charcot encouraged a turn from self-control to release. Still, he was no more interested in the psychology of individuals than the proponents of moral treatment had been: types, not uniquely personal subjects, were his focus; visual ordering and mapping, not language and interpersonal understanding, constituted his method.

Nonetheless, the Salpêtrière in the 1880s offered a kind of window into modern personal life, a space in which dramas of adolescent rebellion, frustrated sexuality, and female outrage were acted out without being understood. As such, it attracted the interest of a wide range of artists and intellectuals. Those in attendance included not only social thinkers like Émile Durkheim and Gustave Le Bon, the police psychologist who wrote *Psychology of Crowds,* but cultural creators like Henri Bergson, Guy de Maupassant, Edmond de Goncourt, Sarah Bernhardt, and Jane Avril (Toulouse-Lautrec's poster subject), and neurologists like Pierre Janet, Morton Prince, and Sigmund Freud.[21] It was these last who transformed Charcot's ideas into a dynamic theory of the subconscious, one that nonetheless remained prepsychoanalytic.

Freud was born in 1856 and came of age at some distance from the great urban centers of the second industrial revolution. He was a second-generation eastern European Jew, whose ancestors had relocated from lands ruled by the tsar to find refuge under the protection of the Austrian emperor. His father, Jacob, was a wool salesman who left Galicia, in southern Poland, the poorest region of European Jewry, to settle in Freiberg, a town of about five thousand inhabitants set amid meadows and forests in Moravia. His mother, Amalie Nathansohn, Jacob's third wife, also emigrated from Galicia. In 1859, when Freud was three, business failure forced his family to move to Vienna. The Freuds thereby joined the waves of migrants—Bohemians, Moravians, Hungarians, Ruthenians, and Croats—who were turning Vienna into the most multinational and polyglot city in Europe, as well as the city with the largest Jewish population outside Warsaw.

A railroad hub, a city of congested and unsanitary housing, seventy-hour workweeks, and a thriving prostitution industry, Vienna also boasted such exemplary Enlightenment institutions as the Parliament, City Hall, and the university. Freud entered the latter in 1873 as part of a dramatic influx of Jewish students and faculty.[22] Originally planning to take a double doctorate in zoology and philosophy, he had a deep interest in psychology

The house in which Sigmund Freud was born
in 1856 in rural Moravia

from the start. He took five courses with Franz Brentano, a lapsed Catholic priest and a founder of phenomenology who had come to Vienna in 1874 propounding an empirical science of consciousness. Freud maintained a friendship with Brentano outside the university and depended upon him for work as a translator, but he did not share the philosopher's religious aims and eventually broke with him.[23]

Freud's education was also shaped by scientist-teachers such as Ernst Brücke, who later oversaw his laboratory research, and Theodor Meynert, who supervised him at the Vienna General Hospital. Themselves influenced by Hermann von Helmholtz, these men were involved in empirical investigations into the processes by which we gain knowledge of the external world. In contrast to many neurologists, however, they did not aim to explain the mind in physiochemical terms (an effort eventually known as psychophysics and integral to academic psychology). Rather, they were neo-Kantians who were redefining Kant's innate or a priori categories and "forms of intuition" as evolutionary products, outcomes of adaptation and of struggle within nature.[24]

In 1876 Freud abandoned the plan of a double doctorate and entered Ernst Brücke's physiological laboratory, where he did research for six years and found, in his words, "rest and full satisfaction."[25] Because of Freud's straitened finances, Brücke urged him to abandon research and become a doctor. After military service in 1879–80, Freud completed his medical degree and began work in the Vienna General Hospital. Only after getting his medical degree did he move out of his parents' home. While working in Brücke's laboratory, he met Josef Breuer, an older, much admired family physician and physiologist who had discovered the function of the semicircular canals of the ear. Breuer mentored Freud and lent him money. In 1885 Freud got a university appointment as lecturer (*Dozent*) in neuropathology and won a fellowship to study with Charcot at the Salpêtrière. There he plunged into the new world of the "nervous diseases," especially hysteria.

At first Freud was caught up in Charcot's charisma. In November 1885 he wrote to his fiancée, Martha Bernays: "My brain is sated as after an evening in the theater . . . no other human being has ever affected me in the same way."[26] After returning from Paris, he began working as a private doctor for nervous diseases, primarily with Jewish and immigrant patients, relying on Breuer for referrals and for loans. Defiantly opening his first office on Easter Sunday, he presented himself as a convert to the French school. He delivered a paper, "On Male Hysteria," before the Viennese Society of Physicians, using Charcot's theories to criticize German and Austrian medicine. In 1887 he told Wilhelm Fliess, the Berlin ear, nose, and throat specialist who would soon become his mentor and rival, that he found hypnotism "positively seductive."[27] The violinist Fritz Kreisler, the son of a doctor friend of Freud's, later remembered him as "by no means the famous man . . . but a practicing *magnétiseur*."[28]

Even in the late eighties, as research tended to discredit hypnotism, Freud refused to abandon the practice, long relying on attenuated forms.[29] He also remained within the framework of the somatic model, even as he criticized standard versions of it. His first book, *On Aphasia* (1891), challenged the then-prevailing idea that aphasia was caused by lesions in identifiable centers of the brain, arguing that it was not possible to determine whether a problem arose in a speech center or in the paths of association between centers. In place of a causal connection between the brain and speech, he postulated a hypothetical "zone of language."[30] But this was not new. A search for psychological explanations characterized most serious neurology in the 1890s.

In 1895 Freud and Breuer published five case studies under the title *Studies in Hysteria*. Although much of what is today thought of as psychoanalysis—repressed memory, the talking cure—can be found in the book, it, too, exemplified the prevailing dynamic psychiatry, according to which the unconscious was an idée fixe or split-off idea located somewhere in the lower or subconscious realms of the psyche, cut off from the conscious ego, inaccessible except by hypnosis. William James summarized: in "the wonderful explorations by Binet, Janet, Breuer, Freud, Mason, Prince and others, of the subliminal consciousness of patients with hysteria, we have revealed to us whole systems of underground life, in the shape of memories of a painful sort which lead a parasitic existence buried outside of the primary fields of consciousness. . . . Alter or abolish by suggestion these unconscious memories, and the patient immediately gets well."[31]

Nevertheless, the book did contain one idea that was truly new: *defense* (*Abwehr*), an idea that was connected to dynamic psychiatry's emphasis on *trauma*. In accord with standard neurological thinking, Breuer and Freud viewed hysteria as a splitting of consciousness, a release of tension, a failure of synthesis.[32] The working hypothesis of *Studies* was that this splitting reflected an excess of stimuli—more stimuli than could be dealt with by consciousness. An event that could not be integrated into consciousness they called a trauma. But while the two authors agreed that trauma caused hysteria, they disagreed concerning what made a person *susceptible* to the splitting of consciousness or breakdown of synthesis that followed trauma. Breuer believed that if an event did not reach consciousness, that was because the hysteric had been in a susceptible or hypnoid state (a fugue state) when the event occurred. A predisposition toward a state of lessened psychological tension, he maintained, was hereditary. Freud, by contrast, believed the splitting occurred because the hysteric *defended* against awareness of the traumatic event; he believed, in other words, that the splitting was motivated.[33]

Freud's emphasis on defense was the thread that led to the idea of the personal unconscious. Dependent on Breuer for a long time, Freud became increasingly unhappy with what he took to be the older man's efforts to dampen his enthusiasm, and with Breuer's attempts to forgive Freud's financial debts. Another source of tension was Freud's conviction that the causes of hysteria were always sexual, an idea that is barely mentioned in *Studies in Hysteria* but that lay behind Freud's insistence on defense. What enabled the break, however, was Freud's intensifying friendship with Fliess. At first, although Fliess was two years younger than Freud, he was the dominant figure in their new twosome. He tolerated and even encouraged Freud's grandiose ambitions and served as Freud's doctor at a time when Freud had death fears and tried to stop smoking. Freud called Fliess "teacher," "the only other, the *alter,*" professing that "I can write nothing if I have no public at all, but I am perfectly content to write only for you."[34]

But Fliess also had a profound intellectual influence on Freud, especially through his view of the nervous system as a conduit of sexual energy. Most neurologists of the time thought of the sexual drive in exclusively genital terms. By contrast, Fliess maintained that infantile sexuality was causally implicated in neurosis, a view that Freud soon took on. The shift in Freud's allegiances can be seen in an 1895 incident. Breuer gave a scientific talk describing himself as "converted" to Freud's sexual theories. When Freud thanked him privately afterward, however, Breuer said, "I don't believe it all the same." Freud reported this incident to Fliess in a letter, commenting, "Do you understand this? I don't."[35]

Until 1895 Freud had pursued an eclectic career, working on brain anatomy, cocaine studies, hypnosis, aphasia, and childhood cerebral paralyses, translating professionally from English and French, and practicing cathartic psychotherapy. After he completed *Studies in Hysteria,* however, the notion of defense "forced its way into the foreground" of his thought.[36] Commenting on a first attempt to sketch a theory of the psyche, he wrote Fliess: "All I was trying to do was to explain defense, but just try to explain something from the very core of nature! I had to work my way through the problem of quality, sleep, memory—in short, all of psychology."[37] Trying to think through the meaning of defense focused his energies. In an 1895 letter he informed Fliess that his character was such that he could not live without "a consuming passion . . . a tyrant." "I have found my tyrant," he continued; "my tyrant is psychology."[38]

In July 1895 he interpreted a dream of his own for the first time. Writing Fliess that someday the event might be commemorated with a plaque, he may well have dreamt the dream with a view to interpreting it. In the year and a half that followed, he wrote out a draft of *The Interpretation of Dreams.*[39] Yet he did not complete the book for three more years. He later explained the delay as the result of his "self-analysis," the introspection and mourning precipitated by his father's death in October 1896. Whatever the reasons, his father's death uprooted him, awakening his past and prompting him to surmise that the death of a father was invariably the most significant event in a man's life.[40] The processes of completing *The Interpretation of Dreams* and of coming to grips with his father's death went on together. The book contains a theory of the mind and records the genesis of the theory in the form of fragments from Freud's dreams. Each fragment illustrates both the theory and the difficulties Freud had in formulating the theory. The latter centered on his relation to his father. The parts of the book he had difficulty finishing were the literature review, which recounted his debts to

Sigmund Freud's 1885 visiting card

others, and the concluding chapter, which put forth his most original ideas. His ability to complete the book depended on Fliess's receptivity to his ideas. When Freud finished the book, he also ended his relations with Fliess.[41]

The greatest innovation of *The Interpretation of Dreams* lay in its subject: a sleeping individual. In contrast to the active, rational subject of the Enlightenment, this subject has no access to the external world; all stimuli arise from within. The ego is in darkness. Only occasionally do perceptual stimuli—light, color, figures, sounds, representational fragments—break in upon it. The book's thesis, heir to the earlier emphasis on defense and not formulated until 1898, was that dreams result when wishes or worries left over from daytime experiences become associated with childhood memories that are forceful enough to disturb sleep. A single, overriding, biologically determined wish (*Wunsch*) lies behind every dream: the wish to remain asleep. The dream protects sleep by portraying the dreamer's wish as fulfilled, but in a disguised form. Thus, the seminal work announcing the

emergence of modern personal life centered on dreaming, a state characterized by withdrawal from reality, the omnipotence of thought, and deeply
introverted and convoluted processes of wish fulfillment.

Freud offered the dream of Irma's injection, which he dreamt in July
1895, as the centerpiece of the book. On the night he had the dream, Freud
and his family were on summer holiday in Berchtesgaden, in southern Germany. Freud planned to give a birthday party for his wife, Martha, who was
pregnant with Anna, their sixth child. Several doctor friends had been
invited, along with some patients. Earlier that year, Freud had recommended that one of the latter, Emma Eckstein (Irma), see Fliess for a rou-
tine, although unnecessary, operation. Fliess almost killed Eckstein by
leaving gauze in her nasal cavity. Freud then compounded the injury by
insisting that her continued symptoms were psychological. Later, a second
operation revealed the truth. On the night of the dream, a doctor friend of
Freud's had informed him that Eckstein was still not responding to treatment. The dream was precipitated by Freud's guilt and anxiety but also by
his desire to triumph over numerous adversities.

It opened in "a large hall—numerous guests, whom we are receiving."
Among them was Irma. Freud took her to the side and reproached her: "If
you still get pains, it's really only your fault." She replied: "If you only knew
what pains I've got." Freud then assumed he was missing an organic problem. He looked down her throat—her "unconscious"—where he saw
"extensive whitish grey scabs . . . curly structures." He called his fellow doctors over. One said: "There's no doubt it's an infection." Not long before,
she had received an injection. The formula for a chemical—trimethylamine—that Fliess believed was the basis of sexuality floated before the
dreamer's vision. "Injections of that sort ought not to be made so thought-
lessly," Freud thought; "probably the syringe had not been clean."

The dream exemplifies the workings of the personal unconscious. It
shows Freud transforming both early and contemporary events of his life
into a meaningful psychical structure in an effort to satisfy his unconscious wishes while sleeping. On the most immediate level, it is motivated
by Freud's guilt. First he blames Irma for the disaster, then the doctors,
and finally trimethylamine. Everyone is responsible except himself. The
thought connections are loose, dynamic, and unpredictable. Thus, the
dreamer worries that his "thoughtless injection" is responsible for Martha's
unwanted pregnancy and for his misguided experiments with cocaine a
decade earlier. At a deeper level, the dream reflects Freud's infantile ambitions, his need to always be right. The medical figures are all incompetent.
Fliess bungled Eckstein's operation and is now caught up in absurd sexual

Emma Eckstein: the "Irma" of the Irma dream (1895)

theories. In contrast to such bungling, the dream reflects Freud's then-ongoing efforts to formulate his theory of the unconscious. It has a tripartite structure—hallway, Irma's mouth, trimethylamine—which anticipates his first model of the mind: preconscious, unconscious, organic. Freud's wish to believe that sexuality was at the root of the neuroses may have been the deepest wish of the dream.[42]

Freud's interpretation of the dream demonstrates the way in which he had already transformed the outwardly ordered, hyperrational, visual space of the Salpêtrière into the internal, dynamic, psychological, and linguistic space of psychoanalysis. Nonetheless, the path from interpreting a dream to developing the theory of the unconscious still lay ahead. To follow it, Freud had to abandon the idea, intrinsic to *Studies in Hysteria* and, indeed, to the whole of late-nineteenth-century psychiatry, that a particular event caused a particular "splitting of consciousness." The beginnings of this shift lay in his relinquishment of what has come to be known as the seduction theory.

In 1896 Freud claimed that, "without exception," hysteria was the result of childhood sexual abuse.[43] Even then, however, he emphasized the transformative effect of unconscious thinking. Whatever its effect on the victim at the time of the incident, the *memory* of childhood sexual abuse took on new importance with the onrush of puberty.[44] This qualification, however, did not suffice to save the seduction theory. Rather, Freud began to modify the theory almost upon its formulation, eventually concluding that "there are no indications of reality in the unconscious, so that one cannot distinguish between truth and fiction that has been cathected with affect."[45] In abandoning the theory, Freud did not reject the significance of external events but only the idea that a *specific* symptom was *always* the result of a *specific* trauma.

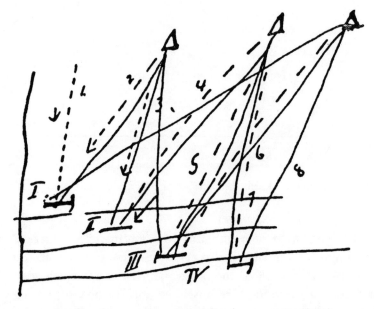

Freud's early attempt to conceptualize the unconscious (1897)

The dynamic psychiatry from which Freud was now disengaging himself still thought of unconscious ideas as "idées fixes" or repressed memories isolated and cut off from "consciousness proper, that is the Ego."[46] By contrast, Freud was beginning to think of the unconscious as an infinite field of associational connections, branches, and pathways, diverging in every possible direction. Analogies include languages, with their rambling and discordant sublanguages, specialized vocabularies, and dialects; cities that branch into diverse neighborhoods, suburbs, and slums; disconnected archaeological strata; the proliferating fields of mathematics; chemical processes; rivers, pastures, and forests; the universe itself; the algorithmically generated spaces of twenty-first-century thought. The unconscious, in Freud's emerging view, was a kind of infinite archive or classification system; consciousness could bring into focus, through perception, only some parts of it, and then only momentarily.[47]

Freud's letters to Fliess between 1896 and 1898 show his developing conception of how the unconscious mind in general works. In December 1896 he informed Fliess that he was working on the assumption that memory developed by a process of stratification. Memory traces, for which Freud used such diverse terms as trace (*Spur*), breaching (*Bahnung*), sign (*Zeichen*), and transcription (*Umschrift*), were subjected to "rearrangement in accordance with fresh circumstances . . . as it were, transcribed." What distinguished his theory from that of his predecessors, Freud explained, was "the thesis that memory is present not once but several times over."[48] In other words, memories derived their meanings from being connected to other memories and not from the events from which they derive.

In 1897 Freud sent Fliess a drawing of the architecture of the mind; an accompanying letter explained the diagram. Consciousness, indicated by the small triangles, was perception. The Roman numerals indicated "scenes." Some were accessible directly, "others only by way of fantasies set up in front of them." The higher Roman numerals referred to levels of decreasing accessibility. The less "repressed" scenes came to light first, "but only incompletely on account of their association with the severely repressed ones." Analysis had to proceed by "loops" (indicated by the Arabic numerals). "Fantasies are formed by amalgamation and distortion analogous to the decomposition of a chemical body which is compounded with another one." A fragment of a visual scene combined with a fragment of an auditory one. The leftover fragment "links up with something else. Thereby"—a key observation—"an original connection has become untraceable."[49]

Here, then, was a step toward a new theory of the unconscious, neither as a disturbance of reason nor as a split-off idea connected to the lower reaches of the nervous system. As Freud took this step, he encountered something that would remain at the center of psychoanalysis throughout its history, namely, the idea of resistance. A dream, he began to theorize, was a compromise between wishes and the *resistance* to revealing those wishes. Since the writing of the book was a deeply personal attempt at emancipation for him, many of his dreams focused on his own resistances, as exemplified in his relations with his father or father substitutes. One records him giving a deceased friend a piercing look under which the friend melted away. This dream reversed an experience in which he came late to work and was humiliated by the accusatory stare of his supervisor, Brücke. In another dream, he saw his father as a political figure among the Magyars; it made him recall how like Garibaldi his father had looked on his deathbed. A late dream in which Brücke gave him the task "of making a dissection of my own body, my pelvis and legs" suggests that even his project of self-analysis was an act of piety. Other dreams reflected larger, political concerns. In one, provoked by seeing a Zionist play by Theodor Herzl, Freud saw himself depressed and almost in tears: "a female figure—an attendant or nun—brought two boys out and handed them over to their father, who was not myself."[50] The dream concerned "the Jewish problem, concern about the future of one's children, to whom one cannot give a country of their own, concern about educating them in such a way that they can move freely across frontiers."[51] Finishing the book and working through his resistance went together. A responsive, nonpurposeful, uncritical state of free-floating attention was the prerequisite to the free association that was necessary to recall, much less interpret, a dream. Attaining that state, Freud wrote, meant taking the psychical energy normally devoted to self-criticism and turning it to self-observation.[52]

Between March 8 and March 10, 1898, Freud had a dream that announced his ability to complete the book by formulating the theory of the unconscious—he had written a botanical monograph, which he saw lying open before him. The dream pivoted around a childhood incident in which his father rebuked him for buying expensive books. Soon afterward he wrote the final, theoretical chapter of *The Interpretation of Dreams*. He was able to finish the book when he conceived of the unconscious as the locus of dynamic, personal motivations arising in infancy: his core insight into modern personal life.

In contrast to preconscious thinking—thinking that is directly available to consciousness—he now described the infinite field of the unconscious in terms of what he called "primary process thought." As he understood it, the primary process was unbound and disorganized, its energies flowing freely between different streams. Not logic, but such mechanisms as condensation, by which like memory traces were combined, and displacement, by which the emotion associated with one trace was transferred onto another, governed its movement. The study of dreams had given Freud a window into primary-process thinking. The primary-process thinking that lay behind a dream was able to enter consciousness only when it took on a visual or aural character and thus attracted a certain degree of intensity to itself. Even so, it had to be revised before the dream became conscious, as in the thought, "This is only a dream."

In calling unconscious thinking "primary," Freud had in mind that it preceded secondary-process or conscious thinking in the evolutionary context. But he thought of it as primary in another sense as well: beginning in infancy, it was associated with the motivational core of the individual. According to Freud's formulation, the dynamics of the personal unconscious took shape when early experiences transmuted the instinctually driven, unmet needs of infancy into *wishes*. The wishes of childhood, moreover, were immortal; a slap suffered by a three-year-old child retained its force undiminished in the unconscious fifty years later. Unconscious wishes were "the core of our being." They were the source of the creativity that erupts in normal discourse and of all mental intensity, that is, of the "extra" affect that adds so much weirdness and unpredictability to daily life. While everyday "entrepreneurial" worries provoked dream thoughts, only infantile wishes could supply the "capital" those thoughts need to create a dream. Freud's Irma dream, for example, took shape when everyday worries about Eckstein combined with infantile wishes for omnipotence and revenge.

To be sure, many late-nineteenth-century thinkers recognized that the mind does not merely mirror reality but rather creatively organizes and reorganizes signs that derive their meaning from their relation to other signs. This was especially true of those thinkers grouped together under the rubric "the linguistic turn," such as Stéphane Mallarmé or Ferdinand de Saussure. But they lacked any conception of motivation. Freud was virtually alone in supplying such a conception. He argued that it was unique wishes and memories, formed in the closest relation to one's parents and siblings, that drove the reconstitution of experience, giving it its personal character.

At first Freud did not grasp the full implications of this idea. When he informed Fliess that he intended to title the concluding, theoretical chapter of his book "Dreams and Neurosis," he made his first explicit observation that the same mechanism—infantile wishes guided by primary-process thinking—underlay both phenomena.[53] Later he extended the idea of the unconscious to explain slips of the tongue, jokes, daydreams, and works of art. All human products, he began to believe, arose in the unconscious and were subtly revised and given representable form as they made themselves conscious.

Even so, finishing the book gave Freud no immediate joy. "Inwardly," he wrote Fliess, "I am deeply impoverished, I have had to demolish all my castles in the air."[54] Nonetheless, completing it changed him dramatically. Earlier, he had dreamt of becoming an exceptional figure; now he claimed to see himself as a man like other men.[55] Completing the book also transformed his writing style; abandoning the persona of professional anonymity, he began to address the reader directly.[56] Completion led him to reject his earlier positivism, although not his love of science. Unlike much of what later became psychoanalysis, which he always understood to be tentative and sometimes speculative, *The Interpretation of Dreams* gave him what he always sought in science: certainty. In his seventies, he wrote: "Whenever I began to have doubts of the correctness of my wavering conclusions, the successful transformation of a senseless and muddled dream into logical and intelligible mental process in the dreamer would renew my confidence of being on the right track."[57]

Freud published *The Interpretation of Dreams* in 1899 but dated it 1900. The book presaged a new way of being human, one that was psychological, interpersonal, and nonjudgmental. All of the new, fin de siècle tendencies—the psychical separation of the individual from concrete time and place, the new encouragement given to instinctual release, the explosive force of sexuality, the building up of complex inner worlds that in no way reproduced an outer reality—were visible in its pages. Soon to be termed "modernism," this new way of being human would transform the nineteenth-century liberal tradition.

To be sure, psychology had occupied a central place in the bourgeois or liberal worldview, especially since the Enlightenment. Thus, psychoanalysis was the culmination of a long history. But in arguing that instincts or drives, which exist at the boundary between the body and the mind, give rise to psychical wishes that constitute the idiosyncratic and particular core of our being, Freud remade that history. The Enlightenment stress on the autonomous, rational subject gave way to the modernist idea of a unique individual, the product of a highly specific and localized history, driven by a complex set of motivations that could not be understood except in the context of a genuinely personal, nonreproducible inner world.

In moving personal, unconscious wishes to the center of psychology, Freud was also tacitly engaging with a second stream of thought, whose influence was at least as strong as that of the Enlightenment. This second stream was Calvinism, which had given nineteenth-century psychology its moral core. Not merely psychiatry, but the whole Enlightenment identification of autonomy with self-control, the injunction to harness one's energies, hold one's passive tendencies in check, keep one's will like a bow always bent: these all descended from the Calvinist idea of the calling. Like Calvinism, psychoanalysis directed introspection toward noninstrumental ends. But whereas Calvinism, the secret philosophy of the first industrial revolution, was focused on detecting any hint of the Devil in oneself, psychoanalysis, the secret philosophy of the second, sought to transmute self-criticism into self-observation.

In its relation to both the Enlightenment and the Protestant ethic, *The Interpretation of Dreams* reflected the optimism that accompanied the second industrial revolution. Personal life was the outcome of an epochal advance: the socialization of production in the nineteenth century, which relieved the family of its most visible economic functions. Encapsulating the possibilities of existence beyond necessity, personal life was the site of deep wishes and utopian imaginings, including the promise of releasing women, young people, and homosexuals from the confines of the family. Reflecting its deep, inner connection to such promises, psychoanalysis would be dogged throughout much of its history by its intimate connection to utopian thinking. Nonetheless, contra Schorske, Freud's idea of a dynamic, personal unconscious did not represent a retreat from the core values of the Enlightenment. On the contrary, as we shall see, in the new conditions of fin de siècle reality only a new conception of *personal*—as opposed to *moral*—autonomy could validate individual strivings for freedom and happiness.

What Schorske's perspective does accurately reflect, however, is that the fin de siècle hopes for personal life were still premature. For the overwhelming majority of men and women, the historic task was not to deepen self-understanding but rather to stabilize the working-class family and community. As a *social* possibility, personal life depended upon political and economic conditions, including a democratic ethos and a secure material basis for childhood. These conditions only *began* to exist in the Fordist, or mass consumption, epoch that followed World War I, and then only in a small part of the world. Until then, psychoanalysis could function only as a charismatic sect, confined to a small segment of the population: the educated middle classes, artists, and bohemians, and others with the freedom to experiment with personal life. In this sense, early psychoanalysis exemplified the pathos of a new understanding available primarily to the few.

An avatar of what H. Stuart Hughes called the "discovery of consciousness," the efforts during the early years of the second industrial revolution to formulate a conception of the active but not merely rational subject to supplant the associationist psychology, *The Interpretation of Dreams* added something unique: the shaping of motivation by the contingencies of early childhood, and even adulthood; thus its intrinsically personal character.[58] Because of that character, what Freudians would soon call "intrapsychic life" constituted a kind of second world, set alongside and complicating modern subjectivity. The Freudian unconscious stood for the *nonreducibility* of the individual to his or her surroundings, a nonreducibility or *surplus* that was itself a social product. This idea alone, however, would not have turned psychoanalysis into a charismatic force. Freudianism became historically powerful because the idea of the personal unconscious was inseparable from a new understanding of sexuality. Sexuality, as Max Weber wrote, loomed in the epoch of mass production as the "gate into the most irrational and thereby real kernel of life . . . eternally inaccessible to any rational endeavor."[59]

Chapter Two

GENDER, SEXUALITY, AND PERSONAL LIFE

The futurists have grasped sharply and clearly that our age, the age of big industry, of the large proletarian city and of intense and tumultuous life, was in need of new forms of art, philosophy, behaviour and language. This sharply revolutionary and absolutely *Marxist* idea came to them when the Socialists were not even vaguely interested in such a question, when the Socialists certainly did not have as precise an idea in politics and economics. . . . It is likely to be a long time before the working classes will manage to do anything more creative.

—Antonio Gramsci, "Marinetti the Revolutionary" (1921)

The reason-centered subject extolled by Enlightenment thinkers was freighted with gendered assumptions: the rational, autonomous, active subject was male; the passive, sensuous, private person, female. In the course of formulating his idea of the unconscious, Freud also challenged those gender assumptions. Just as he found it necessary to reject an inherited schema that opposed self-control to release, so he found it necessary to reject the received basis for distinguishing the sexes. Jettisoning the nineteenth-century view that sexual wishes corresponded directly with gender difference, Freud foregrounded individuality in sexual life. The result was a new conception of sexuality, one that stressed "each person's special individuality in the exercise of the capacity to love."[1] This conception, too, resonated deeply with the new currents of personal life.

Earlier, women and men had labored within a common familial enterprise, albeit at separate tasks. Among the nineteenth-century middle classes, however, they came to occupy different worlds: the public and the private, the economy and the family. Although this division was central to the self-understanding of the Victorian age, it was unstable and contradictory. Women were viewed as dependent on men, yet their labor as wives and mothers laid the basis for men's autonomy. Gender difference also pervaded the cultural order. "Failures" of autonomy, such as labor strikes, were coded as feminine. When imperialists portrayed the globe as inhabited by a family of races and peoples, "the family" took on mythic proportions, while the actual family was emptied of history.[2] In fin de siècle Europe and the Americas, however, this entire way of viewing the world began to crumble.

The key source of pressure on the gender order was the shift from a commercial society to one based on mass production and mass consumption. The first industrial revolution had inaugurated a century-long struggle for the material prerequisites of family life: shorter working hours, housing, sanitation, and social insurance. It moved the mother to the center of working-class family life, while promoting what one observer called the "waning of domestic monarchy."[3] In fact, the working classes pioneered nearly all the innovations in the sphere of personal life: birth control, the sexualization of street and café life, women's open expression of sexual interest.[4] With the second industrial revolution, however, a new middle class appeared. The economic surplus brought the lengthening of infancy, the elevation of childhood, and the elaboration of adolescence as a new stage in the life cycle. New female occupations arose in shops, offices, schools, and the professions. While conservatives criticized women's increased independence, small families, and "spoiled" children, a progressive family critique also emerged. In Ibsen's 1879 play *A Doll's House,* Nora's husband admonished her: "You are first and foremost a wife and mother," to which Nora replied: "I don't believe that any longer."[5]

Like the changes in the meaning of autonomy, the fin de siècle changes in gender relations produced a divided response. Some women lamented the effects of economic progress. In 1895 Marianne Nigg, a Viennese feminist writing in the newly minted journal *Frauen-Werke,* bemoaned what she viewed as the decline in women's power brought about by industrialization. In preindustrial society, she noted, woman was a "universal genius," responsible for kitchen and cellar, fields and garden, linen and embroidery, public and private life. As a result she marched forward "step by step" with men; "That was how it was in the golden age."[6] Many others, however, welcomed "modernity," as embodied in the second industrial revolution. They believed that its technological innovations, opportunities for women to work outside the home, and cultural liberalization would benefit women, especially by freeing them from the family.

Debates over the implications of modernity for gender relations revolved around the cultural roles of two new dramatis personae: the "new woman" and the public male homosexual. Both of them pioneered personal

Emma Goldman: sexual radical, new woman,
anarchist (1910)

life in the sense of life outside of, or at least not defined by, the family. Although both encompassed relatively small numbers, they were highly visible figures who held special significance for psychoanalysis. As we shall see, Freud's intervention transformed these debates, bringing about a new understanding of women's equality, as well as of homosexuality.

Historians generally restrict the term "new woman" to mean the unmarried, middle-class women who entered public space at the turn of the century. The type included social reformers like Florence Kelley, travelers like Jane Dieulafoy, writers like Natalie Barney, photographers like Julia Margaret Cameron, and radicals like Emma Goldman. Despite their differences, all were independent, assertive, self-supporting; some were openly sexual. "Any woman who shows herself dishonors herself," Rousseau had written in the eighteenth century.[7] A century later the entry of the middle-class woman into public space redefined the urban landscape.

The new woman presaged a new strand of gender consciousness, one whose governing norm was *individuality*. Women first expressed this norm in terms of a desire for a life beyond the family. Thus, in her 1892 talk before the U.S. Senate Committee on Women Suffrage, Elizabeth Cady Stanton voiced women's wish to move beyond "the incidental relations of life, such as mother, wife, sister, daughter" to focus instead on what she called the "individuality of each human soul."[8] Closely related to sexuality, individuality was at odds with the organized women's movement, which stressed female virtue and domesticity. Twenty-two years after Stanton's speech, the feminist Edna Kenton wrote: "We have grown accustomed in these years to something known as the Woman movement. That has an old sound—it is old." She went on: "The new, wonderful, final step which woman must take is to enter upon the free unfolding of her personality as an end in itself."[9]

Even more than the new woman, the male homosexual pioneered personal life in the sense of life outside of, or not defined by, the family. He also made explicit its sexual dimensions. The dandy, the *flaneur,* the rake, the fop, the man of feeling prefigured the homosexual, while also anticipating the fin de siècle reorientation to leisure, receptivity, and consumption.[10] Except for a few highly publicized exceptions, the figure of the lesbian tended to fade into that of the new woman, but an explicit male homosexual identity emerged in the 1890s. The three 1895 trials of Oscar Wilde marked the turning point. Even after several young men testified that they had had sex with him, his supporters found the charge inconceivable. "You talk with passion and conviction, as if I were innocent," Wilde exclaimed to the journalist Frank Harris. "But you *are* innocent!" cried Harris in amazement. "No," said Wilde, "I thought you knew that all along." "I did not know," Harris replied. "I did not believe the accusation. I did not believe it for a second."[11]

Just as the new woman rejected a sharp dichotomy between man and woman, so the new homosexual rejected sexual dichotomy. Edward Carpenter, author of the 1896 *Love's Coming of Age,* described his great leap of joy upon reading Whitman and finding there a capacious attitude toward life that accorded with his own. Rejecting Havelock Ellis's defense of homosexuality as a "sport," Carpenter termed homosexuality "perfectly natural, a part of Nature's infinite variety, the diversity and richness of which defies society's crude moral and sexual classifications." Eros was the great leveler; homosexuality existed in all classes. Influenced by the *Bhagavadgītā,* Carpenter cited Krishna: "Only by love can men see me, and know me, and come unto me."[12]

The new woman and the male homosexual were only the most visible figures on the new horizon of personal life. They made explicit norms of individuality that had a wider following. The result was a deepening of the meaning of women's emancipation, one that prepared the way for the redefinition that occurred in the 1920s. Centered on equal rights, Enlight-

Edward Carpenter: pioneer of homosexual
liberation (c. 1910)

enment feminism had maintained that as rational beings men and women
shared a common nature. The nineteenth-century middle classes had
rejected that view, insisting that men and women were fundamentally different. Both views rested on assumptions about women's nature. By
contrast, the new woman and the homosexual presaged the unfolding
of personal life. They aspired to relations whose governing norm was neither sameness nor difference but rather individuality. Psychoanalysis gave
expression to this norm.

That norm, however, was doubly utopian. First, individuality depends
upon a secure childhood, freedom from want, shared cultural institutions,
and rough social equality. Yet the same historical forces that produced the
aspiration toward individuality were undermining its social prerequisites.
In addition, individuality in love could not flourish widely in a period in
which women were denied suffrage, excluded from higher education, and
banned from many professions. Just as the emerging working classes had
limited opportunities for autonomy, so the sexual freedom that came with a
genuinely personal life was still a dangerous option for women. This awareness lay behind Mary Wollstonecraft's cautiously formulated wish that the

difference between the sexes be confined to the sphere of sexual love; in the absence of social equality, she herself had attempted suicide over one love affair and was to die from complications following childbirth in another. Thus, the promise of individuality in sexual and romantic life was premature. As a result, Freud's second contribution to modern personal life, his conception of a personal sexuality, left an ambiguous legacy.

As an upwardly mobile young researcher and doctor, Freud held typical Victorian ideas concerning gender. In 1883 he wrote his fiancée: "The mob gives vent to its appetites, and we deprive ourselves. We deprive ourselves in order to maintain our integrity, we economize in our health, our capacity for enjoyment, our emotions; we save ourselves for something, not knowing for what. And this habit of constant suppression of natural instincts gives us the quality of refinement." Refinement, he continued, presupposed women's place within the home. Scoffing at Harriet Taylor's essay "The Enfranchisement of Women," which he had just translated into German, Freud conceded that "law and custom have much to give women that has been withheld from them, but the position of women will surely be what it is: in youth an adored darling and in mature years a loved wife."[13]

Yet, despite his conventional attitudes, Freud unwittingly hastened the crumbling of the nineteenth-century gender order. Overturning one of its central features, he undid the knot that tied the sexual instincts to the difference between the sexes. From the standpoint of the biology of his time, a man's sexual "instinct" was directed toward women, a woman's toward men. To stress sexuality was to stress the "natural" attraction of men and women toward one another, while also assuming men's activity and women's passivity. These dichotomies had pervaded discussions of hysteria. In Freud's milieu, however, the link between the instincts and heterosexuality was being questioned.

Sexologists, exponents of a new field of study based on the application of Darwinism to sexuality, pioneered the questioning. Havelock Ellis, Iwan Bloch, Albert Moll, and Richard von Krafft-Ebing, Freud's colleague at the University of Vienna, were the best-known researchers in the field.[14] In the 1870s and '80s they developed three new lines of thought that weakened the presumption of innate heterosexuality.

First, the discovery of infantile sexuality loosened the ties between sexuality and the genitals and thereby weakened the idea that heterosexual attraction was built into the instincts. By the 1880s, sexological interest in nongenital impulses had given rise to such terms as "libido," "component instincts," "erotogenic zones," "autoeroticism," "orality," "anality," and "narcissism." Thumb sucking was considered a sexual expression. Fliess's 1897 book, *The Relations Between the Nose and Women's Sex Organs,* presented sobbing and diarrhea, as well as infant male erections, as sexual acts. As we saw, Fliess taught Freud that infantile sexuality was causally connected to the neuroses.[15]

Second, new work on female sexuality, pioneered by Havelock Ellis, loosened the tie to reproduction. Rejecting earlier theories of a reproductive instinct, which he held were "unconsciously dominated by a superstitious repugnance to sex," Ellis sought to identify the distinctive features of women's sexuality. In his 1894 *Man and Woman: A Study in Human Secondary Sexual Characters,* he argued that while male sexuality was predominantly open and aggressive, female sexuality was elusive. The sexual impulse in women was at once larger and more diffuse, involving more of both the mind and the body, whereas male sexuality was focused on a single goal, the ejaculation of semen into the vagina.[16] Such theories were still imbedded in nineteenth-century assumptions concerning men's and women's natures. Nonetheless, they opened the way for an understanding of female sexuality that did not reduce it to the complement of male desire.

Finally, new work on homosexuality and on the "perversions" challenged the assumption of innate heterosexuality. Here the sexologists had been preceded by English Hellenists, who used Plato to redefine male roles, and by French writers who linked homosexuality to modernity. But sexology brought awareness of homosexuality to a new level. The coining of the term "homosexual" in 1869 was followed by other neologisms, such as "urning," "tribade," "third sex," "uranian," "sapphic," and "arcadian." "Invert" (Freud's original usage) was introduced to replace the legal term "sodomite."[17] Krafft-Ebing's 1886 *Psychopathia Sexualis,* originally a brief study published in Latin, mushroomed to 238 case histories and 437 pages by the twelfth edition in 1903, largely as a result of confessional letters sent to the author.[18] Some 320 publications about homosexuality appeared between 1895 and 1905 in Germany alone.[19] Many attributed homosexuality's new prominence to the rise of the cities. In "Berlins Drittes Geschlecht" (1904), published in *Documents of Life in the Big City,* the sexologist Magnus Hirschfeld catalogued the clubs, restaurants, hotels, and bathhouses of gay men. Iwan Bloch's *Das Sexualleben unserer Zeit* (1906) studied the homosexual "vibrations" that emanated from ballrooms, dance floors, cabarets, and city streets.[20]

The emerging awareness of homosexuality could have challenged the presumption of normative heterosexuality. But the twentieth-century meaning of homosexuality did not yet exist. Rather, homosexuality was still subsumed within the general framework of gender difference. The relevant distinction among men, which had come down from antiquity, was not whether one slept with men or with women, but whether one adopted the active or passive sexual role. The receptive partner was stigmatized as a "sissy," "fairy," "pussy-foot," "Miss Nancy," "Mary-Anne," or "she-man," while the man who penetrated another man was simply a man. There was scarcely any mention of the lesbian. A woman who stepped out of her assigned gender role might be termed a new woman, a cross-dresser, or a close friend, but her sexuality was barely remarked upon. Thus, gender structured the entire field of meanings within which sexuality was understood. Sexuality was a function of gender.

Sexologists, too, assumed that gender binarism was the proper frame for analyzing sexuality. That assumption structured the master concept they used to explain homosexuality, namely, *bisexuality*. Bisexuality in the late nineteenth century did not have its present-day meaning of taking sexual partners from both sexes. Rather, it meant androgyny: the condition of an individual with characteristics of both sexes. The idea descends from Plato's *Symposium*. In the 1890s artists and writers revived it as a way of describing deviations from the established gender order. For some, androgyny expressed a new ideal to be distinguished from hermaphroditism, which was considered an aberration of nature. For Oscar Wilde, for example, the androgyne combined the grace of Adonis with the beauty of Helen.[21] For Otto Weininger, by contrast, admixture of the "M" and "W" factors entailed degeneration; the presence of the "W" factor corrupted autonomy, which was found in an unadulterated form only in Plato, Christ, and Immanuel Kant.[22]

Bisexuality was central to the sexologists' thinking.[23] They viewed all human beings as internally divided between the masculine and the feminine. At a time when the endocrine system was unknown, Havelock Ellis argued that each individual contained male and female "germs." Krafft-Ebing analyzed sadism and masochism in terms of the male's activity and the female's passivity respectively; both currents, he maintained, were found in everyone.[24] James G. Kiernan described the primates as bisexual.[25] Other researchers emphasized the feminization or masculinization of the opposite sex: men with breasts, women with facial hair.

The sexologists also used the idea of bisexuality to analyze homosexuality. Karl Ulrichs described the homosexual man as possessing a female brain in a male body. Kiernan wrote of a male homosexual's "femininely functionating brain." Homosexuality, all concurred, was a stepchild, a third or intermediate sex, combining elements of the male and female. Third-sex imagery pervaded Magnus Hirschfeld's Scientific Humanitarian Committee in its early years, as well as Havelock Ellis's six-volume *Studies in the Psychology of Sex.* Hirschfeld and Ellis used this imagery to destigmatize homosexuality and to argue for its decriminalization at a time when Germany and England had harsh nationwide antihomosexuality laws.

Despite its progressive uses, the concept of bisexuality did not challenge the principle of gender binarism. Rather, by describing the individual as composed of masculine and feminine currents, the sexologists *affirmed* gender binarism even as they sought to encourage tolerance for sexual "deviance." Thus, bisexuality as the sexologists used it was a transitional concept. It represented an unstable compromise between the older emphasis on fixed gender differences and the dawning awareness of the idiosyncratic nature of sexuality and love.

In the 1890s Freud took up the sexologists' idea of bisexuality. His innovation was to apply it not to homosexuality but to the neuroses, especially hysteria. Psychoanalysis was born when he failed.

Freud's interest in bisexuality took off around 1895. Part of the excitement that characterized his relations with Fliess lay in the fact that the two men shared what they regarded as the secret of the concept. "I was still lying in bed," Fliess later reminded Freud, when "you told me the case history of a woman who had dreams of gigantic snakes." Freud was quite impressed, Fliess recalled, "by the idea that undercurrents in a woman might stem from the masculine parts of her psyche."[26] Playful allusions to bisexuality were sprinkled throughout their correspondence. At times Freud portrayed himself as a young woman. Approaching a "congress" with Fliess, as they termed their infrequent meetings, Freud described his "temporal lobe lubricated for reception" and his anticipation of the "introduction of a fertilizing stream." In other letters he described himself as waiting for "thrusts and pushes" from his unconscious: "God alone knows the date of the next thrust," he complained.[27]

Fliess's interest in bisexuality centered on its relation to periodicity, the intermittent character of organic development. He believed that all life was regulated by male and female substances, to which temporal cycles corresponded—twenty-three days for the male, twenty-eight for the female. Combinations of these cycles determined the life cycle, including the moment of death. Thus, Fliess saw bisexuality as an organic fact.

At first Freud shared Fliess's conception and sought to use it to explain hysteria. His working assumption, he told Fliess in 1897, was that there were male and female substances in both sexes and that the male substance "produces pleasure."[28] But as his thinking grew increasingly psychological, he gradually dropped the language of substances. In early 1898 the two men quarreled when Freud rejected Fliess's linking of bisexuality to left- and right-handedness. By repudiating that linkage, Freud was questioning the equation of organic and psychological sexuality.[29] Nevertheless, even as he moved to an increasingly psychological conception, he continued at first to think of masculinity and femininity as discrete psychological currents.

Attempting to explain hysteria in terms of masculinity and femininity, Freud brought the gender assumptions of Victorian culture to a new level of explicitness. His guiding idea was that the libido was masculine and that the repressed element in both sexes was feminine. The greater degree of masculinity in men helped explain their intellectual nature as well as their greater propensity toward perversion. Women were more inclined toward repression. Their "natural sexual passivity," Freud elaborated, "explains their being more inclined to hysteria."[30] His equation of libido with masculinity also seemed to explain why women admitted more readily to homosexual experiences than men. For women, an experience with another woman was masculine and therefore not so prone to being repressed. By contrast, a man's experience with another man was linked to femininity and thus likely to be repressed. "What men essentially repress," Freud observed, "is the pederastic element."[31]

As he sought to explain hysteria in terms of the dichotomy between the sexes, Freud found his explanations increasingly unsatisfying. Two months after rejecting the seduction theory, he informed Fliess that he had "given up the idea of explaining libido as the masculine factor and repression as the feminine one."[32] Instead, he turned to the idea that each sex repressed the opposite sex in itself. Then he suggested that both sexes repressed masculinity, in the sense of libido.[33] In 1899 a transitional formulation appeared in a letter to Fliess: "Bisexuality! You are certainly right about it. I am accustoming myself to the idea of regarding every sexual act as a process in which four individuals are involved."[34]

Formulations superficially similar to those of the late 1890s can be found throughout Freud's later writings, but after 1899 they no longer had explanatory force. The reason was that in the course of completing *The*

Interpretation of Dreams, Freud formulated an idea that rendered irrelevant both the nineteenth-century concept of bisexuality and the assumption of fixed gender differences upon which it was predicated. The idea was the personal unconscious.

After formulating his theory of the personal unconscious, Freud stopped trying to explain hysteria in terms of a conflict between the masculine and feminine sides of the individual. Although he would continue to refer to bisexuality throughout his life, he changed the term's meaning. Masculinity and femininity were no longer psychological currents for Freud; nor did he ever again use the dichotomy between them as an explanation. Freud's redefinition of bisexuality began when he started to think about sexuality as distinct from gender.

Throughout much of the 1890s, Freud tended to defer to Fliess on the subject of sexuality. But in 1898, as he was finishing *The Interpretation of Dreams,* he informed Fliess that he did not intend to leave the psychology described in the dream book "hanging in the air without an organic basis."[35] A year later he wrote, "A theory of sexuality may be the immediate successor to the dream book."[36] As he began to work on this theory, the implications of the idea of the personal unconscious were not immediately clear to him. In 1901 he informed Fliess that his next work would be titled "Human Bisexuality." It would be his last and most profound, because repression, the "core problem, is possible only through reaction between two sexual currents," that is, between masculinity and femininity.[37] A month later he asked Fliess to collaborate on the work: everything he knew about the subject he owed to him, he conceded. Then he reiterated: "Repression and the neuroses, and thus the independence of the unconscious, presuppose bisexuality."[38]

Three Essays on Sexuality is the work Freud originally intended to call "Human Bisexuality."[39] Yet it barely mentioned bisexuality. The ostensible reason was that Freud was protecting Fliess's claim to publish on the subject first. In 1903 Otto Weininger's *Sex and Character* had introduced the idea of bisexuality to a wide audience. Fliess felt that Weininger had stolen his ideas, and charged Freud with being the source of the leak, because Freud had commented on an early draft of *Sex and Character* and also because Freud had explained bisexuality to a patient, Hermann Swoboda, who was also a friend of Weininger's.[40] To conciliate Fliess, Freud promised to not to discuss the subject except where unavoidable, as "when I mention the homosexual current in neurotics."[41] In fact, anything resembling Fliess's and Weininger's conception of bisexuality, which Freud had once shared, would have contradicted the basic ideas of *Three Essays*.

In *Three Essays* gender is no longer part of the individual's biological or psychological foundation. Instead, it is the outcome of a complex, precarious, and idiosyncratic psychical process. In place of the nineteenth-century concept of sexual instinct, which assumed an inbuilt tropism aimed at the genitals of the opposite sex, Freud distinguished three things: first, the sexual source, or bodily zone from which a desire emanated; second, the sexual aim, the urge or impulse that seeks satisfaction; and third, the sexual object toward which the urge is directed. An aim could arise in connection with different bodily sources; it could be active or passive; it could be directed at a man, a woman, an animal, or an inanimate object. With this apparently simple threefold distinction, the plurality of sex came into view. An individual's sexuality was driven by the variable history of his or her urges, memories, and emotional constellations. It was not the unfolding of a predetermined process. Sexuality, rather, was personal—in the new, decentered Freudian sense.

In place of the Victorian notion of gendered instincts, then, a new idea emerged, that of *object choice*, meaning whether one chooses to love a man or a woman. To be sure, what Freud called "the great enigma of the . . . duality between the sexes" remained basic to psychoanalysis, but not in the sexologist's sense of a conflict between one's masculine and feminine sides.[42] Instead, the antithesis between the sexes became a sociocultural dichotomy that every infant had to deal with; it was not the source of the infant's sexual inclinations. Indeed, the terms "masculinity" and "femininity," so prominent in Freud's earlier writings, dropped out until 1915, when he added a footnote to a revision of *Three Essays*, remarking on how problematic the terms were. Nor did Freud, in his many revisions of *Three Essays*, ever go back and fill in the material on bisexuality he had supposedly left out to spare Fliess's feelings.

In transforming the meaning of bisexuality from a conflict between masculinity and femininity to a conflict between a male and a female object choice, Freud entered into a complex, unstable, and, above all, psychological terrain. In his writings after 1900, ambivalence and conflict supplanted the dichotomy between men and women, or masculinity and femininity. One could be ambivalent between active and passive wishes, or love and hate, or heterosexual and homosexual object choices. Moreover, and most important, these various dichotomies were no longer correlated in a one-to-one manner. In *Three Essays*, for example, Freud noted that conflicts between sadistic and masochistic aims, on the one hand, and between male and female object choices, on the other, could be *connected* with one another.[43] But they did not *coincide*, as they would have had to according to nineteenth-century thinking.

As the dichotomy of gender began to lose its foundational character, it was replaced by a new dichotomy, however, that between a heterosexual and a homosexual object choice. Thus, "homosexual," as a designation for someone who chooses a sexual partner of the same sex, is a *post*-Freudian concept. Although the consequences of this shift were ambiguous, as we shall see, *Three Essays* constituted an extraordinary moment. With his redefinition of bisexuality, Freud effectively reformulated Wollstonecraft's wish. On the one hand, he limited the relevance of gender to the sphere of sexuality, as she had urged. At the same time sexuality, in its new, extended sense, which led eventually to object choice, supplied much of the shape and motive power of the unconscious, and thereby of the relations between men and women. The consequences became apparent in the "Fragment of an Analysis of a Case of Hysteria," the "Dora" case, in which Freud formulated his solution to the problem of hysteria.

Ida Bauer ("Dora") was a new woman. An eighteen-year-old Jewish student, whom Freud described as "of very independent judgement," she regularly visited the secessionist shows of Klimt and Hoffmann. Apart from her studies, her main interest lay in feminist lectures. Influenced by the General Austrian Women's Association's advice to women, she had sworn not to marry until she was older. She had become severely depressed when she was eight years old (a fact that many of today's political readings of the case tend to ignore), and again in adolescence, when she was treated by electrotherapy. Her father, an industrialist who had emigrated from Bohemia, had himself consulted Freud for tuberculosis and syphilis. In 1900, describing his daughter as moody, hostile, and with a symptomatic cough, he took her to see Freud.

The resulting story is well known. During her adolescence, Ida's father subtly encouraged her relationship with an older man, Herr K., in order that he might pursue a liaison with Herr K.'s wife. Ida became especially upset when Herr K. propositioned her using the phrase "I get nothing from my wife," which she had overheard him use with a servant girl. Freud eventually told Ida that she had been attracted to Herr K., but in the published case study he asserted that she was more deeply in love with *Frau* K., her father's paramour. It is unclear whether he ever discussed the significance of this with Ida. After eleven weeks she broke off treatment.

The case shows the great impact the idea of the personal unconscious had on the nineteenth-century conception of gender. Freud's main interest lay in Ida Bauer's infantile or nongenital sexual wishes. He traced the vicissitudes of those wishes as if they were elements in a dream. For example, aware of the significance of fellatio in the liaison between Frau K. and her impotent father, Freud's "Dora" had displaced genital excitements to her mouth; their repression led to her cough.[44] Freud treated Ida as a fully sexual person—something that was unusual in the context of his times, and that has received much criticism since then. But his main point was that she was unable to consolidate her own sexuality. Inclined toward both Frau K. *and* Herr K., she was unable to decide between them. The conflict between a male and female object choice, Freud argued, was the predominant conflict in hysteria. *This* ambivalence he now called bisexuality.

In "Dora," accordingly, there are no preexisting masculine and feminine currents. Rather, Freud portrayed a woman struggling to consolidate a plurality of sexual aims, impulses, and objects. Ida's conflict was not between masculinity and femininity but rather between choosing a man and choosing a woman. Her hysteria lay in her inability to resolve this conflict, not in the fact that she was inclined in both directions. In breaking off treatment, Freud claimed, she hoped to resolve the conflict. Since she associated Freud with her father, and with men in general, the meaning of the break was: "Men are all so detestable that I would rather not marry. This is my revenge."[45] But this action did not resolve her conflict; she neither became a lesbian nor settled on men.

After "Dora," Freud took hysteria to mean the inability to choose between male and female objects, as the hysteric identified with both. So Freud likened the hysteric to a masturbating man who vacillated between imagining himself as a dominating man and as a submissive woman; or to a female who pressed her dress against her body with one hand while tearing it off with the other. Freud also linked hysterical ambivalence to resistance in the transference; the patient constantly switched associations, "as though on to an adjoining track, into the field of the contrary meaning."[46] Ultimately, however, the roots of bisexuality lay in the structure of the family. As Freud later wrote, a vacillation between male and female "characterizes *every one's* choice of a love-object. It is first brought to the child's notice by the time-honoured question: 'Which do you love most, Daddy or Mummy?' "[47]

By 1900, then, Freud had broken with the conceptual paradigm of nineteenth-century sexology. The sexual instincts were no longer bound to two genders conceived as opposites. The idea that masculinity and femininity were independent psychological currents had given way to the idea of an individual, psychical organization of sexuality. Likewise, the distinction between aim and object undermined any characterization of homosexuals in terms of a set of behavioral traits.[48] In challenging the notion that homosexual men were effeminate, or homosexual women mannish, Freud went far beyond the sexologists.[49] His refusal to believe that an object choice, such as homosexuality, implied any particular psychological traits exemplified the general tendency of analytic thought to break down correlations of individuals with "types," such as man and woman, heterosexual and homosexual, Christian and Jew. It thereby expressed newly salient, sociocultural aspirations for individuality.

Nonetheless, in spite of these potentially emancipatory implications, Ida Bauer walked out on Freud. She apparently did not appreciate being told that her problem was due to her failure to resolve her sexual vacillation. Indeed, to interpret her difficulties exclusively in these terms was misleading and potentially harmful in a time and place when women like Bauer were systematically intimidated and exploited by men. Under these conditions, when women could neither vote nor earn their own living, Freud's exclusive insistence on intrapsychic emancipation seemed one-sided. This goes a long way toward explaining the unfriendly reception he got not only from Bauer but also from the Viennese women activists with whom she was associated.

This point should not be overstated. From the first, women constituted the main group of Freud's readers, as well as of analytic patients. They were drawn to psychoanalysis for the same reason that men were: at the very least it promised release from suffering, when it did not articulate a radically new and deep conception of sexuality and of individuality. Emma Goldman, who first heard Freud speak in Vienna in the mid-nineties, and was present at the Clark University lectures in 1909, is a case in point. Linking the sexual emancipation of younger working-class women to revolution, Goldman felt that the "merely external emancipation" sponsored by feminists turned the modern woman into an artificial being, a "professional automaton." At the same time, however, many other "new women" rejected what Charlotte Perkins Gilman called the "philosophical sex-mania of Sigmund Freud, now poisoning the world."[50] Thus, Phyllis Blanchard, an American psychologist who read Freud in college in the mid-1910s, was shocked to discover that "the necessity of a normal sex life for women was a scientific fact." One of the most disturbing innovations of modernity, she added, was "the emergence of the sex element in marriage."[51]

Women's wariness of sexuality reflected their economic dependence on men and their ties to the family. Accordingly, most women activists of the time were preoccupied with support for motherhood. Certainly, this was a high-priority issue for the Catholic and socialist women's organizations that rejected psychoanalysis. But even activists sympathetic to psychoanalysis sought to connect sexual emancipation with reformed conditions for women's mothering. A paradigmatic example was Grete Meisel-Hess, Freud's most important feminist follower in Vienna. Meisel-Hess's 1909 book, *Die Sexuelle Krise,* used Freudian ideas to argue that patriarchy was based upon sexual repression.[52] But unlike Freud, Meisel-Hess argued that sexual emancipation had to be based on women's economic independence and on social and economic support for motherhood. Similarly, Auguste Fickert was the Viennese representative of Ellen Key, the Swedish educator who propounded a "new love" based solely on the "natural attraction of man and woman to each other."[53] In 1893 Fickert helped found the General Austrian Women's Association, which inspired Ida Bauer's decision not to marry. Fickert also led in building the Bund für Mutterschutz, which demanded social support for women's right to bear children under any circumstances they chose. Freud was a member of the Bund. Yet there was little in his writings that reflected its political and materialist concerns.

The reception of psychoanalysis also reflected more concrete sexual conflicts. Rosa Mayreder, cofounder with Fickert of the General Austrian Women's Association, called Freud "an outstanding dialectician" but a "monomaniac," and wrote a book restating his Oedipal theories in nonsexual terms. For many years her supportive husband, Karl, worked side by side with her in the middle-class women's movement.[54] After 1912, however, Karl suffered from severe depressions and bouts of insanity. Together husband and wife consulted fifty-nine doctors, coming eventually to Freud. According to Harriet Anderson, the leading historian of Viennese feminism, "Freud suggested that Karl's depressions were the expression of a sense of inferiority in the face of a strong, intellectual woman who dominated her husband." Soon after, at breakfast her husband stated: "I have written my obituary. It has the heading: Rosa Mayreder's husband dead." In her diary Rosa wrote: "At first I laughed but then I saw that it confirmed Freud's view that he suffers from my personality because I suppress his masculine prerogative. . . . If I had to admit that, it would be the ultimate martyrdom for me, the complete loss of everything which made our life together valuable." Anderson glosses Mayreder's phrase "masculine prerogative" as "the need of men to feel superior to women."[55] Be that as it may, despite some agreement on the level of intellectual content, Mayreder's feminism and Freud's psychoanalysis were at odds in daily life.

Freud was sometimes retrograde in his attitudes toward women. But the deeper source of his reticence vis-à-vis feminism was that the implications of his work lay elsewhere: in establishing the autonomy of intrapsychic life and the irreducibly personal character of love. For the women's movement, however, the ties that bound women to family relations needed to be loosened and reformed *before* the full range of women's desires, including the full range of women's bisexuality, could flourish. Thus, feminism and psychoanalysis were out of phase. Sociologically premature, Freud's stress on individuality in love was simultaneously attractive and problematic. Yet it was precisely the "decontextualization" of psychoanalysis—the separation of the sexual and the psychical from the social—that gave it such authority.

Given the fact that feminism and psychoanalysis were out of phase, what would be the implications of psychoanalysis for gender? To answer this question, let us return to our analogy with Calvinism. As Max Weber showed, the birth of capitalism was associated with a revolutionary reappraisal of the role of women, based upon heightened respect for their labor within the family. The second industrial revolution, by contrast, promoted *defamilialization,* or the rise of a personal life beyond the confines of the family. To be sure, it was only after the entry of women into the ranks of analysis, and the consequent reorientation of analysis to the role of the mother, that analysis became especially meaningful to the masses of women. But defamilialization had immediate meaning for men. It implied, before anything else, a new consciousness concerning their relation to their fathers, and to other men.

After he published *The Interpretation of Dreams,* Freud founded a small, all-male group, the Wednesday Psychological Society, which met in his house and eventually became the Vienna Psychoanalytic Society. Composed of lower-middle-class Jewish doctors, and expanded gradually to include students from outside Vienna, the society was effectively a *Männerbund,* a circle of younger men drawn to a charismatic father figure and functioning as an alternative to conventional domesticity. As was often the case with such groups, the psychoanalytic *Männerbund* mobilized the passive, dependent, and homoerotic feelings of its members. In that context, Freud continued to work out the implications of his rejection of nineteenth-century gender psychology. The result was a series of new case studies, all of whose subjects were men. Aimed at elucidating general psychical processes yet unwittingly taking the male as the norm, these studies can be read as reinterpretations of masculinity in the context of the dawn of personal life.

Classical bourgeois liberalism of the sort Schorske valorized had set its ideal of masculinity against that of the aristocracy. Whereas the aristocracy esteemed physicality and martial virtues, liberals equated masculinity with reason, loyalty to the domestic family, and self-control. By the late nineteenth century, however, the rise of the corporation and the decline of private productive property had shaken the meaning of masculinity by weakening the bond between father and son. Many regarded this as a loss. Basil Ransom in Henry James's *The Bostonians* complained that "the masculine tone is passing out of the world."[56] When Charcot first encountered *male* hysteria, he noted that his patient behaved "just like a woman." This is something, he added, "that has never entered the imagination of some people."[57] Neurologists commented on young men's "weakness," which they attributed to their inability to refrain from masturbating, the telltale symptom of neurasthenia.[58] Such neologisms of the 1890s as "stuffed shirt," "cold feet," and "sissy" reflected the widespread perception that masculinity was in decline. Boy Scouts, the Olympics, and college athletics were among the antidotes proposed.[59]

Recently, several authors have assimilated Freud to those defending a waning and embattled masculine ideal. Sander Gilman has argued that Freud was so fearful of being viewed as Jewish that he projected onto women the identifying marks (circumcision) and negative traits (emotional lability and insincerity) that the anti-Semitic literature of the time ascribed to the Jews.[60] The result, for Gilman's former colleague Eric Santner, was "an aggressively heterosexual psychoanalytic theory," a "compulsive elaboration . . . of the so-called positive Oedipus complex."[61] There is some truth to these characterizations, but very little. The main point of Freud's case studies was to reject the idea that being a man necessitated being in control. To be sure, Freud's subjects repudiated their passive and submissive wishes. But that was the problem Freud analyzed, not the course of action he recommended.

Far from aggressively promoting heterosexuality, Freud's case studies were early explorations of male *bi*sexuality, concerned not only with ambivalence over object choice but also with boys' identification with their mothers, and with their passivity and narcissistic sensitivity. In their background lay a new awareness of male vulnerability in the epoch of mechanization. Freud's case studies after "Dora" should be read alongside such works as Gustave Caillebotte's 1898 painting of a naked man caught from behind, his anus reflecting openness and frailty, while his posture reflects strength, and Franz Kafka's 1912 "The Judgment," whose hero is driven to his death when his father imitates his son's fiancée: " 'Because she lifted up her skirts,' his father began to flute . . . and mimicking her he lifted his nightshirt so high that one could see the scar on his thigh from his war wound, 'because she lifted her skirts like this and this you made up to her.' "[62] These and other early-twentieth-century works were concerned with male vulnerability, but not with homosexuality as the term is understood today.

Men's vulnerability in relation to other men was hardly unknown to Freud, as we have seen. After completing *The Interpretation of Dreams,* he wrote Fliess: "No one can replace for me the relationship with the friend which a special—possibly feminine—side demands." But in 1910 he informed his disciple Sándor Ferenczi that he no longer had "any need to uncover [his] personality completely. . . . Since Fliess's case . . . that need has been extinguished. A part of homosexual cathexis has been withdrawn and made use of to enlarge my own ego."[63] As in this passage, Freud often used the term "homosexual" to describe men's passive wishes in regard to other men, and especially in regard to what came to be known as "father figures." But he did not mean an *adult* same-sex object choice except where, as in his study of Leonardo da Vinci, he made that sense explicit. Rather, he meant an *infantile* wish, a boy's passive, narcissistic, bisexual desire to be the object of his father's love.

Such wishes, along with the deepening of individuality that can occur when men understand them in themselves, were the focus of the "Rat Man" (1909), "Little Hans" (1909), Schreber (1911), and "Wolf Man" (1915) studies. In each case Freud analyzed what he eventually called the "negative Oedipus complex": the boy's identification with his mother, which leads him to seek to win his father's love through submission rather than through rivalry and achievement.

Freud's first case study after "Dora," the "Rat Man," which he wrote in 1907, was also his first exploration of this "homosexual" dimension in men's psychology. Ernst Lanzer, the patient, was a young lawyer who felt that he had wasted years fighting against his own ideas. Full of doubt and confusion, he found it impossible to recount the simple story of his inability to return a pair of glasses sent him in error. His greatest shame was his excitement over a torture he had read about, in which rats chewed into a prisoner's rectum. While he spoke, Freud felt that Lanzer demonstrated a "horror at pleasure of his own of which he himself was unaware."[64]

Freud argued that Lanzer's maddening and self-contradictory discourse would become comprehensible once it was understood as the outcome of two conflicts. The first was Lanzer's conflict between loving a woman and loving his father. This conflict was hysterical or bisexual in exactly the sense that Ida Bauer's was: it corresponded to a vacillation between male and female objects. At a deeper stratum, however, lay a second conflict—between Lanzer's passive wishes toward his father and his rebellion against them. A conflict between passive and active aims, such as Lanzer's, Freud argued, "can not be described as 'masculine' or 'feminine,' " but it "can persist throughout life and . . . permanently attract a large portion of sexual activity to itself."[65] Lanzer's problem, then, was not that he had passive wishes. It was rather that to him these wishes signified "castration." Not his wishes but his attempt to repudiate them led to his neurosis.

Freud's 1911 account of the case of Judge Daniel Schreber continued this logic. In 1902 Schreber published a memoir while attempting to win release from a mental hospital. The work attracted wide interest among psychiatrists, including Freud. According to the memoir, Schreber was mute during his first few years of hospitalization. Then he began to think of himself as a voluptuous woman chosen by God to be impregnated by Him. Over the years, he felt his male organs retract, his beard and moustache disappear, and his height diminish, and he believed that he was being sexually used by his psychiatrist. Ultimately, he "wholeheartedly inscribed the cultivation of femininity on my banner," admitting that he was voluptuous "from the top of my head to the soles of my feet as is the case only in the adult female body."[66]

In 1911 Freud published his analysis of Schreber's case. As in the case of the Rat Man, Freud did not explain Schreber's problem in terms of "femininity." Nor did he consider Schreber a homosexual in the sense that Leonardo da Vinci, for example, had been a homosexual. Instead, Freud explained Schreber's experience in terms of the judge's narcissism or self-love, as it had taken shape in his early relation to his father. Schreber had had two breakdowns, only the second of which had resulted in hospitalization. Both were provoked by blows to his self-esteem: a humiliating election loss in the first case ("Who is Schreber?" asked the newspapers) and a failure to father children in the second. In Freud's interpretation, Schreber's attempts to compensate for these blows led him back to his infantile, narcissistic relations to his father, whom he identified with his psychiatrist. His paranoia was a defense against this early grandiosity: "A man loves me" became "A man hates me." According to Freud, Schreber's belief that he was a woman was not a worsening of his illness but a step toward recovery, because through it he aimed to retrieve the epoch in which he had been the object of his father's love.

The last of Freud's studies of the "negative Oedipus complex" was his 1914 account of Sergei Pankejeff, the "Wolf Man." Pankejeff, a Russian aristocrat born in 1886, broke down after an attack of gonorrhea. His family consulted several psychiatrists before they sought out Freud in 1910. In childhood Pankejeff had degraded his older sister out of resentment of her intellectual superiority. As an adult, he chose women whose education and intelligence were beneath his own. Nonetheless, Freud explicitly rejected the view that Pankejeff was asserting his "masculinity." Instead he described Pankejeff's basic wishes as passive and masochistic, derived from seeing or imagining his mother having sex with his bullying father. Like Lanzer and Schreber, Pankejeff could not tolerate those wishes because they signified castration to him. A man's wish to suffer or be humiliated, Freud argued, could be at least as powerful as his wish to dominate, and moreover was more likely to be unconscious.[67]

With such formulations, Freud effectively cracked the gender code of nineteenth-century liberal culture. The case studies showed that having "passive" and "submissive" wishes did not make a man a woman, as nineteenth-century psychology had seemed to suggest. Nor did having such wishes in relation to another man make a man a homosexual. Specifically, his work implied that the "problems"—hysteria, passivity, dependency—that Victorians had assigned to women, to the working class, or to "inferior" or "uncivilized" people were universal—and, indeed, were not problems at all but rather universal characteristics of human psychology. Thus, the logic of the distinction between those in control (white businessmen and professionals) and those in need of control (women, blacks, homosexuals, and Jews) began to break down. In a sense, Freud can be described as outing the white male professional's passive and dependent wishes.

Here we see the force of Carl Schorske's emphasis on the introspective roots of psychoanalysis. Analysis was born out of reflection upon experiences of defeat, loss, mourning, and withdrawal. It was not a heroic ethic. What was new in it, as revealed in the letters between Freud and his followers, was the emergence of a language centered on *recognizing* the universality not only of dependency needs but of fear and vulnerability. "I confess this to you with a struggle," Jung wrote to Freud in 1907; "veneration for you is disgusting and ridiculous because of its undeniable erotic undertones."[68] "[I wish you] had torn yourself from your infantile role to place yourself next to me as an equal companion," Freud wrote Ferenczi a few years later; "I would rather have an independent friend but if you make such difficulties, I will have to accept you as a son."[69]

The deepest contribution of psychoanalysis lay not in its ideas but in the range of experiences it made available. Its early studies of masculinity pointed to the universality of such experiences as passivity, vulnerability, and, indeed, the dread of castration. These experiences were not alternatives to reason and control but rather their dark, neglected complement. Far from being especially appropriate to the middle classes, then, in the long run psychoanalysis had the greatest meaning for those who were marginalized or excluded from the dominant sources of power, and onto whom these experiences had been projected: those confined to the family; those who lived in the homosexual subculture, the Jewish ghetto, the ex-slave urban neighborhood; those in conditions of exile, diaspora, and homelessness. It is part of the irony of the history of psychoanalysis that these groups received the least benefit from it. Yet, as we shall see, in the long run the fate of analysis would depend on the powerless and the excluded, whose numbers at times included the analysts themselves.

Like its approach to autonomy, the psychoanalytic approach to gender partook of a broader outlook and sensibility, one that would lead in time to a reformulation of the meaning of women's equality. This outlook—early-twentieth-century modernism—was highly developed in Freud's Vienna. While it did not assume its full stature until after World War I, a common insistence on clarity, directness, and honesty ran through prewar dress reform, architecture, philosophical work, and aesthetic movements, as well as new forms of personal and collective life. As the philosopher Rudolf Carnap later recalled, modernism demanded clarity everywhere but realized "that the fabric of life can never quite be comprehended." It paid careful attention to detail but sought to identify "the great lines which run through the whole."[70]

In describing sexuality as the idiosyncratic expression of the individual's unconscious wishes, Freud partook of this emerging modernist sensibility, but he also distinguished psychoanalysis from it. As we shall see, it was not sexuality so much as *transference*—the infant's early relations to authority as represented by the two parents—that Freud placed at the center of analysis. That, as we shall also see, was the reason for the insistence on the fear of castration. Nonetheless, transference was also the key to the analytic method because only through the creation of the transference could the analyst discern the patient's "special individuality in the exercise of his capacity to love—that is, in the conditions which he sets up for loving, in the impulses he gratifies by it, and in the aims he sets out to achieve in it."[71]

Freud's idea of a personal unconscious, and of a distinctively individual constellation of sexual wishes that first take shape in relation to one's parents, resonated with still broader currents. The Freudian unconscious appeared along with such inventions as the typewriter, film, the moving-picture camera, and the first mass daily newspapers read by both men and women. The new media had, along with crime, two main topics: wars, such as the Spanish-American War, the Boer War, and the Moroccan crisis; and sexual scandals, such as the 1907 Eulenberg scandal in Germany, which revealed that the kaiser was surrounded by a coterie of homosexuals, and the 1889 Cleveland Street scandal in England, which concerned the discovery of a homosexual brothel allegedly run by several lords. Robert Musil's *The Man Without Qualities* captured this emerging world by describing fin de siècle Vienna's fascination with Moosbrugger, a carpenter on trial for cutting up a young girl. "By what qualities did Moosbrugger cause the excitement and gooseflesh that for half of the two million people living in this city amounted to practically as much as a family quarrel?" the hero wonders. "In the last resort all these cases are like a loose end of a thread hanging out, and if one pulls at it, the whole tightly knit fabric of society begins to come undone."[72]

Chapter Three

ABSORPTION AND
MARGINALITY

[In 1911] Walter Lippmann [first] introduced us to the idea that the minds of men were distorted by unconscious suppressions. . . . There were no warmer, quieter, more intensely thoughtful conversations at Mabel Dodge's [salon] than those on Freud and his implications.

—Lincoln Steffens, *Autobiography*

As personal life emerged out of the traditional family, it had an ambiguous relation to the rest of society. As the product of surplus labor—labor beyond what was necessary to simply reproduce the society—personal life pointed beyond political-economic necessity. While the economy called for active and cooperative strivings, personal life was the site of passive and regressive desires—to relax, to rest, to be cared for, to be loved "for oneself." Idiosyncratic though it was, personal life nonetheless had a social meaning. It pointed toward the utopian but increasingly realistic possibility of a society that subordinated economic considerations to human wishes—a post-economic society.

The utopian character of personal life created a dilemma for those who struggled to realize its potential. Either they could remain true to the utopian impulse and risk becoming marginal, elitist, and sectarian; or they could adopt a pragmatic, outward-looking stance and risk being absorbed into a routinized, functionalist regime. Marginality and absorption seemed to represent the mutually exclusive poles of an inescapable choice. Psychoanalysis was not alone in facing this choice. Artistic modernism, the other main charismatic force of the second industrial revolution, also encountered it. Beginning with romanticism, the artist had symbolized the free individual who brought to society not the performance of an assigned function but his or her own expressive and emotional self. During the second industrial revolution, however, the culture industries began to integrate artists into mass-production-based entertainment factories. Avant-garde artists resisted this absorption by defining themselves as unique individuals, "geniuses," thereby encouraging elitism and obscurantism. Thus, artists were caught between absorption and marginality.

Psychoanalysis encountered this dilemma in a particularly sharp form. On the one hand, there was pressure to conform to the norms of the established professions, especially medicine, and to accept a constricted notion of science. (American ego psychology of the 1950s was one outcome of this pressure.) On the other hand, to resist absorption meant to emphasize the unconscious, sexuality, and the instincts, those dimensions of the psyche that were most removed from everyday reality. Absorption and marginality were two horns of the same impossible dilemma, as in the case of art. Either way, the critical dimension of psychoanalysis would be blunted.

In the early years of psychoanalysis, Freud and his followers had some awareness of this dilemma. As the products of a charismatic explosion, Freud's ideas seemed to them to imply something more or other than a therapeutic practice, but there was no consensus as to what. Should psychoanalysis become part of a branch of medicine (psychiatry, neurology), a discipline within the university (psychology), a reform organization, an adjunct to revolutionary politics or avant-garde culture, a new profession, or some combination of the above? The pull toward absorption was reflected in the analysts' search for respectability and scientific acceptance. The pull toward marginality, in contrast, was reflected in the terms that analysts would eventually use to describe the analytic enterprise: *Bewegung,* "movement," and *die Sache,* "the cause."

The dilemma of absorption versus marginality was heightened by the fact that the two main institutions through which psychoanalysis could gain legitimacy, namely, the new therapeutic professions and the research university, were both closely tied to the corporate reorganization that accompanied the second industrial revolution. New theories and disciplines of social reproduction such as eugenics, hygiene, mental health, psychotherapy, psychological testing, social work, and counseling developed in response to immigration and urbanization. Typically preoccupied with "degeneration," racial stereotyping, the prevention of crime and insanity, and the maintenance of gender norms, these disciplines aimed at incorporating the masses into the new industrial order. By World War I, they had assumed tasks of large-scale classification and sorting in the military, in the educational system, and in industry. For psychoanalysis to gain entry into this new array of disciplines and professions, it would have to give up its distinctive concern with personal autonomy and reorient its goals toward social control.

The other means by which psychoanalysis could have become a legitimate discipline was through the research university, especially its medical schools. This, too, posed enormous problems. Like the new disciplines of social reorganization, the research university was a response to the second industrial revolution. Its goal was not merely to advance knowledge but to organize it in a systematic, practical manner adapted to the corporate reorganization of society. In particular, it possessed the authority to certify the scientific status of psychoanalysis. Broadly speaking, empiricism is the basis for all scientific research, but the early-twentieth-century research university tended to define science in a narrowly positivist way. Aiming to separate knowledge into observable, quantifiable facts, and to formulate lawful relations between them, the positivist conception of science had difficulty dealing with many aspects of the study of the human mind, such as the place of motivation, language, and experience. Nor did it allow room for speculation, which is intrinsic to all scientific discovery. Even the most rigorous philosophers of the Enlightenment had a more open, flexible concept of reason, and a more sympathetic understanding of its relation to "sensibility" and "the passions," than did the positivists of Freud's day.[1] As a result, Freud's empirically based but interpretive and sometimes speculative psychology was largely excluded from the university, and from the mainstream of science at that time. The effect was to encourage its tendencies toward grandiosity, paranoia, and defensiveness.

The dialectic of absorption and marginality also reflected the uneven development of Europe and the United States. Late-nineteenth-century Europe was still primarily a continent of landlords and peasants clustered in rural settlements, hamlets, and farm villages. An older order dominated the church, the military, the upper reaches of the state, much of banking and commerce, the universities, the academies, and higher stations of law and medicine. In most countries, kings and emperors remained the centerpieces of authority.[2] In Europe, consequently, psychoanalysis came by its critical stance more or less naturally; like everything "modern," it emerged *against* an older, traditional, patriarchal order, one that persisted until the end of World War II.

In the United States, by contrast, traditional authority, with its feudal and Catholic roots, was weak. Interest in psychoanalysis reflected the ideals of self-management and "empowerment" characteristic of a mass, democratic society. As a result, American analysis became a method of cure and a form of self-improvement rather than a critical stance. The effect was to give the overall history of psychoanalysis a geographical slant: absorption in the United States, marginality in Europe. This generalization should not be overstated: there were marginal and critical currents in the United States; and psychoanalysis gained legitimacy in parts of Europe before the 1960s. Nonetheless, in Europe analysis tended to find its greatest support among intellectuals and elites, while in the United States it became a mass phenomenon, but one that lacked a critical dimension.

Differences between Europe and the United States also shaped the psychiatric professions. In Europe the asylums had originally been connected to churches, and psychiatrists relinquished their connections to traditional authority only slowly.[3] Even as they professionalized, they retained a deeply conservative bias. Influenced by the tradition of psychological healing that had begun with moral treatment, yet drawn to somatic explanations of "degeneration," they were usually not impressed by Freud. Emil Kraepelin, professor of psychiatry at Heidelberg and at Munich and the leading European psychiatrist of Freud's day, is an example. Kraepelin's fame rested on his distinction between dementia praecox, which he deemed the result of external causes (traumas) and possibly treatable through psychological techniques, on the one hand, and hereditary and incurable diseases of the brain, on the other. Since psychoanalysis was removed from any biologically based research protocol, it remained marginal to the mainstream of European psychiatry, even though it offered a psychological approach.

In the United States a different set of circumstances prevailed. There psychoanalysis did not have to contend with an established psychiatric profession. Rather, the medical schools were still struggling to establish their monopoly against popular forms of healing and self-help such as mesmerism, "mind cure," and homeopathy. As in England, professionals sought to distance themselves from the "female emotionalism" of popular therapeutics. Thus, the 1910 Flexner Commission insisted upon the priority of professionalization and credentialing. Open to European ideas, American psychiatrists saw psychoanalysis as a scientific alternative to popular forms of mental healing. For them, the key issue was that any new technique be practiced by M.D.s and not by uncredentialed "amateurs." As a result, American psychoanalysis rode the wave of professionalization, scientism, and the growth of a mass culture characteristic of the second industrial revolution.

Where analysis won institutional acceptance, as in the United States, it tended to become alien in spirit and content to its original insights. Where it remained marginal, as in Europe, it became cultish, grandiose, and schismatic. Thus, psychoanalysis was caught between Scylla and Charybdis. As with the conflicts that surrounded autonomy and gender dualism, it had to find a creative way through. Since absorption would have destroyed the identity of psychoanalysis, marginality seemed to many the better starting point.

By World War I, in any case, the core of analysis was a small, marginal group centered on Freud. Far from destroying psychoanalysis, the discipline's inward-turned character shaped its preoccupation with authority, its self-awareness, its tolerance for speculation, and its intellectual courage. At the same time, marginality led to grandiosity, scapegoating, and division. Freud himself, however, never accepted the marginal status of analysis, and consistently sought to articulate the scientific dimensions of the analytic enterprise.

Much of the response to the first industrial revolution had been pessimistic and reactionary, based on idealization of the preindustrial order. Responses to the second industrial revolution, in contrast, tended toward a future-looking optimism. The years between the turn of the century and World War I saw a dramatic contrast between an older order in which emperors still pretended to rule and a newer one in which the motorcar and airplane were part of everyday life. The result was a terrific rejection of the past and a proliferation of prophetic and utopian thinking, of "arenas and agitation for the announced revolution,"[4] of expressionists and futurists, Narodniks and Bolsheviks, sexual experimenters and communitarians, avant-gardes, manifestos, and sects. Psychoanalysis was born in this environment.

As we saw, its first expression, the Wednesday Psychological Society, was a *Männerbund,* a countercultural alternative to the conventional family, organized around a charismatic male. As such, psychoanalysis resembled other charismatic, male-centered circles in Vienna, including the Secession (Gustav Klimt), twelve-tone music (Arnold Schoenberg), literary modernism (Arthur Schnitzler), Zionism (Theodor Herzl), and the group centered around Karl Kraus's satiric newspaper, *Die Fackel.* Edward Timms has described these circles as "a condensed system of micro-circuits." Circuits overlapped: many of Freud's early associates wrote for *Die Fackel,* and Hugo Heller, Freud's publisher, organized the first exhibit of Schoenberg's paintings.[5] Most such circles met at the university or in cafés. Freud's met in his home, however, suggesting the early association of psychoanalysis with the private sphere.

The analytic circle began in 1902 when Freud sent out postcard invitations to four medical colleagues. Meetings were held weekly in Freud's nondescript, overcrowded, marginally middle-class home at Berggasse 19, a dull street that began at the Tandelmarkt, a Jewish flea market, and ended, on top of the hill, at the University of Vienna.[6] By 1906, there were seventeen members, all male, including Paul Federn, Isidor Sadger, Max Graf, Viktor Tausk, David Bach, Eduard Hitschmann, Hugo Heller, and Fritz Wittels.[7] Apart from Freud, the key figures were Alfred Adler, an eye doctor, born in 1870, Wilhelm Stekel, a publicist and doctor from Czernowitz in Bukovina (in today's Romania), and Otto Rank.[8] Born Otto Rosenfeld in 1884, Rank was a machinist by day and a writer by night when his doctor, Alfred Adler, told him about Freud. Rank met Freud in 1905, became the group's salaried secretary, and attended the gymnasium and university at Freud's urging and expense.

The composition of Freud's circle reflected the shift in the makeup of the middle classes from state-dependent civil servants to self-employed professionals. In contrast to traditional intellectuals who identified with centers of authority such as the church, court, and university, these men were doctors and writers. Their prestige came from their intellect and expertise, not from their social standing. Largely unaffiliated with institutions, they resented the traditional centers of authority and the moneyed interests associated with them. Thus, Paul Federn, Freud's first secretary, described doctors as an "intellectual proletariat."[9] Vienna's Jews were in the vanguard of this shift from traditional to what Antonio Gramsci has called organic intellectuals—intellectuals integral to the emerging system of corporate production. By the 1890s, Jews were close to the majority in law, medicine, and journalism. Disproportionately represented in commerce, manufacturing, and industry, underrepresented in agriculture and primary-goods production, they were closely tied to the new arenas of personal life: urban development, the arts, and the professions.

As Schorske plausibly suggested, the traumatic disintegration of the nineteenth-century liberal tradition in the face of the second industrial revolution was one precondition for the rise of psychoanalysis. In Austria, after an economic crash in 1873, liberalism came under attack. Czech and Hungarian nationalisms challenged liberal principles, while anticapitalist and anti-Semitic feeling mounted. A minority in a multinational state, the liberals were dependent on the traditional power structure. Only the emperor prevented the seating of the populist and anti-Semitic Karl Lueger as mayor of Vienna, and that only until 1897.[10] Freud responded to Lueger's rise, as well as to the Dreyfus affair, by joining B'nai Brith. He stepped down the social ladder, from the medical and academic intelligentsia to a stratum of ordinary Jewish doctors and businessmen who, "if they could not assist or further his scientific pursuits, did not threaten or discourage him."[11] It was from this stratum that he recruited the Wednesday Psychological Society.

The fact that *all* of Freud's early associates were Jewish guaranteed that psychoanalysis would remain marginal. The Jews were the racialized "other" in European life of the period. As the researches of Sander Gilman and others have shown, the Jewish nose, the Jewish foot, Jewish sexuality, the Jewish language, Jewish "greed," and Jewish "disrespect" for community values were matters of obsessive concern for European doctors and social scientists. Even Charcot, who was breaking with racially based theories of neurology, associated Jews with the neuroses, and his student Henry Meige traced the "wandering" of the Jews to their incessant demand for attention.[12] The Jewish male was also often feminized, as in Weininger's ascription of the "W" factor to women, homosexuals, and Jews. Excluded from idealized correlations of masculinity with valor, supposedly imprisoned by the "hyper-trophy of the Jewish family," Jewish men were more likely to be cognizant of the passive, vulnerable, and "homosexual" qualities that lay behind the masculine ideal. Under these conditions, the Jewish composition of psychoanalysis guaranteed that all analysts regarded the dominant culture as hypocritical—an assumption shared by all oppressed or marginalized groups for obvious reasons. As they saw it, much of Austrian politics was a façade behind which the emperor and the aristocracy ruled.

Social democracy offered one possible solution to the problematic social place of psychoanalysis. Austrian socialism opposed anti-Semitism and was less economistic and more oriented toward cultural questions than most socialist traditions.[13] Many of the original figures in Freud's circle were Social Democrats. Alfred Adler's first book, *Health Book for the Tailor Trade* (1898), attacked medicine for ignoring "social illnesses." Wittels met Freud out of a shared commitment to legalizing abortion, and made his name by attacking Jewish converts to Christianity as motivated by economic ambition.[14] Another member, David Bach, organized Vienna's workers' symphonies, served as music critic for *Arbeiter Zeitung,* the socialist newspaper, and advocated a Wagnerian communal theater.[15] Many analytic patients were also socialists. Bertha Pappenheim (Anna O.) translated Mary Wollstonecraft's *Vindication of the Rights of Woman* into German and founded the Jewish Women's Union (*Jüdischer Frauenbund*).[16] Emma Eckstein

(Irma) was an associate of Karl Kautsky, the leader of the German Social Democrats, and the sister of Therese Schlesinger, a Social Democrat who was one of the first female members of Parliament.[17] These ties between social democracy and psychoanalysis reflected not only the politics of class but also an interest in maternalist feminism. In the long run, however, central European socialism was too closely tied to the defense of the traditional, working-class family and community to support the analytic focus on personal life.

In fact, autodidacticism and countercultural pursuits were combined with a socialist sensibility in early psychoanalysis. Discussions at the Wednesday-night meetings ranged over such topics as Nietzsche's *Ecce Homo,* the woman question, the psychology of Marxism, and the sexual enlightenment of children.[18] As in his university course, Freud required every member to participate in discussion, the order determined by choosing slips from an urn. Ideas were deemed common property, to be used without citation. This they called "intellectual communism."[19]

Analytic marginality was socioeconomic as well as cultural. Vienna was a center of European psychiatry. The decriminalization and scientific study of the "perversions" and the first chemical treatments for mental illness both originated there.[20] But Freud was outside the psychiatric establishment, and his only contact with the university was through a course he taught without pay. He had neither jobs to dispense nor patients to refer. The marginality of analysis converged with Freud's oppositional persona and lifelong concerns about money. In 1899 he wrote Fliess: "Money is laughing gas for me. I know from my youth that once the wild horses of the pampas have been lassoed, they retain a certain anxiousness for life. Thus I came to know the helplessness of poverty and continually fear it."[21] In the last eight months of 1899 he had only one new case. In May 1900 he averaged three and a half hours' paid work per day.[22] That same year, one day after his forty-fourth birthday and a few months after publishing *The Interpretation of Dreams,* he would describe himself as "an old, somewhat shabby Jew."[23]

Though marginal in Vienna, Freud's ideas were seriously studied at Burghölzli, the prestigious asylum connected to the University of Zurich. Founded in the 1860s, Burghölzli had among its early directors such well-known psychiatrists as Auguste Forel and Wilhelm Griesinger. Eugene Bleuler became director in 1898 and in a few years transformed it into the foremost psychiatric teaching hospital in the world, outstripping

Carl Gustav Jung: Freud's student, rival, and
the founder of analytic psychology (c. 1910)

Kraepelin's prestigious clinic at the University of Munich.[24] Bleuler followed Kraepelin's view that dementia praecox was psychological in origin.[25] His interest in Freud arose from this contention.

In 1904 Freud heard from Bleuler that his staff, influenced by Bleuler's assistant Carl Jung, had been studying Freud's writings for several years. From an elite family, Jung was brilliant and attractive, with an unusually forceful personality. Although a generation younger than Freud, he was Freud's social and professional superior. In 1902 he had achieved early fame with a series of experiments that demonstrated the existence of unconscious ideational "complexes." By 1905, he was clinical director of Burghölzli and *privat dozent* at the University of Zurich. By 1908, he was wealthy enough to build a large house of his own design.[26] He also had a mystical side that attracted him to psychoanalysis. His father was a pastor who originally wanted to become a Hebraist. His mother was a spiritualist, who used to stand behind her husband as he wrote his sermons to make sure the Devil did not visit him.[27] In 1906 Freud and Jung began to correspond, and Jung visited Freud a year later. The two men were strongly drawn to each other.

In 1905 Freud published *Psychopathology of Everyday Life, Wit and the Unconscious,* "Dora," and *Three Essays on Sexuality.* In response to this out-pouring, other medical men contacted him. Ernest Jones, a Welsh doctor of rural, religious, and working-class background living in London, read the Dora case and was shocked to discover a doctor who "listened closely to every word his patient spoke."[28] He was attracted to Freud, he later wrote, out of his awareness of "the injustices, stupidities, and irrationalities of our social organization."[29] In 1906 Jones began an analytic discussion group in London, but clashes with the medical establishment and accusations of sexual involvement with a patient sent him into exile in Canada.[30] Freud's first impression of Jones was of a fanatic. "He denies all heredity," Freud wrote Jung; "to his mind even I am a reactionary."[31]

Aside from Jones, almost every doctor who came to Freud from outside Vienna came through Burghölzli. Karl Abraham, a stiff and formal Berlin Jew, Max Eitingon, a self-effacing Russian, and Sándor Ferenczi, an engaging Hungarian, encountered Freud's writings as medical students there. Later Eitingon and Abraham joined Magnus Hirschfeld, Europe's leading advocate of the decriminalization of homosexuality, and Iwan Bloch, whose massive study of sexual mores appeared in 1905, in an analytic discussion group in Berlin.[32] "If my reputation in Germany grows," Freud wrote Abraham in 1907, "it will be helpful to you, and if I may designate you directly as my pupil and follower—you don't seem to be the man who would be ashamed of it—then I can energetically [back you professionally]."[33] By 1910, psychoanalysis was well enough known in Berlin for a prominent neurologist to call for its boycott, and subscriptions to psychoanalytic journals were far more extensive than in Vienna.[34]

In Hungary in 1900 Ferenczi had refused to review *The Interpretation of Dreams* for a local medical journal. "Not worth the effort," he had remarked. Jung convinced him to take Freud seriously. Ferenczi was two years older than Jung, a member of a cultivated Budapest family, and a prolific writer of essays and poetry as well as a doctor.[35] His father was a bookstore owner who had emigrated from Poland and "Magyarized" his Yiddish-sounding name (Fraenkel) out of enthusiasm for Hungary's 1848 revolution. His mother was president of the Union of Jewish Women. A member of the *Nyugat* (Occident) circle, which included Georg Lukacs, the Hungarian poet Endre Ady, and composers Béla Bartók and Zoltán Kodály, Ferenczi had a long-standing interest in hypnotism, autosuggestion, and both male and female homosexuality. Before reading Freud, he had served as the Budapest representative of Hirschfeld's International Humanitarian Committee for the Defense of Homosexuals. Bilingual and later a member of the Vienna Psychoanalytic Society, he reproached himself in 1910 for creating "propaganda . . . but no trace of an organization" in Budapest.[36]

At Burghölzli, Freud was widely read. A. A. Brill, the key figure in early U.S. analysis, first encountered Freud's writings there in 1908. A Jewish immigrant from Austria who arrived in New York penniless in 1889 at the age of fifteen, Brill worked his way through medical school by playing chess for money. A brilliant clinician, he loved medicine, worked with the American psychiatrist Adolf Meyer, and translated Kraepelin into English. Ludwig Binswanger, the nephew of Nietzsche's psychiatrist and a founder of existential analysis, also encountered Freud's writings at Burghölzli. Oskar Pfister, a Protestant minister and an associate of Jung's in Zurich, felt upon reading Freud "as if old premonitions had become reality." Freud in turn assured Pfister that "our eroticism includes what you call 'love' in your pastoral care."[37] Even Freud's most radical early follower, Otto Gross, came to him through Burghölzli, where Jung treated him for drug addiction.

Charismatic sects are marked by founding moments and historical turning points that help them consolidate their identity and achieve recognition. For psychoanalysis, the first few years of the twentieth century constituted such a moment. On one hand, Freud gathered around him a group of followers who saw in his thought a breakthrough into a whole new level of civilization. On the other hand, a regressive sense of traumatic hurt, defeat, and exclusion was equally central to the consolidation of analytic identity. Both sentiments were based on identification with Freud and were sustained by the *Männerbund* character of psychoanalysis.

The cement holding the circle together was a shared view of Freud as a "father." Max Graf wrote of the Wednesday Psychological Society that there was an "atmosphere of the foundation of a religion in that room. . . . Freud's pupils . . . were his apostles."[38] But this statement is misleading. Although Freud was clearly central, the minutes suggest a fractious environment with many strong personalities. As we saw, what was historically new about the emerging analytic circle was not Freud's paternal role but the members' attempt to be self-conscious about their relation to it. In fact, personal contact with a teacher was historically necessary to all education involving inward development (*Bildung*). Identification with Freud was a way to learn to think in a new way, "analytically" or self-reflectively, and much analytic theory was generated out of the no doubt flawed filiations between fathers and sons, teachers and students. What also reflected identification with Freud was that ideas drove the movement. Hanns Sachs, a Viennese lawyer who joined the society in 1910, wrote that when he read *The Interpretation of Dreams* he found "the one thing worthwhile for me to live for; many years later I discovered it was the only thing I could live by."[39] Jung transported himself "back to the time before the reformation of my psychological thinking. . . . My thinking in those days . . . now looks like an immense dishonesty towards myself."[40] Identification with Freud also animated one of the deepest and most persistent passions of the analytic movement—the passion to write.

Freud was often uncomfortable with his paternal role. He was drawn to Ferenczi but had trouble with Ferenczi's childlike relation to him. In 1909 Ferenczi complained to Freud: "I'd rather be the way I am . . . I'm at least happy, a happy child. You (Prof. Freud), however, are obviously (intellectually) *so old*, explaining everything, resolving all your own passions into thought, that you cannot be happy."[41] The next summer the two men vacationed together. Freud wrote Jung: "My travelling companion is a dear fellow, but dreamy in a disturbing kind of way, and his attitude toward me is infantile. He never stops admiring me, which I don't like, and is probably sharply critical of me in his unconscious when I am taking it easy." After the trip Freud wrote that he was "not that [psychoanalytic] superman whom we have constructed. . . . I haven't overcome the countertransference. I couldn't do it, just as I can't do it with my three sons because I like them and I feel sorry for them in the process."[42]

As an older, charismatic male, Freud attempted to play the role of the good father. In letters to his followers he discussed their ambitions, rivalries, and competitiveness in a straightforward way that must have been reassuring. When Abraham used the term "neuroticism," Freud commented: "We all have these complexes, and we must guard against calling everyone neurotic."[43] Jones viewed Freud as "a man, who in spite of his authority and rank, would understand and not blame." He told his best friend that Freud was the only man of position he had ever met "who knew what it was to feel young in heart, meaning that [he] had the power of comprehending the trials and difficulties of youth."[44]

The bonds that held the group together also led to its conflicts. Adler told Freud that it gave him no pleasure to stand in his shadow.[45] Jung, who had been abused as a child, described a feeling of inferiority that frequently overcame him. He called a request for Freud's photograph "almost absurd" and, agreeing with Freud that he had a "self-preservation complex," wrote: "Actually—and I confess this to you with a struggle—I have a boundless admiration for you both as a man and a researcher . . . my veneration for you has something of the character of a 'religious' crush. [I] feel it is disgusting and ridiculous because of its undeniable erotic undertones."[46] Sándor Ferenczi, the eighth of eleven children, often alluded to his "brother complex," and Jones queried Freud as to who understood his theories best. As Hanns Sachs observed, rivalry for Freud's acclaim and approbation was the mainspring of the movement's wranglings.[47]

Sometimes Freud verged on the seductive in exposing his vulnerability and loneliness. When Abraham visited him in Vienna, Freud not only gave the younger man gifts but paid for his hotel room. In 1914, smarting, as we shall see, from his break with Jung, Freud wrote gratefully to Abraham: "All my life I have been looking for friends who would not exploit and then betray me, and now, not far from its natural end, I hope I have found them."[48] Part of Freud's attractiveness came from his ability to expose aspects of his weakness selectively. "My prevailing mood," he wrote Abraham during World War I, "is powerless embitterment, or embitterment at my powerlessness." Regularly, his letters were preoccupied with money and with aging. "I didn't answer your last letter," he mentioned on another occasion, because "I was too angry and too hungry."[49] On his fiftieth birthday his closest admirers presented him with a medallion inscribed with a quote from *Oedipus Rex:* "He divined the famous riddle and was a most mighty man." They called him "Professor," though his real title, professor extraordinary, meant only adjunct instructor. An unspoken sense of Freud as a weak, aging, or wounded father, a sense propelled by Freud's own self-perceptions, permeated his inner circle and set in motion a desire to protect him that reinforced the circle's doomed search for recognition and legitimation.

If the circles centered on Freud constituted one pole in the history of psychoanalysis, professional acceptance and mass popularity constituted the other. As it turned out, the fate of the second pole would be decided five thousand miles from the origins of the discipline. Psychoanalysis remained marginal to European psychiatry until after World War II, when Americans brought it back to Europe, but it became central to American culture almost immediately. The reason was the weakness of traditional authority in the United States and the widespread belief in the power of the individual mind to overcome "external" difficulties. In that context, American psychoanalysis became intensely popular. As a result, it was caught up in a process that emphasized personal empowerment, self-regulation, and individual charisma. As we shall see, the actual practice of analysis was less important than its cultural impact. Ultimately American analysis came to mean almost the opposite of the self-reflective exploration of internal limitations that characterized its European counterpart.

An expansive, antinomian sense of self had long been central to American culture. Ralph Waldo Emerson evoked its spirit when he described himself as "standing on the bare ground—my head bathed by the blithe air, and uplifted into infinite space—all mean egotism vanishes."[50] The frontier and mass democracy sustained this sense of boundlessness, which coexisted with self-improvement, sexual prudery, and commercialism. By the middle of the nineteenth century, American receptivity to the idea of mental healing was unparalleled in the world. In 1869 the first purely psychological theory of a neurosis, neurasthenia, was put forth there.

While many factors converged in preparing the way for psychoanalysis, the American faith in mental healing received its greatest boost from the second Great Awakening, the great evangelical Protestant revivals of the nineteenth century that sought to revitalize America's Calvinist or Puritan roots. Although aimed at temperance and the strengthening of the work ethic, the revivals were accompanied by the development of such sects as mesmerism and Swedenborgism, and by the thought of influential eccentrics like Phineas Quimby, who preached the power of words to heal regardless of their content. The result was a widespread American belief in the "subconscious," the impersonal or superpersonal mind, which, as we saw, converged with pre-Freudian dynamic psychiatry. This belief was one-sidedly optimistic. In the 1890s, as many Europeans turned inward toward pessimism, subjectivity, and the world of the dream, Americans, inspired by the pouring in of immigrants, the growth of mass consumption, and the beginnings of America's global hegemony, reaffirmed their conviction of the power of the transcendental mind.

By the time Freud's writings appeared, the belief that the subconscious could cure depression as well as somatic illnesses had swept American society in the form of Christian Science and, more broadly, "mind cure." Converging with American religiosity, mind cure had a special appeal to women. Indeed, the founder of Christian Science was a woman: Mary Baker Eddy. Eddy, like Clara Barton (a founder of the U.S. nursing profession), Dorothea Dix (a reformer of psychiatric asylums), and Jane Addams (a founder of the U.S. social work profession), had been sick when young but then discovered her vocation and went on to lead a rich, healthy, and productive life. By the 1890s, then, the American landscape was home to a vast variety of faith cures, "mental sciences," and "divine healings," which preached the power of surrender through meditation on such slogans as "I am not body." The goal was to become "perfectly passive" to facilitate "the discovery and use of those inexhaustible subconscious powers which have their roots in the Infinite."[51] What held all these currents together, wrote a doctoral student at Clark University in 1899, was the idea of suggestion, "the law that any idea possessing the mind tends to materialize itself in the body."[52]

The mind-cure attitude went far beyond healing. The "New Thought" movement, popular between 1895 and 1915, taught that financial reward depends primarily on "the Personal Magnetism of the seeker after success."[53] The same needs that drove the growth of mind cure drove the new mass culture. Just as mind cure preached the mind's ability to overcome bodily ailments, so the new culture idealized the individual's ability to rise above circumstances through positive thinking, generally abetted by a conversion experience. Dime novels, amusement parks, movies, and sports reflected immigrant and working-class traditions with important democratizing elements. But they also reflected the stress on mental solutions that accompanied the revolution in mass production.[54]

Again, it would be wrong to overstate the contrast between the United States and Europe. American mass culture, like American business methods, was already beginning to permeate European cities, for example, in the form of imported American cowboy and detective stories, penny periodicals, gymnastics, cycling, and department stores. Nonetheless, in contrast to the steel frame of paternal authority that still haunted the European imagination, the individual—generally in the form of a business success, sports hero, or other celebrity—was at the center of the democratic imagination. Mind cure, with its emphasis on psychic power, was ideally suited for democracy. Whereas nineteenth-century psychiatry had functioned by excluding and isolating those deemed "mad," mind cure stressed the universality of the "subconscious." In this way, mind cure's language, codes, and explanatory schemata helped create a consumer market, an audience, and a body of spectators.

The widespread belief in mind cure did not go unnoticed by doctors and other professionals. Large-scale immigration and uprooting had created a need for new forms of classification, ordering, and the adaptation of the individual to contexts beyond those of immediate, face-to-face relations. In the nineteenth century, individuals discussed their personal problems with doctors, lawyers, and clergymen as well as with family members and friends. Psychiatrists managed mental hospitals. The growth of neurology encouraged psychiatrists to reinvent themselves. Turning from asylum management, they emphasized prevention, social adjustment, and the treatment of alcohol- and drug-related diseases with new therapeutic techniques. Warning that nervousness was a way station on the road to insanity, they claimed special expertise in regard to juvenile delinquency. In all these spheres, they worked systematically to co-opt mental healing while attacking its practitioners. As a New York physician declared in 1898, there was no reason to allow "an army of irregulars to carry away the best patients from our business."[55]

The spread of psychiatry was further abetted by the clergy in this period in which church attendance was declining. Just as the social-gospel movement sought to make religion relevant to poverty, crime, and alcoholism, so ministers learned the new medical terminology and combined it with religious advocacy. The two years preceding Freud's Clark lectures were also the high point of the quasi-religious, Boston-based Emmanuel movement, which brought together doctors and ministers in common pursuit of the new therapeutics.[56] Family doctors, too, began advocating that "psychotherapy," as it would soon be called, be applied to the problems of everyday life.

A small group of Boston-based neurologists, psychiatrists, and psychologists had taken up the study of mental healing as early as the 1880s. Participants included important influences on American psychoanalysis such as James Jackson Putnam and G. Stanley Hall, leaders of non-Freudian psychiatry such as Morton Prince and Boris Sidis, and future critics of psychoanalysis such as the psychiatrist Adolf Meyer. William James, also a member, was in some ways the most important figure paving the way for the American reception of Freud. James attacked the attempts of doctors to monopolize mental healing, criticized the positivistic presuppositions of his fellow professionals ("old fogyism," he wrote, seems to begin at the age of twenty-five), and argued that the future of mental healing would depend on popular movements, especially women's movements.[57] His 1890 *Principles of Psychology* challenged mind-body dualism and thereby further legitimized mental healing. As we have seen, his 1901 *Varieties of Religious Experience* described mind cure approvingly as a break with Victorianism, arguing that relaxation should supplant intentness.[58]

With the support of such luminaries, psychiatry quickly absorbed mental healing. The first American advocates of "psychotherapy," Morton Prince and Boris Sidis, were followers of Pierre Janet, Charcot's most important French disciple.[59] In 1906 Prince founded *The Journal of Abnormal Psychology;* that same year the word "psychotherapy" was first listed in the *Index Medicus*. Richard Cabot, a Boston neurologist, wrote: "Psychotherapy is a most terrifying word, but we are forced to use it because there is no other which serves to distinguish us from Christian Scientists, the New Thought people, the faith healers, and the thousand and one other schools which have in common the disregard for medical science and the accumulated knowledge of the past."[60] In 1909 the journal *Psychotherapy* appeared, calling for "sound psychology, sound medicine and sound religion."[61] In the same year Paul DuBois's *Psychic Treatment of Nervous Disorders,* containing an influential attack on hypnosis as degrading to the patient's dignity, was translated into English, further paving the way for the absorption of Freud into the psychotherapy movement.

As American professionals struggled to distinguish their work from the popular forms of mental healing, they betrayed their underlying affinity with them. Hugo Munsterberg's 1909 book, *Psychotherapy,* offers an example. Munsterberg, a professor of philosophy at Harvard, wrote the book to combat mind-cure amateurism. Arguing that the "big marketplace of civilization" had weakened communal ties, he called for "a conscious social program of symbol-building and communal reintegration led by professionals." By "a conscious social program," Munsterberg meant the new forms of social control aimed at the immigrant working class. At the same time he defined psychotherapy's purpose as the inhibition of pain, the suppression of emotion, and the substitution of pleasant ideas "until the normal equilibrium is restored."[62] Similarly, Boris Sidis believed that in every individual there is a suggestible "secondary self" or "hypnoidal state." Upon attaining this state, the individual feels the flood of fresh energies as a marvelous transformation, a "new light," a "new life."[63] What Max Weber called the "iron cage" of instrumental control coexisted easily with an incitement to dream. This was the context surrounding Freud's reception in the United States.

Like the first skyscrapers, Charlie Chaplin's movies, and Thomas Edison's electric bulb, Freud's 1909 lectures at Clark University deserve to be remembered among the signal moments announcing the advent of the second industrial revolution. Like those developments, Freud's lectures marked an occasion that was qualitatively new and transformative. Nonetheless, Freud had mixed feelings when he first received the invitation from Clark's president, G. Stanley Hall. Calling Hall "something of a kingmaker," he complained that the time away would cut into his practice, adding: "America should bring money, not cost money."[64] Unbeknownst to Freud, Hall's first choice had been Wilhelm Wundt, the founder of experimental psychology; Hall had turned to Freud at Jung's urging only after Wundt had refused. Jung now counseled Freud to accept, pointing out that prestige would repay sacrifice. Perhaps he would do as well as Kraepelin, who had just received fifty thousand marks for a single consultation in California.[65]

Freud was simultaneously attracted to and repulsed by the United States. Reflecting on the invitation, he wrote to Jung: "When I started my practice [in 1886] I was thinking only of a two-month trial period in Vienna; if it did not prove satisfactory, I was planning to go to America and found an existence that I would subsequently have asked my fiancee in Hamburg to share. . . . [N]ow, twenty-three years later, I am to go to America after all, not, to be sure, to make money, but in response to an honorable call!"[66] After the dates were rearranged and he had accepted, however, Freud wrote Jung: "There is a good deal to be said about America [but] once they discover the sexual core of our psychological theories they will drop us. Their prudery and their material dependence on the public are too great."[67] With Ferenczi he was more direct. Once the Americans realize the sexual basis of our ideas, he wrote, we'll be "up shit creek."[68]

The Clark lectures were the decisive moment in the eruption of Freud's charisma. Reflecting the close connection between professionalism and popular culture, the audience included a cross section of America's medical and academic elite: William James (philosophy), Edward Titchener (psychology), Franz Boas (anthropology), Adolf Meyer (psychiatry), and James Jackson Putnam (neurology).[69] Jones advised Freud "to aim first at the recognised people, and not to popularise too soon. There is so much vulgarisation and exploitation of everything here, that one has a strong weapon in insisting on the exact scientific side." But, Jones continued, analysis faces problems "peculiar to the Anglo-Saxon race." One must know their "currents and prejudices in order to combat them most successfully . . . a man who writes always on the same subject is apt to be regarded [in America] as a crank . . . if the subject is sexual he is simply tabooed . . . hence I shall dilute my sex articles with articles on other subjects."[70]

On the boat to America, Freud discovered his cabin boy reading *The Psychopathology of Everyday Life.* It occurred to him then that he was about to become a world figure. He had addressed the second edition of *The Interpretation of Dreams* to a "wider circle of educated and curious-minded readers."[71] Now, against Jones's counsel, he aimed his lectures at a true mass audience. He stressed "the practicality, the optimism, the comparative simplicity of psychoanalysis," at times condensing his theories almost to the point of caricature.[72]

The lectures not only constituted Freud's claim to scientific legitimacy; they brought Freudian analysis and the world of mass consumption into their fateful juxtaposition. Within a few years the coverage of analysis eclipsed that of all other therapies in popular magazines, especially those aimed at women.[73] In spite of Freud's ambivalence about the United States, his reception satisfied his deepest wishes. Later he described it as "the realization of an incredible daydream": "In Europe I felt like someone excommunicated; here I saw myself received by the best as an equal." The lectures, he added, were "the first time I was permitted to speak publicly about psychoanalysis."[74]

Of all the early analysts, Jones was the one who best appreciated the opportunities that psychoanalysis faced in the English-speaking world. Although he had been mistrustful of Freud when they first met, the lectures seem to have resolved his doubts. Freud also recalled them as a turning point. "When you left Worcester [Massachusetts] after a time of dark inconsistencies from your side . . . I had to face the idea that you were going away to become a stranger to us," Freud wrote to Jones. "Then I felt it ought not to be so and I could not show it otherwise than by accompanying you to the train and shaking hands before you went away."[75] Earlier Jones had observed: "The originality-complex is not strong with me; my ambition is rather to know, to be 'behind the scenes,' and 'in the know,' rather than *to find out*."[76]

Meeting with the American Therapeutic Society, organized by Morton Prince in the summer of 1909, Jones portrayed free association as "in almost every respect the reverse of treatment by suggestion" or mind cure.[77] All therapies, he held, can be ranged in terms of "the extent to which the patient himself is made actively to bring about changes in his mental functioning."[78] The Freudian version was, of course, the acme. Under Jones's influence, two analytic societies formed in 1911: the New York Psychoanalytic Society, headed by A. A. Brill, and the American Psychoanalytic Society, headed by Adolf Meyer and James Jackson Putnam. From the very first, the U.S. societies were different from those of Europe. Technique-driven and with little interest in psychoanalytic theory, both were composed exclusively of medical doctors; both made a medical license a requirement of admittance.[79]

Alongside the societies, the first Freudian generation of hospital psychiatrists emerged. Younger doctors, such as Smith Ely Jelliffe and William Alanson White, discontented with somatic interpretations of mental illness, were its leaders. White and Jelliffe founded *The Psychoanalytic Review* in 1912, the first journal devoted to psychoanalysis in the United States. They viewed the theory of the neuroses as the "indispensable path to the [treatment of the] psychoses."[80] Successive editions of White's *Outlines of*

Psychiatry, one of the most popular short texts in American psychiatric history, trace Freud's impact. In 1907 White described hysteria as a narrowing of the field of consciousness. In 1911 he denounced suggestion therapy and introduced Freud's theory alongside Janet's. In 1915, when the book was replaced by White and Jelliffe's *Diseases of the Nervous System,* White recommended analysis as the treatment of choice at "higher psychological levels." It could not cure psychotic patients, he conceded, but it could relieve their symptoms.[81]

Psychiatrists particularly appreciated what they took to be Freud's environmental approach.[82] Likening analysis to eugenics, White and Jelliffe stressed the ways in which it could help prevent delinquency and addiction.[83] Largely rewritten in the language of behaviorism after the publication of J. B. Watson's *Behaviorism* in 1914, the American version of Freud was portrayed as a hard-boiled scientific psychology. As Watson explained, when teaching Freudian psychology he omitted "the crude vitalistic and psychological terminology" and stuck to biological factors; "Freud himself admits the possibility of this."[84] Yet even as Freud's thought was incorporated into American psychiatry, psychiatrists remained skeptical of everything that transcended behaviorism. "The main thing," Adolf Meyer remarked, "is that your point of reference should always be life itself and not the imagined cesspool of the unconscious."[85]

Although American analysis remained marginal to European analysis, it was never far from the consciousness of Freud and his associates. By World War I, the United States had the largest number of analysts in the world. Freud sometimes tried to ignore this; Jones never did. In 1908 the two men met with Brill to discuss translating Freud's works into English. In 1909 Brill translated parts of *Studies on Hysteria,* in 1913 *The Interpretation of Dreams,* and in 1918 *Three Essays.*[86] Though cavalier about copyrights, Freud supervised translations, suggested English terms such as "repression," and vetted all important decisions.[87] Understanding that professional approval was the key to mass popularity, the translators were guided by the idea that English, like German, was a vernacular language that did not promote emotive distance. They therefore used a psychiatric terminology drawn from Latin and Greek. While Freud's German was almost colloquial, they encouraged neologisms and technical terms such as "anaclitic," "fixation," "epistemophilia," and "parapraxis." The everyday German *Lust* became "libido." *Trieb* (drive) became the hardwired "instinct." *Schaulust,* pleasure in looking, was translated "scopophilia."[88] *Angst,* another everyday word, became the clinical "anxiety." *Ich* (I) became "ego." *Besetzt,* "taken" or "occupied," became "cathected." To underline the professional legitimacy of analysis, Brill's translation of *The Interpretation of Dreams* warned that sales were "limited to members of the Medical, Scholastic, Legal and Clerical professions." As translations appeared, Jones produced glossaries that standardized a set of terms relied on by all subsequent translators, including James Strachey.[89] As much as any other factor, these translations laid the basis for the later Anglo-American dominance over psychoanalysis.

After the Clark lectures, the conflict between the marginal identity of psychoanalysis and its inflated place in the popular imagination intensified. Public pride confounded private doubts. Freud, normally realistic, began to write: "We must conquer the whole field of mythology . . . we must also take hold of biography."[90] At the same time he recognized the pressing problem of finding an institutional form for analysis and urged that it be discussed at an analytic congress to be held at Nuremberg in 1910.

The obvious solution was for analysis to become part of medicine. Freud called medicine the motherland of psychoanalysis, the "sister" who informed all the sciences about the human organism.[91] When Ferenczi asked him how to stimulate interest in psychoanalysis, Freud counseled him to advertise a course for physicians and others.[92] At the same time, however, Freud believed that analysis should retain its independence from psychiatry. On this point he was more radical than his associates. Editing Freud's preface to the Hungarian edition of Ferenczi's essays in 1909, Ferenczi changed the description of the intended audience from "men of education" to "doctors and men of education." "I don't want the book to be described as 'popular science,' " he explained.[93] After the International Psychoanalytic Association was founded in 1910, Jung urged that the Zurich rule that "only holders of academic degrees can be . . . members" be extended to all analytic societies. Freud, however, disagreed. "The statutes [of the International Association] leave us free," he replied, "although their spirit does not tend toward such exclusiveness." Such a "regressive measure would never be accepted in Vienna and is also displeasing to me personally."[94]

In fact, the horizons opened by Freud's thought stretched far beyond medicine. As we shall see, Freud and his associates had subordinated psychiatric categories to a developmental sequence stretching from earliest childhood through what increasingly came to be called the "Oedipus complex." These works situated the neuroses within a fundamentally philosophical, evolutionary, and anthropological conception centered on the individual's relation to authority. Freud often alluded to their broad social implications, but he was cautious about trying to spell them out. In 1907 he told the Vienna Psychoanalytic Society that from analytic case studies we learn "what is really going on in the world . . . analyses are cultural historical documents of tremendous importance."[95] A few years later he characterized the neuroses as "asocial" structures that attempt "to achieve by private means what is effected in society by collective effort."[96] Thought-provoking as such insights were, the problem of institutional form remained.

Reflecting the powerful thrust toward social reorganization that accompanied the second industrial revolution, many of Freud's associates sought a closer relation between psychoanalysis and social democracy. Alfred Adler was the most prominent. In preparation for the Nuremberg conference, Freud asked Adler to speak to the Vienna Psychoanalytic Society on the question of whether psychoanalysis is compatible with every worldview or whether it entailed adherence to a particular political viewpoint.[97] Ferenczi also urged that the conference discuss the "*sociological* significance of our analyses."[98] In the United States, James Jackson Putnam sought to join analysis with social and moral reform. In Switzerland, Auguste-Henri Forel tried to enlist Freud's support in a reform association devoted to the eradication of syphilis, alcoholism, and other social problems.[99]

Freud at first responded enthusiastically to Forel's proposal, writing to Jung that he was attracted by Forel's willingness "to combat the authority of State and Church directly where they commit palpable injustice."[100] By the time of the congress, however, Freud had rejected this option. His ostensible motive was to protect analysis. In fact, Freudian thought was at odds with the politics of the day, both conservative and left-wing. Conservative parties were founded on the defense of the patriarchal, monarchical, and religious traditions that analysis described in terms of the "father complex." Yet the most important populist alternatives to conservatism were xenophobic and anti-Semitic. Freud's personal politics were liberal in the European sense, stressing secularism and freedom of speech, but his experiences in Vienna led him to be skeptical of this tradition. Meanwhile, social democracy valorized communal principles and tended to reduce injustice to the question of economic organization.

Freud's opposition to proposals to join psychoanalysis to a specific politics reflected its role as a theory and practice of personal life. In his view, for an analyst to affirm or challenge a patient's moral or political stance was not only an unwarranted abuse of authority but also an obstacle to analyzing the motives and meaning of the patient's stance. When Freud told the Viennese society that analytic case studies teach us what is really going on in the world, he meant at the level of motives and meanings, not of politics. In his view, analysis aimed to support individual and cultural self-reflection; it did not imply any particular political practice.[101] In fact, a new interpretation of the ideal of personal autonomy was implicit in the idea of the personal unconscious. Fidelity to that idea put analysis at a level once removed from ordinary political commitments. Instead of focusing directly on the forms of political and social domination in modern society, analysis focused on the internal, psychic preconditions for domination. In this sense, it sought to be metapolitical or "transcendental," a Kantian term then in use by analysts.[102] In the long run, however, as we shall see, the apolitical stance of analysis proved impossible to maintain.

Alongside those who wanted analysis to join with the Social Democrats' efforts at reform, there were countervailing pulls toward the avant-garde, especially in those nations that had not yet established stable, mass democracies: Germany and Russia. One such effort was spearheaded by Otto Gross in Munich's Schwabing district, a center of avant-garde culture that also housed Thomas Mann, Frank Wedekind, Stefan George, and Richard Strauss. Gross was a charismatic bohemian and self-proclaimed analyst who propounded a philosophy of sexual liberation, opposition to patriarchy, and revolution. A forerunner of Wilhelm Reich and Herbert Marcuse, he held that "the immense future of psychoanalysis [is] comprehensible as the soul of tomorrow's revolutionary movement."[103]

In 1907 Gross submitted an article on psychoanalysis to a scholarly German journal. Max Weber, an editor of the journal, rejected the article in a letter that illuminates the categorical break that had occurred between psychoanalysis and the tradition of utopian revolution. Weber began by distinguishing Freud from Gross. Gross asks of a theory only "Can one eat it?—that is, can one construct a practical 'world view' from it?" This was not true of Freud, whom Weber regarded as a scientist, albeit one whose formulations had not yet stood the test of time. Furthermore, according to Gross, "*every* suppression of emotion-laden desires and drives leads to 'repression,' " and therefore calls for revolution. But an ethical life invariably entails repression, Weber argued. The real problem, which Gross ignored, was to distinguish ethical from unethical repression. Gross essentially espoused a "psychiatric ethic": "admit to yourself what you are like and what you desire." This, Weber wrote, was the ideal of the "*nerve-snob.*" Behind the "*specialist* jargon," he added, "the whole article is absolutely bursting with noisy value-judgements."[104]

In Russia, too, a strong effort was made to integrate psychoanalysis into an avant-garde worldview. Translations of Dostoyevsky, the Paris premiere of Vaslav Nijinsky in Sergey Diaghilev's *Ballets Russes,* and Wassily

Kandinsky's *On the Spiritual in Art* had placed Russia at the forefront of early-twentieth-century modernism. Correspondingly, Russian intellectuals turned passionately toward the West. Hungrily interrogating Hegel, Schopenhauer, and Nietzsche, they translated practically everything Freud wrote between 1909 and 1914, generally preceding any other foreign translations.[105] Based on this interest, Moshe Wulff in Odessa (where Freud discerned a "local epidemic of psychoanalysis"), Tatania Rosenthal in St. Petersburg, and Nikolai Osipov in Moscow founded analytic groups or societies.

Along with these groups, the symbolist poets and philosophers were the main Russian advocates of psychoanalysis. Supposedly like psychoanalysis, symbolism distinguished two planes of reality, the visible and the invisible. In addition, there were many other points of apparent contact. Committed to the idea of Russia's special mission, the symbolists sought the dissolution of the ego, and especially of gender distinction, in what the philosopher Vladimir Solovyov described as a "feminine" all-oneness and the symbolist poet Vyacheslav Ivanov called "the realm of bisexual, feminine-masculine Dionysius." In the same vein, Nikolai Berdyaev described sexuality as the painful search for a lost androgyny, apparent in Adam and Christ, while other symbolists espoused a Dionysian transcendence of the self through sexual practices. Christianity, the symbolist poet Sergei Solovyov told Alexander Blok, "at its very core is beyond gender" and can only be attained through sexual release. In fact, these ideals were as incompatible with psychoanalysis as political revolution was, but for a while the two movements occupied a common terrain.[106]

Eschewing sectarian reinterpretations of psychoanalysis, whether political or aesthetic, Freud sought to reassure those analysts who struggled for professional acceptance that they were doing their duty to society: not only were they helping their patients, but they were contributing their "share to the enlightenment of the community from which we expect to achieve the most radical prophylaxis against neurotic disorders."[107] Nonetheless, the desire to align psychoanalysis with social reform persisted. As late as February 1913, Freud would suggest to Ferenczi that the next round of analytic discussions at international meetings center on "the social role of neuroses."[108] But when James Jackson Putnam argued that analysts needed to join with other social forces, Freud responded: "Your complaint that we are not able to compensate our neurotic patients for giving up their illness is quite justified. But . . . this is not the fault of therapy but rather of social institutions . . . the recognition of our therapeutic limitations reinforces our determination to change other social factors so that men and women shall no longer be forced into hopeless situations. Out of our therapeutic impotence must come the prophylaxis of the neuroses."[109]

The fact that analysis was poised between an institutional integration that would destroy its unique contribution and a marginality that could destroy its effectiveness came to the fore at the Nuremberg congress. Whereas the first analytic congress, at Salzburg in 1908, had been an informal gathering, a *Zusammenkunft,* this one gave birth to an independent organization, the International Psychoanalytic Association. Although the aim was to win professional legitimacy, the result was long-term marginality.

Freud's hopes for a permanent organization focused on Jung. Although only in his mid-fifties and in excellent health, Freud was obsessed with the idea of finding a successor. By mail, Freud and Ferenczi concurred that "the [psychoanalytic] worldview does not lead to democratic equalizing": there should be an *elite* along the lines of Plato's rule of philosophers."[110] At the congress they fought to have Jung elected president for life, to give him the power to approve all articles or speeches before presentation or publication, and to have the association's center moved to Zurich. When the Viennese responded to Freud and Ferenczi's proposals by threatening to walk out, Freud offered a compromise: Jung would direct the association, Freud would edit the *Jahrbuch,* Adler would replace Freud as president of the Vienna Psychoanalytic Society, and a new periodical, the *Zentralblatt,* would be edited by Adler and Stekel in Vienna.

At the very moment at which Freud moved to win professional acceptance, he was forced to acknowledge the marginality of analysis. During the conference, he went to the hotel room where the Viennese were meeting without him. Speaking privately to his earliest followers, he explained what he saw as the dilemma: "Most of you are Jews, and therefore incompetent to win friends for the new teaching. Jews must be content with the modest role of preparing the ground. It is absolutely essential that I should form ties in the world of great science."[111] Bitterly, he reminisced: "When I assured my patients that I knew how to relieve them permanently of their sufferings they looked round my modest abode, reflected on my lack of fame and title, and regarded me like the possessor of an infallible system at a gambling-resort, of whom people say that if he could do what he professes he would look very different himself. Nor was it really pleasant to carry out a psychical operation while the colleagues whose duty it should have been to assist took particular pleasure in spitting into the field of operation."[112]

Dramatically throwing back his coat, he declared: "My enemies would be willing to see me starve; they would tear my very coat off my back."[113]

Caught between sectarian isolation with its attendant self-pity and mass popularity with its threatened loss of identity, the sectarian—and Jewish— character of the movement deepened. The year before the Nuremberg congress, while visiting America for the Clark lectures, Jung had developed a theory of an American "Negro complex." Now he presented it at Nuremberg. The Negro's example, he believed, posed a threat to the "laboriously subjugated instincts of the white races."[114] Problematic as this was, it was soon adapted for another purpose. "The persecution of blacks in America," Ferenczi wrote Freud, occurs because "blacks represent the 'unconscious' of the Americans. Thus the hate, the reaction formation against one's own vices. Along with the circumcision/castration complex, this mechanism could also be the basis for *anti-Semitism.* The free, 'fresh' behavior of the Jew, his 'shameless' flaunting of his interest in money, evokes hatred as a reaction formation in Christians, who are ethical not for logical reasons but out of repression. It is only since my analysis that I have understood the widespread Hungarian saying: '*I hate him like my sins.*' "[115] Freud needed little convincing. After the Nuremberg conference, he exploded to Ferenczi about a journal attack that cited his theory of anal eroticism as an example of Viennese decadence: "Viennese sensuality can't be found elsewhere!" Reading between the lines, Freud continued, "We Viennese are not only pigs but also Jews. But that wasn't printed."[116]

The retreat to the predominantly Jewish character of the early analytic group also affected the *Männerbund.* Abraham and Jung had always disliked each other and, after the Nuremberg conference, began an open break.[117] Freud wrote to the "consanguineous" Abraham: "Racial relationship brings you closer to my intellectual constitution, whereas he, being a Christian and the son of a pastor, can only find his way to me against great inner resistances. His adherence is therefore all the more valuable." In another letter he urged Abraham to "develop a little masochism and be prepared to endure a certain amount of injustice. . . . You may be sure that if my name were Oberhüber my new ideas would . . . have met with far less resistance."[118]

The formation of an international organization, the appointment of Jung as its president, the appointment of Adler as the head of the Vienna branch: Freud experienced these primarily as hollow achievements. Returning from the congress, he was depressed. "No doubt, it was an extraordinary success," he wrote Ferenczi, but there was something wrong at its core. "We are both a little at fault." His own aversion to the Viennese circle and Ferenczi's "brother complex," Freud noted, "have had the combined effect of making us shortsighted."[119] A few months later he wrote Jung, "When I look at the situation objectively, I believe I went ahead too fast. I overestimated the public's understanding of the significance of ΨA [psychoanalysis]. I shouldn't have been in such a hurry about founding the I.A. My impatience to see you in the right place . . . also had something to do with it. To tell the truth, we should have done nothing at all."[120]

With the congress, Freud lost his last chance for integration into European psychiatry. At Nuremberg he clashed with an assistant from Kraepelin's clinic in Munich, Max Isserlin. As a result, Kraepelin later attacked Bleuler for his association with Freud.[121] Bleuler, who had wavered for years, told Jung he would not join the society. It was too narrow, too exclusive, one cannot "sit down with everybody." In subsequent letters to Freud, Bleuler elaborated, saying he was "less tempted than you to sacrifice my whole personality for the advancement of the cause" and insisting: "This 'who is not for us is against us,' this 'all or nothing' is in my opinion necessary for religious sects and political parties . . . but for science I consider it harmful."[122] Jung, like Freud, was downcast. "The break with Bleuler has not left me unscathed," he wrote Freud. "Once again I underestimated my father complex."[123]

In fact, the International Psychoanalytic Association had barely been founded before it began to fall apart. Jung never wanted to play the part to which Freud had assigned him, and their difficulties began immediately after the congress. By 1910 the marginality of psychoanalysis was inscribed, and it never lost the traces of its early years. Its classical period would be dominated by three great schisms: one between Freud, Jung, and Adler in the 1910s; a second involving Ferenczi and Rank in the 1920s; and a third between Anna Freud and Melanie Klein in the 1930s and '40s. Afterward, in the period following World War II, its greatest popularity set the stage for its most intense rejection.

Chapter Four

FROM PATERNAL AUTHORITY
TO NARCISSISM

Charismatic fervor is rooted in the attempt to come into contact
with the very essence of being, to go to the very roots of existence,
of cosmic, social and cultural order, to what is seen as sacred and
fundamental.

—Shmuel Eisenstadt, *Max Weber on Charisma and
Institution Building*

Because they aimed at formulating universal laws and moral principles,
Enlightenment thinkers never tried to develop a psychology that could
explain the particularities of an individual's life. Instead, taking Newton's
corpuscular theory as their model, they sought to isolate the elementary
building blocks of mind in general, aspiring to become the "analysts of the
soul," as physicists and chemists were the analysts of the inorganic world.[1]
By contrast, twentieth-century modernity was oriented toward interiority
and subjectivity from the first. Rejecting the idea that the mind was
made up of associated ideas built out of elementary sensations, modernist
thinkers in philosophy and the social sciences, like modernist artists and
writers, sought to evoke deep structures of interiority that could be accessed
only from within.

In the years before World War I, psychoanalysis was already beginning to
serve as a guidepost to this modernist reorientation toward subjectivity, even
among intellectuals who rejected it. Epitomizing the shift from the rational
individual of the Enlightenment to the singularity and contingency of modern personal experience, Freudianism suggested that a dynamic and individual *un*conscious lay beyond the *pre*conscious structures of experience,

myth, and collective representations that modernist thinkers described. In addition, psychoanalysis had a uniquely mass appeal. Like electricity, film, and the automobile—the characteristic innovations of the second industrial revolution—the Freudian unconscious symbolized the freedom of individuals from the confines of space and time. Nonetheless, until the 1920s, psychoanalysis did not have a real alternative to the Enlightenment notion of the rational individual. Indeed, psychoanalysis had no worked-out conception of individual psychology at all.

It took a series of convulsive schisms in the years immediately following the Clark lectures to produce such a conception. In part, these schisms revolved around Freud's place in the analytic movement, and whether there was room within the movement for alternatives to his views. But the schisms also had an important intellectual content: what was the proper attitude to take toward the ego or "I" (*das Ich*), the site of subjectivity, the arena of personal experience, and the only means of gaining access to the interior world? As a consequence of the schisms, the question of the ego or "I" moved to the center of analysis, paving the way for an engagement with the threefold promise of modernity, including, now, the third promise: democracy.

For Freud's first critic, the Viennese doctor Alfred Adler, the ego or "I" was the whole of psychology. Its primary concerns were status, social comparison, and competition. Against Freud's emphasis on sexuality, Adler stressed the importance of aggression, the desire to enhance one's place in the world. In his view, the ego was haunted less by sexual wishes than by the anxiety of being displaced by a rival or humiliated by a putative equal. A social democrat and a feminist, Adler insisted on the social roots of the ego's aggressivity, resentment, and insecurity. Assuming that individuals had an innate sense of dignity and self-respect, he posited that the "neuroses" arose from some insult or affront, including the affront of poverty or discrimination. Like the many American thinkers who welcomed his teachings, he viewed modernity as the unfolding of a long-term process of democratization, and he wanted to assimilate psychoanalysis to reformism, social-democratic politics, and a results-oriented psychotherapy.

For Carl Jung in Zurich, by contrast, the ego was nothing. He despised its petty hurts, its "oversensitivity," its prickliness, its obsession with its standing in the world, all traits for whose tolerance he eventually blamed the Jewish character of psychoanalysis. A man of aristocratic temperament, Jung believed that a valid life was one lived in the shadowed valleys of what he came to call the collective unconscious, the great cosmic formations that harbor the archetypes—transhistorical structures such as the Great Mother, the Anima, and the Shadow. Viewing modernity through the prism of loss and decline, he sought to halt its impoverishment of meaning by restoring contact with the sacred. Accordingly, he aimed to assimilate psychoanalysis to myth and religion, although not to any organized religion of his time.

Freud rejected both approaches. Like Adler, Freud took the aggressivities, hurts, and resentments of the ego seriously, but he did not equate what he called the ego's "secondary revisions" or "rationalizations" with the whole of the psyche. Like Jung, Freud believed that the ego resided in the shadows of a vast realm available only to obscure introspection, but he called that realm the id, not the cosmos. Whereas Adler critically affirmed the ego's strivings, and Jung contemptuously dismissed its weakness, Freud sympathetically grasped its vulnerability, which he traced to the infant's dependence on a primal object. In contrast to animals, which are born with predetermined instincts that lead them to the objects they need, humans depend for their survival on the care of other humans throughout a prolonged period. Because of this lengthy period of biological helplessness, according to Freud, "the value of the object which can alone protect [the infant] is enormously enhanced."[2] Unlike both of his critics, then, Freud placed an intensely personal need for "objects" at the center of his conception of the ego.[3]

Forced to respond to Adler and Jung, Freud went back and rethought the foundations of psychoanalysis, turning the hypotheses of unconscious, infantile wishes, sexuality, and primary-process thinking into a systematic, dynamic, developmental theory. Only in 1912 did he conclude that the Oedipus complex was the "nucleus of the neuroses." In 1913 he put forth his first model of pregenital (oral and anal) stages of sexual development. In 1914 he produced his first attempt at a theory of the "I": his essay on narcissism, a precursor to his theory of the ego, soon to supplant the unconscious as the most important concept within psychoanalysis. Ultimately, as we shall see, Freud's attempt to formulate a theory of the ego or "I" was inextricable from the attempt to transform psychoanalysis into a theory based on the existence of two sexes, an attempt that began to preoccupy analysts during World War I.

But the conflicts with Adler and Jung did more than spur theoretical innovations. They also transformed the psychoanalytic movement. Until the schisms, psychoanalysis was effectively a *Männerbund.* The object of global projections and idealizations, Freud stood at the intersection of an impossible dilemma: he embodied the authority he claimed to analyze. The schisms brought this dilemma into focus, leading Freud to write *Totem and Taboo,* with its startling portrait of the primal father and his murder. Obviously colored by the *Männerbund's* father-son and brother-brother conflicts, *Totem and Taboo* coincided with a further narrowing of the analytic sect: the formation of a secret "Committee" and the expulsion of Jung. In the longer term, however, the schisms set in motion a different trajectory. As the theory of narcissism sparked attempts to understand sexual difference, the effect was to open psychoanalysis to women. The schisms, then, not only presaged the development of the theory of the ego; they precipitated the transformation of the sectarian analytic *Männerbund* into the relatively democratic and mixed-sex movement that we find after World War I.

Born to a middle-class Jewish family, Alfred Adler came from the same milieu as Freud and even attended the same gymnasium. A convert to Christianity, an eye doctor, and a member of the Wednesday Psychological Society since 1902, he first formulated his ideas as a theory of "organ inferiority." In medicine, "organ inferiority" referred to the weakness of a particular organ, such as nearsightedness or a stammer. Sensitivity to the weakness, Adler argued, led the individual to dwell upon it, producing "excess" cerebral activity, a "psychic superstructure." The short person's "Napoleonic complex" is an example.

Adler was married to a Russian-born socialist, Raissa Epstein. An acquaintance of Leon Trotsky, who was then in exile in Vienna, and therapist to another important Bolshevik, Adolf Ioffe, Adler was a regular contributor to Vienna's socialist daily, *Arbeiter-Zeitung*. His first book, as we saw, concerned the social and economic causes of physical illnesses. Clearly, then, Adler's focus on the ego's struggle to gain self-respect made a political statement. In 1909 he argued that psychoanalysis supplied the instinctual complement to Marxism. Sensitivity to slights, Adler reasoned, provided the real basis for class consciousness.[4]

Adler also tied the psychology of inferiority to the struggle for women's rights. Influenced by his wife, and by the close links between social democracy and the women's movement, he reformulated his earlier idea of organ inferiority in terms of the sexologists' conception of bisexuality. By "feminine," he wrote, the neurotic "understands almost anything that is bad, certainly anything inferior." Attempting to "avert what [he or she perceives to be] pathological," that is, passive or "feminine," the neurotic engaged in compensatory forms of self-assertion that Adler called the "masculine protest." Any physician, Adler held, can observe the masculine protest in the transference. When the neurotic loves or needs, he or she feels "I am a slave." As a result, the neurotic patient is in constant rebellion against the physician

Alfred Adler: theorist of the
"masculine protest" (c. 1911)

on whom the patient depends. All neuroses "are derived and obtain their power from the battle between the feminine foundation and the masculine protest." Moreover, Adler added, "one must assume the presence of a masculine protest in all women, without exception," since the devaluation of woman is "the driving force in our civilization." In June 1911 Adler restated his view: "There is no principle more generally valid for all human relationships than 'on top of' and 'underneath.'"[5]

Freud liked Adler's original theory of organ inferiority, especially its emphasis on compensatory strivings, and at first there was much agreement between them. The breach occurred over Adler's insistence that the *invariable* motive for repression was the need to guard against feelings of inferiority. At the most fundamental level, Freud rejected the assumption that the driving force in human life was the wish to repudiate a passive or subordinate position. In a 1914 essay, he used a graphic image to develop a counterargument. He asked his readers to consider one of the fundamental situations in which desire is felt in infancy: a young boy observing the sexual act between his parents. The boy will want to put himself in the place of what he takes to be the active man *and* in place of what he takes to be the passive woman. "Between them, these two impulses," Freud wrote, "exhaust the pleasurable possibilities of the situation." However, Adler's "masculine protest" described only the first.[6] Yet the desire to submit, to be passive or "under," was at least as powerful a source of motivation as the boy's desire to be "on top," and, further, was more likely to be unconscious.

Freud also criticized Adler for "sexualizing repression." By this Freud meant that Adler had cast the repressing force as masculine and the repressed wish as feminine. This, of course, had been Freud's own way of thinking in the 1890s, but now he admonished Adler. "The concepts 'masculine' and 'feminine' are of no use in psychology," Freud stated, since "we do not know what we should call masculine and what feminine." The proper dichotomy was "not between masculine and feminine but between libido and repression." Neurosis in a man, Freud continued, was sometimes the result of the man's desire to disown or overcome currents he perceives as "feminine," but not always. As a counterexample, he cited a case that anticipated his 1914 theory of narcissism. In this case, a "young man was convinced of his great charm (of which he had been persuaded in childhood) and now he thought everyone would do everything to please him." He was not a megalomaniac compensating for feelings of inferiority. On the contrary, there was no trace of a feeling of inferiority.[7]

Freud did not take up for another three decades Adler's idea that the masculine protest had special relevance to women, nor did he appreciate the value of Adler's interpersonal orientation. Nonetheless, Freud acknowledged that Adler's criticisms directly spurred the development of psychoanalysis. In a 1909 letter to Jung he conceded that he had so far described only the repressed, which he called "new and unknown." Adler, in contrast, deserved credit for calling attention to the existence of a repressing agency. But Adler, Freud argued, took the repressing agency's desire for "self-respect" and "independence" at face value, whereas in fact the ego was often making a virtue of necessity, compromising with infantile wishes while assuming an air of command.[8]

Ideally, psychoanalysis should have been able to include both men. But the intense fantasies and group processes triggered by the Clark lectures, along with Freud's insecurities and Adler's ambitions, led to a split. In January 1911 the Vienna Psychoanalytic Society, successor to the Wednesday Psychological Society and by this time large enough to meet in an auditorium, debated the two men's views. In June Adler resigned from the society and founded a new group called the Society for Free Psychoanalysis, which would hold its meetings on *Thursday* nights.[9] According to Hanns Sachs's wife: "The feud broke up long-standing friendships. Wives stopped talking to each other."[10] So bitter did Freud remain that in 1912, when Lou Andreas-Salomé began attending Adler's meetings, Freud pressured her not to discuss either man's work at the other's meetings.

Although the split further isolated psychoanalysis from the medical and scientific community, it also helped consolidate its identity. In correspondence Freud elaborated: one can see, he wrote Jung, how Adler "tries to force the wonderful diversity of psychology into the narrow bed of a single aggressive 'masculine' ego-current," as if a child "had no other thought than to be 'on top' and play the man."[11] Calling Adler's "a nice little case of paranoia," he added: "So far it hasn't occurred to him that with such a theory there can be no explanation for the real sufferings of neurotics, their feelings of unhappiness and conflict."[12]

Needless to say, Freud's ad hominem comments, most of them private, do not constitute an argument. However, they shed light on his and his circle's thinking. Adler, the Freudians believed, could not accept his subordinate relation to Freud. Even in public meetings, Freud complained, all we hear from Adler is "wanting to be on top," "safeguarding," and "covering one's rear."[13] Ferenczi elaborated on Freud's view: "Now I . . . understand Adler's hate theories; he doesn't want to love, and therefore he has to hate and thinks he is being hated; in so doing he projects all this into his theories. It is strange, and certainly no coincidence, that both Fliess and Adler emphasize *bisexuality* in this way; the [unanalyzed] homosexual origin of their character is expressed therein."[14] In such formulations, the ambivalent legacy of psychoanalysis was foreshadowed. As the Freudian circle questioned the sharp gender dichotomies of nineteenth-century culture, it unwittingly helped lay the basis for a new heterosexual/homosexual dichotomy.

After the break with Freud, Adler went on to world fame. When he died in 1938, Freud wrote Stefan Zweig: "the world really rewarded him richly for his service in having contradicted psycho-analysis."[15] But Freud's spiteful remark was too self-centered to do justice to the world's motives. Adler's conception of an ego that strives aggressively for status and recognition, regarding all forms of dependency and expressions of weakness as signs of inferiority, articulated deep currents then taking shape in the new mass democracies: one-sided desires for empowerment and control. Accordingly, when the historian Warren Susman tried to describe the dominant tone of Fordism and mass culture in the United States in the 1920s and '30s, he could find no better rubric than "The Age of Adler."[16] Meanwhile, psychoanalysis itself would incorporate many of Adler's ideas, especially his focus on aggression, which led to the discovery of what was called "the defensive functions of the ego."

As the conflict with Adler was ending, the conflict with Jung erupted. From the start of their essentially epistolary relationship, Freud had idealized Jung. For his part, Jung played the role of an "intermittently unruly . . . favorite son," calling his differences with Freud "neurotic ingratitude."[17] After the Clark lectures, Jung established relations with American doctors critical of Freud, such as Trigant Burrow from the University of Virginia.[18] He made a considerable amount of money in America and returned for regular visits. On the eve of the Nuremberg congress, Freud had panicked over whether Jung would make it back from America in time. "What will happen if my Zurichers desert me?" he asked Pfister.[19] After the congress, as we saw, Jung immediately began disappointing Freud's hopes.

While Adler sought to link psychoanalysis to social democracy, Jung wanted to connect it to myth, especially to the great symbol systems that lay beneath organized religion. His chief interest had always been in Freud's explanations of such meaning-creating mechanisms as condensation and displacement. He believed that while the conscious mind operated through Kantian categories such as space, time, and causality, the unconscious operated symbolically, through analogies, likenesses, and formal resemblances. Freud's contribution, he thought, was the discovery of a symbolic or "analogical" method of organizing mental signs.

Interest in the symbol-creating character of human psychology was intrinsic to modernism and common among analysts. James Jackson Putnam, who shared Jung's emphasis on symbolism, made it the point of his keynote address at a psychoanalytic congress in Weimar in March 1911. Psychosexual conflicts, Putnam argued, expressed the contradiction between man's participation in the infinite and his confinement to the temporal and transitory. Thus, analysis needed to be embedded in idealist philosophy. Freud referred to Putnam's speech as a "decorative centrepiece that all look at but none touch," but Freud was wrong.[20] Putnam's views were shared by many, including American and French psychopathologists who subscribed to a theory of the subconscious: Frederic Myers and his followers in the London Society for Psychical Research; the Geneva psychologist Théodore Flournoy, an early hero of Jung's; and Flournoy's cousin, Édouard Claparède. Adler's 1912 *The Nervous Character* also stressed the symbolic function—the "prospective tendency"—of neurotic symptoms. So did Herbert Silberer's *Problems of Mysticism,* which argued for a dual line of interpretation—psychoanalytic and "anagogic," the latter meaning prospective, forward-looking, or spiritual.[21]

Since Jung thought that the purpose of psychoanalysis was to restore "man" to his place in the cosmos, he never accepted Freud's idea of sexuality. Regularly threatening to "pump" Freud for a definition of libido, Jung complained that "so far I haven't come up with anything satisfactory."[22] His own view, which he communicated to Freud as early as 1906, was that "in nature . . . we see only a continuous life-urge, a will to live."[23]

In 1912 Jung published a long two-part essay, "Transformations and Symbols of the Libido," in the *Jahrbuch,* in which he combined his ideas concerning a unitary, nonsexual life force and the symbol-making character of human psychology with a new stress on the importance of the mother. Drawing upon the anthropology of Aryan solar myths, he posited an early matriarchal age reproduced developmentally in the infant's early attachment to the mother. Incest, he informed Freud by letter, characterized "the early, cultureless period of matriarchy" when the father's role was "purely fortuitous."[24] Behind incestuous wishes are "higher" motives focused on the mother. Among these are the wish to become a child again, as expressed in the myth of being reborn. The Freudian emphasis on sexuality diverts attention from the symbol world in which humans actually live.[25]

Like Adler, Jung drew on sharp gender distinctions in place of Freud's emphasis on the dynamic or personal unconscious. In contrast to Adler, however, Jung was appalled by modern tendencies toward women's rights. After the Clark lectures, he informed Freud that "American culture really is a bottomless abyss; the men have become a flock of sheep and the women play the ravening wolves—within the family circle of course. I ask myself whether such conditions have ever existed in the world before. I really don't think they have."[26]

Be that as it may, Jung found much support for his views in the United States. A 1912 visit there precipitated his break with Freud. Smith Ely Jelliffe invited him to give a series of lectures at Fordham University. "Jung's summons to America shouldn't be anything good," Freud wrote Ferenczi. "A little, unknown *Catholic* university run by Jesuits, which Jones had turned down."[27] In his lectures Jung expanded on his essay. "Obtaining pleasure is by no means identical with sexuality," he asserted.[28] The value of the concept of libido lay "not in its sexual definition but in its energic view."[29]

Just as Adler felt that psychology should be linked to the cultures of social democracy and feminism, so Jung felt it had to be rooted in the deep ethical currents that constitute a *Volk.* When Auguste Forel sought Jung's help in gaining analytic support for an "International Fraternity for Ethics and Culture"—a multi-issue reform organization—Jung informed Freud that he considered social reform "artificial." For a coalition to have "ethical significance," he continued, it "must be nourished by the deep instincts of the race. . . . An ethical fraternity, with its mythical Nothing, not infused by any archaic-infantile driving force, is a pure vacuum. . . . I imagine a far finer and more comprehensive task for ΨA than alliance with an ethical fraternity. . . . We must give it time to . . . revivify among intellectuals a feeling for symbol and myth, ever so gently to transform Christ back into the soothsaying god of the vine, which he was." By contrast, "a syndicate of interests," such as Forel's, "dies out after ten years." Freud replied, "You mustn't regard me as the founder of a religion."[30]

As the two men's differences intensified during 1912, Freud and his associates understood them in the same terms in which they had understood the conflict with Adler: both of Freud's antagonists denied infantile sexuality and the personal unconscious, while also resorting to nineteenth-century gender assumptions, and, in Adler's case, to the pre-Freudian notion of bisexuality. In addition, there was a second similarity that the circle did not notice: while both men stressed the social basis of the ego, neither grasped the discontinuity between the individual psyche and *all* group formations, a discontinuity that was itself a historical product. In both cases, the two men rejected the defining features of Freudian thought.

Freud's response to his critics stretched over several years. He began by answering Jung in *Totem and Taboo* (1912), a book that tacitly conceded Jung's insistence that psychology be based on the anthropology of myth and ritual, not simply on a theory of biological evolution of the sort Freud had inherited from sexology. But whereas Jung's conception of myth was holistic and conservative, *Totem and Taboo* foregrounded the contingency and disrupted character of modern personal life. If *Totem and Taboo* offered an alternative to Jung's emphasis on myth, "On Narcissism" (1914) provided an alternative to Adler's concern with status. Initiating the theoretical trajectory through which analysis incorporated the ego's demand for recognition, "On Narcissism" described the "I" as one element in a complex constellation of unconscious forces. In both cases, Freud sought to rebut his opponents while incorporating key elements of their critique. The result was a major expansion of the scope of analytic thought. Now, Jones wrote, analysis would finally come into its own: it would be "not a mere therapeutic measure that is to replace hypnotism, but . . . a key to the deepest problems of civilization."[31]

F̲reud had thought in terms of a "father complex" at least since the 1890s. In 1897 he had purchased the famous medieval witchcraft manual *Malleus maleficarium,* because he thought he recognized a similarity between witches and hysterics: both were obsessed with "the *pater.*"[32] His interest in archaeology, too, had been linked to his belief that there was a deep and complex history to authority. He had used the phrase "Oedipus complex" intermittently ever since writing *The Interpretation of Dreams.* During the conflicts with Jung and Adler, however, such preoccupations moved to the center of Freud's thought. In 1908 he wrote Jung that he suspected that "myth and neurosis have a common core."[33] Soon after he described himself as "obsessed by the idea of a nuclear complex."[34] Finally, in *Totem and Taboo* he announced "a most surprising discovery": that social psychology, no less than individual, "should prove soluble on the basis of one single concrete point—man's relation to his father."[35] A few years later he set aside the idea of a single father in favor of the idea that there had been a historical epoch, somewhere around the time of the Ice Age, in which "tyrannical primal fathers" ruled. These fathers, he wrote, actually did rob their sons of their "genitals if the latter became troublesome to [them] as a rival with a woman."[36] In response, the sons banded together and murdered their fathers. Remorse over the murders, Freud held, led to the establishment of the incest taboo and the patricentric family.

Freud's focus on paternal authority was not original. The early evolution of bourgeois society was premised on the the critique of patriarchal society and the attempt to establish (male) equality in the realms of politics and contract. Perhaps the most famous assertion of this idea was John Locke's seventeenth-century riposte to Sir Robert Filmer. Filmer, who supported the divine right of kings, argued that paternal power was absolute and always explicitly included the power to castrate. Locke, in contrast, defended the "natural authority" of mothers and fathers within the family but rejected Filmer's notion of "Fatherly power," calling it "this strange kind of domineering Phantom . . . this *New Nothing*."[37] Locke's claim to the contrary, however, the shadow of paternal authority still fell everywhere in Freud's time. It was implicit in the equation of autonomy with masculinity; it haunted the intimate relations of men and women, in which femininity was confused with submissiveness; and it buttressed "modern" economic and political authority, so that employers intimidated subordinates, whites bullied freedmen, and imperials overwhelmed colonials, just as if the father had never been slain by market liberalism and the democratic revolutions.

Nevertheless, Freud's conception of authority differed from both Filmer's and Locke's. In the traditional conception, authority derived from founding moments, social contracts, or divine revelations. By contrast, Freud traced the roots of authority to traumatic events: momentous occurrences that overflowed the capacity of men and women to remember them and that were repeatedly worked over by unconscious processes in the course of time. The myth of the primal murder was such an event. Freud evoked it to explain authority's irrational dimension—for example, the bizarre behavior of such figures as Lanzer, Schreber, and Pankejeff. Lacking a fuller explanation of how that dimension had been transmitted from its prehistorical origins, Freud pointed to the dynamics of the family. Every child relived the unrecoverable primal murder in the Oedipus complex, because every child *wanted* to commit incest and to murder the parents. Every child also recapitulated the resolution of the Oedipus complex, the acceptance of the incest taboo, in the latency period. What analysts observed in the neurotic's unconscious—dread of passivity, fear of castration, guilt—were the pathogenic aftereffects, the repetitions and returns, that occurred when this resolution remained incomplete.

For Filmer and Locke, moreover, the father was the representative of authority *tout court*. For Freud, by contrast, the father was also the primal object on whom all infants depend. Behind authority, then, lay dependence. Closely connected to Freud's insight into the traumatic bases of authority, his focus on the fear, need for protection, and love that runs through the relation to the father greatly modified the tradition of political thought—and social reform—that descended from Locke. Later Freud became increasingly aware of the role of the mother, eventually realizing her centrality. Yet he never dropped his counterintuitive view of the father as the protector of early childhood. Only that view makes Lanzer's, Schreber's, and Pankejeff's internal conflicts and ambivalence comprehensible. They not only feared their father, they loved him, and their love deepened and complicated their fear. True, Freud drove this point home with his fantastic and speculative myth of the primal murder. But what made his "just so" story, as Alfred Kroeber called it, worth listening to were the case studies of the aforementioned individuals whose lives had been profoundly distorted by their love for, and fear of, their fathers. Moreover, in Freud's account, if the primal sons had not also "loved" their father, they never would have been able to turn their murder into a creative, civilizing act.

Totem and Taboo also served to clarify Freud and Jung's differences concerning the relation of psychology to myth and religion. Jung was by no means a sectarian Christian. At the time of the schisms, he was interested in Teutonic mythology; soon thereafter, he broadened his perspective to include non-Western religious and mythological symbols such as the mandala. But Christian or not, he was certainly anti-Semitic. The Jew, he wrote in 1912, because of his "extraordinary fixation to the family," was fixed at the level of "uncontrolled incestuous feeling . . . ungovernableness and surrender to the emotions," whereas "the Redeemer and Physician of that time was he who endeavored to educate man to the sublimation of incestuous libido."[38] Understandably, then, Freud viewed *Totem and Taboo* as a rebuke to Jung, writing Abraham that "the totem job . . . will serve to cut us off cleanly from all Aryan religiousness."[39]

More was at stake than ethnoreligious sensibility. Ferenczi caught the significance of the conflict while writing a review of Jung's *Jahrbuch* articles. Jung's main concern in the articles, he told Freud, was the restoration of the individual to a place in the community. Jung, Ferenczi continued, "identifies confession with psychoanalysis and evidently doesn't know that the confession of sins is the lesser task of ΨA therapy: the greater one is the demolition of the father imago, which is completely absent in confession." Ferenczi also believed that Jung's conception of the analyst differed from Freud's. Jung doesn't want to allow himself to be analyzed, he wrote, but rather wants to remain to his patients "the *savior* who suns himself in his Godlike nature!" Being analyzed would entail exposing "his hidden homosexuality," Ferenczi explained, which appears in Jung's writings as the "Christian community" or "brotherhood." Rather than make his own homosexuality clear to himself, Ferenczi continued, Jung prefers to " 'despise' sexuality" and praise "the 'progressive function of the [unconscious].' "[40] A few months later, Ferenczi reiterated: "The *father* plays almost no role . . . the *Christian community of brothers* takes up all the more room."[41]

Freud responded by reminding Ferenczi of the significance of Enlightenment universalism and secularism: "On the matter of semitism: there are certainly great differences from the Aryan spirit. We can become convinced of that every day. Hence there will surely be different world views and art here and there. But there should not be a particular Aryan or Jewish science. The results must be identical, and only their presentation may vary. . . . If these differences occur in conceptualizing objective relations in science, then something is wrong." But Freud then suggested that Christianity's thrust was integrative, whereas Judaism's was analytic. "It was our [Jewish] desire," he wrote, "not to interfere with their more distant [Christian] world view and religion, but we considered ours to be quite favorable for conducting science. You had heard that Jung declared in America that ΨA was not a science but a religion. That would certainly illuminate the whole difference. But there the Jewish spirit regretted not being able to join in."[42] In other words, Freud maintained that scientific conclusions were culturally neutral, but the cultures that produce science, and that interpret its meaning, varied. Psychological science involved self-consciousness. It was harder for the Christian, who starts from a position (universal brotherhood and "community feeling") that represses and acts out the infantile relation to the father to engage in this science, than for the Jew, who was more self-conscious concerning his—or her—dependence.

In intensifying the regressive, sectarian, and incestuous quality of the analytic circle, the split with Jung also brought to light its *Männerbund* or male-society aspects. The most sensible observation concerning the unfolding break with Jung came from Emma Jung, who, by virtue of being a woman, was an outsider. Toward the end of 1911 she wrote Freud in confidence that she was "tormented by the idea" that Freud's relation with her husband was "not altogether as it should be": "You may imagine how overjoyed and honoured I am by the confidence you have in Carl, but it almost seems to me as though you were sometimes giving too much—do you not see in him the follower and fulfiller more than you need? Doesn't one often give much because one wants to keep much? Why are you thinking of giving up already instead of enjoying your well-earned fame and success . . . you are not so old." Freud was fifty-five. "You should rejoice and drink to the full the happiness of victory after having struggled for so long. And do not think of Carl with a father's feeling: he will grow old but I must dwindle, but rather as one human being thinks of another." Her letter concluded: "Don't be angry with me."[43]

Freud ignored Emma Jung's advice. As Carl Jung became increasingly isolated, Freud and his associates collectively came upon the idea of forming a secret, inner circle. Since the Clark conference, Freud's relations with Jones had deepened. In 1911 Freud congratulated him for, as it were, conquering "America in no more than two years."[44] The next year Jones wrote Freud that he was "a little pessimistic" about the future of analysis: Jung had effectively withdrawn, Stekel was impossible, Rank impoverished, Ferenczi rash.[45] What was needed, he urged Freud, was a small group of men analyzed by Freud personally to "represent the pure theory unadulterated by personal complexes, and thus build an unofficial inner circle." Freud was thrilled: "a secret council composed of the best and most trustworthy among our men," he exulted, "to defend the cause against personalities and accidents when I am no more."[46] Formed the next year, the "Committee," as this sect within a sect was called, included Jones, Rank, Ferenczi, Abraham, Max Eitingon, and Hanns Sachs. To mark the founding, Freud gave each man a Greek intaglio, mounted into a ring, from his collection.

Jung was still the president of the International Psychoanalytic Association. Hence, in May 1913 Freud described himself to Abraham as politically crippled. In August, the International Association met in Munich and almost dissolved as a result of the underlying conflicts. Afterward, however, Freud refrained from action so as not to "lose any position by affective motives." Explaining his willingness to let himself be advised by the four or five people closest to him, Freud remarked: "Since being taken in by Jung my confidence in my political judgement has greatly declined."[47] When Jung did resign from the *Jahrbuch* in October, Freud suspected a ploy and considered having the societies under his own control resign from the International. Jones dissuaded him, pointing out that the Americans would not understand his action. Finally, in April 1914 Jung, along with most other Swiss analysts, unexpectedly withdrew from the International.[48] Although Freud did not know it, Jung had broken down mentally as the split unfolded. Only with the onset of World War I did he begin to recover, interpreting his breakdown as a vision of the impending world catastrophe. As for Freud, he exulted to Abraham: "So we are rid of them at last, the brutal, holy Jung and his pious parrots."[49]

The Committee, in its various manifestations, served as the icon of charismatic authority within the analytic movement until the late twenties. It was then succeeded by a series of institutions and informal groups centered on Freud. The most important of these was the training analysis, the *rite de passage* of every analyst. Reverentially, all analytic literature listed (and still lists) Freud's 1909 walks with Max Eitingon as the first training analysis.[50] Through subsequent training analyses each succeeding generation relived the founding generation's transference to Freud. In the course of all its changes, analysis remained divided between a professional façade and a secret, fantasied, and ambivalent love aimed at Freud.

Ironically, at the very moment (1912) in which Freud articulated the idea of the Oedipus complex, paternal authority was giving way to a new system of social organization reflected in law, economic relations, and government. It was said at the time that the administration of men was giving way to the administration of things, but it is more accurate to say that the locus of control was shifting to science, technology, and bureaucracy. Even the settings of the case studies that followed "Dora" suggest the importance of the new administrative and managerial context. The "Rat Man" was an army officer. Schreber was trying to get out of a mental hospital. If Dora was in flight from the Victorian family, Lanzer and Schreber were fleeing mass, bureaucratic organizations, organizations that relied not on external coercion but on internalized self-control.

The shift explains both the power and the limits of Freud's prewar writings. His spectral image of a castrating father played a role for early-twentieth-century mass democracies analogous to that played by Plato's

The *Männerbund,* or "Committee," in 1922; *left to right standing:*
Rank, Abraham, Eitingon, Jones; *sitting:* Freud, Ferenczi, and Sachs

cave in antiquity or Dante's inferno in the later Middle Ages. Referring to a
past, albeit a past that was still somehow present, it haunted people's imag-
inations. In Raymond Williams's terms, the "castrating father" was a "resid-
ual imago" left over from a previous historical epoch. Freud had discovered
it just as it was losing its grounding in social organization. Under these conditions, analysis would have to adapt its theories to the new democratic
context. No issue would be so crucial to this effort as gender.

Whereas psychoanalysis had been born into a milieu in which the lines
of authority still ran between fathers and sons, the emerging world of mass
production and mass consumption was a mixed-sex world. Modernity, as
we shall see, would foster collegial relations between men and women in the
professions and intimate ones in the family. New modes of child rearing
would aim at providing boys and girls with an early, deep familiarity with
the other sex. Coeducation would become the norm. Dress codes would
shift closer to an androgynous midpoint. As the workplace expanded to
include personnel, social work, and psychological adjustment, women
would pioneer in developing therapeutic approaches that fostered a deeper
understanding of the opposite sex. Above all, as Freud's work demon-

strated, no one was simply a man or a woman; self-knowledge necessitated an understanding of both sexes. As for psychoanalysis, such concepts as castration, homosexuality, and sexual difference could scarcely be broached when discussed by men alone.[51] Insofar as it remained a *Männerbund,* psychoanalysis would never grasp the transformation of the family that gave it its power. Accordingly, the entry of women into the ranks of analysts was the single most decisive shift in its history.

The beginnings, however, were not auspicious. As late as 1907, ten years after women were admitted to the University of Vienna's medical school, the Vienna Psychoanalytic Society was still debating women's capacity to practice medicine. The responses to Fritz Wittels's paper "Female Physicians," which argued that repressed sexuality was the motive behind women's wish for an education, evoke the conflicted character of the analytic milieu. Paul Federn, a socialist, argued that "the importance of work and the concept of giving meaning to life through work have to be taken into account in evaluating women's wish to study." However, he agreed with Wittels that "it is not permissible to have women [doctors] publicly handle men's genitals." Max Graf argued that female physicians lack "the great personal influence, the suggestive power . . . indispensable for the competent physician." No physician can dispense with this bit of priesthood. Freud took an ironic attitude toward the sometimes oafish Wittels, remarking that his article "lacked a sense of justice" and failed to distinguish between repressed sexuality and sublimation. But Freud also questioned whether women would benefit from increased opportunities for education.[52]

Nevertheless, within a few years, women began to practice analysis. The first active woman analyst was Dr. Margarete Hilferding, the wife of Rudolph Hilferding (the author of *Finance Capital,* the book Lenin took issue with in his *Imperialism*). Margarete Hilferding applied to the Vienna Psychoanalytic Society in 1910. The issue was debated before she was allowed to join. Freud and Alfred Adler spoke in her favor, and the vote was twelve in favor, two opposed. She played an active role until withdrawing during Freud's conflict with Adler in 1911. The minutes of the society record her speaking on three occasions. During a discussion of a child's psychic fear of the color blue-green, she pointed out that the fear might have a real, social (i.e., not psychogenic) cause, since copper implements were frequently used in working-class households. Her second intervention must be among the earliest public discussions of the intricacies of female masturbation. Her third was a lecture on mothers' ambivalence toward their children.[53]

Hilferding notwithstanding, women still figured in analysis largely as the objects of men's sexual attention. Much of the point of Freud's early

analyses of men's unconscious submission to paternal authority was to analyze inhibitions on men's sexual relations. Thus, it was especially in the
study of the transference that sexual difference came to the fore. In fact,
many of the early analysts became involved with female patients. Gross and
Stekel were involved with several. Jones was accused of sexually abusing
patients (in one case, a child) in both England and Canada and was paying
blackmail. Jung had an affair with Sabina Spielrein, schizophrenic at the
time, while he was her doctor at Burghölzli. Ferenczi was involved for years
with two patients: Gizella Pálos, whom he eventually married, and her
daughter Elma. Writing to Freud, he remarked that "the thought occurred
to me that it is not right to use the same couch for one's occupation and for
making love . . . a person with a fine sense of smell could sense that something took place there."[54]

At first these relations resembled the classic scenario of the exchange of
women. Thus, Freud, at Ferenczi's request, analyzed Elma Pálos. Ferenczi,
at Freud's suggestion, analyzed Jones. Freud, at Jones's request, analyzed Loe
Kann, Jones's lover. First Jones wrote Freud gratefully: "I have much less
tendency to abase myself before her as previously, and after all no woman
can altogether demand this in her heart from a man, in spite of friend
Adler."[55] But, in contrast to the classic *Männerbund,* loyalties formed
between men and women. Thus, Loe Kann's analysis with Freud led her to
separate from Jones, and Jones's relations with Freud actually deepened as a
result. Freud was also able to form a good, paternal relationship with Spielrein while at the same time reassuring Jung, who had been terrified about
Freud's reaction. Nevertheless, Freud counseled Jung: these experiences
"help us to develop the thick skin we need and to dominate 'countertransference,' which is after all a permanent problem for us. . . . The way these
women manage to charm us with every conceivable psychic perfection until
they have attained their purpose is one of nature's greatest spectacles."[56]

In the absence of a genuinely mixed-sex community of analysts, analytic
thinking remained one-sided. Nevertheless, even before the large-scale entry
of women into their ranks, the nearly all-male community of analysts was
struggling to redefine psychoanalytic theory so as to incorporate the difference between the sexes. Thus, in 1909 Karl Abraham asked Freud whether
he was convinced that the father was always the predominant influence in
psychological development. In some of his analyses, Abraham said, the
mother plays the key role; in others, the father. It seems to depend on individual circumstances. Freud agreed: "I have previously believed the parent
of the same sex to be more important for the person concerned, but can reconcile myself to greater individual variations."[57]

The beginnings of a transition to a worldview that included both sexes, as well as the beginnings of the theory of the ego, occurred with the formulation of the theory of narcissism. Beginning in 1909, Freud had used the concept of narcissism as a virtual synonym for homosexuality, but as the intensity of his conflicts with Adler and Jung waned, he began to apply it to female sexuality as well. Two new relations with women provided the catalyst. One was the aforementioned Elma Pálos, whom Freud saw in analysis in 1912 and (unethically) discussed with Ferenczi. In a letter to Ferenczi that contains Freud's first tentative schema of female sexual development, he wrote that he had brought to light Elma's disappointment with her father, her identification with him, and her "striving to do to others what she has suffered through him." But now he noticed another "surface current" (*Oberströmung*) that had "mobilized repression without accomplishing anything proper itself." Connected with the image of her mother and "genuinely feminine," meaning that it was directed toward men, this current proved resistant to analysis. Two weeks later Freud wrote again to Ferenczi: "Things have come to a total halt with [Elma] and I think I know where, in narcissism."[58]

Soon Freud was arguing for a connection between narcissism and female psychology. Lou Andreas-Salomé, a Russian writer in her fifties who attended meetings of the Vienna Psychoanalytic Society from October 1912 to April 1913, was another source for this idea. Andreas-Salomé brought Freudian analysis into contact with the Viennese feminist circle of Helene Stöcker, but she was also "one of Europe's leading *femmes fatales,*" known for her relations with Nietzsche and Rilke, as well as for her 1910 treatise, *Die Erotik.*[59] An only girl with five older brothers, Andreas-Salomé recalled in a memoir that "the feeling of being open and trustful and tied to men by fraternal bonds was so evident for me in the family circle that it radiated out to all men in the world."[60] Andreas-Salomé not only wrote about narcissism; she is said to have served as one model for Freud's portrait of female narcissism in his "On Narcissism," written in "seventeen delicious days" during a 1913 trip to Rome.[61]

In a letter to Ferenczi, Freud called the essay "the scientific settling of accounts with Adler."[62] The view of life reflected in the Adlerian system, he continued, "was founded exclusively on the aggressive impulse; there is no room in it for love." By contrast, the theory of narcissism described the personal unconscious in libidinal and affective terms. Whereas earlier Freud portrayed the mind in terms of a conflict between self-preservation and sexuality, he now wrote that "narcissism and egoism . . . coincide; the word 'narcissism' is only intended to emphasize the fact that egoism is a libidinal

Lou Andreas-Salomé: one prototype for
the theory of female narcissism (c. 1914)

phenomenon as well."[63] Narcissism, or self-love, Freud believed, was a stage
in the development of sexuality. Whereas the earliest sexual aims were fragmentary and uncoordinated, narcissism, in which the baby takes the "I" as
his or her own love object, represented a first, but transitional, synthesis,
presaging object choice. To prove that such a stage existed, Freud offered
many examples, including autoeroticism, paranoia, megalomania, hypochondria, sleep, and pain, as well as the apparent self-sufficiency of actors,
criminals, humorists, cats, beautiful women, and, especially, "his majesty,
the baby." Whatever the differences between these phenomena, Freud
wrote, taken together they suggest a stage in the evolution of love in which
the human being is his or her own object.[64]

"On Narcissism" initiated the process that would be at the center of psychoanalysis in the postwar world: the complication and radicalization of the
threefold promise of modernity, beginning with the first and most basic of
these promises—autonomy. For the Enlightenment, let us recall, autonomy
meant liberation from external authority via universal reason. At the time
of the schisms, by contrast, autonomy was acquiring a more personal and

psychological cast. Whereas Jung regarded this shift as a sign of modernity's superficiality, and Adler viewed autonomy solely in terms of status anxiety, Freud's theory of narcissism highlighted the passive, regressive, and utopian constellations in which early personal life first appeared. With its strong focus on the need to be loved, it recognized the importance of passive strivings and thereby opened them to critical reflection. Problematizing the "I" by situating it in a larger, unconscious psychological field, the theory of narcissism paved the way for the new conception of *personal* autonomy pioneered by psychoanalysis in the 1920s.

In addition, the theory of narcissism led Freud to elaborate on his refusal to base psychology on "masculine" and "feminine" currents. Earlier, when we examined Freud's final case history of a man, the "Wolf Man," we saw that while Pankejeff had spent much of his life degrading women, Freud argued that Pankejeff's true feelings were passive and masochistic. But Freud had not then been able to explain why "masculinity," or the masculine protest, was so important to the patient. The essay on narcissism suggested an explanation. Not simply the fear of castration but the desire to preserve his narcissism motivated Pankejeff's insistence on his masculinity. The ego, Freud concluded, "has no sexual currents, but only an interest in its own self-protection and in the preservation of its narcissism."[65] "Masculinity," he later added, was an "empirical and conventional" cultural ideal, not a libidinal force at all.[66] In the 1920s, as we shall see, psychoanalysis converged with a new approach to gender equality, one that subordinated gender difference to personal individuality.

Finally, the theory of narcissism contributed to a critical approach toward modern democratic society. During the stage of narcissism, Freud argued, we develop an idealized image of the self. But this image also "has a social side; it is the common ideal of a family, a class or a nation." That which the individual "projects ahead of him as his ideal is merely his substitute for . . . the time when he was his own ideal."[67] Just as the concept of transference implied a critique of hierarchical authority, so the concept of narcissism implied a critique of the forms of group identity that develop in democratic societies: groups based on an idealized identification with others—that is, groups made up of people who follow the same leader, who belong to the same nation or religion, who have the same gender or sexual orientation, or even, in the context of mass culture, are caught up in the same passions. In such groups, every member is presumed equal. Exclusion supplants subordination as the method of control. Thus, the theory of narcissism also paved the way for the psychoanalytic critiques of anti-Semitism, mass culture, and fascism that flourished after World War I.

A few months after completing the essay, Freud wrote Andreas-Salomé that his depiction of narcissism would someday be called metapsychological, the word he later used for his description of the psyche in terms of agencies (id, ego, and superego) instead of regions.[68] In fact, the essay initiated the thinking that led to the revised or structural theory. Transference and narcissism may seem like different phenomena, one "interpersonal," the other "intrapsychic." But in Freud's view they were internally related. Transference was unconscious attachment to a parental figure; narcissism was "libidinal cathexis of the self." But narcissism also developed through *identification* with the parents, specifically, as Freud later wrote, with the parents' own idealized self-images. Accordingly, if on the one hand, the theory of narcissism led to the realization that identification was the basic means through which the ego developed, on the other hand, it encouraged a more object-relational point of view. One year after writing the essay Freud criticized a manuscript of Abraham's for emphasizing instincts (sadism and anal erotism) without bringing out "unconscious object cathexis."[69] In "Mourning and Melancholia" (1915), he described mourning with the phrase "the shadow of the object fell upon the ego," suggesting the process by which the ego would be built up out of lost or abandoned love objects. Such formulations anticipate Freud's later revisions.

Freud had written "On Narcissism" in an exultant state, but World War I soon intervened. Tracing the German military fortunes in the paper daily, Freud was at first as caught up by it as he had been during the Franco-Prussian War, when he was a boy. By December 1914, however, he described himself to Ferenczi as living in a "primitive trench."[70] "What Jung and Adler have left intact of the movement is now perishing in the strife among nations," he wrote Jones.[71] In the same month he wrote Andreas-Salomé: "I and my contemporaries will never again see a joyous world. . . . And the saddest thing about it is that it has come out just as from our psychoanalytic expectations we should have imagined."[72] In a dream, Freud saw his son at the front: "His face or forehead was bandaged."[73] By 1917 he described himself as neutral in the struggle between the Entente and the Quadruple Alliance. The only thing that gave him any pleasure was "the capture of Jerusalem and the British experiment with the chosen people."[74] Besides writing "Mourning and Melancholia," Freud used the enforced leisure of World War I to write a set of metapsychological essays, most of which he later destroyed. In some random notes titled "Thoughts for the Times on War and Death," he expressed bewilderment in the face of worldwide irrationality. The war, he conceded, required more explanation than analysis was able to provide.

Freud's study

The Great War, as it was then called, spelled the end of the nineteenth-century liberal dream of reason, *Bildung,* and inner development that Schorske evoked through the statue of Athena. It convinced all Westerners that there were unconscious pathogenic elements in civilization, as well as in individuals, and that a new conception of the human psyche was necessary. On the eve of the war, Stravinsky's *Rites of Spring* had provoked riots in Paris. In 1916, after the war had raged for two years, the first dada performance was given at the Café Voltaire in Zurich. It was a contrapuntal recitative in which three voices spoke, sang, and whistled simultaneously, along with background sounds, banging, and sirens. Hugo Ball later noted, "The human voice represents the soul, the individuality in its errant journey accompanied by demonic guides. The noises provide the background—the inarticulate, the fatal, the determining . . . a world that threatens, strangles and destroys, whose speed and noise are inescapable."[75] In the same year, the apparently endless Battle of the Somme came to symbolize what seemed to be the destructiveness and paralysis of Western civilization. Nonetheless, a genuine cultural break was beginning to take shape, and psychoanalysis would be at its center.

Part Two

───────

FORDISM, FREUDIANISM, AND THE THREEFOLD PROMISE OF MODERNITY

Chapter Five

THE GREAT WAR
AND THE BOLSHEVIK
REVOLUTION

A generation that had gone to school on a horse-drawn streetcar now stood under the open sky in a countryside in which nothing remained unchanged but the clouds, and beneath these clouds, a field of force of destructive torrents and explosions, was the tiny, fragile human body.

—Walter Benjamin, *Reflections*

The Great War was the first total war. Centered in Europe, it was global in scope. Battles were fought in city streets as well as country fields; civilians perished along with infantrymen; women participated alongside men; colonials fought alongside their rulers. The air and sea, as well as the earth, were polluted. Precipitated by imperialist conflicts over colonies and markets, as well as over the disintegration of the older empires, the war's conflicts persisted throughout the interwar period, with fateful implications for psychoanalysis.

In the course of the war, Western civilization died and was reborn. No longer could anyone doubt the furies that underlay it. Ten million people were killed or maimed during five years of combat: two million casualties per year, six thousand per day. In 1916 the Battle of the Somme claimed a half million casualties in four months; the ten-month Battle of Verdun, seven hundred thousand. To an age not yet inured to mass slaughter, the destruction was impossible to grasp. What overwhelmed contemporaries was not so much the unprecedented scale of the disaster as the defensive stalemate symbolized by the trenches. A new psychic as well as geographic landscape resulted: caves, exploding mines, the fear of being buried alive,

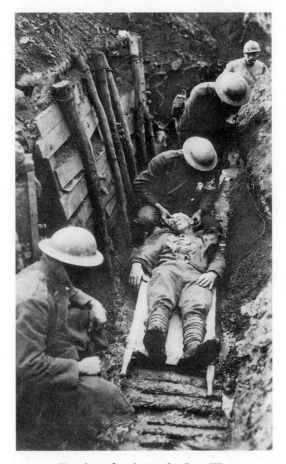

Trench warfare during the Great War

deafening sound and vibration, the insidiousness of gas, disorientation, fragmentation, the lack of visual clues, the disappearance of the distinction between night and day, identification with the enemy, the narrowing of consciousness. Stalemate also bred new images of escape: the aviator, the equation of wounds with flowers, an obsession with the sky.

The war not only shattered the nineteenth-century liberal worldview, it transformed the identities of those who lived through it. "No one will come out of this war who has not become a different person," wrote one soldier. Anyone who returns "will have become different in every respect."[1] After Picasso saw Braque off to fight in 1914, he commented, "We never saw each other again," meaning that they were so different afterward. For Camille Mauclair, a French art critic, the war "dug a trench between yesterday's ideas and those of today. . . . We have all been thrown outside ourselves by a tremendous shock."[2] Peter McGregor, a British soldier, wrote to his wife: "I am all right—just the same as ever—but no—that can never be." Marc Boasson, a French infantryman, admitted to his wife: "I'm changed terribly. I didn't want to tell you about the frightful weariness that the war has produced in me, but you force me to. I feel crushed, diminished."[3]

The war also transformed women's identities. On the home front, vivid, detailed descriptions of rape and violation regularly filled the newspapers. Women's suffrage became a war aim.[4] When Vera Brittain began nursing at the front in 1915, she had "never looked upon the nude body of an adult male," but "from the constant handling of their lean, muscular bodies," she not only found herself at home with physical love but also was led "to think of the male of the species not as some barbaric, destructive creature who could not control his most violent instincts but as a hurt, pathetic, vulnerable, patient, childlike victim of circumstances far beyond his control."[5] The war, Ernst Jünger summarized, was "father of us all." When it ended, he commented: "Never before has a generation stepped out into the light from a door so dark and immense as from out of this war."[6]

The war triggered the vogue for psychoanalysis that marked the 1920s, but the ground had already been prepared by the second industrial revolution. In nineteenth-century Europe, the sense of personal identity had been rooted in class membership. For the aristocracy, class and family relations coincided. For the bourgeoisie, identity corresponded to an ethical ideal: "individual effort (culture, moral tenor), family effort (profit, patrimony), social effort (propriety, personal merit), political effort (authority, competence)," one Frenchman wrote.[7] And for the working class, identity derived from the workplace and from the Social Democratic party with its leisure-, family-, and community-centered activities. In each case, class connoted a way of life rather than a set of interests. All this changed in the wake of the Great War. The war led European states to rationalize their economies, introduce planning, and attempt to balance the claims of business and labor. Laissez-faire gave way to corporatism. Increasingly, men and women saw themselves as bearers of interests rather than as members of classes with moral identities. But interest could not moor identity in the way that class had. As a result, new forms of personal identity replaced those based on class.

The war also underlined the sense of vulnerability, with its roots in early infancy, that was at the heart of analysis and that connected it to the contingency of personal life. It focused attention on the dangers that Freud traced to the darkest, most private, and earliest sources of family life: the instincts. The war's violence, and the sense of total crisis to which the violence was linked, also gave rise to two deeply irrational political currents whose history became entwined with that of psychoanalysis. The first was Bolshevism, which insisted on the priority of history and social practice, just as psychoanalysis insisted on the priority of the individual. The other was fascism, which appealed to individuals as consumers, as people with savings accounts, or as members of a national audience, rather than as workers. Fascism not only served as a reminder of the role that violence plays in modern society but, when combined with mass anti-Semitism, led to the destruction of continental European analysis.

As the war ended, analysis became decisively intertwined with "modernity," "the light" into which Ernst Jünger claimed the younger generation now stepped. The term "modernity," ubiquitous in the early twenties, encompassed far more than artistic modernism. Bound up with a vast expansion of personal life, the modernity of the 1920s entailed a radically new acceptance of contingency and a new, ethical awareness of subjectivity, especially among the young. Courage and honesty in facing oneself were highly prized. Few things seemed more contemptible than hypocrisy. This attitude sometimes seemed apolitical: what counted was the individual, not one's class, race, or gender. But it could deeply affect politics, as in W. E. B. Du Bois's reproach to Booker T. Washington: "The way to truth and right lies in straightforward honesty, not in indiscriminate flattery." The dominant tone, analytic in spirit, was antiromantic. Since the war, such terms as "honor" and "glory" had become obscene, Ernest Hemingway noted; henceforth, the artist's proper subjects would be "the concrete names of villages, the numbers of roads, the names of rivers."[8] Nevertheless, the artist remained an exemplar of personal life. When Proust rewrote what he regarded as his overly sociological first novel, *Jean Santeuil,* he commented in his journal: "I knew perfectly well that my brain was like a rich basin to be mined, wherein lay vast and extraordinarily diverse precious beds. But would I have time to exploit them? I was the only person capable of doing it."[9]

To many, Freudianism symbolized the new, modernist ethic of personal life. Certainly, Freud seemed to epitomize the Zeitgeist with statements like "All those who are able to overcome their own inner resistance to truth will wish to count themselves among my followers and will cast off the last vestige of pusillanimity in their thinking."[10] Shedding its sectarian trappings, analysis became an influential profession and a mainstay of social organization, affecting psychiatry, advertising, and film. At the same time, its inner life, the practice of analysis, also changed. From the almost exultant discovery of the unconscious, attention shifted to resistance, the death instinct, and the sense of guilt. Thus, the dialectic of absorption and marginality took a new turn.

The Great War was the first revelation of the catastrophic potentialities inherent in modernity. Preparing to meet its dangers involved a profound rethinking of human psychology, in the arts, political thought, and public opinion. The importance of psychoanalysis to this rethinking first became apparent when the "war neuroses" burst on the scene, signaling the decline of an older warrior ethic, a revolution in sexual and gender roles, and a massive shift toward psychological thinking.

"Shell shock" (*Granatschock*)—the experience of men so shattered by the war that they could not function—gained widespread public attention in 1915.[11] Within a few months, hundreds of thousands of sufferers were counted on both sides. As the term suggests, shell shock was originally explained as an impairment of the nervous system resulting from an explosion, but as incidents multiplied this hypothesis began to crumble.[12] At a 1915 medical congress in Hamburg, the symptoms of shell shock were successfully removed by hypnosis. By the end of the year, 40 percent of the British injuries in the combat zone were being diagnosed as psychological in origin.[13] Even so, many army psychiatrists rejected the turn toward psychology. Treating shell shock as their predecessors had treated hysteria, they described it as a weakness or malady of the will, introducing such terms as "greed neurosis" and "pension-struggle neurosis" in order to undermine its validity. Treatment by electric shock or nakedness, they promised, would increase "the activity of the individual in unheard of fashion."[14]

Shell shock signaled the psychological devastation precipitated by the war, a devastation that the older psychiatry was unable to comprehend. As one soldier wrote, "Whoever has been in these trenches for as long as our infantry . . . must at least have lost feeling for a lot of things. Too much of the horrific, too much of the incredible has been thrown at our poor chaps. . . . Our poor little brain simply can't take it all in."[15] Ernst Simmel, a young German student of Freud's, elaborated: "It is not only the bloody war which leaves such devastating traces . . . it is also the difficult conflict in which the personality finds itself. . . . Whatever in a person's experience is too powerful or horrible for his conscious mind to grasp and work through filters down to the unconscious levels of his psyche. There it lies like a mine, waiting to explode."[16] Across the Maginot line, a French medical student, André Breton, had an even more pregnant insight. Treating a traumatized

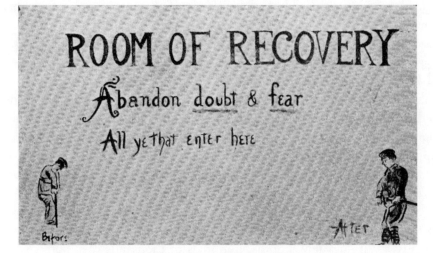

Shell shock and its treatment: "Before" and "After" (1919)

soldier who believed the war was a fake, the wounded cosmetically made up, the corpses rented from medical schools, he began to formulate what he called surrealism.[17]

The situation was ready-made for psychoanalysis. Because it fully accepted the psychological dimension, it could present itself as the humane, noncoercive alternative to the older psychiatry. All of Freud's close associates worked with shell-shock victims. Abraham headed a clearinghouse for psychiatric cases on the eastern front. Ferenczi organized the psychiatric section at a military hospital in Budapest. Ernst Simmel was in charge of a psychiatric field hospital in Posen. Viktor Tausk served as a psychiatric expert at a military court in Lublin and as an advocate for soldiers court-martialed as deserters.[18] Abraham exemplified their approach: "I disregarded all violent therapies as well as hypnosis" in favor of "a kind of simplified psychoanalysis."[19] Meanwhile, Simmel complained that nonanalytic psychiatrists "make a torture of the treatment."[20] "Fate would seem to have presented us . . . with an unexampled opportunity to test the truth of Freud's theory of the unconscious," summarized British doctor W. H. R. Rivers.[21]

Psychoanalysis was welcomed not only because of its psychological theories; its unique approach to gender was equally important. By 1916 psychiatrists' favored explanation for shell shock was the soldiers' enforced "passivity." According to Rivers, shell shock was rooted in the fact that "men in the trenches were often passive and helpless for long periods of time."[22] For W. M. Maxwell, a "high degree of nervous tension is commonest among men who have . . . to remain inactive while being shelled. For the man with ordinary self-control this soon becomes a matter of listening with strained attention for each approaching shell, and speculating how near it will explode. . . . An hour or two . . . is more than most men can stand."[23] The British War Office also concluded that the primary cause of shell shock was "prolonged danger in a static position." Such explanations seemed vindicated when the incidence of neuroses plummeted after the German offensives of 1918.[24]

"Passivity," of course, was a code word for femininity. Contemporary military psychiatrists viewed shell shock as a failure of masculinity, just as earlier psychiatrists had viewed hysteria as a failure of femininity. Garfield Powell, a British army diarist incensed by antiwar talk during the Somme offensive, wrote: "Shell shock! Do they know what it means? Men become like weak children, crying and waving their arms madly, clinging to the nearest man and praying not to be left alone."[25] Captain McKechnie in Ford Madox Ford's *Parade's End* pleaded: "Why isn't one a beastly girl and privileged to shriek?" Even though Freud had broken with the idea that masculinity was an independent psychological factor, the same language could be found among analysts. At the Budapest psychoanalytic congress of 1918, Abraham noted that at the front soldiers are forced to endure peril through "a purely passive performance." As a result, they "show the traits of complete feminine passivity in the way they abandon themselves to their suffering. In their symptoms they relive over and over again the situation which caused the outbreak of their neurosis, and try to gain the sympathy of others."[26]

The war had been possible only because an older, aristocratic, warrior ethic centered on masculine honor, self-sacrifice, and physical force still seemed viable in 1914. When the war turned out to be a matter of mass, insensate violence rather than individual heroism, the older ethic wore thin. Shell shock was the symptom of this fraying.[27] In spite of Abraham's language, psychoanalysis led the way in breaking the spine of the older ethic, with its valorization of self-control and of the strict difference between the sexes. The magnitude of the change is well captured by the novelist Pat Barker, in her reconstruction of W. H. R. Rivers's reflections as he began to apply analytic methods:

> In leading his patients to understand that breakdown was nothing to be ashamed of, that horror and fear were inevitable responses to the trauma of war, and were better acknowledged than suppressed, that feelings of tenderness for other men were natural and right, that tears were an acceptable and helpful part of grieving, [Rivers] was setting

himself against the whole tenor of their upbringing. They had been trained to identify emotional repression as the essence of manliness. Men who broke down, or cried, or admitted to feeling fear, were sissies, weaklings, failures. Not *men*. And yet he himself was a product of the same system. . . . In advising his young patients to abandon the attempt at repression and to let themselves *feel* the pity and terror their war experience inevitably evoked, he was excavating the ground he stood on.[28]

It has often been said that Freud's theory of the death instinct was a response to the Great War. There is truth to this assertion, but not the simple, reflexive truth that is usually intended. Rather, shell shock raised several problems for the older theory, leading to its thoroughgoing reformulation.

For one thing, the priority of an external, environmental factor in precipitating the neurosis was obvious. The problem was in the soldier's present experience, not in some repressed or infantile past. How was this to be explained in light of the theory of the unconscious? In addition, the war neuroses could not be explained in terms of the older repression model. Far from repressing their experiences, the victims of shell shock repeated them compulsively, for example, in dreams. How could the repetition of a painful experience be reconciled with Freud's pleasure principle, which presumed that the psyche took any path, including the bypassing of reality, to discharge tension?

Just as the reformulation of the meaning of gender had made the discovery of the unconscious possible, so it made the revised theory possible. In attempting to explain shell shock, Freud reasoned that all of its victims, regardless of their sex, repeated traumatic experiences because they were attempting to master them. In the case of shell shock, the stricken soldiers went back repetitively to the period before the shell exploded because they were attempting to prepare for a new blow. But this "preference for the active role" had more general relevance. In infancy, when the ego was still weak, even micro-upsets could be traumatic. Thus, Freud's grandson compulsively repeated the experience of being left by his mother by inventing a game in which he alternately hid and produced a ball, repeating *da/fort*, here/gone. The motive for the repetition was the child's wish to master his suffering. "At the outset," Freud noted, his grandson "was in a *passive* situation—he was overpowered by the experience; but, by repeating it, unpleasurable though it was, as a game, he took on an *active* part."[29]

Freud's sensitivity to repetition had arisen from the difficulties of the analytic situation. Patients feared being in a passive, vulnerable position that was modeled on a traumatic infantile prototype. They expressed their "resistance" to analysis by refusing to *remember* their infantile experiences; instead they *repeated* them. The repetition was a misguided attempt to master the original trauma, aimed at forestalling an event that had already occurred. The same compulsion to repeat could be observed in adult life. Freud cited a woman who married three men, each of whom died soon after. The compulsion to repeat had something "daemonic" about it. Nonetheless, it was also so general—we see it in children's play, for example—as to suggest organicity.

The repetition compulsion, Freud later wrote, "put [him] on the trail of the death instinct."[30] By this he meant to convey his belief that the compulsion to repeat unpleasant experiences, and the difficulty of remembering the unconscious prototype for these experiences, could not be fully explained by a dynamic conflict. Rather, it reflected something in the nature of the instinctual life itself, namely, its "conservative" character: its tendency to undo what the ego strove to accomplish. The death-instinct hypothesis was an attempt to explain this tendency. What Freud had previously described as the pleasure principle—the attempt to rid the mind of tension—he now described as the death instinct, a term meant to connote decomposition, entropy, and the return to an inorganic state. What he had previously understood as the sexual and self-preservative instincts he now subsumed under the term "life instincts" or *eros*, instincts that, because of their inner relation to death, also contained a regressive pull toward decomposition.

The attempt to think through the implications of trauma and repetition led Freud to the revised or structural theory. Instead of the distinction between conscious and unconscious, he proposed the division among id, ego, and superego. The ego (*das Ich*), as Freud began to conceive of it during the war, was still the "I" of narcissism, a love object for the instincts. But he increasingly also thought of it as an agency within the mind that mediated between the instincts and the outside world. In both senses, the ego was endangered by "shocks" external to it. These shocks could come from the outside world, or they could be eruptions from within, albeit a "within" external to the ego. If in war the main danger was an external "shock," Freud wrote, in peace the enemy against which the ego defended itself was normally *eros* or the libido, "whose demands seem to it to be menacing."[31] Anxiety (*Angst*), which Freud had previously described as repressed sexuality, he now viewed as a signal that a shock was coming. Trauma occurred when the anxiety signal failed.[32] Ultimately, he predicted, the focus on trauma would help explain the severe neuroses and the interpersonally constructed psychoses, notably paranoia.

Thus, the war set psychoanalysis upon a new path. It wrote finis to the Victorian view of the family as a "haven in a heartless world" by situating trauma and repetition at the core of sexual and emotional life. Self-preservation, which had disappeared with the theory of narcissism, would soon be restored to a central place but given a different—defensive—inflection. The practice of analysis was about to shift from the interpretation of the unconscious to the uncovering of the resistance. Because the dread of passivity seemed so powerful, the passive, "feminine" elements in women's love would appear difficult to comprehend. From a current of thought that coexisted easily with social democracy and social reform, psychoanalysis was evolving into a theory that found its deepest applications in the attempt to understand fascism.

Two years after the war ended, Thomas Mann, reading a newspaper review of Freud's *Beyond the Pleasure Principle,* wrote in his diary that the book signaled the "end of Romanticism [including] a weakening and dying of the sexual symbolism that is virtually identical with it."[33] Mann's note went to the heart of the matter. Romanticism, especially in its German variant, did indeed exemplify an older exaltation of the self. The sexual symbolism to which Mann referred was the goal of transcendence, of the merger of the self with a great, all-encompassing event such as the war. Although Mann was still ambivalent about Freud's thought, in the course of the twenties he came to see it as a bulwark against what he regarded as the rebirth of romanticism in twentieth-century Germany, namely, National Socialism, itself another product of the war.

The Great War was a catastrophic upheaval amid which utopian currents flowed. The Bolshevik revolution, by contrast, was a utopian upheaval that contained a catastrophe. Ironically, the war and the revolution implied each other. For years the men and women of Europe had sent their sons into trenches, face-to-face, with the sole intent of killing one another, and with no hope of victory or retreat.[34] For years they had watched them fall from the air in flames, or drown slowly in "the dark recesses of the sea."[35] The original appeal of the Russian Revolution came not only because Lenin understood the depth of the crisis but because he appeared to have a way to act upon it. Destructive though the Bolsheviks were, Robert Musil confided to his diary, "[o]ne must concede one thing to them: they have looked into the abyss."[36]

Marxism and psychoanalysis had crossed paths before—for example, in the period leading to the Nuremberg conference—but the Bolshevik revolution inspired a new field of relations. The reason was a hidden strain of likeness. Like psychoanalysis, Bolshevism was a product of the second industrial revolution, whose technological achievements seemed to enable the leap into communism. Just as the war inspired the hopes for communism, so it inspired faith in psychoanalysis. The moment of deepest abyss was also the moment at which the two currents first touched. After the Bolsheviks seized the Winter Palace in Moscow in 1917, uprisings followed in Vienna, Prague, Germany, and Bulgaria. In Hungary, Communists briefly took power. As a result, the first analytic congress since 1913 was held at the invitation of the Béla Kun Communist regime in September 1918. Inspired by the war neuroses—the new Hungarian government planned to build a clinic to treat them—the regime reserved an elegant new hotel, the Gellert, for the visiting analysts and provided a special steamer for trips up the Danube.[37]

The Budapest congress adopted two resolutions that shaped the postwar history of analysis: first, to prepare for "mass," that is, publicly financed, therapy, and second, to require that every analyst be analyzed.[38] Both resolutions arose from the crisis provoked by the war. The first was based on the idea that psychotherapy should be considered an entitlement. In Hungary the Communist government nationalized hospitals, sanatoriums, and drug companies, sponsored free medical care for children, improved salaries and conditions for teachers, and introduced sex education in the public schools, removing crucifixes and forbidding school prayer.[39] It assured Freud of state support for psychological clinics. As the analytic congress passed a resolution to prepare for publicly financed therapy, Freud explained: "The poor man should have just as much right to assistance for his mind as he now has to the life-saving help offered by surgery . . . the neuroses threaten public health no less than tuberculosis."[40] At the same time, analytically oriented outpatient clinics, aimed at patients unable to afford private fees, such as the Tavistock in London and Bellevue in New York, were being founded abroad.[41]

Reflecting the resolution on mass analysis, European analysis had a socially oriented cast throughout the twenties and thirties. February 1920 saw the opening of the Berlin outpatient Polyclinic on Potsdamerstraβe, financed by Eitingon, housed in a building renovated by Freud's son Ernst, and offering low-cost, government-supported psychotherapy.[42] Simmel, the head of Berlin's Socialist Physicians Union, remarked that society "makes its poor become neurotic and lets its neurotics stay poor."[43] Three years later Freud added that low-cost analysis was a social necessity since the intellectual strata, "especially prone to neurosis, are sinking irresistibly into poverty."[44] During the 1920s, 14 percent of the Berlin patients were blue-collar workers. In Vienna the figure was 24 percent, and in Budapest by the late twenties, anyone "who was ill had the right to get help."[45]

Mass analysis also meant that analysts would play an educative role as part of the social-democratic culture of the time. In Berlin the Polyclinic provided such courses as "The Psychoanalytic Theory of Crime" and "Psychoanalytical Aspects of Dealing with People."[46] In Vienna, analysts distributed *Das Psychoanalytische Volksbuch* to the working classes, while an appreciative city government offered them land on which to build an institute.[47] Siegfried Bernfeld, a prominent Vienna analyst, moved from directing the Children's Home for War Orphans to organizing the socialist Hashomer Hatzair in Palestine.[48] In England and Austria the term "applied analysis" emerged to describe analytic work in nursery schools, child-guidance clinics, teenage consultations, and social work.[49] Analysts spoke against corporal punishment, urging those who dealt with children "to reflect rather than be angry," and published such progressive and widely read works as August Aichhorn's *Wayward Youth* and Hans Zulliger's *From the Unconscious Life of Our School Youth*.[50]

In addition to endorsing public clinics, the Budapest congress also endorsed the requirement of a training analysis for every analyst.[51] The purpose of the resolution was to secure the independence of analysis by gaining control over training and licensing. It aimed to distinguish analysis both from popular techniques, for which no training was necessary, and from psychiatry, which required a medical degree. The prerequisites for becoming an analyst, according to Freud, were "psychological instruction and a free human outlook."[52] To be sure, most European analysts in 1918 were doctors, but European doctors did not enjoy the elevated status that doctors in the United States had already successfully claimed. Many analysts had no medical degree, including Oskar Pfister (minister), Hermine Hug-Hellmuth, Anna Freud, and Barbara Low (teachers), Lou Andreas-Salomé and Otto Rank (writers), Hanns Sachs (lawyer), Ella Freeman Sharpe (literature professor), August Aichhorn and Siegfried Bernfeld (social workers), and Ernst Kris (art historian). Of the eight members of the soon-to-be-founded Moscow Analytic Society, only three were doctors.[53] Although pressure to medicalize began soon after the Great War, European analysts remained broadly educated at a time when Freud, accurately, attributed the

Sándor Ferenczi and Sigmund Freud, 1918

very existence of a psychoanalytic movement "to the exclusion of psycho-analysis from Universities."[54]

The resolutions on mass analysis and on training were attempts to establish a place for analysis in the postwar world. At the same time, the congress reaffirmed psychoanalysis's austere but exalted conception of personal life. In his keynote address, Freud returned to James Jackson Putnam's desire to place psychoanalysis "in the service of a particular philosophical outlook on the world [and to] urge this upon the patient for the purpose of ennobling his mind. In my opinion," Freud said, this is "only to use violence, even though it is overlaid with the most honorable motives." Devoting his address to refuting yet again the prewar ideas of Jung and Adler, he called "psycho-synthesis" "an empty phrase" and boasted: "We refused . . . to turn a patient who puts himself into our hands in search of help into our private property, to decide his fate for him, to force our own ideals upon him, and with the pride of the Creator to form him in our own image and see that it is good." Then he added: "I have been able to help people with whom I had nothing in common—neither race, education, social position nor outlook upon life in general—without affecting their individuality."[55]

The revolutionary ethos that surrounded analysis encouraged attempts to communicate on a mass basis, but the content of the communication was respect for individual autonomy. In an article written for a Budapest magazine, Freud attempted to explain the popular appeal of analysis. Its key propositions, he wrote, were not original to it. Schopenhauer's "will" was "equivalent to the mental instincts of psychoanalysis," for example. What distinguished psychoanalysis, he argued, was not the *abstract* affirmation of its propositions but its insistence that they "touch every individual personally and force him to take up some attitude towards these problems."[56] The fact that Freudian concepts, writings, and insights were derived from the concrete practice of individual analyses was the ultimate source of its appeal.

Psychoanalysis followed a different course in the Bolshevik and the social-democratic regions of the postwar world. Its fate in the Soviet Union reflected not only the totalizing presuppositions of communism but also the predominantly peasant character of the Russian and eastern European family. In contrast, Western social democracy and psychoanalysis evolved in tandem, converging in the creation of the Keynesian welfare state during World War II.

During the Bolshevik revolution, the patriarchal family had been viewed as the "conservative stronghold of all the squalors of the old régime," but the New Economic Policy, which began in 1921, was accompanied by attempts to liberalize middle-class family life. The result was the rebirth of Russian psychoanalysis. Analytic groups sprang up in Moscow, Petrograd, Kiev, Odessa, Kazan, and Rostov.[57] In Kazan the Analytic Society published a journal on "the psychophysiology of labor." In Moscow it sponsored an experimental home for children.[58] In 1922 Soviet analysts established the world's second analytic institute, gaining the simultaneous approval of both the International Psychoanalytic Association and the Soviet government.[59] In the same year one-eighth of the members of the IPA were in the Soviet Union. The government-run Psychological and Psychoanalytic Library translated, published, and mass-distributed analytic works in cheap editions. Lenin complained that Freudianism had become a fad.[60]

The excitement reflected the Bolshevik hope that psychoanalysis could be annexed to communism. Thus, such products of the revolution as

Nadezhda Mandelstam's memoirs, Nikolai Yevreinov's Freudian-influenced "theater therapy," and Mikhail Bulgakov's *The Master and Margarita* contrasted psychoanalysis to hypnotism, a relic of despotism associated with the old regime and symbolized by the power of Rasputin over the czar's family. According to Fyodor Stepun, "We walked into every office as if it was an institute of psychoanalysis," meaning a new world of words and gestures that needed to be decoded, not controlled from above. Mikhail Bakhtin and Sergei Eisenstein undertook lifelong dialogues with Freudian thought.[61] In 1923 Bernard Bykhovskii called for a "Freudian Marxism," sparking a widespread debate. Younger neuropsychologists, such as Alexander Luria and Lev Vygotsky, argued that "psychoanalysis decisively breaks with the metaphysics and idealism of the old psychology, and gives a new perspective . . . [that] of an organic process, which unfolds in the human organism taken as a whole."[62]

Nonetheless, even in the heyday of the New Economic Policy, there was a fundamental contradiction between Bolshevism and psychoanalysis. The difference was not only a matter of free speech; the Bolsheviks lacked a concept of personal life. Leon Trotsky exemplifies the problem. In the whole history of analysis, there has been no other political figure of comparable rank who was so seriously involved with analysis. He met with Alfred Adler and other analysts in Vienna between 1909 and 1911. He attended analytic meetings and studied analytic texts with Adler's Russian patient Adolf Ioffe, a Bolshevik. Despite Stalin's increasing enmity, he covertly supported the analytic societies, funneling resources to them and diverting attacks. Yet Trotsky rejected the very idea of personal autonomy.[63] After the Bolshevik coup, he boasted that "the revolution had dealt with [Ioffe's] nerves far better than psychoanalysis. . . . [It] lifted him [and] straightened him out." Trotsky's interest in analysis intensified when he faced an unanticipated problem: the resistance of the Russian people to Bolshevism. Marxism, he reasoned, had only subordinated the *social* unconscious; it needed psychoanalysis to subordinate the *psychological* unconscious.[64] Thus, for Trotsky, the unconscious needed to be socialized and subjected to control.

In the West the experience of revolutionary councils inspired a different line of reasoning, one that sought to use psychoanalysis to complicate the socialist worldview. Thus, Otto Gross, citing the communal feeling produced by the councils, argued that in a society based on maternal love, aggression would disappear.[65] Paul Federn's "The Fatherless Society" ("Die Vaterlose Gesellschaft")—delivered as a talk to the Vienna Psychoanalytic Society in 1919—analyzed Vienna's political struggles in terms of the relation to the father. The majority Social Democrats, "strongly tied to the basic attitude of the son," allied with bourgeois militarists in hope of gaining protection, while the revolutionary Spartacists turned the "original tie to the father . . . into . . . instinctual hate."[66] In England, where the war wound down without revolutionary councils, M. David Eder, a psychoanalyst, an activist in the British Labour Party, and a Zionist, described the League of Nations as an attempt to create coequal authority. Noting that "the band of brothers does not easily exist without a father," he insisted that questions of authority had to be reconstrued in light of the increased political activity of women, which was bringing the mother into the political realm. Over time, Eder's lecture proved prophetic. When war clouds gathered again, the League of Nations arranged for Albert Einstein and Sigmund Freud to correspond over the causes of war, and invited analysts such as Edward Glover to lecture on the war's instinctual roots.[67] During World War II, analysis moved to the center of a democratic, antifascist consciousness.

Ultimately, the close connections between Marxism and psychoanalysis reflected their common origins in utopian wishing. Their utopianism differed, however. For Marxists, personal life was an illusion, a mere diversion from the dream of a communal society in which nothing would be private and everything would be shared. The appeal of psychoanalysis, by contrast, reflected its unprecedented understanding of the depth and value of personal life. While psychoanalysis drew deeply from utopian sources, its inner character was profoundly anti-utopian, constantly striving to leaven the dreams of personal life with the grain of reality. The fact that in developed societies, where the family was no longer a unit of production, personal life was itself a social product was grasped by neither current. Marxists did not realize that without respecting individual autonomy they could never develop a convincing conception of socialism, while analysts were unable to see how quickly the "merely external" political realm would affect their project—and, indeed, destroy it.

Freud dealt with the dual impulses at play in psychoanalysis— utopianism and realism, respect for the power of the instincts and belief in the possibilities of reason—by tacking between them. His sense of being an outsider, which he never lost, was his strongest ally. Certainly, he had only guarded sympathy for what he called in 1926 "the great experiment in civilization . . . now in progress in the vast country that stretches between Europe and Asia."[68] Told by a Communist that seven years of war, famine, and misery would be followed by seven years of peace, prosperity, and harmony, he conceded that he believed the first half of the prophecy. But he had equally little sympathy for the American "invasion" of Europe that began in 1917. "America the good Samaritan healing the wounds of war-torn Europe" was how the publicity expert J. Ward Moorehouse in John Dos Passos's *1919* put it, adding, with a funny, deprecatory smile, "And the joke of it is, it's true."[69]

Freud's alienation from politics increased with the Paris Peace Conference. Although Woodrow Wilson understood that the war necessitated a new understanding of psychology, along with new forms of communication and knowledge, Freud regarded Wilson as a fool and lent his name to a muckraking psychobiography by William Bullitt, Freud's patient, who apparently quit the American delegation at Versailles when Wilson refused to consider Lenin's offer to confine Communist rule to Moscow and St. Petersburg in return for a place at the peace table.[70]

Analysis was Freud's only motherland. While all the world was celebrating the armistice, he wrote Ferenczi, referring to the shell-shock episode, "Bad luck, no sooner had [analysis] begun to interest the world . . . than the war comes to an end." Ferenczi responded stoically, "Our position as outsiders will continue for the time being."[71] Of course, there were other reasons for pessimism. Freud, like many Austrians, was devastated financially; he accepted potatoes for fees and hired an English-language tutor in case he had to emigrate to avoid financial ruin.[72] The influenza epidemic, which killed his daughter Sophie in 1920, the death by cancer of his patron and friend Anton von Freund, and more distant events such as the suicide of Viktor Tausk led Freud to ask Jones: "Can you remember a time so full of death?"[73]

As the war ended, Freud tried to reunite the Committee—Abraham, Ferenczi, Rank, Jones, Eitingon, and Sachs—but found it torn by rivalries. Rank had moved to Cracow, assumed the editorship of the official publication of the Austrian Army, and married, all of which strengthened his independence from Freud. After the war, he managed the publishing house Internationaler Psychoanalytischer Verlag, considered by Freud the most important institution of analysis.[74] In May 1919, during the Communist interregnum, Ferenczi had finally received a professorship and became director of the Batizfalvy sanatorium. Three months later, the Communists were ousted, and Ferenczi's medical license was revoked for "collaboration."[75] Until the late twenties he lived a kind of floating existence. Freud wanted to set him up in Vienna and thought he might replace Jones as the international representative of analysis, but neither hope materialized. Meanwhile, Jones and Rank were at each other's throats over the Verlag.

Shaken by these and other tensions, and resolved to avoid a repeat of the prewar schisms, the *Männerbund* agreed to communicate by means of

Rundbriefe, internal newsletters.[76] They vowed that no one would leave the Committee without the concurrence of the others. Their last face-to-face meeting occurred in September 1921, when the seven men, without their families, toured the Harz Mountains in eastern Germany for a week, staying in comfortable hotels and visiting collections of antiquities. Freud read aloud a paper he had written on telepathy. Like students of the occult, he said, analysts had received "contemptuous and arrogant treatment by official science." This was not surprising, since analysis "stands in opposition to everything that is conventionally restricted, well-established and generally accepted."[77] His followers warned him that the article was too controversial to publish; he took their advice and suppressed it.[78]

Analytic pessimism notwithstanding, by 1921 a sustained mood of optimism, largely sparked by economic recovery, swept through every Western capital. Simultaneously reflecting the end of wartime horrors and the new possibilities unleashed by mass production, this was the moment in which the term "modernity" became ubiquitous. The emergence of the Labour Party in England, the beginnings of a center-Left coalition in France, and the growth of the Social Democrats in Germany encouraged the new mood. Meanwhile a new generation, born in the 1880s and '90s, had constituted itself through opposition to the war: dadaists in neutral Zurich and then in Paris, New York, and Munich; socialists in Russia, Germany, central Europe, and the United States; sexual reformers and conscientious objectors in London and Berlin; pacifist suffragists in London and New York. Among this generation, enthusiasm for psychoanalysis burst out everywhere.

Some of those who turned to psychoanalysis as the twenties began were veterans. These included most of Freud's immediate associates, as well as artists such as André Breton and Max Ernst, who returned from battle convinced that a new literature and painting had to be based on the unconscious. Blaise Cendrars, who lost an arm, and John Dos Passos, who served in an ambulance unit, returned to write about depth psychology. Siegfried Sassoon began a memoir, which culminated in his treatment for shell shock by W. H. R. Rivers. Suicidal, wounded, deranged, he recalled Rivers walking into his hospital room: "Without a word he sat down by the bed; and his smile was benediction enough for all I'd been through. 'Oh Rivers, I've had such a funny time since I saw you last!' I exclaimed. And I understood that this is what I had been waiting for."[79]

Others had been students during the war. Adrian Stephen, Virginia Woolf's younger brother, who had been studying medieval law at Cambridge, "suddenly threw the Middle Ages . . . out of the window." He and his wife, Karin, both moved to Vienna to become analysts.[80] Jean-Paul Sartre, seventeen years old and studying Descartes's "I think therefore I am" for his *bachot* degree, came upon Freud's *Psychopathology of Everyday Life*, "with its substitutions, combinations and displacements." "It took my breath away," he later wrote.[81] Another philosophy student, Theodor Adorno in Frankfurt, began a dissertation attempting to integrate Kant and Freud.[82] Wilhelm Reich and Helene Deutsch, newly minted psychiatrists, showed up at the Vienna Psychoanalytic Society for training. Jane Harrison, a classicist at Cambridge who had originally been "sickened" by Freud's "sexual mud," suddenly found that "the light broke," leading to a "sense of release. Here was a big constructive imagination; here was a mere doctor laying bare the origins of Greek drama as no classical scholar had ever done."[83]

For many, the ending of the war opened new vistas of emancipation. André Gide wrote in his journal: "Freud. Freudianism . . . for the last ten years, or fifteen, I have been indulging in it without knowing it." And then, a few lines later, the publication of *Corydon*—Gide's exposure of his own homosexuality beyond a narrow audience—is "long overdue."[84] Kurt Tucholsky, editor of *Die Weltbühne*, the leading left-wing Weimar journal, saw hypocrisy as Weimar Germany's key problem. Reforms, he wrote, "are of no use if a basic honesty (*Redlichkeit*) does not permeate the country." A picture of Freud hung in his study.[85] George Bernard Shaw, responding to the wartime banning of D. H. Lawrence's *The Rainbow*, called Freud the "fugleman" (standard bearer) for free speech.[86] Romain Rolland believed that the war betokened "the beginning of a great catastrophic era in which shall disappear a great part of our old 'white' civilization." Along with translations and biographies of Rabindranath Tagore, Swami Vivekananda, Swami Ramakrishna, and Mahatma Gandhi, he began a correspondence with Freud, centered on the problem of nonviolence. Meanwhile, Rolland's prophecies of the end of white domination were translated and published in *The Crisis*, the newspaper of America's NAACP.[87]

If one had to name the postwar book most closely tied to the intense new fascination with analysis, it would be Lytton Strachey's 1918 *Eminent Victorians*. According to Cyril Connolly, *Eminent Victorians* was "the first book of the 'twenties.' " Articulating the postwar revolt against "Victorianism," "it struck the note of ridicule which the whole war-weary generation wanted to hear. . . . Using the weapon of Bayle, Voltaire and Gibbon" against the creators of the Red Cross and the public-school system, it appeared to postwar young people "like the light at the end of a tunnel."[88] The book, Leon Edel later noted, was written in "a new kind of ink—the ink of Vienna, of Sigmund Freud."[89] A few years later Lewis Namier, emigrating from Poland to England, made his own translations of Freud and invented a new approach to political history by demonstrating that political ideologies, such as liberty, were rationalizations of deeper interests and passions.[90] Literary London also discovered Freud about 1920. According to the poet Bryher (Annie Ellerman), "People did not always agree but he was always taken in the utmost seriousness."[91]

Finally, there was the United States, alien in spirit from Freudian analysis yet already home to the largest number of analysts in the world. Just as many Americans went to Paris to write or paint after the war, so many went to Vienna and Berlin to become analysts, among them Abram Kardiner, Clarence Oberndorf, Joseph Wortis, Roy Grinker, and Ruth Mack Brunswick. As a true American avant-garde emerged, interest in Freud was at its center. Max Eastman "read Freud and every book on Freud then available in English, rehearsing" their doctrinal points and becoming "a kind of amateur specialist."[92] Floyd Dell called himself "a sort of missionary on the subject."[93] Susan Glaspell complained: "You could not buy . . . a bun without hearing of someone's complex." Sherwood Anderson reported that "all the young intellectuals were busy analyzing each other. . . . They psyched me. They psyched men passing in the street."[94] And, as noted, Lincoln Steffens recalled one evening discussion in 1911 at Mabel Dodge Luhan's Greenwich Village salon, "led by Walter Lippmann, [which] introduced us to the idea that the minds of men were distorted by unconscious suppressions. . . . There were no warmer, quieter, more intensely thoughtful conversations at Mabel Dodge's than those on Freud and his implications."[95]

Paul Johnson, reflecting a later generation's disillusionment with psychoanalysis, has described this postwar explosion of interest: "Not for the first time, a prophet in his fifties, long in the wilderness . . . suddenly found a rapt audience of gilded youth."[96] But "gilded youth" tells us more about Johnson than about Freud's postwar readers. Their interest must be understood against the background of the war. That unimaginably obscene catastrophe had also directed a shaft of light into the depths at which the global order was being remade. If, on the one hand, the war signaled an entirely new level of danger, on the other, it opened the way for unprecedented possibilities. Psychoanalysis captured both impulses and was in turn captured by them. As the fantastic productive capacities of the second industrial revolution opened onto a new promised land, the war remained in the background of people's minds. Carl Jung's recollections illustrate this. In 1926 he dreamt that he was "driving back from the front line with a little man, a peasant, in his horse-drawn wagon. All around us shells were exploding and I knew that we had to push on . . . for it was very dangerous." Later Jung analyzed his dream: "The shells falling from the sky were . . . missiles coming from the 'other side.' They were therefore effects emanating from the unconscious, from the shadow side of the mind." Awakening, he scribbled, "The war, which in the outer world had taken place some years before, was not yet over, but was continuing to be fought within the psyche."[97]

Chapter Six

FORDISM, FREUDIANISM, AND MODERNITY

Our Ford—or Our Freud, as for some inscrutable reason he chose
to call himself whenever he spoke of psychological matters.

—Aldous Huxley, *Brave New World*

Henry Ford, not Woodrow Wilson or Vladimir Lenin, proved the
great symbol of the postwar era. As a result of Ford's innovations,
capitalism's irrationality seemed to have been tamed, its great machinery
no longer turned obsessively inward to extract a surplus from factory workers but now also turned outward to create mass purchasing power. The
Americans, noted a British commentator, had "solved the elementary
problem . . . still convulsing Europe": they had created a mass-production
economy while ameliorating class conflict.[1] Because of its drive toward
planning and rationalization, many took Fordism to mean conformity,
standardization, and the rule of the machine. Paradoxically, however, it also
turned personal life into a mass phenomenon. The result was a fatal convergence between Fordism and Freudianism.

It is ironic that Henry Ford gave his name to the new epoch, since he
was a perfect representative of an older drive toward regimentation, order,
and planning. Obsessed with holding down costs, Ford began in 1914 to
monitor his workers' family life, in hopes of reducing lateness, absenteeism,
turnover, and "soldiering," or relaxing on the job. As John R. Lee, his labor
expert, said: "Mr. Ford believes, and so do I, that if we keep pounding away

Fordism and the assembly line, c. 1940

at the root and the heart of the family in the home . . . we are going to make better men for future generations, than if we simply pounded away at the fellows at their work."[2] But Fordism could not be reduced to planning and regimentation. For one thing, postwar Fordist managers encouraged a new level of personal attention to factory workers, castigating the earlier, Taylorist system of scientific management for reducing workers to cogs.[3] In addition, the iron fist of rationalization wore the velvet glove of mass consumption. Ford's "five-dollar day," which made it possible for the workers to purchase the Model T's they built, symbolized the new regime.

Mass consumption reflected the coming of age of the second industrial revolution. In the first industrial revolution the requirements of production determined the level of consumption. Thus, consumer goods were produced only in order to reproduce the labor force that produced raw materials, machinery, and factories. The second industrial revolution reversed that relationship: consumer demand drove the economy. Henceforth the goal of the system was to expand, not restrict, consumption. Expanding consumption coincided with the increased importance of the managerial class, technicians, and educated labor.

The result was a new focus on psychology. In the workplace, managers were urged to find out "what the employee thinks . . . what are the worker's satisfactions and aspirations?"[4] In the marketplace, concerted efforts to entice consumers spawned such new enterprises as advertising, film, and survey research. Radio turned the home into a concert hall, a theater, and an aural billboard. To be sure, many of the techniques that informed the new consumer economy came from nonpsychoanalytic fields, such as social psychology, behaviorism, and testing. Nevertheless, Freudianism fueled the overall drive toward psychological thinking and provided the dominant, if sometimes implicit, conception of the mind.

Mass consumption also unleashed a flood of utopian imaginings. The prewar avant-gardes had already envisioned a society no longer determined by scarcity. The futurists had identified the automobile, the defining technological innovation of the second industrial revolution, with modernity because it implied freedom from the restrictions of space and time.[5] After the war, the utopian celebration of dynamism took new forms. Advertising, credit financing, and marketing exploded. Unending "sensations" materialized: jazz, nudism, aviation, professional sports, organized crime. Artists like Picasso and performers like Josephine Baker attained unprecedented celebrity. Even in prison, the Italian Communist Antonio Gramsci was struck by the "Fordist fanfare . . . exaltation of big cities, overall planning for the Milan conurbation . . . the affirmation that capitalism is only at its beginnings and that it is necessary to prepare for it grandiose patterns of development."[6] On the eve of the Bolshevik revolution, cubo-futurist painters Mikhail Larionov and Natalya Goncharova had written: "We exclaim: the whole brilliant style of modern times—our trousers, jackets, shoes, trolleys, cars, airplanes, railways, grandiose steamships—is fascinating, is a great epoch, one that has known no equal in the entire history of the world."[7]

Fordism thus gave rise to a paradox: beginning as an attempt to regiment both work and family, it generated the utopian idea that human life need no longer be subordinated to the imperatives of production. Writing from a fascist jail cell in 1928, Gramsci brilliantly caught the relation of psychoanalysis to this paradox. Like all attempts at planned societies— Gramsci cited Campanella's *City of the Sun*—Fordism placed the sexual question at the center of its project. Attempting to produce "a new type of worker," one who subjugated "natural (i.e., animal and primitive) instincts to new, more complex and rigid norms and habits," "Fordised" industry relied upon "increased moral coercion exercised by the apparatus of the state." Coercion alone, however, could not succeed. Fordism needed Freudianism because Freudianism articulated the inner longings of the worker. Recapitulating the role played by primitivist fantasies during the Enlightenment, Freud had created "a new myth of the [noble] 'savage' on a sexual basis (including relations between parents and children)," a myth appropriate to consumer society.

The loosening of sexual restrictions during the war had supplied the soil in which this myth had germinated, according to Gramsci. After the war, mass consumption encouraged a further relaxation. Conservatives attacked Fordism for its "cold," "soulless" home life; American women, they were pained to report, no longer considered housework a *Beruf,* a calling. Gramsci, by contrast, scorned anti-Americanism and praised Fordism for producing "a new form of sexual union" shorn of bohemianism and "romantic tinsel," and "a new feminine personality" that embraced both employment and men. Nevertheless, he insisted, capitalism blocked its own emancipatory potential. Therein lay the significance of Freudianism. Freudianism inspired men and women to pass beyond Fordism's capitalist integument, but only in the realm of thought.[8]

Fordism, then, was the site of a paradox. Driven by a passion for standardization, it inspired individuality; materialist in form, it was animated by a vision of freedom. Films like King Vidor's 1928 *The Crowd* made the paradox apparent. The protagonist, John Sims, born on July 4, 1900, had a lifelong dream of becoming "special," a "big man," a dream expressed through contempt for the "losers" he encounters at work and in the streets. After numerous setbacks, he abandons his dream and accepts his place as a member of the crowd. In the final scene he takes his family to a vaudeville show as the camera fades to show the ultimately indistinguishable faces of the audience. The film's brilliance lies in the complex way it questions Sims's dream. Accepting his place in the crowd *is* a kind of triumph for Sims, as well as a heart-sickening defeat.

Postwar psychoanalysis found itself entangled in this paradox. Ultimately an attempt to turn society into a factory, Fordism worked because of a sleight of hand that led individuals to locate their real identity outside work. Psychoanalysis was Fordism's sleight of hand. A marginal, charismatic, and extra-economic force, psychoanalysis both trumped and deepened the logic of rationalization. Far from being an agent of adaptation or conformity, as often charged, psychoanalysis became so important precisely because it did foster individuality. On the one hand, it excavated pathways to an inner world and released the primary-process thinking without which rationalization would have remained external. On the other hand, it became a stable part of social organization, helping to incorporate personal life and sexuality into the very fabric of planning and order.

The relation of psychoanalysis to the family was at the heart of this paradox. With the advent of mass consumption, the family continued to lose its core identity as a productive unit based on the ownership of property. At the same time, it received new meaning as the realm of personal life, the sphere of society in which one expected to be understood and valued "for oneself." As individuals lost their sense of belonging in an integrated system of social labor, Freudianism gave them a new sense, according to which individuality was rooted in one's unconscious, one's desires, and above all, one's childhood. Thus, the economic and sociological coordinates of traditional marriage opened onto a new horizon, one suffused with ardor, mystery, and romance. Originally an agent of defamilialization, psychoanalysis subtly began to acquire a refamilializing role.

To be sure, the integration of psychoanalysis into the fabric of capitalist social organization proceeded unevenly. In the industrial working class, consumerist innovations that were expected to break down communal solidarities, such as motion pictures, chain stores, and radio, were actually adapted by families and communities in order to keep local cultures alive. Working-class personal life germinated, as Lizabeth Cohen has written, "within the intimacy of the community."[9] By way of contrast, Freudianism appealed directly to Fordism's vast new middle classes, whose members often worked in professions influenced by it.

These new professionals included "human-relations specialists," such as social workers, marriage counselors, sex-education specialists, juvenile-court consultants, and psychotherapists, on the one hand, and those who worked in the new mass culture, on the other. Freudianism was as important to the self-definition of these new professionals as Calvinism had been to capitalism's earliest pioneers. Informing their self-understanding as a "lost generation" rather than a new social class, Freudianism sanctioned their view of the family as the arena of personal fulfillment. It infused their ideas of child rearing and progressive education, which celebrated creativity and diversity. It permeated their business culture, which was prone to liken an imaginative jingle to an impulse from the verdant woods. It underwrote their group-based models of authority and organization, which described corporations and governments in terms of homeostatic self-regulation rather than top-down control. It encouraged their scorn for biologistic racism, even as it inspired the cult of primitivism that grounded their new notions of ethnicity and culture. Because of its "unmasking" characteristics, it even informed their Menckenesque contempt for mass culture and mass democracy, a contempt that was, paradoxically, ubiquitous.

The second industrial revolution's drive for control stood behind the human-relations professions. The Salpêtrière provided the template. Often directed at the working class and the poor, psychological ordering techniques aimed to preselect and pretreat the mentally ill, school disrupters, or those unfit for military service. Older techniques of managing conflict, such as law and religion, were considered heavy-handed and coercive. By contrast, analysts, as they frequently boasted, imposed nothing but simply responded to the client's desire. This, of course, made analytic techniques infinitely more effective. Encouraging "an increased flexibility of relational structures, a loosening of the familial vise," psychoanalysis helped shape many professions into conduits for relational norms.[10]

Psychoanalysis also jump-started modern office psychotherapy, premised on the then-innovative idea that personal life was an autonomous sphere that needed its own specialists. In the United States, Morton Prince described post–World War I Freudian therapy as flooding the field like a full rising tide, leaving other approaches "submerged like clams buried in the sands at low water."[11] In England, the war-neurosis episode turned the Tavistock Institute into a vanguard of socio-Freudianism. In France, the state-run Ligue Nationale Française d'Hygiène Mentale began to substitute Freudian-derived psychologies for hereditarian, "external" markers of mental illness. Analytically influenced therapists, in turn, prided themselves on "eclecticism." Freud complained of "the many psychiatrists and psychotherapists who warm their pot of soup at our fire" but "without being very grateful for our hospitality."[12]

If the psychoanalytic influence on the therapeutic professions contributed to the downward reach of the state, it also encouraged the diffusion of a newly psychological way of thinking. Increasingly the term by which psychological thinking was designated, Freudianism not only reflected but also helped construct a new object: personal experience. Inventing a new language of self-description, it introduced or redefined such words as "oral," "anal," "phallic," "genital," "unconscious," "psyche," "drives," "conflict," "neurosis," "hysterical," "father complex," "inferiority complex," "ego-ideal," "narcissist," "exhibitionist," "inhibition," "ego," "id," and "superego." In so doing, it encouraged people to regard much of what they experienced as arising within themselves, thereby contributing to the process of inward development that is the only secure basis for progress.

If the human-relations professions reflected the drive toward control, mass culture reflected the utopian impulse that accompanied and sought to escape control. But whereas psychoanalysis was directly incorporated into the human-relations professions, its contributions to mass culture were indirect. Two stand out. First, it portrayed individuals as infinitely desiring, rather than capable of satisfaction, an image that was indispensable to the growth of mass consumption. Second, it supplied the culture with a stock of mythological characters and scenarios, such as the primal scene and the Oedipus complex, which portrayed the individual at war with nature and not with history.

The idea that the unconscious constituted an insatiable but also manipulable well of desire was crucial to the development of consumer culture. Beginning with Walter Dill Scott's *The Psychology of Advertising* (1908), advertising textbooks overflowed with a debased analytic language: the "herd instinct," "mesmerization," "suggestion." The consumer, one agency head summarized, "nearly always purchases in unconscious obedience to what he or she believes to be the dictates of an authority which is anxiously consulted and respected."[13] Effective advertisements broke down consumer "resistances," added Edward Bernays, Freud's nephew and the self-professed "father of U.S. public relations."[14] When *Printer's Ink,* the advertising industry's journal, sought to summarize the history of the profession in 1938, it described its relation to the new psychology as follows: "The first advertising sold the name of the product. In the second stage, the specifications of the product were outlined. Then came emphasis upon the uses of the product. With each step the advertisement moved further away from the factory viewpoint and edged itself closer to the mental processes of the consumer."[15]

The mythmaking function of psychoanalysis—a function that led Nathanael West to designate Freud the modern Bulfinch—made its greatest contribution to film.[16] The first of the new technologically based art forms to emerge with the second industrial revolution, film became central to consumer society after World War I.[17] Whereas the prewar narrative films had been moralistic, Freudianism pervaded the mass-entertainment cinema that flourished in the twenties. The vastly popular Cecil B. DeMille films in which one marriage partner tires of the other's Victorianism and toys with the idea of an extramarital fling provide one example. In the 1923 *Flaming Youth,* "the film that packaged the 'flapper' for a mass audience," the movie star Colleen Moore was filmed reading a book by Freud. Offscreen, her publicity agents stressed that she actually did read Freud. John Barrymore prepared for a torrid theatrical production of *Hamlet* by self-consciously consulting an analyst, Smith Ely Jelliffe.[18] In Europe, Freudianism gave bite to surrealist and expressionist films, such as *The Blue Angel,* with its withering view of patriarchal authority. But in the classic Hollywood film, analysis was domesticated and ironized. In *Carefree* (1938) Fred Astaire told his reluctant patient, Ginger Rogers, "I'm only trying to help you find yourself." "If I ever get lost I'll call on you," she replied.[19]

Recognizing the entwinement of psychoanalysis and cinema, many filmmakers sought to capture analysis. D. W. Griffith's *The Criminal Hypnotist* (1908) portrayed the first movie psychiatrist. Léonce Perret's 1912 *Le mystère des roches de Kador* presented the "application of the Cinematographe to psychotherapy" as a form of "mental medicine" that worked through images. Fritz Lang's 1922 *Dr. Mabuse* centered on a psychoanalyst who used his extraordinary powers to manipulate the stock exchange, the gambling tables, and an extensive underground of blind counterfeiters, as well as to drive a patient to suicide. The film provoked Paul Federn to urge the Vienna Psychoanalytic Society to counter popular misrepresentations of analysis, but Federn's fellow analysts saw no danger. In 1924 Sam Goldwyn sailed for Europe, announcing that he would offer Freud one hundred thousand dollars to assist in devising "a really great love story," or, failing that, would get Freud to "come to America and help in a 'drive' on the hearts of this nation." Who better than Freud? queried Goldwyn, Freud with his insight into "emotional motivations and suppressed desires." The next year Karl Abraham, Hanns Sachs, and Siegfried Bernfeld were approached by Goldwyn and by the German film producers UFA for help in making a psychoanalytic film.

Freud cautioned against participation, advising Abraham that "plastic representation of our abstractions is not possible. We do not want to give our consent to anything insipid."[20] Still, in a context in which Lou Andreas-Salomé argued that film was the only "technique . . . which allows a rapid succession of images approximating to our own imaginative activity, even imitating its volatility," in which Otto Rank praised film for using the "clear and sensuous language of pictures" to describe phenomena that the speaker is "unable to render in words," and in which Hanns Sachs insisted it "would be monstrous to ignore this medium," Freud's advice was rejected. The film, *Secrets of the Soul,* was made by G. W. Pabst with Goldwyn financing and with Abraham and Sachs serving as "scientific advisors."[21] "We think we have succeeded in principle in presenting even the most abstract concepts," claimed Abraham.[22] Despite his refusal to participate, Freud praised Goldwyn for the intention of sticking "to the aspect of our subject that can be plastically represented very well, that is to say love."[23] Meanwhile, to Jones he wrote: "Perhaps we are all too conservative in this matter."[24]

Perhaps Freud *was* conservative, but psychoanalysis was not. Whereas arbiters of taste still insisted that culture be uplifting, that it encourage out-

Stills from *Secrets of the Soul* (1926)

ward, ethical, and social capacities, rather than inward, corporeal, and private ones, psychoanalysis denied that the mind could be understood apart from the body or that the moral sense constituted the steering mechanism for the psyche as a whole. Supplying, as Gramsci discerned, a new myth of the noble savage, psychoanalysis facilitated the massive democratization of culture that took root in the 1920s. At the same time analysis itself became debased. By 1917, the Hearst press had already serialized an analysis, that of Mabel Dodge Luhan, whose Greenwich Village salon had housed the earliest analytic group discussions in the United States.[25] Ten years later, William Randolph Hearst tried to get Freud to come to Chicago "at any price" to "analyze" the young murderers Leopold and Loeb.[26]

Freud never returned to the United States after the Clark lectures, but there was no lack of movement in the opposite direction. Just as nineteenth-century British hegemony over the world capitalist system rested on banking, international law, and insurance, so twentieth-century American hegemony rested on film, cars, and cheap, standardized products for the home. Because Freudianism so deeply infused the mythic structure of Fordist culture, Freudianism and consumerism became hopelessly enmeshed. Analysis seemed to exemplify the idea, as one American coed put it, that "the average young person of today is not bound by the strict conventions" of previous generations.[27] Freudianism laced Americanization with modernity. It became one of many phenomena—others include social science, analytic philosophy, and pizza—invented in Europe but transformed in the United States and then reimported.

Psychoanalysis, then, supplied Fordism with an indispensable utopian dimension, facilitating a wave of rationalization that would have been much more difficult to achieve, and very different in character, without it. Psychoanalysis, however, was not the only utopian current of the 1920s. On the contrary, the culture as a whole was caught up in the epochal upheaval of "modernity," the redefinition of what Enlightenment liberalism had called the "subject," from the locus of universal reason to a contingent individual, located in a concrete time and place, and characterized by a deeply individualized consciousness. Fordism, assisted by Freudianism, turned this conception of the individual into a mass phenomenon, especially in the United States. In doing so it vulgarized it but also politicized it, asking in effect what difference it would make if the Enlightenment subject were a woman, an immigrant, or an ex-slave. As new social movements erupted— the "new woman," the "new homosexual," the "new Negro"—their relation to analysis became important. Two sites were particularly relevant.

The first was the family at the moment at which it was being transformed into a discrete sphere of sexual tensions and personal intimacy. The second was the new mass culture, which was then taking on its demotic, global, and multicultural characteristics, and which developed a deep investment in the "primitive." Both sites witnessed a massive engagement with psychoanalysis. To be sure, the involvement of psychoanalysis with the inner recesses of family and culture bolstered its charisma and facilitated its transformation into a mass, utopian outlook. At the same time, the new social movements of the Fordist twenties were often ambivalent about psychoanalysis. After all, flappers, homosexuals, radical intellectuals, and racial modernists all drank from the same nonproductivist, charismatic, underground streams as Freud did. Believing that psychoanalysis was the carrier of a genuine discovery, the unconscious, a discovery as significant as the Calvinist discovery of the individual soul, they also often felt they understood Freud's message better than he did.

Consider, first, women's love/hate relationship with analysis, which arose from the transformation of the family. As we saw, even before the First World War, many women experienced their own role and stature as diminished when compared with that of their mothers and grandmothers, women who had labored within the family unit defined by private productive property. Thus, in a letter to Jane Addams, Charlotte Gilman described the modern woman's sense of living secondhand, of getting life in translation, of finding herself unready and afraid in the "face of experience." Similarly, the sociologist Mary Roberts Coolidge mourned her "manufacturing grandmother," who enjoyed "an immense and stimulating field of action" at a time when the family was a "miniature factory." Feminists who shared this sentiment sought the solution to the woman question in social labor and not in sexuality. Accordingly, they constituted an enormous reservoir of anti-Freudianism. Charlotte Gilman, for example, the most anti-Freudian of the early-twentieth-century feminists, believed women's exclusion from social labor was the cause of hysteria and called the "non-productive" and "parasitical" housewife "oversexed."[28]

After the war a new generation of women experienced the vogue for psychoanalysis as a further diminution. As housewives, and especially as mothers, they became the focus of the Fordist aspiration for personal happiness, responsible for sexuality, the emotional tone of family life, and child rearing. Far from being a refuge for women, the family was a workplace. Yet Freudianism encouraged the illusion that women were outside the dominant material processes and class relations of their time. Masked as a return to "natural" affections, women's responsibility for personal life rested on the ancestral equation of women with intuition and sensuality, an equation that analysis seemed to sanction. The "new mother," wrote Havelock Ellis in 1922, "regards motherhood as a relationship of loving and natural intimacy." No longer guided "by obedience to outworn traditions, she has learnt how to become the friend of her children."[29]

Nonetheless, many women were drawn to analysis after the First World War, and for reasons that specifically had to do with their condition as women. In part, this reflected women's profound interest in the transfer of production out of the household. Psychoanalysis arose along with such innovations as the refrigerator, the vacuum cleaner, the radio, the washing machine, linoleum, and indoor plumbing. Women were attracted to it for the same reason they were attracted to short hair, Kotex (invented in 1920), and aviation: it promised release from the material weight of family life. In addition, however, psychoanalysis spoke to a specific problem that postwar women faced, the problem of "women's difference," which in the 1920s came down to the question of women's sexuality.

On the surface, the prewar women's movement, focused on suffrage, had neglected "women's difference." Beneath the surface, the movement was obsessed with sexuality but understood it only in the form of sexual exploitation. English and American suffragists spoke regularly of the "sex war," called marriage "legalized prostitution," and argued that women, "denied the right to earn their living, were reduced to contracting their person for support, while men, bound by no such constraints, took advantage of a double standard." Cicely Hamilton, an English militant, became a suffragist when she encountered the story of Lucretia, the Roman woman who committed suicide after being raped, and realized that "her 'honour' was not a moral but a physical quality," which any man sufficiently brutal might take from her. Plagued by the double standard, prewar suffragists upheld the nineteenth-century presumption that women were responsible for morals. Accordingly, in both England and the United States, suffragism overlapped with woman-led campaigns against prostitution and in favor of prohibition, film censorship, and restrictions on lower-class voting.[30]

The war shattered that women's movement, in part because of the new experiences it fostered among women, and in part because suffrage victories meant that diverse demands could no longer be united in the struggle for the vote. Although many historians of women describe the postwar vogue for psychoanalysis as a "counterrevolution," the truth is that the war, and the economic changes that followed it, brought to the fore women's desires that had been obscured by the earlier movement.[31] The suffragists' achievement, especially their emphasis on women working, was not forgotten, but many "new women" of the 1920s rejected the characterization of male-female relations as a "sex war." In particular, while suffragists had insisted "that the majority of human attributes are not sexual," many women of the new generation accepted the idea that the scope of sexuality in human life was as large as Freud insisted.

They did so because they, along with men, were drawn to the new family ideal, according to which marriage involved a deeply experienced, genuinely personal sexual relation. Family size decreased and contraception usage increased as women's work outside the home expanded. Closely watched partnerships, such as those of Neith Boyce and Hutchins Hapgood, or of Louise Bryant and John Reed, pioneered the "invention of heterosexuality." Psychoanalysis crystallized the new ideal. What was new was not so much the well-documented sexual conflicts that accompanied the new heterosexuality but rather the Freudian-inspired consciousness concerning the psychosexual roots of these conflicts, and women's expectation of sexual fulfillment.[32]

Women's attraction to the new ideals of personal life and sexual freedom brought them into conflict with their mothers' generation, above all with their mothers' role as guardian of morals. Birth control, which prewar feminists eschewed because they feared it would allow men to force women to have sex, became a key demand.[33] The popular 1925 movie *Stella Dallas* portrayed the embittered mother as living vicariously through her emancipated daughter. The flapper, the *New York Times* enthused, could "take a man's view as her mother never could."[34] Ultimately, the resonance between the new woman and Freudianism was so intense as to transform analysis. Nevertheless, the Freudian impact was ambiguous. As we shall see, the abstract and utopian character of popular Freudianism facilitated its convergence with more concrete sexual ideologies. As Susan Kent has argued, "In embracing radically new—and seemingly liberating—views of women as human beings with sexual identities, many feminists . . . accepted theories of sexual difference that helped to advance notions of separate spheres for men and women."[35]

Psychoanalysis also appealed to the "new homosexual." In Harlem and Greenwich Village—not to mention Paris, Schwabing, and Chelsea—homosexual subcultures, cafés, and performances coexisted naturally with a Freudian culture. In Weimar Berlin, the city in which Freud's writings were most fully studied by the intelligentsia, Magnus Hirschfeld's Institute for Sexual Science and the Berlin Psychoanalytic Institute sponsored joint seminars. The classics of sexology, such as Auguste Forel's *The Sexual Question* and Iwan Bloch's *Sexual Life of Our Time*, were read along with *Beyond the Pleasure Principle*; and such films as *Anders als die Andern* (1919) and *Mädchen in Uniform* (1931), which circulated positive images of homosexuals, were screened on the same program with *Secrets of the Soul.* "Come to Berlin. Berlin means boys," Christopher Isherwood telegraphed W. H. Auden in London, even though in Bloomsbury, which was a center of psychoanalysis, "*ménages à trois, à quatre, à cinq*" were a regular part of the family circle.[36]

Psychoanalysis appealed to homosexuals for the same reason that it appealed to women: it stood for the emancipation of sexuality from reproduction. At the same time, homosexuals were drawn to the ideal of the same-sex community and not to what Judith Butler later called the "pathos of heterosexuality." In his World War I memoir, *Seven Pillars of Wisdom,* T. E. Lawrence described his "friends quivering together in the yielding sand with intimate hot limbs in supreme embrace," and wrote that such experiences taught him "the truth behind Freud."[37] By this Lawrence meant that Freud saw latent homosexuality everywhere, which Freud certainly did not. Similarly, according to Hans Blüher, an editor of Weimar's homosexual journal *Der Eigene,* Freud's theories implied that "beyond the socializing principle of the family that feeds off the Eros of male and female . . . a second principle is at work in mankind, masculine society [*die männliche Gesellschaft*], which . . . finds its expression in male-bonding [*Männerbunden*]*.*" Eventually, however, Blüher rejected Freud, finding him too tolerant of the "hypertrophy of the family" and the resulting "weakness in male-bonding" that Blüher associated with Judaism.[38]

For the same reason—their commitment to the same-sex community—many homosexual women of the twenties also rejected psychoanalysis. Gertrude Stein broke with her brother, Leo, as a result of his decision to be analyzed. Looking forward to an un-Freudian twenty-first century, "when everybody forgets to be a father or to have one," she disdained the self-conscious Freudian twenties, insisting that "if you write about yourself for anybody it sounds as if you are unhappy but generally speaking everybody . . . has a fairly cheerful time in living."[39] The Cambridge classicist Jane Harrison was strongly influenced by Freud, but citing archaeological evidence for mother goddesses and James Frazer's *The Golden Bough,* she likened the Freudian vogue of the twenties to the Doric invasion of pre-Homeric Greece. In both cases an "archpatriarchal *bourgeois*"—Zeus and Freud—had imposed the heterosexual family on a matriarchal, chthonic, woman-centered order.[40]

The ambivalence of flappers and homosexuals reflected the fundamental antinomies of the Fordist epoch. Psychoanalysis was bisexual in a way that homosexuality was not: it stood for identifications and object relations with both sexes, not for sexual relations with both sexes. Yet psychoanalysis as a profession was not itself fully "bisexual"; although far more progressive than most other professions, it was male-dominated and did not accept homosexuals. As a result, women and homosexuals would remain conflicted about this new myth of the noble savage.

Along with turning the family into a sphere of personal life, Fordism transformed the meaning of culture. In 1934, the American editor Henry Seidel Canby recalled his rural upbringing, writing that his small town was not Athens, but that his life had been "rich and deep." By the time he was fourteen, he had acquired "what anthropologists call a culture, which is quite different from culture. He had made himself by easy and natural experience part of a conscious, an organized, a unified society."[41] Canby's use of the word "culture" looked back to its nineteenth-century meaning, that of a whole way of life. By the twenties, however, amid the cosmopolitan, polyvocal "heteroglossia" of the great metropoles, the term had acquired a nostalgic tinge. Just as women were identified with nature, intuition, and sensuality, so the small town, the ethnic community, or the place of origins signified roots, depth, and authenticity. At times nostalgia shaded into primitivism as men and women became interested in African sculpture, Irish theater, and the Mexican Revolution, along with such primary or "primitive" realms as those of the child, the dream, and the "subconscious."

Just as psychoanalysis served as a vehicle for exploring modern family life, so it served as a vehicle for exploring modern culture. Some equated analysis with primitivism, reinforcing the myth of the noble savage, but many innovations, such as the ethnographic experiments of the surrealists, the rewriting of analytic theory in the decolonizing world, and the growth of the "culture and personality" school in the social sciences, testify to the seriousness of these explorations. Before the rethinking sparked by National Socialism and associated with Frankfurt School critical theory, the most extensive engagement between psychoanalysis and modern culture took place in New York. Uniquely cosmopolitan due to its location, its numbers and variety of immigrants, and its role as the center for the new, globally organized culture industries—such as publishing, music, and film distribution—New York was also the capital of Black America, the mother lode of "primitive" aesthetics, sexuality, and music. Housing the commingled intelligentsias of Greenwich Village and the Harlem Renaissance, it boasted more analysts than any other city in the world. Freudianism was, and would remain, central to its identity.

The overall goal of the New York intellectuals of the 1920s was to develop a genuinely American culture, emancipated not only from Europe but from New England. Thus, New York intellectuals drew on psychoanalysis in the first instance as a counterweight to Calvinism or, as its Anglo-American variant was called, Puritanism, as symbolized not only by white, New England Protestant arbiters of culture but also by their lineal descendants in the South and the West. In the 1950s anti-Puritanism fell into disrepute, largely because the scholarship of Perry Miller demonstrated the depth and complexity of Puritan religious thought. But what was at stake in the twenties was not religion but culture, specifically the hard-bitten culture of early capitalism, which seemed to have settled the country at the cost of extinguishing its spirit. Many believed that Fordism had made a new, more expressive culture possible, but that the older mores persisted, especially at the level of the family.

Drawing on Freudianism to contest these mores, intellectuals viewed psychoanalysis first as a kind of immanent critique of Puritanism, preserving the Calvinist emphasis on instinctual renunciation but shedding Calvinism's ascetic, compulsive, and hypocritical character. After all, in the psychoanalytic situation, only a distant, unapproachable, incomprehensible, analytic "God" was present, one whose dicta could not be answered but could at best be grasped internally. The keyword of analysis, Freud repeatedly insisted, was "abstinence." No advice, no "mothering," no attempts at intersubjective understanding. Only one thing mattered: not worldly success, not sensory satisfaction, not "self-esteem," but, as with the Calvinists, the state of one's soul.

In addition, intellectuals redefined the aforementioned "discovery of heterosexuality" to bring out its historical and cultural grounding. According to Floyd Dell, the New York thinker most deeply engaged with analysis, the resilience of Puritanism could be traced to the older, self-sufficient, economically based family. So long as women and young people were economically dependent on the family, paternal authority persisted. When mass production eliminated the familial basis for Puritanism, "socially acceptable mores" were transformed into neuroses.[42] Against "the old patriarchal family institution," Dell upheld "a love-marriage . . . which arose whenever and wherever property considerations were removed." Dell associated this "love-marriage" with bohemia, a Fordist innovation that the police condemned as the haunt of "radicals, Freudians, androgynes [and] narcissi" but that Dell recognized as a space in which paternal authority had receded and economic life had been reduced to appropriately minimal proportions. Significantly, Dell did not support "free love" but rather aimed to reform marriage as part of the reform of culture.[43]

The New York intellectuals also drew on psychoanalysis to encourage integrity and depth in the new mass culture itself. Amid the proliferation of small magazines and serious publishers, Van Wyck Brooks revived interest in Herman Melville and Mark Twain, victims of Puritanism whose dark views foretold Freud's. Others introduced tragedy into American theater, which until then knew only melodrama, musical comedy, and farce. Acclaiming Eugene O'Neill's proto-Freudian dramas, they likened the shallow proscenium to consciousness while the vastly larger backstage seemed like the unconscious, within which unbearable fantasies of incest, patricide, and racial tortures unfolded.[44] Initiating experimental theater through the Provincetown Players, they launched Broadway's "psychoanalytic era" with Susan Glaspell's 1916 *Suppressed Desire*.

Much of the twenties' criticism of Puritanism was aimed at making room for Jews, Italians, and other immigrants, but the intellectuals of the Harlem Renaissance—white and black—viewed the African-American experience as crucial.[45] For one thing, America had no other "folk," no "peasant soil" on which to ground a genuine culture. As W. E. B. Du Bois maintained, Black America was the sole oasis of spirit "in a dusty desert of dollars and smartness."[46] Furthermore, insofar as Puritanism signaled the dark, unconscious American past, there were no darker currents than those produced by slavery. And yet, what relevance could psychoanalysis have to a people so directly and externally oppressed, especially since psychoanalysis followed a logic of defamilialization, whereas the most determined African-American effort had gone into the preservation of the family?[47]

Nonetheless, there were two reasons psychoanalysis played a role in the Harlem Renaissance. For one thing, Harlem intellectuals were also grappling with Puritanism in the form of Booker T. Washington's ideology of self-help and respectability. As Jean Toomer, the most important African-American modernist, complained, "We who have Negro blood in our veins, who are culturally and emotionally the most removed from Puritan tradition, are its most tenacious supporters."[48] In addition, the deep embeddedness of the African-American family in African-American society encouraged the attempt to combine psychoanalysis with a theory of culture. Zora Neale Hurston offers an example.

Born in Alabama in 1891, the daughter of a sharecropper father and a schoolteacher mother, Hurston first read Freud in a Columbia University seminar devoted to psychoanalysis taught by Franz Boas in 1925. Boas taught psychoanalysis as a contrast to nineteenth-century racial science. In addition, though, Hurston was influenced by the ethnographic method itself, a method that was dialogic and interpretive but that aspired to the status of science, and that thereby paralleled psychoanalysis. She was also influenced by Edward Sapir, a colleague of Boas, who believed that analysis supplied the "invaluable kernel" of anthropology and defined culture as an unconscious resource that "embodies the national genius."[49]

After leaving Columbia, Hurston voyaged through the African-American South, viewing herself as an analytic ethnographer. According to her, the Black South's dialect, tales, humor, and folk mores constituted a "racial unconscious," meaning a collective, aural catalogue of the past, a past that was still insistently present. The racial unconscious had its own language. Thus, "the white man thinks in a written language and the Negro thinks in hieroglyphics." Her best-known work, *Their Eyes Were Watching God,* described the efforts of a black woman to work through her traumatic experiences by drawing upon the language, folk patterns, and collective memories of the Deep South. In 1939 Hurston responded to the complications that Freud had introduced into the idea of identity when he described Moses as an Egyptian: she did so by retelling the Hebrew exodus story as the African-American exodus from white-imposed slavery. Not only did Hurston (like Freud) contest racial essentialism, she also extended Freud's view that freedom posed greater challenges to the African-American people than slavery did. Freedom, her Moses repeatedly tells his people after they have fled Egypt, is an inner state, "not a barbecue."[50]

Hurston's contemporary Jean Toomer also utilized the concept of a racial unconscious. The scion of an aristocratic family of "yellow" New Orleans and Washington, D.C., African-Americans, Toomer resisted any definition of himself as black or Negro, which in his view ignored the American sources for his identity. Nonetheless, in a review of Eugene O'Neill's 1920 play *The Emperor Jones* Toomer wrote: "The contents of the unconscious not only vary with individuals; they are differentiated because of race. . . . Jones lived through sections of an unconscious which is peculiar to the Negro. Slave ships, whipping posts, and so on. . . . [H]is fear becomes a Negro's fear, recognizably different from a similar emotion, modified by other racial experience." *The Emperor Jones,* Toomer concluded, is "a section of Negro psychology presented in significant dramatic form."[51]

The Harlem Renaissance came to an end with the Great Depression of the 1930s, but the involvement of black intellectuals with psychoanalysis did not. The sociologist Horace Cayton, coauthor (with St. Clair Drake) of *Black Metropolis,* wrestled his entire life with the contradiction between individuality and race. Eventually, he underwent a five-year analysis with

Helen V. McLean, a Chicago analyst whose withered arm and female sex made him feel that she would understand his "handicap." In the early stages of his analysis, Cayton came to see that race was a "convenient catchall," a rationalization for personal inadequacy, a "means of preventing deeper probing." Only later did he realize that race "ran to the core of [his] personality, . . . formed the central focus for [his] insecurity": "I must have drunk it in with my mother's milk," he asserted. Psychoanalysis changed his sociological theories, leading him to understand how central racial hatred and self-hatred were to modern society.[52]

Richard Wright, who worked with the psychiatrist Frederic Wertham to found the Laforgue Mental Health Clinic in Harlem, was another black modernist who used psychoanalysis to complicate the meaning of race. According to Wright, cultures were "screens" that men and women use to divide "that part of themselves that they are afraid of [from] that part . . . they want to preserve." Linking bisexuality and ambivalence to aggression, Wright's novels provoked James Baldwin's observation that in black literature the place usually filled by sexuality tends to be taken by violence. A character in Wright's *The Long Dream,* observing a castrated, mutilated victim of lynching, comments to his friend: "You have to be terribly attracted to a person, almost in love with 'im to mangle 'im in this manner. They hate us, Tyree, but they love us, too, in a perverted sort of way, they love us."[53] Given such terrible insight, even W. E. B. Du Bois, who originally had viewed "race prejudice [as] based on wide-spread ignorance," eventually conceded that he had not been "sufficiently Freudian to understand how little human action is based on reason."[54]

The cultural experiments of the twenties were aborted after the Great Depression. Nonetheless, the idea of culture in the modern sense of the word had been born. That idea, as Lionel Trilling later wrote, "developed concomitantly with certain new ways of conceiving of the self." It referred to the "style" of society, a style that is visible in society's "conscious, intentional activities, in its architecture, its philosophy, and so on, but also to its unconscious activities . . . its unexpressed assumptions—the unconscious of society." Psychoanalysis, evolving in the context of a great social transformation, was crucial in creating this notion of culture. It taught that even as the surrogates of culture were established in the mind, the mind itself passed beyond them.

Finally, alongside its involvement with the "new woman," the "new homosexual" and the "new Negro," Jazz Age psychoanalysis became caught up with artistic modernism. This encounter was the most conflictual of all, essentially because European artistic modernism and analysis so clearly arose from a common source and had common stories to tell.

In the nineteenth century the romantic artist, recently freed from patronage to sell his or her talents in the marketplace, embodied the then-new idea of personal sentiments and experiences cut loose from a fixed place in the division of labor.[55] By the 1890s, diverse avant-gardes had defined a common goal: "guiltless revelation of the unconscious . . . radically free play with material to reveal the force of unconscious feeling." Like the early analysts, the early avant-gardes saw their work as non- or post-economic. As the painter Paul Gauguin remarked, "The self-esteem one acquires [from artistic creation is] the only consolation. . . . Income, after all—most brutes have that." The avant-garde artist and the psychoanalyst also shared an orientation toward the "primitive" as the source of identity. "My hands were covered with blood," Gauguin wrote of his painting, "the old residue of my civilized emotions utterly destroyed."[56] The analytic view that the revelation of the unconscious entailed withdrawal from the object world paralleled a series of artistic innovations culminating in the discovery of abstraction. Thus, in 1913 the Russian suprematist painter Kazimir Malevich described his "desperate struggle to free art from the ballast of the objective world." That "was no empty square I had exhibited," he wrote, "but rather the experience of objectlessness."[57] Each of these steps reflected the new possibilities unleashed by the new productive forces—possibilities of forms of thought no longer confined within Newtonian limits and no longer constrained by material necessity.

The "second modernity" of the 1920s deepened the resonance between modern art and psychoanalysis. The great literary works published between 1921 and 1924 include Pirandello's *Six Characters in Search of an Author* (ambiguity, identity); Proust's *Remembrance of Things Past* (the equation of the self with memory); Mann's *The Magic Mountain* (disease, the breakdown of civilization); Woolf's *Mrs. Dalloway* (interiority, stream of consciousness); and Joyce's *Ulysses* (the linguistic subconscious, the interplay of the mythic and the everyday, the cultural outsider). T. S. Eliot's *The Waste Land* described modernity as "a heap of broken images, where the sun beats, and the dead tree gives no shelter." In a great variety of guises, *some* conception of the unconscious was at the center of every modernist innovation.

At the same time, although psychoanalysis and modern art arose from the same terrain and shared many preoccupations, Fordism brought them into conflict. Mass production not only exalted the artist but turned him or her into an employee, as radio, film, book clubs, the mass arts, journalism, and design all became subject to the technical requirements of mass reproducibility. As we have seen, artists often responded by mystifying creativity and insisting on the idea of the "genius." Needless to say, grandiosity, a narcissistic preoccupation with a unique "founder," and painful dramas of isolation and "misunderstanding" were not unknown among analysts. Nevertheless, both psychoanalysts and modern artists, children of the same parents, preferred to regard themselves as self-created. When analysts went further and pretended to *explain* art, artists naturally rebelled. The early twenties were the moment of rebellion.

The first novel about psychoanalysis, Italo Svevo's *The Confessions of Zeno* (1923), portrayed the relation between analysis and literature as the attempt of science to subordinate art.[58] Virginia Woolf's "Freudian Fiction" criticized Freud's transformation of "characters" into "cases" and his doctrinal "key" that "simplifies rather than complicates."[59] In Joyce's *Finnegans Wake,* an accusation of incest is called a "freudful mistake," Freud appears as a "traumconductor," and another character is described as "jung and easily freudened."[60] Thomas Mann had not yet read Freud when he wrote *The Magic Mountain,* but he had Hans Castorp collapse into hilarity when he heard about psychoanalysis at the Berghof Sanatorium. Although Mann later credited Freud with giving him the courage to write his homoerotic *Death in Venice,* he also remarked that artists felt "disquieted and reduced" by analysis: "The artist is being X-rayed by Freud's ideas to the point where it violates the secret of his creative art."[61] The classic statement of the artist's suspicion was Roger Fry's 1924 essay "The Artist and Psychoanalysis," which characterized the distinctive component of art as "disinterested . . . contemplation of formal relations detached from the emotions evoked by representation."[62] Freud, by contrast, thought that formal relations supplied a kind of "forepleasure," facilitating the wish fulfillment that the content of art provided. From his standpoint, Fry's position looked like a form of repression.[63]

D. H. Lawrence offers the paradigm case of an artist intensely involved with psychoanalysis yet also repelled by it. In *Women in Love,* written during the war, Lawrence described the terrible impact of Fordist mass production: "Expert engineers were introduced in every department . . . New Machinery was brought from America . . . the miners were reduced to mere mechanical instruments."[64] Mass production, Lawrence believed, had rendered the realistic novel, based on the "old stable ego of character," obsolete. Seeking to describe "another ego, according to whose action the individual is unrecognizable," Lawrence nonetheless equated psychoanalysis with scientific management. In 1924 he informed Mabel Luhan: "I know what lies back" of the fascination with psychoanalysis—"the same indecent desire to have everything in the *will* and the *head*. Life itself comes from elsewhere." "I hate therapy altogether," he added on another occasion. Neurotics assume "perfect conscious and automatic control when they're cured. . . . I would prefer that the neurotics died."[65] He added, "At last I begin to see the point of my critics' abuse of my exalting of sex. They only know one form of sex: the nervous, personal, disintegrative sort, the 'white' sex . . . the current sort of sex is just what I *don't* mean."[66]

Lawrence's loathing of analysis did not simply reflect his defense of the autonomy of art; rather, he had a profoundly different conception of personal life. For Lawrence, sexuality was the ground of being; rationality was invariably defensive, a form of intellectualization. At root, beneath his rejection of psychoanalysis, lay his difficulty in recognizing a thinking woman as a sexual being. Wyndham Lewis was another writer who identified Freud with an emancipation of women that would destroy the manly virtues. Mocking Sherwood Anderson as "a poor, henpecked, beFreuded, bewildered White [man], with a brand new 'inferiority' complex," Lewis, like Lawrence, sought sympathy for the powerless male child. "Stirred up against his papa by his feminist mama," he wrote, the boy wonders whether "he shall slay and eat him."[67]

The most productive engagement of modern artists with psychoanalysis occurred among the surrealists. The reason was that the surrealists viewed modern society as organized through the uniquely unbound and pseudo-individualized release of desire.[68] This insight led them to minimize and downgrade the special role of the artwork, which they saw as an institution aimed at containing and channeling desire. After all, they had watched the futurists open up the marvelous world of electricity and radio, the cubists problematize the division between art and mass culture, and the Russian avant-gardes explore the contribution of art to a democratizing and industrializing people. Yet, by the 1920s, the avant-gardes' works hung in museums, their transgressions gelded. Conceding that "paintings arouse emotion," Breton insisted that "in this epoch it is reality itself that is in question." He wanted to create not artworks but the sense that reality itself was charged with unconscious contents.[69]

Like analysts, the surrealists adopted a predominantly intellectual—but not intellectualizing—stance. *Pace* much current opinion, their main interest was not restricted to sexuality but also included the unconscious mind: its strange logic and associational principles; its lack of any grammar; its acceptance of contradiction; its ignorance of time, death, or negation; and its preference for an imagistic vocabulary. The dadaists (who preceded them in rejecting

Max Ernst, *The Robing of the Bride:* surrealist painting, 1939

the artwork) considered chance a magical procedure transcending causality, but the surrealists called chance "Freud's 'unconscious mind.' "[70] They saw in Freud's analysis of the dreamwork "the superior reality of certain forms of association heretofore neglected." Automatic writing, found objects, a preference for "indexical" media such as photography, which seemed to bypass the processes of signification, the linking of apparently unrelated images (umbrellas, sewing machines, operating tables) were all attempts to describe the non- or superrational logic of the unconscious.[71] Of course, the war had inspired their efforts. Max Ernst, the surrealist most deeply influenced by Freud, gave his autobiography as "Died August 1, 1914; resuscitated, Nov. 11, 1918 (the armistice)" and produced oneiric paintings whose elements resisted interpretation or harmonization, thus articulating a permanent "identity crisis."[72]

Freed from the limitations of professional medicine, the surrealists sometimes improved on psychoanalysis. At a time when analysts were debating penis envy, they mocked the bourgeois family and exalted female parricides,

The grave of Antonio Gramsci, founder of the
Italian Communist Party and originator of
the idea that psychoanalysis was a new theory
of the noble savage

mystics, and prostitutes, even as the subculture they created remained far
more homophobic and sexist than that of analysis.[73] Similarly, André Breton attacked "the blind and intolerant prejudice under which works of art
[are] produced in asylums."[74]

There was one great difference between psychoanalysis and surrealism,
however. For Freud, words and images required interpretation, while the
surrealists viewed words and images as incantations with magical power.[75]
Freud sought to translate dreams into the language of waking life; the surrealists criticized Freud for distinguishing dream and reality, instead of
combining the two into an absolute reality or surreality. In 1928 Louis
Aragon and Breton celebrated one of Charcot's cases as "the fiftieth anniver-
sary of hysteria, the greatest poetic discovery of the latter part of the [nine-
teenth] century."[76] The point was to celebrate, not to analyze, hysteria.

Like the Freudians, the surrealists could not escape the dialectic of
absorption and marginality. The more the surrealists attacked the art insti-

tution by tying art to gesture and everyday experience, the more vulnerable they became to integration into mass culture, advertising, and film. The more they sought to expose city streets and shopping arcades as dream-scapes of repression, the more they inspired dancing Coke-bottle ads, banana headdresses, and, soon enough, TV psychodramas. So broad was their influence that to understand modern culture one must speak not of the surrealists but of a surrealist impulse. Yet, although Freud met Breton and Dalí, he had little understanding of their project, calling them in a personal letter "complete fools," or "let us say 95%, as with alcohol."[77]

The encounter between psychoanalysis and modern art was the most telling of all the encounters of the twenties. Since the Enlightenment, artists had been thought of as possessing unique access to reality, coequal with and not reducible to scientific knowledge. Freud's insistence on analyzing art revealed a major limitation of analysis: difficulty in knowing when to let go. At the same time, the defensiveness of artists suggested an unsuspected fragility in the modernist persona, one that time increasingly would reveal.

Like Gramsci in prison, then, flappers, homosexuals, and artists caught the deep truth of Fordism: that it relied on the everyday wishes of the masses, even as it mobilized, distorted, diverted, and betrayed them. Catching this truth, they inevitably grappled ambivalently with analysis. In the late 1960s, as we shall see, their ambivalence was resolved in a negative direction. Feminism supplanted analysis as a theory and practice of personal life; analysis was redefined as an art, not a science; and radical politics, after embracing Freudianism under the slogan "The personal is political," went into terminal decline. Nevertheless, while these movements lasted, they gave the analytic profession much of its aura and affected its practice, albeit unconsciously; they thereby contributed to its reformulation of the threefold promise of modernity.

Chapter Seven

AUTONOMY AND RESISTANCE

The greatness of our time rests in the fact that freedom, the peculiar possession of the mind whereby it is at home with itself, is
recognized.

— G. W. F. Hegel, *Philosophy of History* (1837)

I n 1783 Immanuel Kant responded to the question "What is Enlightenment?" by answering "autonomy" or "emancipation from self-imposed
immaturity." By autonomy Kant meant *intellectual* and *moral* autonomy.
On the one hand, he wanted individuals to get out from under the tutelage
of priests and lords, and to think for themselves. On the other hand, he
wanted them to rise above their desires and act in accord with moral norms
that they themselves formulated by exercising their reason. For Kant, moreover, norms formulated in this way would be universally applicable. Thus,
from the Kantian point of view, one's race, gender, and social situation, to
say nothing of the particularities of one's personal life, were irrelevant.
Bringing such specificity to bear on moral decisions could only derail the
pursuit of autonomy.

In the nineteenth century, however, thinkers such as John Stuart Mill
envisioned an alternative conception—that of *personal* autonomy. From
their point of view, an autonomous individual was one who lived a life of
his or her own devising, took responsibility for that life, and regarded it as a
life worth living. Central to modernity, the ideal of personal autonomy was
frequently linked to the idea that a person's life could be viewed as a self-

authored narrative or work of art. Moral issues did not disappear from this perspective, but they were restricted to matters that were appropriately governed by universal norms. Beyond them lay the realm of personal choices. Such choices could not be dictated by moral reflection but required self-scrutiny of another, more personal kind.

The sea change wrought by the second industrial revolution made personal autonomy something more than a philosophical question. Moral autonomy was closely linked to the nineteenth-century property system and to the liberal assumption that certain individuals (Western, white, male, property-owning) could turn aside their own interests to think in terms of the common good. World War I brought the older liberal order to an end. Modernism was, at root, the search for a new ideal of civilization to replace that of nineteenth-century liberalism. In the course of that search, autonomy was redefined so that it no longer rested on property and family position. Instead, it came to be understood as a new, inward relation to oneself. The result was a profound interrogation of the meaning of autonomy during the interwar years, one in which psychoanalysis played a major role.

There were three areas in which this interrogation unfolded. First, autonomy was considered one of the psychological prerequisites of democracy. As we saw, the weakening of the liberal order did not result in stable democratic regimes. Rather, nineteenth-century liberalism was succeeded by Fordist and communist attempts to mold human nature; by authoritarian regimes based upon traditional conservative values, for example, in Hungary; by organic and corporatist models of society, such as those the Catholic church sponsored in Portugal, Spain, and Austria; and by fascism, which used the techniques of mass democracy for authoritarian ends. In that context, many believed that the future of democracy depended on autonomous citizens socialized to oppose authoritarianism. Freud's writings addressed this concern. As World War II approached, his thinking inspired an enormous literature on family, education, culture, and politics, all aiming to specify the psychological prerequisites of a democratic citizenry.

Second, psychoanalysis proved relevant for understanding the new type of society that accompanied mass democracy. Consumer society—or, as it was then beginning to be called, mass society—equated personal autonomy with market choice. Psychoanalysis, in contrast, probed beneath the level of choice to its roots in unconscious instincts and wishes. Much of the interest in analysis came from those, such as Walter Lippmann and the Frankfurt School theorists, who rejected consumerism and mass culture as the moral basis of modern civilization, seeking either to return to nineteenth-century ideas of autonomy or to redefine those ideas in the context of mass democracy.

Finally, analysis influenced efforts to extend the practice of self-reflection to the entire realm of individual choices that were not dictated by morality. As ties to place, kin, and ritual weakened; as freely chosen, extrafamilial lifeworlds proliferated; as men and women gained a new, secular access to their inner lives, there was a need for institutions, practices, and ideas that helped individuals reflect upon and evaluate their immediate wants and impulses in light of deeper values and long-term goals. The growth of psychotherapy mirrored the felt need for such practices. But psychotherapy could become a servant of consumer society, which is systematically organized to appeal to unreflective wants. Psychoanalysis, in contrast, seemed to offer a kind of reflection that could not be so easily recuperated.

Freud's revised or structural theory, even more than his theory of the unconscious, was at the center of the interest in autonomy. Freud expounded this theory in a series of brief volumes—*Beyond the Pleasure Principle* (1921), *Group Psychology and the Analysis of the Ego* (1921), and *The Ego and the Id* (1923)—and was still working out its implications in his subsequent essays on female sexuality. Written during a few explosive years after World War I, these works described the psyche in terms of agencies (id, ego, superego) rather than regions (conscious, preconscious, unconscious). They also elaborated the new instinct theory, which revolved around the conflict between the drive to reduce tension, the "death instinct," and the drive to synthesize or create higher and more complex levels of organization, the "life instinct," or *eros*. Addressed not only to analysts but also to "the wider circle of educated people . . . able to appreciate the science of the human mind," these works reflected the new interest in personal autonomy.[1]

A theory of the ego or "I," the successor to Freud's theory of narcissism, was at the center of Freud's revised theory. The ego, as Freud conceived it, arose where the instincts encountered the external world. Associated with perception or consciousness, as well as with preconscious thought and memory, its main effort was devoted to quieting or regulating tension. Reflecting the origins of the theory in the shell shock episode, Freud maintained that the greatest danger the ego faced was "an experience of helplessness . . . in the face of an accumulation of excitation."[2]

The ego developed the capacity to sustain tension, and thus to promote autonomy, in several different ways. At the most primitive level, it defended itself against excess excitement through projection, treating urges, impulses, or other messages arising from within as if they were external. Later, it modeled itself on somatic processes such as ingestion or expulsion as a way of mastering those processes. Next, it induced the id to give up its earliest attachment to parents and siblings by identifying with them; through identification, the ego developed influence over the id, deepening its relations with it while also appeasing it: "Look, you can love me too—I am so like the object."[3] Finally, the ego relied on the external world, beginning with the parents, to gain influence over peremptory internal demands.

The crucial moment in the ego's development was the Oedipal crisis: the uniquely human encounter with authority. In earliest childhood, behavior was motivated by fear of the loss of love or the loss of protection. During the Oedipal crisis, however, the individual gained control over his or her wishes by diverting them, through identification with the parents' superegos, into an internal agency that oversees the ego, a superego or *Über-Ich*. The superego had the character of the id. Unlike the ego, it was neither shaped by external influences nor responsive to external intervention. It was the result, rather, of the turning of the sadistic wishes of infancy against the ego, a process Freud chillingly depicted in his 1919 "A Child Is Being Beaten." The theory of the superego reflected the disjuncture between intrapsychic and sociocultural reality. After the Oedipal crisis, not only acts but thoughts and wishes were censored; the renunciation of forbidden acts did not lessen guilt but tended instead to increase it.

This portrait of the ego had profound implications for personal autonomy. For Kant, as we saw, autonomy meant distancing oneself from one's inclinations as well as from one's social context in order to act from duty alone. For Freud, in contrast, the ego was not only the agency of rational thought; it was also the precipitate of inclinations, drives, love objects, and identifications. Thus, reason could not finally be separated from contingent experiences but rather was a kind of "soft" but "persistent" voice that could be heard along with them. Likewise, attaining critical distance from desires, identifications, and object cathexes did not mean attaining a universal viewpoint. Rather, it entailed a hermeneutic process of introspection that in principle could never be completed.

In addition, the kind of reasoning that Kant advocated to attain moral autonomy was formal and logical: the test of a moral maxim was its capacity to be universalized without contradiction. For Freud, in contrast, introspection required concrete self-reflection. To attain autonomy in personal life meant working through the specific, idiosyncratic, contingent features of the individual's life history and narratively constructed identity. By showing that the ego disappears into, and draws resources from, the id, Freud's theory reflected the widespread modernist questioning of ratio-

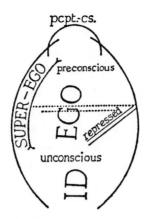

Freud's structural theory,
taken from his
New Introductory Lectures

nalization, planning, and control. As R. P. Blackmur wrote: "Reason had above all . . . the labour of associating the elements of a sensibility believed to be dissociated empirically." The modernist project involved "reason in madness, operating and drawing from madness; it was reason controlling madness."[4]

Freud's distinction between the ego and the superego, and his arguments concerning the irrational roots of the superego, also dovetailed with the general loosening of morality that accompanied mass consumption. By linking the superego to the id, Freud highlighted the rigid, compulsive, and punitive character of much that passed for morality. Weber had already traced not only Benjamin Franklin's utilitarianism but Kant's pietism to their Calvinist roots. Now Freud, theorizing the superego as the heir to the castration complex, equated Kant's "categorical imperative"—his universal moral principle—with the superego: "what seems to us so grandiose about ethics, so mysterious and, in a mystical fashion, so self-evident, owes these characteristics to its connection with religion, its origins from the will of the father."[5] The morality that came from the superego, in Freud's view, needed to be tempered by the identifications that reside near the id and by the ego's realism, consultative capacities, and propensity for judgment.

Freud's revised theory reflected the emergence of a new social terrain that lay beyond both the traditional community, which had no room for autonomy, and classical liberalism, with its decontextualized and impersonal idea of moral autonomy. In this new terrain, individuals moved among different types and levels of obligations. Autonomy no longer meant control over the self, as in Kant; rather, it meant reflective equilibrium among different and conflicting demands. To be sure, some demands could be universal and moral, thus trumping others. Nonetheless, an autonomous life was one that looked in many directions simultaneously: toward personal life, the sphere of personal autonomy per se, as well as toward family, the community, religion, and science. The ego's task was to mediate among different psychical environments, dealing at once with cravings and internal demands, self-criticisms, and representations of the social world. These environments were not only different; they were irreconcilable because they were different in kind. Some were close to reflexes, others were interpersonal, still others were the products of culture and collective action.

In line with this conception, Freud began to formulate an increasingly complex psychology. He portrayed the mind as "a hierarchy of superordinated and subordinated agencies, a labyrinth of impulses striving independently of one another towards action, corresponding with the multiplicity of instincts and of relations with the external world, many of which are antagonistic to one another and incompatible." He compared the regions of the psyche to areas of color in modern painting that are not bounded but "melt into one another."[6] The new conception was unfamiliar, perhaps even more unfamiliar than the unconscious. As Anna Freud wrote, it took her a long time to think of the psyche in terms of "aims and functions, id, ego, and superego each pursuing their aim in life to the best of their possibility," but eventually it "gave [her] a real sense for the purpose of life, or rather for the conflicting purposes in human life which are inevitable once a higher development of the personality is attempted and reached." Such a theory was necessary, she continued, if we are to explain why "the parts of the mind" were often in "such a muddle—as if they were not only at cross-purposes with each other but also speaking different languages and acting out their intentions in a totally different medium."[7]

Before the war, psychoanalysis had been mixed up with many other forms of psychotherapy, such as mind cure, Jungianism, Adlerianism, and mental hygiene, as psychiatry was increasingly called. Freud's revised theory led to a sharp distinction between psychoanalysis and the rest. While there were many ways to characterize this distinction, Freud drew the line with his assertion that *the ego was the locus of resistance*. Deeply rooted in his thought, this idea became central to the modernist redefinition of autonomy, as well as to the practice of psychoanalysis itself.

Freud's starting point had been the riddle of the neurosis, a force that he viewed as "inexpedient, and running counter to the flow of life." From the beginning, Freud believed that patients did not come to analysis to get well; they came, rather, to serve neurotic ends. For this reason he insisted on "abstinence." Through the analyst's refusal to palliate the patient's situation, the neurotic need would be frustrated, intensified, and brought into sharper focus. Frustration brought the transference into sharper focus, but it was especially in the *negative* transference that the underlying neurosis emerged. In 1915 Freud asked why this was so. His answer was that as the neurotic conflict came increasingly into focus, a two-sided imperative intensified: the patient sought to satisfy simultaneously both the underlying wish and the *resistance* against that wish. Nonanalytic therapies relied on the positive transference, which served them as the vehicle of cure. But only psychoanalysis brought to light the negative transference or resistance, the obstacle to cure. The negative transference had to be turned into insight or self-understanding before one could speak of analysis proper.

The observation of the war neuroses deepened this line of thought. The predominant fact in the war neuroses was the repetition of frustrating or unsatisfying behaviors. But this was exactly what occurred in the analytic situation when patients repeated frustrating infantile scenarios that they supposedly came to analysis to end. Freud attempted to explain this phenomenon by recourse to the death instinct. Allied with the superego, the death instinct set up a vicious circle in defense of the neurosis. As the patient got better, the superego attacked the improvement because infantile satisfactions, not the wish to be relieved of guilt, drove the analysis.[8] Freud's earlier view, that the basic conflict in the mind was between consciousness and the repressed unconscious, had implied that the repressed was "afraid to be discovered." But the fact of repetition suggested that the repressed was constantly trying to break through to consciousness. It was not the repressed but the *ego* that prevented it from doing so. The result was a paradox: resistance to gaining knowledge of the unconscious came from the ego, and yet the ego was also the locus of reason and self-reflection, the "one beacon-light in the darkness of depth-psychology."[9]

It is often said today that psychoanalysis is "pluralistic" or "polycentric," that it has no agreed-upon core theory. Perhaps. But until the end of the sixties, it did have a core theory: the analysis of the resistance. All the classical theories, such as object relations, North American ego psychology, and Lacan's theory of narcissism, were devoted to this goal. Over time theoretical languages changed, but in practice all analysts concentrated on analyzing the negative transference or resistance. No other therapy did this, at least not in a systematic fashion. This was why there was psychoanalysis at all, and not just psychotherapy.

Freud sought to distinguish psychoanalysis in this way at a time of enormous ferment in the analytic world. The number of analysts had increased sharply, as did the number and length of analyses, the demand for technical guides and procedures, and the increasing awareness that many analyses failed to reach any resolution.[10] Rejecting the earlier idea that the analyst's job was to interpret the unconscious, Freud argued that it was to analyze the resistance. In a typical contemporary response, Max Eitingon wrote to Melanie Klein: "This is putting dynamite to the house."[11] Nevertheless, the effect of Freud's structural theory was to open a host of new clinical possibilities expressed in a series of new terms: "resistance analysis," "character analysis," the "metapsychological" approach, "defense analysis," and "ego psychology."

Ego psychology, with its focus on the resistance, was the outcome of Freud's earlier dispute with Adler and the formulation of the theory of narcissism. Karl Abraham noted this in 1919 when he observed the "narcissistic inaccessibility" of patients mired in long, frustrating, and unproductive analyses. The "pretended compliance" of these patients was a defense, Abraham wrote, because analysis was "an attack on the patient's narcissism . . . that instinctual force upon which our therapeutic endeavours are most easily wrecked."[12] In setting ego psychology apart from other therapies of the time, psychoanalysis gave a name to its alternatives: "mind cure." Mind cure was any therapy that suppressed the negative transference and, in that sense, denied internal conflict. In the most basic sense, mind cure was positive thinking, as exemplified by Annie Payson Call's 1918 *Nerves and the War*, which called shell shock "the product of negative thinking," and urged soldiers not to "take the war into your mind" and to "rouse the will to direct the brain into wholesome channels."[13]

In a 1924 paper Abraham cited the ideas of Emile Coué, a French radio therapist whose *Self Mastery Through Conscious Auto-Suggestion* was a runaway bestseller in the United States, as an example of mind cure. Coué had given his followers a formula, the mantra "Every day, in every way, I'm getting better and better." In Abraham's view, Coué had successfully mass-marketed Adler's masculine protest. The key to Coué's effectiveness, Abraham argued, was his followers' belief that he gave each of them the same "gift," the ritual formula. In other words, Coué was a good father: he didn't favor any of his children; he treated them all equally. This encouraged their identification with one another and flattered their narcissism or "self-mastery," as Coué called it, with its "optimistic denial . . . of inferiority, real or imaginary."[14] Psychoanalysis, by contrast, did not flatter its patients. Rather, it sharpened their sense of inferiority, challenged their narcissism, and made them aware of their envy and resentment of others.

The most anguished of all psychoanalytic ideas, the idea that the self-reflecting ego was also the seat of resistance, transformed both the self-understanding and the public perception of the analyst. It changed the analyst from a "helper" into someone who, in his or her daily work, served as the target of the deepest paranoia, defensiveness, and rage. Some analyses disintegrated into sadomasochistic double binds, prompting demands for a return to a time when the analyst was a simple doctor. Freud even admitted in the 1930s that analysis could precipitate a psychosis.[15] The focus on resistance also sanctioned analysts' "know-it-all" attitudes and their "depreciation of patients' self-perceptions," giving popular portrayals of analysis a hostile edge.[16] In the long run, the effects unleashed by the issue of resistance proved at least as important in determining the ultimate standing of psychoanalysis as its epistemological status or Freud's personality. Yet, there was no question that the focus on resistance was at the heart of the analytic contribution to modernity.

The subtlety of Freud's conception lay in the idea that the ego, the part of the mind devoted to self-reflection, was also the locus of the resistance. Almost immediately, two alternative approaches appeared. One, originated by Wilhelm Reich, saw the ego solely as the sphere of the resistance and aimed, by confronting the patient, to turn the ego into a "symptom" and analyze it away. The other approach, associated with Otto Rank and Sándor Ferenczi, sought to bypass the "intellectualizations" of the ego and address the "real" person—the id—directly. Both approaches abandoned the characteristic Freudian stress on the two-sidedness of the ego, but they led in different directions. Reich's was revised to become mainstream ego psychology, while Rank and Ferenczi's became a persistent alternative to classical psychoanalysis, eventually largely supplanting it.

Wilhelm Reich, the founder of "character analysis," was born in Galicia in 1897 to an assimilated Jewish family, and in the early twenties was the youngest instructor at the Vienna Institute in spite of Freud's personal dislike of him.[17] Reich's experiences working in the Vienna Psychoanalytic Polyclinic, which had a predominantly working-class clientele, convinced him that the neuroses arose from poverty and the accompanying lack of privacy, health care, and birth control. They had to be addressed through political change and not by individual therapy alone. How could one justify individual therapy, he asked, when "in a city like Berlin there are millions of people who are neurotically ruined in their psychic structure"?[18]

Reich viewed analysis as a method that would "break through" socially necessitated repressions. To describe how, his lectures at the Vienna Institute, first published as *The Impulsive Character* in 1923 and later expanded into *Character Analysis,* distinguished symptoms from "character." Symptoms, Reich argued, such as a tic or a nervous cough, emanate from the id. Patients experienced symptoms as alien and welcomed help against them. By contrast, character traits, such as irony, stiffness, or an attitude of superiority, were part of the ego. Patients experienced them as part of themselves, and therefore resisted having them analyzed.[19] The problem of the resistance, of the "negative therapeutic reaction," was for Reich the problem of analyzing character, that is, of turning it into a "symptom." When Freud read Reich's manuscript, he was enthusiastic: Reich's book, he wrote its author, reinforced the idea that "the relations between the ego and superego will be a realm of research for us similar to that hitherto studied . . . between the person (ego and superego) and the object."[20]

Reich's idea of character anticipated his later attempts to link psychoanalysis and Marxism, but it also made an independent contribution to psychoanalysis. Viewing character as a system of safeguards against the breakthrough of instinctual drives, Reich described the "character armor" or "character resistance" in which the underlying conflict was "frozen."[21] *Character Analysis* supplied the first technical rule of what first became known as defense or character analysis and then ego psychology: "Make the first approach to any material from the side of the ego. . . . In other words, the defense or resistance has to be dealt with before the unconscious content is told to the patient."[22]

Reich's formulations constituted a breakthrough in understanding resistance. When viewed from the Freudian perspective, however, they appeared one-sided. In Freud's perspective, the ego was the source not only of resistance but also of reason, self-knowledge, and instinctual modification. For Reich, in contrast, the ego was solely the locus of resistance; the instincts, by contrast, were wholly benign. Nonetheless, in revised forms, character analysis became the basis of the first systematic, clinically based analytic theory. Worked out and revised at the Berlin Kinderseminar, the theory was codified by linking the forms of resistance to the stages of infantile sexuality.[23] Character analysis also became the subject of the first "international symposium on the theory of technique and therapy," held at Salzburg in 1924. Later, Hanns Sachs sought to integrate character analysis into a "metapsychological" approach, emphasizing the contribution of all three psychical agencies to the resistance.[24] That Freud was not wholly comfortable with these changes is suggested by a 1922 letter to Abraham, in which he stated that he found "character analysis . . . more difficult" than the older techniques.[25]

The other alternative to Freud's structural theory emerged from Budapest and Vienna, where Ferenczi and Rank objected to what they saw as the "cold" and "intellectual" theories coming out of Berlin. Their opposition centered on two points. First, in their jointly authored *Development of Psychoanalysis* (1923), they argued that the resistance could be bypassed through an "active therapy" in which the analyst facilitated the repetition of a trauma through a "language of gesture."[26] After all, by definition, they pointed out, a trauma had not been experienced consciously and therefore could never be remembered. Rather, as Ferenczi elaborated, the analyst must take an *active* role, prohibiting activities such as masturbation and daydreaming, or else enjoining patients to fantasize, even suggesting the content of their fantasies.[27] "Active therapy," based on the cooperation of patient and analyst, differed from the insight gained through remembering. Knowledge, after all, "is something entirely different from the healing factor." Active therapy, Rank added, would promote rapid cures. "We see the process of sublimation, which in ordinary life requires years of education, take place before our eyes."[28]

The proponents of "active therapy" also emphasized the significance of the mother in early development. In a 1918 remark that anticipated his later orientation toward touch and holding, Ferenczi explained the Moro reflex, the clasping of the fist in infants under the age of three months, as the evolutionary outcome of the "little shock (or traumatic) neurosis" that originated when the young monkey was "compelled . . . to hold fast with the fingers to the mother's fur while she climbs about trees."[29] In 1919, moved by his wife's pregnancy, Rank remarked to Ernest Jones that "men were of no importance . . . the essence of life [is] the relation between mother and child."[30] In 1923 Rank's *Trauma of Birth* linked the mother to the resistance or, more specifically, to the single traumatic childhood experience from which all resistance arose, namely, birth. All neuroses, Rank held, were attempts to master that "primal castration," the prototype for all later anxiety. There is only one fixation point, he continued—the maternal body. Therefore, "there is . . . no need to ascertain the 'pathogenic traumata' . . . by the lengthy way of analytic investigation. . . . Analysis is now in a position to free itself to an extensive degree from the work of investigation, since we know from the outset . . . the whole content of the Unconscious."[31]

Freud's revised theory sought to give the individual some freedom from impulses, from social pressures, and from impersonal representations of internalized authority. His critics both advanced and retarded this program. On the one hand, they set in motion long-term developments: in the case of Reich, the theory of the defenses; in the case of Rank and Ferenczi, the view that the therapeutic relationship, not insight, was the healing factor in analysis. At the same time, Reich's view of the ego as merely defensive threatened to short-circuit self-reflection, while Rank and Ferenczi risked bypassing the negative transference, turning analysis into a variant of mind cure.

In April 1923 Freud was diagnosed with cancer. Although he survived for another sixteen years, fears that his death was imminent helped precipitate the disintegration of the earlier circle. In a process that one analyst described as fraught with "outbursts of id forces and reaction-formations against them," the transformation of psychoanalysis from a *Männerbund* into a profession became entwined with debates over the ego.[32]

When Freud first heard Rank's ideas about the birth trauma, he called them "the most important progress since the discovery of psychoanalysis." "Anyone else would have used such a discovery to make himself independent," he told Jones.[33] But in February 1924, in response to criticism from Berlin, Freud wrote a long circular letter, explaining his agreements and disagreements. Praising Rank's stress on the strength of passive or "regressive" longings, complimenting him for raising the question of "the biological background of the Oedipus complex," Freud nevertheless insisted that Rank had not explained how the ambivalence directed at the mother was transferred to the father and other objects. Rank's emphasis on birth, Freud complained, made sexuality "*a priori,* i.e., biologically, ambivalent." For himself, in contrast, the main causes for ambivalence lay in the conditions of early childhood, especially the incest taboo. Although the taboo's origins lay in "the primordial history of the human family," it had to be re-created anew in every individual. Thus, for Freud, "the actual father [is] the real obstacle that recreates the incest barrier in each new individual."[34]

In the same letter Freud questioned innovations aimed at speeding up analysis. Having learned while ill that his beard took six weeks to grow back, he doubted that the "deeper layers of the unconscious" could be changed in six months. He could not understand, he wrote Rank, "how the magic formula of leading back all libido to the mother should produce a therapeutic effect."[35] Later he called *The Birth Trauma* and *The Development of Psychoanalysis* children of their time, "conceived under the stress of the contrast between the postwar misery of Europe and the 'prosperity' of America, and designed to adapt the tempo of analytic therapy to the haste of American life."[36] Having urged that analysts "renounce any short-sighted therapeutical ambition," Freud envisioned an analytic subject able to tolerate frustration and postpone gratification.[37] Rank and Ferenczi, by contrast, were beginning to imagine the typical recipient of therapy in the emerging world of mass consumption.

Freud's increasingly critical reaction to Ferenczi's work, and Ferenczi's growing unhappiness over what he felt was the failure of Freud's analysis of him, led Ferenczi to withdraw. For a while he thought of emigrating to America, at least for long enough to build up a cash reserve. When he lectured at the New School in 1926, Harry Stack Sullivan dubbed him the "genius of the psychoanalytic movement."[38] In the end, however, Ferenczi elected to remain in Budapest, where he became increasingly critical of Freud.

Like Ferenczi, Rank also had enormous difficulty breaking away from the enchanted circle of Freudian charisma. For several years after publishing *The Birth Trauma,* he went back and forth between Paris and New York, alternating between breaking with Freud and returning to the fold. Buoyed by adulation on a 1924 trip in America, he exclaimed, "*Im Gegenteil, die Mutter!* On ze contrary, ze mozer!"[39] Yet as late as 1926 he was apologizing to Freud, "From a state which I now recognize as neurotic, I have suddenly returned to myself."[40] Meanwhile, Abraham died unexpectedly in 1925, Eitingon turned slowly toward Palestine, eventually emigrating, and Sachs became increasingly marginal.

Through it all, Freud hoped the Committee would replace him. "Only try," he wrote to Abraham in 1920, and "you will see that you will manage without me."[41] After the discovery of his cancer, he proposed that the Committee "learn to achieve harmony without him." He called himself "unfit to function as a despotic, ever wakeful censor." For half a dozen men of different characters to agree on all matters of detail was neither possible nor desirable, he had pointed out in his *Rundbriefe.* And because for him, Freud, it was so difficult to feel his way into new lines of thought, if they waited for his approval they "would run the risk of growing very old first."[42]

Despite these appeals, the *Männerbund* disintegrated. Ever since the war, Jones and Rank had struggled over control of the *Verlag.* Rank feared that Jones sought to "unite the Anglo-Saxon world under [his] sceptre." Jones complained to Abraham that Freud lacked any objectivity in regard to Rank.[43] In 1924, after the birth-trauma controversy, Anna Freud wrote Eitingon "that the question of whether Rank can be checked is the question of whether the publishing house and the magazines will continue to exist." Rank in turn called the analytic movement "a fiction."[44] In 1924 the Committee was dissolved and reconstituted. The new members, reflecting the attempt to move beyond the *Männerbund,* were all women: Anna Freud, Lou Andreas-Salomé, Marie Bonaparte (Napoleon's great-grandniece and a leader of the newly founded French Psychoanalytic Society), and Loe Kann (Ernest Jones's ex-partner). In 1926 the reconstituted Committee, too, was dissolved.[45] Freud wrote Ferenczi: "I have survived the committee that was to be my successor. Perhaps I shall yet survive the International Association. I only hope that psychoanalysis will survive me."[46]

What replaced the *Männerbund* was the "psychoanalytic movement," a diverse collection of national societies, all seeking to turn the circle around Freud into a discipline or profession. The size and diversity of the movement is suggested by the first postwar congress, held in The Hague in September 1920, a meeting with the character of a reunion. One hundred twelve individuals participated: sixty-two from Austria and Hungary, sixteen from Holland, fifteen from Britain, eleven from Germany, seven from Switzerland, and one from Poland.[47] Four years later, the International Psychoanalytic Association had a total membership of 263. Until World War II its membership was small enough to be printed with individuals' addresses at the back of the *International Journal of Psychoanalysis.* Although the Americans were absent from the 1920 congress, psychoanalysis's center of gravity had already shifted toward England and the United States. In 1919 the largest single analytic society (over forty members) was in London and the largest national membership (fifty-three) was in the United States. Freud, sarcastically quoting the chancellor of defeated Germany, spoke of "our new orientation towards the West."[48]

The task faced by the analytic movement was to routinize Freud's charisma, that is, to move from Freud's personal authority to open, rational, collegial forms of self-governance. In the interwar years, many attempted to accomplish this by establishing psychoanalysis in the university, including Sándor Ferenczi at the University of Budapest, Karl Abraham at the University of Berlin, Franz Alexander at the University of Chicago, and Max Eitingon at the Hebrew University in Jerusalem. Freud supported these efforts but sought to guard the autonomy of psychoanalysis, which, he insisted, was subject to the general protocols of science but not reducible to existing paradigms such as organic psychiatry or experimental psychology. He need not have worried. All attempts to gain a foothold in the university failed.[49]

Stymied in their efforts to win legitimacy from the university, and capitalizing on the popularity of analytic practice, analysts created a separate profession, developing a core curriculum, standardized forms of practice, and regularized mechanisms of succession to replace the Committee. To this end, they established "institutes," all-purpose centers that combined a society, a clinic, and formal training through course work, supervised clinical practice, and didactic or "training" analyses. Ego psychology, because it lent itself to systematization and to teaching, was central to the process of professionalization.

After the disintegration of the *Männerbund,* an inner circle centered on Vienna, Berlin, and London—which is to say on Freud—persisted but became increasingly peripheral to the main thrust toward professionalization. From this circle substantial control passed to a new generation distinguished from the *Männerbund* in terms of age, gender, sexuality, and political orientation.

The age differences were dramatic. Whereas Freud had been born in 1856, Melanie Klein was born in 1882, Otto Rank and Helene Deutsch in 1884, Karen Horney in 1885, Franz Alexander in 1891, and Wilhelm Reich, a prodigy, in 1897. They were all still young in the 1920s and recognizably "modern" in their sensibilities and values. Freud, by contrast, had negative feelings about such exemplary products of modernity as the radio, the telephone, film, feminism, abstract art, and U.S. culture. When he saw *Secrets of the Soul* advertised as "a psychoanalysis picture . . . soon to be made in Vienna, supervised by Professor Freud and explaining his system," he told Ferenczi that he could no more avoid the film than he could bobbed hair, but in neither case would he participate.[50] The distinction between old and young inflected many debates of the period, including those over brief therapy, female sexuality, and the place of the United States in the analytic movement.

The gender composition also shifted dramatically. The number of female analysts rose from two before World War I to approximately fifty in the immediate postwar period. By 1929 the majority of new trainees were women. Many had been teachers, and many were mothers. As we shall see, the changing gender composition of the movement encouraged a dramatic shift in its preoccupations to the mother/infant relationship, the mother/daughter relationship, and female sexuality.

The shift concerning sexuality is more difficult to trace, but two incidents of the immediate postwar period are revealing. In 1920 an openly homosexual doctor applied for membership in the Dutch Psychoanalytic Association. Its members turned to Jones for advice, and he counseled

PROF. Dr. FREUD   WIEN, IX. BERGGASSE 19.

April 9th 1935

Dear Mrs ▮▮▮▮

I gather from your letter that your son is a homosexual. I am most impressed by the fact that you do not mention this term yourself in your information about him. May I question you why you avoid it? Homosexuality is assuredly no advantage, but it is nothing to be ashamed of, no vice, no degradation, it cannot be classified as an illness; we consider it to be a variation of the sexual function produced by a certain arrest of sexual development. Many highly respectable individuals of ancient and modern times have been homosexuals, several of the greatest men among them (Plato, Michelangelo, Leonardo da Vinci, etc). It is a great injustice to persecute homosexuality as a crime, and a cruelty too. If you do not believe me, read the books of Havelock Ellis.

By asking me if I can help, you mean, I suppose, if I can abolish homosexuality and make normal heterosexuality take its place. The answer is, in a general way we cannot promise to achieve it. In a certain number of cases we succeed in developing the blighted germs of heterosexual tendencies which are present in every homosexual, in the majority of cases it is no more possible. It

is a question of the quality and the age of the individual. The result of treatment cannot be predicted.

What analysis can do for your son runs in a different line. If he is unhappy, neurotic, torn by conflicts inhibited in his social life, analysis may bring him harmony, peace of mind, full efficiency, whether he remains a homosexual or gets changed. If you make up your mind he should have analysis with me — I don't expect you will — he has to come over to Vienna. I have no intention of leaving here. However don't neglect to give me your answer.

Sincerely yours with kind wishes

Freud

P.S. I did not not find it difficult to read your handwriting. Hope you will not find my writing and my English a harder task.

Letter from Sigmund Freud to the mother of a homosexual
(1936), later donated to the Kinsey Institute

against admittance. Sachs, Abraham, and Eitingon urged from Berlin that this was a matter for the individual society to determine, although, they added, there should be a presumption that any homosexual was neurotic, unless analysis demonstrated otherwise.[51] Even Ferenczi, long a champion of the legalization of homosexuality, insisted that "these people are too abnormal" to be analysts.[52] Freud, in contrast, recommended acceptance but conceded that the matter was ultimately to be determined by the local analytic society. In 1921, in another incident, Ernest Jones wrote Freud informing him that he was refusing psychoanalytic training to a homosexual. Freud again disagreed: "We cannot exclude such persons without other sufficient reasons, as we cannot agree with their legal persecution. . . . a decision in such cases should depend upon a thorough examination of the other qualities of the candidate."[53]

Politically, the ethos of the analytic movement became more democratic. Whereas in 1910 Freud had argued for an elite "along the lines of Plato's republic," by the twenties he advocated local autonomy, as just noted. When Ferenczi welcomed Eitingon to the Committee in 1919, he told him that the idea was "to keep Freud's work *unchanged* as much as possible. . . . Everything must be cared for with a kind of dogmatism. . . . The ability to give up one's own idea in favor of a central idea [was the] chief qualification for membership."[54] But such views were not held by younger analysts and were soon abandoned by Ferenczi himself. After World War I, moreover, disagreements did not necessarily provoke schisms. Rank and Ferenczi left the analytic movement voluntarily, albeit amid turmoil; they were not excluded. In 1927 when the International Training Commission tried to impose lay analysis on the New York Psychoanalytic Society, Anna Freud led the opposition, calling it an obvious injustice.

In the postwar period, however, there were important antidemocratic exceptions. One was Freud's tragic attempt to impose Horace Frink on American analysis, which Freud regarded as "leaderless." Frink was a handsome, non-Jewish patient of Freud's. In the course of his analysis, Freud urged Frink to leave his wife and children and marry a wealthy married woman whom Frink believed he loved. In 1921 Freud told Frink: "Your complaint that you cannot grasp your homosexuality implies that you are not yet aware of your phantasy of making me a rich man. If matters turn out all right let us change this imaginary gift into a real contribution to the Psychoanalytic Funds." While Freud's meaning may not be wholly clear, he was certainly exploiting his patient's vulnerability. Frink had episodes of insanity for the rest of his life and blamed Freud for not realizing that analysis had to be restricted to the neuroses.[55] This was the case that led Freud to admit to Abram Kardiner that analysis could precipitate a psychosis. All American analysts knew this story, and it deepened their alienation from the man they sometimes called "the Pope in Vienna." Another antidemocratic incident, described in a later chapter, was the exclusion of Wilhelm Reich from the analytic movement in 1934, an event that shows the power of anticommunism to corrupt liberal values.

The task that the analytic societies faced in the 1920s was to establish stable, legitimate, professional institutions. The 1918 Budapest resolutions specified the means: mass therapy and the didactic or training analysis. Ego psychology—the analysis of the resistance—provided a practice-oriented theory that facilitated training and certification. The first analytic institute to implement the Budapest resolutions was also the center of postwar theorizing: the Berlin Institute.

Supported by government funds and recognized by the medical community, the Berlin Psychoanalytic Institute was the flagship for the entire movement. Run by Karl Abraham, Max Eitingon, and Ernst Simmel, benefiting both from proximity to and distance from Vienna, sponsoring the influential *Kinderseminar*—the discussion group of younger analysts such as Otto Fenichel, Käthe Friedländer, Edith Jacobson, and George Gerö—the institute pioneered in ego psychology.[56] Others trained there include Erich Fromm, Franz Alexander, Karen Horney, Sándor Rádo, Melanie Klein, Theodor Reik, Therese Benedek, Helene Deutsch, and Edward and James Strachey. By the fall of 1928, sixty-six analysts had graduated and thirty-four were in training.[57] Berlin also housed the *Verlag* and the *Internationale Zeitschrift*, edited by Rádo. Spurred by its example, societies were developing in Dresden, Hamburg, Frankfurt, Heidelberg, and southwest Germany when the ascent of the Nazis to power effectively destroyed German psychoanalysis.

International analytic politics took shape around the London and Vienna societies along with Berlin. The London Psychoanalytic Society, with about fifty-five members, counted among its members Ernest Jones, a central figure in the IPA who maintained close relations not only with Sigmund and Anna Freud, but also with the far-flung parts of the former British empire, especially the United States. It benefited from a relatively democratic and woman-friendly environment and was also associated with a substantial publishing effort: Leonard and Virginia Woolf's Hogarth Press, which published the English edition of the *International Journal of*

Psychoanalysis, the English translations of Freud, and the International Psychoanalytical Library.[58] Like Berlin and London, the Vienna Psychoanalytic Society was a hub of training. By the early thirties, the number of candidates had grown to thirty-five. Freud signed diplomas, until stopped by protests from other societies.[59]

Reflecting its inaugural place in the history of psychoanalysis, Vienna also produced ego psychology's definitive formulation. Written as an eightieth-birthday present to her father, Anna Freud's 1936 *Ego Psychology and the Mechanisms of Defense* recast Reich's idea of character as a theory of the defenses. While a one-sided concentration on the id characterized "the now obsolete situation of hypnosis," Anna Freud concluded, it is only when analysts move back and forth between the ego's defenses and the free associations that arise from the id "that we can speak of *psychoanalysis.*"[60] After the rise of the Nazis, this modified version of ego psychology spread to England and, especially, the United States.

Alongside mainstream ego psychology, three important variations emerged in London, Paris, and Budapest. In each case, the idea of personal autonomy underwent a revision. The first variation was associated with Melanie Klein, who proposed an *object-relational* view of the ego. According to Klein, one incurred obligations not by virtue of being generically human, as in Kant and Freud, but because one was inseparably connected to others by the peculiar circumstances of one's life. The most important of these connections, the one that shaped all future relations, was with the mother. Developing an ethic of responsibility rather than an ethic of justice, providing what some have called a feminine alternative to Freud, Klein's thought resonated with a new, middle-class orientation to the problem of building up and sustaining personal relations, as opposed to the problem of autonomy implicit in the theory of the Oedipus complex. Klein emigrated to London in 1926 and delivered her inaugural lecture in the home of Virginia Woolf's brother. Her thought reflected the influence of the philosopher G. E. Moore, who argued that immediate situated relations—for example, to friends, family, and community—took precedence over abstract ideals.

In 1936 Jacques Lacan developed a second alternative to ego psychology in his famous "mirror stage" article. According to Lacan, the ego or "I" was a defensive response to the traumatic discovery of emptiness, an imaginary "crystallization or sedimentation of images of an individual's own body and of self-images reflected back to him or her by others."[61] Having no basis in what Freud had called the instincts, the ego was better thought of as an object than an agent. According to Freud, the statement "Where id was there shall be ego" defined analysis, but Lacan insisted that the purpose of analysis was not to strengthen the ego but to relax it, wear down its defenses, and encourage it to adopt a detached attitude toward its own narcissism. If Klein contrasted responsibility to autonomy, Lacan encouraged an ironic acceptance of one's divided nature, one that in many ways went back to the original idea of the unconscious. Emerging from the Société Psychanalytique de Paris, founded in 1926 with twenty members and two journals (*L'Evolution psychiatrique* and *Revue française de psychanalyse*), Lacan's alternative reflected the distinctness of French psychoanalysis, which drew upon earlier traditions of French moral thought, Heideggerian philosophy, and surrealism.

Finally, in Budapest, Ferenczi became the favored doctor and central figure in a freelance, café-based intellectual circle. In contrast to Freud's emphasis on the difficulty of achieving autonomy, Ferenczi argued that the original state of the newborn was one of expecting to receive without having to give anything in return.[62] Passive receptivity, not agency, was the driving force of development. However implausible, his argument had ethical force. Whatever the original psychological state of human beings, they *deserve* to start life with their fundamental needs met. Because nearly all the Hungarian analysts eventually emigrated, Ferenczi's deeply felt rejection of Freud's insistence on abstinence had profound long-term effects. Those inspired by Ferenczi include Istvan Hollós and Imre Hermann, who drew on primatology to theorize the need to cling, and Alice and Michael Balint, early researchers into the mother/child relationship.[63] Ultimately, Ferenczi's thought lies behind Heinz Kohut's theory of narcissism. Those in Ferenczi's debt believed that analysis should provide a "corrective emotional experience," not insight per se.[64]

In its emphasis on the ego's vulnerability, in the way the ego was formed out of its own love relations, and, above all, in viewing the ego as the site of resistance and defensiveness, Freud's structural theory was at the center of the rethinking concerning autonomy that occurred in the 1920s. The variations that developed—object relations, the mirror stage, and passive object love—variations to which we will return in subsequent chapters, further contributed to this modernist redefinition. Klein complicated the ideal of autonomy by linking it to responsibility to concrete others. Lacan questioned whether the wish for autonomy was not simply a defense against the unconscious. Ferenczi insisted that autonomy, responsibility, and subjectivity all rested on a fundamental, quasi-innate demand for what would soon be called recognition. The result was a profound interrogation of one of modernity's central ideals.

Meanwhile, the psychoanalytic movement grew. In 1935 Freud boasted of its range: "In addition to the older local groups (in Vienna, Berlin, Budapest, London, Holland, Switzerland, and Russia)," he stated, "societies have since been formed in Paris and Calcutta, two in Japan, several in the United States, and quite recently one each in Jerusalem and South Africa and two in Scandinavia."[65] Yet, as psychoanalysis spread, it encountered new difficulties. "Resistance" was a psychological concept: it described something "inside" individuals. But resistance was also embodied in social institutions, cultural prejudices, and the organization of knowledge. During the interwar period, attacks on psychoanalysis came from conservatives, fascists, and Bolsheviks, but also from liberal defenders of scientific orthodoxy.

The unremitting opposition of the Catholic church, which effectively postponed the large-scale entry of analysis into France, Italy, Spain, Portugal, Latin America, and parts of eastern Europe until after World War II, was especially important. Even in Vienna, analysts lived in fear of the church. High church officials, such as Father Agostino Gemelli, a Milanese architect of Catholic/fascist cooperation, and Father Wilhelm Schmidt, director of the Lateran Ethnological Museum in Rome, were passionate anti-Freudians. Schmidt was prominent in Viennese academic life.[66] Much of the embittered opposition to Wilhelm Reich came from the conviction that by entering politics Reich risked drawing the wrath of the church. Freud postponed publishing *Moses and Monotheism* out of the same fear. The church's shadow helps explain the "hierarchical, correct and courteous" aura of the Vienna Psychoanalytic Society.[67] French antagonism to a theory "applicable only to Jews, [Freud's] racial brothers, predisposed to libidinal pansexualism," stemmed in part from the same source.[68] Catholicism and anti-Semitism also retarded the efforts of Ludwig Jekels to establish a society in Poland.[69] In Ireland the church had psychoanalysis banned.[70]

Catholic opposition, however, could also give analysis an edge. The first collected works of Freud in any language began publication in Madrid in 1922 as a result of José Ortega y Gasset's initiative.[71] The paintings, films, and assemblages of Salvador Dalí and Luis Buñuel reflect Freud's influence in Spain. Analytic reading groups began in Mexico, Brazil, and Peru in the late twenties. Angel Garma, who trained in Berlin and emigrated to Argentina, sparked a belated but explosive post–World War II expansion.[72]

After Edoardo Weiss's lectures were published in Trieste in 1931, Italian analysis also began to take off.[73] In England, meanwhile, Samuel Beckett drew on Jesuit metaphysics to influence his analyst, Wilfred Bion. Nonetheless, overall, the church's opposition to the project of personal autonomy, as well as to nonmarital sexuality, retarded analysis.

Institutionalized Marxism was a second center of resistance to psychoanalysis. As we saw, even those Bolsheviks who embraced analysis rejected the idea of personal autonomy. Stalin's defeat of Trotsky in the late twenties ended the clandestine support Trotsky had funneled to Vera Schmidt and other analysts. Stalinism portrayed itself as an alternative to "bourgeois" psychology: "For Freud, man exists entirely in the past. . . . For Freud, the conscious is subordinate to the unconscious. For Freud, man is a pawn of internal, elemental forces."[74] The last translation of Freud into Russian appeared in 1930.[75] Freud wrote Nikolai Osipov, his Prague-based Russian translator: "From somewhere the Bolsheviks have caught the opinion that psychoanalysis is hostile to their system. You know the truth that our science is not able to be put into the service of any party, but that it needs a certain liberal-mindedness [*Freiheitlichkeit*]."[76]

Yet another source of resistance was the increasing rationalization of science and medicine. Before World War I there were alternatives to Newtonian notions of causality, quantification, and prediction. Physics had broken down and been reconstructed to incorporate relativity, uncertainty, the subatomic, and the cosmological. Biology had become a full-fledged science by incorporating contingency and particularity. Positivism was in retreat, despite efforts to rebuild it in Vienna and Cambridge. In that context, Freud's insistence on the scientific character of psychoanalysis had been widely accepted. Albert Einstein himself had engaged in a well-publicized correspondence with the founder of psychoanalysis.

The second industrial revolution, however, encouraged the rise of foundation-sponsored "big science," which placed a premium on prediction and control. Behaviorism swept the social sciences, including psychology. The Rockefeller Foundation financed behaviorist child-study research in several European capitals, including London and Vienna. At first psychoanalysis benefited from the new boom in empirical research. For example, Charlotte Bühler directed a Rockefeller-funded research center at the University of Vienna.[77] Although Bühler despised psychoanalysis and banned discussion of it in her classroom, many prominent analysts, among them René Spitz, Else Fraenkel, Marie Jahoda, Rudolf Ekstein, Bruno Bettelheim, and Edith Weisskopf, began their careers by studying with her. Analysts also benefited from the institutionalization of empirical child study in Geneva. There they founded two analytic societies, including one at the Institut Rousseau of the University of Geneva, one of the leading pedagogical laboratories in the world.[78] Jean Piaget, a member of one Geneva society, sought to add a cognitive theory to psychoanalysis. But the two worlds were also in tension. Undergoing a didactic analysis with Sabina Spielrein, Piaget abruptly realized what transference was, announced "*J'ai compris,*" and walked out.[79]

"Big science" meant that psychoanalysis had to be translated into measurable variables and testable hypotheses. The Viennese logical positivist Richard von Mises conceded that analysis was grounded in "incontestable observations" but suggested that its regularities might better be described in statistical terms.[80] In the United States, John Dollard's 1939 *Frustration and Aggression* used laboratory experiments on rats to demonstrate that "aggression is always a consequence of frustration."[81] Even sympathetic behaviorists could not conceal their condescension. Clark Hull never tired of reiterating "that there was something of importance in [psychoanalytic] theory." Lewis Madison Terman considered the Freudian concepts "even . . . discounted . . . ninety percent . . . one of the two most important contributions to modern psychology, mental tests being the other."[82] Analysts responded to such "compliments" ambivalently. When Saul Rosenzweig sent Freud data purporting to confirm his theories, Freud responded that analysis did not lend itself to experimental testing, but he added, "Still, it can do no harm."[83] As we shall see, Freud was wrong.

Medicine, too, was transformed after World War I, becoming professionalized, more dependent on laboratories and hospitals, and far more prestigious. Holistic, theory-based treatment went into decline in favor of demonstrable, measurable alteration of the statistically probable course of a specific disease. Bacteriology supplied the model. Family intervention, sexual policy, and pronatalism (the encouragement of childbearing) proliferated in new "Ministries of Health" aimed at serving the *Volksgemeinschaft*, the national or racial community. These changes put increasing pressure on analysts to be doctors and to coordinate their theories with those of the laboratory-based sciences.

As a result, European psychoanalysis became increasingly medicalized. The Dutch Psychoanalytic Society, founded with twelve members in 1917 by Johann H. W. van Ophuijsen and Westerman Holstijn, was restricted to M.D.s.[84] The major obstacle the Soviets faced in gaining acceptance by the IPA in the early twenties came from the fact that few of its leaders were doctors. IPA analysts had special difficulty accepting that Otto Schmidt, vice president of the Moscow Psychoanalytic Society, was a mathematician.[85] Of course, medical domination was contested. Conflicts over lay analysis led to the founding of a second Dutch society in Leyden, as well as to a split in the Belgian society.[86] But the tendency toward medicalization was consistent and was vastly intensified by the weight the United States had in the analytic world.

Nowhere else had doctors achieved the status and financial benefits that they enjoyed in the United States. By using licensing to limit the supply of doctors, as recommended in the Flexner Report, they had revolutionized their position. American psychoanalysts followed suit. In 1925 the American Psychoanalytic Association passed a regulation requiring a medical degree for every analyst.[87] Freud protested immediately, describing medicalization as "the last mask of resistance against psychoanalysis, and the most dangerous of all," and predicting a "gloomy future [for] analysis if it does not succeed in creating an abode for itself outside of medicine."[88]

The effects of medicalization were exacerbated by the financial dependence of European analysis on the United States. By 1919, 60 percent of Freud's personal caseload consisted of Americans, and he often conducted his analyses in English.[89] Keeping a safe in his office for dollars, he urged Rank to charge the "savages" high fees.[90] In 1920 he insisted that Abraham defer to the American refusal to hold an analytic congress in Berlin, noting that without American support "we shall not be able to keep the German journals alive for more than a year."[91] As late as 1932, the *Verlag* was so dependent on American subscriptions that its managers opposed the formation of the English-language *Psychoanalytic Quarterly*.[92] Commenting on the American insistence on medicalization, the analyst Hermann Nunberg remarked, "In our ranks, as elsewhere, the economic struggle finds its ideology."[93]

In spite of Freud's opposition, analysis moved inexorably toward requiring a medical degree. In 1927, when the *International Journal of Psychoanalysis* published a one-hundred-page symposium on lay analysis, the majority of analysts opposed Freud. Ferenczi, Freud's most loyal ally, organized a group of lay analysts in the United States and applied to the International as a test case, but the group dissolved.[94] In 1929 Jones got the British Medical Association to define the Freudian version of psychoanalysis as the only legitimate one, thus further sanctioning the principle of medical regulation. Freud called himself a "Commander-in-Chief without an army" and hoped the conflict over lay analysis would bring about what he called "a friendly separation with the Americans."[95]

In fact, the reverse occurred. In 1930 a phalanx of younger, American-born analysts seeking a more "professional" approach led a revolt against the older generation of eastern European Jews, especially Brill.[96] Taking the

Berlin Psychoanalytic Institute as their model, this "tough-minded American elite" courted Franz Alexander, known as a revisionist ego psychologist with a "modern" approach.[97] The next year Hanns Sachs moved to Boston and Hermann Nunberg to Philadelphia. In 1932, after Alexander became head of the Chicago Psychoanalytic Society, Karen Horney became his assistant. Sándor Rádo came to New York to organize an institute on the Berlin model. The amount of money raised for Rádo's venture—forty thousand dollars—was unheard-of in European analytic circles.[98] Even before the triumph of the Nazis, then, the homeland of the second industrial revolution began reclaiming its prodigal offspring.

Observing the growth of American power in the psychoanalytic world, Freud vented common strains of anti-Americanism intensified by his own neurotic fear of poverty, but also containing an element of truth. Sneering at "dollar country," "Dollaria," and that "crazy anal *Adlerei,*" he told Rank that analysis "suits Americans as a white shirt suits a raven."[99] His fullest discussion of the relation of analysis to U.S. culture was excised from *The Question of Lay Analysis,* the 1925 work he wrote to defend his position, because Jones and Sachs feared it would provoke the Americans to secede from the International. Recently published, the excised passages equate America with Calvinism, mind cure, and, although Freud does not use the word, Fordism.

Freud was skeptical, he wrote, of a nation whose highest ideal was "efficiency, fitness for life," especially when it omitted to take "precautions when appointing a helper for their psychic troubles." "Time is indeed money," he continued, "but it is not entirely clear why it has to be transformed into money in such a hurry. . . . In our Alpine lands, a common salutation when two acquaintances meet or part is: Take your time. We have poured much scorn on this formula, but in view of American haste, we have come to realize how much worldly wisdom it contains. Yet the American has no time. He has a passion for large numbers, for the magnification of all dimensions, but also for cutting the investment of time to an absolute minimum. I believe the word for this is 'record.' " At the end he added: "The American superego seems greatly to mitigate its severity toward the ego where the interests of earning money are concerned. But perhaps my readers will find that I have now had enough wicked things to say about that country, before which we have learned to bow down in the last decade."[100]

After the entry of women, the most consequential event in the history of psychoanalysis was the debate over medicalization, a debate that ultimately involved the scientific status of psychoanalysis. While it is often said today that the claims of psychoanalysis to scientific standing have been disproven, the deeper question is what is meant by science. Reflecting Kantian as opposed to Baconian thinking, Freud did not regard science as a problem-solving enterprise aimed at meeting human desires. Rather, he believed the development of science would bring about a change in human nature itself, namely, the modification of desire by reason. In this sense, the reduction of science to behaviorist parameters and of psychoanalysis to psychiatry implied the shrinking of autonomy to choice, losing the element of self-reflection. Observing this process in his own time, Freud complained that men and women were "ready to accept the results of scientific thinking, but without the change having taken place in them which scientific thinking brings about in people."[101]

Finally, as psychoanalysis spread, many rejected it as a Western theory with little relevance to the vast masses of Africa, Asia, and the Middle East. This resistance reflected the fact that psychoanalysis, like Christianity, first pene-trated beyond the West as part of imperialism. In the Philippines, analyti-cally influenced colonial doctors taught soldiers and administrators who earlier had been "unnerved" by "tropical neurasthenia," "Philippinitis," and "brain-fag" that "nervousness indicated not an over-permeable outer mem-brane but a rotten core."[102] The New Zealand psychoanalyst Claud Dangar Daly's "Psychology of Revolutionary Tendencies" counseled colonial ad-ministrators that the anti-British movement was motivated by no less infan-tile emotions than the Irish or suffragist rebellions had been.[103] Géza Róheim's ethnographic expeditions, which introduced psychoanalysis to Australia, were also made possible by imperialism. As a result, colonial sub-jects who pioneered in introducing analysis to the non-Western world had understandably mixed feelings about it.

T. Girindrasekhar Bose, born in 1886, the son of a maharajah and by his own description "the second self-analyzed analyst in the history of psycho-analysis," is an example. Bose founded the Indian Psychoanalytic Society in Calcutta in 1922.[104] Of fifteen original members, nine were academics and five were doctors. Bose conducted his analyses in Bengali and wore tradi-tional clothes. Autonomy, as understood in Europe, was not a high value for Bose. Rather, he drew on Hindu introspective techniques, as well as on yogic and tantric visualizations, to prescribe an actively didactic stance for the analyst. Basing his technique more on the model of the guru than on that of the analyst, he considered even Ferenczi too nondirective. The rea-son for his stance, as he explained in the *International Journal of Psycho-*

analysis and in his correspondence with Freud, was that psyche, body, and community were not invariant across cultures. In nations that had not experienced the West's psychological revolution, and in which individuals believed that psychic disturbances were caused by black magic, karma, or disturbed humoral equilibrium, external direction was the necessary prelude to an inward orientation.[105]

Bose also countered imperialist uses of psychoanalysis. Owen Berkeley-Hill was a psychiatrist and member of the Calcutta society who had been analyzed by Ernest Jones. Partly responsible for the quick recognition of the Calcutta society by the IPA, Berkeley-Hill, a student of yogic sphincter control, traced the supposed dislike inspired by Hindus to their anal fixations. Bose contemptuously rejected this theory, stressing instead the mother over the father, object relations over sexuality, and a positive approach to Indian culture over a condescending one. To do so he drew upon India's "core fantasy of the split mother" to argue that an intense but interrupted period of maternal fusion predisposed Hindu men to be more accepting of their "maternal feminine component," less prone to castration anxiety, and more likely to accept a negative/submissive solution to the Oedipal crisis.[106]

Each non-Western nation followed its own path to analysis. Whereas Bose was self-taught, Heisaku Kosawa, the main figure in Japanese analysis, studied at the Vienna Psychoanalytic Institute from 1929 to 1933 and was analyzed by Freud. And whereas Bose was often reacting against English medicine, Japanese psychoanalysis was relatively self-directed. Kosawa taught at the University of Tohoku in Sendai in the northeast, where the first Japanese analytic society started. Yaekichi Yabe, a psychologist, and Kenji Otsuki, a writer, founded a second society at Tokyo in 1932, along with the first Freudian review in Japanese, *Seishin-Bunseki.* The two societies were the center of East Asian analysis, their translations studied at Seoul Imperial University in Korea as well as in the Chinese coastal cities. As we shall see, Kosawa, like Bose, developed an alternative to the Oedipal theory, the "Ajase complex," focused on the boy's relation to the mother.[107]

China, where Western psychiatry had been introduced by missionary societies, presented a third variation. Here there were few if any attempts to synthesize indigenous and Freudian thought. Instead, analysis entered China as part of the Western-imported modernity of the May Fourth movement. After 1919, in the so-called New Period, Zhang Shenfu translated Freud to counter behaviorism in *New Tide,* one of the most important journals of the Chinese Enlightenment.[108] "Freud" also served as a code word for sexuality to advertise such novels as *Diary of a Young Girl.*[109] Most

A Japanese translation of Freud printed over
a letter written by Freud to Kenji Otsuki

important, psychoanalysis was linked to the need for revolution. A 1936 newspaper letter explained: "In modern times, the main obstacle to human instincts is the social system itself. Social property is in the hands of a handful of people." To preserve their privileges, these people institute "religious doctrines and moral rules." Meanwhile, "the instincts cry out for satisfaction. . . . Such a situation is particularly common among us women."[110]

In the Islamic world, psychoanalysis remained largely undeveloped. The main exception was Ataturk's Turkey, to which, in the late thirties, psychoanalyst Edith Vowinckel-Weigert accompanied her labor-economist husband. Vowinckel-Weigert's first patients were Jewish refugees from Germany, but Turkey soon developed an indigenous analytic tradition. The first translation, Hans Zulliger's *From the Unconscious Life of Our School Youth,* influenced educational reform. In addition, French psychiatrists worked in Tunisia, Morocco, Algeria, and Senegal, eventually establishing a society in Lebanon. Moustapha Safouan, a follower of Lacan, produced the first Arabic translation of *The Interpretation of Dreams* in 1958: *Tafsir el ahlam.*[111] The French tradition of African and Middle Eastern psychoanalysis, however, was the one that Frantz Fanon attacked in his writings on the Algerian revolution, arguing that only violence could remediate the psychical damage done by colonialism.

The attitude of Western psychoanalysts toward non-Western psychoanalysis was complex. The *ur*-text on this question, Wulf Sachs's 1937 *Black Hamlet,* an intimate account of the exchange between a Jewish émigré psychoanalyst and a Rhodesian healer who has lost faith in his father's methods of traditional healing, was at root an attack on colonial psychiatry's distinction between black and white psyches.[112] Freud took his Asian interlocutors seriously. He urged Zhang Shizhao, a government official seeking to introduce psychoanalysis into China, to "test our hunches concerning archaic forms of expression against the material of your language."[113] He boasted to Andreas-Salomé that his Indian followers were "learned Hindus," not white expatriates, colonial administrators, or native dilettantes. And he responded to Bose's objections to psychoanalysis at length, conceding that psychoanalysis had neglected the coexistence of opposite wishes from three sources—bisexuality (male/female), ambivalence (love/hate), and activity/passivity.[114] On the other hand, he told Romain Rolland that "Hellenic love of proportion, Jewish sobriety, and philistine anxiety" kept him away from Asian thought. And when a Calcutta professor of philosophy asked to visit him in 1926, he commented: "My need of Indians is for the present fully satisfied."[115]

Freud's suspicion of Asian thought was not due to an aversion to cultural pluralism. On the contrary, he criticized Marxism because it lacked an understanding of how "racial variations and . . . cultural transformations" interacted with economics.[116] Freud's attitude reflected the priority he assigned to the ideal of personal autonomy, an ideal that would have to be reformulated and reconceptualized outside the Western context. Symptomatically, although his 1930 *Civilization and Its Discontents* mentions the loss of ego consciousness in yoga as one route to happiness, Freud told Romain Rolland that he was unable to experience the "oceanic" feeling—the "feeling of an indissoluble bond, of being one with the external world"—that Rolland associated with Indian mysticism and called "the true source of religious sentiments." The oceanic sentiment, Freud suggested, may simply be a remnant of primary narcissism.[117]

The breadth and diversity of the analytic societies of the 1920s and '30s suggest the extent to which the psychoanalytically influenced ideas of autonomy and resistance were important to the first mass, self-conscious experience of modernity. Wherever analysis penetrated, an analytic milieu developed, if not at odds with, then at least distinct from, the dominant culture. In these milieus, the relatively small number of people who went into analysis, seeking either a profession or a "cure," made honesty in relation to oneself their most strongly held group value. In 1920, when Anton von Freund, the greatest financial donor to psychoanalysis in his time, was dying of cancer at the age of forty, Freud visited him daily, writing at the end to Eitingon that Freund "bore his hopelessness with heroic clarity, did not disgrace analysis."[118] Thus, in spite of professionalization, psychoanalysis still possessed the character of a sect, with a distinctive identity, overlapping identifications, and core values, such as stoicism and truthfulness. In what D.W. Winnicott later called a "facilitating environment," such values contributed to much larger processes of social change. Where the environment was less facilitating, as increasingly in Germany and eastern Europe, psychoanalysts supplied a dark, pessimistic counter- or ultramodernism that lowered the register of the music of the Jazz Age, almost as if its practitioners sensed the coming catastrophe.

Chapter Eight

THE TURN TOWARD
THE MOTHER

The process which has been described refers, as has been expressly said, to male children only. How does the corresponding development take place in little girls? . . . Here the feminist demand for equal rights for the sexes does not take us very far.

—Sigmund Freud, 1924

Just as the second industrial revolution inspired a change from moral to personal autonomy, so it inspired a change in the meaning of women's emancipation. The classical liberal conception of women's emancipation, which originated in the Enlightenment, emphasized equal rights. Grounded in the idea of a common human reason, it focused on emancipation in the public sphere. In the 1920s, however, advocates of women's emancipation viewed the struggle for equal rights as largely completed. Refusing to rest content with the assertion of a common human reason, they explored gender difference—then understood as "women's difference"—especially in regard to two questions: mothering and sexuality.

Women's new relation to the family underlay this change. As production left the household, as the war economies mobilized women, and as women won the vote, women were drawn into public life. At the same time they found themselves at the emotional center of the new, family-based consumer economy. Thus, their ties to the family were simultaneously loosened sociologically and reconstructed at a psychological level. Accordingly, they sought to complete the struggle for equality in the public realm while drawing on psychoanalysis to explore gender difference in the sphere of personal life.

Two changes were especially important. First, whereas maternal responsibilities had previously been invoked to justify confining women to the family, many now argued that mothering involved social, not just private, responsibilities. For example, Robert Briffault's *The Mothers* (1927) argued that all forms of social organization arose from the need for prolonged maternal care, and Lewis Mumford's *Technics and Civilization* (1934) portrayed the maternal village as the basis for the paternal town.[1] As a result, attention to women's mothering often implied emancipation rather than privatization. In the words of H. G. Wells, "the discipline of cooperation" implied the emergence of women "from the cell of the home" and pointed toward a new culture in which men would be more "more social and cooperative" and women "less cloistered."[2]

Second, while the Victorian notion of the mother was that of a desexualized "angel in the house," married women of the twenties were openly interested in sexual satisfaction. According to the Jungian analyst Beatrice Hinkle, the postwar woman differed from the suffragist in that she based her feminism on "the necessities of . . . personal life."[3] The great discovery of the age, opined the neo-Freudian *Modern Quarterly*, was "that woman wants sex love as men want it, desperately."[4] Nor was women's sexuality confined to the family. Whereas in the 1890s female homosexuality had still been largely invisible, in the twenties a lesbian identity was elaborated in popular works like Radclyffe Hall's *The Well of Loneliness* (1928). Lesbian subcultures imagined and portrayed the female genitalia and female sexuality in ways far in advance of the medical and psychological sciences. For some, a new culture "neither masculine nor feminine but specifically and peculiarly homosexual" was emerging.[5]

In this context, the stage was set for a new encounter between women and psychoanalysis. Ida Bauer walked out of Freud's consulting room in 1900 in part because she had no vote, no chance for gainful employment, and no culture supportive of her needs as a woman. Women drawn to analysis in the 1920s, however, were no longer so impoverished. Suzanne LaFollette published Freudian essays in *The Freeman* because she worried that an "empty emancipation" might lead women to live "without the exercise of the reflective intellect, without ideas, without ideals, and in a proper use of the word without emotions."[6] In Salt Lake City a circle of about twenty-five lesbians read and discussed Freud's essays in an effort to destigmatize their way of life, while in Paris Madeleine Pelletier, a psychiatrist, cross-dresser, and feminist, regularly cited Freud to support women's sexual freedom.[7] As we have seen, many women pursued psychoanalysis to help them separate not only from their fathers but also from their mothers, whose "grotesque solicitude" could smother their independence. The psychoanalyst Helene Deutsch, for example, allied with Freud to gain, as she put it, "liberation from the tyranny of the mother."[8] In all these cases, psychoanalysis helped recast the meaning of women's emancipation in the context of personal life.

After World War I, moreover, large numbers of women became psychoanalysts, altering the character of Freudian discussions and the focus of analytic concerns. Whereas Freud had originally assumed a single, undifferentiated path of psychic development for boys and girls, the entry of women brought the issue of sexual difference to the fore. Whereas Freud had sometimes tacitly adopted the boy's trajectory as the norm, analytic attention now turned to the girl, to female sexuality, and to lesbianism. As in the analysis of personal autonomy, the analysis of female sexuality centered on obstacles to self-fulfillment, especially on women's resistance to femininity, meaning sexual love for men. But explaining these obstacles turned out to be more difficult and far-reaching than anyone at first suspected. The effort led by the 1930s to a major shift in the analytic paradigm: from the father to the mother, from castration to separation, from authority to dependence. At the same time, the heart of the Freudian discovery—namely, men's and women's common experiences of passivity, fear, and, indeed, "castration," and the importance of sexuality to those experiences—threatened to be lost as a new "female psychology" emerged.

The exploration of women's difference in the 1920s was part of a broader social process: the entry of women into paid labor and the professions. Psychoanalysis offered an especially dramatic example of this process. In the first decade of analytic history, from 1902 to 1909, there had been 80 male and 2 female analysts. In the period between 1910 and 1919 there were 221 men and 39 women. By 1929 there were 219 men and 92 women.[9] Thus, women accounted for all of the growth in the 1920s. As we have said, at the end of the decade the majority of the younger adherents were women.[10]

Psychoanalysis in the early twenties was considerably more open to women than comparable professions. In Germany the percentage of women lawyers rose from 0.4 percent in 1925 to 1.3 percent in 1933.[11] In the latter year the percentage of women doctors was 6.5 percent.[12] Among analysts, in contrast, the figure was about 40 percent and growing. Helene Deutsch's examiner in internal medicine at the University of Vienna refused to allow her to attend his lectures and routinely addressed her as "Mr. Deutsch." When she became an analyst, in contrast, she almost immediately became director of training at the Vienna Psychoanalytic Institute. Only in the "helping professions" and a few enclaves in the social sciences did women have remotely comparable professional opportunities.

The shift was not only a matter of numbers. By 1930, women were among the dominant figures in analysis: Marie Bonaparte in France, Jeanne Lampl–de Groot in Holland, Alfhild Tamm in Sweden, Sabina Spielrein in the Soviet Union, and Melanie Klein in England are examples. Karen Horney played an important role in Germany and a central one after emigrating to the United States. Anna Freud increasingly acted as her father's proxy after he developed cancer in 1923. Other important women analysts of the 1920s included Alice Balint, Clara Thompson, Frieda Fromm-Reichmann, Ruth Mack Brunswick, and Barbara Low.

At the same time, however, these women often depended for their positions on powerful men, such as Freud, Jones, or Abraham. Moreover, often women were not simply analysts unmodified. Rather they specialized in child analysis or "applied analysis," that is, education or social work, spheres that were coded as feminine. Often, too, their theoretical work centered on the specificity of female development and the role of the mother. Anna Freud and Melanie Klein, for example, the leading figures in the next generation, distinguished themselves by their practical experience with children. One was a mother, the other a teacher. Both were child clinicians. Neither was a doctor.

Freud's writings reflected the changed composition of the movement. His 1925 essay on female sexuality was ostensibly written without regard to the sex of his audience. But his "Femininity" lecture of 1933 was marked by what Sarah Kofman has called, with only a little exaggeration, an attempt "to establish complicity with the women analysts so as to clear himself of the suspicion of 'anti-feminism.' "[13] In it he credited women analysts for their innovations: Ruth Mack Brunswick was the first "to describe . . . a fixation in the pre-Oedipus stage"; Jeanne Lampl–de Groot "established the incredible phallic activity of girls towards their mother"; Helene Deutsch showed that relations between homosexual women reproduce relations between mother and baby. Evoking the presence "of our excellent women colleagues in analysis," Freud almost apologized for the fact that some comparisons "seemed to turn out unfavorable to their sex."[14]

Nevertheless, the growth in women's participation did not introduce what a later generation would have called a feminist sensibility into analysis. When, in the 1980s, Nancy Chodorow asked surviving female analysts how their gender affected their experience in the 1920s and '30s, they frequently claimed not to understand her question. "There are many professional women in the world; why shouldn't they be analysts too?" was a typical remark. One woman responded to Chodorow's "What did the women do?" with "I don't know, what did the women eat?" In answer to the question "Did it make a difference that so many of the leading analysts are women?" another woman answered: "I find it difficult to *lump* together women. . . . I can think of *special* women; it would have been different without *them*. But women, when you *lump* them into a *whole*, I don't know." Another remarked: "I didn't know anything about feminist movements, feminist activity . . . it seemed to be pretty easy as a woman to do what you wanted." For still others, "We were all analysts," "Training was so easygoing; people were consumed by [their] interests in psychoanalysis"; and "The thing that struck me the most and was hardest for me was doing all this in German, seeing as I didn't know German."[15] Chodorow's evidence can be extended from other sources. Charlotte Wolff, a Berlin psychiatrist, reminisced: "[We women] never thought of ourselves as . . . second-class citizens. We simply were ourselves, which is the only liberation which counts anyway."[16]

Grasping the difference between Chodorow's outlook and those of her subjects is crucial to understanding the history of psychoanalysis. For Chodorow, gender was a *social* distinction; she assumed that women's outlook would reflect their *collective* identity. Her subjects, by contrast, saw gender as subordinate to their *personal* projects, their self-authored being. The two outlooks lead to different theoretical orientations. Chodorow was interested in the differences between the sexes *as such*. Her subjects, by contrast, were interested in the psychical significance of sexual difference *in the minds of individuals*. Bisexuality, in its new Freudian sense, enabled them to focus this interest. Thus, just as the first male analysts had been self-conscious regarding their relations to "father figures" and to other men, so these women were self-conscious regarding what they called their masculine and feminine identifications. To have a successful personal life involved accepting one's masculine and feminine sides and forming a satisfactory sexual relation. This problem was the psychical counterpart to the practical problem women faced in the 1920s: the need to combine career and motherhood.

The analytic literature first took up this problem in discussions of the "anomaly" of the professional woman: a woman for whom it was important to have a sexual relation with a man and perhaps to have children, while also functioning in a public world that was still culturally homosocial or "neutral," that is, covertly male-dominated. Joan Riviere, one of the translators of Freud's *Collected Papers,* defined the problem in a 1929 paper, "Womanliness as a Masquerade." In the past, Riviere held, intellectuality in women was associated almost exclusively with "an overtly masculine type." But today one constantly meets professional women who fulfill every criterion of "complete feminine development." They are "excellent wives and mothers" and "capable housewives" with "no lack of feminine interests, e.g. in their personal appearance." They play the part of "mother substitutes" among relatives and friends at the same time as "they fulfill the duties of their profession at least as well as the average man. It is really a puzzle to know how to classify this type psychologically," Riviere wrote.[17]

Among the early female analysts, one repeatedly observes this effort to operate in the professional world without undue regard to gender, while remaining a woman—whatever that may mean—in their personal relations. Helene Deutsch was a case in point. A Polish Jew born Helene Rosenbach in 1884, Deutsch was her jurist father's favorite, mistreated by her authoritarian mother and abused by her brother. Her first paper, delivered at The Hague in 1920, concerned "a highly ambitious and intellectual [woman who] lived in a constant state of conflict between her strong masculine aspirations and the feminine role she had assumed as housewife and mother." The paper was favorably received, but afterward Deutsch went alone to a park and cried because she felt she was failing in her maternal duties to her son.[18] In another lecture she explained George Sand's feminism as a reaction to her failure to live up to her feminine aspirations. In her autobiography Deutsch credited the three great liberations of her life— from her mother, from capitalism, and from the unconscious—to the influence of powerful men: her father, her first lover, and Freud.[19]

Many other female analysts also utilized a relation with a father figure to free themselves from difficult relations with their mothers. Born in Vienna in 1882, Melanie Klein grew up, like her later rival, Anna Freud, an unwanted child competing against older, favored sisters. Her mother's death led her to enter analysis with Ferenczi in Budapest, where she had moved with her husband. After her marriage disintegrated, she moved again with her three children to Berlin and became an analyst under the mentorship of Karl Abraham. Alix Strachey described her in Berlin as taking "the high conventional line—a sort of ultra heterosexual Semiramis in slap-up fancy dress."[20] Despite Klein's early dependence on Ferenczi and Abraham, after moving to London she came into her own as an impassioned intellectual who saw herself as Freud's real successor. Yet she continued to rely on Jones's protection.

Born in 1895, Anna Freud exemplified both the daughter's devotion to the father and the single woman's responsibility for other women's children. The sadness surrounding her early life was foreshadowed in Freud's anxieties over Martha's pregnancy in the Irma dream. According to Elisabeth Young-Bruehl, "[Anna] and psychoanalysis were twins who started out competing for their father's attention." Relatively little is known of her relations with her mother, Martha, but they were undoubtedly complex. In 1920 Anna began accompanying her father to analytic congresses, and a few years later, after having been "analyzed" by her father, she described herself to Lou Andreas-Salomé as "pulled apart, analyzed, published, and in every way mishandled and mistreated."[21] In 1925, with her father sick from cancer, Anna Freud read "Some Psychical Consequences" for him at the Hamburg congress. It contains such passages as: "After a woman has become aware of the wound to her narcissism, she develops, like a scar, a sense of inferiority."

Other female analysts bonded strongly with their mothers. Karen Horney, born in Berlin in 1885, was the child of a Norwegian sea captain, a repressive patriarch whom she hated and feared. Her dynamic mother, twenty years younger than her husband, urged Horney to become a doctor. As an adolescent, Horney read the Swedish feminist and exponent of motherhood Ellen Key, likening her to a "lustrous star toward which [her] soul directed its way."[22] Later, however, when her parents divorced, Horney felt that her mother interfered and competed with her. Herself a divorced mother who raised three daughters alone, Horney met Abraham in 1907 and became influential in the Berlin Psychoanalytic Society during World War I, partly because most of the male analysts were at war.[23]

In some cases the bond to the mother was linked to feminism. Helene Stöcker, the head of the Bund für Mutterschutz and a member of the Berlin Psychoanalytic Society, strove toward a "higher synthesis" for women, the union of motherhood and career.[24] A follower of Charlotte Gilman and a passionate maternalist, Stöcker challenged Freud's emphasis on aggression by claiming to demonstrate, in a 1928 experiment, that well-fed ants would not fight.[25] Joan Riviere also came into her own through the ascendancy of a woman, Melanie Klein. In 1918 she wrote to her analyst, Ernest Jones, who may also have been her lover, of "the long tragedy of my relationship with you," while Jones described her as "the worst failure I ever had."[26]

In spite of the reluctance of some female analysts to "lump women together," analytic societies did encompass informal female-centered networks. In Berlin one such network reached beyond analysis proper to include nonanalytic female doctors such as Charlotte Wolff, the biographer

Edith Jackson, analytic pediatrician (left), Melanie Klein (center),
and Anna Freud (right), c. 1935

of Magnus Hirschfeld.[27] In the British society, a female network centered
on Melanie Klein. In the society's records, one frequently finds remarks like
that of Sylvia Payne to Klein: "I have known from the first day that I met
EG [Edward Glover] that he feared and defended himself against and was
jealous of the successful intellectual, i.e. rival, woman."[28] One indicator of
gender consciousness lay in the choice of an analyst. Sigmund Freud, in his
1920 analysis of a female homosexual, urged that his client see a female analyst because she did not trust men.[29] In 1941, by contrast, a female patient
complained to Klein that working with a woman would increase her husband's defensiveness, because he thinks we are "in league against him." In
addition, the patient confided, she herself did not trust women. Klein
replied, "The best thing you could do is to be analyzed by a woman,"
implying that the woman's lack of trust for other women was precisely what
needed analysis.[30]

Nonetheless, given their struggle to subordinate gender loyalty to personal autonomy, it is no surprise that Chodorow's subjects had mixed feelings about forms of feminism that made gender difference the foundation
of their thought. Even Horney, the most feminist of all analysts by today's

standards, refused to apply the term to herself. Yet a remark by Helene Deutsch suggests the effort analysts made to accommodate feminist concerns: "If we replace the expression 'turn toward passivity' by 'activity directed inward,' the term 'feminine passivity' acquires a more vital content. . . . The term 'activity directed inward' indicates a function, expresses something positive, and can satisfy the feminists among us who often feel that the term 'feminine passivity' has derogatory implications."[31] Finally, one did not have to be female to be feminist. Freud concedes in his 1931 essay "Female Sexuality" that not only women but "men analysts with feminist views" might disagree with him.[32]

Its ranks swelled by such women, postwar psychoanalysis vigorously debated the nature of female sexuality and the role of the mother in psychical development. The result was the second most commented-upon episode in the history of psychoanalysis, after Freud's "discovery of the unconscious." Betty Friedan, Julia Kristeva, Juliet Mitchell, Luce Irigaray, and Judith Butler followed the lead of Simone de Beauvoir in reading the debates through the lens of second-wave feminism, which focused on such questions as whether femaleness is innate or constructed, and whether Freud was a sexist, smuggling Victorian prejudices into a new science, or a feminist manqué, providing, against his own wishes, a prototheory of patriarchy. To be sure, such questions can be discerned in the texts of the 1920s and '30s, but they were peripheral. Other concerns drove the debate. Beginning with the concepts of the ego, resistance, and trauma, analysts were struggling to change analysis from a male-centered theory to one that took both sexes into account. In particular, they were pioneering in the exploration of women's personal lives: loosening female sexuality from its heterosexual teleology, considering the mother-child relationship in its full complexity, and reinterpreting aggression and envy as normal components of psychical life.

The background of the debate lay in the large-scale crisis in "sex-roles" provoked by World War I. During the war, psychoanalysis advanced a new understanding of male psychology, yet it was itself susceptible to a broader cultural backlash provoked by the successes of the women's movement, as when Freud pondered the origins of the emancipated woman's "hostile bitterness against the man."[33] During the late war years the term "masculinity complex" increasingly appeared in analytic literature. Karen Horney defined it as "the entire complex of feelings and fantasies that have for their content the woman's feeling of being discriminated against, her envy of the male, her wish to be a man and to discard the female role."[34] This tendentious background prejudice, reflecting the overwhelmingly male character of the prewar movement, shadowed the subsequent debate, so that analysts of both sexes found themselves regularly apologizing for some prior misunderstanding.

The debate itself began with a single question: since the mother is the original object, "there is no cause for surprise that boys retain that object in the Oedipus complex. But how does it happen that girls abandon it and instead take their father as an object?"[35] Karl Abraham's 1920 article "Manifestations of the Female Castration Complex," the essay that dominated the first phase of the debate, provided an answer. According to Abraham, what provoked the young girl to shift her love interest from her mother to her father was her discovery that she lacked a penis, which led her to seek a child as compensation.[36] The masculinity complex, characterized by envy and resentment of men, resulted when this process misfired.

As we shall see, several women, including Helene Deutsch and Karen Horney, produced alternative theories almost immediately. Freud, however, both built upon Abraham's line of thought and modified it. Freud's first article on female sexuality, his 1925 "On the Psychical Consequences of the Anatomical Distinction Between the Sexes," differed from Abraham's on two grounds. First, Abraham implied that in turning to her father, the girl repudiated her mother. Freud, by contrast, believed that the turn to the father did not end the relation to the mother.[37] Thus, Freud was concerned with the woman's *bisexuality,* not her heterosexuality, a term that Freud almost never used. In addition, Abraham believed that girls literally envied boys' penises, because of real advantages such as ease of exhibitionism or masturbation. For Freud, however, castration concerned not the anatomical penis but the *phallus,* a psychical representation of the erect penis.[38] Most important, whereas Abraham held that the girl's discovery of anatomical difference was the motive behind her envy, Freud held that the discovery was not the "motive" but only the "trigger."

To be sure, Freud never dropped his insistence on the castration complex. Thus, he claimed that the female dread of a castrating father led girls to make the same "tender object-cathexis" that boys repudiated because it signaled castration. In other words, girls constructed themselves as passive objects of their father's desires, while boys avoided this response to the fear of the father. But once he began writing alongside female analysts, Freud came to the view that castration can never have the force, or "content," for girls that it has for boys.[39] Rather, in trying to understand what was distinctive about female development, he began to plumb girls' early relations with their mothers. What girls feared, he concluded, was not so much external punishment—castration—as separation from the mother or loss of the mother's love.

It soon emerged that the problem of separation was larger than the problem of female sexuality that had inspired it. After his 1925 essay, accordingly, separation became more important to Freud's thought. In his 1926 *Inhibitions, Symptoms and Anxiety* he responded to Rank's *Birth Trauma* by arguing that separation was the cause of infant anxiety. He thereby demoted castration—the pivot of the Oedipus complex—to one form of separation in a sequence that included birth, weaning, and social isolation. One result was a further revision of his theory of anxiety. Previously Freud had linked anxiety to the dread of castration. In 1926, however, he wrote that anxiety originated when the mother was absent in earliest childhood. Because the infant believed that an external object "can put an end to the dangerous situation which is reminiscent of birth," the loss of that object caused anxiety.[40]

More important, in the course of trying to understand female sexuality, Freud was led to the importance of the mother not just as the infant's sexual object but as the sustaining ground of psychical life. From its focus on authority, psychoanalysis subtly shifted to a focus on dependence. Thus, though Freud never abandoned his insistence on bisexuality, fear of castration, and the phallic stage, his work converged with that of the new generation of female analysts. Nonetheless, he fell silent on the question of female sexuality for six years.

Freud developed the theories of the phallic stage, the castration complex, and the Oedipal crisis in part to explain female sexuality, but no sooner did he apply them than it became clear how little of female sexuality they actually explained. A deeper understanding depended on the study of the girl's early relations with her mother, study largely undertaken by the female analysts. So massive were the implications of their work that it swept the whole of psychoanalysis into its path. A psychic landscape dominated by an *Urvater*, a primal crime, and an incest taboo now appeared as an episode in an older and more fundamental story.

Earlier discussions of the significance of the mother, for example, by Rank or Reich, tended to be apocalyptic or schematic. Thus, for Rank separation from the mother was everything: nothing else affected development. For Reich, maternal love was pure and ideal. Once female analysts entered the discussion, however, the character of the discussion changed. Their accounts reflected not only an introspective warmth born of experience but also knowledge gleaned from the new discipline of child analysis, which interpreted children's play instead of verbal free associations. So extensive were these investigations that Freud wrote that children had replaced neurotics as "the main subject of psychoanalytic research." The researchers included Hermine Hug-Hellmuth and Melanie Klein in Berlin and Sophie Morgenstern in Paris, conducting the first child analyses; Susan Isaacs teaching at the Malting House nursery school at Cambridge; Vera Schmidt directing an experimental school in Moscow; and Edith Sterba running a child-guidance clinic in Vienna.[41]

The effect of such work was to overturn a central assumption of early Freudianism: henceforth, the mother supplanted the father as the dominant figure in early childhood. Increasingly understood as the source of all early nurturance and recognition, as the child's first and strongest love object, and as the prototype for all later love relations, the mother moved to center stage. The Oedipus complex, by contrast, tended to become secondary. Thus, the investigation of female sexuality with which—in the form of hysteria—psychoanalysis had begun once again revolutionized analysis, sparking the most important paradigm shift in its history.

What precipitated the shift was the attempt to understand the emergence of women's sexual desires for men, given the depth of their bonds with their mothers. Helene Deutsch proposed a simple solution: what turned the girl's sexuality toward men was her *identification* with her mother. For Deutsch, accordingly, the experiences that mothers and daughters shared—"menstruation, defloration, intercourse, pregnancy, infertility, childbirth, lactation, menopause"—laid the basis for female heterosexuality.[42] Melanie Klein pioneered an alternate line of reasoning. Female heterosexuality, she argued, arose from the infant girl's awareness of her vagina. For her, accordingly, women were interested in men because they were interested in babies. Karen Horney articulated the common point in these and other responses to Freud: rather than focusing on "the genital difference between the sexes," psychoanalysis should look to "the different parts played by men and by women in the function of reproduction." In men, she argued, the discovery of this difference led to "womb envy," the wish to give birth. As for women, Horney cited Ferenczi's claim that women lacked "any real primal impulse to coitus," and commented, "At this point I, as a woman, ask in amazement, and what about motherhood?"[43]

The attempt to locate the roots of female sexuality in the girl's early relationship to her mother challenged three icons that had governed sexuality during the epoch of the *Männerbund:* the primacy of the phallus, the distinction between sexuality and nonsexual needs such as self-preservation and recognition, and the presumption of heterosexuality.

The primacy of the phallus had been based on the assumption that the father was both protector and authority. But the work of the 1920s cast the mother in both of these roles. In 1926 Klein wrote: "In both sexes it is the mother who in the deepest strata of the unconscious is specially dreaded."[44] In place of Freud's vision of a castrating father, Klein described a maternal dominion, evoking such figures as Kali, the Indian goddess of destruction, and Lilith, who haunts both the Hebrew and the Christian Bibles. At the same time, Klein described the mother, and especially the fantasy of the mother's teeming womb, as the source of all "supplies": milk, children, feces, the father, love. The result was an enormous augmentation of the mother's role and, by extension, of femininity. Until the female analysts of the 1920s began to write on the subject, female sexuality had been defined in terms of a series of *lacks:* penis envy, ignorance of the vagina, the need to subordinate the clitoris, the need to turn away from the mother, the centrality of envy to female development, and so forth.[45] Beginning in the twenties, however, analysts like Klein described the *presence* of the clitoris, vagina, and the fertile womb, if not yet the labia and the buttocks, directly, explicitly, and without shame, as they were simultaneously being represented in the arts of the twenties, for example, by Georgia O'Keeffe, Josephine Baker, and Anaïs Nin.[46]

The prevalence of maternal imagery in the fantasies of early infancy also turned the psychoanalytic view of sexuality away from the phallic stage, which Freud had prioritized. Now the infant's dependent needs, such as the need for food and the need to be held, came into focus. As a result, analysts began to view sexuality as arising during a psychical epoch in which sexual needs could not be distinguished from nonerotic needs. Being held, being recognized, being fed, maintaining the security of the body image—these all appeared to play a much greater role in sexuality than the focus on the genitals had allowed. This was especially true for women, analysts claimed, since the early attachment to the mother tended to last longer in girls, while the Oedipal phase occurred later and was of less significance. Genitality, they concluded, was less important to girls than to boys. Similarly, the anxieties of infancy were different from those that arose during the Oedipal stage. Reading fairy tales anew so that "the man-eating wolf, the fire-spewing dragon, and all the evil monsters out of myths" were seen as representations of the mother, analysts hypothesized that children feared being displaced by siblings, or being abandoned, or not being fed, before they feared being castrated.[47]

Finally, the new work on the mother decentered heterosexuality by stressing the bisexual component in all love relations. This in turn led to the formulation of the first analytic theory of homosexuality in today's sense of the term, namely, as sexual object choice. Thus, Deutsch sought to show that the lesbian bond reproduced the mother-daughter bond, while Freud suggested that the male homosexual identified with his mother and so cast about for a love object similar to her love object—similar, that is, to himself. In addition, women's relation to their mothers—in other words, women's bisexuality—was shown to illuminate the ambivalence, conflict, and even torment that sometimes accompanied heterosexual love.

Consider in this regard Melanie Klein's 1932 description of her six-year-old patient "Erna." Identifying with her mother, "Erna pretended to be a queen before whom everyone bowed down. . . . It was always the child who got the worst of it." Everything Erna did in the role of her mother—"the tenderness she showed to her husband, the way in which she dressed herself up and allowed herself to be admired—had one chief purpose, which was to arouse the child's envy and to wound its feelings." Seeking solace from her painful relations with her mother, Erna designated her analyst, Klein, "the king." One day she celebrated her marriage with Klein and called for Klein to lie down beside her. When Klein refused to do so, Erna insisted that Klein sit on a little chair by her side. Taking Klein's hand, she made a fist out of it and hit the sofa with it. "This she called 'churning,' and it meant copulating."[48] It was against the background of such descriptions that Freud argued that "many women who have chosen their husband on the model of their father, or have put him in their father's place, nevertheless repeat toward him, in their married life, their bad relations with their mother. The husband of such a woman was meant to be the inheritor of her relation to her father, but in reality he became the inheritor of her relation to her mother."[49]

The distinctive contribution of the European female analysts' work emerges sharply when compared with that of contemporaneous Asian psychoanalysts who criticized Freud's emphasis on the Oedipus complex as a misguided, Western-centered illusion. In 1929, for example, Girindrasekhar Bose wrote that he did not "deny the importance of the castration threat in European cases but believed that in India the real struggle lies between the [man's] desire to be male and . . . the desire to be a female."[50] Just as Freud had turned to Oedipus, so Bose turned to what Sudhir Kakar has called the "hegemonic myth of Indian culture," namely, the myth of the split mother. According to this myth, a terrifying, sexual mother passes through a series of transformations that render her yielding, soft, and pliable to a man.[51]

Similarly, in Japan Heisaku Kosawa proposed the "Ajase complex" as an alternative to the Oedipus complex. According to the medieval tale from which Kosawa drew, an aging queen tries to abort her son, Ajase, who is actually a soothsayer. When the son reaches adolescence, he tries to revenge himself but is stricken with disease until rescued by Buddha. Both Bose and Kosawa were concerned with the boy's ability to overcome his fear of a mother perceived as dangerous and potentially violent. But what is striking about the Asian theories is that they paid no attention to *female* development. Rather, they aimed to help men overcome their fears of phallic, omnipotent, and dangerous mother figures and thus sought to bolster male authority in the traditional Asian family.

Above all, the women analysts differed from their Asian counterparts, as well as from both male and female modernist homosexual communities, in the high value they placed on intimate relations between men and women. That value was distinctively modern. It characterized the epoch of personal life, which was also the epoch of psychoanalytic hegemony. The women analysts studied the mother against the background of a historically unprecedented intimacy.[52] Their appreciation of female bisexuality, their focus on the richness and complexity of female ardor, and their sense that women's relations with men were haunted by their involvement with their mothers were probes into modern personal life. At the same time as they explored girls' relations to their mothers, their work converged with Freud's emphasis on the role of early helplessness in creating both the permanent danger situations and the need to be loved that accompany people of both sexes throughout life.

In spite of these gains, however, there remained the problem with which the debates had begun: women's "resistance to femininity." From the beginning, this problem had constituted the painful knot at the center of the debates. For women's anger against men had been defined as something negative, something that had to be overcome. But as psychoanalysis incorporated the experience of women, the question emerged: why shouldn't women be angry at men? If, from one point of view, women's anger sometimes exceeded its social causes, setting women against their fathers, brothers, and husbands, and, above all, against themselves, from another point of view the entire analytic enterprise could appear as a sophisticated attempt at patriarchal control, systematically diverting attention from the social basis of women's anger.

It was not until well into the 1920s that the problem of giving fair weight to both the social and the intrapsychic dimensions of women's psychology came explicitly to the fore. The reason was that until then personal life still retained its utopian character. As a result, the Freudian claim that intrapsychic reality could never be reduced to an existing political program, such as socialism or feminism, actually enhanced utopian thinking, even though this was scarcely Freud's intention. Thus, Freudianism and radicalism both flourished. By the late 1920s, however, personal life was beginning to be adapted to pro-natalism and to a conservative familialism, one that was often linked to racism and nationalism. In that context, the autonomy of intrapsychic reality increasingly connoted an *a*political and *anti*political outlook. After the Great Depression, and especially after the rise of German fascism, an increasing number of analysts began to agree with Wilhelm Reich that it was necessary to bring a social and political perspective to their work.

In the 1930s Karen Horney brought that program to bear on the question of women. Ultimately, she concluded that women needed both a political movement and a political perspective on their own lives. Horney reached this conclusion after years of wrestling with the conundrum of gender. In 1920 she had broken off her analysis with Karl Abraham when he tried out his theories of penis envy on her. In 1922 she published the first of several attacks on his theory, maintaining that femininity had its own intrinsic line of development. In 1926 she argued that masculine narcissism, far from being the expression of phallocentrism as Freud had argued, was a defense against womb envy. Men, she observed, were apparently "under a greater necessity to depreciate women than conversely"; otherwise, how could one explain the male analyst's notion that "one-half of the human race is discontented with its sex"?[53] Finally, as the threat of fascism loomed in the early thirties, Reich's long-standing influence on Horney intensified. Just as Reich sought to adapt an increasingly conservative psychoanalysis to antifascist ends, so Horney sought to adapt it to women's emancipation.

Horney was also responding to increasing cultural conservatism. Along with sexual and familial experimentation, the twenties had generated pro-natalist sentiment because of the desire to replenish the populations lost during the war. French politicians criticized "beings without breasts" and "civilization without sexes," while praising *la mère de famille nombreuse.* The Weimar constitution banned abortions and the display of contraceptive methods. English suffragists complained that the state treated women as if they were permanently pregnant. With the Depression, pro-natalism intensified. A 1930 papal encyclical forbade marital sex that lacked the intent to procreate. In the United States, fewer women worked; fewer young people left home when they married. Italy and Germany ordained women's duty to

Karen Horney: pioneering feminist critic
of Freud (1952)

reproduce. Virginia Woolf feared that the investigations into the mother's role that had enthralled her in the twenties had been co-opted by the Right.[54]

In 1932 Horney emigrated to the United States, a move she later credited with deepening her awareness of social and external influences. Franz Alexander, her student in Berlin, became her supervisor in Chicago. Erich Fromm joined her the next year, and the two moved together to New York, where they joined a flourishing seminar of social scientists and analysts at Columbia University. In this period, American social scientists had a strong interest in primary institutions such as the family, and thus in psychoanalysis. Psychoanalysis, for its part, was a charismatic sect and esoteric doctrine desperately in need of depersonalization and external exchange. The encounter of the two incubated influential amalgams including "neo-Freudianism" and the "Culture and Personality" school of anthropology.[55] Works of the period reflecting the neo-Freudian influence include Horney's *Neurotic Personality of Our Time* (1937), Fromm's *Escape from Freedom* (1941), Harry Stack Sullivan's *Conceptions of Modern Psychiatry* (1940), Abram Kardiner's *Individual and His Society* (1939), Ruth Benedict's *Chrysanthemum and the Sword* (1946), Margaret Mead's *Male and Female* (1949), and Erik Erikson's *Childhood and Society* (1950).[56]

As we saw, the emphasis on culture in American thought was connected to race and ethnicity. In the neo-Freudian milieu, Horney refashioned it into a profound riposte to the psychoanalytic theory of women. Like Freud, she held that culture was the source of repression, but she added the view that cultures varied. Different cultures repressed different emotions: sexual desire, or fear, or aggression. Anxiety was the awareness of a repressed impulse, the expression of which would involve an external danger. Anxiety arose from the frustration of any basic need, not just sexuality, and the extent to which a repressed impulse caused anxiety was "largely dependent on the existing cultural attitude." The neurotic, then, was a cultural product, a "stepchild" of the culture, whose problems would be divested of their "fantastic and abstruse character" when one saw that he or she repressed culturally specific needs in ways that differed only in intensity from the so-called "normal person."[57]

Even before emigrating, Horney noted that women, too, were being pathologized, as the titles of her preemigration essays suggest: "The Problem of the Monogamous Ideal" (1928), "The Distrust Between the Sexes," (1931), "Problems of Marriage" (1932). A 1926 essay called frigidity a "determined rejection of the female role" but argued that it had to be explained by "supra-individual, cultural factors." Frigidity was a weapon expressing women's "inner bitterness against the male as the privileged one—similar to the concealed hostility of the worker against his employer." Just as we see guerrilla warfare every day in the employee's relation to the boss, so, too, we see it in marriage. Women do not reject sex, Horney insisted, they reject the female role.[58]

After she came to the United States, Horney's social perspective deepened. Her 1934 essay "The Overvaluation of Love" described the modern woman's conflicts as arising when she seeks to be independent but is "unwilling to pay for her daring with the renunciation of her femininity." This was the same problem that Riviere had described, but Horney reformulated it historically. The patriarchal ideal "of woman as one whose only longing is to love a man and to be loved by him" arose with the advent of field agriculture and the restriction of women to the home. Now that women were leaving the home, the traditional ideal persisted. Analysts' emphasis on heterosexual experience could blind them to the "neurotic overvaluation of and overemphasis upon [the exclusively sexual] sphere."[59]

Integrating a feminist sensibility with Popular Front leftism, Horney rejected the analytic description of women's resistance to femininity as a problem. In *The Neurotic Personality of Our Time* she argued that capitalism had made competitive strivings and "diffuse hostile tension between individuals" pervasive. The need for cooperation, and especially for affection, was repressed and thereby intensified. Since for cultural, not biological, reasons women represented affection, they became the fulcrum of consumerist culture. Women's real problem was dependency, not penis envy. They had been taught that only by giving love and minimizing their own needs could they gain happiness, security, and prestige. *Contra* Freud, masochism was not sexual; it was an attempt to gain satisfaction in life through being inconspicuous. "In our culture it is hard to see how any woman may escape becoming masochistic to some degree."[60]

Thus, Horney proposed what she understood to be a post-Freudian perspective on female sexuality. For her, sexual needs were less important than needs for security, recognition, and worldly achievement. Women's problems arose not in infancy but rather in adulthood, when women were faced with a cultural double bind. The conflict was not between instincts and culture, as in Freud, but between cooperation and competition. Tasks of affection, nurturance, and support that were denied broader cultural expression had been restricted to women. Freud's focus on sexuality diverted attention from this problem. Masochism, for example, did not originate in early bodily impulses, as Freud believed; it was a cultural message that could be resisted once its external origins were understood. Sexual desire, hostility, and misunderstanding were not the only factors permeating the relations between the sexes, as one might conclude from Freud. Power was also relevant. Women needed to reject the insistence on their femininity and validate their own competitiveness and desire for security.

These were powerful theses, but they did not necessarily contradict classical psychoanalysis. For one thing, Freud had repeatedly pointed out that the analytic debates referred only to the sphere of a woman's sexuality, not to the whole of her psychology. More to the point, understanding the cultural double binds that oppressed women as a gender and understanding the unconscious mechanisms that made oppression personal could have been pursued as complementary rather than contradictory activities. Nevertheless, Horney emphasized the incompatibilities. Under the influence of American social psychology, she rejected the idea that there was an intrapsychic world that could be understood in distinction from the self's relations to others. Along with Fromm, and in typical Popular Front terms, she boasted: "Man for us was no longer an instinct-ridden creature, but a being capable of choice and responsibility. Hostility was no longer innate but reactive. . . . Human nature was no longer unalterable but could change."[61]

Horney's break with psychoanalysis was part of a larger turning point in the always ambivalent relations between psychoanalysis and feminism. In the 1930s many women who had never accepted the turn toward "difference," and who regarded maternalism with horror, became outspoken in their criticisms of psychoanalysis. Rebecca West, deeply influenced by psychoanalysis in her study of Balkan culture, nonetheless complained in 1933 that when Freud spoke of women he "suddenly goes into a keepsake plane," describing them as passive beings for whom "to be loved is a stronger need than to love."[62] Observing her women friends struggling with their hostility toward men, she complained of "the modern timidity about mentioning that there is such a thing as sex-antagonism." Two years later she added:

> I am an old-fashioned feminist. I believe in the sex-war. . . . When those of our army whose voices are inclined to coo tell us that the day of sex-antagonism is over and that henceforth we have only to advance hand in hand with the male I do not believe it. . . . When [a postwar feminist] says in a speech that "women must learn to work with men," I disagree. I believe that women know how to work with men. But I believe that it is the rarest thing in the world for a man to know how to work with women without giving way to an inclination to savage his fellow workers of the protected sex. . . . The woman who forgets this, who does not realize that by reason of her sex she lives in a beleaguered city, is a fool who deserves to lose (as she certainly will) all the privileges that have been won for her by her more robustly-minded sister.[63]

West was not alone in her hardheaded intuition that psychoanalysis, having been co-opted into an eroticized consumerism in the twenties, was in danger of evolving into a tendentious maternalism in the thirties. The suffragist Winifred Holtby blamed Freud for the postwar "dethronement of reason" in favor of "nerves and memory."[64] Virginia Woolf, who had published psychoanalytic texts since World War I but never really read them (wondering while handling proofs why "these Germans think it proves something—besides their own gull-like imbecility"), finally read Freud in the thirties.[65] Her goal, she wrote, was "to enlarge the circumference, to give my brain a wider scope: to make it objective; to get outside." Pleasantly surprised, she found Freud's emphasis on the father bracing, given the prevalence of the image of the maternal body in fascist propaganda. But after praising Freud for insisting on "the falseness of loving one's neighbor," she claimed that he had neglected the specifically male nature of aggression. Aggression, Woolf wrote, was not a universal instinct in Freud's sense but was a trait specific to men who "desire other people's fields and goods perpetually . . . make frontiers and flags, battleships and poison gas . . . offer up their own lives and their children's lives."[66]

In a dozen years, then, psychoanalysts had generated three successive approaches to "women's difference." First, Freud portrayed the moment in which a woman is young, vulnerable, and beginning to turn to a male love object. Next, the female analysts portrayed the psychology of the mother, especially the sexual mother, newly aware of her own powers. Then Horney portrayed the "post-Freudian" woman as a worker or a wife, someone for whom sex was a very restricted concern, someone who had interests of her own and was prepared to defend those interests. Finally, six years after his initial article, Freud intervened in the femininity debates once again.[67]

In two new articles, "Female Sexuality," written after the death of his own mother in 1931, and "Femininity," written in 1933, Freud described the child's early passionate and exclusive attachment to the mother. Calling this period of attachment the "preoedipal stage," he compared it to the "discovery, in another field . . . of the Minoan-Mycenean civilization behind the civilization of Greece." Everything "in the sphere of this first attachment to the mother seemed . . . so difficult to grasp in analysis—so grey with age and shadowy . . . that it was as if it had succumbed to an especially inexorable repression."[68] Its effects, he wrote, lasted much longer than previously thought, especially in girls. Nonetheless, its dynamics were identical in both sexes.

So strongly did Freud now emphasize the child's early attachment to the mother that Jones wrote warning him against a "one-sided . . . discounting of the father." Freud replied: "That I am supposed to have forgotten the father is generally not like me." But the father, he claimed, played no role, or a negligible one, in the first developmental phase. By calling the earliest stage pre-Oedipal, however, he emphasized its difference from the Oedipal stage, when the knowledge of sexual difference became significant. In Freud's model, one moved chronologically from issues of separation and dependence to issues of authority and sexual difference. In Kleinian circles, he complained to Jones, "this chronological order is neglected . . . too many disparate elements are thrown on to the same plane."[69]

Bringing this perspective to bear on female development, Freud's essays of the early thirties suggested a wide range of motives for the collapse of the girl's early relations with her mother and her reorientation to her father. These included resentment of siblings, a feeling of being inadequately fed, and a fear of being poisoned. So intense are the earliest needs that it is as if "our children had remained forever unsated, as though they had never sucked long enough at their mother's breast."[70] The mother inadvertently aroused the girl's sexual feelings and then forbade them, and so, Freud surmised, she turned out to be the seducer who lay behind the hysteric's fantasies, discovered in the 1890s.[71] In addition to these "pre-Oedipal" difficulties, however, Freud continued to insist on a traumatic moment in which the difference between the sexes was discovered: fear of castration in the case of the boy; penis envy in the case of the girl. Yet he also wrote: "The sight of the penis and its function of urination cannot be the motive, only the trigger of the child's envy."[72]

What, then, was the motive? To answer this question, it is necessary to go back to an epoch before the sexes were even aware of each other, and reconsider the role of infantile traumas, repetition, and resistance in form-ing the ego. According to Freud there is an "unmistakable revolt against passivity and . . . preference for the active role" in the earliest years of *both sexes*. Responding to interlocutors' claim that the infant girl was already "feminine" and "receptive," Freud observed that little girls made their mother into their object and behaved as the active subject toward her. In this regard girls and boys were identical; when a child of either sex received an impression passively, it "trie[d] to do itself what ha[d] just been done to it." For example, children played at being doctors in order to treat a younger child as they had been treated. Thus, playing with dolls had been frequently cited as an example of the girl's awakening femininity, but, Freud noted, it was the *active* side of femininity that finds expression there.[73]

In stressing both sexes' preference for activity over passivity, Freud was positing the ultimate commonality of the sexes. But he also held that the common preference took two different paths in the Oedipal period. It was during that period, under the sign of castration, that activity and passivity assumed the connotations of masculinity and femininity. In the boy, the preference for activity normally led toward "masculinity"; in the girl, the same preference was suppressed. Here, then, was the crucial moment in which a long line of preceding ideas—the irreducibility of the activity/pas-sivity dichotomy, the biological prematurity of the ego, the revolt against passivity—were brought into relation with the difference between the sexes.

After the Oedipal period, men were required to dissimulate their pas-sive, regressive, infantile longings. In his 1929 essay on fetishism, Freud described one way in which this could miscarry. There the subject used a piece of fur or a shoe to protect himself from the fear of being castrated, that is, of being a "woman." Citing the Chinese custom of "mutilating the female foot and then revering it like a fetish after it has been mutilated," Freud remarked: "It seems as though the Chinese male wants to thank the woman for having submitted to be castrated."[74] As for women, they were required to dissimulate their active strivings. "Penis envy"—the condition of the woman who acted out her dissatisfaction with femininity—was one possible outcome. Joan Riviere, in her characterization of professionally successful women as putting on "a mask of femininity," gave another. In her account, professionally successful women would undermine their public roles by "flirting and coquetting . . . in a more or less veiled manner." According to Riviere, they had to treat the situation of displaying their active wishes "as a 'game,' as something 'not real.' "[75]

Freud returned to the subject of female sexuality one last time in his 1937 "Analysis, Terminable and Interminable." By the time he wrote this essay, German analysis had been destroyed, the Americans had become the most powerful group in the International, pro-natalism had absorbed much of the pioneering exploration of the mother, and Viennese psychoanalysis was surviving only through the sufferance of the church. The subject of the essay was the resistance, the difficulty of analyses, and their high rate of failure. In its background lay many disappointing experiences, including Freud's analysis of Ferenczi, who had turned against him. Ferenczi's reflections on analysis provoked Freud's return to the question of female sexuality.

Ferenczi, who had remained an analytic utopian, proposed the following criteria for terminating analysis: "Every male patient must attain a feeling of equality in relation to the physician as a sign that he has overcome his fear of castration; every female patient . . . must emotionally accept without a trace of resentment the implications of her female role." Freud's essay offered many reasons for believing that these goals were impossible: the strength of the instincts, the persistence of early traumas, the impossibility of treating conflicts unless they were present and active, the pervasiveness of resistance. But Freud concluded by emphasizing one point above all. What appeared in the man as a refusal "to subject himself to a father-substitute" and in the woman as depression, the result of "an internal conviction that the analysis will be of no use," derived from the same cause. Something, he wrote, "which both sexes have in common has been forced . . . into different forms of expression."

This "something" was the compulsive attempt to overcome the traumas of early childhood through activity. In men this attempt took the form of a repudiation of castration and a striving to be masculine. That fear of castration was the cause of this striving was shown in the fact that what men repudiated was not passivity in general but passivity in regard to other men. The same man who balked at submissiveness in regard to a man may "display a masochistic attitude—a state that amounts to bondage—towards women." As for women, their whole development—the separation from the mother, the turn toward the father, the reorientation of their sexuality toward male objects—was aimed at ensuring that their "masculinity," their preference for the active role, succumbed to a "momentous process of repression." "Masculinity complex," "penis envy," "frigidity"—all the "diseases" of femininity—were proofs that this momentous process often misfired.

Freud also returned to the early debate with Adler, who had died a few months before. Adler's term "masculine protest," Freud now conceded, "fits the case of males perfectly," since for men the repudiation of castration coincided with the assertion of masculinity. In contrast, the term did not well describe women's development, since women repressed or obscured their active or "masculine" strivings. The best term, Freud concluded, was "repudiation of femininity," because it covered both sexes.[76] Unsatisfying as this formula may have been, it was his last contribution to a continuing attempt to deepen and complicate the meaning of women's equality. As Freud was writing it, events were catching psychoanalysis up in a new constellation of fascism and war.

Chapter Nine

FASCISM AND THE DESTRUCTION OF CLASSICAL EUROPEAN ANALYSIS

After spending years pondering this matter, I remain convinced that our critics have never quite understood our dilemmas in the 1930s.

—Peter Gay, *My German Question: Growing Up in Nazi Berlin*

Just as men and women used psychoanalysis to deepen ideals of autonomy and women's emancipation during the interwar years, so they used it to deepen the ideal of democracy. Above all, they drew on analysis to revise the liberal distinction between the public and the private, a distinction that is crucial to democratic society. Whereas nineteenth-century liberals such as John Stuart Mill sought to maintain a clear separation between the public and private spheres, modern intellectuals influenced by Freud were struck by the traffic between them. They did not always use the terms "public" and "private" in their contemporary sense, speaking instead of "mass society" and "the individual." Nonetheless, they were convinced that the erosion of the distinction, especially the *psychological* distinction, between the public and the private undermined modernity.[1] In the context of the rise of fascism, moreover, their work assumed a political cast.

The new concerns responded to the massive changes set in motion by the second industrial revolution. Freudians called attention to the interpenetration of public and private just as mass production subverted the division between them. Alongside corporate intervention into private life, increased government regulation of business overrode the liberal separation of the private economy from the public state. State intervention in such areas as childhood, health, and education belied the myth of the private family's independence from the state. The rise of a sexualized mass culture scrambled the classical division between public and private, as did the entry of women into public life. Previously, family-based productive property had underpinned identity. Now individuals had to find their identities in civil society, through personal relations and group affiliations. Thus, psychoanalytic ideas influenced discussions of the public and the private in the context of an institutionally expanded and experientially freighted personal life.

Much of this discussion was permeated by fears that large-scale forms of social organization such as communism, fascism, and even Fordist planning eroded individual freedom. Fascism in particular promised to reunite what the second industrial revolution had thrust asunder: communal symbols, on the one hand, and the intrapsychic life of individuals, on the other. All of its innovations—a tribal nationalism based on biological determinism; a philosophy of action based on intuition, élan, and heroism; a reinterpretation of socialism in which the national community replaced the working class—were directed toward this end.[2] As Mussolini's favorite philosopher, Giovanni Gentile, explained, fascism aimed at establishing a new form of authority, one that "penetrates the soul and rules there incontestably." Although World War I had already generated large-scale, *public* organizations with the power to intervene in private life, the Great Depression inspired the idea that total mobilization was necessary for recovery. Some called for a führer capable of awakening an entire population; torch-lit parades, mass assemblies, and the worship of youth and the body became commonplace.

Freud wrote *Group Psychology and the Analysis of the Ego* (1921), the locus classicus for all subsequent analytic discussions of the public and the private, in the wake of World War I, with its unprecedented mass mobilizations.[3] In it he used the army and the church as paradigmatic examples of group psychology. Although he later wrote that it "was not easy . . . to introduce the idea of the unconscious into group psychology," the task flowed logically from ego psychology because of its roots in the theory of narcissism and its focus on the early familial constellation.[4] As Freud stated, "In the individual's mental life someone else is invariably involved, as a model, as an object, as a helper, as an opponent; and so from the very first, individual psychology . . . is at the same time, social psychology."[5]

Like much of psychoanalysis, *Group Psychology and the Analysis of the Ego* revised a prior Enlightenment tradition, one that extolled the individual and viewed socialism, trade unionism, and even mass culture as examples of "herd" thinking. At the Salpêtrière, Hippolyte Taine's condemnation of the role of the "mob" in the French Revolution of 1789 had been considered a classic, and witchcraft outbreaks, dancing manias, and female suggestibility were cited as examples of group hysteria. As a student, Freud imbibed this way of thinking, writing to his sister-in-law Minna that the French were "the people of psychical epidemics, of historical mass convulsions."[6] In *Group Psychology and the Analysis of the Ego* he drew upon the leading exponent of Salpêtrière group psychology, Gustave LeBon, a police psychologist who described urban masses and striking workers as "extraordinarily credulous and open to influence."[7] Like his predecessors, Freud aimed at elucidating the regressive processes unleashed by groups.

But there was a crucial difference. Whereas the Salpêtrière theorists explained the psychology of groups in terms of *imitation,* Freud explained it in terms of *identification.* Imitation was not a depth-psychological concept but a simple propensity of human nature. Identification, by contrast, was based on the psychology of early infancy, and thus paved the way for a complex and nuanced analysis. For Freud, identification, especially with the parents, was the chief mechanism through which the ego developed. Groups, he argued in *Group Psychology,* facilitated a regression from a mature ego to the state of narcissism. The reason was the power that groups bestowed on their leaders. As members projected their own qualities onto the leader, they abandoned their autonomy and *identified* with one another. This gave them surcease from internal conflicts, thus swelling their narcissism, but at the cost of true self-respect.

Freud's book gave voice to the widespread worry that large-scale forms of social organization such as communism, fascism, and Fordist planning eroded the individual's ability to think freely and undermined the bases of democracy. But its argument was not universally accepted. Within psychoanalysis, three major alternative psychologies of the public/private division were produced in the years before World War II: one by Wilhelm Reich, another by the thinkers of the Frankfurt School, and still another by Freud himself, just before his death. (During World War II, as we shall see, a fourth alternative was developed by British object-relations theorists, the subject of the next chapter.)

In the 1930s both fascism and communism challenged the liberal separation of the public from the private, albeit from opposite directions. World War I had brought fascist governments to power in Italy and Hungary, while sparking strong right-wing movements in Germany, Austria, France, and in eastern Europe. In 1933–34 fascists gained power in Germany and Austria, raising the specter of a massive synchronization of the public and private, extending from the highest reaches of the state into the intimacies of birth, sexuality, and death. Fascination with the charismatic order-inspiring individual surged through European culture. Often the model was the hypnotist, as in Freud's writings, Bulgakov's *The Master and Margarita,* and, perhaps most memorably, Thomas Mann's "Mario and the Magician," where the political alarm raised by a baby running naked on the beach signified incipient fascism.

In a very different spirit, the Left also challenged the liberal division between the public and the private. Extolling the working class rather than the nation, most Marxists had long viewed the public/private distinction as ideological, a mask for social injustice. Within psychoanalysis, the most important exponent of the Marxist position was Wilhelm Reich. Having learned through his work in the Vienna Psychoanalytic Polyclinic to think of neuroses as social diseases, he insisted that the view that societal repression caused the neuroses was implicit in Freud's writings but that Freud had become too old, too compromised, and too worried about organizational survival to develop it.[8]

Reich did not invent the idea of a politics centered on sexuality, health, abortion, maternity, housing, sex therapy, and psychiatric reform. These issues had been central to European politics since the late nineteenth century; and after World War I they inspired struggles among doctors, moral-purity campaigners, pro-natalists, sexual reformers, and feminists.[9] Reich's innovation lay in the idea that psychoanalysis offered a new approach to these issues. Liberalism, for him, reflected the surface level of consciousness, while fascism mobilized the secondary drives, such as sadism, envy, and greed. In contrast, a psychoanalytically informed revolution would penetrate to the deepest layer, the instincts themselves.

Reich's radicalism brought him into conflict with the social-democratic movements of his time. These movements, reflecting the logic of first-wave industrialization, had made "Red Vienna" famous throughout the world for its working-class apartment blocks (one of them named for Freud), schools, libraries, community centers, social insurance, and swimming pools, all aimed at creating *neue Menschen.*[10] But Reich criticized the implicit conservatism of this attempt to strengthen the working-class family and protect young women from the effects of industrialization. In his view, the working-class family was "a factory for authoritarian ideologies and conservative character structure." Attacking socialism's "sexual abstinence" literature, he called for the sexual liberation of youth and women.[11]

Freud did not share the Reichean vision. The rise of an active right wing forced the differences between the two men into the open. In April 1927 the Austrian Social Democrats won a large electoral victory, depriving the conservative Catholic government of its majority. The optimism that followed was shattered when three rightist *Frontkämpfer* on trial for the murder of a Social Democratic supporter and an eight-year-old boy were acquitted. Spontaneous mass demonstrations led to a riot. The police barricaded themselves in the Palace of Justice; the crowd set it on fire; gunfire prevented firefighters from intervening; eighty-five workers were left dead and hundreds injured. The Right treated the incident as a show of strength, while socialists feared that the confrontation would threaten electoral support.[12]

Working as an assistant at the Polyclinic hospital, Reich observed the police shooting at workers. The crowd's behavior, it struck him, refuted Freud's group psychology. He saw not a herdlike mass in search of an authority figure but a leaderless mass seeking justice. The crowd, he insisted, acted out of spontaneous outrage, while the police behaved mechanically. He visited Freud to discuss the incident. "It seemed to me," Reich later wrote, that Freud "lacked all understanding of the revolt and viewed it as a catastrophe similar to a tidal wave." Groping for an alternative, Reich read Engels's *Origins of the Family, Private Property and the State.*[13]

Reich was not the only figure who turned against Freud in the face of the collective mobilizations of the late 1920s and 1930s. Fifty-five years later, Elias Canetti also remembered the burning of the Palace of Justice in Vienna: "The agitation . . . is still in my bones. It was the closest thing to a revolution that I have physically experienced. . . . I became a part of the crowd, I fully dissolved in it, I did not feel the slightest resistance to what the crowd was doing." Canetti went home and read Freud's *Group Psychology.* The book repelled him from the first and repelled him no less fifty-five years later when he reread it. Freud and the writers in his tradition "had closed themselves off against masses, crowds; they found them alien or seemed to fear them; and when they set about investigating them, they gestured: Keep ten feet away from me! A crowd seemed something leprous to them, it was like a disease. . . . It was crucial for them, when confronted with a crowd, to keep their heads, not to be seduced by the crowd, not to melt into it." In contrast to Freud, Canetti wrote, "I knew the crowd from the inside. . . . I saw crowds around me, but I also saw crowds within me. . . . What I missed most in Freud's discussion was *recognition* of the phenomenon."[14]

Like Reich, Canetti concluded that crowds did not need leaders. On the contrary, he stressed the feeling of equality in crowds, writing: "One might even define a crowd as a state of absolute equality."[15] Crowds were organic phenomena, characterized by rhythm, pulsation, and a drive to destroy. Freud failed to recognize the primal quality of crowd experience: "It is only in a crowd that man can become free" of his most elemental fear, the fear of a touch that comes from the unknown. Describing paranoia as a crowd phenomenon, Canetti revisited Daniel Paul Schreber's *Memoirs of a Neuropath,* calling attention to Schreber's view, ignored by Freud, that the Germans were God's chosen people.[16] Thus, where Freud saw a herdlike mass in search of authority and Reich saw a leaderless band seeking justice, Canetti saw a pulsating, omnivorous horde capable of absorbing everything in its path. None of the three, however, had ever experienced the forms of collective mobilization characteristic of democratic societies, such as the highly disciplined labor-union mobilizations then unfolding in western Europe and the United States.

Behind the preoccupation with the crowd lay the drastic consequences of the 1929 economic collapse. In Austria unemployment nearly doubled between 1928 and 1932, much of it among youth under the age of twenty-five. Struck by the susceptibility of young people to antidemocratic appeals, Reich and others began to open sexual-consultation clinics, staffed by analysts and midwives, in working-class districts. The clinics provided free abortions, sex education, and counseling on sexual problems and child rearing.[17] So popular were Reich's ideas that Freud felt he had to defend himself in *Civilization and Its Discontents:* "Anyone who has tasted the miseries of poverty . . . and has experienced the indifference and arrogance of the well-to-do, should be safe from the suspicion of having no understanding or good will towards endeavours to fight against the inequality of wealth."[18]

Responding to the massive mobilizations of the time, Reich turned to Engels's theory of the origin of the family. In early societies, Reich held, there was no distinction between public activities, such as labor, and the quasi-biological activities of the household, such as sexuality. Terming matriarchy the familial system of "natural society," Reich cited Malinowski's claims that in the Trobriand Islands children freely engaged in sexual play with no other regulation than the incest taboo, that parents were not authoritarian, that women were active and expressive in their sexuality, and that there were no neuroses or perversions. According to Reich, "The amazing thing about matriarchy is the natural self-regulation of sexuality that it entails," a form of sexual life to which humanity would return after the abolition of private property.[19]

In 1928 Reich joined the Communist Party, and the next year he toured the Soviet Union, visiting nursery schools and pedagogical centers.[20] Lecturing in Moscow, he distinguished psychoanalysis as a theory of psychology (which, he argued, the Soviets should embrace) from the "Freudist" worldview, psychologization (which he urged them to reject). He corresponded with Trotsky, met with Sergei Eisenstein, and had a lecture published with critical comment by party officials.[21] His report on the visit, *The Sexual Revolution*, praised the undermining of patriarchal authority in the Soviet collective farms but warned that threats to ban homosexuality and abortion foretold the revolution's collapse.[22] His experiences reinforced his conviction that social change had to precede psychotherapy: "Go back to the unspoiled protoplasm," he advised.[23] In response to Reich's reports, published in analytic journals, the psychoanalyst and Russian émigré Moshe Wulff criticized the attempt "to prove that psychoanalysis can be acceptable to Marxists." Wulff observed, "Where there is no freedom of speech, there can be no psychoanalysis."[24]

After returning to Vienna, Reich helped organize Revolutionäre Sozialdemokraten, a party faction aimed at preparing for armed struggle.[25] In 1930 he moved to Berlin. There he published his most important book, *The Mass Psychology of Fascism*. That year the Nazis became the second-largest party in Germany. In the wake of this disaster, socialist and communist discussion revolved around whether the middle class would support fascism or join the proletariat in its expected opposition to the Nazis.[26] Having in mind the small middle class of government officials, white-collar workers, and semi-independent professionals characteristic of nineteenth-century capitalism, and not the consumption-oriented middle classes born in the 1920s, Reich predicted that the middle class would ally with the bourgeoisie. Drawing on the Oedipal theory, he likened the white-collar worker to an eldest son with a powerful father: "While subordinate to the top, he is to those below him a representative of . . . authority and enjoys, as such, a privileged moral (not material) position. The arch personification of this type . . . is to be found in the army sergeant."[27]

In Berlin, family and sexual politics were intensely contested. One-third of the labor force was female. On the one hand, socialists and feminists demanded free medical services, maternity benefits, and child care for women at work. On the other hand, a savage pamphlet by a Lutheran pastor denounced "Sexual Bolshevism."[28] Reich's Association for Proletarian Sexual Politics (sometimes termed SEXPOL), which united sex reformers, sexologists, and Communists, claimed forty thousand members at its height.[29] Yet when the German Communists began building an antifascist popular front, they refused to distribute works published by Reich's publishing house, the Verlag für Sexualpolitik. In March 1933 Reich was expelled from the German Communist Party and returned to Vienna.

Given the growth in the power of National Socialism, Reich's activities created a crisis in the analytic world. In 1932 he submitted a paper, "The Masochistic Character," to the *International Journal of Psychoanalysis,* in which he argued that sexual repression turned a neutral drive toward mastery into aggression. Freud agreed to publish it but criticized its "nonsensical statement that what we have called the death instinct is a product of the capitalistic system." He wanted to add an editorial comment disassociating psychoanalysis from any political interests and identifying Reich as a Bolshevik, but his fellow editors stopped him, arguing that such a statement "would be equivalent to a declaration of war against the Soviets."[30] To pacify Freud, Siegfried Bernfeld wrote a refutation.

Letters exchanged between Ernest Jones and Anna Freud detail the turmoil. Jones saw Reich as going back to the early Freud, especially to the idea of "actual neurosis," a neurosis caused by dammed-up libido. Reich's Communism, Jones informed Anna Freud, was "not so much economic" as an attempt to give sex reform a better chance. Anna Freud agreed: Reich was honest and had a deep understanding of analysis but was also unhappy and psychologically sick, and he greatly overestimated his support among analysts, which was limited mostly to Otto Fenichel and to Reich's wife, Annie. Her father, she added, was willing to see analysis persecuted for being analysis but not for a politics it did not share. Reich could be the match that lights "the barrel of gunpowder."[31]

This was her father's view as well. After Hitler became chancellor in January 1933, Max Eitingon banned Reich from the offices of the Berlin Psychoanalytic Society, apparently at Freud's suggestion. By the end of the year, Reich's name was secretly stricken from its membership rolls.[32] Although the documentation drops off, we know that in 1934 Reich learned that he would not be listed as a member of the IPA. In August his membership was debated at the Lucerne congress, and he was almost certainly expelled. The transcripts of the congress are no longer available, but the persecution of Reich shows how fearful and repressive psychoanalysis was becoming.[33]

Reich himself became increasingly unbalanced. When he was twelve he had discovered that his mother was having an affair. His father found out, probably through Reich, and his mother committed suicide. Reich believed this incident had formed his character, and he returned to it obsessively all his life. Edith Gyömröi, a Hungarian analyst, described a walk she and Fenichel took with Reich in 1933. Reich talked endlessly about his new theory, centered on the magical energy of the orgone: "Fenichel and I did not dare to look at each other, and had cold shivers. Then Reich suddenly stopped, and said . . . 'Children, if I were not so certain of what I am working on, it would appear to me as a schizophrenic fantasy.' We didn't say anything. Not even on our journey back. It was for us both a great loss and a great sorrow."[34] Reich emigrated to Denmark and Norway, where he was initially welcomed by students at the University of Oslo, only to be driven out a few years later by conservative opponents. He finally settled in the United States in 1939 and died in prison, where the Food and Drug Administration had sent him for making bogus scientific claims.[35] Thus, Reich lived out, in his personal tragedy, the impossibility of ever fully reconciling what later came to be called the "personal" and the "political." His belief that they could be fully reconciled was the mirror opposite of the equally deluded conviction among many analysts that the public and private could be kept wholly separate.

On January 31, 1933, Adolf Hitler became chancellor of Germany. On February 1 the Communists were suppressed. On February 27 the Reichstag burned. On April 1 Hitler ordered a boycott of Jewish shops. One month later the trade unions were outlawed. On May 10 Freud's books were burned in a public square in Berlin. By the end of May, birth-control and sex-counseling clinics had been shut down and physicians associated with sex reform forced into exile. At this point there were a half-dozen analytic institutes in Germany. In October analysis was attacked as a Jewish science and banned from a congress of psychology in Leipzig. The censors held that Freud had perverted the ideas of the creators of depth psychology such as Novalis, Goethe, and Nietzsche, turning psychology into a business aimed at rich hysterics. Freud struck "the Nordic race at its most sensitive spot, its sex life."[36]

When a crystal breaks, it cracks along lines of preexisting weakness. The Berlin Psychoanalytic Society was one important weak point in the analytic response to fascism. After Karl Abraham's death in 1925, the society had lost some of its cachet. In the ensuing polycentric period, Horney, Reich, Klein, and Alexander each had followings. In April 1933 the government ordered that no Jews could serve in an executive function in a medical organization. Both Max Eitingon and Ernst Simmel, the two directors of the society, were Jewish, as was 80 percent of the membership. Felix Boehm, a leading non-Jewish analyst, wanted Eitingon and Simmel to "voluntarily" step down and visited Freud to enlist his support. Although Freud warned that this would not ensure the survival of the society, he agreed.[37] In response to a written report from Boehm, he made two requests: Harald Schultz-Hencke, a revisionist analyst who would play a leading role after World

War II, should not be part of the new leadership; and "Free me from [Wilhelm] Reich" (*Befreien Sie mich von Reich*).³⁸ Boehm and another non-Jew, Karl Müller-Braunschweig, took over the leadership of the society. Jewish analysts began leaving Germany, among them Hanns Sachs, Otto Fenichel, Siegfried Bernfeld, Karl Landauer, and Ernst Simmel. By 1934 more than half the institute's former members had fled. Membership dropped from 65 to fewer than 15, and the number of students dropped from 222 in 1931 to 34 in 1934. "The word 'hara kiri' was repeatedly used," Boehm wrote Jones.³⁹

The analytic response to these developments is difficult to comprehend for someone who did not live through them. In 1934 Anna Freud praised Jones for his remarks at the international meeting opposing "the combination of analytical with political activities," referring specifically to Ferenczi and Reich. Commenting on the German events, she insisted that "the [Nazi] government never made an attack on analysis or restricted its activity in any way. The twenty-five members who left, did so because they were Jews, not because they were analysts."⁴⁰ Müller-Braunschweig asked Jones, then head of the IPA, to help collect money that the emigrated Jewish analysts owed the student-loan fund. Resentment, he remarked, does not free debtors of their moral obligations.⁴¹ Jones, in turn, wrote Boehm denouncing what he called the "ultra-Jewish attitudes" that persisted among German-Jewish analysts.⁴²

At the heart of these responses lay a dread of politics that went far beyond caution. In 1935 patients of three German analysts were arrested as suspected Communists. In response, the German Psychoanalytic Society, as it was then called, resolved that analytic treatment should not be offered to any politically engaged patient. That year Edith Jacobson, one of the last Jewish analysts in Berlin, was arrested. Analysts told one another that the arrest resulted from her having treated a Communist. According to some reports, this led to her being discharged from the society. Boehm convinced Jones and Anna Freud to cease international agitation on her behalf, lest they alienate the Nazis. Anna Freud attacked all politically involved analysts: "Care for the well being of the organization is foreign to them." When Jacobson was accused of lending her apartment for political activities, no analyst believed the accusation. "It seems unlikely that this can be anything very serious unless she is quite crazy," wrote Jones to Anna Freud.⁴³ In fact, Jacobson had been involved with a resistance group for two years. She had lent her apartment for political work and spoken at gatherings there. Convicted of treason but granted temporary release for a medical operation, she fled Germany in 1937. Fourteen years later, even after she published *Observations on the Psychological Effects of Imprisonment on Female Political Prison-*

ers, most analysts still believed she had been convicted because of a patient's work in the underground, not because of her own.

By 1935 *Gleichschaltung* (synchronization) had advanced to the point that existing organizations were merged with state and party agencies. The organization of German psychotherapists was rechristened the German Medical Society for Psychotherapy. Matthias Heinrich Göring, a neurologist who was both a disciple of Alfred Adler and a cousin of Field Marshal Hermann Göring, was put in charge. In Zurich, Jung headed an international umbrella organization dominated by the German Psychoanalytic Society. There he argued that the difference between German and Jewish psychology should no longer be glossed over: Freud had applied "Jewish categories to Christian Germans or Slavs."[44] He added: "The Jews have this peculiarity in common with women: being physically the weaker they have to aim at the chinks in their opponent's armor."[45]

Members of the German Psychoanalytic Society never questioned whether they should seek membership in the Göring Institute. Upon request, they immediately made their records available, forcing the remaining Jews into the open. In November 1935 Jones wrote to Anna Freud: "All Jews have to resign from Berlin Society. Deplorable as it would be, I should still say that I prefer psychoanalysis to be practiced by Gentiles in Germany than not at all, and I hope you agree."[46] To facilitate the society's "integration," Jones, Brill, Boehm, and Müller-Braunschweig met with Göring. Psychoanalysis, Jones assured Göring, was not "*Weltanschaulich fremdartig,*" unfriendly to Nazism in its worldview. Fear pervaded the entire analytic world, not just Berlin. Although Jones offered the refugee analysts membership in the IPA, other societies were not welcoming. The Dutch Psychoanalytic Society refused to take in refugees. Van Ophuijsen wrote Jones: "The members are afraid to suffer both financially and narcissistically."[47] The Americans denounced what they called a "free-floating membership."[48] New York analysts routinely rewrote appeals to help "German-Jewish" analysts to read "German analysts."[49] Fenichel alone advised Jones that the German Psychoanalytical Society had gone far beyond what was necessary: "This dutiful show will not save them."[50]

In 1936 the German Psychoanalytic Society joined the Göring Institute. Freudian ideas were melded into an outlook called *Seelenheilkunde,* "soul-healing," and the goal of therapy was redefined as the treatment of "weaklings." At first the society retained some autonomy. In November 1936 Anna Freud wrote Ernest Jones: "Strange to say the work is flourishing. New candidates are arriving, the courses are attended, the various hospitals are sending patients galore for treatment. Even official bodies believe in the

Group photo of the most important members of the Göring Institute
in 1941. Werner Kemper is second from left, Matthias Göring is
ninth from left, Felix Boehm is twelfth, and Karl Müller-Braunschweig
is on the far right.

seriousness of analysis and in its therapeutic efficacy. This bit of success
in the outside world naturally makes it really difficult for [Boehm] to dis-
solve everything and give up."[51] Indeed, Boehm's specialty was homosexuality, and as advisor to the armed forces, he effectively opposed the most
punitive methods such as internment, at least until 1944.[52] As for Müller-
Braunschweig, he wrote many essays proving that analysis was not un-
German but, in the right hands, could transform unfit softlings into people
energetically engaged in life. In 1938 the German Psychoanalytic Society
was dissolved. Even so, a group within the Göring Institute claimed to
remain loyal to Freudian ideas.[53]

Through all this, Freud's stance must be described as opportunistic. In
1936, when Boehm visited him to discuss the absorption of psychoanalysis
into the Göring Institute, Freud told him: "You may make all kinds of sac-
rifices but are not to make any concessions."[54] In 1938 Boehm again came to
Vienna, this time to propose dissolving the Vienna Psychoanalytic Society
and merging it into a newly formed German Institute. Freud said he would
neither forbid nor support the action.[55] Obviously self-serving, these state-

ments cannot be fully interpreted now because the Freud-Boehm correspondence remains closed. Nonetheless, it was recognized at the time that racial exclusion violates the spirit of free and open inquiry. The Dutch Psychoanalytic Society, although unwelcoming to Jewish refugees in the mid-thirties, resigned en masse after the Nazi occupation. So did the Norwegian society under the leadership of Harald Schjelderup. Yet until his death in 1939, Freud continued to communicate with the Berlin group as if they represented psychoanalysis in Germany, apparently believing that psychoanalysis could survive in a fascist context.

As fascism triumphed, psychoanalysis crumbled. In 1935 Édouard Pichon, a right-wing militant and member of the royalist, anti-Semitic Action Française, became the president of the French Psychoanalytic Society. Analysis *à la française* had prevailed. Rudolph Loewenstein and Heinz Hartmann, both Jews, fled to the United States, where they became leaders of American ego psychology. Nevertheless, the French society was abolished when the Nazis entered Paris.[56] In no nation was analysis so corrupted as in Germany, but France had its own symptomatic episode. René Laforgue, a founder of the Société Psychanalytique de Paris, was an Alsatian who had fought on the German side in World War I and become a French citizen in 1918. Overwhelmed by the German victories in 1939–40, he tried to resume his original nationality and approached Göring with the idea of creating an "aryanized institute" in Paris. The initiative came to nothing, since the Germans never trusted Laforgue—and with good reason. Having been a member of the League Against Anti-Semitism earlier in the 1930s, he soon turned to protecting Jews.[57]

Everywhere, survival was the overriding motive. Giovacchino Forzano was a cabinet minister in the Italian government and coauthor with Mussolini of several plays. In 1933 the leading Italian analyst, Edoardo Weiss, who was treating Forzano's daughter, brought her and her father to Vienna for a consultation with Freud. Forzano asked Freud for an inscribed book for Mussolini. Freud chose *Why War?*, his exchange of letters with Albert Einstein. Stating that he intended to recognize Mussolini's role in excavating Italian archaeological sites, he inscribed it: "Benito Mussolini, with the respectful greetings of an old man who recognizes in the ruler the champion of culture." Two months later, Mussolini complained about his difficulties with the Communists: to understand them, he said, "one needs to be competent in the new science or imposture called psychoanalysis."[58] Italian analysis was put out of business by the anti-Semitic laws of 1938. Nonethe-less, that spring Mussolini apparently offered to intervene with Hitler on Freud's behalf and to give him refuge in Italy.[59]

The scapegoating and death of Ferenczi in 1932 should also be situated in the context of the moral disintegration of psychoanalysis. Ferenczi's fore-most disciple, Michael Balint, described the increasingly isolated Ferenczi of the late 1920s as proud of his position as an enfant terrible, "but it was a bitter pride. His favourite story . . . was the fantasy of the 'wise baby' who though still in the cradle, is wiser than the whole family."[60] Trying to pre-serve Ferenczi's friendship while criticizing his revisions, Freud wrote him in 1931: "Since you like to play the tender mother role toward others, per-haps you are doing it toward your self. So you should hear the reminder from the brutal father's side that . . . you were no stranger to sexual games with your patients in your pre-analytical period."[61] To Eitingon, he was blunter: "First one [person] then another turns out to be unusable or unguidable. Ferenczi's obstinacy with his suspect technique, Reich and Fenichel's attempt to misuse the journals for Bolshevik propaganda. . . . Everything shows that under the corrosive influence of these times charac-ters rapidly decompose."[62]

Ferenczi's criticisms of psychoanalysis, like Reich's, were not so easily dismissed. Like many analysts of the time, he had returned to the actual and the social as opposed to the psychical. Thus, he argued that the analytic sit-uation, because of its emphasis on abstinence and privation, reproduced the infant experience of deprivation and trauma. He complained of "unconcern regarding the length of the analysis, indeed the tendency to prolong it for purely financial reasons: if one wants to, one turns the patients into taxpay-ers for life."[63] He urged the analytically trained to "found an association which would combine the greatest possible personal liberty with the advan-tages of family organization." He returned to Freud's abandoned seduction theory of the 1890s.[64] Michael Balint described his mood during his final illness as "a severe depression . . . a feeling that nobody could love him, especially not his master, and a gnawing fear that once again his enthusiasm had carried him away . . . and that he had lost forever the respect and esteem of his colleagues."[65] By the time he died in 1932, many analysts con-sidered him insane. Freud's unkind obituary notice commented: "His need to heal and help had become imperious."[66]

Although analytic work—congresses, theoretical production, visits be-tween societies, especially London and Vienna—continued throughout the thirties, everything took place in the German shadow. In the Soviet Union, Stalin had condemned analysis in 1927, but it had remained legal.

After the Nazi victory in 1933, Soviet repression deepened: the remnants of the Moscow Psychoanalytic Society disbanded, and in 1936 analysis was banned. After 1939, when Germany controlled the Continent, the Hungarian society passed into "non-Jewish" hands; meetings had to be reported to the police in advance. In the Netherlands, training continued in secret. Only in neutral Switzerland did analytic societies continue to operate openly. There, French-speaking analysts such as Henri Flournoy and Raymond de Saussure remained oriented toward Paris, while German speakers, such as Ludwig Binswanger and Medard Boss, began the development of existential analysis (*Daseinsanalyse*).[67]

Reichean radicalism survived. After 1933 the leadership of the analytic Left devolved onto Otto Fenichel, who had emigrated to Prague when the Nazis came to power in Berlin. A group of analysts centered around him sought to resist the Nazification of German analysis and to prevent discrimination against Marxist psychoanalysis in analytic journals.[68] To this end, Fenichel coordinated a newsletter, also termed a *Rundbriefe*. Its general theme was that instinctual life varies historically. Articles on anti-Semitism, national character, and the psychology of money appeared, along with attacks on Ferenczi, American psychoanalysis, Klein ("an exaggeration of biology"), and Reich ("completely *meschugge*"). In 1938 Fenichel, fleeing Prague, was asked to identify the most pressing question in analytic research. Whether the Nazis come to power in Vienna, was his answer. Later, in America, Fenichel continued to send out the *Rundbriefe*. In its last and briefest issue, July 14, 1945, the journal stated that the fight was not for a social psychoanalysis but for the "very existence of Freudian psychoanalysis." The next year, at forty-eight, Fenichel died of an aneurysm.[69]

Most poignant, certainly, were the experiences of analysts and analysands in concentration camps. Some struggled to maintain an analytic perspective even there, testifying to the extraordinary ability of the analytically oriented to suspend consideration of the external environment in order to focus on the intrapsychic. Analyst-prisoners analyzed symptoms away, lectured secretly, and sought to explain the social psychology of the camps. Karl Landauer, founder of the Frankfurt Institute, "practiced" analysis at Bergen-Belsen before he died there. Ernst Federn, the son of Paul Federn, who was in Buchenwald from 1938 to 1945, lectured to inmates on such subjects as homosexuality.[70] Bruno Bettelheim, also in Buchenwald for almost a year, used analytic introspection to develop the analysis of camp psychology that made him famous.

Many analysts perished. After the Germans invaded Hungary in 1944, Jozsef Mihály Eisler (a member of the Hungarian Psychoanalytic Society since 1919), Miklos Gimes, Zsigmond Pfeifer, and Géza Dukes died in the camps. The Yugoslav analyst Nikola Sugar, also a member of the Budapest society, died at Theresienstadt. David Oppenheim, a classics teacher with whom Freud had coauthored his first piece on folklore and who parted with Freud over the Adler controversy, was murdered in a camp.[71] Auguste Watermann had fled Hamburg in 1933 but was never fully accepted by the Netherlands society. After the Germans invaded Holland, he was arrested with his wife and child and deported to Wremdelingen at Westerbork, then to Theresienstadt, then to Auschwitz, where all three were killed. Ernst Hoffman, a Jew from Vienna, had fled to Antwerp in 1933 and trained the future founders of the Belgian Psychoanalytic Society before he was deported in 1942 to a camp in Gurs, France; he died soon after.[72] Sabina Spielrein was shot to death during a forced march, along with her two daughters, in a ravine outside Rostov. Fugitives from German occupation forces included Leo Eitinger in Norway and Hans Keilson in the Netherlands. Camp survivors included Eddy de Wind, Elie Cohen, and Viktor Frankl.[73] Leopold Szondi, who coined the term "destiny-analysis," survived Belsen and lived until 1986.[74] Raoul Wallenberg's intervention saved the Hungarian Jewish analyst Istvan Hollós. Gottfried R. Bloch, a Czech analyst, survived Auschwitz and lives at the time of this writing in Los Angeles.[75] John Rittmeister, a Communist psychoanalyst and member of the Resistance, executed by the Gestapo in Berlin in 1943, was remembered by East Germans as a hero and by West German analysts as a Bolshevik spy.[76]

Although Nazism destroyed many analytic societies, its victims created new ones. Eitingon emigrated from Berlin to Palestine in 1933 and along with Moshe Wulff founded an institute in Jerusalem.[77] Chaim Weizmann recalled immigrants from Galicia arriving in Palestine with no clothes but with copies of *Das Kapital* and *Die Traumdeutung* (*The Interpretation of Dreams*) under their arms.[78] Fritz Perls, the founder of Gestalt therapy, greatly influenced by his analyst, Wilhelm Reich, left Germany and along with Wulf Sachs founded the South African Institute of Psychoanalysis in 1935, before coming to the United States in 1945.[79] Under Reich's influence, Sachs revised *Black Hamlet* as *Black Anger:* Chavafambira's greatest need, he now wrote, "was not to know more of his repressed unconscious, but to know the society he lived in, to recognize its ills, and to learn how to fight them."[80] Adolf Josef Storfer had been director of the *Verlag* since 1925 and coeditor of *Imago, Psychoanalytische Bewegung,* and *Almanach der Psychoanalyse.* One of eighteen thousand German-speaking émigrés to Shanghai, he founded the émigré journal *Gelbe Post* and used it to popularize analytic ideas in China.[81]

The Palestine Institute
of Psychoanalysis

WAS OPENED ON OCTOBER 15
by the
"Chevra Psychoanalytith b'Erez Israel"
(THE PSYCHOANALYSIS SOCIETY OF PALESTINE)

Under the direction of Dr. Eitingow

138, Abyssinian St. ——————— Jerusalem

COMPLETE LIBRARY OF BOOKS ON PSYCHOANALYSIS
WHICH MAY BE BORROWED (BY PERSONS FROM
ALL PARTS OF THE COUNTRY AGAINST A SMALL
SECURITY AND A SMALL FEE

Hours: Monday to Friday, 8—10 a.m.

ביום 15 לאוקטובר פתחה

„חברה פסיכואנליטית בא"י"

מכון לפסיכואנליזה

בהנהלה ד"ר מ. איטינגון (לשעבר ברלין)
ירושלים, רח' החבשים 138

על יד המכון נמצאת ספריה משוללמת של
ספרות פסיכואנליטית. ספרים אפשר להשיג
במקום ונשלחים לכל מקומות בארץ נגד.
בערבון ותשלום מינימלי.

השעות 8-10 לפני הצהרים
בכל ימי השבוע מלבד שבת וראשון

Announcement of the opening of the Palestine
Institute of Psychoanalysis, printed
in English and Hebrew in the *Internationale
Zeitschrift für Psychoanalyse,* 1934

Several Spanish analysts fled the Franco victory, among them Miguel Prados, who emigrated to Canada, and Gonzalo Lafora, who went to Mexico. Angel Garma, a product of the Berlin Psychoanalytic Institute and the first Spanish-speaking analyst in Latin America, arrived in Buenos Aires in 1938.[82] Two Viennese analysts, Max Langer and Marie Langer, members of the Communist Party, joined the International Brigade during the Spanish Civil War. After the Franco victory they emigrated and, with Garma, formed the Argentine Psychoanalytic Association in 1942. Helped by the growth of civil aviation, the Argentinians spread psychoanalysis throughout Latin America. As for Marie Langer, she remained an analyst, a feminist, and a Marxist activist as late as the Sandinista revolution of the 1980s.[83]

In the United States, interest in Freud had at first seemed to decline with the Great Depression. Articles such as "Farewell to Freud" and "The Twilight of Psychoanalysis" appeared. *Fortune* opined, "Sex is no longer news. And the fact that it is no longer news is news."[84] In fact, analytic psychiatry was exploding. Franz Alexander was among the key figures. Forging connections to psychosomatic medicine, he promoted the sleek modern office, analytic popularization, and the adaptability of analysis to acceptable forms of cultural criticism. His 1938 presidential address to the American Psychoanalytic Association contrasted America, where "emotional resistance against psychoanalysis has become less and less evident," to the "ivory tower" of European analysis. He deplored the use of the term "movement" for psychoanalysis and called for "more precise, more quantitative knowledge . . . more exact experimental evidence."[85] In the words of Kurt Eissler, Alexander "made analysis a common-sense science, [adapting] it to the horizon of the medical man."[86]

Because the bulk of the émigrés headed to the United States, its "merging of analysis into psychiatry" loomed large for psychoanalysis as a whole. Since the early thirties the Americans had operated largely independently.[87] By the end of the thirties they barely participated in the International. Calling for the abolition of the International Training Committee, they formulated their own standards for training. If the war had not intervened, they would have seceded.[88]

The continued absorption of analysis into psychiatry in the United States was the counterpart to its destruction in Europe. Analysis survived but was thoroughly transformed. Freud agreed with Jelliffe "that Psychoanalysis has spread in the US more widely than deeply."[89] What Franz Alexander saw as American "openmindedness," Freud ascribed to the culture's "lack of emotional investment in genuine understanding"; the pride they take in their "*broad-mindedness*" only demonstrates their "lack of *judgement*."[90] Freud's belief that the analytic spirit could disappear, even as analysis triumphed as a profession, was revealed in many well-known statements (though those were not explicitly directed at the United States): "My discoveries are not primarily a heal-all. My discoveries are a basis for a very grave philosophy. There are very few who understand this."[91] Nevertheless, in 1939 Freud advised Arnold Zweig to emigrate to the United States rather than to England. "America seems to me an Anti-Paradise, but it has so much room and so many possibilities, and in the end one does come to belong to it. Einstein told a friend recently that at first America looked to him like a caricature of a country, but now he feels himself quite at home there."[92]

As psychoanalysis disintegrated, the resulting fragments were transformed, sometimes through amalgamation with other currents. In Germany, the Institute for Social Research—the Frankfurt School—became a more faithful successor to German psychoanalysis than the Göring Institute, albeit one that combined psychoanalysis with critical social theory. The result was another attempt to apply psychoanalysis to the problems of understanding both fascism and mass democratic society.

Frankfurt had been a center of the 1848 liberal uprising and was the German city with the highest proportion of Jews. The University of Frankfurt was known as "one of the few in Germany where the Nazis could be sure of getting their heads bloodied if they [provoked] clashes with the left wing or Jewish students."[93] In 1923 Felix Weil, a Marxist millionaire, founded the Institute for Social Research there. Among its earliest associates were Max Horkheimer and Theodor Adorno, Jewish intellectuals whose fathers were wealthy businessmen. From the first, the institute had a close relation to psychoanalysis. Beginning in 1929, it housed the Frankfurt Psychoanalytical Institute, led by Karl Landauer and Heinrich Meng. Owing to this relationship, the Frankfurt Psychoanalytical Institute became the only one in Germany that could offer university lectures. Demonstrating its esteem for analysis, the city of Frankfurt awarded Freud the Goethe Prize for literature in 1930.[94]

The early thought of the Frankfurt School followed Reich in tracing the roots of fascism to a corrupted family structure. After the 1930 elections, Erich Fromm, a former rabbinical student who was director of social psychology at the institute, conducted surveys of family life to explain the Nazi gains.[95] Like Reich, Fromm contrasted the individual prone to fascism, characterized by a strict superego and a submissive attitude toward paternal authority, to the individual likely to resist, characterized by "optimistic trust in mother's unconditional love." The middle-class, patricentric family, Fromm argued, defined duty as the central concern of life.[96] Class society reproduced the familial situation. Because the workers experienced their rulers as all-powerful, rebellion seemed pointless, and they sought goodwill through submission. The Great Depression led to further regression, strengthening the sense of duty and the "demand for heroic action."[97]

Following the appointment of Hitler as chancellor in 1933, the Frankfurt Institute moved to Columbia University in New York City. Like Reich and

Fromm, Horkheimer and Adorno had originally been interested in Freud because of his insights into the decline of the middle-class family. In the United States, however, they also began to view him as one of the "dark thinkers" of the Enlightenment, someone who illuminated the Enlightenment's totalitarian propensities. Beneath the differences among fascism, communism, and Fordism, they believed they discerned a common element: the Enlightenment-inspired wish to create a mass utopia through planning and control. Whereas in Germany the state took the leading role in organizing society, in the United States Horkheimer and Adorno were struck by the power of the media. They turned to Freud as a thinker who could illuminate this phenomenon.

The German social theorist Siegfried Kracauer pioneered the attempt to apply psychoanalysis to the study of the mass media. As he explained in his 1927 essay "The Mass Ornament," the chorus line was the "American distraction factory's" complement to the assembly line. The assembly line abstracted from social labor to produce generic, interchangeable units of labor-time, just as the market abstracted from concrete "use values" to create generic exchange values. The chorus line celebrated this process of abstraction: "Not only were [the chorus lines] American products . . . they demonstrated the greatness of American production. . . . When they formed an undulating snake, they radiantly illustrated the virtues of the conveyor belt; when they tapped their feet in fast tempo, it sounded like *business, business.*"[98] The aesthetics of the chorus line constituted "the daydream of society." Its harmonious rhythms mirrored the "secret mechanism" of capitalist control, in which instrumental-commodity relations eroded depth while feeding unconscious fantasies of plenitude and power.[99]

After Horkheimer and Adorno moved to New York, they elaborated on Kracauer's initiative. Even in the midst of the Depression, they were struck by the fact that film, magazines, and advertising had co-opted the surrealist program of charging reality with unconscious content. Department stores were deliberately organized to disorient customers, defamiliarize everyday objects, and render commodities sublime and monumental. Magazine design picked up on modernism's attention-commanding diagonal, off-center layout and expressive distortion.[100] Advertisements portrayed commodities such as cigarette boxes as autonomous beings.[101] King Kong and Tarzan movies generated a kind of "psychoanalysis in reverse," supplying new myths of the noble savage, displayed on the screen but not traced to the mind. Mass culture, not the family, the émigrés concluded, supplied the crucial link between the individual and modern society; commodity fetishism, not the Oedipus complex, provided the key to understanding advanced capitalism. In 1935 Adorno, pursuing graduate study at Oxford, marked the shift when he wrote to Horkheimer at Columbia: "I consider the decisive mediation between society and psychology not to be the family, but the commodity character."[102]

Eventually, Horkheimer and Adorno applied their analysis of mass culture to psychoanalysis itself. In Freud's theory, the ego acquired strength by confronting, as well as by identifying with, parental authority. Under Fordist mass production, however, socialization increasingly occurred through the culture industry. The result, according to Adorno's 1942 essay, was the appearance of a new psychological type, characterized not by repression but by the substitute gratification provided by mass culture.[103] Idealization of the "mass idol" fostered "narcissistic regression" and allowed powerless individuals to secure "infinite celebrity." As a result, the ego lost its living space and became incapable of remaining distinct from the id. Mass support for fascism, like the power of consumer culture in the United States, demonstrated that "psychological motivation in the old liberalistic sense" had nearly disappeared. Freud's *Group Psychology and the Analysis of the Ego* had caught this postpsychological, deindividualized flattening-out of psychology, "the turning point where psychology abdicates."[104]

After World War II, Adorno and Horkheimer connected the decline of psychoanalysis to changes in the family. The small property owner, they wrote, constituted the "psychological corner shop" of the early capitalist system, the "dynamic cell of economic activity." Psychoanalysis embodied the outlook of this small businessman. It portrayed the individual ego as enjoying some freedom, although "the friction surfaces [were] large and neuroses—the *faux frais* [incidental costs] of this instinctive economy—inescapable." In the consumerist epoch, in contrast, economic decisions had been taken over by administrators, and the private sphere had been integrated into mass culture. The masses, they wrote, "are more effectively shaped by the guidance of their impulses [by mass culture] than they ever could have been by their restraint."[105] The result, Adorno and Horkheimer predicted, would be the obsolescence of psychoanalysis and of the Freudian vision of man.

Although prophetic, Adorno and Horkheimer's work was one-sided. They grasped the dystopic possibilities that the second industrial revolution had unleashed, but they failed to see the openings it had created for redefining the promise of modernity. Until Herbert Marcuse wrote in the 1960s, the one member of the Frankfurt School who did grasp this opening was Walter Benjamin, whose *Passagen-Werk,* left unfinished when Benjamin died in 1942, had inspired the idea that the commodity form had supplanted the family as the crucial mediation between the individual and society.

Like his Frankfurt School colleagues, Benjamin wanted to analyze the "dreamworld" of twentieth-century capitalist society. To do so he returned to its origins in mid-nineteenth-century Paris. Unlike Kracauer, Benjamin did not believe that the collective unconscious of Parisian consumer culture could be understood through a single controlling image, such as that of the chorus line. Instead, he hoped to arrange the "small, superficial symptoms" of the epoch in the form of a collage, hoping thereby to preserve a sense of its contradictory and discontinuous character. Announcing his goal as "graphicness" (*Anschaulichkeit*), Benjamin investigated such categories as plushness, interiors, fashion, advertising, prostitution, *flâneurs,* gamblers, and boredom. He drew on the surrealists because they had been engaged in "the uncontrolled, passionate use of the drug: *image.*" Politics, he added, was "a sphere reserved one hundred percent for images."[106]

Influenced as much by Hasidic and cabalistic mysticism as by Marxism, Benjamin wanted to translate the "wish images" of the twentieth-century mass utopias into "dialectical images" capable of awakening the world "from the dream of itself." In spite of his enthusiasm for the surrealists, he believed that they were not interested in awakening but wanted to remain within the dream. "I'm going to take up Freud in the near future," he wrote Adorno. "Does anything in him or his school having to do with a psycho-analysis of awakening come to mind?" When he did read Freud, he was struck by Freud's paradoxical view that memory fragments are most power-ful and enduring when the incident that left them behind had not been per-ceived. The more "consciousness registers these [unconscious] shocks," Benjamin wrote, "the less likely are they to have a traumatic effect." For Benjamin, such "shocks" characterized modernity. At the same time, he wanted "awakening" to mean something more than reflective understand-ing; he wanted it to mean epiphany: incantation with revelatory power. Like the surrealists, however, Benjamin failed to find this in Freud.[107]

As refugees poured out of Germany and central Europe, Freud refused to believe the Nazis would enter Austria. In 1934 the Austrian constitution was annulled, the Socialist Party banned, and Engelbert Dollfuss, Austria's authoritarian chancellor, gunned down in his office by local Nazis. These blows did not convince Freud to flee. Yet in 1935 he explained to Lou Andreas-Salomé that he could not risk publishing *Moses and Monotheism* because "it is only . . . Catholicism which protects us from the Nazis."[108] In

November 1937 he described the future to Stefan Zweig as grim, adding, "What I have wanted was to come close to you in a human way rather than be admired like a rock against which the waves break in vain."[109] The next year he told Marie Bonaparte that flight from Vienna would signal the dissolution of psychoanalysis.[110]

Through the protracted difficulties of the interwar period, Freud had not been unresponsive to the general crisis that followed the collapse of classical liberalism. On several occasions he took up the question of Marxism, which Reich, as well as the Frankfurt theorists, had placed at the center of psychoanalysis. In 1932 he wrote: "We must not forget that the mass of human beings who are subjected to economic necessities also undergo the process of cultural development—of civilization, as other people say— which, though no doubt influenced by all the other factors, is certainly independent of them in its origin. . . . If anyone were in a position to show in detail the way in which these different factors—the general inherited human disposition, its racial variations and its cultural transformations— inhibit and promote one another under the conditions of social rank, profession and earning capacity—if anyone were able to do this, he would have supplemented Marxism so that it was made into a genuine social science."[111]

Civilization and Its Discontents, one of the great anti-utopian works of the thirties, centered on the painful, inevitable limit to all attempts to harmonize the public and the private, focusing on the examples of Christianity and Marxism. The Christian golden rule, "Love thy neighbor as thyself," was an attempt to transcend selfishness and reconcile individuals with one another. The problem, Freud pointed out, was that a neighbor is not only a potential helper or sexual object, but also a potential exploiter, a thief, a rapist, a humiliator, and a murderer. "Anyone who calls to mind . . . the horrors of the recent World War," he added, "will have to bow humbly before the truth of this view."[112] Marxism was even more ambitious than Christianity in its Enlightenment-inspired attempt to order, plan, and harmonize. But to the Marxist view that human beings are benign except insofar as they have been corrupted by property, Freud rejoined that property was the tool of aggression, not its cause. We see aggression "in the nursery almost before property has given up its primal, anal form."[113]

Aggression, Freud continued, was the result neither of childhood frustration nor of faulty but remediable social institutions. The fatal inevitability of guilt is the heart of all aggression and the reason we can never be rid of it. The guilt derives from the murder of the father, but there must have been something prior to the murder to explain the guilt. The prior condition is the ambivalence of instinctual life itself. Thus, the sons both loved and hated their father; after the murder they transformed both instincts into guilt. Their renunciation of aggression, their turning inward upon themselves, their burden of guilt, were reborn in every childhood. At a private meeting with analysts, Freud claimed that *Civilization and Its Discontents* had been widely misunderstood. It has been said, he insisted, "that I am trying to force the death instinct upon analysis." However, he maintained, "I wrote the book with purely analytic intentions, based on my former existence as an analytic writer, in brooding contemplation, concerned to promote the feeling of guilt to its very end. The feeling of guilt is created by the renunciation of aggression. . . . I consider this [idea] the most important progress in analysis."[114]

In the lengthening darkness of the German shadow, even technical works took on a political cast. Thus, Anna Freud's 1936 *Ego Psychology and the Mechanisms of Defense* included veiled political criticisms of Ferenczi and Reich for assuming that drives originally have only positive and loving aims and attitudes, and that hatred and destructiveness are simply the result of frustration. One year later a closely related work, Heinz Hartmann's *Ego Psychology and the Problem of Adaptation,* rejected "the malaise of our time," which Hartmann defined as "the fear that a surfeit of intelligence and knowledge will impoverish and denaturalize man's relationships to the world." Hartmann added, "No period in history has had a detrimental excess of knowledge or intelligence."[115]

Freud, aging, sick, and surrounded by destructive forces, continued to develop his theory of the ego with brilliant late fragments on splitting and "constructions in analysis." But he also returned to his great theme of paternal authority. In 1936, in an open birthday letter to Romain Rolland, he recalled the odd sadness he had felt when he first visited the Acropolis in 1904. Reading mythology and history as a child, he had dreamt of visiting Greece. When he realized his dream, however, he became inexplicably depressed. The cause of the depression, he now realized, was "*filial piety*": "a sense of guilt . . . attached to the satisfaction in having gone such a long way." His father, he informed Rolland, "had been in business, he had had no secondary education, and Athens could not have meant much to him." The 1904 incident came into his mind, Freud added, because he had grown old himself, and was "in need of forbearance and [could] travel no more."[116]

Moses and Monotheism, Freud's last completed book, wrestled with the same classic, indeed biblical, theme. A meditation on the nature of tradition and on charisma, the basis of tradition's "special power," the book asserted that it was impossible "to dispute the personal influence upon

Freud, 1938

world-history of individual great men." Granting the significance of objective forces such as economics and demography, Freud nonetheless insisted that one man, the Egyptian Moses, fleeing the destruction of Egyptian monotheism, had created the Jews. The reason the Jewish people believed themselves to be "chosen" was that Moses had chosen them.[117] Charismatic figures like Moses were often those "in whom one of the human impulsions has found its strongest and purest, and therefore often its most one-sided, expression." Such figures gave a people or an epoch its cultural superego.[118] Writing and rewriting a book he hid from the censors, Freud restated his basic idea: "We know that in the mass of mankind there is a powerful need for an authority who can be admired, before whom one bows down, by whom one is ruled and perhaps even ill-treated. We have learnt from the psychology of individual men what the origin is of this need of the masses. It is a longing for the father felt by everyone from his childhood onwards."[119]

But even as Freud returned to the theme of paternal authority, he expanded it with a new insight, one that stressed the traumatic roots of group identity. What drove this third revision of Freud's group psychology was his attempt to understand Judaism, especially his own Judaism. In 1935 he told Thornton Wilder: "Hitherto I have said that religion is an illusion;

now I say it has a truth—it has an historical truth."[120] What he meant was that the truth of religion, in the sense of the compelling emotional power that lay behind it, rested on actual but forgotten events. The Jews, Freud believed, had chafed under Moses' stern, demanding ethical principles. Finally, they murdered him. But the truth that Moses embodied for them, the monotheistic ideas he studied at the court of Ikhnaton, returned in the later history of Judaism, for example, in the age of the prophets. As Freud wrote to Andreas-Salomé: "Religions owe their compulsive power to the *return of the repressed;* they are reawakened memories of very ancient, forgotten, highly emotional episodes of human history . . . the strength of religion lies not in its *material,* but in its *historical* truth."[121]

An unconscious group identity, then, such as that shared by the Jews, was not only based on identification with a common history or ideal; group identity also reflected a compulsion to repeat and work through traumatic group experiences. While this insight could deepen and complicate religious or national identity, it also undermined loyalty and piety. In the case of Judaism, to claim that Moses was an Egyptian, and that the Jewish people murdered him, was, as Freud wrote to Jones in 1936, nothing less than "a denial of the Jewish national myth."[122] In place of that myth Freud asserted that otherness and antagonism were at the center of Jewish identity. Challenging the Hebrew Bible's account of Jewish history, Freud compared the distortions that the biblical text had undergone to a murder: "The difficulty is not in perpetrating the deed, but in getting rid of its traces."[123] The traumas that had constituted the Hebrew people—the fact that their founder was an Egyptian, the fact that they had murdered him, the fact that they had merged with an entirely different people, and so forth—had left behind so many fixations, compulsions, defensive reactions, avoidances, inhibitions, and phobias that it was impossible to assign a clear, positive content to the fact of being a Jew.

One question remained. In 1934 Freud wrote Arnold Zweig: "In view of the renewed persecutions I am asking myself again how the Jew . . . has drawn upon himself this undying hatred."[124] Like everything else in psychoanalysis, Freud's answer returned to the evolution of the family with its decisive impact on human psychology. Ultimately, he argued, we know our mothers through direct sensory perception, but to establish a connection to our fathers requires cognition. Egypto-Hebraic monotheism with its strong emphasis on the father-centered family signified the "victory of intellectuality [*Geistigkeit*] over sensuality [*Sinnlichkeit*]." "All [such] progress in spirituality results in increasing self-confidence, in making people proud so that they feel superior to those who have remained in the bondage of the senses." *Pride* had led the Jews to eschew the Christian solution to "the ancient ambivalence in the relation to the father," namely, the erecting of the son into a new God. In refusing to join in this step, however, the Jews had brought down "a tragic load of guilt upon themselves."[125] Jewish intellectuality and pride, then, in tandem with Jewish guilt, had made Jews the target of Christian ingratitude, envy, and contempt.

Meanwhile, in Austria, where anti-Semitism had been the single most persistent force in twentieth-century politics, the Nazis came to power. In February 1938 Adolf Hitler summoned the Austrian chancellor, Kurt von Schuschnigg, to Berchtesgaden, the resort town where *The Interpretation of Dreams* was largely written. After a few weeks, Hitler replaced Schuschnigg with the head of the Austrian Nazi Party, who proclaimed the Anschluss, or union with Germany. According to a contemporary historian, "The spontaneous anti-Semitic riots accompanying the Anschluss were so violent that they shocked even the Germans."[126] On March 11 the Germans marched without opposition across Austria's northern border and into Vienna, destroying Freud's fantasy that Hitler would be stopped at the city gates. Two days later, the board of the Vienna Psychoanalytic Society decided that all members should flee the country and establish the future headquarters of the society wherever Freud went. On March 22 the Gestapo visited the Freud household and took Anna Freud away for seven hours of questioning concerning the *Verlag*. When she returned home, still composed, her father wept.[127]

Freud's focus on the uncanny or *unheimlich* otherness that is at the center of Jewish identity did not stop him from affirming his own Judaism. In 1926 after describing his language, culture, and attainments as German, Freud added that since he had "noticed the growth of anti-Semitic prejudices in Germany," he preferred to call himself a Jew.[128] In his 1930 preface to the Hebrew translation of *Totem and Taboo,* he wrote:

> No reader of [the Hebrew version of] this book will find it easy to put himself in the emotional position of an author who is ignorant of the language of holy writ, who is completely estranged from the religion of his fathers—as well as from every other religion—and who cannot take a share in nationalist ideals, but has yet never repudiated his people, who feels that he is in his essential nature a Jew and who has no desire to alter that nature. If the question were put to him: "Since you have abandoned all these common characteristics of your countrymen, what is there left to you that is Jewish?" he would reply: "A great deal, and probably its very essence." He could

not now express that essence clearly in words: but some day, no doubt, it will become accessible to the scientific mind.[129]

A sometime opponent of Zionism who once warned against the "baseless fanaticism" of the settlers, Freud nonetheless insisted in 1935 that he had "never pretended to be anything but what I am: a Jew from Moravia whose parents come from Austrian Galicia."[130] When, upon arriving in England, he was asked by a British periodical to comment on the growth of anti-Semitism in that country, he responded: "After 78 years of assiduous work I had to leave my home, saw the Scientific Society I had founded, dissolved, our institutions destroyed, our Printing Press ('Verlag') taken over by the invaders, the books I had published confiscated or reduced to pulp, my children expelled from their professions. Don't you think you ought to reserve the columns of your special number for the utterances of non-Jewish people, less personally involved than myself?"[131]

The coming of the Nazis to power seemed to bring to an end the great redefinition of the Enlightenment that had characterized the modernity of the 1920s and '30s. But, in fact, it had sparked a profound interrogation of the third great ideal of modernity: democracy. In contrast to those who had propounded the classical liberal separation of public and private life, the thinkers of the 1930s recognized the unavoidably psychological and cultural character of modern politics, and thus the impossibility of separating the problems of democracy from those of personal autonomy, gender and sexuality, group identity, and the commodification of everyday life. Psychoanalysis had been central to this recognition, as we can see from Freud's theories of group formation, Reich's explorations of the role of the family, the Frankfurt School's investigations of mass culture, and Freud's final insights into the traumatic bases of identity. These accomplishments left an enormous legacy.

Running through both the prewar and the postwar analytic interrogations of modernity was one problem: the place of the family, and of the new phenomenon of personal life, under the conditions of large-scale planning released by the second industrial revolution. That revolution had made possible an economic surplus, and with it the transformation of the family and the rise of personal life. Beneath the vicissitudes of political upheaval, emigration, and even war and destruction lay a change of world-historical proportions. The family, historically the site of society's most painful, compelling, and regressive material processes, was now giving rise to society's most transcendent hopes. Psychoanalysis may have expressed those hopes in an ideological form, presenting human beings as ends only insofar as they had been abstracted from their real conditions of social life, but the fact that it expressed them at all had made it central to the twentieth century's redefinition of modernity.

Meanwhile, psychoanalysis expired in its central European birthplace. Soon after Hitler entered Vienna, Ernest Jones and Marie Bonaparte helped bring thirty-eight Viennese analysts, including Sigmund and Anna Freud, to London.[132] The elder Freud never recovered from the move. Yet, when he died a year later, W. H. Auden remarked that Freudianism was no longer the thought of one man but had become a whole "climate of opinion." This climate was integral to the great coalition that defeated fascism. At its moment of collapse, then, the analytic movement was poised on the verge of an extraordinary expansion of analysis in its "object relations" and "ego psychology" forms.

Part Three

FROM THE PSYCHOLOGY OF AUTHORITY TO THE POLITICS OF IDENTITY

Chapter Ten

THE MOTHER-INFANT RELATIONSHIP AND THE POSTWAR WELFARE STATE

[She] is conceived as any small child would in essence think of his mother, not as small and frail, but as the one large, secure, solid background to life.

—Walter Hussey

Like the Great War, World War II provoked a series of efforts to rethink the nature of the modern subject in light of the dangers that modernity had brought in its wake. Unlike the first war, however, which was waged by morally comparable nations and empires, the second war was waged against a monster state. Its conclusion brought the revelations of the Hiroshima deaths and the Holocaust, and ushered in the so-called cold war. Powerful new media—photojournalism, film, TV—dispatched images of horror around the globe. Thus, if the first postwar generation had been preoccupied with the problem of death, the World War II generation was preoccupied with the problem of evil. As before, psychoanalysis was at the center of its reflections.

This was a very different psychoanalysis, however, one increasingly centered on the mother. Introduced with Freud's structural revisions, inspired by the attempt to turn analysis into a theory that accounted for both sexes, and reinforced by the shift from central Europe to Britain and the United States, concern for the pre-Oedipal infant moved to the center of analytic thinking. In this regard, too, psychoanalysis resonated with the deepest currents in the culture. Thus, during the worst battle of World War I, Freud had called the mother's body "the former *Heim* of all human beings," adding, "Whenever a man dreams of a place or a country and says to himself, while he is still dreaming: 'this place is familiar to me, I've been here before,' we may interpret the place as being his mother's genitals or her body."[1] Similarly, when the Great Depression intensified the longing for home—as memorialized in John Steinbeck's *Grapes of Wrath*, which ends with a young mother breast-feeding a starving vagrant—the mother symbolized a wish for nurturance, peace, and security amid the dangers and disappointments of the time.

World War II completed the process by which the mother moved to the center of the democratic imagination. Whereas Freud's 1916 comment evoked an uncanny, spectral absence, in 1943, when Henry Luce proclaimed the twentieth century the "American Century," Luce's readers all assumed that a citizenry capable of defeating the Nazi brute required the mother's *presence*. By that time, such analytically influenced public intellectuals as Erik Erikson, Margaret Mead, Ruth Benedict, and Geoffrey Gorer were tracing fascism and militarism to deficiencies in early mothering. Liberal social reform—not only the attempt to reduce crime and "deviancy" but the new focus on racial injustice—was taking an increasingly psychological turn. And "Momism," as Philip Wylie called the new, mother-centered regime in 1942, was to be the basis of democratic strength, even though Wylie feared it had become a source of weakness.

For a while this project was a success. Indeed, historians term the period between the 1940s and the 1970s a "Golden Age" because of the prosperity made possible by the newly created welfare states.[2] Much of Wilhelm Reich's program—housing, privacy rights, the expansion of social and psychological services, birth control, and legal abortion—was enacted by the Beveridge welfare state in England, the New Deal in the United States, and the social-democratic welfare states of continental Europe, themselves generally modeled on the New Deal. Newly focused on the dependent state of earliest childhood, and on the building up of trust and cooperative object relations, the new, welfare-state-based generation of analysts began to regard their prewar predecessors as "paleoFreudian," as English analyst Charles Rycroft put it. Many of the suppressed or defeated elements of the earlier period—Adler's focus on equality, Ferenczi's emphasis on recognition, Reich's emphasis on the crowd or group—now came into their own.

Nonetheless, there is a crucial contradiction that runs through this final phase in the history of classical psychoanalysis. The outcome of a century of struggle, the culmination of the second industrial revolution, the welfare state was premised on the idea that human beings were interdependent and responsible for one another.[3] At the same time, it confined this idea to a limited, privatized form. Its "family wage" model—a male breadwinner and a full-time mother—was already obsolescent in the 1940s, both because of the increasing numbers of women working outside the home and because in freeing individuals from economic dependence, the welfare state also began to free them from the family. As psychoanalysis was integrated into the welfare state, then, it too became obsolescent. This two-sided process began in Britain, to which so many analysts had fled in the 1930s.

As the heartland of the first industrial revolution, England was also the heartland of a social-democratic culture that valorized the working-class family, the working-class community, and the working-class mother. Thus, especially during the Popular Front period of the 1930s, British object-relations psychoanalysis and the Beveridge welfare state grew from a common soil. Popular Front culture stressed interpersonal connection and social solidarity. Examples include George Orwell's writings on working-class culture; the documentary-film movement, which instructed the English in how interdependent they were by, for example, showing how many individuals participated in moving a letter from its author to its addressee; and the idea of the Popular Front itself. The experience of World War II introduced a new stress on ruptured connections and a corresponding drive to establish or repair relations. Newspapers anxiously worried over the effects on evacuated London children of being separated from their parents. Maternally coded images of home and homeland proliferated, as did the concepts of "culture" and "the organic." Images of the mother pervaded portrayals of the working-class family.

In that context, the relation to the mother came to dominate analytic theory. "Ego," "sexuality," and the "individual" gave way to "object," "mother," and "group." Along with an emphasis on rupture from, and reconnection with, "the mother," British analysis developed a new "relational" view of the ego as ethically responsible. Ethical responsibility was less a matter of observing universal moral norms than of meeting concrete obligations to particular others. At first, the relational ego was associated with personal life beyond the family: the terrain of friends, colleagues, and neighbors. Not accidentally, Bloomsbury, with its ethic of transfamilial sociality, played an important role in this stage of object-relational thinking. Later, however, when analysis became increasingly integrated into British society, the focus shifted to include larger complexes, such as "the group" and the national "family."

Several specific features of the English context shaped the emergence of the object-relations perspective. First, social-democratic, pragmatic, and Fabian traditions, which stressed democratic control at the base, provided a different political culture than that promoted by the Leninist party. "Mass-Observation"—a collective, participatory project of self-observation focused on such subjects as the "behavior of people at war memorials," "bathroom behavior," "beards, armpits and eyebrows," and "female taboos about eating"—suggests the feel of English social-democratic culture in the thirties, a culture that hoped to expand both solidarity and self-knowledge. "Mass-Observation," one organizer wrote, was "in the tradition of Darwin, Marx, Freud and Breuer."[4] In contrast to continental Marxists, English writers had a propensity to think about economics in moral or psychological terms. John Maynard Keynes, for example, argued that "dangerous human proclivities can be canalised into comparatively harmless channels by the existence of money-making."[5]

Alongside a strong working class with powerful collective traditions, the second industrial revolution began to reach England after World War I, producing a new middle class.[6] Technical, scientific, commercial, and symbol-using, working for a salary rather than a wage, the middle class constituted close to 25 percent of the population in the thirties and would grow larger after World War II. Simultaneously mobile and home-owning, it experienced a new level of separation between work and home, which brought greater intimacy and intensified but restricted sociability. According to the historian Ross McKibbin, in the working-class neighborhood "there were acquaintances in every direction, [but] little discrimination was made between degrees of social intimacy." In the middle class, by contrast, "friend[ships] were few but comparatively close" and not based on geographical location.[7] While working-class friendships were still rooted in class affiliation, the middle class depoliticized personal relations. The Labour Party, the middle classes complained, "dragged" politics into everything.

The core perceptions of the new middle class were given sharpened expression by the Bloomsbury circle. Bloomsbury represented a new conception of interpersonal ethics, one for which the society itself was generating a need. The point of reference was not "the generalized other," as in Kant and Freud, but the concrete, particularized other. G. E. Moore was the key thinker in this regard. Moore argued that immediate situated relations—for example, to friends, family, and community—took precedence over abstract ideals. Said Leonard Woolf, "We were and always remained primarily and fundamentally a group of friends."[8] Said E. M. Forster, "If I had to choose between betraying my *country* and betraying my *friend,* I hope I should have the guts to betray my country."[9] According to Keynes, "We entirely repudiated a personal liability on us to obey general rules. We claimed the right to judge every individual case on its merits, and the wisdom to do so successfully. . . . We were, that is to say, in the strictest sense of the term, immoralists. . . . Nothing mattered except states of mind . . . chiefly our own."[10]

The Popular Front emphasis on solidarity and the middle-class emphasis on personal relations both flowed into the country's strong feminist tradition, which encompassed not only suffragism but also maternalist social reform, lesbianism, and cultural experimentation. The "great mother" was no stranger to this tradition. Bronislaw Malinowski's anthropology, Jane Harrison's matriarchy-centered work on classical tragedy, and James Frazer's twelve-volume compilation of fertility myths, *The Golden Bough,* had all provoked serious and widely discussed challenges to Freud's father-centered Oedipal theory.[11] Melanie Klein and her followers represented a strong expression of "difference feminism" within psychoanalysis, a current that emphasized the importance of women's reproductive role. The lay ethos of the British Psychoanalytic Society brought many opportunities for women. In 1930 the society was 40 percent female, and many of the women were mothers. With the British romantic poets and Victorian novelists in their background, many female analysts had a strong interest in early childhood. These include M. N. Seal, Barbara Low, Susan Isaacs, who ran the Malting House nursery school at Cambridge, and Ella Freeman Sharpe, who ran a teachers' training center before studying analysis.[12]

Finally, the reorientation to the mother drew on Britain's strong empirical and meliorist tradition. There was a legacy of careful and direct observation but little tolerance for theory. The Tavistock Institute, a center of analytic innovation during World War II, described itself as a mixture of Freud, managerial innovation, and sociology. Proclaiming its credo to be "No doctrine, only aims," its "new psychology" stressed "the whole person." Tavistock psychologists such as Laura Hutton wrote the sex manuals that diffused Freudianism into the working classes, encouraging "the vague but powerful idea that sex was . . . central to existence." Religion also played an important role. Known informally as the "parson's clinic," Tavistock sponsored Ian Suttie's 1935 book, *The Origins of Love and Hate,* which argued that Christianity was a "system of psychotherapy" in which matriarchal elements were central. Suttie emphasized the social over the individual, the external over the internal, the altruistic over the "selfish." The Freudian emphasis on the father, Suttie concluded, was "a disease." Until the 1938 emigration the British Psychoanalytic Society was unusual among analytic societies in having almost no Jewish members.[13] The emigration changed all that. In 1975 Charles Rycroft expressed relief that with the passing of the older analysts, it had "become possible for a gentile to criticize classical psychoanalysis without being accused of being anti-Semitic."[14]

Of all the factors bringing about the reorientation to the mother, feminism was the most important. The history of British object relations in this period is in large part the history of a conflict between two women, Melanie Klein and Anna Freud. Although both women distinguished themselves from Sigmund Freud by their practical experience with children, they otherwise represented different daughterly relations to a common father figure. Klein was a brilliant, ambitious rebel whose true rival was Sigmund, not Anna. Anna Freud, by contrast, was a dutiful daughter, sometimes overwhelmed by her sense of responsibility to and for her father. The conflict between them dominated the history of analysis until well into the 1960s.

As we saw, Melanie Klein was born in 1882 in Vienna, was analyzed by Ferenczi in Budapest, and studied with Abraham in Berlin, where her personal eccentricities and unorthodox ideas earned her the condescension of many of the younger analysts. At the Berlin Psychoanalytic Institute she met Alix Strachey, a British analyst and the wife of Freud's English translator. At Strachey's urging, she emigrated to London in 1926. Described by Phyllis Grosskurth as "squat, Jewish, and *déclassée,*" she delivered her inaugural lecture in Virginia Woolf's brother's house on Russell Square. "Nowhere else . . . have I experienced this feeling of a very strong sympathy and an ability in me to adapt to the strange and unknown," she wrote soon afterward.[15]

In Berlin Klein had been one of the first to practice analysis on children, whose "presenting symptoms" were typically school problems. Viewing early learning as directed at the mother, she interpreted inhibitions on learning as resulting from the child's fear of retaliation for what the child perceived as its hostile wishes.[16] From this Klein concluded that the mother, not the father, was the original authority figure. Claiming that "the man-eating wolf, the fire-spewing dragon, and all the evil monsters out of myths and fairy-stories" were frequently mother figures, she argued against Freud that what drove female development was girls' rivalrous and often embittered relations with their mothers.

It was not until the late twenties, however, after having settled in England, that Klein began developing an alternative to the Freudian paradigm.

Melanie Klein, 1902

Today the shift is often described as a move from "instinct" theory to "object relations," but this is misleading for several reasons. For one thing, Freud's theory was always object-relational, as his focus on transference would suggest. For both Freud and Klein, moreover, the term "object" referred to an *internal* representation and not, as in most later object-relations theories, to an interpersonal or intersubjective relation.[17]

The most important difference between Freud and Klein lay elsewhere: in their implied understandings of personal life, as reflected in their theories of the ego. For Freud, the ego came into existence long before the superego and maintained some critical, reflective distance from the latter's imperatives. For Klein, in contrast, there was no real distinction between the two psychic agencies. What she called the superego overlapped with what Freud called the ego. Far from being the distanced agency of moral imperatives, the Kleinian superego was the deeply embedded center of ethical concerns. I use the term "ethical" here, as opposed to "moral," because Klein did not focus on universal moral norms. Rather, like her Bloomsbury associates, she attributed responsibility to concrete others, beginning with the mother and extending outward to particular communities.

Klein's key move was her insistence, contra Freud, that the superego originated in early representations of the mother, long before the Oedipus complex came into being.[18] This innovation had far-reaching implications. First, it implied that the formative conflicts for the individual were often very primitive, closely tied to biological survival. For Klein, accordingly, aggression, guilt, and responsibility were components of the earliest dependence. Associated with feelings of being denied satisfaction of basic material needs, they were not subject to the ego's self-critique. This represented a major departure from Freud, who believed that material frustrations became meaningful only later, after they had been reconfigured as moral imperatives.[19]

Second, Klein's view of the inner object world was strikingly different from Freud's. For Freud, there was always a third agency—the superego—that stood apart from the ego and judged it. For Klein, in contrast, all relations were saturated with ethical and moral content, but there was no independent or impersonal viewpoint. Rather, the Kleinian inner world was a complex, three-dimensional, differentiated landscape of gratifying and frustrating, rivalrous and supportive, "part" and "whole" objects. The result, Klein claimed, would be "a new understanding of the unconscious and of internal relationships as they have never been understood before apart from the poets."[20]

Finally, Klein's view implied a different diagnosis of the fundamental problem facing modern men and women. For Freud, the key problem had been to strengthen the ego so as to give the individual some freedom from the superego, from the demands of the id, and from society. For Klein, in contrast, the problem was to build up an internal world of whole objects, that is, to forge and sustain personal connections.

Klein always described her emphasis on internal objects as an elaboration of Freud's theory of the superego. In 1942 she claimed that the starting point of her thought was a passage in *The Ego and the Id* asserting that the superego resulted from sadism projected onto the parents, who were thus "established in the superego as . . . persecuting figures." She asked, "Who can doubt that the superego was a new beginning" toward object-relational thinking?[21] But these statements were misleading. Freud conceptualized the superego as a psychic agency to be understood in terms of its place within a structure, not as a personification. Klein, by contrast, viewed psychic structure—id, ego, and superego—as composed wholly of object representations.

All British object-relations thinking descends from Klein's notion of the "depressive position." She proposed this idea in a 1934 presentation that has been described as one of the most exciting in the history of psychoanalysis. In a paper provoked by her son's death while mountain climbing, she took the experience of mourning, in which we *identify* with lost objects, as the starting point for explaining how an inner object world was built up.[22] To conceptualize this inner world, Klein introduced the concept of a "position," which she defined as a "specific grouping of anxieties and defenses." A position can be contrasted with a neurotic conflict. A neurotic conflict is localized, even if its effects are pervasive; a position, in contrast, describes a stance or attitude of the mind as a whole.

Klein described early development—indeed, the whole of life—as the story of a shift between two positions: the paranoid position and the depressive position. These corresponded respectively to the state of not being related to an intersubjective, ethically meaningful world, on one hand, and the state of being related to such a world, on the other. In its earliest phase, according to Klein, the psyche was in the paranoid position: experience was fragmentary and discontinuous; thoughts and feelings happened to the subject; persecutory anxiety predominated. The great human accomplishment lies in achieving the "depressive position," although persecutory anxiety is never fully supplanted. Normally achieved in the first year of life, the depressive position consists of setting up the mother as an internal object. Based on the recognition that the mother is separate, it constitutes the beginning of subjectivity. Since, in Klein's conception, subjectivity involved object loss, mourning, and sadness, she also called this the "pining" position. Subjectivity, for Klein, was inseparable from the recognition that one has harmed or damaged the internal object on whom one depends.

Thus, there was no distinction for Klein between subjectivity and conscience. The human problem is to build up and maintain access to an internal object world. Whereas in the paranoid position relations are formed to "part objects," the depressive position involves an effort to represent "whole objects," in other words, to recognize others as subjects.[23] Since introspection involves an awareness of vulnerability, dependence, and guilt, it gives rise to "manic" attempts to avoid depression, especially through unreflective action. According to one commentator, the "heart of the depressive position is the realization that security can only be achieved through responsibility." The awareness that one can hurt an object upon whom one depends, and has done so, spurs efforts at "reparation," which is the only goodness we can know.

Klein's insistence on the inseparability of the ego from concrete relationships as opposed to universal moral considerations can be seen in her essay on Orson Welles's 1941 film *Citizen Kane.* The film's plot is set in motion by young Kane's violent separation from his mother. The sled he uses to defend himself—"Rosebud"—is the secret to his life. His dying word referred, Klein argued, to "the breast," whose sustenance Kane needed but could never allow himself to attain. This sustenance was not mere milk, of course; what he needed, rather, was to reconnect with and heal his painfully aborted relation to his mother. Kane, Klein wrote, is a person whose "depressive feelings [are] overlaid and kept at bay by manic mechanisms," that is, mechanisms of control. What is good in Kane—both in his politics and in his love life—stems from his effort to connect. Thus, he becomes a reformer not out of a principled sense of right and wrong but rather through a sense of compassion and concrete obligation to individuals and groups. Because of his traumatic uprooting, however, he cannot sustain this effort: "Long forgotten are the wishes to further the interests of poor people. These . . . soon changed into ways of controlling them." Similarly, he is attracted by his wife Susan's poverty and helplessness, which reminds him of his own devastated inner state, but after he marries her his feelings "turned into attempts to control." Klein noted: "The more his capacity for love proves a failure, the more the manic mechanisms increase."[24]

By the late thirties, Klein had created a new language centered on the problems of building up an internal object world capable of sustaining a complex and deeply felt personal life. This language implied a different way of conceptualizing modernity from Freud's, one concerned less with universal moral issues than with the effort to maintain small, meaningful, interpersonal communities. Klein's vision provided her contemporaries with a new vocabulary for describing culture. D. W. Winnicott described the modern city as organized around the manic defense: "the wireless that is left on interminably," the noise that never ceases. Adrian Stokes explained the reassurance given by arts such as sculpture and architecture as the relief that whole objects provide from persecutory anxiety. The gallery viewer, Donald Meltzer wrote, has "the aim of carrying out an infantile introjection, with the hope . . . of obtaining something in the nature of a reconstructed object."[25]

Klein's work also implied a reformulation of analytic practice, especially the problem of resistance. A 1936 essay by her associate Joan Riviere, "A Contribution to the Analysis of the Negative Therapeutic Reaction," exemplified the revision. Whereas for Freud the primary source of resistance was unconscious guilt, for Riviere it was the impaired transition to the depressive position. For Freud, the goal of analysis was autonomy; all that really mattered was for the patient to gain self-knowledge. For Riviere, the aim of analysis was to foster connection by enabling the patient to rediscover the internal object. For Freud, the analyst maintained distance and neutrality to model the ego's reflective capacity. For Riviere, in contrast, the analyst had to be available as an object. Both Freud and Riviere located the roots of resistance in narcissism, but their accounts of narcissism diverged. Freud assumed that narcissism prevented analysis by impeding transference. For Riviere, in contrast, the analyst needed to penetrate the narcissistic surface to the depression that inevitably lay beneath it. "The love for the internal object must be found behind the guilt," she wrote.[26]

For both Freud and Klein, then, the individual struggled to achieve a certain goodness. But for Freud the struggle was Kantian and moral, whereas for Klein it was concrete and relational. For Freud, the superego was a depersonalized categorical imperative; for Klein, the superego referred to particularized and concrete others. For Freud, internal life was dominated by the problem of finding one's individual place in the world; for Klein, it was dominated by responsibility to particular others to whom one had incurred obligations, not by virtue of being generically human, as in Kant, but because one found oneself in specific relations and circumstances. For Freud, the moral core of the person was formed in conflicts deriving from the "laws" that constitute our humanity, especially the incest taboo; for Klein, the core conflicts reflected frustrations of basic material needs and the rage and envy that invariably result. Potentially, Klein's focus on concrete obligations to others enriched and complicated Freud's focus on autonomy. Everything depended on how it would be interpreted.

In English analytic circles of the mid-thirties, Klein's work caused enormous excitement. Winnicott recalls his analyst, James Strachey, breaking into a session to tell him about it.[27] Later, when Klein was under attack, she reminded the British Psychoanalytic Society of how proud they had once been of her work. She published continually, stirring resentment. Jones wrote that when people said she was going too far, they meant she was going too fast. She was also, always, an outsider, squat and Jewish, as we have seen, whereas her Bloomsbury companions were tall and angular.[28]

The reception of Klein's work was also colored by her conflict with Anna Freud, which arose when they both wrote on child analysis.[29] Behind Anna stood Sigmund. After visiting London in 1927, Ferenczi informed Freud of Klein's "domineering influence," which Ferenczi considered "directed toward Vienna." Publicly, Freud remained neutral. In letters to Jones, he presented his criticisms of Klein as criticisms of Joan Riviere. Privately, however, he blamed *Jones,* whom he charged with "organizing a veritable campaign in London against Anna's child analysis" and "go[ing] too far with [his] tolerance" for Klein.[30] To Eitingon, Freud wrote: "Compared to the opinions of Klein, [Anna's] are conservative, one might even say reactionary, but it looks as if she is right."[31] Nonetheless, he later conceded that "the sphere from which [Klein] has drawn her observations is foreign to me." In the last few months of his life he seems to have worked on a never-completed critique of Klein's work.[32]

The prospect of a struggle between London and Vienna was momentous. Following the Nazi victories in 1933, these were the two most important analytic societies in Europe. The Vienna society was strongly anti-Kleinian. In 1935 Jones arranged a series of exchanges between the two societies aimed at discussing Klein's work. Many of the Viennese criticisms of Klein were based on the view that psychoanalysis needed to be brought into conformity with child-development protocols. For example, Robert Wälder criticized Klein for overstating the cognitive potential of earliest infancy and ignoring infants' realistic fears.[33] Klein was also scapegoated by the old guard. When the "Controversial Discussions," as they were called, continued during World War II, a new argument was directed against Klein—namely, that she had added nothing original. Walter Schmideberg (Klein's son-in-law) said that when he came to London ten years earlier he met his "old friends . . . under new names. Even 'Boehm's hidden penis' (that is how we used to call the phantasy of the father's penis hidden in the mother) was found . . . in Mrs. Klein's luggage. Will anybody please, who comes across it, return it to its rightful owner, Dr. Felix Boehm, Berlin, Tiergartenstrasse 10?"[34] In other words, Klein was wrong; besides, what she had to say was already well known.

In the late thirties Klein's ranks thinned. Klein and Riviere's 1937 *Love, Hate and Reparation* received little comment in *Die Internationale Zeitschrift.* Otto Fenichel and Michael Balint, among others, attacked her work, and key British analysts such as Nina Searl, Ella Sharpe, John Bowlby, and John Rickman kept aloof. Klein's daughter, Melitta Schmideberg, who was not only an analyst but a doctor, attacked her mother publicly for failing to grasp the true nature of maternal love. Edward Glover, Schmideberg's analyst, backed his patient publicly. Klein later described herself as "inclined to regard Melitta's attacks more in the way of a naughty child . . . only so bad because the society did not know how to deal with it."[35] Descriptions of Klein at this time capture her difficulties. Diana Riviere, Joan's daughter, remembers Klein as "always in a dreamy state," constantly preoccupied; "if spoken to, she would react as though she had been startled out of a trance." To Donald Woods Winnicott, "she was always having ideas . . . and they were tremendously important to her when she had them."[36] Virginia Woolf described her in 1939 as "a woman of character & force, some submerged—how shall I say?—not craft but subtlety: something working underground. A pull, a twist, like an undertow; menacing. A bluff grey haired lady, with large bright imaginative eyes."[37]

Thus, it was a fractured analytic community that Sigmund Freud entered in 1938 when he, together with his family and thirty-eight other analysts, arrived in London. The next year, Leonard and Virginia Woolf visited him at Hampstead, encountering a "screwed up shrunk very old man: with a monkey's light eyes, paralysed spasmodic movements, inarticulate: but alert . . . an old fire now flickering."[38] His mood was introspective.[39] When a grandchild visited him in the summer of 1939 and said he would see him at Christmas, Freud told him he would not be there. Told that World War II would be the last war, Freud remarked, "Let's say it will be *my* last war." In late August 1939 he wrote in his notebook: "Mysticism is the obscure self-perception of the realm outside the ego, of the id."[40] Less than a month later he asked his physician, Max Schur, to fulfill his promise to help him die. Schur writes: "I indicated that I had not forgotten my promise. He sighed with relief, held my hand for a moment longer, and said: *Ich danke Ihnen* ('I thank you'), and after a moment of hesitation he added: *Sagen Sie es der Anna* ('Tell Anna about this')."[41] Anna Freud later told a friend: "There is nothing worse than to see the people nearest to one lose the very qualities for which one loves them. I was spared that with my father."[42] Mercifully, Freud did not know that he was to lose four of his five sisters two years later. They were taken from Vienna to Theresienstadt in 1941 and to Auschwitz the following year.[43]

Freud's death in 1939 brought the conflict between Klein and Anna Freud to a head. In 1940 there were forty-eight active members of the British Psychoanalytic Society in London (many refugees having gone elsewhere in Britain or to the United States). Competition for patients was fierce.[44] Klein's opponents charged that she and her followers aimed to take over the British society. Its deputy president, Edward Glover, wrote: "The Society has got very far away from Freud in recent years, and . . . after all, the purpose of the Society is Freud's work." Klein responded by calling the society "weak and without initiative," its members lacking "more than average discrimination." She raised the issue of Sigmund Freud's "proper successor" in a letter to Jones. "Having reached his climax in *Inhibitions, Symptoms and Anxieties,*" she wrote, Freud "not only did not go further, but rather regressed. In his later contributions to theory some of his great findings were weakened or left aside, and he certainly did not draw the full conclusions from his own work. That might have had many reasons in himself, such as age, his illness, and the fact that there might be a point beyond which no person, no matter how great a genius, can go with his own discoveries. I am convinced though that Anna's influence was one of the factors that held him back. . . . It is tragic," she concluded, "that his daughter, who thinks that she must defend him against me, does not realize that I am serving him better than she."[45] In addition, Klein accused Jones of having "done much harm to psychoanalysis" by helping Freud and his circle emigrate to London. Some of the emigrants, she told him, had volunteered "that they had every possibility to go to America and would have done so had you not invited and encouraged them to come to England." Perhaps it was this kind of confrontational style that led Anna Freud's biographer, Elisabeth Young-Bruehl, to speak of Klein's "imaginative verve, her ambition, and her startlingly uninhibited egoism."[46]

The conflict continued throughout the war. Young-Bruehl compared Anna Freud's followers to a hierarchical convent and Klein's to a charismatic cult. John Bowlby put the same point differently when he said that Anna Freud worshipped at the shrine of St. Sigmund, while Melanie Klein worshipped at the shrine of St. Melanie. According to Young-Bruehl, it was as intolerable for Anna Freud in the years after her father's death "to think of any rearrangement of his theoretical house as it was to think of rearranging his study," while James Strachey asserted that Anna Freud regarded analysis as "a game Reserve belonging to the F. family."[47] In 1944 Sylvia Payne, the newly elected president of the British Psychoanalytic Society, complained to Jones that Anna Freud had inherited her father's "determination to keep psycho-analysis isolated. . . . Unfortunately, we have the same omnipotence in Melanie and this is really why her work has made so much trouble."[48] For her part, Klein maintained that Anna Freud "had no point of view of her own. She made it clear that she represented her father's views (which according to her are absolutely binding for all who claim to be psychoanalysts)."[49]

Freud's death also initiated a prolonged period of mourning. Anna Freud inherited not only her father's papers but his aura. Seven years after his death, her father appeared to her in a series of dreams: "He is here again. All of these recent dreams have the same character: the main role is played not by my longing for him but rather his longing for me. . . . In the first dream of this kind he openly said: 'I have always longed for you so.' The main feeling in yesterday's dream is that he is wandering about (on top of mountains, hills) while I am doing other things. At the same time, I have an inner restlessness, a feeling that I should stop whatever I am doing and go walking with him. Eventually he calls me to him and demands this himself."[50]

The conflicts that swirled around Klein had a gender subtext that became more pronounced over time. As we saw, Sylvia Payne believed that leading anti-Kleinians such as Edward Glover feared and envied "the successful intellectual, i.e. rival, woman."[51] After Freud's death, Klein withdrew from the main, mixed-sex analytic arena into an all-female analytic circle. Encompassing women we can safely call feminists, such as Joan Riviere, as well as those we can call protofeminists, such as Payne, the Kleinian circle was preoccupied with "the mother."

Just as Freud's early circle lived, as well as studied, father/son relations, the circle around Klein lived and studied the mother/daughter relationship. Their study takes on additional meaning when it is set against the background of the English working-class family. In contrast to the middle-class idea of "companionate marriage," many working-class women's closest relations were with their mothers. One woman told a sociological investigator that she knew her marriage was no good within the first week. When she became pregnant, she kept praying: "Let it be a girl. She'll be my companion. She'll be my companion. I'll never be lonely any more." Likewise, the historian John Prest, entering the RAF in 1947, was struck by the fact that his fellow servicemen spoke of their mothers with intense warmth, but often despised their "wastrel" fathers.[52] This sense of an absent father also permeated Klein's circle.

A letter from Joan Riviere to Melanie Klein, written in June 1940, while the Battle of Britain raged, reveals how Klein had become a mother figure for some younger female analysts, while also suggesting how the shift to a mother-centered theory affected analytic thinking concerning gender. Riviere wrote to Klein:

> When the first official mention of invasion began, the possibility of our work all coming to an end seemed so near, I felt we should all have to keep it in our hearts . . . as the only way to save it for the future. . . . Of course, I was constantly thinking of the psychological causes of such terrible loss and destruction as may happen to mankind. So, I had the idea of your telling me (and then a group of us) everything you think about these causes. . . . First what you think about the causes of the German psychological situation, and secondly, of that of the rest of Europe and mainly the Allies, since the last war. To me the apathy and denial of the Allies, especially England, is not clear. (I never shared it.) How is it connected with what I call the "Munich" complex, the son's incapacity to fight for mother and country? . . . One great question is why it is so important to be brave and to be able to bear whatever happens? Everything in *reality* depends on this.[53]

Riviere's letter can be found among Klein's papers, filed with an essay by Klein entitled "What Does Death Represent to the Individual?" in which she describes Hitler's weapon as a "destructive and dangerous penis." In men, Klein wrote, "hidden, passive homosexual phantasies, plotting and scheming with the destructive father, come to the fore. . . . The guilt about the sadistic alliance with the dangerous father is one important reason for denial." When the unconscious relation to a sadistic internal father figure was not understood, it was likely to dominate. For example, a man's insistence on remaining on the offensive "expressed the drive towards active and dangerous homosexuality as reaction against the desire and fear of being buggered."[54] In her letter, Riviere, too, had described the British male apathy as the expression of "homosexual leanings."

Certainly, these formulations are repugnant—not least because of what we know about the persecution of English homosexuals in this period. Nonetheless, they reveal the subtle but important interplay between feminism, the Popular Front, and psychoanalysis. The familial imagery is matricentric. The most striking fact is Riviere's wish that Klein instruct, and in so doing protect, her children in the face of the emergency. The mother's role has expanded to encompass education and protection. Correspondingly, the image of the good, strong, protective father—a father who plays a very important role in Freud's writings—has disappeared. The most significant male role is that of the son, who has inherited the paternal obligation to protect. The key question is whether the son has the capacity to fight for his mother and his sisters and their children, which is to say, for those who are vulnerable. The son should have learned from his own vulnerability in childhood—his depressive position, his relation to his mother—to feel responsibility for others. But the English sons are "absent," caught up in sadomasochistic relations, phallic displays, and manic efforts at "control." The "homosexual leanings" to which Riviere refers are men's passive relations to a phallic, "hard," or threatening figure, like Hitler. The same weakness that leads to British men's unconscious complicity with fascism prevents them from recognizing their responsibilities to women and children.

The homophobia of these documents is indisputable, to be sure, but the point for Riviere and Klein was not to condemn homosexual object choice. For one thing, much of their milieu was openly gay; for another, the Kleinian imaginary was largely desexualized. In this exchange, both Riviere and Klein were focused on male/female relations, but not because they were enthralled by heterosexuality. Rather, their aim was to redefine manliness as the son's ability to protect the mother/child relationship. Within the Kleinian worldview, recognizing the relation to the mother, for both sexes, meant recognizing vulnerability and dependence. For both sexes, the relation to the mother was the key to ethical responsibility.[55]

The Kleinian worldview was prefeminist, of course. One might rightly ask why Klein and Riviere take for granted that protecting the "motherland" from the Nazis is predominantly men's responsibility, especially since we know that the significance of sexual difference faded dramatically in the hurly-burly of wartime England. But again, the point was not to subordinate women. Rather, Klein and her followers valued cross-sex obligations as ethical acknowledgments of human vulnerability and of the importance of child rearing in society. Their outlook can be instructively contrasted to that of the post–World War II American analysts, who blamed "castrating mothers" for homosexuality. Meanwhile, Riviere's foreboding sense of the transformative power of world politics proved accurate.

The outbreak of war transformed the conditions for the development and reception of Klein's thought. On the one hand, the war produced tremendous suffering. Three-quarters of a million Englishmen died, out of a total population of thirty-eight million. About a third of the dead were married.

Sheffield, England, 1941

Public grief was common. Often there was no site for a funeral. The entry of analysts into the inner worlds of bombed civilians, devastated soldiers, and bereaved children precipitated the long-developing shift of psychoanalysis away from Freud's theory of the ego to the Kleinian themes of connection and rupture. In the words of Peter Homans: "The metapsychology [i.e., id, ego, and superego] collapsed in [wartime] London. Under the impress of . . . social structural change and augmented by national mourning over the losses inflicted by a terrible war, it virtually withered away, to be replaced by clinical and theoretical concerns with attachment, loss and the social world of patients, many of whom were soldiers and children."[56]

On the other hand, the war released enormous integrative energies. Whereas World War I had exposed the internal contradictions of European societies, World War II generated a sense of unity, shared purpose, and national confidence, at least among the Allies. The 1939–40 German bombing of London, wrote one observer, was experienced as "almost a natural disaster which fosters a single spirit of unity binding the whole people together." In October 1940 the documentary filmmaker Humphrey Jennings wrote his wife: "Some of the damage in London is pretty heartbreaking but what an effect it has on people! What warmth—what courage!

Londoners sleeping in a tube station during the Blitz, 1940

what determination."[57] The liberating effects on young people and on women were particularly striking. Class barriers seemed to decline in importance, especially after the East End was bombed and 3.5 million children and mothers of infants, many poor, evacuated to the countryside.[58] Perhaps the most dramatic images of the Blitz, memorialized in Henry Moore's drawings, were of the individuals and families who occupied the London tubes, against official orders, during the bombing. These drawings symbolized the mingling of public and private in a city under siege, as well as the attempt to care for children in a semicommunal environment.

The English response to the bombing also rested on an almost mythic sense of identification with core Western values. Whereas during World War I German music had been frowned upon and even banned, during World War II the Allied symbol for victory was the opening bars of Beethoven's Fifth Symphony ("V" in Morse code). Lunchtime concerts were held at the National Gallery (emptied of paintings), bombs sometimes exploding overhead. In one of the most famous, filmed by Jennings, the pianist Myra Hess played Beethoven's "Appassionata" Sonata followed by Bach's "Jesu, Joy of Man's Desiring." Kenneth Clark reminisced: "In common with half the audience, I was in tears. This is what we had all been waiting for—an assertion of eternal values."[59]

The image of the English people as a family, an image that transcended the distinction between Left and Right, lay behind this assertion. George Orwell's essay "Socialism and the English Genius," written in London at the height of the bombardment, used familial imagery to argue for the welfare state. What was needed, Orwell argued, was a democratic revolution that would "break the grip of the monied class." Otherwise, he continued, Britain would remain "a family with the wrong members in control: . . . A rather stuffy Victorian family . . . its cupboards bursting with skeletons. It has rich relations who have to be kowtowed to and poor relations who are horribly sat upon, and there is a deep conspiracy of silence about the source of the family income [the British empire]. It is a family in which the young are generally thwarted and most of the power is in the hands of irresponsible uncles and bedridden aunts. Still, it is a family. It has its private language and its common memories, and at the approach of an enemy it closes ranks."[60]

In the creation of this "family," the image of the mother played a key role. The most celebrated work of art produced during the war, Henry Moore's *Madonna and Child,* was unveiled in 1943 at St. Matthew's Church in Northampton. The sculpture resulted from the initiative of the Reverend Walter Hussey, who wanted to see the Church of England retake its leading role in the arts. Moore's shelter drawings seemed to Hussey "to possess a spiritual quality and a deep humanity as well as being monumental and suggestive of timelessness." At the dedication of the sculpture, Hussey told the congregation: "The Holy Child is the centre of the work, and yet the subject speaks of the Incarnation—the fact that the Christ was born of a human mother—and so the Blessed Virgin is conceived as any small child would in essence think of his mother, not as small and frail, but as the one large, secure, solid background to life."[61]

The image of the mother was also at the center of the welfare state. The *Beveridge Report,* with its focus on mothers and children, was published in 1942, the darkest year of the war. After the bombing of the East End, the queen announced her support for socialized medicine, remarking, "The people have suffered so much."[62] In 1943 Winston Churchill called for "a National Health Service [and] national compulsory insurance for all classes for all purposes from the cradle to the grave."[63] When the National Health

Service was finally created in 1948, it was the first health system in any Western country to provide free health care to the entire population, the first based not on the insurance principle, in which entitlement follows contribution, but on the principle of social citizenship.[64] The result was more than a form of material help. It universalized the basis of entitlement and helped sustain a mother-centered, working-class way of life.

Analysts joined in the general spirit. In 1938 a report by psychiatrists predicted that air raids would be devastating and that psychiatric casualties—shell shock—would exceed physical casualties by three to one. In fact, the air raids led to a decreased use of mental hospitals and clinics. Suicides and drunkenness also declined. Edward Glover disbanded the Psychoanalytic Clinic a month after it opened for lack of patients.[65] As Glover explained, the terrific morale of the English people rendered it unnecessary.

Instead of shell shock, the focus of psychiatric attention was on evacuated, orphaned, and homeless children. In December 1939, in response to the bombing of London, three British psychoanalysts, D. W. Winnicott, John Bowlby, and Emmanuel Miller, wrote a letter to the *British Medical Journal* stating that "the evacuation of small children between the ages of two and five introduces major psychological problems."[66] This letter was widely distributed. An important strand of English and American philanthropy had long focused on the child. Once the United States entered the war, a transatlantic network formed around such figures as Walter Langer, William Bullitt, Bettina Warburg, and Joseph Kennedy, the U.S. ambassador to England. They helped analysts emigrate to the United States, while also supporting research into child welfare and development, especially through the American Foster Parents' Plan for War Children. Anna Freud became the director of Hampstead Nurseries, a complex of residential homes for homeless children. Her 1944 *Infants Without Families,* written with Dorothy Burlingham, centered on the practice of involving absent parents with institutionalized children.[67]

Along with the focus on the infant, enthusiasm for teamwork epitomized the new, public face of British analysis. A younger generation, exemplified by Donald Woods Winnicott and John Bowlby, took over the leadership of the British Psychoanalytic Society. Deeply influenced by Klein but not themselves Kleinians, they channeled analytic energies into the war effort, conducting group-psychology experiments on "morale-building." Taking psychoanalysis public, they stressed Klein's great themes of "the mother," "ethical responsibility," and "connection" but gave them a different spin. Dropping Klein's conception of a personal life lived independently of, and potentially in opposition to, the dictates of large-scale institutions, the neo-Kleinians began to turn analysis into an instrument of social ratio-nalization and integration.

The key move was a new, positive—but abstract—focus on "the group." Whereas Freud had described groups as mindless masses seeking father-leaders, the neo-Kleinians treated groups as the natural matrices for indi-viduals. Freud, Wilfred Bion argued, had taken a wrong turn after explaining hysteria as a conflict over object choice. He had failed "to real-ize . . . the nature of the revolution he himself produced when he looked for an explanation of neurotic symptoms, not in the individual, but in the individual's relationship to objects."[68] The connection between the infant and the group was not merely contingent. Just as the infant must find its way to the breast, so, Bion wrote, the "adult must establish contact with the emotional life of the group."[69]

There were two practical reasons for the focus on the group. The first was the concern for morale, the word that, more than any other, haunted wartime politicians, civil servants, and generals. As Edward Glover wrote: "For the first time . . . the Ministry of Information has established that group feeling is a medico-psychological concern."[70] The goal was not "parade-ground efficiency and obedience to officers, but a quasi-democratic 'group spirit.' . . . The rallying cry is 'Teamwork': 'millions of us, all stick-ing together. . . . There's nothing to stop us, only ourselves.' "[71] In addition, group therapy was used to treat shell shock, which, of course, increased as time went on.

British analysts, deeply involved in the war effort and inspired by their work with groups, had the sense of breaking out of an artificially imposed restriction to an "inner" world. One participant wrote that the Russians are mistaken "to think that the social is something external and not an internal part of the individual. . . . The social and cultural element is deeply ingrained in the individual and is to a large extent unconscious."[72] When Jacques Lacan visited England in 1947, he was struck by the British analysts' experiments in group psychology. The war, he wrote, had left him "with a vigorous sense of the atmosphere of unreality within which the collectivity of the French had lived it," but the English victory "has a moral source . . . a truthful relation to the real." He found himself especially impressed by the influence of British analysts among psychiatrists and the "Child Guidance" movement. With the experiments of Bion and others, he claimed to have "rediscovered the feeling of the miracle that accompanied the first of Freud's steps." As he later explained, "Bion deliberately con-structed a group without a leader . . . so as to force the group to take account of the difficulties of its own existence, and to render it more and more transparent to itself."[73]

The new salience of psychoanalysis transformed the British Psychoanalytic Society. John Bowlby returned from two years in the army to describe the interest in analysis among military psychiatrists. "The Society has been insulated," he asserted; "there is far more demand for psycho-analysis than is appreciated."[74] In 1943 the society formed a committee to prepare for socialized medicine. By 1944, Freudians controlled the psychiatric division of the armed forces in England.[75] In 1945 the Labour Party won the national elections. The National Health Service, including psychotherapy, was created three years later.

After the war, the English and American focus on the mother/infant relationship intensified. In 1945 a new journal, *The Psychoanalytic Study of the Child,* was founded. Edited by Anna Freud in London and Heinz Hartmann, Ernst Kris, and Rudolph Loewenstein in New York, it was soon one of the most influential analytic journals in the world. Its articles on mothering were widely cited in the "maternal employment" literature of the late 1940s, which sought to demonstrate the danger to children of mothers working outside the home. In 1953 John Bowlby's *Maternal Care and Mental Health,* written for the World Health Organization, described the discovery that the young child could be scarred by separation as "comparable in magnitude to that of the role of vitamins."[76] Even Melanie Klein stopped calling the mother a "dreaded castrator" and began describing the "good breast" as "the prototype of maternal goodness, inexhaustible patience and generosity as well as creativity."[77] One vocabulary fell away from analytical writing and a new one appeared. Terms such as "Oedipus conflict," "superego," and "guilt" appeared less and less often; "mourning," "envy," "gratitude," and "responsibility" became prevalent. Lacan noted that the term "sadistic" had essentially vanished.[78]

The effect of these developments was a sea change in analytic culture, reflected in those who personified it. The emblematic analyst was no longer Melanie Klein, in whom Virginia Woolf had discerned something menacing. A new breed of analytic spokesperson emerged: nonphallic, benign, avuncular "advocates" for children and their "moms"; Donald Woods Winnicott in Britain and Benjamin Spock in the United States are examples. Winnicott, born in 1896, the son of a successful merchant and politician, described himself as "an only child with multiple mothers," meaning older sisters, a nanny, and a governess. During and after the war he became well known for his BBC broadcasts addressed to parents and for courses for social workers at the London School of Economics.[79] Benjamin Spock was a key figure in the child-study movement, whose other members included Margaret Mead, Kurt Lewin, Elton Mayo, George Homans, and Lawrence Frank. The movement sought "to create a society that was more cooperative, more consensus-oriented and more group conscious."[80] Whereas Winnicott was known as an analyst but emphasized his pediatric background, Spock so thoroughly downplayed his analytic identity that he could almost be described as closeted. Perhaps in part for this reason, his 1946 *Common Sense Book of Baby and Child Care* sold more copies than any other book first published in the twentieth century: forty million.[81] Thus, the war brought about a remasculinization of British analysis, if not in numbers, then in the face that it presented to the public. Ironically, these analysts were the good, responsible sons for whom Klein and Riviere had longed.

In general, then, the war experience refamilialized psychoanalysis. This was a contradictory affair. On one hand, analysts contributed to a historic democratization of psychological knowledge. Previously, child-rearing advice, like education, social work, and the juvenile-justice system, had been a middle-class domain that looked down on and criticized working-class practices. Analysts, however, promoted a shift toward intuition and emotion rather than control that validated the everyday, untutored practices of the working-class mother. Thus, Winnicott developed his theory of the "good enough mother," one who provides the frustration optimal for development rather than one who follows a "perfect" regime. Affirming what he called the "ordinary devoted mother," he portrayed her as a working-class woman who "feels" rather than as a middle-class woman who reads childcare manuals and directs servants.

Yet this same contribution also entrenched the full-time mother within the home as the ideal of the coming welfare state. Dropping the "dark" strands that suggested the genuine difficulty of an authentic personal life, postwar British analysis reinforced conventional sex roles in the traditional working-class family. Furthermore, as the cold war developed, and as Western "respect" for the family was counterposed to Soviet "totalitarianism," the identification of women with mothering contributed to the uncritical glorification of the West. Thus, for Winnicott: "The ordinary good home is something that defies statistical investigation. It has no news value, is not spectacular, and does not produce the men and women whose names are publicly known."[82] In both respects—the recognition of dependence and the construction of an idealized view of the mother—psychoanalysis dovetailed with the emerging pattern of the Beveridge welfare state. The war, Richard Titmuss later recalled, had changed everything, creating a new contract between the parties and between the people and the government, one that lasted until the 1970s. That contract was economically progressive but culturally conservative, and thus problematic for building the postwar order.

In spite of the special place that it occupies in the history of psychoanalysis, the British Psychoanalytic Society never fully overcame the traumatic disruptions provoked by World War II. The "Controversial Discussions," which stretched from 1942 to 1944, bore the weight of the knowledge that the British society was the last surviving analytic society in Europe. At the end of the war, the members mooted their differences by forming three training paths taught by associates, respectively, of Klein (group A), Anna Freud (group B), and a middle or independent group, which included such figures as D. W. Winnicott, Michael Balint, and W. R. D. Fairbairn. Often touted as a triumph of English rationality, moderation, and compromise, the solution had the effect of marginalizing Klein's thought, especially as American ego psychology expanded as part of the postwar U.S. hegemony. To be sure, many of Klein's ideas were imported into ego psychology, but they were not acknowledged as hers.

The same centripetal tendencies that brought the society's members into a powerful but short-lived alliance during the war propelled them into disparate, centrifugal orbits afterward. Jones retired to tend the society archives and write a biography of Freud. Strachey undertook the *Standard Edition*. Bowlby left analysis for psychiatry and ethology. Glover, having gradually ceased persecuting Klein for deviationism, turned to his deepest interest, criminology. Bion pursued his work largely outside the context of the society. Balint in Manchester and Fairbairn in Edinburgh stayed away from London. Melitta Schmideberg emigrated to the United States and never reconciled with her mother. Paula Heimann, the pro-Kleinian analyst portrayed in Nicholas Wright's play *Mrs. Klein*, rebelled against Klein over a technical issue in 1949, describing her previous self as enslaved. Klein died in 1960, just after having begun work on her memoirs. By the end of the century, the still-vital British society had 405 members out of a population of 60 million: one of the thinnest ratios in the developed world.

Despite the dispersion, English analysts continued to work within the Kleinian paradigm. Two new contributions were particularly important. The first was Winnicott's 1953 theory of the transitional object. Claiming that we know a great deal about what goes on *inside* individuals (through psychoanalysis) and *outside* individuals (through the social and behavioral sciences) but almost nothing about what goes on *between* them, Winnicott argued that an object-relational approach could explain the relation between individuals and their cultures. Tracing "the capacity to be alone" to the experience "of being alone, as an infant and small child, in the presence of mother," Winnicott conceived psychical development as providing a "transitional space" between individuals who share something vital while remaining separate. To describe this "in-between" area, he invoked the bit of torn blanket many children carry with them. For the child, the blanket may be a *substitute* for the mother, since, like her, it is warm, sensuous, and comforting. Freud's theory, Winnicott believed, was essentially a theory of such "substitutes." A transitional object was not a substitute, however, but a meeting ground between "inner psychic reality" and "the external world as perceived by two persons in common." Likening this transitional space to play, Winnicott stressed its creative, paradoxical character and the fact that it belonged to neither person alone.[83] In fact, he insisted that the question of whether it is "inside" or "outside" the individual ought not to be asked.

Largely forgotten today, Michael Balint's 1959 *Thrills and Regressions* is equally important. Balint posited two ideal psychological types, both of them pathological in their extreme state: one person's inner world consists "of objects, separated by horrid empty spaces," the other's of "friendly expanses dotted more or less densely with dangerous and unpredictable objects." In formulating this idea, Balint revised his previous view, derived from Ferenczi, that the "need to cling," characteristic of the person who dreads empty space, is primary. In analysis, he wrote, we "offer ourselves to our patients incessantly as objects to cling to, and interpret anything contrary to clinging as resistance, aggressiveness, narcissism, touchiness, paranoid anxiety, castration fear, and so on."[84] But "the need to cling," Balint now realized, like the corresponding need to avoid objects, "is a reaction to a trauma, an expression of . . . the fear of being dropped or abandoned." The real aim "can never be achieved by clinging. The real aim is to be held by the object and not to cling . . . to it. . . . The profoundly tragic situation is that the more efficiently one clings, the less is one held by the object."[85]

After the war, the need to be held by the mother appeared to many English analysts as the enabling condition of psychoanalysis, the condition that Freud had presupposed but never articulated. Ego psychology, wrote Winnicott, "only makes sense if based firmly on the fact of dependence."[86] Freud, he added, did not write much about the early mothering situation, but it "turned up in his provision of a setting for his work, almost without his being aware." The analyst "would be reliably there, on time, alive, breathing," and "preoccupied with the patient."[87] According to Masud Khan, the mother was the protective shield discussed by Freud in *Beyond the Pleasure Principle*. The analyst, for Christopher Bollas, provided a "maternal sound—a kind of verbal humming" that was more important than interpretations. In Bollas's summary: "What Freud could not analyse in himself—his relation to his own mother—was acted out in his choice of the ecology of psychoanalytic technique."[88]

Not everyone agreed. Anna Freud lived at the Freud residence at 20 Maresfield Gardens in London until her death in 1982. Although Jones once described her to Klein as a "tough, perhaps indigestible morsel," there was an inescapable sadness to her later life that reflected her feeling that her father's work was slipping away.[89] In 1947 she wrote that object relations missed the essence of psychoanalysis, which was "conflict within the individual person . . . aims, ideas, and ideals battling with the drives to keep the individual within a civilized community." It has become modern, she continued, "to water this down to every individual's longing for perfect unity with his mother, i.e., to be loved only as an infant can be loved. There is an enormous amount that gets lost this way." Guilt, for example, was a relation not between two people but between "parts of the . . . mind, that is, an anxiety felt by the ego with regard to the superego." Psychoanalysis, she added, is, above all, drive psychology. "But for some reason people do not want to have that."[90]

Chapter Eleven

CHARISMA OR RATIONALIZATION? U.S. PSYCHOANALYSIS IN THE EPOCH OF THE COLD WAR

> My generation invested personal relations with an intensity they could hardly support, as it turned out; but our passionate interest in each other's lives cannot very well be described as a form of emotional retreat. We tried to re-create in the circle of our friends the intensity of a common purpose, which could no longer be found in politics or the workplace.
>
> —Christopher Lasch, *The True and Only Heaven*

During the same crisis of fascism and war that brought British psychoanalysis into its fateful relationship with the Beveridge welfare state, nearly two hundred refugee psychoanalysts, most of them Jewish, arrived in the United States from Austria, Germany, and France. After the war the influence of psychoanalysis exploded. Erich Heller, writing of the United States in the 1950s, observed that analysis was "more than merely one among many possible theories about the psyche; rather it comes close to being the systematic consciousness that a certain epoch has of the nature and character of its soul."[1] Heller's observation was somewhat overstated; currents like existentialism and existentialist theology were also important. But psychoanalysis had an extraordinary resonance with U.S. culture in the 1950s. As in England, it derived much of its appeal from the opposition to totalitarianism, but, in contrast to England, in the United States collective traditions were vulnerable and psychoanalysis bore the mark of its mind-cure predecessors. Partly for these reasons, postwar psychoanalysis became a veritable fount of homophobia, misogyny, and conservatism, central to the cold war project of normalization. Yet when many of the most profound thinkers of the fifties—Lionel Trilling, Philip Rieff, Norman O. Brown, and Herbert Marcuse among them—sought to criticize social control and conformity, they turned to psychoanalysis. Both strands of psychoanalysis—the rationalizing or social-control strand and the critical or anti-rationalizing strand—were rooted in the matrix of Freudian charisma.

As we saw, this charisma arose from Freud's ability to articulate the historically new experience of having a personal identity distinct from one's place in the family, society, or division of labor, but charisma becomes institutionalized. With its routinization, it congeals into organizational structure. But it may also reemerge in new antinomian, anti-institutional upsurges that seek to revivify the dying spirit.

By World War II, psychoanalysis was being institutionalized in the United States. Like Weber's Protestantism, it was becoming a "this-worldly program of ethical rationalization," one with links to such normalizing agencies as the social-service professions, the social sciences, and the welfare state. Yet even as it was being routinized, analysis retained its connections to its charismatic, anti-institutional origins, partly through "the aura of close association with the founding fathers," partly through its relations to art and religious experience, but especially through its associations with sexual love, which, as Weber wrote, appeared as "a gate into the most irrational and thereby real kernel of life."[2] During the 1950s, U.S. analysts drew on these associations to resanctify the heterosexual family, investing domesticity with deep personal, ethical, and sexual meanings previously attached to extrafamilial forms of personal life. In so doing, they invoked charismatic forces they could not always contain. By the 1960s, antinomian upsurges linked to analysis would overflow the boundaries of the analytic profession, the heterosexual family, and the welfare state. Simultaneously normalizing and fueled by charismatic sources, then, U.S. analysis was at the center of *both* the growing rationalization of personal life unfolding in the 1950s *and* the looming critique of rationalization, the charismatic rejection of the mundane, that came to the fore in the 1960s.

The rationalization of psychoanalysis began before the wartime emigration. In 1907 the American sociologist Edward Ross coined the term "social control" to describe a broad, general, and desirable shift from external coercion to internalized self-control. Ross's central idea was that the citizen or worker was a free, self-determining agent, not a passive object to be commanded. In Michel Foucault's terms, social control meant a shift from "repressive" to "productive" forms of power, forms that elicited the active cooperation of their subjects. The project, accordingly, was ambiguous. On the one hand, it meant a vastly increased space for individual and collective decision making. On the other hand, largely aimed at industrial-era class conflict, it implied adjustment, psychologization, and the rise of a new, professional class.

By the Fordist period, many U.S. social planners had connected psychoanalysis to the project of social control. In 1927 the political scientist Harold Lasswell, seeking to dispel the "tumult" and "rhetoric" of "class politics," cited Freud for the idea that politics was often driven by needs that originated in the private sphere.[3] The same idea informed the famous Hawthorne experiments, which purported to show that workers were more interested in whether anyone paid attention to their complaints than in their actual conditions of work.

These efforts, however, took the Freudian idea of the unconscious as their point of departure. The professionalization of American psychoanalysis in the 1930s, and the emigration of such Berlin analysts as Franz Alexander, connected a very different current of analytic thought, namely, ego psychology, to social control. As we saw, the core idea of ego psychology was that the ego was two-sided: simultaneously an agent of rational self-reflection and the locus of the resistance to self-reflection. Thus, analysis had to work both *through* and *against* the ego. In the U.S. reception and development of the theory, however, this two-sided character was lost. The view of the ego as the locus of resistance receded, and the ego increasingly appeared as the agent of reason and control.

The principal architect of this shift was Heinz Hartmann, whose 1937 lecture "Ego Psychology and the Problem of Adaptation" laid out much of the framework developed by U.S. ego psychologists in the 1940s and '50s. Born in 1894, Hartmann came from Vienna's assimilated Jewish elite. One grandfather had been a deputy in the Frankfurt assembly of 1848; another was, in Freud's words, "the most eminent of all our Vienna physicians." Hartmann's father had been a historian at the University of Vienna; his tutor became Vienna's mayor; his wife was a pediatrician. Hartmann himself was intellectually distinguished. Having attended Max Weber's 1918 lectures in Vienna, he maintained contact with the circle of logical positivists, studied experimental psychology, and was analyzed by Freud at Freud's invitation. One can imagine his prestige among analysts.[4]

Hartmann's main theme was the "strength" of the ego: its ability to adapt and thereby master the external world. Claiming that the earlier generation of analysts had overemphasized the power of the drives, he hoped to turn psychoanalysis into a general psychology that could explain such functions as thinking, memory, and perception. His 1937 lecture described the ego as an apparatus of regulation and adaptation whose central function, thought, was made possible by neutralized or desexualized energies. Although he was careful to cite Freud for the existence of these energies, Hartmann maintained, contra many Freudians, that not every adaptation to the environment was the result of a defensive conflict. Thus, the ego could transform an attitude that originally arose as a reaction formation against a drive, such as generosity, into an independent source of motivation. Even experiences that seemed to emanate directly from the drives, such as orgasm, might be better understood as "the ego-controlled suspension of certain ego functions," or, as the idea later came to be known, "regression in the service of the ego." Because Hartmann's main interest was not the ego's relations to the id but its relations to social norms, mind-sets, and demands, he became the favorite psychoanalyst for those who sought to harness psychoanalysis to social planning. In 1963 Bruno Bettelheim and Morris Janowitz praised him for breaking with the dominant view of the ego as "devoid of energy and initiative." Not only had Hartmann shown that the ego was more powerful than Freud realized; he had also shown that the id can be influenced by society, that "reality shapes not only the ego but even the underlying drives."[5]

With its stress on the power of the ego, ego psychology dovetailed neatly with the project of social control. The thinker who best grasped the possibilities was Talcott Parsons. In the late thirties Parsons sought to theorize democratic forms of character and social organization able to withstand "fascistic" and "communistic" appeals. Participating in a reading group in Boston with such refugee analysts as Edward and Grete Bibring, Parsons learned from psychoanalysis that self-control could be strengthened when external authority did not intervene. When World War II broke out, he urged the government not to respond to antiwar protests "hysterically," as it had during World War I. A propaganda agency, Parsons wrote, should assume a "disinterested" role and decline to respond "to hostile interpretations of government policy—thus defeating them in the manner of a therapist whose non-responsive behavior [undermines] a patient's neurotic perceptions by withholding confirmation from them." Avoid partisan politics, identify with integrative national symbols, cultivate a reputation for integrity. Franklin Roosevelt's handling of the Great Depression supplied the model. Roosevelt was certainly conscious of being "the object of 'negative transference,' " Parsons noted, but his speeches were "analogous to the interpretations of a psychoanalyst. . . . One of the most interesting things for a very high executive to learn is not to speak publicly too much, too often, or at the wrong times."[6]

Like social control generally, the implications of Parsons's approach were ambiguous, suggesting both democratization and enhanced autonomy on the one hand, and psychological manipulation, on the other. This ambiguity was inherited by the new corps of experts—aptitude counselors, forensic specialists, school psychologists, guidance counselors, industrial psychologists, urban planners, and above all doctors—who turned social control into a large-scale program of social reorganization during and after World War II.

Analysis was at the center of this project. As in England, the American entry into the war precipitated a new alliance between analysis and the state. During World War I only 2 percent of all American recruits were excluded for psychiatric reasons. During World War II the corresponding figure was 8–10 percent. During the first war, the chief reasons for psychiatric rejection were mental insufficiency and psychosis; during the second, neurosis was the leading ground for rejection.[7] A key reason was that Brigadier General William Menninger, head of the neuropsychiatry division of the Surgeon General's Office during World War II, ordered that every doctor in the military be taught the basic principles of psychoanalysis.[8] Altogether, one million men and women were rejected from military service for mental and neurological reasons, and 850,000 soldiers were hospitalized for neuroses.[9]

When doctors could not meet the demand for treatment, the newly founded professions of clinical psychology and psychiatric social work stepped into the breach. Psychology became an established discipline during World War I through the development of intelligence and aptitude testing aimed at large-scale tasks of sorting, regimentation, and classification. During World War II, however, its clinical or therapeutic branch expanded exponentially. Carl Rogers's 1942 *Counseling and Psychotherapy* sparked the change. Rogers contrasted counseling to classical psychoanalysis, advocated "mirroring," or nonjudgmental recognition, rather than interpretation, and pressed for the use of the term "client" rather than "patient." Largely as a result of his influence, psychologists won authorization to use psychotherapy to treat veterans.[10] Similarly, social work had developed its casework approach in the 1920s under Freudian influence. During the war, however, casework became more closely associated with psychiatry through the creation of the subfield of psychiatric social work.[11]

Nevertheless, the postwar growth of analysis was almost wholly based on the expansion of psychiatry. In 1940 there had been only 2,295 psychiatrists in America, two-thirds practicing in public hospitals.[12] By 1948 the figure was 4,700 and growing rapidly. In 1945, 60 percent of the patients in

V.A. hospitals were confined for psychiatric reasons; 50 percent of all disability pensions were paid to psychiatric casualties. By the mid-fifties, half the hospital beds in the country were occupied by mental patients, a fact the 1955 Hoover Commission called "the greatest single problem in the nation's health picture." The National Institute of Mental Health (NIMH), the fastest-growing division of the National Institutes of Health, subsidized psychiatric research into juvenile delinquency, suicide, alcoholism, and TV violence. By 1976 there were 27,000 psychiatrists in the United States.[13]

To a significant extent, the approximately four hundred U.S. psychoanalysts practicing by the end of the forties dominated this vast host. The reason was that postwar psychiatry expanded as a reform or "psychodynamic" discipline that rejected its earlier custodial image. Often sparked by conscientious objectors, muckraking exposés of the mental hospitals attacked the older psychiatrists' reliance on drugs and electroshock therapy. Albert Deutsch's *Shame of the States* compared mental hospitals to concentration camps. By contrast, "talking therapy" exemplified reform. Since psychiatrists were department heads in hospitals and oversaw social workers and clinical psychologists, the reach of analysis was vast. Such disciplines as counseling, testing, welfare, education, personnel, and law, especially new branches such as juvenile and domestic relations and criminology, were transformed.[14] Virtually every practice that centered on children, adolescence, and the family was deeply affected.[15] So, too, was religion, which became a locus of psychological counseling.[16] But the most important effect was on medicine in general, which shifted its emphasis from the treatment of specific diseases to the management of the social and interpersonal dimensions of illness. In this shift, too, the formulations of psychoanalysis served as the guideposts.[17]

In all areas, then, analysis was central to postwar social reorganization. In contrast to earlier forms of social intervention, which were now stigmatized as "paternalist," the newer disciplines aimed, according to the sociologist Morris Janowitz, at "the enriching of personal control by means of the development and reinforcement of autonomous ego controls."[18] Operating "through the element of subjectivity," the new analytically informed "agencies and mechanisms of regulation" treated the ego as a rational, self-regulating actor whose maturation would be facilitated by forms of intervention that *refrained* from external direction.[19]

The new regime was represented in the rash of postwar psychiatric films such as Anatole Litvak's *The Snake Pit* (1948), which invariably contrasted the analytically coded doctor to the old-style psychiatrist. Typically, the turning point in these films occurs when the analyst does *not* retaliate against the patient's anger, thus facilitating the patient's self-control.[20] These films record the coming into maturity of the distinctively modern form of power that Foucault identified in the 1970s as working "not from the outside but from within . . . not by constraining individuals and their actions but by producing them."[21]

While Foucault described the new form of power as wholly negative, the results were actually ambiguous. On the one hand, the expanding regime of psychological experts in 1950s America gave ordinary people new vocabularies and practices of self-reflection and empowered them against earlier forms of community control. On the other hand, it gave unprecedented new powers not only to doctors and therapists but to human-relations-oriented supervisors, personnel experts, ministers, rabbis, and high school guidance counselors. The treatment of homosexuality exemplifies the ambiguity.

Before the war, homosexuals in the military were imprisoned. Conviction for oral sex could and did lead to fifteen years behind bars. Psychiatric reformers, led by analysts, successfully fought to change the designation "sodomist" to "homosexual" and to reduce the punishment to discharge. At their urging, President Roosevelt pardoned a naval officer charged with homosexuality. Progressive though it was, this reform extended the scope of surveillance within the military, transferring the supervision of homosexuals from the criminal-justice system to the psychiatric profession and laying the groundwork for the heightening of discrimination that occurred after the war. In explicit contradiction to Freud's view, homosexuality was redefined as an illness.[22] Considered more humane at the time, that alternative may have been more insidious than legal prosecution, since it was likely to affect homosexuals' self-perceptions more deeply.

The importance of the "internal" dimension in social reorganization found broader cultural expression in a new stress on individual privacy. Given the close proximity of Nazism and Stalinism, freedom in the private or personal realm was touted as the indispensable ground for freedom in public life. That point was central to such exemplary works as Hannah Arendt's 1951 *Origins of Totalitarianism* and her 1958 *Human Condition*. But analysts invested it with charismatic depth.

Perhaps no contemporaneous document is so illuminating on this question as Bruno Bettelheim's 1943 memoir, "Individual and Mass Behavior in Extreme Situations."[23] Born in 1903, Bettelheim had been in analysis in Vienna when he was arrested and sent first to Dachau and then to

Buchenwald, where he spent one year. Having apparently bribed his way out of the camps, he came to the United States in 1939. His memoir of this experience was published in 1943 in the *Journal of Abnormal and Social Psychology,* edited by the Harvard psychologist Gordon Allport. In 1945 Eisenhower had it distributed to all U.S. officers in occupied Germany. Dwight Macdonald reprinted selections in the journal *Politics.* Hannah Arendt discussed it in her *Origins of Totalitarianism.* Bettelheim made it the centerpiece of his 1960 book, *The Informed Heart.* It deeply influenced such crucial works of the period as Stanley Elkins's *Slavery* (1954) and Betty Friedan's *The Feminine Mystique* (1963). In short, it attained iconic status.

The theme of Bettelheim's memoir is the survival of the individual personality in an environment aimed at destroying it. "According to the well-known ideology of the Nazi state," Bettelheim wrote, "the individual as such is either nonexistent or of no importance." The camp was set up "to break the prisoners as individuals," as well as to provide the Gestapo with an "experimental laboratory in which to study the effective means of breaking civilian resistance." Writing in a calm, logical, social-science style, Bettelheim distinguished three types of camp behavior—individual, mass, and private—but gave only one example of the last: his own self-reflection during his imprisonment. This, he claimed, was the key to his survival: he had divided himself into an observing and an observed ego.

An ego psychologist, Bettelheim introduced many themes that later became standard in the literature of the Holocaust, such as the initial shock, the experience of deportation and transportation, and the differences between old and new prisoners. Most riveting, however, was his account of the prisoners' psychological regression. Deprived of all adult rights, especially privacy, required to ask permission to use the latrine, forced to address one another as "*du,*" treated en masse whenever possible, and regularly threatened with torture, the prisoners grew ashamed of being punished, especially if the punishment was minor. To be sure, they fantasized impossible revenges. But, of deeper significance, they imitated the guards, shared the latter's contempt for "unfit" prisoners, criticized ex-prisoners who had condemned the camps in the world's newspapers, and sewed and mended their uniforms to resemble the Gestapo's, even when punished for doing so. The guards treated the prisoners with utter contempt, but the prisoners imagined that the guards were secretly on their side. Once, when a guard cleaned his boots before entering a barracks, the prisoners discussed it excitedly for weeks, arguing over whether it was a sign of respect.

Bettelheim's account was later challenged by other inmates, but its accuracy is not the issue here.[24] More important is how it was received. Bettelheim claimed that his observations applied not only to the camps but also to "the concentration camp of Greater Germany." His readers extended the scope of his account even further: they read the essay as a generalized account of the factors that threatened autonomy in all modern societies. Like Bettelheim, who had based his analysis on Freud's theory of groups, they were struck by the individual's difficulty in maintaining autonomy when treated solely as a member of a group.[25] And they followed Bettelheim in identifying a single, crucial means for keeping one's soul intact in such an environment: psychoanalytic self-reflection.

What made the camp so terrible, in Bettelheim's account, was that there was no retreat from the guards and therefore no division between public and private. This emphasis on the sanctity of that division pervades the great works of American social science of the 1950s. In Arendt's *Origins of Totalitarianism,* the destruction of private life distinguished totalitarianism from earlier forms of tyranny that left the private sphere essentially undisturbed. In Elkins's *Slavery,* it was the absence of a private space—ability to own property, a house and garden, literacy, the right to travel—that made North American slavery so much more virulent and destructive than that of Brazil or Haiti, where slaves did have some space of their own. And for Friedan and those who followed her, it was the then-new awareness that women had no private space—that the home had become a prison—that made the condition of women so oppressive.[26]

The stress on privacy fostered a turn from politics to interiority. The historian Carl Schorske, with whom our journey began, returned from military service, became a teacher, and watched his students' interests shift from economics, politics, and sociology to literature and philosophy.[27] Even the great works of engaged social science of the period, such as Gunnar Myrdal's *An American Dilemma,* (1944), were founded on the assumption that "the moral struggle goes on within people and not only between them."[28] For most, the agony of McCarthyism lay not in the struggle of worldviews but in the demand that individuals betray their conscience, and their friends.[29] Many observers also believed that the atomic age required deeper insight into psychology than the Popular Front had allowed. Writing in the *Saturday Review,* Norman Cousins described "a primitive fear, the fear of the unknown [which] has burst out of the subconscious and into the conscious, filling the mind with primordial apprehensions."[30]

Often, the stress on privacy shaded into a new emphasis on domesticity. The dominant ideology of the postwar family stressed its private character, the way in which it protected its members from the external world, including even the American government. The ideology reflected the shift from a class- and community-based industrial society to a family-centered "post-industrial" society, oriented toward mass consumption.[31] With hitherto undreamt-of possibilities for private consumption, personal life, previously associated with countercultural and transfamilial milieus, became the ideology of the masses. Propelled by its ideals, the postwar generation lowered the age of marriage for both sexes, reduced the divorce rate, and increased the number of children, a trend that lasted until the end of the sixties. Meanwhile, advertising and Hollywood invested not just specific commodities but the entire project of domestic consumption with the charisma of utopian desire. Whereas powerful ethnic communities and industrial-union drives had organized working-class life in the 1930s, in the postwar period prefabricated suburban homes, washing machines, refrigerators, and "luxury" goods for the masses further eroded class-based identities. National chains supplanted local, ethnically based stores; networks edged out local radio programming; and television discovered in the working-class family the material of sitcoms.

In this context, a new ethic of "maturity," "responsibility," and "adulthood" unfolded, simultaneously shaped by, and in turn shaping, psychoanalysis. In Erik Erikson's definition, the mature person was "tolerant of differences, cautious and methodical in evaluation, just in judgement, circumspect in action, and . . . capable of faith and indignation."[32] Reflecting women's historic stress on the significance of the family, and middle-class as opposed to working-class norms, "maturity" implied men's rejection of the homosocial, adolescent world of "mates" or "buddies," their reorientation to the heterosexual dyad, and their acceptance of the responsibilities of marriage. Maturity also implied the acceptance of limits. In Philip Rieff's formulation, it meant "resign[ing] yourself to living within your moral means, suffer[ing] no gratuitous failures in a futile search for ethical heights."[33]

Key elaborators of the ethic of maturity, psychoanalysts tied it to domesticity. Infusing the private, familial realm with charismatic meanings associated with sexuality, the deep self, and personal life, they resanctified heterosexual love and marriage. Whereas in the New Deal epoch, the family had been mundane, a sphere of resisted authority for men and of unremunerated work for women, in the 1950s it became an intensely invested sphere of personal meaning, perhaps especially for women. While there is some truth in the later feminist portrait of the 1950s as a time when "Rosie the Riveter" was unwillingly pushed back into the home, women continued to make up a majority of Freud's readers and of analytic patients.[34] Many believed in the new ideals of the home, the profound significance and rewarding character of child rearing, the ethical value of a lifelong commitment, and the associated goal of maturity. In the 1956 movie *The Man in the Gray Flannel Suit,* the wife (Jennifer Jones) longs for a nicer house and pushes her husband (Gregory Peck) to earn more money. Yet her insistence on personal integrity is counterposed to the shallow, empty "yes man" he encounters in his new job in public relations. And the wife "matures" in the course of the film. At the climax, having learned of her husband's wartime affair with a Roman woman, she overcomes her hurt feelings, recommits to her marriage, and agrees to accept financial responsibility for her husband's war child, thus symbolizing America's financial responsibility for Italy in the mid-1950s.

Masculinity, too, was further transformed during and after World War II. Previously, conservative pundits had worried that the New Deal was producing dependent "weaklings." In 1943 General George C. Marshall wrote, "While our enemies were teaching their youths to endure hardships," ours had learned to depend on government. Even William Menninger conceded that American society was at an "immature stage of development, characterized by 'I want what I want when I want it.' "[35] In 1943, however, Dwight Eisenhower censured General George Patton for striking soldiers who had been hospitalized for psychiatric reasons. "Shut up that Goddamned crying!" Patton had shouted at one. By the time the story reached the newspapers, Patton, not the patients, was viewed as the one with the psychological problems.[36] After the war, the Veterans Administration helped produce films like *The Men,* (1950), which centered on Marlon Brando's struggle to accept his paraplegia. Discharged from an all-male V.A. hospital against his will but for his own good, he is shown in the final scene dragging his useless body up the walk of his single-family suburban home. His wife asks if he needs help. "Please," he replies.[37]

In general, then, the postwar period brought major social and cultural transformations. A new sense of individual responsibility pervaded the military, the workplace, and the professions, while the associations of personal life invested marriage and family with intensified value. In these transformations, charisma and rationalization were inextricably intertwined. On the one hand, charismatic associations gave deep personal meaning to such apparently external developments as the reorganization of work and the new reign of science. On the other, the resanctification of domesticity grounded rationalization in the individual's life cycle. The result was to destroy preexisting communities and group solidarities and to create new bureaucratically and technically organized forms of order—psychiatry, medicine, the welfare state, the multiversity, the military, and the family— against which the 1960s generation would rebel.

Psychoanalysis pervades mass culture, 1955

U.S. psychoanalysts were agents of rationalization. Yet they were themselves transformed by it. Ostensibly the key factor was medicine—in particular the requirement that every analyst hold a medical degree. At a deeper level, there had always been a special resonance between psychoanalysis and American mind-cure culture, the culture that sustained the project of social control. Emigration brought the two into fateful conjuncture. The worst tendencies in European psychoanalysis—perfectionism, a worship of science, authoritarianism—received a new and characteristically American inflection.

Rationalization began in the early years of the Depression, when, as we saw, "a new generational phalanx" of younger American analysts, including Ives Hendrick, Ralph Kaufman, Bertram Lewin, Gregory Zilboorg, and Lawrence Kubie, seized power from the Eastern European–dominated New York group centered around Abraham Brill.[38] The key idea of the younger analysts was to build professional institutes combining education, clinical work, and popularization. That idea dovetailed with the psychiatrists' quest for legitimacy, as reflected in the many foundations that sponsored analytic training for psychiatrists.[39] The thirties saw the growth of local institutes, most of them night schools with an intense in-group life. Meanwhile, psychiatric residencies in elite institutions became "psychodynamically" oriented.[40] By the mid-1930s, all candidates for psychoanalytic training were expected to have completed a psychiatric residence in an approved institution.[41]

The arrival of the refugees strengthened the tendency toward medicalization. Most came from the Berlin Psychoanalytic Institute, which led the initial push toward professionalization. The refugees were all pioneering ego psychologists who shared the younger analysts' views; indeed, many of them had been the Americans' analysts earlier, in Austria and Germany. Key figures included Sándor Rádo, who went to Columbia University, and Ernst Simmel, who founded the first psychoanalytic society in Los Angeles in 1934, where he was later joined by Otto Fenichel and Martin Grotjahn.[42] Against Freud's wishes, Helene Deutsch left Vienna in 1935 for Boston, where she joined Hanns Sachs and was herself later joined by Edward and Grete Bibring. Theodor Reik fled Berlin in 1933, first to The Hague and then to New York City. Rudolph Loewenstein, the Polish Jew who had been Lacan's analyst, Ernst Kris, the assistant curator at the Vienna Kunsthistorische Museum who had helped Freud with his collection of antiquities, and Heinz Hartmann, who in 1941 became director of research at the New York Psychoanalytic Society, also emigrated to New York, as did Annie Reich, Hermann Nunberg, Edith Jacobson, Käthe Wolf, and Marianne Kris. When the market in New York became overcrowded, émigrés went elsewhere: Robert Wälder to Philadelphia, Richard and Edith Sterba to Detroit, Else Fraenkel-Brunswick to San Francisco, David Rapaport to the Menninger Clinic in Topeka, and Frieda Fromm-Reichmann to the Chestnut Lodge Sanitarium in Maryland.[43]

The refugees brought tremendous prestige to what was otherwise still a rather colorless profession. Analysis, wrote one, developed against the background of "the unfolding of images and ideas from Sophocles through Shakespeare and Goethe."[44] How, asked another, can one do analysis when one does not understand that the word "gay" can mean homosexual? Many émigrés adopted a pose of fashionable superiority. Abram Kardiner called them "*bei unsers,*" referring to "*Ja, bei uns war es anders*"—"Where we come from one did things differently." Often they expressed a "derisive judgement of American psychoanalysis" as "service-oriented, and rather mindless."[45] Dorothy Burlingham (née Tiffany) complained to Anna Freud of the "big business" methods of the Americans.[46] American-born psychiatrists sometimes reciprocated in kind. Thus, in 1938 Karl Menninger congratulated Franz Alexander: "You are a very flexible person, an international person . . . not aligned with the Jews." And William Menninger told his brother: "I don't know of any medical group that has as many 'queer birds' . . . as the [recently immigrated] psychoanalytic group. . . . I don't feel any great urgency to identify myself . . . with them. . . . I would much rather be identified . . . with the American Psychiatric or the American College of Physicians."[47]

As immigration gave way to assimilation, the requirement of a medical degree was enforced with ever-intensified devotion. At the William Alanson White Institute, nonmedical therapists had to sign a statement promising they would not practice analysis.[48] Elsewhere, analysts were not allowed to participate in reading groups that included nondoctors. Lionel Trilling was refused an analytic honor because he was not a doctor. Paul Federn, Freud's personal secretary, was not allowed to become a member of an analytic society until he became a physician seven years after he immigrated.[49] Freud sent an outraged, impotent protest. Erik Erikson, Siegfried Bernfeld, and even Anna Freud were discredited by their lack of medical credentials. Karen Horney, who founded her own association when the New York Psychoanalytic Society disqualified her as a training analyst, expelled Erich Fromm because he was not a licensed physician.[50] Theodor Reik, whose lay status had been the occasion for Freud's 1926 *Lay Analysis,* wrote: "I was the author of more than 14 books and countless articles in psychoanalytical journals. I really was expecting a royal welcome. I soon found out that all this counted for nothing, because I was not a doctor of medicine. They offered me a miserable job on the condition that I did not start a practice. I often did not even believe myself that I was competent in psychoanalysis in comparison with my medical colleagues."[51]

As analysts conquered psychiatry, they increasingly absorbed its values. The key to success, Ives Hendrick told his fellow analysts in a presidential address to the American Psychoanalytic Association (APA) of 1955, was the "victory" over Freudian dogmatism. American psychoanalysts "refused to be stifled by theoretical dogma. As pragmatists they favored that which endures because it is serviceable."[52] Franz Alexander's 1948 *Fundamentals of Psychoanalysis* argued that it was no longer desirable to study the history of analytic theory since "the conventional historical presentation is often confusing." A text should present a "comprehensive view of the present stage of psychoanalytic knowledge."[53] In 1965 Alexander published Freud's correspondence with Eugene Bleuler in order to demonstrate that psychoanalysis had gone wrong when Freud turned away from the official psychiatry.[54]

As the boundary between analysis and psychiatry weakened, analysts gained enormous prestige and financial reward. Of all the émigrés, the analysts were the most successful. By contrast, for example, Wolfgang Koehler, Max Wertheimer, and Kurt Koffka were never able to rebuild Gestalt psychology.[55] The year 1947, according to Nathan Hale, was "something of a gold rush."[56] In his 1953 presidential address to the APA, C. P. Oberndorf remarked: "Psychoanalysis has finally become legitimate and respectable." Two years later Ives Hendrick called analysis "the brand that (ostensibly, at least) dominates the market," and noted that its membership was "growing by geometrical rather than arithmetical progression." He added: "Our success, hugely magnified . . . by the esteem of other medical groups, has given us unsought and unexpected powers": faculty appointment, student selection, and powers over curriculum and accreditation among them.[57] Even Wilhelm Reich prospered, setting up a lucrative practice in Forest Hills, New York, before dying insane in a federal penitentiary after his conviction for fraud under the Food and Drug Act.[58] Analysis, Alfred Kazin noted in 1956, was a "big business and a very smooth one."[59]

The absorption of psychoanalysis into the American welfare state was something more than the familiar tale of the talented outsider corrupted by the American greed-machine. An unexamined convergence between American traditions of religious conversion, mind cure, and self-help, and the utopian strains in psychoanalysis, inspired the long-standing American love affair with analysis, as well as fueling the postwar program of social reorganization. Insofar as analysis remained a predominantly marginal, countercultural force, this convergence produced few baneful effects. By contrast, the integration of analysis into the welfare state—emblematized by its obsession with the medical degree—lent it state power and authority. Especially in the context of the cold war, its preexisting tendencies toward authoritarianism, scientism, and grandiosity took on a sinister hue.

To begin with, the integration of analysis into the welfare state wedded it to a positivistic notion of science that was soon to be used against it.[60] In 1997 Alan A. Stone remembered that during his postwar training in Boston, his teacher had compared analytic work to the great collective labors of the past. A half-century later, with the charisma of analysis dissipated, Stone reported that he had come to believe that psychoanalysis was not a science, not cumulative, not always based on observable data, and not subject to prediction.[61] Stone's impoverished notion of science would have excluded almost every way of studying human beings not directly modeled on physics; indeed, physics is more complex. The subordination to an idealized and unduly restrictive conception of the natural sciences, the exclusion of critique and speculation, the refusal to ask when empirical verification was necessary and when it was impossible to obtain, the neglect of the fact that the subject under study was not an object but a free being, capable of self-transformation through the process of being studied—all of this was consolidated in the rationalization of the late forties.[62]

Second, a scientistic culture sanctioned analysts in not reflecting upon themselves, either individually or collectively. Nothing could be less analytic, yet analysis was a far less efficacious treatment than its practitioners claimed. As a result, psychoanalysis was often a community in bad faith, boasting of successes and ignoring failures, distorting classroom presentations, and denying itself the means for self-correction. The matter is no doubt complicated. As a charismatic force, analysis made great demands on its practitioners and its patients. Nonetheless, there were far more "failures," second and third analyses, and lives tragically distorted than was publicly admitted. There is truth in Frederick Crews's later condemnation of analysis: "its deliberate coldness, its cultivation of emotional regression, its depreciation of the patient's self-perceptions as inauthentic, its reckless dispensation of guilt, its historic view of women's moral inferiority and destined passivity, and its elastic interpretive license, allowing the analyst to be right every time."[63] This stance was stiffened by internal authoritarianism. According to one analyst's recollection of his training, "if any student asked any question whatever, he was put down and told he was resistant."[64]

Third, medicalization encouraged depoliticization, and even reaction. Ideals of "professionalism" and "analytic neutrality" took on a different meaning when analysts were allied to official power. As the cold war unfolded, claims to be "above" politics became especially pernicious. The most egregious example occurred in Brazil. Werner Kemper, a leading representative of German psychoanalysis during the Third Reich, was among the founders of the Psychoanalytic Institute of Rio de Janeiro in 1946. Much later, but with an outlook formed by medicalization, Amilcar Lobo, an analytic candidate supervised by an analyst trained by Kemper, helped torturers by watching over the psychic and physical state of the victim. Despite repeated requests for intervention, the IPA minimized the significance of the case.[65]

In England, anticommunism subtly shaded an analytic tradition deeply shaped by the Popular Front, but in the United States even liberal analysts acquiesced in McCarthyism. Arthur Miller recalled that his difficulties "were surely personal," but he could "not help suspecting that psychoanalysis was . . . being used as a substitute not only for Marxism but for social activism of any kind."[66] Some analysts urged their patients to cooperate in the HUAC and McCarthy hearings.[67] When the actor Sterling Hayden, whose analyst was himself an ex-Communist, reported that "the FBI isn't going to let me off the hook without my implicating people who never did anything wrong," his analyst advised him that "the FBI would probably treat this information confidentially." When Hayden said his attorney told him not to trust the FBI, his analyst suggested that he "try another attorney." Later the analyst told him: "There's really not much difference between talking to the FBI in private and taking the stand in Washington. You have already informed after all. You have excellent counsel, you know, and the chances are that the public will—in time perhaps—regard you as an exemplary man, who once made a mistake."[68]

Analysts had once stood for a more nuanced notion of the ego than the dominant culture provided; now they identified themselves uncritically with the West's "respect for the individual." In 1948 UNESCO sponsored a conference in Paris at which Harry Stack Sullivan and others debated Eastern European social scientists led by Alexander Szalai of Budapest. The American defense of Western psychology easily defeated the orthodox Marxist insistence that it was impossible to change individual consciousness without first changing social conditions, but that should have been the beginning of the discussion, not the end.[69] Moreover, the Americans adopted a self-serving missionary stance that strengthened cold war triumphalism. Karen Horney advised the United States to adopt "long-term planning for emotional stability," Sullivan called for a "worldwide mobilization of psychiatry," and Henry A. Murray argued that social scientists needed to "invade . . . the realm of values" and become "physicians to society."[70]

The ambiguities of a government-supported psychoanalysis emerged most clearly in the realm of foreign affairs. During the occupation of Japan, Masao Maruyama, a Marxist theorist, linked Japanese militarism to the weakness of what he called "the modern ego" in that country. In Germany, Alexander Mitscherlich, a second-generation critical theorist, exposed the complicity of German psychoanalysis with National Socialism. The American authorities ignored both initiatives. Under the impact of the cold war, they encouraged the development of analysis as a way to *forget* the past. In Germany, as early as October 1945, analysts, including Felix Boehm and Karl Müller-Braunschweig, got a government-backed insurance company to pay for psychotherapy, producing what Edith Kurzweil has called a "psychoboom." Within a decade the Germans had become among the largest groups in the IPA, just as Germany became the United States' main cold war partner. As the history of the Göring Institute was buried, analysts revised "their own recent histories, stressing their earlier 'ambivalence' about the Nazis and the hardships they had suffered, and contacting Jewish analysts in America and England with whom they formerly had been friendly."[71] Thus, U.S. analysts wound up exporting a sanitized version of Freudianism as part of the larger process by which the United States sought to export to both countries its own way of life.

Even as they were caught up in the process of routinization, connection to a charismatic source of meaning shaped the inner life of American analysts and distinguished them from their fellow doctors. No mere economic rewards could explain the discipleship, the self-denial, the years of training, the night classes, the monastic demeanor, the secrecy, and the dedication that produced the analyst. Psychoanalysis, before it was anything else, was a *vocation*. Analytic education, wrote Michael Balint, was "strongly reminiscent of the primitive initiation ceremonies," with esoteric knowledge, dogmatism, and "authoritative techniques." At its center was the training analysis, the deep, one-on-one bond with an individual whose authority ultimately descended from Freud. Its aim, as in the training of any priesthood, was "to force the candidate to identify himself with his initiator, to introject the initiator and his ideals, and to build up from these identifications a strong superego which will influence him all his life."[72] The trauma of emigration intensified the intensity of these dyadic attachments but also drove them underground.

As analysis merged into the welfare state, the most important resource analysts had for maintaining their inner identity was their "shared ego ideal, the idealized imago of Freud." Lionel Trilling, speaking at a dinner in 1955, congratulated psychoanalysis for having "its whole history before its eyes . . . made actual and dramatic in the person of Freud." The Freud centenary in 1956 was guided by a single principle: to do nothing of which Freud would have disapproved. Ruth Thomas commented: "It seemed as if after all we found our one point of agreement in veneration of Freud." Ernst Kris prepared Anna Freud for her visit to the United States: "Everyone will be at your feet. Not because you are Freud's daughter, but nonetheless in a sense because you are." He continued: "If you prefer, you may assume that the positive aspect of their ambivalence toward him is intended for you."[73]

Apart from the training analysis, there were two additional means by which the charismatic tie to Freud was reproduced.[74] The first was through reading Freud's work, especially *The Interpretation of Dreams*. As Heinz Kohut remarked, the study of this text led students to identify with Freud by participating "in the workings of the most intimate recesses" of his mind; "such empathic closeness with total sectors of another person's mind, extending from conscious to unconscious levels, is not available to us in our day to day relationships, not even with those we are closest to—the members of our family and our friends." The second means for reproducing identification with Freud was by assuming his core identity and becoming a writer. In 1945 Ernst Kris called for "authoritative statements of what we believe to be true Freudian psychoanalysis." Writing from London, he sent a "MEMORANDUM—Free Associations to the Topic What to Do Next?" Nothing, he wrote, "is, at the present time, as important" as writing.[75]

The wish to guard and protect Freud's legacy was reflected in a new epoch of systematization. Among its products were Hartmann, Kris, and Loewenstein's regularly appearing articles in *The Psychoanalytic Study of the Child*, David Rapaport's 1959 *Structure of Psychoanalytic Theory*, and the *Hampstead Psychoanalytic Index*, conceived by Dorothy Burlingham and cosponsored by Anna Freud, which sought to record analytic data in a way that made systematic comparisons possible.[76] In mourning, Melanie Klein remarked, one tidies the house.[77] At the same time, systematization served the drive toward medicalization and positivism. Where Freud had spoken of the superego's approval or disapproval of the ego, preserving an experiental dimension, Hartmann, Kris, and Loewenstein "corrected" Freud's language to refer to "degrees of tension" between the two agencies.[78]

The most important projects of this generation—Ernest Jones's three-volume biography of Freud and James Strachey's *Standard Edition of the Complete Psychological Works of Sigmund Freud*—were simultaneously works of mourning and of revision. Jones's biography, dedicated to Anna Freud, "true daughter of an immortal sire," began to appear in 1954. So potent was Freud's imago that analysts attributed Jones's supposed mellowing in the last decades of his life to his immersion in the materials.[79] Seeking to buttress the scientific credentials of analysis, Jones emphasized Freud's relation to Brückean materialism, reporting that while Freud attended Franz Brentano's philosophy lectures, the fact does not "seem of any importance."[80] Still struggling with the aftereffects of a charismatic upheaval, Jones minimized the intensity of the *Männerbund* experience, ignored all connections between analysis and politics, settled old scores with Rank and Ferenczi, and in general exemplified what Peter Homans has called the "*ur-anxiety*" of psychoanalysis—that it would be seen as a religion.[81]

The twenty-four-volume *Standard Edition,* prepared by a small, international team of analysts, was begun in 1946 and completed twenty years later, the fulfillment of Jones's early promise to Freud.[82] There is no comparable edition in English for any other major modern European thinker, not even Marx, Weber, or Nietzsche. Prepared in England, it was largely financed by the American Psychoanalytic Association, which guaranteed the purchase of five hundred copies.[83] Strachey reworked earlier translations, especially those of Joan Riviere and Katherine Jones, with the intent of producing a text of "absolute credibility and overweening authority."[84] He described the imaginary model of the reader he kept before him as "some English man of science of wide education born in the middle of the nineteenth century."[85]

The translation is a monument of the English language, but it also reflects the drive toward medicalization. One casualty was Freud's use of everyday language. Freud used the term *Ich,* "I," to refer to both a psychic structure *and* the experienced self, thus giving it a double meaning. Strachey's translation of *Ich* as "ego" eliminated this duality. Strachey's preference for classicized terms, itself a medical bias, deepened the problem. "Good" became "appropriate," "need" became "exigency," "at rest" became "in a state of quiescence." Affect-laden, active, and dynamic constructions gave way to neutral, passive, and static ones. Freud's present tense, often integral to his effort to capture the timelessness of the unconscious, was replaced with the simple past.[86] The adoption of a standardized glossary underlined Anglo-American dominance over analysis. To this day, the Strachey translation remains the international standard.

Other translations and editions of the period also served to prettify and obscure. The 1960 English translation of an 1883 letter has Freud informing Martha Bernays that he planned to live more "like the gentiles—modestly . . . not striving after discoveries and delving too deep." Freud's German, however, refers to *Gojim*—goyim—not gentiles.[87] In Freud's letters to Fliess, published as *The Origins of Psychoanalysis* in 1954, Ernst Kris omitted, among other passages, Freud's description, in a 1897 letter about "the intrinsic genuineness of infantile trauma," of a father's heartbreaking abuse of his two-year-old daughter.[88] Attempts to "protect" Freud by excising such passages ended up rendering the whole analytic tradition vulnerable to accusations of dishonesty.

In fact, there was a great deal of ambivalence in these efforts. Many of the leading figures who would later seek to discredit Freud and psychoanalysis were either disciples or followers of orthodox analysts: Paul Roazen of Helene Deutsch, Jeffrey Masson of both Anna Freud and Kurt Eissler. Frederick Crews, the chief maligner of Freud's person and thought, was

Psychoanalysis, women, and mass consumption
(*Mademoiselle*, October 1953)

once among America's leading psychoanalytic literary critics. Robert Wallerstein, a leading American analyst writing in 1983, offered an explanation: American analysts "never fully mourned Freud, incorporated their ambivalence toward him, or consolidated their identifications with him."[89]

The harnessing of analytic charisma to cold war normalization had its deepest impact in the sexual realm. Analytic influence in postwar U.S. society rested on its unique ability to scrutinize and influence the inner life of the family. Analysts possessed this ability because individuals trusted them. A medicalized profession often betrayed this trust by pathologizing the aspirations of women, homosexuals, and others.

The rise of American ego psychology to predominance within the international psychoanalytic movement had coincided with the entry into analysis of a large number of women, their emergence as leaders, and the shift to the mother-infant paradigm they brought about in analytic theory. But once in power, ego psychologists effectively remasculinized analysis.

Medicalization brought about a steep reduction in the number of female analysts. In the United States, where only 6 percent of medical students in the 1940s were women, the number of female analysts declined dramatically, from 27 percent in the 1930s to 9 percent in the 1950s. Medicalization made this decline inevitable.[90] Since the United States dominated the international organization and led the rebuilding of analysis abroad, this shift in gender composition affected the entire movement.

Remasculinization was not merely a matter of numbers. Equally important were shifts in orientation and tone. Originally initiated and pursued by women, in the interests of women, the analytic theory of the mother-infant relationship became a medical theory directed *against* women. Female patients were discouraged from pursuing careers and urged to please their husbands, even by older female analysts who pursued successful careers themselves. Social problems were traced to what Abram Kardiner called the "uterine" family structure, meaning women's excessive power within the family, and the consequent decline of the paternal role. "Narcissistic" mothers were blamed for juvenile delinquency; "schizophrenogenic" mothers were blamed for mentally ill children; the "weak, mother-centered family" was blamed for the black male's supposed lack of self-esteem; the "silver cord" was blamed for male homosexuality; and "Momism" in general was blamed for what Philip Wylie called "the mealy look of men today."[91] Ironically, then, analysis became a male domain amid a revolutionary cultural shift in gender and sexual relations that it itself had helped set in motion. If psychoanalysis arose along with all the ardor and mystery of twentieth-century sexuality, it declined when it took on the task of normalization.

This is not to say that there were no weaknesses in the mother-infant paradigm. On the contrary, analytic texts typically cast the mother as an ontological category incapable of varying culturally or historically. In addition, Klein's equation of the ego with concrete obligations had elided the problematic of self-reflection and autonomy at the center of Freud's project. Translated into American ego psychology, the mother-infant paradigm tended to devolve into a straightforward developmental psychology.

Nonetheless, male analysts of the time did not aim to remedy these problems. Rather, like Jacques Lacan, they sniped that the postwar movement had become "matriarchal" or, like Ernest Jones and Edward Glover, "woman-ridden."[92] Anna Freud, in particular, encouraged the remasculinization of psychoanalysis. Her father, she wrote, "was convinced that anatomy determined whether predominantly male or female qualities would be developed and sought to prepare the individual for his or her differing future life tasks." As late as 1977 she argued against feminists that "the anatomical equipment of the female child puts her at a disadvantage in relations to the possessor of the phallus," never questioning how it is possible to possess a representation.[93]

Nevertheless, the influence of the women's emancipation tradition that had emerged after World War I persisted in some analytic quarters. Phyllis Greenacre and Grete Bibring "encouraged their female patients to free themselves from their customary subjugation to men."[94] Helene Deutsch's 1950s writings on the mother/daughter relationship influenced the feminist sociologist Nancy Chodorow. Viola Klein's *The Feminine Character* (1949) integrated Freudianism with Margaret Mead and William I. Thomas's feminist social science.

These, however, were exceptions. As such, they had little impact on the 1960s perception that psychoanalysis was uniformly hostile to feminism. A telling case is the reception of Ferdinand Lundberg and Marynia F. Farnham's 1947 book *Modern Woman: The Lost Sex.* This was the book that Betty Friedan singled out in her 1963 *The Feminine Mystique* as representative of the postwar psychiatric worldview. Indeed, Lundberg and Farnham had written that "feminism was at its core a deep illness. . . . It is not in the capacity of the female organism to attain feelings of well being by the route of male achievement."[95] Subsequently the work gained widespread notoriety in women's liberation circles and in women's studies programs, where it was taken as exemplary of the Freudian viewpoint. In fact, Lundberg and Farnham were not analysts. Moreover, when Frances Arkin reviewed the work for *Psychoanalytic Quarterly*—the only psychoanalytic journal to review it—she complained that "the authors' constricted vision is most disheartening. . . . [They] turn the clock back to the days prior to the industrial revolution."[96]

If postwar U.S. analysis was not uniformly antifeminist, it tended nevertheless to enforce gender and sexual normalization. All of the analysts I have just cited as friendly to feminism—Phyllis Greenacre, Grete Bibring, Helene Deutsch, Viola Klein, and Frances Arkin—were women. Until Roy Schafer's 1974 critique of Freud, it was hard to find a male analyst in the United States with a sympathetic word for feminism.[97]

As always, the most egregious crimes occurred in the treatment. In a not untypical experience, Annie Parsons, Talcott Parsons's daughter, after distinguishing herself in psychology at Swarthmore and Radcliffe; studying in Paris with Lévi-Strauss, Lacan, and Piaget; and doing research at Harvard Medical School, applied to train as an analyst at the Boston Psychoanalytic Institute. The response of her "extremely orthodox analyst" to her deep unhappiness, she later wrote, was to say "nothing at all." He gave no "indication that her status as a candidate was in doubt," writes the historian Winifred Breines. In 1963 she was rejected for "failure to come to terms with her basic feminine instincts." She never recovered, and committed suicide at the age of thirty-three.[98]

Women were not the only victims. Many memoirs and biographies of the period record nightmarish analyses. One of Lionel Trilling's analysts, Ruth Mack Brunswick, was a drug addict. In Trilling's recollection, "the five years in which I was in treatment with Dr. Brunswick were the hardest in my life. Not only when I was at her office but through long sleepless nights I tried to make sense of her bewildering behavior."[99] Calvin Trillin's memoir of "Denny," who appeared on the cover of *Life* magazine in the 1950s but later committed suicide, reveals that Denny was a homosexual who went through analysis, although the details are not given.[100] At the end of the writer Dan Wakefield's "long and dispiriting psychoanalysis," he found himself "lying on the floor of [his] analyst's office in such a state of devastation [he] didn't think" he could get out by himself.[101]

The homosexual was often a special target. In 1956 Anna Freud appealed to the journalist Nancy Procter-Gregg, asking her to not reprint her father's famous 1935 letter to the mother of a homosexual (reproduced on page 178), which dissociated homosexuality from any stigma of illness. According to Anna Freud, analysts now had the means to cure homosexuality, and her father's letter would discourage homosexuals from pursuing that solution.[102] The analyst Lawrence Kubie was among those who specialized in this "cure." Moss Hart's 1941 paean to psychoanalysis, *Lady in the Dark,* ran for 467 performances on Broadway, but Kubie's attempt to end Hart's homosexuality may have caused Hart's depression and early death. Apparently not averse to behavioral techniques, Kubie urged one patient, Vladimir Horowitz, to lock himself in a room when he felt homosexual urges coming on, and had another, Tennessee Williams, end the best relationship of his life.[103] Yet, in Rome in the late forties, the poet James Merrill found an American analyst, Thomas Detre, who accepted and supported his homosexuality.[104] In 1950 Allen Ginsberg went to a "lady psychiatrist" who "called up my father and told him my parents must accept the fact that I like men." The bisexual actor Montgomery Clift vacationed with his semicloseted gay neo-Freudian analyst, William Silverberg, an associate of Harry Stack Sullivan, who was himself a homosexual.[105] And the psychoanalyst Robert Lindner wrote in 1956 that most of his colleagues had come to abandon the "naive" though "humanitarian" view that homosexuality was an illness, coming increasingly to see it as "a rebellion of the personality that seeks to find—and discovers—a way in which to obtain expression of the confined erotic drives."[106]

The career of the term "bisexuality" is especially revealing. As we saw, Freud's redefinition of the concept was intrinsic to the birth of analysis, and the term had always retained its connotations of freedom from prescribed gender roles. In 1940, however, Sándor Rádo at Columbia University asserted that the concept had "outlived its scientific usefulness." The theory rested on an "arbitrary leap from the embryological to the psychological . . . with almost negligible exceptions, every individual is either male or female." Returning to the pre-Freudian notion of a heterosexual instinct, Rádo reasoned that being one gender or the other necessarily implied having a particular sexuality. Therefore, "every homosexual is a latent heterosexual."[107] Ernest Jones and Anna Freud were also among those who believed that Sigmund Freud had "over-stressed" the bisexual disposition of all human beings.[108] As Kenneth Lewes, the historian of the psychoanalytic theory of male homosexuality, summarized: what had been ambiguous in Freud became simple and doctrinaire.[109]

In 1948 when Alfred Kinsey and other researchers described homosexuality among animals, societies in which homosexuality was normal, and happy adjusted homosexuals, analysts were their leading detractors. Edmund Bergler was doubtless an extreme case, but his work was never publicly repudiated. His 1951 *Neurotic Counterfeit Sex* argued that homosexuals only *appeared* to be interested in sex. In fact, they were "injustice collectors [with] Kinsey-hewn chips on their shoulders." Kinsey's "erroneous conclusions," he argued, will be "used against the United States abroad, stigmatizing the nation as a whole in a whisper campaign."[110] Similarly, according to the mainstream analytic thought of Charles W. Socarides, homosexuals feared merging with the "preoedipal mother. . . . They hope to achieve a 'shot' of masculinity in the homosexual act. Like the addict [the homosexual] must have his 'fix.' "[111] Such insights led the American Psychiatric Association in 1952 to classify homosexuality as a sociopathic personality disorder in its first *Diagnostic and Statistical Manual of Mental Disorders* (*DSM-1*).[112] For such reasons, Lewes has rightly, even generously, characterized the postwar period in terms of a "psychoanalytic tradition of moral safeguarding."[113]

Every charismatic sect that survives long enough to become institutionalized eventually becomes rigid, ossified, and text-bound. By the middle of the 1950s, U.S. psychoanalysis had reached this point. Appealing to the most private and unsocialized dimensions of individuality, it had become an agent of rationalization, a virtual emblem of the "organization man" conformism and cookie-cutter domesticity the age so dreaded. Insiders like Anna Freud conceded that psychoanalysis was not in a "creative era": "If my father were alive now, he would not want to be an analyst."[114] As in the history of religion, renewal would have to come from the outside—in this case, from writers and social theorists. But the outsiders appealed to the same charismatic sources as the rationalizers.

Anti-rationalization took two forms: conservative and radical. The dividing point was the status of institutions. Conservative anti-rationalizers, such as Lionel Trilling and Philip Rieff, defended the need for institutions, professions, and political authority, while invoking the instinctual and sexual bases of individuality as correctives to bureaucratization and conformity. Radicals, such as Norman O. Brown and Herbert Marcuse, were anti-institutionalists. They hoped to liberate the depths of individuality from the limits imposed by repressive institutions, especially the heterosexual family.

Both currents had links to the New York intellectuals of the 1950s, among whom nonmedical interest in psychoanalysis flourished.[115] Although highly diverse, this group shared a sense of the exhaustion of Marxism and the limits of New Deal liberalism. Having long rejected Stalinism, they had also moved away from the Popular Front. Reasoning that the conflict between the individual and society had become more important than the conflict between workers and capitalists, they concluded that economic forms of struggle were no longer primary. Some moved to the Right, but others turned to modernism, existentialism, and psychoanalysis in order to criticize "mass society" and "mass culture."[116]

In a period in which medical analysts had sucked the lifeblood out of Freudianism, the intellectuals in the New York milieu resurrected the modernist view that the genuinely personal—as revealed in sexuality, creativity, and spontaneous action—was a permanent resource against rationalization. That view informed the action paintings of the abstract expressionists, Clement Greenberg's and Irving Howe's critiques of mass culture, and Hannah Arendt's philosophy of political action.[117] *Partisan Review,* which had begun as a communist literary journal, came to view early-twentieth-century modernism as a charismatic source of resistance to both rationalization and Stalinism. Modernism, William Barrett wrote, was not so much a matter of literature as an effort to keep "a certain kind of consciousness alive in a society inert or hostile to it."[118] Middlebrow culture, "kitsch," the welfare state, what Arendt called "the social" could only be resisted by an avant-garde in touch with the deeper, darker currents of personal life.

Like the participants in the Harlem Renaissance before them, many postwar New York intellectuals drew upon African-American music, literature, and protest thought to criticize normalization. For many, racial injustice exemplified the dehumanization, loss of identity, and duplicity that characterized modern society more generally. Ralph Ellison's *Invisible Man*, Richard Wright's pioneering attempts to link modernity and racial identity, and James Baldwin's early explorations of the interplay of racial and sexual identity reflected this view.[119] For some, moreover, African-American culture offered resources for transcending dehumanization: the intensely personal spontaneity of jazz, the sadness and ambivalence of the blues, the freedom and sensuality made available by marijuana.

In spite of the conservatism of the analytic establishment, Freud was at the center of this return to the personal. For many, psychoanalysis was the true heir to an ossified Marxism. A 1948 article in *Commentary* contended that "when the political cliques of the 30s lost their passion and died, they never really died, but rose to the bosom of the Father and were strangely transmogrified. Psychoanalysis is the new look."[120] In his autobiography, Arthur Miller recalled the intense fascination with psychoanalysis that swept New York in the late forties. The city, he wrote, "was swollen with rivulets of dispossessed liberals and leftists in chaotic flight from the bombarded old castle of self-denial, with its infinite confidence in social progress and its authentication–through–political correctness. As always, the American self . . . needed a scheme of morals to administer . . . this time the challenge handed lost ones like me was not to join a picket line or a Spanish brigade but to confess to having been a selfish bastard who had never known how to love."[121] The New York milieu constituted a critical bridge between the "old" (Marxist) Left of the 1930s and the "new" (Freudo-cultural) Left of the sixties, but, as Miller's remark suggests, the radical spirit of psychoanalysis could sometimes contribute to moralism and self-righteousness as well.

Paul Goodman—homosexual, communitarian, anarchist—was a pioneering figure in the rediscovery of Freud's radical potentialities. As World War II was ending, he argued that, like the New Deal, ego psychology had fostered a "rationalized sociolatry, . . . the smooth running of the social machine *as it exists*." Wilhelm Reich alone understood "that analysts who do not lend their authority to immediate general sex-liberation in education, morals, and marriage are no true doctors." C. Wright Mills criticized

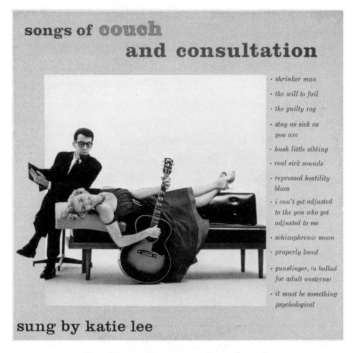

Freud enters the counterculture through
Tom Lehrer's folk music (1961)

Goodman's "gonad theory of revolution," but he too drew on psychoanalysis for his critique of white-collar society and the power elite.[122]

Lionel Trilling dominated the New York intellectual reading of Freud. A professor of English at Columbia University and one of the first Jews on that university's faculty, Trilling had long understood the limits of Marxism as an outlook for modern, middle-class men and women. Conceding "the historic role of the working class and the validity of Marxism," and acknowledging that he was not being "properly pious," he confessed that he shared the middle class's overwhelming preoccupation, born with romanticism, with "the self in its standing quarrel with culture." That quarrel, Trilling held, was the great achievement of modernity. For an "intense conviction of the existence of the self apart from culture is, as culture well knows, its noblest and most generous achievement."

Psychoanalysis, Trilling argued, constituted the apotheosis of that conviction, in part because of its connection to art. Freud's writings, Trilling wrote, constitute "the only systematic account of the human mind which, in point of subtlety and complexity, of interest and tragic power," deserves to stand beside literature.[123] By the whole tendency of his psychology, [Freud] establishes the *naturalness* of artistic thought."[124] At the same time, Freud's contribution goes beyond that of the artist. His emphasis on sexuality, Trilling wrote, "far from being reactionary, is potentially liberating: It proposes to us that culture is not all-powerful. It suggests that there is a residue of human quality beyond the reach of cultural control, and that this residue of human quality, elemental as it may be, serves to bring culture itself under criticism and keeps it from being absolute."[125]

Philip Rieff's 1959 *Freud: The Mind of the Moralist* also contrasted the analytic defense of the personal, not only to totalitarianism but also to the oversocialized, overadministered society of the 1950s. But for Rieff the gap was sharper than for Trilling. Rieff described Freud as the spokesman for "psychological man," the last of the character types—after the political (ancient), the religious (medieval), and the economic (bourgeois)—that have dominated Western civilization. In contrast to Trilling's evocation of the artist, Rieff's description was strikingly antiheroic. The direct descendant of "homo economicus," but no longer preoccupied with the production of wealth, psychological man had inherited "the nervous habits of his father." Freud was a sort of "investment counselor . . . of the inner life, aiming at shrewd compromises," teaching his patients to carefully count their "satisfactions and dissatisfactions." The payoff, however, was entirely internal. Through psychoanalysis, Rieff wrote, the individual learned to "withdraw from the painful tension of assent and dissent in his relation to society by relating himself more affirmatively to his depths. His newly acquired health entails a self-concern that takes precedence over social concern and encourages an attitude of ironic insight on the part of the self toward all that is not self." Psychological man, Rieff added, in a phrase that helped inspire this book's focus on personal life, was "no longer defined essentially by his social relations."[126]

The radical anti-rationalizers agreed. But rather than value the tension or discontinuity between the psyche and social institutions, as Trilling and Rieff did, they believed that the forces uncovered by depth psychology could overflow and even transform institutions. Like their more conservative counterparts, Brown and Marcuse rejected ego psychology. But they also rejected the implications of heterosexual "maturity" and domesticity that Trilling and Rieff at least tacitly endorsed. In 1959 two students of Trilling's who were working in publishing, Jason Epstein and Norman Podhoretz, came upon Norman O. Brown's *Life Against Death,* which had just been published by Wesleyan University Press. Epstein asked Podhoretz if it was worth reprinting. "*Worth* reprinting?" Podhoretz later recalled. "By the time I had read the first few chapters I was overwhelmed, and by the time I had finished I was convinced that we had stumbled on a great book by a major thinker." Having been taught that Freud was a conservative thinker and refuter of liberal and Marxist illusions of progress, Podhoretz was shocked by Brown's arguments. Brown disdained the "cheap relativism" of Freud's early critics such as Karen Horney and Erich Fromm and understood that "the only way around a giant like Freud was through him." Freud's pessimism, Podhoretz now realized, was not necessitated by Freud's theory. Indeed, a whole new way of life was implicit in Freud's vision of polymorphous perversity, a life of play and instinctual freedom.[127]

Brown's vision was antinomian and mystical: he sought to use psychoanalysis as a gateway into trans- or superpersonal experiences such as those known to religious and artistic adepts. Marcuse, by contrast, was a political thinker who believed that psychology could contribute to the project of social transformation. Like Trilling and Rieff, Marcuse located this transformation in the new possibilities released by the increasingly automated, mass-consumption society that emerged after World War II. As we shall see in the next chapter, Marcuse placed two charismatic dramatis personae in the vanguard of social transformation: the artist and the homosexual, both of whom pointed beyond the production-oriented and father-dominated heterosexual family. Although Marcuse and Brown's books were published in the fifties, they anticipated many of the anti-institutional themes of the New Left, especially that of the emancipatory energies of personal life.

Marcuse and Brown were gratified by the developments of the 1960s, while Trilling and Rieff were appalled. But both radicals and conservatives appealed to the same charismatic sources of sexuality, individuality, and the personal unconscious. So, moreover, did the ego psychologists. Thus, it would be a mistake to read the history of this period as one of bad rationalizers versus good heretics, or to play off a conformist 1950s against a rebellious 1960s. Rather, charisma and rationalization were always intertwined: charisma inspired motivational energies and ethical commitments, while rationality guided these energies and commitments into and through institutions. In both decades, the new possibilities of personal life were the grounds for this charisma. Thus, there was an underground continuity between the 1950s ideals of domesticity and the 1960s politics of personal liberation.

Just as seventeenth-century capitalism had required the sacralization of family life, and just as nineteenth-century industrialization had required a new work discipline, so the rise of an automated, mass-consumption society required analogous vehicles for the transformation of subjectivity. Psy-

"I will, however, say this for Freud—he got a lot of people thinking."

choanalysis was one of the most effective of these vehicles. During what might be called "the long 1950s," it triggered internal, charismatically originated motivations that encouraged individuals to transform the family from the tradition-bound and production-oriented unit that it still tended to be in the New Deal period into the carrier of expressive individuality in the epoch of globalizing, postindustrial capitalism. In that transformation, the ego psychologists' stress on reason, maturity, and the ego's capacities to organize the inner and outer worlds proved as necessary as the emancipation of sexuality to which—as the anti-rationalizers seemed to intuit—it was about to give way.

Chapter Twelve

THE 1960s, POST-FORDISM, AND THE CULTURE OF NARCISSISM

The capitalist system, even while built on the operations of the market, had relied on a number of proclivities which had no intrinsic connection with that pursuit of the individual's advantage which, according to Adam Smith, fueled its engine. . . . The family became an integral part of early capitalism because it supplied it with a number of these motivations. . . . As we take for granted the air we breathe, and which makes possible all our activities, so capitalism took for granted the atmosphere in which it operated, and which it had inherited from the past. It only discovered how essential it had been, when the air became thin. . . . It was the cultural revolution of the last third of the century which began to erode the inherited historical assets of capitalism and to demonstrate the difficulties of operating without them. . . . The market claimed to triumph as its nakedness and inadequacy could no longer be concealed.

—Eric Hobsbawm, *The Age of Extremes*

The cultural horizon that confronted psychoanalysis in the 1960s was laced with an explosive new utopianism. In the longest period of uninterrupted economic growth in their history, North Americans experienced an unprecedented sense of power and possibility. Images of "the affluent society," "cybernation," and "the conquest of space" intimated a golden age of scientific progress and economic prosperity. Almost abruptly, the family-centered mass consumption of the 1950s appeared dowdy and the ethic of maturity repressive. Nor was this spirit restricted to North America. Fordist-style mass consumption surged through Western Europe; reformers emerged in the Communist world; Asia and Latin America saw a reduction in the ranks of the peasantry under the impact of the green revolution, small-scale industry, and birth control. Reflecting a warm sense of historic possibilities, as well as the glacial blockage of the cold war, a global student movement emerged, reaching its peak in 1968.

One last time, psychoanalysis found itself at the center of a vast historical transformation. As an inspiration to the student movements of the sixties, its ideas reached the highest point of influence in their history. At the same time, the psychoanalytic profession collapsed, at least in its classical or Freudian form. Certainly, creative new centers emerged in France, Italy, Spain, and Latin America, inspired by a new, charismatic leader: Jacques Lacan. But elsewhere the profession lost most of its coherence and drive. Having served as the Calvinism of the second industrial revolution, it became an "old light" congregation of aging believers as that revolution waned. Having presided over the refamilialization of personal life in the 1950s, it was at a loss to deal with the transfamilial forms that erupted in the following decade. Having served to buttress antidemocratic forces at the height of the cold war, it was disoriented, and eventually displaced, by the democratizing forces of the 1960s. Above all, having valorized the reality-oriented, adaptive ego, it found itself bewildered and in some cases absorbed by the explosive reorientation toward recognition and identity.

The paradoxical fate of Freudianism in the 1960s—mass diffusion and precipitous decline—reflected its twofold character. As the first important theory and practice of personal life, Freudianism was in but not of this world. Implicit throughout its history, this duality now came to the fore. On the one hand, an orthodox Freud seemed to authorize the ego psychologists' adaptation to reality: to American world hegemony, to the modern organization of the sciences, and to the welfare state. On the other hand, a second charismatic Freud remained available, a Freud for whom reason arose from madness and could not be so easily separated from it. This Freud, excluded from professional canons but never wholly banished, inspired such figures as Paul Goodman, Norman O. Brown, and Herbert Marcuse. For this second, demonic Freud, personal life served as a point of critique and transcendence. When the 1960s generation turned to him, it exploded the constraints of the "maturity ethic" and, in the process, classical psychoanalysis itself.

An epochal change in the character of capitalism conditioned this explosion. Four factors were particularly important. First, the great megaliths of the Fordist period—the automobile industry, consumer durables, steel, oil, and electricity—began to be disintegrated, dispersed, outsourced, and subcontracted. Dispersal weakened Fordism's large-scale, impersonal, production-based backdrop, against which the Fordo-Freudian family, and modern personal life, had emerged.

Next, goods production aimed at the masses ceded ground to services tailored to the individual. Stratification by class gave way to market segmentation, demographics, and "psychographics," all premised on the now commonplace insight that "targeting slightly different products to different groups of consumers is significantly more effective than manufacturing one uniform product for everyone."[1] Capitalism appeared less like a factory and more like an emporium. Brand image and consumer identity merged. A new attunement between the inner needs of individuals and the service capacities of capitalism foretold a redefinition of personal life, one that no longer perceived any significant disjuncture between intrapsychic and external reality.

Third, the Fordist division between a white male, unionized, primary workforce, on the one hand, and women, racial minorities, and the Third World, on the other, began to break down. The end of colonial empires and the rising importance of global trade brought racial, ethnic, and national differences to new prominence. The changing nature of the working class encouraged a shift from the second industrial revolution's focus on economic redistribution to new demands for the recognition of difference.[2] The 1960s witnessed the end of the "family wage" ideal, the emergence of the two-earner family, and the resurgence of feminism. As one woman worker complained during a German strike in 1968: "The labor movement had a patriarchal structure": it could only see women as "workers, co-creators of socialism. . . . their autonomous claims as women to subjectivity were not acknowledged." The great, normalizing categories of the Fordist-Keynesian welfare state—"homosexual," "maternal employment," "racial minority," "social disorganization"—now came under attack, as did the psychoanalysts who helped establish them.

Finally, market forces helped consolidate a generationally specific youth identity, as advertisers tapped the purchasing power of the student cohort. Emblematized by blue jeans, rock music, and recreational drugs, youth culture arose along with a new, desocialized technology of color TV and electronic games. Intensely commodified, it was demotic and antinomian. Like feminism, it overflowed the family, producing explosive results in the culture. The poet Philip Larkin wrote that sexual intercourse began in 1963; for the novelist Harold Brodkey, to see his heroine in the sun "was to watch Marxism die." If the nineteenth century's fin de siècle witnessed a shift from "control" to "release," then the twentieth century's fin de siècle, which began in the 1970s, witnessed a shift from introspection to expressiveness, from the unconscious to the surreal, from thought to action.[3]

As Fordism, with its intricate, underground connections to psychoanalysis, went into decline and a new, post-Fordist culture began to emerge, the middle-class family—the historic locus of analytic practice—went into crisis. Sharp rises in divorce rates, in married women working outside the home, and in the number of people living alone, along with the emergence of explicit homosexual themes in fashion, entertainment, and the arts, fomented a cultural war. Self-appointed pundits celebrated "do your own thing" antinomianism, while conservatives condemned "permissive" child rearing. Psychoanalysis was caught up in that war. On one side stood the representatives of the maturity ethic, who viewed the new struggles for identity, recognition, and familial change as regressions to a pre-Freudian epoch. On the other stood those sympathetic to cultural revolution.

The reconstruction of the family in the 1960s and '70s was accompanied by efforts to reconstruct psychoanalysis, all of which pivoted around the concept of narcissism. Almost as if the culture was undergoing a massive, if potentially creative, regression, the emphasis on the ego gave way to an emphasis on the *self.* The structural theory returned to its roots in Freud's 1914 essay on narcissism. The analysis of the resistance succumbed to a "two-person" or "relational" practice. At the same time, much of the charisma of analysis was absorbed into a brilliant new cohort of women's liberation, identity politics, and postmodernist literature and thought. The process spanned a decade and can be thought of as a reformation: the crumbling of the great and unitary psychoanalytic church, the holy, catholic outlook of the Fordist period, which had touched every individual personally at the moments of birth, coming of age, marriage, confession, and death.

In 1950 David Riesman's *The Lonely Crowd* introduced a rich new idea: that the "other-directed" personality had been born the same year (1947) that Henry Ford died.[4] What Riesman meant was that an earlier ideal of autonomy had given way to a new need for mirroring and recognition. In Riesman's metaphor, a gyroscope, an internal steering device that keeps one on course regardless of external influences, had become a radar beam, scanning the external environment. Reflecting the influence of the Frankfurt School, Riesman attributed the change to the declining importance of the family and its replacement by the peer group and the mass media.

Riesman's argument was complicated, but it ultimately rested on the view that the Western world was undergoing a fundamental shift from an industrial society, based on manual labor and goods production, to a postindustrial society based on service and technology. This view converged with evolving ideals of social justice set in motion during and after World War II. In particular, the struggle against fascism had rendered previously existing forms of racial discrimination and anti-Semitism anathema. Although traditional Fordist concerns with economic injustice certainly persisted, there was an intense new focus on decolonization and desegregation. In these struggles, the demand for *recognition* became prominent. The new salience of this demand also affected analysis.

Racism, many noted, had exacted not only material but psychic costs. Thus, in 1954 the U.S. Supreme Court decided the issue of segregated schools on the basis of their injury to black students' self-esteem, not their interests or rights. Similarly, Aimé Césaire, a surrealist poet in Martinique, protested that colonialism had skillfully injected millions "with fear, inferiority complexes, trepidation, servility, despair, abasement."[5] French psychoanalysis, influenced by Sartre's existentialism and faced with the Algerian revolution, was especially open to this line of reasoning. Octave Mannoni, for example, criticized the Communist Party for not realizing that objective inequalities were "embodied in struggles for prestige, in alienation, in bargaining positions and debts of gratitude, and in the invention of new myths and the creation of new personality types."[6] Frantz Fanon, a Martinique psychiatrist working in Algeria, argued that racial distinction structured the entire phantasmagoria of colonialism. Hailed on the street as a " 'Dirty nigger!' or simply, 'Look a Negro,' " the black African was sealed into a "crushing objecthood." Those who suffered from such *mis*recognition did not need psychoanalysis, they needed the purgative violence of revolution.

The growing awareness of the psychic damage caused by misrecognition suggested a shift in psychoanalysis, from a paradigm of intrapsychic autonomy to a paradigm of intersubjectivity. Such a shift had also been developing independently among mainstream ego psychologists. In particular, Erik Erikson responded to the increasing self-awareness of middle-class youth by introducing the concepts of "identity" and "identity crises" in 1956. According to Erikson, adolescence was a historically new stage of life precipitated by the end of the family's role in production. Although Erikson did not explicitly develop the theme of recognition, he explained identity as the outcome of childhood identifications that were selectively repudiated, assimilated, and reconfigured *in relation to others,* not just the parents but the community, religion, economic institutions, and the state. The goal of these interactions was inner consistency and continuity, which was what Erikson meant by identity, and which, he insisted, could never be achieved simply in relation to oneself.[7]

Erikson had scant influence on mainstream analysis, but the move in the direction of intersubjectivity also unfolded in more orthodox quarters. Thus, in 1946 Heinz Hartmann, Ernst Kris, and Rudolph Loewenstein urged analysts to replace the word "ego" in Freud's text on narcissism by the word "self." They explained: "Freud's use of the word is ambiguous; he uses 'ego' to refer to a psychic organization and to the whole person." Narcissism, they pointed out, was not the libidinal investment of the *ego* as opposed to the id but of the *self* as opposed to the world.[8] Contingent though it may have been, the introduction of the concept "self" was pregnant with meaning. Returning to Freud's 1914 theory of narcissism, it brought together three separate notions: narcissism as self-love, narcissism as a stage in the development of the ego, and narcissism as entailing a new form of object relation, namely, recognition.

The explosive possibilities introduced by the concept of the self also reflected the shift toward the mother/infant paradigm pioneered by British psychoanalysts during World War II. Responding especially to Melanie Klein's vast though unacknowledged influence on ego psychology, Edith Jacobson described in 1953 how the boundary between "the self and the object world" was built up through the mother's touching, handling, feeding, watching, listening, seeing—in a word, recognition—of the child.[9] Soon analysts were describing the psyche as an "inner representational world," built up of self and object representations.[10] The ego psychologists' attempts to reconcile psychoanalysis with academic psychology and philosophy also led in the direction of recognition. While psychoanalysis was a drive psychology, academic psychology and philosophy spoke of affects or feelings, not drives; but feelings, as opposed to drives, are intrinsically oriented toward representations of the self and of others.[11]

As American psychoanalysis turned from the ego to the self, the distinction between analytic and nonanalytic approaches became blurred. By 1969 George S. Klein could note with approval that analytic language had shifted from "conflict" to "dilemma," from "defense" to "adaptation," and from "sexual and aggressive drives" to "motivation in general." The overall effect, Klein concluded, was "explanatory parity for conscious intention."[12] A frequently encountered phrase of the 1950s, "the widening scope of psychoanalysis," had referred to its expanding influence. By the sixties, however, the same phrase signaled the disappearance of analysis into eclectic psychotherapy. Even the word "psychoanalysis" declined in use, gradually supplanted by such euphemisms as "dynamic psychology," "dynamic psychiatry," and "psychodynamic therapy."

Although ego psychologists adjusted their theory to the Zeitgeist, they resisted its lifestyle changes, including women's rejection of traditional family roles and the growing self-assertion of homosexuals. Thus, in a period of increasing politicization, they attacked the "narcissism" of 1960s culture, arguing that the declining credibility of Oedipal authority strengthened the primitive, sadistic, self-destructive impulses of earliest childhood.[13] Not content with general observations, Bruno Bettelheim condemned the anti-war movement as "oedipal acting out," implying that those who supported the war in Vietnam were exemplars of maturity. In 1968, at the height of the War on Poverty, Lawrence Kubie criticized his colleagues in a community mental health center for harboring "the Russian fantasy that all psychiatric illnesses are due to social inequities."[14] Not surprisingly, ego psychology fell out of favor.

By 1960 the American Psychoanalytic Association was receiving fewer applications from individual candidates and from societies seeking affiliation. The average age of members was rising sharply, and the number of patients was declining. In 1966, for the first time, a major meeting was canceled for lack of interest. The APA's president, Leo Rangell, reported on a "change in the hospitality, ranging up to sharp hostility, in the scientific and intellectual community, in medicine and in the public press."[15] A series of interviews conducted in the late sixties did not find one senior analyst with an optimistic word for the profession. Several cited Hartmann as an especially depressed figure whose brilliance had been destroyed by his subservience to Freud.[16] A 1972 questionnaire found that most analysts believed that no major discoveries had been made since Freud's death.[17] Kurt Eissler summed up the mood: "In his autobiographical sketch, Freud records . . . that the First World War passed without damage to the psychoanalytic movement. Alas, the same cannot be said of World War II."[18]

The declining prestige of American analysts was reflected in the broader culture. In contrast to the image of analytic integrity in the films of the 1940s and early '50s, analytic corruption became a leitmotif in films of the 1960s and '70s. This was not surprising, since the sixties also witnessed a rise in "boundary violations," the technical term for the breakdown of the norms supposed to regulate the analyst/patient relationship. Thus, in 1963 Elaine May married her analyst, David Rubinfine, and the story was retold in *Lovesick,* in which the ghost of Freud, played by Alec Guinness, returned to criticize the errant analyst.[19] Milton Wexler cowrote Hollywood screenplays with a patient, just as "Donnie," Diane Keaton's analyst in Woody Allen's *Manhattan,* phoned his patients late at night to weep. George Pollock was sued for bilking a patient of money, while Erica Jong's *Fear of Flying* described the "black-bearded Dr. Stanton Rappaport-Rosen who recently gained notoriety in New York analytic circles when he moved to Denver and branched out into 'Cross-Country Group Ski-Therapy.' "[20] Marshall Brick-man's "Neimann Fek" celebrated the solution offered by absorbent-paper company Kimberly-Clark to the problem of the "schmutz" left by the patient on the couch: "It took seventy years before we perfected the beard and the fee. Now finally the napkin. No one need ever be crazy again."[21]

Poised yet again between absorption into a therapeutic, "feel-good" culture and relegation to its margins as its carping critic, the analytic church underwent one last convulsive schism. On one side stood proponents of internal reform. Like the great monastic movements—the Cluniacs, Dominicans, and Franciscans—that preceded the Protestant Reformation, the analytic reformers sought to adapt analysis to the needs of the age. On the other side stood defenders of orthodoxy. Like the clerical establishment that opposed reform, they sought to resist adaptations that would effectively destroy psychoanalysis as they knew it.

Not surprisingly, matters came to a head in the concept of narcissism. Since Freud's 1914 essay, narcissism had had a negative connotation, standing for an infantile moment in the passage to maturity. In the sixties the analytic establishment continued to use the term in this sense, invoking it to signal the purported inability of the sixties generation to make commitments, engage in long-term projects, and sacrifice the self for larger purposes. The reformers, in contrast, sought to accommodate sixties culture by revaluing narcissism. Heinz Kohut, a Chicago-based analyst born in Vienna, was the first analyst to grasp this point.

An affirmative attitude toward narcissism, Kohut claimed, developed naturally out of ego psychology. Whereas in the classical neurotic "a repressed drive element . . . is seeking satisfaction," in the newer borderline or narcissistic patients "an injured narcissistic ego [seeks] reassurance." These patients suffered from "intense hunger for a powerful external supplier of self-esteem and other forms of emotional sustenance in the narcissistic realm." Sexuality was often in the service of that hunger. Rather than tracing demands for recognition to infantile traumas, analysts should recognize the legitimacy of patients' needs to be mirrored, or to idealize a "self-object" who made them feel whole and important.

Like the humanistic reformers of the waning Middle Ages, Kohut at first sought to update the church. Insisting that recognition had replaced sexuality as the defining issue of the age, he argued that the psychoanalytic establishment had become an obstacle to salvation. Ego psychologists' "courageously-facing-the-truth morality," their "health-and-maturity morality," led them to interpret legitimate demands for recognition as defenses against autonomy. Analytic sadism and condescension reflected the analysts' denial of their own narcissistic needs, a denial manifest in Freudworship, which reserved all recognition for the founder. Denying the validity of narcissistic needs, analysts saw only one solution to life's problems: marriage, children, a calling. A respect for narcissism would lead them to another attitude: sympathy with those who rejected the family, who pursued satisfying activities that did not serve a social purpose, or who struck out on their own intellectually.[22]

Kohut's argument seemed to imply the dissolution of psychoanalysis into the new "do-your-own-thing" culture. Pursuing his own logic, he eventually called for an end to analysis and its replacement by a psychology of the self, one whose basic motif would be tragedy, not guilt. Not surprisingly, his initiatives called forth a counterreformation, led by Otto Kernberg. Whereas Kohut sought to break the association of narcissism with pathology, Kernberg reasserted it.

Also born in Vienna, Kernberg had emigrated to Chile and been trained by Kleinians. A product of the long evolution of the 1950s and '60s, which had transformed ego psychology into the theory of an "inner representational world," he defended the power of that psychology to comprehend the new narcissistic culture.[23] For him, the narcissistic patient was not an insecure person who needed recognition but a deeply disturbed individual, driven by oral greed and by the anguish of ruptured connection. Thus, the narcissist's superficial charm masked an explosive rage that would erupt as soon as one failed to mirror his or her grandiose self. Buoyed by drugs, casual sex, and irresponsibility, the intrapsychic world of the narcissist consisted of a "grandiose self" and devalued, shadowy images of others. Internally, narcissists saw themselves as wolves. Far from needing affirmation, they needed the steady, objective distance that generations of analysts had provided. Yet the fact that they could not form genuine relations with others made them almost impossible to analyze. Only the profound suffering they experienced as they aged made the effort worthwhile.

Like Kohut, Kernberg viewed narcissistic pathologies as a result of changes in the family, but for Kernberg these changes were mostly negative. In Kernberg's reasoning, a genuine sexual relation required maturity in the sense of access to one's infantile emotions and the ability to experience and overcome one's own aggression. Both the permissive culture of the sixties and the protofeminist "marital affection" and "companionate marriage" literature that followed denied the existence of aggression within the couple. Such a denial, Kernberg wrote, "transformed a deep love relation into a superficial and conventional one that lacks the very essence of love." Sexual love, he insisted against the permissive culture of the sixties, "is always in open or secret opposition to the group." It "is by nature nonconventional," reflecting "a deep conviction and attitude shared by the couple regarding its freedom from submission to the pressures of its surrounding social group . . . an internal attitude that cements the couple, often in very subtle ways, and that may be masked by surface adaptation to the social environment."[24]

By the 1970s, then, analysts like Kernberg had propounded alternatives to a youth- and appearance-centered culture, but their defense of "abstinence" and "maturity" was a rearguard one. Kernberg's later career, which featured Herculean explications of analytic theory, sometimes bore the marks of a counterreformation or restoration, such as the Council of Trent, which attempted to hold off the collapse of the decaying church by systematizing and ordering its doctrines.[25] Meanwhile, the creative spirit of psychoanalysis had passed from reformers and clerics inside the cathedral to heretics and revolutionaries at the gates. Among the polycentric, globally dispersed, revolution-oriented student and youth groups known collectively as the New Left, the notion of recognition was about to explode into a communal and utopian attempt at self-transcendence.

The tensions surrounding ego psychology reflected the duality of analysis. While orthodox Freudians grappled with whether the classical theory could be salvaged, the second, demonic Freud was assisting a cultural revolution, one that would decimate the analytic establishment as a whole. Although brief, the student movement's encounter with psychoanalysis constituted a critical moment in that revolution. During the Reformation, "extremist" sects such as the Anabaptists, Diggers, and Holy Rollers sought to experience salvation on earth. During the 1960s, New Left extremists rejected the very idea of a disjuncture between the external world and intrapsychic reality, the founding premise of psychoanalysis. They turned to the second—utopian—Freud, not to explore the unconscious but to reconnect the unconscious with the social and political world. In doing so, they served as a kind of shock troop, not only demonstrating how frayed the hold of the maturity ethic had become but limning the horizon of a new society.

The New Left's interest in the second Freud arose from its place at the cutting edge of a new, post-Fordist, "postindustrial" culture. Thus, the early intellectual influences on the New Left, such as Jane Jacobs's *Death and Life of the Great American Cities* (1961), Rachel Carson's *Silent Spring* (1962), and Ralph Nader's *Unsafe at Any Speed* (1965), were criticisms of corporate-inspired regimentation. Similarly, C. Wright Mills's "Letter to the New Left" challenged the view that the industrial working class would be the vehicle of revolution. The key New Left student movements, such as the SDS in Germany, SDS in the United States, and Zengakuren in Japan, began by rebelling against labor-movement-based "youth organizations." In short, the New Left began by rejecting what it termed the "warfare-welfare state."

In rejecting Fordism, the New Left also rejected Fordism's myth of the noble savage—namely, personal life—propounding its own myth instead. Unlike Fordism, it evoked a world in which there was no distinction between what is inside and what is outside, what is home and what is not home, what is civilized and what is natural. In seeking to obliterate distinctions, to keep everything and everyone together, and to transform the world as a whole, the 1960s generation turned to such utopian Freudians as Wilhelm Reich, Herbert Marcuse, and Norman O. Brown, as well as to R. D. Laing and Ken Kesey, who described society, not the individual, as mad. The New Left myth of oneness and harmony was responsible for its greatest achievements, such as the intense feelings of solidarity it forged with peoples of the Third World. But it also explains its grandiosity and evasion of the problem of institutional reform.

The New Left drew on the utopian current in psychoanalysis in at least three different areas. First, it rejected what it regarded as the suffocating conformity of the family, which had led to the privileging of genital sexuality, and the suppression of homosexuality and the "perversions." Eros, the New Left reasoned, needed to be liberated; it needed to find expression in work and politics, in the streets and in other arenas of public life. Women, in particular, at first welcomed the larger eros as a contrast to domesticity.[26] So, too, did homosexuals. Communes; drug use; attacks on monogamy; rock music; the performance onstage of what previously took place only backstage, such as nudity, informal dress, and self-disclosure; an activist culture, whose only regulative ideal was "participation": these all constituted a social basis for the utopian reading of Freud.

Second, the New Left rejected repression and sublimation in favor of authenticity, expressive freedom, and play. In place of what now appeared to be the gray, regimented order of the Fordist epoch, the New Left opened the way for a world pulsating with color, vibrancy, and the primal rhythms of the unconscious id. Heir to the older avant-gardes, student radicals facilitated the breakthrough to a demotic, post-Fordist mass culture in such areas as rock music, poster design, TV, film, and fashion. The New Left's rejection of the inevitability of repression also led to an insistence that it know the truth about everything, that there be no secrets, an insistence that made itself felt in the antiwar movement, the Catholic church, and the universities, and in the exposé of West Germany's continued complicity with Nazism.

Finally, the New Left drew upon the utopian Freudian tradition to reject instrumentalism and the achievement ethic. Work, student activists argued, should satisfy the individual, not serve merely as a means of earning a living. This reflected the students' place in the emerging post-Fordist "information economy," an economy in which the university replaced the automobile as its driving force. Amid dystopic visions of a wholly administered future society and McLuhanist predictions that technology would unilaterally liberate consciousness, New Left intellectuals such as André Gorz, Serge Mallet, and Tom Nairn portrayed creativity, knowledge, and technical capacities as intrinsically dialectical and social.[27] Behind their "new working-class" theories, as they were called, lay the understanding that it was impossible to develop the new economy without developing the individual psyches of which it was composed.

Along with Norman O. Brown's *Life Against Death,* the most important work wedding the utopian strain in psychoanalysis to the New Left was Herbert Marcuse's *Eros and Civilization.* The book, widely translated, turned Marcuse from an aging German-Jewish refugee professor—a member of the Frankfurt School—into an international icon of the New Left comparable to Che Guevara or Frantz Fanon. In Marcuse's reading of Freud, *Ananke*—scarcity—lay behind repression. But the enormous technological possibilities originally released by the second industrial revolution made it possible to distinguish between necessary and *surplus* repression. While *some* repression was inevitable, much was necessitated by class domination. Read historically, therefore, Freud's writings contained a hidden, revolutionary conception of a nonrepressive society, one that became more and more relevant as the sphere of necessity shrank.

As part of his vision of a nonrepressive society, Marcuse introduced an explosive rereading of the concept of narcissism, the very concept that analysts were using to condemn the New Left. Ignoring the ego psychologists' concept of the self, he went back to Freud's idea of a *primary* narcissism characteristic of the earliest infant/mother relationship. Primary narcissism was pre-objectal; it existed *prior* to the emergence of the "I." Far from producing a psychic investment in the self, primary narcissism characterized intrauterine life, sleep, and the loss of self that mystics know. Described by Freud as an "oceanic feeling," it reflected the ego's original, "inseparable connection with the external world."[28]

Marcuse contrasted primary narcissism to the rational, autonomous ego extolled in the Fordist epoch, the ego that had underpinned the maturity ethic. The ego that undertook the rational transformation of the environment, Marcuse argued, was "an essentially aggressive, offensive subject, whose thoughts and actions were designed for mastering objects. It was a subject against an object. . . . Nature (its own as well as the external world)

Herbert Marcuse lecturing to students at the Free University
of Berlin, 1968

was 'given' to the ego as something that had to be fought, conquered, and even violated."[29] The "autonomous ego" was "antagonistic to those faculties and attitudes which are receptive rather than productive, which tend toward gratification rather than transcendence [and] which remain strongly committed to the pleasure principle." Primary narcissism, by contrast, constituted "a fundamental relatedness to reality." It pointed the way, Marcuse reasoned, "from sexuality constrained under genital supremacy" to eroticization of the entire body, and from instrumental rationality toward art, play, and narcissistic display. Allowed free scope, primary narcissism might generate "a comprehensive existential order."

Articulating the utopian element in narcissism, Marcuse helped demolish the production-centered myths of the Fordist epoch. In place of Prometheus, Marx's hero from the ancient world who stole the secret of fire, Marcuse enthroned the poet/musician Orpheus, who introduced homosexuality to human society. Like Narcissus, Orpheus rejected "the normal Eros, not for an ascetic ideal, but for a fuller Eros." Brown's *Life Against Death* also defended "polymorphous perversity" against the genitally based "ego of mastery," a formation "not yet strong enough to die." Like Marcuse, Brown valorized "feminine" motifs. Rejecting "pseudo-individuation" as "based on hostile trends directed against the mother," he sought to rescue what he saw as the critical aspect of Bachofen's matriarchal discoveries from "the Jungian *Schwärmerei*."[30]

By the 1960s, then, the "second modernity," in which analysis had played so important a part, seemed to have ground to a halt. Just as the intensity of early Calvinism gave way to the "iron cage" of bureaucracy and material goods, so the Freudian-inflected threefold promise had disintegrated into instrumentalism, the privileging of genital heterosexuality, and the cold war state. Yet the utopian possibilities of psychoanalysis had not been exhausted. Marcuse, Brown, Laing, and others still found a hidden strain in psychoanalysis, one that could facilitate the move beyond the maturity ethic. Giving voice to the lived critique of the communes, they provided an analytic underpinning to the New Left's critique of instrumental reason, its desire for a new connectedness with nature, and its attempt to liberate sexuality from its genital, heterosexual limits.

Just as "extremist" sects paved the way for the Protestant religions that reinvented Christianity, so the New Left's apocalyptic interpretation of Freud paved the way for Jacques Lacan's explosive reinvention of psychoanalysis. But while Marcuse's vision of primary narcissism reflected the early New Left's critique of privatism, Lacan's "return to Freud" reflected the waning of the New Left and the end of its hopes for a Marx/Freud synthesis. Lacan, too, remade analysis around the theme of narcissism. For him, however, narcissism was not a basis for liberation but a snare and a delusion.

Born into an upper-class family in 1901, Lacan received a Jesuit education. Trained as a psychiatrist, he joined the Société Psychanalytique de Paris in 1934. Divided between an orthodox faction, led by Marie Bonaparte, and a nationalistic opposition, led by the anti-Semitic, proto-fascist grammarian Édouard Pichon, the society in its early years was highly politicized. Lacan's early career centered on his opposition to Pichon. Becoming president of the society in 1937, Lacan observed that it was because Vienna "was the melting pot of the most diverse forms of the family from the archaic to the most evolved . . . [t]hat a son of the Jewish patriarchy imagined the Oedipus complex" there.[31] In 1940 the society was abolished in the wake of splits provoked by the war.[32] At the end of the war, with many of the original members discredited for collaboration, Lacan emerged with Sacha Nacht and Daniel Lagache as one of a troika that ran the reconstituted society. In 1951 he began the weekly seminars on Freud that would continue until just before his death in 1981.

Jacques Lacan in the 1960s: critic of ego psychology
and advocate of the linguistic turn

As we saw, Lacan began his career by questioning Freud's theory of the ego. Freud had described the ego as a psychical agency, originating in the systems of perception and consciousness and serving the drives toward self-preservation and sexual release. Beginning with his famous "mirror-stage" lecture, delivered to the Marienbad psychoanalytic congress in 1936, Lacan rejected Freud's characterization of the ego as an agent. Psychical development, Lacan argued, began not with agency but with primal lack, terror, or the emptiness of nonexistence. The "ego of narcissism," as Lacan called the "I," was a defensive response to the traumatic discovery of this emptiness, an imaginary construction, a "crystallization of images."[33]

Deriving his basic orientation from surrealism, which characterized the unconscious in linguistic and imagistic rather than in instinctual terms, Lacan described the ego of narcissism as born into *discourses,* meaning unconscious, multivoiced streams of associations governed by their own rules of exclusion, prohibition, and privilege. Examples of discourse include the "name of the father," the "desire of the mother," and larger social discourses such as those of religion, nationality, and politics. Neuroses were discourse knots: hysteria was a hieroglyph; inhibition was an enigma; character equaled "armorial bearing." The analyst performed exegeses. Manipulating and guiding a force far greater than the ego, the analyst aimed to foster not autonomy but subjectivity, meaning the ability to allow the flow of desire to express itself and to hear the flow of the desire of others as it mixed with one's own desire, punctuated as desire always is by ellipses, redundancy, syncopation, rhetorical trope, and metaphor.

In the 1950s the long-delayed crumbling of an older order of small producers, and the rapid emergence of a mass-consumption society, gave French psychoanalysis a lift. Lacan's seminars reflected the new self-confidence. Seeking to rescue the unconscious from the prevailing "confused, unitary, naturalistic conception of man," Lacan defended Freud's death-instinct hypothesis as a reminder that "in man, there's already a crack, a profound perturbation of the regulation of life."[34] To foreground that "crack," Lacan located the ego of narcissism at the intersection of three different "orders" or "registers." The imaginary order generated the illusion of unity that underwrote the "I." The symbolic order of language, culture, and paternal law produced the "desiring subject," the split subject of psychoanalysis. Finally, the "real," meaning the order of contingency, meant that the subject was always unstable.

In his 1953 "Rome Discourse," a private lecture given to friends and associates in the midst of an official analytic congress, Lacan contrasted his notion of the split subject to both ego psychology and object relations. Emigration to America and "the absence of the social 'resistances' in which the psychoanalytic group used to find reassurance," he argued, had led ego psychologists to repress the "living terms" of analytic experience; they had become obsessionally preoccupied with technique, "handed on in a cheerless manner." Only because they had such an impoverished understanding of the unconscious had they felt the need to invent the idea of the self. And while the Kleinians had opened up important new areas, such as "the function of the imaginary" (phantasy), object relations (existential phenomenology), and countertransference (the analyst's transference), the naturalistic British emphasis on dependency and maternal care also vitiated Freud's discovery.[35]

By the mid-fifties, French psychoanalysis rode the wave of Marshall Plan mass consumption. Buoyed up by the infusion of funds, Lacan patterned his lifestyle after that of his American counterparts: Right Bank tailors, private barbers, luxurious hotels.[36] Unlike them, however, he found in the "short session" (at times as short as five minutes) a new way to finance his enterprise and expand his corps of followers. According to his biographer, Elisabeth Roudinesco, "he could eat an entire meal during a session, make a show of being rushed, pace back and forth, emit a few grunts, utter an enigmatic comment or sit down at his desk to finish off an article." When a patient protested he would reply: "But, *mon cher,* it doesn't interfere with my listening in the slightest." Lacan's actions were inexcusable, to be sure, but they were also unconscious parodies, especially of the North American analyst's professional pretenses. Just as Melanie Klein's speculative ambitions had begun to blow psychoanalysis's positivist cover, so Lacan's grandiose and self-centered performances ridiculed its uptight medical façade.[37]

In the 1960s Lacan's idiosyncrasies assumed their larger meaning. In 1951 Lacan and others had formed the Societé Française de Psychanalyse (SFP) and applied to the IPA for admission. An IPA committee, headed by Winnicott, rejected the SFP because of Lacan's notorious clinical practices. In 1963 the IPA made the exclusion of Lacan a precondition for recognizing the new society. Comparing himself to Spinoza, Lacan termed the decision an excommunication. When most of his students and associates decided to abandon him and accept the IPA's condition, he screamed: "You're absolutely insane . . . to leave me at a time when I am about to become famous."[38]

Exclusion made Lacan into a New Left icon, comparable to Marcuse but with greater staying power. At the invitation of the Marxist philosopher Louis Althusser, he moved from Saint Anne Hospital to the École Normale Supérieure, where his first seminars drew audiences of five hundred.[39] Soon thereafter he echoed Martin Luther by founding l'École Freudienne on his own authority—"as alone as I have always been in my relation to the psychoanalytic cause." Just as Luther had returned to the biblical text, so Lacan claimed to return to Freud. And just as Luther had rejected the clerical hierarchy, so Lacan rejected the training analysis: "L'analyste ne s'autorise que de lui-même" (The analyst is authorized by no one but himself"). His break with the analytic church opened what became known as *le champ freudien*—the freeing of psychoanalysis from medicine and its integration into the social, cultural, and lifestyle changes that characterized the 1960s.

Associated with the slogan "the death of the subject," *le champ freudien* resonated with the broader left-wing shift from production and the economy to ideology, culture, and the media. Claiming to replace Descartes's *Cogito* or "I think" with "*Ça parle*," where *ça* meant language, Lacanianism articulated the growing sense that it was through media images and discourse, rather than in the workplace, that social domination was secured. The emphasis on the illusory character of the "I" made it possible to understand the ideological effect of a particular text not simply in terms of its content (e.g., capitalism, racism, sexism) but rather through the way it sustained an imaginary sense of wholeness and unity. By focusing attention on the reader, film viewer, or museumgoer, rather than on the author or supposed content of a work, Lacanianism encouraged a dramatically new approach to what previously had been termed the "superstructure."[40]

Nonetheless, the moment of Lacanian radicalism soon passed. Whereas Marcuse articulated the communal experiences that characterized the early and mid-sixties, Lacan spoke for the detached, ironic, privatized culture taking shape by the end of the decade. Addressing demonstrating students in 1968, he told them, "What you as a revolutionary aspire to is a master. You will have one."[41] If Freud's typical patient struggled to achieve integrity, and if a whole line of analytic patients stretching from Ferenczi through Kohut viewed the analyst as a source of narcissistic supplies, then the typical Lacanian analysand was a highly developed student of signs, linguistic systems, spin, someone who took pride in knowing how to decode films, political events, and mass culture. If Lacan initiated a post-Freudian psychoanalysis, no longer linked to what some took to be the obsolete world of instincts, this shift coincided with the new, post-Fordist empowerment of the consumer. Reflecting this coincidence, the Lacanian world was a well-dressed one, valuing appearances precisely because it understood that they are "only" appearances.

After the defeat of the 1968 French general strike, a few younger French intellectuals repudiated Lacan's "return to Freud." Thus, Gilles Deleuze and Felix Guattari's 1972 *Anti-Oedipus* likened psychoanalysis to "the Russian Revolution; we don't know when it started going bad." Nonetheless, that moment soon passed. Although Lacan turned to mathematical formalism, seeking to describe the "impossible spaces" of the mind through Möbius strips, toruses, Escher objects, and Borromean knots, he retained his audience. In 1978, after a minor car accident, he seemed diminished. At the opening session of his seminar for the new academic year, in the presence of a silent and stunned audience, he lost his capacity to speak. According to Roudinesco: "Everyone stared at the old man, deprived of the sublime voice that had held Freudian France breathless for thirty years. . . . 'It doesn't matter,' the audience responded, 'we still love you.' "[42]

Lacan's vast and still continuing influence derived from his creative response to the crisis that psychoanalysis faced in the 1960s. Ego psychology, the center of psychoanalysis since the 1920s, was in irreversible decline. Like other theorists of the period, Lacan realized that the psychology of authority had collapsed back into the theory of narcissism. But unlike Kohut, whose affirmative attitude toward narcissism spelled the final dissolution of psychoanalysis into mass culture, and unlike Marcuse, with his utopian privileging of primary narcissism, which in principle could never be institutionalized, Lacan devised a shrewd and practical strategy aimed at preserving the critical function of psychoanalysis. In doing so, he effectively contributed to the further complication of the threefold promise of modernity. With regard to autonomy, he rejected the demands for recognition and affirmation in favor of a nuanced and critical attitude toward narcissism. With regard to women's equality, he rejected the efforts to transform psychoanalysis into a mother-centered theory of child development, reintroducing the significance of the father and sexual difference. And with regard to democracy, he rejected Marcuse's Marxist-inspired mythology of plenitude, grasping the need to resituate psychoanalysis in a new social field, that of democratic, consumerist capitalism.[43]

Like the great, practical clerics, such as the Anglicans and the Lutherans, who recognized that the extremist sects of the Reformation could not reform Christianity, Lacan understood that if the insights of the "second Freud" were to be preserved, psychoanalysis needed to make its peace with the state. But he also recognized that the explosions of the sixties could not be undone. Just as Luther destroyed the papacy's claims to universal sovereignty while legitimating national churches, Lacan destroyed the IPA's hegemony (its St. Peter's Cathedral located in New York City) while facilitating the growth of psychoanalysis in southern Europe and Latin America. Coinciding with the political counterrevolution that followed the sixties, the ambiguities, paradoxes, and hermetic language that Lacan placed at the center of psychoanalysis helped it to survive in Latin America under the dictatorships. Thus, Lacan accomplished what neither Luther nor Freud ever could: he helped introduce a genuinely personal ethic into the Catholic world.

By 1968 the psychoanalytic church stood rigid, orthodox, ossified, and nakedly hypocritical. Ideas it had once bravely pioneered had become doxa. Efforts at internal reform had failed. Calls to move beyond Freud, to historicize Freud, or to return to Freud had largely foundered. At the gates of the church, the rebellious dissenters, the protestants, the saints all gathered. As in the history of religion, there were finally two alternatives: the antinomian, who goes to the depths of the self, seeking a deeper, more genuine truth, and the Arminian, who goes outward to reform morals and collective behavior.

During the 1960s, the question of personal life had primarily taken the antinomian form of alternative lifestyles, drugs, music, sexuality, and sanctified communities or communes. Beginning around 1968, however, the surrealist, countercultural, and carnivalesque elements of the New Left reached their high point. It was as if the private was becoming public; the issues that Freud described as intrapsychic and familial were acted out on a social scale and on a political stage. As previously private and repressed experiences—sexuality, family, gender—were externalized, antinomianism gave way to Arminianism, that is, to the attempt to build political movements. Psychoanalysis, historically, studied "individuals." By the early seventies, however, the actors involved in the politics of the family were no longer individuals but *groups* with identities centered on gender, sexuality, and race. Increasingly essentialized—understood as rooted in the body and not in the mind—these identities served as the basis of the new politics.

The transition from antinomianism to Arminianism occurred against the background of world-shattering events. The fiery war in Vietnam, memorialized in such quasi-surreal works as Michael Herr's *Dispatches* and Tim O'Brien's *The Things They Carried,* reached an acme in the January 1968 Tet offensive. April brought an uprising in Prague, May a worker/student general strike in Paris. By the end of the year, De Gaulle had lost power in France, and in the United States the New Deal coalition had collapsed and Martin Luther King Jr. and Robert Kennedy had been assassinated. In Mexico City, left-wing students were massacred at the university. Soon afterward in Chile, Paraguay, Brazil, Argentina, and Uruguay, New Left activists were "disappeared," in some cases thrown live from military aircraft. Against such a background, and under the saturated light of TV and film cameras ("the whole world is watching"), a final effort was made to transpose the Freudian view of the psyche onto the sociological and political plane.

Narcissism again served as the guiding concept—this time, however, under the rubric of identity. Narcissism, in the Freudian lexicon, had referred not just to the individual but also to groups based on identification: one's race, nation, or ethnic origin. The fact that individuals shared a common ego ideal is what made them members of a group, rather than a collection of individuals. But psychoanalysis looked at group identity from a first-person perspective. The crucial point about the sixties focus on identity was its third-person point of view. As Jean-Paul Sartre argued in *Anti-Semite and Jew,* it was the *other* who defined the individual as "black," "gay," or "female." As a new politics emerged, centered on the self or identity, it confronted, transfigured, and absorbed much of classical psychoanalysis.[44]

Anticipated by the turn toward "other-directedness" and recognition, the New Left's utopian fusion of the unconscious and the communal precipitated the shift from psychoanalysis to identity politics. The "antipsychiatry" movement of the 1950s was a critical turning point. As we saw in chapter 1, modern psychiatry began with the idea that madness was a "mind-forged manacle." Antipsychiatry, which conflated psychoanalysis

with psychiatry, repudiated the idea that madness was a psychical disturbance at all.

The roots of antipsychiatry lay within psychoanalysis. Anglo-American
antipsychiatry, exemplified by Ronald David Laing, descended from British
object-relations theory. Trained as a psychiatrist at the University of Glas-
gow, Laing joined the staff of the Tavistock Clinic in 1956, where he worked
with D. W. Winnicott, Melanie Klein, and Susan Isaacs, and underwent an
analysis with Charles Rycroft. For Laing, psychoanalysis was "the first lifting of the veil—the first detachment from the objects of consciousness to
look at consciousness itself." At the same time, Erving Goffman's work
taught Laing "how effective a force for control benevolent institutionalization could be."[45] In the early sixties, with Thomas Szasz and others, Laing
began to describe schizophrenia as a condition imposed on the individual
by the psychiatrist, not as an intrapsychic condition.[46]

Michel Foucault was the other great exponent of antipsychiatry. His
first full-length book, *Madness and Civilization* (1963), described psychiatry as "a monologue of reason about madness," rather than a dialogue in
which the voices of unreason spoke for themselves.[47] The common thread
linking the psychiatrist and the psychoanalyst, according to Foucault,
was that both were representatives of order. Nonetheless, psychoanalysis
had added something new. Whereas earlier forms of control, such as hypnosis, reduced their subjects to objects, Freud had invented a technique
through which free subjects reduce themselves to slavery, abjectly seeking
an ever-receding and impossible self-knowledge. Deeply ambivalent about
Freud, Foucault called his entire oeuvre—which covered prisons, military
institutions, clinics, scientific institutions, and hospitals—an "archaeology
of psychoanalysis."

The redefinition of madness in interpersonal and social terms was only
the first step in the undoing of psychoanalysis. Just as the Enlightenment
discovery of the psychological character of madness had paved the way for
modern psychiatry, so a psychological approach to the new woman (i.e., the
hysteric) and the homosexual (i.e., the bisexual male) had paved the way for
psychoanalysis. In the 1960s, however, such concepts as femininity, hysteria,
and, indeed, repression, as well as homosexuality, perversion, and infantile
sexuality, all came under attack. The result was a second great step toward
the politics of identity.

As early as the 1930s, Benjamin Spock had stopped practicing analysis
because of his disquiet over an "intensely feministic" female patient who
"argued fiercely against every interpretation for over two years."[48] But
Spock encountered his patient at a time when the family system still pre-

sumed a full-time mother, and when living outside the family could be difficult and unusual. By the sixties, however, the late-twentieth-century revolution in family life was well under way. In that context, a New York analyst told Betty Friedan that for twenty years he had repeatedly found himself "having to superimpose Freud's theory of femininity on the psychic life of my patients" in a way that he was no longer willing to do. He treated one woman for two years before facing "her real problem—that it was not enough for her to be just a housewife and mother. One day she had a dream that she was teaching a class. I could not dismiss the powerful yearning of this housewife's dream as penis envy. . . . I told her: 'I can't analyze this dream away. You must do something about it.' "[49]

Second-wave feminism politicized this analyst's realization. Asserting that it would deal with the realms of sexuality and personal life that first-wave feminism (the suffrage movement) had neglected, second-wave feminism initially defined itself against analysis. Thus, according to Kate Millett's 1970 *Sexual Politics,* psychoanalysis had been "a superbly timed accusation" against twentieth-century feminism and against "any woman unwilling to 'stay in her place.' "[50] For Shulamith Firestone, the patriarchal family had a "Freudian structure," which feminists needed to dismantle. And for Gayle Rubin, psychoanalysis was a "feminist theory *manqué.*"[51]

Whereas psychoanalysis was a theory of intrapsychic reality, Millett, Firestone, and Rubin called for an attack on the social and political structures of male oppression. Simultaneously, the women's movement turned to "consciousness raising," group discussions of the oppression women shared; "individual explanations" were officially discouraged. What had been forbidden or suspended within psychoanalysis—"acting out"—became privileged. The Oedipus complex was reinterpreted as a "power psychology." Penis envy was actually "power envy."[52] Because she had supposedly seized control of her destiny in rejecting psychoanalysis, Freud's Dora became a feminist icon. For Hélène Cixous, she was "the one who resists the system, the one who cannot stand that the family and society are founded on the body of women, bodies despised, rejected, bodies that are humiliated once they have been used."[53] The farewell of Erica Jong's heroine to her analyst in Jong's 1973 *Fear of Flying* was emblematic: " 'Don't you see that men have always defined femininity as a means of keeping women in line? Why should I listen to you about what it means to be a woman? Are you a woman? Why shouldn't I listen to myself for once? And to other women?' . . . As in a dream (I never would have believed myself capable of it) I got up from the couch (how many years had I been lying there?), picked up my pocketbook, and walked . . . out. . . . I was free!"[54]

Women's liberation: successor to psychoanalysis
as a theory and practice of personal life (1970)

In fact, twentieth-century women had been too deeply involved with psychoanalysis to simply reject it. Thus, within a very few years a new, feminist psychoanalysis emerged. In 1974 Juliet Mitchell's *Psychoanalysis and Feminism* challenged the then-prevailing feminist orthodoxy by arguing that Freud's theories provided an analysis of a patriarchal culture, not a defense of one.[55] Criticizing the overemphasis on the external, Mitchell castigated such thinkers as Millett and Firestone for getting "rid of mental life." For them, she wrote, "it all actually happens . . . there is no other sort of reality than social reality." Nonetheless, Mitchell herself characterized the patriarchal unconscious as the reflection of a patriarchal social structure centered on kinship. The main point—namely, the way in which the rise of personal life changed the relations between the social and the psychological, and therefore the meaning of gender difference—tended to be ignored.

Gay identity also drew on older criticisms of psychoanalysis. After World War II Alfred Kinsey, perusing the newly published notes of the Wednesday Psychological Society, found himself "appalled . . . to read how these early analysts treated masturbation as though it were a sickness and a sign of immaturity."[56] But while feminists were ambivalent about psychoanalysis, gay men considered it the enemy incarnate.[57] In a not untypical case, Howard Brown, commissioner of health in New York City, had been told by his analyst that he "was inherently impaired because of his sexual orientation." "If I could not change it," he said, "I was doubly a failure."

Brown "left analysis convinced that [he] had no talents." It took him twenty years to recover. At a 1973 meeting of the American Psychiatric Association, a roomful of psychiatrists heard a paper on the use of aversive conditioning techniques for sexual deviation. Shouts of "Vicious!" "Torture!" and "Where did you take your residency, Auschwitz?" filled the air. As the paper ended, demonstrators exploded: "We've listened to you, now you listen to us."[58] Urged by analysts such as Judd Marmor, who had long sought to change analytic thinking concerning homosexuality, the APA dropped the classification of homosexuality as a disease in 1973.

In classical psychoanalysis, one could understand a homosexual object choice psychologically, but there was no such entity as "a homosexual." In the course of the seventies, however, homosexuals began to understand themselves as persons with a distinct way of life who belonged to a historically specific community.[59] In that context, efforts to understand the psychology of homosexuality began to seem bigoted, like efforts to understand the psychology of race. The last thing homosexuals felt they needed was psychoanalysis; they needed services, community institutions, and political organizations. Psychotherapy could be useful, but only if it began by understanding the social determinants of seemingly individual problems. So powerful was the pull of identity that many female homosexuals rejected even feminist reworkings of psychoanalysis because they theorized women in relation to men. Adrienne Rich's "Compulsory Heterosexuality and Lesbian Existence" asserted that the "woman-identified woman" or lesbian had no reference to any larger whole and had nothing to do with sexuality. Rather, lesbianism was an identity based on membership in a community.

During the 1920s Freud had predicted that the analytic movement would suffer a "lingering death" after he passed on.[60] By the late seventies, the psychoanalytic category that had first linked sexuality to modernity, namely, hysteria, had disappeared as a clinical entity. In its place stood not only identity movements and communities but also chronic fatigue syndrome, recovered-memory syndrome, multiple-personality syndrome, satanic ritual abuse, and alien abduction. As new churches emerged, the psychoanalytic hegemony faded into history.

A mere four decades passed between the time Martin Luther nailed his ninety-five theses to the cathedral door and the years in which the Counter-Reformation stalled Protestantism's expansive outward thrust. By then, the sects had all fallen to quarreling among themselves and even Protestants agreed that the Reformation itself needed reforming. So it was with psychoanalysis. By the end of the sixties, the great Freudian church had given way to a new, desacralized, "married" clergy. Three great bodies of thought

existed—ego psychology, object relations, and Lacanianism—but they had lost any sense of their relations to one another. Outside the vastly diminished realm of psychoanalysis, authority had shifted to the laity, especially to women and gays. While Freud's imago remained potent, it was cut off from any effective basis in social institutions and would prove unexpectedly vulnerable to attack. Nevertheless, as with the Protestant Reformation, the Freudian upheaval had established a permanent point of reference in the inner life of the West, one to which later upheavals would return.

PSYCHOANALYSIS
IN OUR TIME

Patricide is a bad idea. . . . It is not necessary to slay your father, time will slay him, that is a virtual certainty. Your true task lies elsewhere. . . . You must become your father, but a paler, weaker version of him. . . . Your contribution will not be a small one.

—Donald Barthelme, *The Dead Father* (1975)

In its great days, psychoanalysis stood at the confluence of two distinct currents. One was scientific. Its most important point of reference was the Darwinian vision of the human being as an organism driven by internal needs that it sought to satisfy in specific environmental settings. This current expressed itself in the close relations between psychoanalysis and neurophysiology: for example, in the idea that the instincts were on the "border" between the soma and the psyche, or in the idea that the mind discharged tension or acted reflexively, in ways that were similar to the nervous system. It also led to the view that such characteristics of the psyche as the developmental stages of sexuality, or the functions of the ego, were the product of a long evolutionary history, the continual adaptation of inner and outer realities.

The other stream was humanistic. Its most important expression was the analytic focus on the moral struggle of the human being, a struggle that arose in relation to the parents and that ended in the confrontation with death. This stream drew on literary sources such as the Hebrew Bible and the Greek tragedians, on Shakespeare, Goethe, and Dostoyevsky, and on modernist literature and philosophy, even when psychoanalysis disavowed them; and it also responded to the need for an everyday or "folk" under-standing of psychological life. Freud fused these two currents into an extra-ordinary new synthesis, neither wholly scientific nor wholly humanistic. What made this synthesis both coherent and compelling was the discovery of a new object: the idiosyncratic, meaning-saturated, morally inflected psychical life of the human being. This new conception of the human sub-ject resonated with the forms of personal life that emerged on a mass scale with the second industrial revolution.

The psychoanalytic conception of the human subject both complicated and deepened the Enlightenment project. In its origins, the Freudian stress on contingency and idiosyncrasy was aimed at uncovering the limits, the "mind-forged manacles," that constrained the Enlightenment's active, rational subject. In fact, however, Freudianism vastly extended the Enlight-enment sense of individual responsibility to cover not only deliberate, con-scious, rational decisions but also thoughts and actions that are intentional but unconscious. Encouraging the capacity to look at oneself objectively—"analytically"—and to enter empathically into another person's inner world, analysis promoted an enormous expansion of the moral capacity. The vanguard of an epochal social transformation, it generated a new ethic, one that assumed that a meaningful life necessitated self-reflection in depth. In the period of analytic hegemony, this ethic was imbued with the passion of a calling.

Always embattled, the psychoanalytic conception of the human subject was drastically weakened during the 1960s. By the following decade, the analytic focus on individual responsibility and self-knowledge had given way to group-oriented projects of recognition and identity. Much of his-toric analysis disappeared into a new world marked by the ubiquity of the therapeutic mode, the predominance of celebrity and confession, the colos-sal, dreamlike screens of 24/7 spectacle, and a new porosity between the public and the private. Together, these developments weakened the coher-ence of the broader analytic project.

That project had drawn its strength from its ability to integrate its sci-entific and its humanistic currents. In the 1970s these currents parted ways. Psychoanalysis divided into two divergent projects: a quasi-medical thera-peutic practice aimed at treating mental and emotional disorders, and a set of new approaches to the study of culture. The two new projects—the "therapeutic" and the "hermeneutic"—underwent separate development. The scientific lineage of psychoanalysis gave way to neuroscience, brain research, and psychopharmacology, at first in the United States and then, more slowly, elsewhere. The humanistic and literary lineage gave way to cultural studies, feminist theory, and "queer" theory, and to the study of identity, narrative, and representation. The ethic of self-reflection fell away entirely as new versions of mind-cure "empowerment" triumphed. The history of psychoanalysis since 1968 is a history of this dispersion.

Paradoxically, the ego psychologists had sowed the seeds for the transformation of psychoanalysis into neuroscience and pharmacology when they validated the medical model for psychological conditions. The medical model is based on a sharp distinction between the illness and the patient. Diagnosing the illness on the basis of symptoms or tests, it specifies treatment accordingly. Analysis, by contrast, had always been relational. It sought to bring insight, work through a transferential relationship, or give support, not simply to remove symptoms and modify behavior. Ironically, as we saw, the more the U.S. ego psychologists claimed the mantle of the medical model, the more their critics attacked them as unscientific.

Some psychiatrists had always protested that analysis failed to meet the criteria of medicine, but in the 1960s these voices were strengthened. Earlier, Freud had embarrassed psychoanalysts by ignoring genetics and holding to Lamarckianism.[1] By the sixties, child-development researchers had thrown such analytic notions as "primary narcissism" and "the early breast" into question by showing that the newborn responds to the outside world almost immediately, is stimulus-seeking as well as tension-reducing, and responds to a gestalt rather than to an isolatable experience such as "sucking" or "the breast."[2] Needless to say, the furor surrounding penis envy, and the fact that the American Psychoanalytic Association decided the question of the medical standing of homosexuality by a vote of the membership, did not strengthen the aspirations of psychoanalysis to scientific standing.

In 1980 the bible of North American psychiatry, the *Diagnostic and Statistical Manual of Mental Disorders* (*DSM*), was revised to take account of the critics. Whereas *DSM-II,* published in 1968, was largely psychoanalytic, *DSM-III* tried to assimilate the medical and the psychodynamic models. Explicitly citing Freud's psychiatric predecessor, Emil Kraepelin, whose stock now rose, it distinguished two main diagnostic categories. Axis I was primarily biological and included schizophrenia, depression, bipolar disorder (manic depression), and obsessive-compulsive disorder. Axis II was more psychodynamic and included the narcissistic, schizoid, borderline, and antisocial personalities. Complaining that analysts had deprecated "the basic psychiatric technique through which so much progress was made in the 19th century," most psychiatrists viewed *DSM-III* as a "defense of the medical model as applied to psychiatric problems."[3]

Drugs, infinitely more cost-effective than analysis, and converging with tendencies toward social pacification, marked the turning point. Thorazine, the first important antipsychotic medication, was introduced in 1954, but it was a crude instrument with onerous side effects. Research into the neuro-transmitters led to the marketing of Prozac (fluoxetine hydrochloride) in 1987, followed quickly by Paxil and Zoloft, for treatment of depression. The side effects of these drugs were more easily tolerated than those of earlier treatments, and the drugs were highly effective at removing symptoms. Meanwhile, the scientific standing of psychoanalysis was also subject to legal tests. A landmark case involved an internist, Rafael Osheroff, who had been treated for depression by analysts in 1979 at Chestnut Lodge without success. After seven frustrating months, his family pulled him out and sent him to a nonanalytic mental hospital, where medications quickly lifted his spirits. The family sued, and in 1988 the case was settled to the embarrass-ment of the analysts.

Breakthroughs in neuroscience completed the transition to the medical model. Magnetic resonance imaging (MRI) and positron emission tomog-raphy (PET) made it possible to observe the brain during mental opera-tions. Steven Hyman and Eric Nestler's 1993 *Molecular Foundations of Psychiatry* posited the neural structure of the brain as the guidepost to treat-ment.[4] One psychiatrist recorded his reaction to this book's "really coherent view of brain function and the way it affects speech. I couldn't believe that anyone could still believe, as [analysts] did, that stuttering was rooted in childhood conflict. I mean you'd see psychoanalytic interpretations of ulcers, that the introjected mother was eating the stomach lining, before they realized that ulcers were caused by bacteria."[5]

During the eighties, psychiatrists pursued a pluralist approach, combin-ing drugs with psychodynamic and psychosocial treatments. In the nineties, managed care ended pluralism. Adolf Grünbaum's 1984 *Founda-tions of Psychoanalysis* seemed to many to settle the matter.[6] Viewing science exclusively as a series of testable hypotheses and not as a means of investi-gating a conceptual object, Grünbaum excluded psychoanalysis from the realm of science, thereby reinforcing managed care's reliance on quantita-tive comparative-outcome studies, behavioral techniques, and psychophar-macology.[7] From this perspective, the explanatory foundation of mental disorders lay not in the unique life each person leads but rather "beyond person-hood, in biological microstructures that escape uniqueness."[8]

If psychoanalysis has not fared well as a scientifically grounded medical practice, it might seem to have done better as a cultural hermeneutic. After

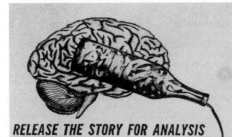

Psychiatric-drug advertisement drawing
on psychodynamic language (*American Journal
of Psychiatry*, August 1952)

the sixties, the application of analytic concepts to cultural phenomena such as gender, nationality, and sexual identity proliferated in almost every area of the humanities. Far from challenging the reduction of psychoanalysis to behaviorism and pharmacology, however, these "cultural studies" effectively complemented it. Praising Freud as an artist, the culturalists concurred that he was no scientist. For example, Harold Bloom asserted that Freud's only literary rivals were Plato, Montaigne, Shakespeare, and "the anonymous primal narrator of Genesis, Exodus and Numbers."[9] But Bloom's goal was to exalt the humanities *against* science, whereas Freudianism had sought to make reasonable connections between the two.

As we saw, Freud's grip on the imagination of men and women until the late sixties derived from the fact that, like Dostoyevsky, Shakespeare, and the authors of the Hebrew Bible, he focused on such core aspects of human life as childhood, sexuality, love, family, and finitude. By contrast, the sixties generation placed its hopes on a radical political culture, and on the relationships that culture sustained. The great post-Freudian texts of the sixties preached the relative insignificance of the individual per se. Although their aim was to enhance personal life by insisting on its social and political dimensions, they inadvertently ushered in group-oriented theories that supplanted analysis. As one great slope of the psychoanalytic edifice disappeared into psychopharmacology, the other slid into identity politics.

The effect was to absorb psychoanalysis into a new "recognition" or "other-directed" paradigm that was *un*psychological and *anti*psychological. This absorption proceeded in two steps. First, analytic concepts were restated in behavioral and interpersonal terms. Thus, the meaning of bisexuality shifted from different identifications and inclinations *within* the individual to the question of which sex the individual slept with. Homosexuality lost its connotation of a universal, infantile, sexual current and came to mean an object choice *tout court.* The focus on infancy and psychical conflict was abandoned at the same moment as the need to attain a universal or impersonal point of view was scorned. Too often the results were studies of male/female relations focused exclusively on what divided men and women, ignoring their common experiences, including the experience of having to deal with sexual difference.

The second step sought to redeem psychoanalysis, but as a theory that "deconstructed" the individual. Seeking to dispel the "essentialism" of the first step, the second wave of cultural theorists sought to submerge individual identity in "discourse." Thus, Leo Bersani praised Freud's texts for making "problematic the identity of the thinker 'in' or 'behind' the discourse."[10] Julia Kristeva replaced the "tacitly male ego" in Freud's texts with "a series of shifting identities, held in check . . . only by the arbitrary imposition of paternal law."[11] For such theorists, the destabilization of identity was taken as a harbinger of a more progressive society.

As with neuroscience and pharmacology, the turn toward cultural studies produced advances: new approaches to the psychology of women, the lifting of the taboo on homosexuality, and sensitivity to racial and cultural difference. Perhaps one of the most enduring of these advances will prove to be Jacques Derrida's deconstruction. In 1964 Derrida criticized Foucault's *Madness and Civilization* for arguing that madness exemplified a principle of rebellion and transgression located outside society. Madness, Derrida insisted, was *inside* the "empire of reason," which could only be critiqued from within. In later works Derrida applied this analytic insight to psychoanalysis itself. Madness and transgression, he argued, had been suppressed

Freud crushed under the weight of identity politics
(*Der Spiegel,* 1998)

within psychoanalysis because of its overly sharp distinctions between internal and external, real and false, conscious and unconscious. Although Derrida was not an analyst, he has invented a new mode of writing, one that dramatizes the way in which the unconscious interrupts, postpones, contradicts, distracts from, and intensifies all intended flows of meaning.[12] Yet, in his work, too, the concreteness and specificity of the psychological realm tend to disappear in the endless play of linguistic ambiguity.

Since the 1960s, therefore, the once-daunting psychoanalytic project has fragmented. With the splitting apart of its scientific and cultural dimensions, Freudianism as such has been cast adrift. Yet the analytic profession has done more than merely survive. As in the Reformation, during which clerical power passed to ordinary men and women, humbled analysts continue to minister to everyday life. In fact, the long-postponed de-idealization of psychoanalysis is finally occurring, as newly modest analytic societies turn inward, reinvent themselves at the margins, and develop a new eclecticism.

The destruction of North American ego psychology's hegemony over psychoanalysis was a prerequisite for this shift. As the sixties waned, and as U.S. ego psychologists lost their fortress in medicine, they also seemed to lose their sense of having anything unique to say. In a 1979 letter to the *New York Times,* Alan J. Eisnitz, president of the New York Psychoanalytic Association, defended Freud by listing his "influential ideas," such as sibling rivalry, the special role of dreams, and "insights into imagination and creativity," but made no attempt to articulate any conception of the analytic project as a whole.[13] A decade later, Robert Wallerstein, president of the International Psychoanalytic Association, described the theoretical positions of analysts—ego psychology, object relations, Lacanianism—as "large scale explanatory metaphors . . . symbolisms, . . . pluralistic . . . articles of faith."[14] Mary Douglas compared North American psychoanalysis to "a ship at anchor, once fitted out for a great voyage, but sails now furled, ropes flapping, motion stilled. It is not as if theoretical winds were lacking to drive it. But the motive to go somewhere is missing."[15]

As its medical center crumbled, women and gays made strides toward taking over the U.S. analytic profession. In 1988 a long-resisted class-action suit forced analytic institutes to admit non-M.D.s, most of whom were women. Although a medical wing survives, the strongest voices in North American psychoanalysis today are feminists and supporters of gay liberation. The dominant approach is "relational," premised on "correcting" Freud's mistakes. In 1996 the weak identity of American psychoanalysis became shockingly apparent when Frederick Crews unleashed a series of well-promoted attacks on Freud and analysis that went largely unanswered.[16]

The situation elsewhere was more upbeat. In France, by 1974 there were three important analytic groups, each with its own journal: the official Société Psychanalytique de Paris (publisher of *Études Freudiennes*), with nearly five hundred members, among the largest analytic societies in the world; Lacan's École Freudienne (publisher of *Scilicet*); and the French Psychoanalytic Association, centered around Jean Laplanche and Jean-Bertrand Pontalis, with its publication (*La Nouvelle revue de psychanalyse*). Thanks to Lacan's influence, every intellectual in France today reads Freud seriously. New thinkers, such as Didier Anzieu, Piera Aulagnier, Janine Chasseguet-Smirgel, Julia Kristeva, and André Green, have expanded the parameters of both analysis and philosophy. In 1994, when the official International Psychoanalytical Association had fewer than nine thousand members, about three thousand of whom were North Americans, France boasted about five thousand non-IPA analysts, four-fifths of them Lacanian.

Most striking has been the extraordinary development of psychoanalysis in Latin America, which in 1994 registered 2,200 analysts in the IPA. As we saw, Freudianism was introduced into Buenos Aires in the forties and fifties by Jewish refugees from Hitler. It witnessed explosive growth and schisms in the sixties, first under the influence of Hannah Segal's Kleinianism, and then through the Lacanianism that flourished under the dictators. After the return of democracy, Buenos Aires billed itself as the "world capital of psychoanalysis." When the IPA met there in 1991, it commanded a level of news coverage comparable to that which the International Chess Association commands in Moscow, or the World Series in New York. As for Brazil, it currently has eleven flourishing societies and has produced its own biographies of Freud and studies of psychoanalysis, eschewing the North American and Western European biases.

Along with decentralization and theoretical pluralism, the history of psychoanalysis since the sixties has been marked by the return of difficulties that were never mastered during the classical period. One of these, the Jewish origins of psychoanalysis, and the influence of Jewish history and thought on the analytic ethos, underwent a kind of normalization.[17] Thus, in 1977 Hebrew University in Jerusalem established the world's first chair of psychoanalysis.[18] Anna Freud, eighty-two years old and the single most important link to the founding father, sent a paper conceding that analysis was a "Jewish science." This "can serve as a Title of Honour," she added blithely.[19] Meanwhile, Jewish analysts had always refused to allow the IPA to meet in Germany. In 1985 they relented. An exhibit illustrating the history of the Göring Institute dominated the meeting, held at Hamburg. A German analyst remarked, "Thank God that you have been willing to come; for 40 years we have been living alone with our shame."[20] Even so, the Jewish question remained symptomatic for some. Thus, in his 1988 autobiography, *The Long Wait*, the English/Punjabi analyst Masud Khan described exulting at throwing off his "Yiddish shackles," and complained that the "Judaic-Yiddish-Jewish bias of psychoanalysis" had always cramped his "personal ethnic style."[21]

Normalization progressed in other senses as well. In 1979 the profession founded an internal historical organization led by Alain de Mijolla, even as its larger history was being written by outsiders, such as Paul Roazen, Henri Ellenberger, Peter Gay, Michael Molnar, Elisabeth Roudinesco, Frank Sulloway, Alexander Etkind, and Carl Schorske. New journals, notably *Psychoanalysis and History*, replaced hagiography with established methods of historical research. Peter Gay produced the first post-transferential biography of Sigmund Freud. The British, French, and German societies built major research collections. The figures that Ernest Jones tried to exclude from the canon, such as Otto Rank, were restored; and for many analysts, especially in the United States, Sándor Ferenczi's reputation came to rival Freud's. New translations of Freud's works were launched, providing alternatives to Strachey's *Standard Edition.*

But what, actually, is meant by normalization? Perhaps more than many other histories, the history of psychoanalysis is punctuated by traumas— that is, by catastrophes that remain "actively vital and yet incapable of resolution."[22] These include personal violations, misshapen lives, wasted years, destroyed documents, secret archives, forgotten lapses, and inexplicable ruptures. Normalization has not unfolded smoothly. The most explosive example of this has been the attempt to understand the single most important catastrophe in the history of psychoanalysis: not the rise of the Nazis but the weak response of analysts to the Nazis and, indeed, to the Holocaust itself.

Prior to the sixties, acceptance by the IPA had been taken as proof of a "place among the persecuted" for German analysts, allowing them "to escape from the burden of [their] national past." When radicals of 1968 became analysts, however, that cover became subject to critical scrutiny. In 1980, at a conference at Bamberg, the younger analysts exploded: "Who was your analyst?" "What were you doing?" "From what has come this feeling of mysteries, lies, the pathology of the reality sense?" Helmut Dahmer, Regine Lockot, Geoffrey Cocks, and others unearthed the history of the Göring Institute and the exclusion of Reich. In 1997 a leading German analyst, Werner Bohleber, attributed the absence of important theoretical developments in post-1968 German psychoanalysis to the fact that German analysts remained so utterly preoccupied with their past.[23]

The true soul of Latin American psychoanalysis can also be found in the experiences of torture, exile, and loss that the sixties left in their wake. Analysts driven into exile include Juan Carlos Volnovich, forced to flee Argentina and still practicing psychoanalysis in Cuba; Marcelo and Maren Viñar, tortured and then driven into exile from Uruguay for treating a Tupamaro; Elizabeth Lira, who worked with the church to restore democracy in El Salvador; Ignacio Martín-Baró, Central America's most important social psychologist, assassinated by U.S.-trained Salvadoran soldiers in 1989; and Marie Langer and other analysts of the Marxo-Freudian Performa and Defensa schools.[24] Many other analysts remained and practiced under the dictatorships. Today reconciliations are occurring. For example, Julia Braun, Marcelo Viñar, Emilio Rodriguez, Elizabeth Jelin, and others are studying the psychology of the "disappeared." Others use analysis to study the hybrid or mestizo identities and the misshapen masculinities that resulted from the colonial trauma. An analytic culture pervades these attempts to grapple with memory and history. In 1995 the Argentine army chief of staff apologized by referring to the "collective unconscious," the "work of mourning," and the need for "working through."[25]

The *samizdat* and other anticommunist movements that triumphed in 1989 allowed another broken cord of analytic history to be picked up. In Russia in 1979 Aron Belkin drew on analysis to explain the national malaise, suggesting that "identification with the Supreme Guide [Stalin] had crushed the family father figure, forced the individual to regard as diabolical any alternative . . . , and eventually caused the death of thought." Another reformer described "the obsessive identification with the father who had disappeared, the feeling of shame towards the father who had been deported or eliminated as an enemy of the people, and the solitude and wanderings of the son."[26] With glasnost, Freud's works were published in Russian for the first time since the early thirties. Andrei Zagdansky's 1989 film *Interpretation of Dreams* celebrated the event by counterposing readings from Freud's texts with archival film from Soviet history. Even in contemporary China, the banned postmodern novelist Wei Hui describes the heroine of his eponymous novel, *Shanghai Baby,* as promiscuous, aspiring to fame, and reading Freud.

In general, then, a psychoanalytic profession has survived both the psychopharmacological assault and the cultural turn. What may not have survived, however, is the analytic ethic of self-exploration of which psychoanalysis was once a part. How important, finally, would this loss be?

By its nature, a period of self-exploration such as the one described in this book will be short-lived. The normal direction of the mind is outward. Thus, the passing of intense interest in psychoanalysis—the interest that characterized its golden age—was to be expected. The question that has to be addressed now is what has been learned. It is not enough to reaffirm a belief in individual uniqueness and diversity. Personal life cannot survive unless it is embodied in actual practices, institutions, and ongoing attempts to gain systematic knowledge of individual psychology. Since psychoanalysis is unlikely to play the same role in the twenty-first century that it played in the twentieth, we may have to invent new institutions that encapsulate and build upon its insights if we want to preserve its achievements. To what extent we continue to rely on psychoanalysis, to what extent we invent successors to it, and what those successors might look like remain open questions.

However we answer those questions, it is not so much a mode of treatment as a set of understandings that we need to protect: that each

Time magazine in 1993: the question remains unanswered.

individual has an inner world that is, in good part, not only unconscious but repressed; that the individual's relations with others, especially loved ones, are permeated by the images and wishes of this unconscious world; that, psychologically, being a man or being a woman is the outcome of an idiosyncratic and precarious process, and that no one is simply one sex or the other; that there is, ultimately, an irreducible gap between the intrapsychic lives of individuals and the cultural, social, and political world in which they otherwise live; that when we speak of the unique value of the individual, it is the concrete, particular, and contingent individual, not an abstract locus of rights and reason, that we have in mind; that society and politics are driven not just by conscious interests and perceived necessities but also by unconscious motivations, anxieties, and half-spoken memories, and that even great nations can suffer traumas, change course abruptly, and regress.

The charisma of psychoanalysis, the enormous idealization it attracted, was a way of protecting these and related understandings, a way of protecting personal life itself. Can such understanding survive the decline of psychoanalysis? Have the global speedup, the near collapse of the boundary between the public and the private, and computerization, which reduces the psychology of meaning to the transfer of information, eviscerated intrapsychic experience? Do our new insights into race, nation, and gender obviate the need for individuals to understand their own unique individuality? Does our wish to be more attentive to "difference" mean that we no longer need a common notion of what it means to be a human being, or even a common language with which we can discuss the question? If so, we are facing a drastic impoverishment. We risk paying lip service to "older" ideals of personal life while embracing an empty conception of "rational choice." We risk congratulating ourselves on knowing our own minds at the very moment when we are being most effectively manipulated into compliance and assent.

Certainly, the present status of the threefold promise of modernity does not give cause for optimism. Autonomy, in the psychoanalytic era, implied a complex, lifelong awareness of interiority, not "empowerment" or utilitarian problem-solving. Women's equality meant the deepest possible engagement of the sexes with each other, not the celebration of femininity or the aspiration of women to become like men. Democracy entailed the capacity for self-reflection and self-criticism, not patriotic self-congratulation and partisan rapacity. The optimism that propelled psychoanalysis during its early history—an optimism associated with the first mass economic surplus in human evolution—is no longer easily available. When we search for optimism today, we need to look inward. In doing so, we will reveal once again our debt to the golden age of psychoanalysis from which we have so recently emerged.

Notes

Works frequently cited in the notes have been identified by the following abbreviations:

Freud–Abraham   Sigmund Freud and Karl Abraham. *A Psycho-analytic Dialogue: The Letters of Sigmund Freud and Karl Abraham, 1907–1926.* Edited by Hilda C. Abraham and Ernst L. Freud. Translated by Bernard Marsh and Hilda C. Abraham. New York: Basic Books, 1965.

Freud–Ferenczi   Sigmund Freud and Sándor Ferenczi. *The Correspondence of Sigmund Freud and Sándor Ferenczi.* Edited by Eva Brabant, Ernst Flazeder, and Patrizia Giampieri-Deutsch. 3 vols. Cambridge, Mass.: Harvard University Press, 1993.

Freud–Fliess   Sigmund Freud and Wilhelm Fliess. *The Complete Letters of Sigmund Freud to Wilhelm Fliess, 1887–1904.* Edited and translated by Jeffrey Moussaieff Masson. Cambridge, Mass.: Harvard University Press, 1985.

Freud–Jones   Sigmund Freud and Ernest Jones. *The Complete Correspondence of Sigmund Freud and Ernest Jones, 1908–1939.* Edited by R. Andrew Paskauskas. Cambridge, Mass.: Belknap Press of Harvard University Press, 1993.

Freud–Jung   Sigmund Freud and Carl G. Jung. *The Freud-Jung Letters: The Correspondence Between Sigmund Freud and C. G. Jung.* Edited by William McGuire. Translated by Ralph Manheim and R. F. C. Hull. Cambridge, Mass.: Harvard University Press, 1988.

Freud–Salomé   Sigmund Freud and Lou Andreas-Salomé. *Sigmund Freud and Lou Andreas-Salomé: Letters.* Edited by Ernst Pfeiffer. Translated by William and Elaine Robson-Scott. New York: Harcourt Brace Jovanovich, 1972.

Jones   Ernest Jones. *The Life and Work of Sigmund Freud.* Vol. 1, *The Formative Years and the Great Discoveries, 1856–1900;* vol. 2, *Years of Maturity, 1901–1919;* vol. 3, *The Last Phase, 1919–1939.* New York: Basic Books, 1953–57.

LSF   Sigmund Freud. *The Letters of Sigmund Freud, 1873–1939.* Edited by Ernst Freud and Lucie Freud. Translated by Tania and James Stern. New York: Basic Books, 1960.

SE   Sigmund Freud. *The Standard Edition of the Complete Psychological Works of Sigmund Freud.* Translated under the general editorship of James Strachey, in collaboration with Anna Freud, assisted by Alix Strachey and Alan Tyson. 24 vols. New York: Norton, 1976.

Introduction

1. Carl E. Schorske, *Fin-de-siècle Vienna: Politics and Culture* (New York: Knopf, 1980).
2. A more precise formulation would distinguish kinship, household, and family in this regard. In general, see Eli Zaretsky, *Capitalism, the Family, and Personal Life*, rev. ed. (1976; New York: Harper & Row, 1986).
3. Philip Rieff, *The Triumph of the Therapeutic: Uses of Faith After Freud* (New York: Harper & Row, 1966).
4. Claude Lévi-Strauss, "The Effectiveness of Symbols," in *Structural Anthropology* (Chicago: University of Chicago Press, 1983), pp. 186–205.
5. Marc Bloch, *The Royal Touch: Sacred Monarchy and Scrofula in England and France*, trans. J. E. Anderson (London: Routledge & Kegan Paul, 1973).
6. Max Weber's *The Social Psychology of the World's Religions* (1920–21) contrasted the Calvinist sense of responsibility to ethics premised on a pregiven fit between a larger, cosmic pattern and the inner world of the individual, such as Confucianism. But Weber did not contrast the Calvinist ethic to the twentieth century's sense of personal or psychological autonomy.
7. *SE*, vol. 15, p. 18.
8. S. N. Eisenstadt, ed., *Max Weber on Charisma and Institution Building: Selected Papers* (Chicago: University of Chicago Press, 1968).
9. The term "second industrial revolution" is sometimes ascribed to Patrick Geddes's *Cities in Evolution* (London: Williams & Norgate, 1915). Important discussions can be found in David Landes, *The Unbound Prometheus* (Cambridge, U.K.: Cambridge University Press, 1969), which emphasizes technological change and financial innovation, and Eric Hobsbawm, *Industry and Empire* (London: Weidenfeld & Nicholson, 1968), pp. 144–49, which points to the new role of science, the assembly line, and consumerism. Other useful discussions include N. Rosenberg, "The Growing Role of Science in the Innovation Process," in *Science, Technology and Society in the Time of Alfred Nobel*, ed. Carl Gustaf Bernhard et al. (Oxford: Oxford University Press, 1982), pp. 231–46; Peter Temin, "The Future of the New Economic History," *Journal of Interdisciplinary History* (Autumn 1981): 179–97; and James P. Hull, "From Rostow to Chandler to You: How Revolutionary Was the Second Industrial Revolution?" *Journal of European Economic History* 25 (Spring 1996): 191–208.

Chapter One

1. For the classic statement and "petty spite" quotation, see John Ruskin, *Sesame and Lilies: Two Lectures Delivered at Manchester in 1864* (New York: J. Wiley & Son, 1865).
2. William James, *Varieties of Religious Experience* (Cambridge, Mass.: Harvard University Press, 1985), pp. 6, 108–9.
3. "Almost liquid" is from Ruth B. Caplan, *Psychiatry and the Community in Nineteenth-Century America: The Recurring Concern with the Environment in the Prevention and Treatment of Mental Illness* (New York: Basic Books, 1969), p. 8. See also Robert Young, *Mind, Brain and Adaptation in the Nineteenth Century: Cerebral Localization and Its Biological Context from Gall to Ferrier* (Oxford: Clarendon Press, 1970), p. 15.
4. Dugald Stewart as quoted in Peter Gay, *The Enlightenment: An Interpretation* (New York: Knopf, 1966–69), vol. 2, p. 168. Voltaire extolled Locke for eschewing "romances of the soul," producing instead the means for writing its history. His *Lettres sur l'Anglais* is quoted in Ernst Cassirer, *The Philosophy of the Enlightenment* (Boston: Beacon Press, 1955), p. 94.
5. Marcel Gauchet and Gladys Swain, *La Pratique de l'esprit humain: L'institution asilaire et la révolution démocratique* (Paris: Gallimard, 1980). Psychiatrists, before this, had been custodians of asylums. Samuel Tuke, a Quaker, founded the first modern British asylum.
6. Long aware that legendary physicians elicited confidence through charisma, they now real-

ized that the ordinary doctor could be trained to elicit submission. Earlier Pinel stressed the unique personal gifts of Francis Willis, physician to George III. See Jan Ellen Goldstein, *Console and Classify: The French Psychiatric Profession in the Nineteenth Century* (Cambridge, U.K., and New York: Cambridge University Press, 1987), p. 86.

7. Benjamin Rush, *Medical Inquiries and Observations upon the Diseases of the Mind* (New York: Hafner, 1962), pp. 174–78.

8. The mind, Percy Shelley wrote, is its own place; it can make a heaven of hell and a hell of heaven. In general, see Meyer Howard Abrams, *The Mirror and the Lamp: Romantic Theory and the Critical Tradition* (New York: Oxford University Press, 1953).

9. Leon Chertok and Raymond de Saussure, *The Therapeutic Revolution, from Mesmer to Freud* (New York: Brunner/Mazel, 1979), pp. 5–14, 34–35; Henri Ellenberger, *The Discovery of the Unconscious: The History and Evolution of Dynamic Psychiatry* (New York: Basic Books, 1970), pp. 72, 155–56.

10. The technique, observed a magnetizer, utilized "the dominance that nature has given one sex over the other in order to attach and arouse." Ellenberger, *Discovery*, p. 160.

11. William James, *The Principles of Psychology*, 2 vols. (New York: H. Holt, 1890).

12. Jose M. Lopez Pinero, *The Historical Origins of the Concept of Neurosis* (London: Cambridge University Press, 1958), p. 58. Neurasthenia was first described by George Beard in an address to the American Neurological Society: see *Medical and Surgical Journal* 3, no. 217 (29 April 1869); James Gilbert, *Work Without Salvation: America's Intellectuals and Industrial Alienation, 1880–1910* (Baltimore: Johns Hopkins University Press, 1977), p. 33; Charles E. Rosenberg, "The Place of George M. Beard in Nineteenth-Century Psychiatry," *Bulletin of the History of Medicine* 36 (1962): 245–59; Gillian Brown, "The Empire of Agoraphobia," *Representations* 20 (Fall 1987): 148. For "Bovaryisme," see Yannick Ripa, *Women and Madness: The Incarceration of Women in Nineteenth-Century France* (Minneapolis: University of Minnesota Press, 1990), p. 62. For "amok," see Mardi Horowitz, ed., *Hysterical Personality Style and the Histrionic Personality Disorder* (Northvale, N.J.: Aronson, 1991).

13. In general, see Alan Krohn, *Hysteria: The Elusive Neurosis* (New York: International University Press, 1978).

14. Valéry is quoted in Theodore Zeldin, *France* (New York: Oxford University Press, 1979), vol. 2, p. 338. For Baudelaire, see Eugen Weber, *France: Fin de Siècle* (Cambridge, Mass.: Harvard University Press, 1986), p. 12. Breuer is quoted in Elaine Showalter, *The Female Malady: Women, Madness and the English Culture, 1830–1980* (New York: Pantheon Books, 1987), p. 158.

15. *The Diary of Alice James*, ed. Leon Edel (New York: Dodd, Mead, 1964), 26 October 1890 and 4 December 1891. Ruth Bernard Yeazell, *Sex, Politics, and Science in the Nineteenth-Century Novel* (Baltimore: Johns Hopkins University Press, 1986), p. 37.

16. Edward Shorter, "The First Great Increase in Anorexia Nervosa," *Journal of Social History* 20, no. 1 (Fall 1987): 77 ff.; Barbara Sicherman, "The Uses of a Diagnosis: Doctors, Patients, and Neurasthenia," *Journal of the History of Medical and Allied Sciences* 22, no. 1 (January 1977): 41. Originally called "nervous" or "functional illnesses," the neuroses, in Freud's later summary, "were considered with increasing certainty to be consequences of disturbances in emotional life." *SE*, vol. 12, p. 329.

17. *SE*, vol. 1, p. 10.

18. George Rosen, "Freud and Medicine in Vienna," in *Freud: The Man, His World, His Influence*, ed. Jonathan Miller (Boston: Little, Brown, 1972), p. 35. Of course, the French also attempted to demonstrate lesions postmortem.

19. Jan Goldstein, "The Hysteria Diagnosis and the Politics of Anticlericalism in Late-Nineteenth-Century France," *Journal of Modern History* 54 (June 1982): 216.

20. Daniel Pick, *Faces of Degeneration: A European Disorder, 1848–1918* (Cambridge, U.K.: Cambridge University Press, 1989), p. 100. Hippolyte Taine used Morel's theories to explain the "degeneracy" supposedly exemplified in the French Revolution and the Paris Commune.

21. Martha Evans, *Fits and Starts: A Genealogy of Hysteria in Modern France* (Ithaca, N.Y.: Cornell University Press, 1991), p. 21. For Le Bon, see Robert Gildea, *Barricades and Borders: Europe, 1800–1914* (New York: Oxford University Press, 1987), p. 388.

22. By 1889, 48 percent of the medical faculty, 22 percent of the law faculty, and 15 percent of the philosophy faculty were Jewish. In 1885, three years after Freud received his medical degree, 41.5 percent of Vienna's medical students were Jewish. Robert S. Wistrich, *The Jews of Vienna in the Age of Franz Joseph* (Oxford: Oxford University Press, 1990); Fredrich Heer, "Freud, the Viennese Jew," in Miller, *Freud,* pp. 1–20.

23. There is still an unpublished correspondence. James Barclay, "Franz Brentano and Sigmund Freud," *Journal of Existentialism* 5, no. 17 (Summer 1964): 8; John Toews, "Historicizing Psychoanalysis: Freud in His Time and for Our Time," *Journal of Modern History* 63 (September 1991): 538–41.

24. Toews, "Historicizing." As Frederick Gregory has written, late-nineteenth-century thinkers accused Kant "of ignoring the facts in his defense of innate ideas. Causality, space, time, number etc., had their origin not in the structure of the mind, but from man's experience in the world." Gregory, *Scientific Materialism in Nineteenth-Century Germany* (Dordrecht, Holland, and Boston: D. Reidel, 1977), p. 147.

    Kant's influence runs through Freud's whole life; he read and understood him as a teenager. William J. McGrath, *Freud's Discovery of Psychoanalysis: The Politics of Hysteria* (Ithaca, N.Y.: Cornell University Press, 1986), describes Freud's letter to his friend Silberstein of 11 April 1875 as revealing his "highly sophisticated grasp of the Kantian framework." In 1882, the year after receiving his medical degree, Freud purchased and extensively annotated *The Critique of Pure Reason.* His private library, which can be visited in London, is arranged historically; it begins with archaeology and ancient history, proceeds to modern literature, and ends with science, sexology, and psychoanalysis. But the *Critique,* along with Locke's *Essay Concerning Human Understanding,* is shelved out of order, amid archaeology and prehistory, reflecting his view that the categories of the mind arose out of the species' struggle with nature. Later Freud described the unconscious as "an extension of the corrections begun by Kant." Just as Kant warned us not to take time or extension as identical with external reality, "so psychoanalysis bids us not to set conscious perception in the place of the unconscious mental process which is its object." Sigmund Freud, "The Unconscious," in *General Psychological Theory* (New York: Collier Books, 1963), p. 121.

25. *SE,* vol. 20, p. 9.

26. Freud to Bernays, 24 November 1885, *LSF,* p. 185.

27. Freud to Fliess, 28 December 1887, *Freud–Fliess,* p. 17.

28. Quoted in Peter J. Swales, "Freud, His Teacher and the Birth of Psychoanalysis," in Paul E. Stepansky, *Freud, Appraisals and Reappraisals: Contributions to Freud Studies* (Hillsdale, N.J.: Analytic Press, 1986), vol. 1, p. 49.

29. In 1889 he visited Nancy in France for further training. Hippolyte Bernheim taught him the "concentration" and "pressure" techniques. When a patient was unable to recall, Freud applied pressure to his forehead and assured him that while the pressure lasts, he will "see before him a recollection in the form of a picture" or idea. When Freud stopped the pressure, he would ask quietly, as if there could be no question of disappointment: "What did you see?" or "What occurred to you?" 31 October 1883, quoted in Jones, vol. 1, p. 247. In his *Autobiographical Study* (1925), Freud points to this visit as encouraging his break with hypnotism. Frank Sulloway, *Freud, Biologist of the Mind: Beyond the Psychoanalytic Legend* (New York: Basic Books, 1979), pp. 48, 73. See also *SE,* vol. 20, p. 17.

30. See the discussion, but not the quote, in Sulloway, *Biologist,* pp. 271–72.

31. William James, " 'Üeber den Psychischen Mechanismus Hysterischer Phänomene' by Josef Brauer and Sigmund Freud (1894)," *Psychological Review* 1 (March 1894): 199.

32. In the language of the time, neurosis was "retraction of the field of consciousness; weakness of psychological synthesis, lessening of psychological tension." Hysteria was "a malady of

the personal synthesis." Pierre Janet, "Psychoanalysis," *Journal of Abnormal Psychology* 9 (1914–15): 1–35, 153–87.

33. In 1909 Freud contrasted his view to Janet's: "We do not derive the psychical splitting from [the hereditary weakness of] an incapacity for synthesis on the part of the mental apparatus; we explain it dynamically, from the conflict of opposing mental forces." See *SE*, vol. 11, pp. 21, 25–26.

34. In general, see *Freud–Fliess*, pp. 15, 27, 73, 87, 301, 313, 412. I have followed the translation in Marie Bonaparte, Anna Freud, and Ernst Kris, eds., *The Origins of Psychoanalysis* (New York: Basic Books, 1977).

35. Peter Gay, *Sigmund Freud: A Life for Our Time* (New York: Norton, 1988), p. 68.

36. See also *SE*, vol. 2, pp. 268–69.

37. Freud to Fliess, 16 August 1895, *Freud–Fliess*, p. 136. The same thought pervaded his published writings. In 1896 he made defense the dividing point between the "neuroses of defense" or "psychoneuroses," which included hysteria and the obsessions, on the one hand, and the somatic or "actual neuroses," which were caused by masturbation, abstinence, or coitus interruptus, on the other. See *SE*, vol. 3, pp. 162–85.

38. Freud to Fliess, 25 May 1895, *Freud–Fliess*, p. 129.

39. According to Freud, *Interpretation* "was finished in all its essentials at the beginning of 1896 but was not written down until the summer of 1899." *SE*, vol. 14, p. 22.

40. His soul was "revolutioned [*sic*]." Gay, *Freud*, p. 390. For example, he was late for his father's funeral. The night after the funeral he dreamt: "I was in a place where I read a sign: You are requested to close the eyes." Freud to Fliess, 2 November 1896, *Freud–Fliess*, p. 202.

41. Thus, the internal connections between the psychology of authority and the psychology of narcissism can be anticipated in Freud's experiences during the late nineties. "Behind-the-couch distance and invisibility [was] replaced by the distance between Vienna and Berlin." Heinz Kohut, "Creativeness, Charisma, Group Psychology," in *The Search for the Self* (New York: International Universities Press, 1978), pp. 806–7.

42. For a further comment on the dream, see Freud to Abraham, 9 January 1908, *Freud–Abraham*, p. 20. My discussion is indebted to Didier Anzieu, *Freud's Self-Analysis*, trans. Peter Graham (Madison, Conn.: International Universities Press, 1986). The tripartite structure of the dream is repeated in the formula of trimethylamine:

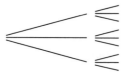

which also anticipates Freud's emerging theory of the tripartite structure of the psyche.

43. Freud's private doubts concerning the seduction theory were much stronger. Gerald N. Izenberg, "Seduced and Abandoned: The Rise and Fall of Freud's Seduction Theory," in *The Cambridge Companion to Freud*, ed. Jerome Neu (New York: Cambridge University Press, 1991), p. 28.

44. "A posthumous action [*Nachträglichkeit*] by a sexual trauma," he wrote, operates "as though it were a contemporary event." *SE*, vol. 3, p. 154; see also pp. 166–67; *SE*, vol. 1, pp. 233, 356–59.

45. In January 1897 he dropped the idea that the content of the trauma determined the type of neurosis. In May he wrote that it was impulses, not memories, that were repressed. In September he jettisoned the theory altogether. Freud ended the letter in which he renounced the theory by commenting: "In this collapse of everything valuable, the psychological alone has remained untouched. . . . It is a pity that one cannot make a living, for instance, on

dream interpretation!" Freud to Fliess, 24 January, 2 May, and 21 September 1897, *Freud–Fliess,* pp. 226–28, 239, 264–66. Freud did return to the theory at times after that.

46. The quote is from Charcot. Ellenberger, *Discovery,* p. 149. See also Nathan G. Hale, *Freud in America,* vol. 1 of *Freud and the Americans* (New York: Oxford University Press, 1971), p. 125.

47. Freud began to draw the distinction between memory and perception in *Studies in Hysteria,* where he likened perception to the mirror of a reflecting telescope and memory to a photographic plate. He continued it in his unpublished 1895 "Project," where he characterized perception as open to new stimuli, whereas memory was characterized by ineradicable traces, but it is fundamental in *The Interpretation of Dreams. SE,* vol. 2, p. 189.

48. Freud to Fliess, 6 December 1896, *Freud–Fliess,* p. 207.

49. Freud to Fliess, included with letter of 25 May 1897, *Freud–Fliess,* pp. 246–47.

50. *SE,* vol. 5, pp. 421–22, 427–28, 441–42.

51. Ibid., p. 442; Sander L. Gilman, *Freud, Race, and Gender* (Princeton, N.J.: Princeton University Press, 1993), p. 12, gives "the worry about the future of one's children, whom one could not give a homeland."

52. *SE,* vol. 4, pp. 101–2.

53. Freud to Fliess, 3 January 1899, *Freud–Fliess,* p. 338.

54. Ibid., 23 March 1900, p. 405.

55. According to biographer Didier Anzieu, Freud now "realized just how attached every individual is to all that is personal to him—his name, his style, his works." Anzieu, *Self-Analysis,* p. 516.

56. Key aspects of his style can be discerned in his adolescent letters: "Some Early Unpublished Letters of Freud," *International Journal of Psycho-Analysis,* 50 (1969): 419–27. His conscious literary model was Gotthold Lessing, the eighteenth-century German critic and dramatist, who advocated a style that revealed the thinker thinking. On Lessing's influence, see Joseph Wortis, "Fragments of a Freudian Analysis," *American Journal of Orthopsychiatry* 10 (1940): 848; Walter Kaufmann, *Discovering the Mind,* vol. 1: *Goethe, Kant, and Hegel* (New Brunswick, N.J.: Transaction Publishers, 1990). An immigrant at the start of his life and a refugee at the end, Freud achieved many of his deepest human contacts through writing, and the history of psychoanalysis is in one sense the history of the transferences that Freud received as a writer.

57. *SE,* vol. 22, p. 7. In a 1907 letter to Jung, he described himself as clinging to *The Interpretation of Dreams* as to "a rock in the breakers." Jones, vol. 2, p. 112.

58. H. Stuart Hughes, *Conciousness and Society: The Reconstruction of European Social Thought, 1890–1930* (New York: Vintage, 1961), passim.

59. Hans Gerth and C. Wright Mills, *From Max Weber: Essays in Sociology* (New York: Oxford University Press, 1946), pp. 345–47.

Chapter Two

1. *SE,* vol. 12, p. 99. I have followed the translation in Philip Rieff's edition of Freud's collected papers: 10 vols. (New York: Collier Books, 1963).

2. Anne McClintock, *Imperial Leather: Race, Gender, and Sexuality in the Colonial Contest* (New York: Routledge, 1995), p. 44.

3. W. Arthur Calhoun, *A Social History of the American Family* (Cleveland: Arthur H. Clerk Company, 1919), vol. 3, pp. 157–58.

4. Edward Shorter, *The Making of the Modern Family* (New York: Basic Books, 1975); Kathy Peiss, *Cheap Amusements: Working Women and Leisure in Turn-of-the-Century New York* (Philadelphia: Temple University Press, 1986); Christine Stansell, *City of Women: Sex and Class in New York, 1789–1860* (New York: Knopf, 1986); George Chauncey, *Gay New York: Gender, Urban Culture, and the Makings of the Gay Male World, 1890–1940* (New York: Basic Books, 1999).

5. Rudolph Binion, "Fiction as Social Fantasy," *Journal of Social History* 27, no. 4 (Summer 1994): 679–99.

6. Quoted in Harriet Anderson, *Utopian Feminism: Women's Movements in Fin-de-Siècle Vienna* (New Haven, Conn.: Yale University Press, 1992), p. 5.

7. Quoted in Michelle Perrot, "Stepping Out," in Georges Duby and Michelle Perrot, *A History of Women in the West* (Cambridge, Mass.: Belknap Press of Harvard University Press, 1992–), vol. 4, p. 463.

8. Elizabeth Cady Stanton, "Solitude of the Self," address before the U.S. Senate Committee on Woman Suffrage, 20 February 1892, reprinted in *The Concise History of Women's Suffrage,* ed. Mari Jo Buhle and Paul Buhle (Urbana: University of Illinois Press, 1978), pp. 325–26.

9. Edna Kenton, "Feminism Will Give . . . ," *Delineator* 85 (July 1914): 17; George Burman Foster, "The Philosophy of Feminism," *Forum* 52 (July 1914): 16. Both quoted in Mari Jo Buhle, *Feminism and Its Discontents: A Century of Struggle with Psychoanalysis* (Cambridge, Mass.: Harvard University Press, 1998), p. 2.

10. Oscar Wilde's *An Ideal Husband* defended its hero against the accusation of leading an idle life: "He rides in the Row at ten o'clock in the morning, goes to the opera three times a week, changes his clothes at least five times a day, and dines out every night. . . . You don't call that leading an idle life, do you?" See also Rita Felski, *The Gender of Modernity* (Cambridge, Mass.: Harvard University Press, 1995), pp. 103–5.

11. Quoted in Alan Sinfield, *The Wilde Century: Effeminacy, Oscar Wilde, and the Queer Movement* (New York: Columbia University Press, 1994), p. 1.

12. The quote beginning "perfectly natural" is from Tony Brown, ed., *Edward Carpenter and Late Victorian Radicalism* (London and Portland, Ore.: Frank Cass, 1990), p. 10. The reference to Whitman is from Carpenter's 1916 *My Days and Dreams;* the "great leveler" is from Carpenter's 1897 *Sexual Inversion;* and the *Bhagavadgītā* is quoted from Juan Morasco's 1962 translation. All are quoted in Brown, *Edward Carpenter,* pp. 10–12. A generation later Christopher Isherwood credited psychoanalyst John Layard with helping him accept his homosexuality by advising him: "There is only one sin: disobedience to the inner law of our own nature." See Noel Annan, *Our Age: English Intellectuals Between the World Wars— A Group Portrait* (New York: Random House, 1990), p. 119.

13. Freud to Bernays, 29 August 1883, *LSF,* pp. 50, 76. I have modified the translation slightly.

14. As with neurology, sexology had important relations to forensic medicine. For example, Krafft-Ebing's 1886 *Psychopathia Sexualis* developed out of his responsibility for proving the "degeneracy" of sexual offenders dragged before the court. See Judith Walkowitz, "Dangerous Sexualities," in *A History of Women in the West,* ed. Geneviève Fraisse and Michelle Perot (Cambridge, Mass.: Harvard University Press, 1993), p. 395.

15. Frank J. Sulloway, *Freud, Biologist of the Mind: Beyond the Psychoanalytic Legend* (New York: Basic Books, 1979), pp. 172, 277, 146.

16. Havelock Ellis, *Studies in the Psychology of Sex* (1905; repr., New York: Random House, 1942), vol. 1, part 2, pp. 189, 249, 256; vol. 3, pp. 15–17.

17. The term "homosexual" was apparently coined by the German-speaking doctor K. M. Benkert. Note the frequent Hellenic point of reference. "Urning," for example, referred to Plato's *Symposium,* in which same-sex love is linked to Aphrodite, daughter of Uranus. See Robert Nye, *Masculinity and Male Codes of Honor in Modern France* (New York: Oxford University Press, 1993), p. 108.

18. This, Jeffrey Weeks has written, marked the "eruption into print of the speaking pervert, the individual marked or marred by his (or her) sexual impulses": Weeks, *Sexuality and Its Discontents* (London: Routledge & Kegan Paul, 1985), pp. 67, 91; Estelle Freedman and John D'Emilio, *Intimate Matters: A History of Sexuality in America* (New York: Harper & Row, 1988), p. 226. For the history of "heterosexuality" as a concept, see Jonathan Katz, "The Invention of Heterosexuality," *Socialist Review* 20 (March 1990): 7–34.

19. George Mosse, *The Image of Man* (New York: Oxford University Press, 1966), pp. 90–91.

20. Bloch is quoted in George L. Mosse, *Nationalism and Sexuality: Respectability and Abnormal*

Sexuality in Modern Europe (New York: Howard Fertig, 1985), p. 32. In general, see Chauncey, *Gay New York.* The study of these phenomena was also part of the shift toward psychologization. Thus, sexologists debated whether "perversion" was to be understood in psychological or biological terms. Medical illustrations shifted from drawings of genitals to drawings of faces. Arnold I. Davidson, "How to Do the History of Psychoanalysis: A Reading of Freud's *Three Essays on the Theory of Sexuality,*" *Critical Inquiry* 13 (Winter 1987): 152, and "Sex and the Emergence of Sexuality," *Critical Inquiry* 14 (Autumn 1987): 16.

21. For the sexologist L. Von Römer, the androgynous ideal was manifest in artists who combined feminine sensibility with active creative force. Natalie Barney longed "for a past age which made its Apollo effeminate and its goddesses virile, leading to the triumph of the androgyne." Quoted in Mosse, *Image of Man,* pp. 92–93. Colette extended the idea of androgyny by identifying sexual ambiguity, uncertainty, and dissimulation as the qualities that made any person attractive.

22. Otto Weininger, *Sex and Character* (New York: Howard Fertig, 2003), pp. 320, 73, 406. The extent to which such ideas were shared should not be underestimated. The book went through 25 editions in 22 years according to Eric Hobsbawm, *The Age of Empire* (New York: Vintage, 1989), p. 206. Weininger's 1903 suicide in Beethoven's house electrified readers throughout Europe. The impact of the book reflects the fact that it combined older idealizations of masculinity with the theme of bisexuality. August Strindberg wrote that Weininger's "awe-inspiring book . . . has probably solved the most difficult of all problems." D. H. Lawrence, James Joyce, Giorgio De Chirico, and the Italian futurists were all deeply affected by it. Bisexuality, in Weininger's sense, pervades *Ulysses.* No less a figure than Wittgenstein reread the book throughout his life, frequently recommending it to friends and associates. Although Weininger propounded emancipation at the expense of women and homosexuals, even Rosa Mayreder and Magnus Hirschfeld cautiously praised his work. See Emile Delavenay, "D. H. Lawrence, Otto Weininger, and a Rather Raw Philosophy," in *D. H. Lawrence: New Studies,* ed. Christopher Heywood (Houndmills, Basingstoke, Hampshire: Macmillan, 1987); Ray Monk, *Ludwig Wittgenstein* (New York: Penguin Books, 1990), p. 19; Alan Janik, *Essays on Wittgenstein and Weininger* (Amsterdam: Rodolphi, 1985). For Mayreder, see Anderson, *Utopian Feminism,* p. 150; also see Magnus Hirschfeld, *The Sexual History of the World War* (New York: Falstaff Press, 1937), p. 58.

23. In *The Descent of Man* Darwin had speculated that "some remote progenitor of the whole vertebrate kingdom appears to have been hermaphrodite or androgynous." Charles Darwin, *The Descent of Man* (New York: American Home Library, 1902), vol. 1, pp. 215–16. Freud's first laboratory studies in the late 1870s, investigations of the eel's sex organs, were directed by Carl Claus, famous for his research on bisexuality in crustacea. In 1886 Richard von Krafft-Ebing, Freud's colleague at the University of Vienna, published *Psychopathia Sexualis.* Krafft-Ebing cited Claus on bisexuality as well as psychiatrist James G. Kiernan on "the rudimentary female organs of the male" (for example, nipples) and female "masculinization" (for example, facial hair). Sulloway, *Biologist,* p. 159.

24. George Chauncey, Jr., "From Sexual Inversion to Homosexuality: Medicine and the Changing Conceptualization of Female Deviance," *Salmagundi* 58–59 (Fall 1982): 131. Richard von Krafft-Ebing, *Psychopathia Sexualis* (New York: Physicians and Surgeons Book Co., 1933), pp. 137–38; Lawrence Birken, *Consuming Desire: Sexual Science and the Emergence of a Culture of Abundance, 1871–1914* (Ithaca, N.Y.: Cornell University Press, 1988), pp. 101–2.

25. Sulloway, *Biologist,* p. 292.

26. Fliess to Freud, 26 July 1904, *Freud–Fliess,* pp. 465–66.

27. Peter Newton, "Freud's Mid-Life Crisis," *Psychoanalytic Psychology* 9, no. 4 (1992): 468–69; Freud to Fliess, 15 July 1896, *Freud–Fliess,* p. 195. Masson translated "*befruchtenden Stromes*" as "stimulating current," but *befruchten* also means fertilize or pollinate.

28. Freud to Fliess, 6 December 1896 and 25 May 1897, *Freud–Fliess,* pp. 211, 246. Freud also agreed with Fliess that these substances should be understood in terms of long-term

rhythms organized according to 23-day and 28-day cycles. He used the idea in the seduction theory to explain which early sexual experiences give rise to unpleasure.

29. Ibid., 4 January 1898, p. 292. According to Paul Roazen, this quarrel is apocryphal (personal communication).

30. Ibid., 1 January 1896, p. 169.

31. "Draft M: The Architecture of Hysteria," attached to letter, Freud to Fliess, 25 May 1897, *Freud–Fliess*, p. 246. The translation in *The Origins of Psychoanalysis*, ed. Marie Bonaparte, Anna Freud, and Ernst Kris (New York: Basic Books, 1977), is: "The essential repressed element is always femininity." Masson's translation is: "The element essentially responsible for repression is always what is feminine." Although Freud's German is ambiguous, the validity of Kris's translation is brought out by the next sentence, which both translate in the same way: "Women as well as men admit more readily to experiences with women than with men. What men essentially repress is the pederastic element."

32. Freud to Fliess, 14 November 1897, *Freud–Fliess*, p. 281.

33. Freud, *Origins*, p. 224; Freud to Fliess, 25 May 1897, *Freud–Fliess*, p. 245.

34. Freud to Fliess, 1 August 1899, *Freud–Fliess*, p. 364.

35. Ibid., 22 September 1898, p. 326.

36. Ibid., 11 October 1899, p. 379.

37. Ibid., 7 August 1901, p. 448.

38. However, he also wrote: "One cannot simply say, 'the conscious is the dominant, the unconscious the underlying sexual factor,' without grossly oversimplifying the very much more complicated matter, even though that is of course the basic fact." Ibid., 19 September 1901, pp. 450–51.

39. We cannot trace the evolution of Freud's thought in the early 1900s, as we can in the 1890s, since the correspondence with Fliess dropped off. Nonetheless, although Freud published *Three Essays* in 1905, it summarized the way of thinking about sexuality found in the works he wrote as he was finishing *The Interpretation of Dreams: The Psychopathology of Everyday Life, Wit and the Unconscious,* and especially "Fragment of an Analysis of a Case of Hysteria" or "Dora," which was basically completed in 1900.

40. When Swoboda complained to Freud about fantasies of being overcome, Freud told him that such fantasies were rooted in a universal bisexuality. Peter Heller, "A Quarrel over Bisexuality," in *The Turn of the Century,* ed. Gerald Chapple and Hans Schulte (Bonn: Bouvier, 1981), p. 98. I believe Heller first identified early psychoanalysis as a *Männerbund.*

41. In an episode later added to *The Psychopathology of Everyday Life* (1901), he gave as an example of everyday forgetting a time that he presented to Fliess as original some of Fliess's own ideas concerning bisexuality. See *SE,* vol. 6, pp. 143–34 and fn. 1. So contrite was he, explained Freud, that he was unable to complete *Wit and the Unconscious* because it, too, was dependent on the idea of bisexuality. Freud to Fliess, 23 and 27 July 1904, *Freud–Fliess,* pp. 464–68.

42. *SE,* vol. 23, p. 188.

43. Ibid., vol. 7, p. 160.

44. Ibid., p. 278.

45. Ibid., p. 120.

46. Ibid., vol. 9, p. 166.

47. Ibid., vol. 10, p. 238.

48. Ibid., vol. 7, pp. 156–67. All human beings, Freud remarked in a footnote added to *Three Essays* in 1915, are capable of making a homosexual object choice because all have unconsciously done so. Ibid., p. 145.

49. Magnus Hirschfeld confused "the distinction between inversion of object and of person." Freud to Ferenczi, 20 May 1910, *Freud–Ferenczi,* vol. 1, p. 175 fn. 2. Commenting ironically on Karl Ulrichs's description of male homosexuality as a "feminine brain in a masculine body," Freud stated that we have no idea what characterizes a feminine brain.

50. Quoted in Buhle, *Feminism,* p. 50.

51. While not necessarily "an attack upon the family," it led to antagonism and required adjustment. Ellen Herman, "The Competition: Psychoanalysis, Its Feminist Interpreters and the Idea of Sexual Freedom, 1920–1930," *Free Associations* 3, part 3, no. 27 (1992): 391–97.

52. It was Meisel-Hess who introduced the Russian Bolshevik feminist Alexandra Kollontai to Freud's writings.

53. This was Havelock Ellis's characterization. Buhle, *Feminism,* p. 40.

54. Contrary to well-known arguments by Nancy Cott, the primary origin of the term "feminism" lay in describing men such as Karl Mayreder, who attached themselves to the women's movement.

55. Anderson, *Utopian Feminism,* pp. 134–35.

56. Henry James, *The Bostonians* (London: Everyman, 1994), p. 300.

57. Quoted in Mosse, *Image of Man,* p. 85.

58. Masturbation, wrote Krafft-Ebing, resulted in "artificially produced pederasts." Mosse, *Nationalism and Sexuality,* passim.

59. Gail Bederman, *Manliness and Civilization: A Cultural History of Gender and Race in the United States, 1880–1917* (Chicago: University of Chicago Press, 1995).

60. Sander L. Gilman, *Freud, Race, and Gender* (Princeton, N.J.: Princeton University Press, 1993), p. 167, quoted in Eric Santner, *My Own Private Germany: Daniel Paul Schreber's Secret History of Modernity* (Princeton, N.J.: Princeton University Press, 1996), p. 116.

61. Santner, *Private Germany,* pp. 121, 117.

62. Caillebotte's *Man at the Bath* is discussed in Tamar Garb's *Bodies of Modernity: Figure and Flesh in Fin-de-Siècle France* (London: Thames and Hudson, 1998). Kafka is quoted in Mark M. Anderson, *Kafka's Clothes: Ornament and Aestheticism in the Habsburg Fin de Siècle* (Oxford and New York: Oxford University Press, 1992), p. 89.

63. Jones, vol. 2, p. 83.

64. *SE,* vol. 10, p. 167.

65. Ibid., vol. 7, pp. 198–99.

66. According to Schreber: "I have to imagine myself as a man and woman in one person having intercourse with myself . . . which perhaps under other circumstances may be considered immoral but which has nothing whatever to do with any idea of masturbation or anything like it." He added, "If I can get a little sensual pleasure in this process, I feel I am entitled to it." Daniel Paul Schreber, *Memoirs of My Nervous Illness* (1902; repr., Cambridge, Mass.: Harvard University Press, 1988), pp. 147–49, 204–10.

67. *SE,* vol. 17, pp. 100, 110–12.

68. Jung to Freud, 28 October 1907, *Freud–Jung,* p. 95.

69. Freud to Ferenczi, 2 October 1910 and 17 November 1911, *Freud–Ferenczi,* vol. 1, pp. 215, 314. I have followed the earlier translations for the first quote.

70. Rudolf Carnap, *The Logical Structure of the World,* trans. Rolf A. George (Berkeley: University of California Press, 1967), p. xviii, quoted in Richard Bernstein, *Praxis and Action* (Philadelphia: University of Pennsylvania Press, 1971), p. 238.

71. *SE,* vol. 12, p. 99.

72. Robert Musil, *The Man Without Qualities* (1930; repr., New York: G. P. Putnam, 1980), vol. 1, pp. 139, 312, quoted in Robert A. Nye, *Crime, Madness, and Politics in Modern France: The Medical Concept of National Decline* (Princeton, N.J.: Princeton University Press, 1984), pp. 338–39.

Chapter Three

1. H. Stuart Hughes, *Consciousness and Society: The Reconstruction of European Social Thought, 1890–1930* (New York: Vintage Books, 1961), pp. 27–29.

2. Arno Mayer, *The Persistence of the Old Regime: Europe to the Great War* (New York: Pantheon Books, 1981), p. 25 and passim.

3. Paul Weindling, *Health, Race, and German Politics Between National Unification and Nazism, 1870–1945* (New York: Cambridge University Press, 1989), pp. 80–81.

4. Renato Poggioli, *The Theory of the Avant-Garde* (Cambridge, Mass.: Harvard University Press, 1968).

5. "Condensed system of micro-circuits" is in Edward Timms, *Karl Kraus, Apocalyptic Satirist: Culture and Catastrophe in Hapsburg Vienna* (New Haven, Conn.: Yale University Press, 1986), p. 9.

6. Bruno Bettelheim, *Freud's Vienna and Other Essays* (New York: Knopf, 1990), pp. 20, 46: "For a Jewish family of the 1880s to have lived in a flat of six rooms meant [their conditions] were excellent when compared with the near-ghetto existence from which Freud's father escaped."

7. Peter Gay, *Sigmund Freud: A Life for Our Time* (New York: Norton, 1988), p. 176.

8. Phyllis Bottome, *Alfred Adler: Apostle of Freedom* (London: Faber and Faber, 1939); Bertha Orgler, *Alfred Adler, the Man and His Work* (New York: Liveright, 1963); William Stekel, *The Autobiography of William Stekel: The Life History of a Psychoanalyst* (New York: Liveright, 1950).

9. Paul Federn, "Zur Reform des Ärztlichen Spitaldienstes," *Wiener Klinische Rundschau* 15 (15 April 1901), quoted in Louis Rose, "The Psychoanalytic Movement in Vienna: Toward a Science of Culture" (Ph.D. diss., Princeton University, 1986), p. 53.

10. David S. Luft, *Robert Musil and the Crisis of European Culture: 1880–1942* (Berkeley: University of California Press, 1980), pp. 8–12. See also John Boyer, "Freud, Marriage, and Late Viennese Liberalism: A Commentary from 1905," *Journal of Modern History* 50 (March 1978): 91–99.

11. Carl E. Schorske, *Fin-de-siècle Vienna: Politics and Culture* (New York: Knopf, 1980), p. 186. Freud was a member of B'nai Brith from 1897 to 1902.

12. Jan Goldstein, "The Wandering Jew and the Problem of Psychiatric Anti-Semitism in Fin-de-Siècle France," *Journal of Contemporary History* 20, no. 4 (1985): 521–52.

13. G. D. H. Cole, *The Second International, 1889–1914*, vol. 3 of *A History of Socialist Thought* (London: Macmillan, 1956), part 2, p. 592: "The Austrian, or at any rate the Viennese, Socialists became the most highly cultured and instructed body of proletarians in the entire world."

14. Louis Rose, *The Freudian Calling: Early Viennese Psychoanalysis and the Pursuit of Cultural Science* (Detroit: Wayne State University Press, 1998), p. 34.

15. Edward Timms, " 'The Child-Woman': Kraus, Freud, Wittels, and Irma Karczewska," in *Vienna 1990: From Altenberg to Wittgenstein*, ed. Edward Timms and Ritchie Robertson (Edinburgh: Edinburgh University Press, 1990), p. 88; Paul E. Stepansky, *In Freud's Shadow: Adler in Context* (Hillsdale, N.J.: Analytic Press, 1983); Henri Ellenberger, *The Discovery of the Unconscious: The History and Evolution of Dynamic Psychiatry* (New York: Basic Books, 1970).

16. Pappenheim is a key figure in the history of German social work and the author of *The Jewish Problem in Galicia*. See Marion A. Kaplan, *The Jewish Feminist Movement in Germany: The Campaigns of the Jüdischer Frauenbund, 1904–1938* (Westport, Conn.: Greenwood Press, 1979); Ellen Jensen, "Anna O.: A Study of Her Later Life," *Psychoanalytic Quarterly* 39 (1970): 269–93.

17. Lisa Appignanesi and John Forrester, *Freud's Women* (New York: Basic Books, 1993), pp. 78, 138.

18. Hermann Nunberg and Paul Federn, *Minutes of the Vienna Psychoanalytic Society* (New York: International Universities Press, 1962–75).

19. Freud to Jung, 7 April 1907, *Freud–Jung*, p. 28.

20. Manfred Joshua Sakel, a Polish neurophysiologist, discovered insulin coma therapy for schizophrenics and other mental patients in 1927, while a young doctor in Vienna.

21. Freud to Fliess, 21 September 1899, *Freud–Fliess*, p. 374.

22. Jones, vol. 1, p. 338.

23. Freud to Fliess, 7 May 1900, *Freud–Fliess*, p. 412.

24. John Kerr, *A Most Dangerous Method: The Story of Jung, Freud, and Sabina Spielrein* (New York: Knopf, 1993), p. 38.

25. Bleuler believed "dementia praecox" referred to not one but several diseases.

26. Ellenberger, *Discovery*, p. 668. Partly this was the result of his wife's money. On Jung's background, see Richard Noll, *The Jung Cult* (Princeton, N.J.: Princeton University Press, 1994).

27. Kerr, *Dangerous Method*, p. 46; Carl Gustav Jung, *Memories, Dreams, Reflections* (New York: Pantheon Books, 1973).

28. Jones, vol. 2, p. 257; Peter Homans, *The Ability to Mourn: Disillusionment and the Social Origins of Psychoanalysis* (Chicago: University of Chicago Press, 1989), pp. 176 ff.

29. Ernest Jones, *Free Associations: Memories of a Psychoanalyst* (New York: Basic Books, 1959), p. 153.

30. There he ran into the same problems when a patient complained to the local Sexual Purity League. Ernest Jones to Sigmund Freud, 8 February 1911, *Freud–Jones*, p. 88. For early British psychoanalysis, see Adam Phillips, *D. W. Winnicott* (Cambridge, Mass.: Harvard University Press, 1988), p. 39; Pearl King, "Early Divergences Between the Psycho-Analytical Societies in London and Vienna," in *Freud in Exile: Psychoanalysis and Its Vicissitudes*, ed. Edward Timms and Naomi Segal (New Haven, Conn.: Yale University Press, 1988); Edith Kurzweil, *The Freudians: A Comparative Perspective* (New Haven, Conn.: Yale University Press, 1989), p. 52; Elizabeth Abel, *Virginia Woolf and the Fictions of Psychoanalysis* (Chicago: University of Chicago Press, 1989), pp. 15–17.

31. Freud to Jung, 3 May 1908, *Freud–Jung*, p. 145.

32. Iwan Bloch, *The Sexual Life of Our Times in Its Relations to Modern Civilization* (London: Rebman, 1906, 1910); Kerr, *Dangerous Method*, p. 129. The Bund für Mutterschutz (Association for the Protection of Mothers), whose organizers included Max Weber and Werner Sombart, was also founded in 1905.

33. Freud to Abraham, 10 August 1907, *Freud–Abraham*, p. 9. See Kurzweil, *Freudians*, pp. 39–40. Hirschfeld left the society in 1911, after attending the Weimar congress. See Charlotte Wolff, *Magnus Hirschfeld: A Portrait of a Pioneer in Sexology* (New York: Quartet Books, 1986), p. 101.

34. In 1910 Hermann Oppenheim, a prominent Berlin neurologist speaking at the Society of German Neurologists, called for a boycott of clinics in which psychoanalysis was practiced. See *Freud–Ferenczi*, vol. 1, pp. 152, 241 fn. 2, 376.

35. He wrote for the journal *Gyógyászat*. Martin Stanton, *Sándor Ferenczi: Reconsidering Active Intervention* (Northvale, N.J.: J. Aronson, 1991), p. 10; Paul Harmat, *Freud, Ferenczi und die ungarische Psychoanalyse* (Tübingen, 1988); Ilse Barande, *Sándor Ferenczi* (Paris: Petite Bibliothèque Payot, 1972).

36. Ferenczi to Freud, 5 February 1910, *Freud–Ferenczi*, vol. 1, p. 131.

37. Freud to Pfister, 9 February 1909, quoted in Peter Gay, *A Godless Jew: Freud, Atheism, and the Making of Psychoanalysis* (New Haven, Conn.: Yale University Press, 1987), p. 73.

38. Max Graf, "Reminiscences of Professor Sigmund Freud," *Psychoanalytic Quarterly* 2 (1942): 471–72.

39. Hanns Sachs, *Freud, Master and Friend* (Salem, N.H.: Ayer, 1944), pp. 3–4, 25–27.

40. Jung to Freud, 24 May 1907, *Freud–Jung*, p. 49.

41. Ferenczi to Freud, 5 October 1909, *Freud–Ferenczi*, vol. 1, p. 76.

42. Freud to Ferenczi, 6 October 1910, ibid., p. 221. Apparently Freud actually wrote, "I am that psychoanalytic superman that we have constructed." The German edition inserts the "not," in brackets. An interesting slip!

43. Freud to Abraham, 3 June 1912, *Freud–Abraham*, pp. 118–19.

44. Jones to Freud, 30 January 1912, *Freud–Jones*, p. 130.

45. Marthe Robert, *The Psychoanalytic Revolution: Sigmund Freud's Life and Achievement* (New York: Harcourt Brace & World, 1966), p. 244.

46. Robert Steele, *Freud and Jung* (London and Boston: Routledge & Kegan Paul, 1982), p. 206.

47. Sachs, *Freud,* p. 57.

48. Freud to Abraham, 26 July 1914, *Freud–Abraham,* p. 186.

49. Freud to Abraham, 27 August 1918, ibid., p. 278. As late as 1920, when Freud tried to get Theodor Reik established in Berlin, Abraham told him there were not enough patients.

50. Ralph Waldo Emerson, *Nature* (Boston: James Monroe, 1836), p. 13.

51. Donald Meyer, *The Positive Thinkers: A Study of the American Quest for Health, Wealth and Personal Power from Mary Baker Eddy to Norman Vincent Peale* (Garden City, N.Y.: Doubleday, 1965), p. 14. On women's relation to mind cure, see Ann Douglas, *Terrible Honesty: Mongrel Manhattan in the 1920s* (New York: Farrar, Straus and Giroux, 1995), pp. 242–43.

52. Henry H. Goddard, "The Effects of Mind on Body as Evidenced by Faith Cures," *American Journal of Psychology* 10 (1899): 431–502, quoted in Eric Caplan, *Mind Games: American Culture and the Birth of Psychotherapy* (Berkeley: University of California Press, 1998), p. 87.

53. Reinhard Bendix, *Work and Authority in Industry: Ideologies of Management in the Course of Industrialization* (New York: John Wiley, 1963), p. 259.

54. Lary May, *Screening Out the Past: The Birth of Mass Culture and the Motion Picture Industry* (New York: Oxford University Press, 1980), p. 61.

55. Quoted in Caplan, *Mind Games,* p. 64.

56. Andrew Abbott, *The System of Professions: An Essay on the Division of Expert Labor* (Chicago: University of Chicago Press, 1988), pp. 280–314. According to Nathan G. Hale, *Freud and the Americans: The Beginning of Psychoanalysis in the United States, 1876–1917* (New York: Oxford University Press, 1971), pp. 248–49, the Emmanuel movement, founded by Elwood Worcester, "functioned as a transition from the supernaturalism of the mind cure cults to scientific psychotherapy."

57. Caplan, *Mind Games,* pp. 98–99. Urging an alliance of the "feminine mystical mind" and the "scientific-academic mind," William James wrote that any "science" of the mind that denies the therapeutic efficacy of the mind-cure practices "lies prostrate in the dust before me." Quoted in Douglas, *Terrible Honesty,* pp. 217–18.

58. William James, *Varieties of Religious Experience* (Cambridge, Mass.: Harvard University Press, 1985), pp. 6, 108–9.

59. Hale, *Freud and the Americans,* pp. 127–28. Prince's *The Dissociation of a Personality* (1906; repr., New York: Greenwood Press, 1969), a study of a multiple personality, describes Prince's effort to re-repress the personalities of which he disapproved.

60. Richard C. Cabot, "The American Type of Psychotherapy," in William Belmont Parker, *Psychotherapy: A Course Reading in Sound Psychology, Sound Medicine, and Sound Religion* (1908), p. 1, quoted in Caplan, *Mind Games,* p. 4.

61. For *Psychotherapy,* see Hale, *Freud and the Americans,* p. 231.

62. Hugo Munsterberg, *Psychotherapy* (New York: Moffat, Yard, 1909), p. x; Hale, *Freud and the Americans,* pp. 127, 140.

63. Boris Sidis, *The Psychology of Suggestion* (New York: D. Appleton, 1898); Robert Fuller, *Americans and the Unconscious* (New York: Oxford University Press, 1986), pp. 102, 106.

64. Freud to Ferenczi, 10 January 1909, *Freud–Ferenczi,* vol. 1, p. 33.

65. Jung to Freud, 7 January 1909, *Freud–Jung,* p. 194; Kerr, *Dangerous Method,* p. 209.

66. Freud to Jung, 9 March 1909, *Freud–Jung,* p. 210. A copy of the Declaration of Independence hung on the wall of his office.

67. Freud to Jung, 17 January 1909, ibid., p. 196: "Jones's observations are shrewd and pessimistic, Brill sees everything through rose-colored spectacles. I am inclined to agree with Jones."

68. Freud to Ferenczi, 10 January 1909, *Freud–Ferenczi,* vol. 1, p. 33.

69. Emma Goldman, who had first heard Freud speak in 1895 or 1896, was in Worcester giving a talk of her own and also attended. Among the descriptions of the Clark lectures: Dorothy Ross, *G. Stanley Hall: The Psychologist as Prophet* (Chicago: University of Chicago Press,

1972), and Saul Rosenzweig, *Freud, Jung, and Hall the Kingmaker: The Historic Expedition to America (1909)* (Seattle: Hogrefe & Huber, 1992). Also present was Howard W. Odum, the southern sociologist. See Daniel Joseph Singal, *The War Within: From Victorian to Modernist Thought in the South, 1919–1945* (Chapel Hill: University of North Carolina Press, 1982), p. 141. For a fictional version, see E. L. Doctorow, *Ragtime* (1975; Toronto: Penguin, 1996).

70. Jones to Freud, 7 February 1909, *Freud–Jones,* p. 13 ff.; Vincent Brome, *Ernest Jones, Freud's Alter Ego* (London: Caliban, 1982), p. 66.

71. *SE,* vol. 4, p. xxv. I owe this reference to John Forrester.

72. Hale, *Freud and the Americans,* p. 5. It is true that the lectures were delivered in German.

73. Lewis A. Coser, *Refugee Scholars in America: Their Impact and Their Experiences* (New Haven, Conn.: Yale University Press, 1984). Perhaps the most important popularization was that of Max Eastman in *Everybody's Magazine* in 1915. Among the early popularizations: James Jackson Putnam's *Human Motives* (1915), William A. White's *Mental Hygiene of Childhood* (1916), Isador Coriat's *What Is Psychoanalysis?* (1917), A. A. Brill's *Fundamental Conceptions of Psychoanalysis* (1921). Freud's books sold poorly in the United States until the 1930s.

74. Gay, *Freud,* p. 207.

75. Freud to Jones, 24 February 1912, *Freud–Jones,* pp. 132–33.

76. Jones to Freud, 19 June 1910, ibid., p. 61.

77. Frederick H. Gerrish, ed., *Psychotherapeutics* (Boston: Badger, 1909), p. 101; Sanford Gifford, "The American Reception of Psychoanalysis: 1908–1922," in *1915: The Cultural Moment,* ed. Adele Heller and Lois Rudnick (New Brunswick, N.J.: Rutgers University Press, 1991).

78. Ernest Jones, *The Treatment of Neuroses* (1920; repr., New York: Schocken, 1963), p. 56. The final phrase is in italics in the original.

79. Coser, *Refugee Scholars,* pp. 43–45; Jones, vol. 2, p. 119. Shortly thereafter, societies were started in Boston and Washington/Baltimore.

80. "Indispensable" is from Ernest Jones, quoted in Hale, *Freud and the Americans,* p. 442. In 1909 A. A. Brill was 35, Jones 30, Smith Ely Jelliffe 43, William Alanson White 39, Edward J. Kempf 24; Putnam, 63, was the exception. Gerald Grob, *Mental Illness and American Society, 1875–1940* (Princeton, N.J.: Princeton University Press, 1983), pp. 120–21. Murray H. Sherman, ed., *Psychoanalysis in America: Historical Perspectives* (Springfield, Ill.: C. C. Thomas, 1966). The earliest American psychiatrists to use Freudian techniques in mental hospitals were probably Kempf, White, and Jelliffe.

81. Hale, *Freud and the Americans,* pp. 443–44.

82. Freud's calls for attention "to the purely human and social circumstances of our patients," as well as to the somatic, sanctioned this view. See *SE,* vol. 7, p. 18.

83. Beginning around 1915, psychiatric casework, intended to supplement hospital-based psychiatry, became important in social work, penology, and law. William Healey's *The Individual Delinquent* (1915) and Bernard Glueck's *Studies in Forensic Psychiatry* (1916) were the turning points. A social-work textbook of the twenties asserted: "All social case work, in so far as it is thorough and in so far as it is good case work, is mental hygiene." Quoted in Roy Lubove, *Professional Altruist: The Emergence of Social Work as a Career* (New York: Cambridge University Press, 1965), p. 113.

84. Hale, *Freud and the Americans,* pp. 324, 355; J. B. Watson, *Behaviorism* (New York: Macmillan, 1914), pp. 106–8. Edwin Holt's *The Concept of Consciousness* (1914), the first American popularization of psychoanalysis, defined "wish" as a "motor set of the organism."

85. Helen Swick Perry, *Psychiatrist of America: The Life of Harry Stack Sullivan* (Cambridge, Mass.: Belknap Press of Harvard University Press, 1982), p. 237.

86. Riccardo Steiner, " 'Die Weltmachtstellung des Britischen Reichs': Notes on the Term 'Standard' in the First Translations of Freud," in Timms and Segal, *Freud in Exile,* p. 182.

87. Jones later wrote that Freud was "distinctly cavalier about the copyright of his translations. [He] would give us the full copyright in English, then hand over the American rights to his

nephew Edward Bernays, restore them to us for a limited period, then get Rank to dispose of them during his visit to America, and so on." See Jones, vol. 3, p. 50; Frederick J. Hoffman, *Freudianism and the Literary Mind* (Baton Rouge: Louisiana State University Press, 1967), pp. 49–50.

88. James Strachey, "Obituary of Joan Riviere (1883–1962)," *International Journal of Psychoanalysis* 44 (1963): 229.

89. Steiner, " 'Die Weltmachtstellung des Britischen Reichs,' " pp. 182–83, 184, 186–87; Darius Ornston, "Freud's Conception Is Different from Strachey's," *Journal of the American Psychoanalytic Association* 33, supp. (1985): 379–412; Michael Balint, *Problems of Human Pleasure and Behaviour* (New York: Liveright, 1957). For *Lust,* see *SE,* vol. 7, pp. 135, 212.

90. Freud to Jung, 17 October 1909, *Freud–Jung,* p. 158. For similar remarks concerning psychiatry, see ibid., p. 126.

91. Freud to Jung, 22 January 1911, *Freud–Jung,* p. 338; Jones to Freud, 15 March 1912, *Freud–Jones,* p. 135.

92. Freud to Ferenczi, 12 April 1910, *Freud–Ferenczi,* vol. 1, p. 160.

93. Ferenczi to Freud, 7 December 1909, ibid., p. 111.

94. Freud to Jung, 29 and 31 October 1910, *Freud–Jung,* pp. 363, 367–68.

95. Nunberg and Federn, *Minutes,* vol. 1, p. 251 (27 November 1907).

96. The neurotic "replaces by his own symptom formation the great group formations from which he is excluded [creating] his own world of imagination for himself, his own religion, his own system of delusions and thus recapitulat[ing] the institutions of humanity in a distorted way." The quoted phrase is from *SE,* vol. 13, p. 73, but an almost identical formulation can be found in Nunberg and Federn, *Minutes,* vol. 1, p. 251 (27 November 1907).

97. Editor's note, in *Freud–Ferenczi,* vol. 1, p. 146 fn. 1.

98. Ferenczi to Freud, 22 March 1910, ibid., pp. 153–54. Italics in original.

99. Jones, vol. 2, pp. 67–68; Freud to Jung, 13 February 1910, *Freud–Jung,* p. 295; Auguste Forel, *Out of My Life and Work* (New York: Norton, 1937).

100. Freud to Jung, 13 February 1910, *Freud–Jung,* p. 295; Jones, vol. 2, pp. 67–68.

101. In preparation for the Nuremberg congress, Ferenczi urged Freud to consider the "sociological significance of our analyses." He did not mean alignment with a party. He wrote of a typesetter, in whom he could see the "terrorism that so horribly oppresses the individual worker from the side of the [Marxist] party, and . . . that mocks all 'brotherliness,' " and a printer, with "all his swindles." Ferenczi to Freud, 22 March 1910, *Freud–Ferenczi,* vol. 1, pp. 153–54.

102. When Freud first discussed his intention of writing a "metapsychology" in 1910, Viktor Tausk argued that "the term should not be meta but . . . 'transcendental psychology' . . . i.e., a psychology that discloses unconditional functions." Nunberg and Federn, *Minutes,* vol. 2, p. 332 (24 November 1909).

103. Otto Gross quoted in Nicholas Sombart, "Max Weber and Otto Gross: On the Relationship Between Science, Politics, and Eros in Wilhelmine Germany," *History of Political Thought* 8, no. 1 (Spring 1987): 140. Gross's hard-line criminologist father, Hans Gross, had his son arrested in a case that became a cause célèbre. The anarchist periodical *Revolution* published a special issue on the question. Franz Kafka was among those transfixed by it.

104. Max Runciman, ed., *Max Weber: Selections in Translation* (New York: Cambridge University Press, 1978), pp. 383 ff. See also Marianne Weber, *Max Weber: A Biography* (New York: Wiley, 1975), pp. 375 ff.

105. Magnus Ljunggren, "The Psychoanalytic Breakthrough in Russia on the Eve of the First World War," in *Russian Literature and Psychoanalysis,* ed. Daniel Rancour-Laferriere (Amsterdam: John Benjamins, 1989), pp. 173–91; Dr. Sara Neidietsch and Dr. Nikolai Ossipow, "Psychoanalysis in Russia," *International Journal of Psychoanalysis* 3 (1922): 514–17; Martin A. Miller, *Freud and the Bolsheviks: Psychoanalysis in Russia and the Soviet Union* (New Haven, Conn.: Yale University Press, 1998), p. xi.

106. Alexander Etkind, *Eros of the Impossible: The History of Psychoanalysis in Russia,* trans. Noah and Maria Rubins (Boulder, Colo.: Westview Press, 1997), pp. 3, 4, 29, 52, 58, 66, 71.

107. *SE,* vol. 11, p. 151.

108. Freud to Ferenczi, 2 February 1913, *Freud–Ferenczi,* vol. 1, p. 465.

109. Freud to Putnam, 5 December 1909, in *James Jackson Putnam and Psychoanalysis: Letters Between Putnam and Sigmund Freud, Ernest Jones, William James, Sándor Ferenczi, and Morton Prince, 1877–1917,* ed. Nathan G. Hale (Cambridge, Mass.: Harvard University Press, 1971), p. 338.

110. Ferenczi to Freud, 5 February 1910, *Freud–Ferenczi,* vol. 1, p. 130.

111. Fritz Wittels, *Sigmund Freud: His Personality, His Teaching, and His School* (London: Allen and Unwin, 1924), pp. 139–40.

112. *SE,* vol. 11, p. 146. At the Wednesday meetings, Viktor Tausk argued that Darwinism had needed no organization for its dissemination. Tausk held that Vienna was the perfect soil "for the dissmination of Freud's teachings . . . because it is a sick soil. It [won't] do to consider psychoanalysis merely from the medical standpoint." Nunberg and Federn, *Minutes,* vol. 2, pp. 465–67 (6 April 1910); Rose, *The Freudian Calling,* pp. 211–12. Wittels stated: "The Zurichers are trained clinically to become Freudians; they would probably champion any other doctrine with the same righteousness and the same tearful tone. The Vienna society, on the other hand, has grown historically; each one of us has a neurosis, which is a necessary entry into Freud's teachings; whether the Swiss have is questionable." Nunberg and Federn, *Minutes,* vol. 2, p. 468 (6 April 1910).

113. Jones, vol. 2, pp. 69–70. In Stekel's version, quoted in Paul Roazen, *Freud and His Followers* (1974; repr., New York: New York University Press, 1984), p. 183: "They begrudge me the coat I am wearing; I don't know whether in the future I will earn my daily bread." Tears were streaming down his cheeks.

114. Editor's footnote, in *Freud–Jung,* p. 223 fn. 6.

115. Ferenczi to Freud, 9 July 1910, *Freud–Ferenczi,* vol. 1, pp. 186–87.

116. Freud to Ferenczi, 24 April 1910, ibid., p. 165.

117. Jung did not consider Abraham a gentleman, whereas Abraham considered Jung a fake.

118. Freud to Abraham, 3 May 1908, *Freud–Abraham,* p. 34. Freud: "I was almost going to say it was only his emergence on the scene that has removed from psycho-analysis the danger of becoming a Jewish national affair."

119. Freud to Ferenczi, 3 April 1910, *Freud–Ferenczi,* vol. 1, pp. 154–55.

120. Freud to Jung, 10 August 1910, *Freud–Jung,* p. 343.

121. Kerr, *Dangerous Method,* pp. 284, 290.

122. Eugene Bleuler to Sigmund Freud, 19 October 1910 and 11 March 1911. Quoted in Gay, *Freud,* p. 215. See also Franz Alexander and Sheldon Selesnick, "Freud-Bleuler Correspondence," *Archives of General Psychiatry,* vol. 12 (Chicago: American Medical Association, 1965), p. 5.

123. Jung to Freud, 17 June 1910, *Freud–Jung,* p. 328.

Chapter Four

1. Ernst Cassirer, *The Philosophy of the Enlightenment* (Boston: Beacon Press, 1955), p. 94.

2. *SE,* vol. 20, pp. 154–55.

3. What distinguished Freud's account from that of later theorists of "object relations" and intersubjectivity was the view that the need for the object qua object is not innate but rather originates and grows under conditions of profound vulnerability. As a result, the human need for objects was more feverish, ambivalent, and complex than it would have been if humans, like animals, were innately object-oriented.

4. Alfred Adler, "On the Psychology of Marxism," in *Minutes of the Vienna Psychoanalytic Society,* vol. 2: 1908–1910, ed. Hermann Nunberg and Ernst Federn (New York: International Universities Press, 1962–75), pp. 172–78 (10 March 1909). See also the minutes of 2 June 1909.

5. Adler's main presentation before the Vienna society was on 23 February 1910. Nunberg and Federn, *Minutes,* vol. 2, pp. 423–27. Alfred Adler, "Der psychische Hermaphroditismus im

Leben und in der Neurose," in *Heilen und Bilden* (Frankfurt, 1973), has been translated as "Masculine Protest and a Critique of Freud," in Alfred Adler, *Cooperation Between the Sexes,* ed. Heinz C. Anbacher and Rowena R. Anbacher (New York: Anchor, 1978), p. 59. It is not clear when Adler began to use the term "inferiority complex," which he apparently adopted from Janet.

6. *SE*, vol. 14, pp. 52–55. Translation follows the Rieff edition of Freud's collected papers.

7. Nunberg and Federn, *Minutes,* vol. 2, p. 541.

8. Freud to Jung, 19 December 1909, *Freud–Jung,* pp. 276–78.

9. Three members of the society left with Adler, and seven others protested Adler's resignation as "unquestionably provoked." Bernhard Handlbauer, *Die Adler-Freud Kontroverse* (Frankfurt a.M.: Fischer Tasdenbuch Verlag, 1990), p. 157.

10. John Kerr, *A Most Dangerous Method: The Story of Jung, Freud, and Sabina Spielrein* (New York: Knopf, 1993), p. 354.

11. Freud to Jung, 3 December 1910, *Freud–Jung,* p. 376.

12. Freud to Jung, 22 January 1911, ibid., p. 387.

13. Nunberg and Federn, *Minutes,* vol. 3, p. 148 (1 February 1911).

14. Ferenczi to Freud, 19 December 1910, *Freud–Ferenczi,* vol. 1, p. 245. Italics in original.

15. Quoted in Phyllis Grosskurth, *Melanie Klein: Her World and Her Work* (New York: Knopf, 1986), p. 211.

16. Warren Susman, *Culture as History: The Transformation of American Society in the Twentieth Century* (New York: Pantheon Books, 1984).

17. Peter Gay, *Sigmund Freud: A Life for Our Time* (New York: Norton, 1988), p. 227; Kerr, *Dangerous Method,* pp. 219, 227. In general, Kerr, *Dangerous Method,* greatly influenced my understanding of Jung.

18. Jung to Freud, 25 December 1909, *Freud–Jung,* p. 280; Kerr, *Dangerous Method,* p. 269; Jacques Quen and Eric T. Carlson, eds., *American Psychoanalysis: Origins and Development* (New York: Brunner/Mazel, 1978), p. 91. Eugene Taylor, "C. G. Jung and the Boston Psychopathologists, 1902–1912," *Voices: The Art and Science of Psychotherapy* 21, no. 2 (1985): 132–45.

19. Freud to Pfister, 17 March 1910, quoted in *Freud–Jung,* p. 304 n.

20. Jones, vol. 2, p. 86; F. H. Matthews, "The Americanization of Sigmund Freud: Adaptations of Psychoanalysis Before 1917," *Journal of American Studies* 1, no. 1 (April 1967): 258.

21. Herbert Silberer, "Mantik und Psychoanalyse," *Zentralblatt für Psychanalyse* 2 (1912); Kerr, *Dangerous Method,* pp. 110–11.

22. Jung to Freud, 2 December 1909, *Freud–Jung,* p. 270.

23. Jung to Freud, 5 October 1906, ibid., pp. 4–5; Carl C. Jung, *Freud and Psychoanalysis, Collected Works of Carl C. Jung,* ed. Gerhard Adler et al., trans. F. Hull (Princeton, N.J.: Princeton University Press, 1961), vol. 4, p. 123.

24. Jung to Freud, 8 May 1912, *Freud–Jung,* p. 503. According to Richard Noll, *The Jung Cult* (Princeton, N.J.: Princeton University Press, 1994), p. 119: "*Wandlungen* is an attempted syncretism of psychoanalysis and the German sciences most devoted to the study of Aryan culture. It is . . . a syncretic blend of sexual mythology and solar mythology as the two major theories of the human soul and of human culture." Johann Jakob Bachofen's 1861 *Das Mutterrecht* was the original source for most Germanic theories of matriarchy, but Jung avoided mentioning Bachofen's work because it was scorned by the anthropologists of the day.

25. Jung's *Transformations and Symbols of the Libido* (1911–12) was first translated into English as *Psychology of the Unconscious* in 1916 (1916; repr., New York: Dodd, Mead, 1947). Jung's work during his period of collaboration with Freud is in vol. 4 of his collected works, *Freud and Psychoanalysis;* see especially pp. 155 ff. Paul E. Stepansky, "The Empiricist as Rebel: Jung, Freud, and the Burdens of Discipleship," *Journal of the History of Behavioral Sciences* 12 (1976): 225.

26. Jung to Freud, 8 November 1909, *Freud–Jung,* p. 258.

27. Freud to Ferenczi, 23 June 1912, *Freud–Ferenczi,* vol. 1, p. 387.

28. Jung, "The Theory of Psychoanalysis," *Collected Works,* vol. 4, pp. 121–26. This work is based on Jung's New York lectures.

29. Linda Donn, *Freud and Jung: Years of Friendship, Years of Loss* (New York: Scribners, 1988), p. 148. In 1913 the inaugural issue of Jelliffe and White's *Psychoanalytic Review* contained a letter from Jung identifying the main issues facing psychologists: the effort to "explain psychic manifestations as equivalent energy transformations," and "symbolism, the structural analogy of . . . intellectual functions in their onto- and phylogenetic evolution." See Gerhard Adler and Aniela Jaffé, eds., *C. G. Jung Letters* (Princeton, N.J.: Princeton University Press, 1973), p. 29; Jung, *Collected Works,* vol. 4, pp. 83 ff.

30. Jung to Freud, 11 February 1910, and Freud to Jung, 13 February 1910, *Freud–Jung,* pp. 294–95.

31. Jones to Freud, 15 March 1912, *Freud–Jones,* p. 135.

32. Freud to Fliess, 17 and 24 January 1897, *Freud–Fliess,* pp. 224–28. The reason for hysterical symptoms, Freud informed Fliess at the time, was "the height from which the father lowers himself to the child."

33. Freud to Jung, 13 August 1908, *Freud–Jung,* p. 169.

34. Freud to Jung, 11 December 1908, ibid., p. 186.

35. *SE,* vol. 13, p. 157.

36. Sigmund Freud, *A Phylogenetic Fantasy* (Cambridge, Mass.: Belknap Press of Harvard University Press, 1987), pp. 89, 99.

37. John Locke, *Two Treatises of Government: First Treatise* (London: A. Churchill, 1690), chap. 2, sec. 6, chap. 6, secs. 59, 72.

38. Carl Jung, "Transformations and Symbols of the Libido," part 2 (1912), in *Psychology of the Unconscious: A Study of the Transformations and Symbols of the Libido: Contribution to the History of the Evolution of Thought,* trans. Beatrice Hinkle (New York: Moffat, Yard, 1916), p. 432.

39. Freud to Abraham, 13 May 1913, *Freud–Abraham,* p. 139.

40. Ferenczi to Freud, 25 October 1912, *Freud–Ferenczi,* vol. 1, p. 417. Italics in original.

41. Ferenczi to Freud, 26 December 1912, ibid., p. 450. Italics in original.

42. Freud to Ferenczi, 8 June 1913, ibid., pp. 490–91.

43. Emma Jung to Freud, 30 October 1911 and 6 November 1911, *Freud–Jung,* pp. 452, 456–57.

44. Freud to Jones, 9 August 1911, *Freud–Jones,* p. 112.

45. Jones to Freud, 30 July 1912, ibid., p. 146; R. Andrew Paskauskas, "Freud's Break with Jung: The Crucial Role of Ernest Jones," *Free Associations* 11 (1988): 7–34.

46. Freud to Jones, 1 August 1912, and Jones to Freud, 30 July 1912, *Freud–Jones,* pp. 146 ff. The inner circle, according to Ferenczi, would "serve as centres where others (beginners) could come and learn the work."

47. "It is quite remarkable," Freud noted, "how each one of us in turn is seized with the impulse to kill, so that the others have to restrain him." Freud to Abraham, 13 May and 9 November 1913, 25 March 1914, *Freud–Abraham,* pp. 139, 157, 168.

48. Jones, vol. 2, p. 150; Kerr, *Dangerous Method,* pp. 465–66.

49. Freud to Abraham, 12 July 1914, cited in Gay, *Freud,* p. 241. To Ferenczi, Freud conceded that his efforts to amalgamate "Jews and goyim in the service of ΨA" had failed. "They are separating like oil and water." Freud to Ferenczi, 28 July 1912, *Freud–Ferenczi,* vol. 1, p. 312.

50. Michael Balint, *Primary Love and Psychoanalytic Technique* (New York: Liveright, 1965), pp. 275–76; Freud to Jung, 17 October 1909, *Freud–Jung,* p. 252; and Freud to Ferenczi, 22 October 1909, *Freud–Ferenczi,* vol. 1, p. 85. Also see Ernest Gellner, *The Psychoanalytic Movement* (London: Paladin, 1985), p. 55: The "central emotional bond holding the [analytic world] together is a striking network of intense binary relations of analysand to analyst. . . . It is both sad and astonishing that little research has gone into establishing a full map of these relationships."

51. An interesting predecessor to the attempt to bring men and women together in order to discuss sexuality was the London "Men and Women's Club" of the 1880s, which included such accomplished women as Olive Schreiner, Annie Besant, and Eleanor Marx-Aveling, and which sought to formulate a new, nonprocreative heterosexual norm for marriage. It eventually collapsed in recriminations because, from the women's point of view, the men overestimated the maternal instinct, underestimated women's sexual needs, and especially "denied the validity of female subjective experience" in sorry efforts to appear scientific. Judith Walkowitz, *City of Dreadful Delight* (Chicago: University of Chicago Press, 1992), pp. 135, 145–46. But if a sexist organization could not engage in a sustained investigation into personal life, neither could an all-female group such as the General Austrian Women's Association, which allowed only "supportive" men such as Karl Mayreder into its ranks. Such a group was in no position to generate the egalitarian, mixed-sex exchanges, and the reflective relation to authority, that an understanding of personal life necessitated. What was necessary was a new kind of social milieu, certainly not sexist, but not restricted to women either.

52. Nunberg and Federn, *Minutes,* vol. 1, pp. 195–201 (15 May 1907).

53. Ibid., vol. 2, pp. 49, 514; vol. 3, pp. 112–15.

54. Ferenczi to Freud, 17 August 1910, *Freud–Ferenczi,* vol. 1, p. 206.

55. Jones to Freud, 25 April 1913, *Freud–Jones,* p. 199.

56. Freud to Jung, 7 June 1909, *Freud–Jung,* p. 231. A few years later he called for an essay on the subject of countertransference, adding, "Of course, we could not publish it, we should have to circulate copies among ourselves." In 1909, however, Freud called countertransference a "blessing in disguise." Freud to Jung, 6 July 1909 and 31 December 1911, ibid., pp. 230–31.

57. Abraham to Freud, 7 April 1909; Freud to Abraham, 27 April 1909, *Freud–Abraham,* pp. 76–78. The exchange was provoked by an article of Jung's: "Die Bedeutung des Vaters für das Schicksal des Einzelnen," *Jahrbuch für psychoanalyse* 1 (1909).

58. Freud to Ferenczi, 18 March 1912, *Freud–Ferenczi,* vol. 1, p. 360. For Freud's theory of female development, see his letter of 3 March 1912.

59. Lisa Appignanesi and John Forrester, *Freud's Women* (New York: Basic Books, 1993), p. 240.

60. Quoted ibid., p. 243. According to her brother's recollection, one of her lovers reminisced: "Looking at you with her radiantly blue eyes she would say, 'The reception of the semen is for me the height of ecstasy.'" H. F. Peters, *My Sister, My Spouse: A Biography of Lou Andreas-Salomé* (New York: Norton, 1962), p. 263.

61. Gay, *Freud,* p. 338.

62. Freud to Ferenczi, 17 June 1913, *Freud–Ferenczi,* vol. 1, p. 492.

63. *SE,* vol. 14, p. 223.

64. Ibid., pp. 88, 91, 95–97; and vol. 12, p. 318.

65. Ibid., vol. 17, pp. 100, 110–12. Freud wrote the case up in the winter of 1914–15, though he did not publish it until 1918.

66. For "empirical and conventional," see ibid., vol. 23, p. 188.

67. Ibid., vol. 12, p. 318.

68. Freud to Andreas-Salomé, 31 January 1914, *Freud–Salomé,* pp. 26–29; Lou Andreas-Salomé, *Looking Back: Memoirs* (New York: Paragon, 1991).

69. Freud to Abraham, 4 May 1915, *Freud–Abraham,* p. 220.

70. Freud to Ferenczi, 15 December 1914, *Freud–Ferenczi,* vol. 2, p. 36, gives "private trench."

71. Freud to Jones, 25 December 1914, *Freud–Jones,* p. 309.

72. Freud to Andreas-Salomé, 25 November 1914, *Freud–Salomé,* p. 21.

73. *SE,* vol. 5, pp. 559–60.

74. Freud to Abraham, 10 December 1917, *Freud–Abraham,* p. 264. Actually, Freud's attitude toward Zionism—at least before the Nazi takeover in Germany—was nuanced. In 1930, Dr. Chaim Koffler solicited Freud for a position at the newly opened Hebrew University in Jerusalem. In his response of 26 February 1930, Freud wrote: "I do not think that Palestine could ever become a Jewish state, [nor] that the Christian and Islamic worlds would ever be

prepared to have their holy places under Jewish care. It would have seemed more sensible to me to establish a Jewish homeland on a less historically-burdened land." The letter comes from the Schwadron Collection of Autographs at Jewish National University and Library in Jerusalem and is available on the Web site of the Freud Museum in London.

75. Ball quoted in Friedrich A. Kittler, *Discourse Networks 1800/1900,* trans. Michael Metteer with Chris Cullens (Stanford, Calif.: Stanford University Press, 1990), p. 302.

Chapter Five

1. Eric J. Leed, *No Man's Land: Combat and Identity in World War I* (New York: Cambridge University Press, 1979), p. 1.
2. Kenneth Silver, *Esprit de Corps: The Art of the Parisian Avant-Garde and the First World War, 1914–1925* (Princeton, N.J.: Princeton University Press, 1989), pp. 27, 3.
3. Modris Ecksteins, *Rites of Spring: The Great War and the Birth of the Modern Age* (Boston: Houghton Mifflin, 1989), p. 212.
4. Women won the vote in Austria in 1907, in Britain in 1918 (if over the age of thirty), in the United States in 1920, and in India in 1925. In Germany the principle of women's equality was written into the Weimar constitution.
5. Vera Brittain, *Testament of Youth: An Autobiographical Study of the Years 1900–1925* (New York: Macmillan, 1933), pp. 165–66; Susan Kent, *Making Peace* (Princeton, N.J.: Princeton University Press, 1993), pp. 72–73.
6. Enst Jünger, "Kampf als inneres Erlebnis," quoted in Leeds, *No Man's Land,* p. 153. I have slightly modified the translation.
7. Charles Maier, *Recasting Bourgeois Europe: Stabilization in France, Germany, and Italy in the Decade After World War I* (Princeton, N.J.: Princeton University Press, 1988), p. 32.
8. Hemingway's 1929 *A Farewell to Arms* quoted in Paul Fussell, *The Great War and Modern Memory* (New York: Oxford University Press, 1975), p. 21.
9. Marcel Proust quoted in Michael Sprinker, *History and Ideology in Proust* (London: Verso, 1988), p. 175.
10. Quoted in Ann Douglas, *Terrible Honesty: Mongrel Manhattan in the 1920s* (New York: Farrar, Straus and Giroux, 1995), p. 31.
11. The railroad neuroses, generally termed "hysterical," offer the nearest precedent. According to Harold Merskey: "Perhaps no single topic can have had as many branches as 'shell shock,' and as many consequences for psychiatry, for medicine, and for society," Merskey, "Shell-Shock," in *100 Years of British Psychiatry,* ed. German Barrios and Hugh Freeman (London: Gaskell, 1991), p. 246.
12. In 1915 Hermann Oppenheim, a German psychiatrist, published the standard work, supposedly proving the physical nature of shell shock. See Jose Brunner's *Freud and the Politics of Psychoanalysis* (Oxford, U.K., Cambridge, Mass.: Blackwell, 1995), pp. 106–22.
13. Elaine Showalter, "Hysteria, Feminism and Gender," in Sander Gilman et al., *Hysteria Beyond Freud* (Berkeley: University of California Press, 1993), p. 321.
14. Brunner, *Freud and the Politics,* p. 109; the French and British characterized these methods as examples of German bestiality, but they also questioned the legitimacy of the complaints.
15. Quoted in Ecksteins, *Rites of Spring,* p. 172.
16. Ernst Simmel, *Kriegs-Neuroses und "Psychisches Trauma"* (Munich: Otto Nemnich, 1918), pp. 5–6, 82–84.
17. Hal Foster, *Compulsive Beauty* (Cambridge, Mass.: MIT Press, 1993), p. xi.
18. See Tausk's 1916 article "On the Psychology of the War Deserter," translated and published in *Psychoanalytic Quarterly* 38 (1969): 354–81, and reprinted in Paul Roazen, *Tausk, Sexuality, War, and Schizophrenia: Collected Psychoanalytic Papers* (New Brunswick, N.J.: Transaction, 1991), pp. 141–65. In it Tausk wrote that the psychologist "is not concerned with whether or not the consequences that follow from his investigations harmonize with the requirements of the army," p. 354.

19. Brunner, *Freud and the Politics,* p. 113. Of course, under wartime conditions, analytic treatment was greatly simplified. Thus, in 1918 Freud explained to Simmel: "Your therapy should be termed cathartic rather than psychoanalytic. You take essentially the point of view of the *Studies in Hysteria.*" David Brunswick and Ruth Lachenbruch, "Freud's Letters to Ernst Simmel," trans. Frances Deri and David Brunswick, *Journal of the American Psychoanalytic Association* 12, no. 1 (January 1964): 93–109.

20. Leed, *No Man's Land,* p. 176.

21. W. H. R. Rivers in 1917, cited in Ronald W. Clark, *Freud: The Man and the Cause* (New York: Random House, 1980), p. 385. For England, also see Jones, vol. 2, p. 253; *SE,* vol. 17, pp. 209–10.

22. Ted Bogacz, "War Neurosis and Cultural Change in England, 1914–1922: The Work of the War Office Committee of Enquiry into 'Shell Shock,' " *Journal of Contemporary History* 24 (1989): 239.

23. W. M. Maxwell, *A Psychological Retrospect of the Great War* (London: Macmillan, 1923).

24. Leed, *No Man's Land,* pp. 181–83.

25. Quoted in Ecksteins, *Rites of Spring,* p. 173.

26. Karl Abraham, "Psychoanalysis and the War Neuroses," in *Clinical Papers and Essays on Psychoanalysis* (New York: Brunner/Mazel, 1955), pp. 61–63.

27. As Freud noted, the epidemic resulted from the recruitment of a conscript as opposed to a mercenary army. Unlike the professional, the draftee was a divided soul, facing "a conflict . . . between the soldier's old peaceful ego and his new warlike one . . . which [the old ego] sees as threatening its life." *SE,* vol. 17, p. 209. Also see Freud to Jones, 18 February 1919, *Freud-Jones,* pp. 334 ff.

28. Pat Barker, *Regeneration* (London: Dutton, 1992).

29. *SE,* vol. 18, p. 16.

30. Ibid., p. 56.

31. Ibid., vol. 17, p. 209, has "which it sees is threatening its life."

32. Trauma or fear of trauma was "to be found at the bottom of every case of transference neurosis (*Übertraggs-neurose*)." Freud to Jones, 18 February 1919, *Freud-Jones,* p. 334.

33. Thomas Mann, *Diary* (London: Robin Clark, 1984), 24 May 1921, p. 115.

34. François Furet, *The Passing of an Illusion* (Chicago: University of Chicago Press, 1999), p. 48.

35. Winston Churchill, *The World Crisis, 1911–1918* (London: Thornton Butterworth, 1931), pp. 19–20.

36. Robert Musil, *Diaries, 1899–1941,* selected, translated, and annotated by Philip Payne from the original German version of the *Diaries* edited by Adolf Frisé, ed. Mark Mirsky (New York: Basic Books, 1998), p. 271.

37. Paul Johnson, *Modern Times: The World from the Twenties to the Eighties* (New York: Harper & Row, 1983), pp. 5–6; Jones, vol. 2, p. 223. Neutrals, such as the Dutch, were present, but no one from France, England, or the United States.

38. This assertion is found in many scholarly works, and perhaps especially in Bertram Lewin and Helen Ross, *Psychoanalytic Education in the United States* (New York: Norton, 1960). However, in a private letter, Paul Roazen has written to me: "The Budapest Congress beat back the idea that all analysts be analyzed. Rank and Tausk opposed it. . . . Lewin and Ross are simply wrong." Roazen's forthcoming work may lead me to modify this assertion.

39. Frank Eckelt, "The Internal Policies of the Hungarian Soviet Republic," in *Hungary in Revolution, 1918–1919,* ed. Iván Völgyes (Lincoln: University of Nebraska Press, 1971), pp. 61–88.

40. *SE,* vol. 17, p. 167. Freud added that even though the "gold" of analysis would be alloyed with the "copper" of suggestion, the most important ingredients of all popular therapies would "remain those borrowed from strict and untendentious psycho-analysis."

41. H. V. Dicks, *Fifty Years of the Tavistock Clinic* (London: Routledge, 1970), p. 1.

42. Elisabeth Young-Bruehl, *Anna Freud: A Biography* (New York: Summit Books, 1988), p. 92; Michael Balint, "On the Psychoanalytic Training System," in *Primary Love and Psychoanalytic Technique* (New York: Liveright, 1965), p. 168.

43. Quoted in Susan Quinn, *A Mind of Her Own: The Life of Karen Horney* (New York: Summit Books, 1987), p. 196. Walter Laqueur, *Weimar: A Cultural History, 1918–1933* (London: Weidenfeld and Nicholson, 1974), p. 215. See also *SE*, vol. 17, p. 167; Peter Gay, *Sigmund Freud: A Life for Our Time* (New York: Norton, 1988), p. 462. Other members of the Union included Heinrich Meng and Angel Garma.

44. *SE*, vol. 19, p. 285.

45. Hungarian analysis of the twenties, Balint added, was "a very left-wing thing." Interview with Michael Balint, 6 August 1965, Oral History Collection, Columbia University Library; Gay, *Freud*, pp. 462–63. By contrast, American analysis was fee-for-service. Even in the midst of the Depression there were only two low-fee analytic clinics in the United States—in Chicago and Topeka, Kansas. Nathan G. Hale, "From Bergasse XIX to Central Park West," *Journal of the History of Behavioral Sciences* 14 (1978): 302.

46. Hannah S. Decker, "Psychoanalysis in Germany," *Comparative Studies in Society and History* 24, no. 4 (October 1982): 591; Edith Kurzweil, *The Freudians: A Comparative Perspective* (New Haven, Conn.: Yale University Press, 1989), pp. 44–47; Elisabeth Roudinesco and Michel Plon, *Dictionnaire de la psychanalyse* (Paris: Fayard, 1997), p. 30. In 1930 Eitingon drew up a ten-year balance sheet documenting 1,955 consultations, including 721 analytic treatments.

47. Sheldon Gardner and Gwendolyn Stevens, *Red Vienna and the Golden Age of Psychology* (New York: Praeger, 1992), p. 126. The society had to decline the gift, since it lacked the funds to build. An institute was not established until 1935. See also Gay, *Freud*, p. 458.

48. Bernfeld developed the concept of "social location" as an alternative to Reich. Siegfried Bernfeld, *Antiautoritäre Erziehung und Psychoanalyse: Ausgewählte Schriften*, 3 vols., ed. Lutz von Werder and Reinhart Wolff (Darmstadt: März-Verlag, 1969); and "Der sociale Ort und seine bedeutung für Neurose, Verwahrlosung und Pädagogik," *Imago*, 1929. See Philip Utley, "Siegfried Bernfeld's Jewish Order of Youth, 1914–1922," in *Leo Baeck Institute Yearbook*, 1979.

49. Denise Riley, *War in the Nursery: Theories of the Child and Mother* (London: Virago Press, 1983), p. 71; Anna Freud, *The Psychoanalytic Treatment of Children: Technical Lectures and Essays*, trans. Nancy Procter-Gregg (London: Imago, 1947), preface, p. x. On Anna Freud's connection to Montessori, see *LSF*, pp. 319–20; Kurzweil, *Freudians*, p. 134. For child analysis in Budapest, see Ferenczi to Freud, 31 May 1931, *Freud-Ferenczi*, vol. 3, p. 411.

50. *SE*, vol. 12, p. 305; Ernst Federn, son of Paul, writes: "Were we brought up psychoanalytically? Certainly corporal punishment was excluded." Ernst Federn, *Witnessing Psychoanalysis: From Vienna Back to Vienna via Buchenwald and the USA* (London: Karnac, 1990), p. 283.

51. Balint, "Psychoanalytic Training," pp. 168, 261; Lewin and Ross, *Psychoanalytic Education*, p. 29.

52. *SE*, vol. 12, pp. 330–31.

53. Other lay analysts include Robert Wälder, J. C. Flugl, and James Strachey. See Gay, *Freud*, p. 492; Elisabeth Roudinesco, *Jacques Lacan and Co.: A History of Psychoanalysis in France, 1925–1985*, trans. Jeffrey Mehlman (Chicago: University of Chicago Press, 1990), p. 39.

54. *SE*, vol. 17, p. 171.

55. Ibid., pp. 161, 164–65.

56. Ibid., p. 144.

57. In 1912 Freud reported to Jung that there was an "epidemic" of interest in Odessa. Quoted in Alexander Etkind, *Eros of the Impossible: The History of Psychoanalysis in Russia*, trans. Noah and Maria Rubens (Boulder, Colo.: Westview Press, 1997), p. 115.

58. The home was headed by Moshe Wulff and Vera Schmidt. Caresses were supposedly replaced by more "rational" exchanges. Other societies formed in Petrograd, Kiev, Odessa,

and Rostov. Another key figure was I. D. Ermakov, a psychiatrist and literary critic. Vera Schmidt, *Psychoanalytic Education in Russia* (n.p., 1924); Roudinesco, *Lacan & Co.,* p. 39; Jones, vol. 2, p. 76; E. James Lieberman, *Acts of Will: The Life and Work of Otto Rank* (New York: Free Press, 1985), p. 186; Dr. Sara Neidietsch and Dr. Nikolai Ossipow, "Psychoanalysis in Russia," *International Journal of Psychoanalysis* 3 (1922): 514–17. Sabina Spielrein "jump-started" Russian interest, not only in Freud but in Jung and Piaget. See also Lisa Appignanesi and John Forrester, *Freud's Women* (New York: Basic Books, 1993), p. 225; Mireille Cifali, "Une femme dans la psychanalyse: Sabina Spielrein, un autre portrait," *Le Bloc—Notes de la Psychanalyse* 8 (1988): 253–66.

59. Martin A. Miller, *Freud and the Bolsheviks: Psychoanalysis in Russia and the Soviet Union* (New Haven, Conn.: Yale University Press, 1998), p. 59.

60. Etkind, *Eros,* p. 179. Instead of the present "hypertrophy in sexual matters," Lenin advocated "healthy sport . . . bodily exercises of every kind" in his 1920 conversations with Clara Zetkin. See Beatrice Farnsworth, *Alexandra Kollontai: Socialism, Feminism, and the Bolshevik Revolution* (Stanford, Calif.: Stanford University Press, 1980), pp. 356–57. Of course, the repressed returned, as in Lenin's characterization of left-wing communism as "an infantile neurosis," or his characterization of the Social Revolutionaries as "hysterical."

61. Etkind, *Eros,* p. 179.

62. Quoted in Alex Kozulin, *Psychology in Utopia: Toward a Social History of Soviet Psychology* (Cambridge, Mass.: MIT Press, 1984), pp. 87–88; Martin A. Miller, "Freudian Theory Under Bolshevik Rule: The Theoretical Controversy During the 1920s," *Slavic Review* 44, no. 4 (1985): 628. Vygotsky's first published work was an introduction to Freud's *Beyond the Pleasure Principle.* His view that there is no presocial or prelinguistic form of thought developed in tacit dialogue with Freud.

63. According to his biographer Isaac Deutscher, Trotsky "studied psychoanalytic issues deeply and sympathetically, and therefore knew the method's shortcomings." Quoted in Etkind, *Eros,* p. 232.

64. Man first drove "the dark forces" out of industry, Trotsky explained, then out of politics, then out of the family, and finally would drive them out of the individual psyche. "The man of today, with all his contradictions and lack of harmony, will open the road for a new and happier race." See Etkind, *Eros,* chap. 7. Trotsky liked the emphasis on reflex because it broke down the distinction between psychology and physiology. He asked Pavlov whether "the doctrine of conditioned reflexes did not include Freud's theory as a particular instance." David Joravsky, *Russian Psychology: A Critical History* (Oxford, U.K., and Cambridge, Mass.: Blackwell, 1989), pp. 211, 217, 235–36, 248. For Trotsky's meeting with analysts in Vienna in 1909, see Roudinesco, *Lacan & Co.,* p. 35. "Reflexology" was associated with ambivalent defenders of analysis such as A. R. Luria, L. S. Vygotsky, and A. B. Zalkind.

65. Gross had lived in a commune whose ideals included free love, women's control over their own sexuality, and cooperative child rearing. Martin Stanton, "Otto Gross's Case Histories: Jung, Stekel, and the Pathologization of Protest," in *Carl Gustav Jung: Critical Assessments,* ed. Renos K. Papadopoulos (London and New York: Routledge, 1992), vol. 1, pp. 200–208; Otto Gross, *Über Psychopathische Mindewertigkeiten,* pp. 49–52, cited in Arthur Mitzman, "Anarchism, Expressionism, and Psychoanalysis," *New German Critique* 10 (Winter 1977): 77–104. Gross's close associate Franz Jung identified the crucial struggles, left over by the Russian Revolution, as those for women, youth, and free thought.

66. Paul Federn, *Zur psychologie der Revolution: Die Vaterlose Gesellschaft* (Wien: Anzengruber-Verlag Brüder Suschitzky, 1919); Rudolf Ekstein, "Reflections on and Translation of Paul Federn's 'The Fatherless Society,'" *Reiss-Davis Clinic Bulletin,* 1971–72. I have modified the translation.

67. Luisa Passerini, *Europe in Love, Love in Europe: Imagination and Politics Between the Wars* (London: Touris, 1999), pp. 82–87.

68. Sigmund Freud, *The Future of an Illusion* (New York: Norton, 1961), pp. 10–11.

69. John Dos Passos, *1919* (New York: Harcourt, Brace, 1932).

70. This is the contention of Etkind, who in *Eros* cites W. C. Bullitt, *The Bullitt Mission to Russia,* testimony before the U.S. Senate Committee on Foreign Relations (1919) (New York: Hyperion, 1977).

71. Cited in Jones, vol. 2, pp. 201, 215.

72. Young-Bruehl, *Anna Freud,* p. 91; Ann Douglas, *Terrible Honesty,* p. 123; Gay, *Freud,* p. 380.

73. Freud to Jones, 12 February 1920, *Freud-Jones,* p. 370.

74. Freud to Abraham, 27 August 1918, *Freud-Abraham,* p. 278; Jones, vol. 3, p. 7; Young-Bruehl, *Anna Freud,* p. 92; Balint, "Psychoanalytic Training," p. 168. Peter Homans, *The Ability to Mourn: Disillusionment and the Social Origins of Psychoanalysis* (Chicago: University of Chicago Press, 1989), pp. 155, 165, 168.

75. For the history of psychoanalysis during the *Räteregierung* (the Communist interregnum), see Paul Harmat, *Freud, Ferenczi und die ungarische Psychoanalyse* (Tübingen: Edition Dikord, 1988), pp. 72–76.

76. The *Rundbriefe* appeared approximately every ten days at first; 327 were written over five years. They are available at Columbia University in New York, and a translation is in progress.

77. *SE,* vol. 18, pp. 175, 178.

78. Phyllis Grosskurth, *The Secret Ring: Freud's Inner Circle and the Politics of Psychoanalysis* (Reading, Mass.: Addison-Wesley, 1991).

79. Quoted in Fussel, *Great War,* p. 102.

80. Leonard Woolf, *Downhill All the Way: An Autobiography of the Years 1919–1939* (New York: Harcourt, Brace, 1967), p. 164; Jan Ellen Goldstein, "The Woolfs' Response to Freud: Water Spiders, Singing Canaries, and the Second Apple," in *Literature and Psychoanalysis,* ed. Edith Kurzweil and William Phillips (New York: Columbia University Press, 1983), pp. 235–36.

81. Jean-Paul Sartre, "An Interview," *New York Review of Books,* 26 May 1970, p. 23.

82. Theodor Adorno, "Der Begriff des Unbeussten in der Transzendentalen Seelenlehre" (1924), in *Gesammelte Schriften* (Frankfurt a.M.: Suhrkamp, 1973) vol. 1, cited in Martin Jay, *Marxism and Totality: The Adventures of a Concept from Lukács to Habermas* (Berkeley: University of California Press, 1984), p. 245.

83. Jane Ellen Harrison, "Reminiscences of a Student's Life," *Arion* 4 (Summer 1965), originally published London: Hogarth Press, 1925, quoted in part in Sandra J. Peacock, *Jane Ellen Harrison: The Mask and the Self* (New Haven, Conn.: Yale University Press, 1988), pp. 237, 179–223. Also see Elizabeth Abel, *Virginia Woolf and the Fictions of Psychoanalysis* (Chicago: University of Chicago Press, 1989), p. 27.

84. He goes on: "Ah, how embarrassing Freud is! And how easily it seems to me we should have discovered his America without him!" André Gide, *Journal* (New York: Vintage, 1956), 4 February 1922, p. 349; 19 June 1924, p. 379. Gide was in his forties when he was initiated into analytic thought by Eugénie Sokolnicka, a Pole, with a sympathetic audience in *Nouvelle revue française* circles. Sokolnicka appears as Mme. Sophroniska in Gide's *Les faux-monnayeurs.* There she introduces the adolescent hero to dream analysis and free association and criticizes his mother for having tried to suppress his masturbation. Jean Delay, *The Youth of André Gide* (Chicago: University of Chicago Press, 1963), pp. 100–101; André Gide, *Les faux-monnayeurs* (Paris: Gallimard, 1997), pp. 176–80; André Gide, *Journal des faux-monnayeurs* (Paris: Gallimard, 1927); Michel Gourévitch, "Eugénie Sokolnicka," *Medecine de France* 219 (1971): 17–22.

85. Harold L. Poor, *Kurt Tucholsky and the Ordeal of Germany, 1914–1935* (New York: Scribner's, 1968), p. 67.

86. In 1915 Lawrence's *The Rainbow* was declared obscene, the remaining copies seized and burned; in 1928 Radclyffe Hall's *The Well of Loneliness;* and in 1933 *Ulysses.* Michael Holroyd, *Bernard Shaw,* vol. 3 (New York: Random House, 1988), p. 170.

87. Rolland quote from George Hutchinson, *The Harlem Renaissance in Black and White* (Cambridge, Mass.: Harvard University Press, 1995), p. 106.

88. Quoted in Michael Holroyd, *Lytton Strachey: A Critical Biography* (London: William Heinemann, 1967), vol. 2, p. 329. A genealogy of the term "Victorian" appears in Michael Mason, *The Making of Victorian Sexuality* (New York: Oxford University Press, 1995).

89. Leon Edel, *Bloomsbury: A House of Lions* (Philadelphia: Lippincott, 1979), p. 228.

90. Linda Colley, *Lewis Namier* (New York: St. Martin's Press, 1989). Namier was analyzed by Theodor Reik in 1921.

91. "The theories were the great subject of conversation wherever one went." Elizabeth Abel, *Virginia Woolf*, pp. 15–17.

92. Nathan G. Hale, *Freud and the Americans* (New York: Oxford University Press, 1971), p. 399.

93. Douglas, *Terrible Honesty*, p. 124.

94. Sherwood Anderson, *Memoirs* (New York: Harcourt, Brace, 1942), p. 243.

95. Lincoln Steffens, *The Autobiography of Lincoln Steffens* (New York: Harcourt, Brace, 1931), pp. 655–56.

96. Johnson, *Modern Times*, p. 8.

97. Quoted in Fussell, *Great War*, p. 113.

Chapter Six

1. Philip Kerr, "Can We Learn from America?" *Nation and Athenaeum* [London] 40 (1926): 76–77, quoted in Daniel T. Rodgers, *Atlantic Crossings: Social Politics in a Progressive Age* (Cambridge, Mass.: Belknap Press of Harvard University Press, 1998), p. 375.

2. Stephen Meyer III, *The Five Dollar Day: Labor Management and Social Control in the Ford Motor Company, 1908–1921* (Albany: SUNY Press, 1981), pp. 123–24.

3. Stephen P. Waring, *Taylorism Transformed: Scientific Management Theory Since 1945* (Chapel Hill: University of North Carolina Press, 1991).

4. Lizabeth Cohen, *Making a New Deal: Industrial Workers in Chicago, 1919–1939* (New York: Cambridge University Press, 1990), p. 173.

5. "The racing automobile with its bonnet adorned with great tubes," Marinetti wrote in *The Futurist Manifesto*, was "more beautiful than the Victory at Samothrace."

6. Antonio Gramsci, "Americanism and Fordism," in *Selections from the Prison Notebooks of Antonio Gramsci*, ed. Quintin Hoare and Geoffrey Nowell Smith (New York: International Publishers, 1971), p. 287.

7. Quoted in John E. Bowlt, ed., *Russian Art of the Avant-Garde: Theory and Criticism, 1902–1934* (New York: Viking Press, 1976), p. 89. The quote dates from 1913.

8. Gramsci, "Americanism," pp. 277–321. Even on the assembly line, Gramsci added, it was only the "physical gesture" that was mechanized. "The brain of the worker, far from being mummified, [had] ever greater opportunities for thinking."

9. Cohen, *New Deal*, p. 129.

10. As Jacques Donzelot has written, psychoanalysis cast suspicion on the "family of origin, with its defects, and replaced faulty appraisals of this family with the concept of the family as a horizon for individuals to conquer." Donzelot, *The Policing of Families* (New York: Random House, 1979), pp. 208–9, 233.

11. Quoted in Lewis A. Coser, *Refugee Scholars in America: Their Impact and Experience* (New Haven, Conn.: Yale University Press, 1984), p. 45.

12. *SE*, vol. 22, p. 8.

13. Jackson Lears, *Fables of Abundance: A Cultural History of Advertising in America* (New York: Basic Books, 1994), pp. 139, 208.

14. In his 1928 book, *Propaganda*, Bernays promoted advertising as a revolutionary break with authority; thus, cigarettes became "torches of freedom" when smoked in public by women. See Stuart Ewen, *Captains of Consciousness* (New York: McGraw-Hill, 1976), pp. 160–61.

15. Quoted in Ewen, *Captains,* p. 80.

16. Nathanael West, "Some Notes on Miss L.," *Contempo* 15 (May 1933). Freud was cited more in the lovelorn columns than in the news pages.

17. By the early 1920s, the United States boasted 18,000 movie theaters, England 4,000, Germany 3,700, and France about 2,500. See Kristin Thompson, "The End of the 'Film Europe' Movement," in *History on/and/in Film,* ed. T. O'Regan and B. Shoesmith (Perth: History and Film Association of Australia, 1987), pp. 45–56.

18. Irving Schneider, "The Theory and Practice of Movie Psychiatry," *American Journal of Psychiatry* 144, no. 8 (August 1987): 996; Ann Douglas, *Terrible Honesty: Mongrel Manhattan in the 1920s* (New York: Farrar, Straus and Giroux, 1995), p. 123 and passim.

19. Schneider, "Movie Psychiatry," p. 999.

20. Not that Freud was immune to commercial blandishments, having recently solicited an offer from *Cosmopolitan.* See Jones, vol. 3, p. 29.

21. Freud was dimly amused by the "primitive films" he saw in 1909 in New York, but Jones reports that Ferenczi chased them down "in his boyish way." When Melanie Klein's ten-year-old patient asked her if she was going to the movies, she told him she was planning to read. Jones, vol. 2, p. 56; *The Freud Journal of Lou Andreas-Salomé* (New York: Basic Books, 1964), pp. 101–3; Melanie Klein, *Narrative of a Child Analysis* (London: Virago, 1989), p. 343. For both references, as well as Rank's, see Stephen Heath, "Cinema and Psychoanalysis," in *Endless Night: Cinema, Psychoanalysis, Parallel Histories,* ed. Janet Bergstrom (Berkeley: University of California Press, 1999), pp. 26, 51.

22. Abraham to Freud, 18 July 1925, quoted in Heath, "Cinema," p. 53. In his Clark lectures, Freud had explained repression and analysis by using an image of a noisy intruder being forcibly ejected from a lecture hall and then persuaded to return more peacefully. But when Abraham and Sachs wanted to use this image in their film, he cautioned against it.

23. Freud to Abraham, 9 June 1925, *Freud-Abraham,* p. 384; Barbara Eppensteiner, Karl Fallend, and Johannes Reichmayr, "Die Psychoanalyse im Film 1925/26 (Berlin/Wien)," *Psyche* 2 (1986); Irving Schneider, "The "Psychiatrist in the Movies: The First Fifty Years," in *The Psychoanalytic Study of Literature,* ed. Joseph Reppen and Maurice Charney (New York: Academic Press, 1985).

24. Freud to Jones, 13 December 1925, *Freud-Jones,* p. 586.

25. Lois Palken Rudnick, *Mabel Dodge Luhan: New Woman, New Worlds* (Albuquerque: University of New Mexico Press, 1984), p. 139; Nathan G. Hale, *Freud and the Americans: The Beginnings of Psychoanalysis in the United States, 1876–1917* (New York: Oxford University Press, 1971), especially pp. 399, 346; June Sochen, *Movers and Shakers: American Women Thinkers and Activists, 1900–1910* (New York: Quadrangle Books, 1973); Catherine Covert, "Freud on the Front Page: Transmission of Freudian Ideas in the American Newspaper of the 1920s" (Ph.D. diss., Syracuse University, 1975). Brill was Luhan's analyst. He apparently told her "that 'normality' was a difficult achievement that she need not despise until she had attained it." See especially Mabel Dodge Luhan, *Intimate Memories* (New York: Harcourt, Brace, 1936), vol. 3, pp. 505–12.

26. Jones, vol. 3, p. 103; Douglas, *Terrible Honesty,* p. 123. Hearst was not the first to call for Freud's counsel in a murder case. Theodor Lessing, a defense attorney in the 1924 trial of the serial murderer Fritz Haarman in Hanover, Germany, was dismissed by the judge when he called for expert testimony from Freud, Alfred Döblin, Alfred Adler, and Ludwig Klages. "What sort of psychological questions could possibly be asked?" queried the judge. See Maria Tatar, *Lustmord: Sexual Murder in Weimar Germany* (Princeton, N.J.: Princeton University Press, 1995), pp. 48–50, 192.

27. Paula Fass, *The Damned and the Beautiful: American Youth in the 1920s* (New York: Oxford University Press, 1977), p. 291.

28. Scott and Nellie Nearing also grieved in 1912 that once the home had been "a complete economic unit." Daniel T. Rodgers, *The Work Ethic in Industrial America* (Chicago: University of Chicago Press, 1974), pp. 190–96.

29. Quoted in Eli Zaretsky, *Capitalism, the Family and Personal Life*, rev. ed. (New York: Harper & Row, 1986), pp. 85, 87.

30. In England in 1913 Christabel Pankhurst called for "Votes for Women, Chastity for Men," insisting that 80 percent of all men in England suffered from venereal disease, a figure so grotesquely exaggerated that it did great harm to her cause. Susan Kent, *Sex and Suffrage in Britain, 1860–1914* (Princeton, N.J.: Princeton University Press, 1987), pp. 3–13.

31. For one example of the counterrevolution, or "backlash," thesis, see Karen Offen, *European Feminisms, 1700–1950: A Political History* (Stanford, Calif.: Stanford University Press, 2000), p. 274.

32. For the opposing viewpoint, see Ellen Kay Trimberger, *Intimate Warriors: Portraits of a Modern Marriage, 1899–1944/Selected Works by Neith Boyce and Hutchins Hapgood* (New York: Feminist Press at the City University of New York, 1991).

33. Birth control was also a free-speech issue that linked feminism to artistic modernism, for example, after D. H. Lawrence's *The Rainbow* was declared obscene in 1915, and to lesbianism when Radclyffe Hall's *The Well of Loneliness* was banned in 1928.

34. *New York Times,* 16 July 1922, quoted in Douglas, *Terrible Honesty,* pp. 246–47. Guardians of their daughters' sexuality, mothers could smother their daughters through "the threat of castration imminent in [their] overwhelming love." This was a major theme in the culture of the twenties, as suggested by the 1925 movie *Stella Dallas,* which portrayed the mother as a vampire, needing to live vicariously through her daughter. See Douglas, *Terrible Honesty,* p. 245; articles in *The Nation* in 1926 spoke of the "injurious strain of my mother's devotion."

35. Susan Kent, *Making Peace: The Reconstruction of Gender in Interwar Britain* (Princeton, N.J.: Princeton University Press, 1993), p. 6.

36. Isherwood quoted in Anton Gill, *A Dance Between Flames: Berlin Between the Wars* (New York: Carroll and Graf, 1993), p. 230; Alex Zwerdling, *Virginia Woolf and the Real World* (Berkeley: University of California Press, 1968), p. 168. According to Virginia Woolf, "The word bugger was never far from our lips." Quoted in Leon Edel, *Bloomsbury: A House of Lions* (Philadelphia: Lippincott, 1979), p. 149. As for Berlin, the Weimar censorship law, though strict, was the least repressive in Europe. German films like *The Blue Angel* could not be shown in Paris or London. But Robert Graves and Alan Hodge, *The Long Week-end: A Social History of Great Britain, 1918–1939* (1940; repr., New York: Norton, 1963), testify to the openness of homosexuality, common-law marriage, and contraception in interwar London.

37. Quoted in Niall Ferguson, *The Pity of War* (New York: Basic Books, 1999), p. 349.

38. Blüher is quoted in Andrew Hewitt, *Political Inversions: Homosexuality, Fascism, and the Modernist Imaginary* (Stanford, Calif.: Stanford University Press, 1996), pp. 112, 123; see also Harry Oosterhuis and Hubert Kennedy, eds., *Homosexuality and Male Bonding in Pre-Nazi Germany* (New York: Haworth, 1991), p. 243.

39. Douglas, *Terrible Honesty,* pp. 134–35, 139.

40. The conjugal bond, Harrison believed, suppressed women's ties to one another. Thus, her 1921 *Epilegomena to the Study of Greek Religion* seconded Freud's insistence that "sexual desires do not unite men but divide them," but, in contrast to Freud, Harrison drew antisexual, or at least antiheterosexual, conclusions from this observation. See Jane Ellen Harrison, "Reminiscences of a Student's Life," *Arion* 4 (Summer 1965), originally published in London by Hogarth Press in 1925; Sandra J. Peacock, *Jane Ellen Harrison: The Mask and the Self* (New Haven, Conn.: Yale University Press, 1988), pp. 237, 179–223; Elizabeth Abel, *Virginia Woolf and the Fictions of Psychoanalysis* (Chicago: University of Chicago Press, 1989), pp. 27–28.

41. Henry Seidel Canby, *The Age of Confidence: Life in the Nineties* (New York: Farrar and Rinehart, 1934).

42. Floyd Dell, *Love in the Machine Age: A Psychological Study of the Transition from Patriarchal Society* (New York: Octagon, 1973), p. 7. According to Casey Blake's *Beloved Community,* Thorstein Veblen described the instinct for workmanship in behavioral terms, but in his

works on Twain and James, Van Wyck Brooks used Bernard Hart's *Psychology of Insanity* to redo Veblen's concept psychoanalytically.

43. Douglas Clayton, *Floyd Dell: The Life and Times of an American Rebel* (Chicago: Ivan R. Dee, 1994); Floyd Dell, *Homecoming: An Autobiography* (Port Washington, N.Y.: Kennikat Press, 1969), pp. 249–50, 271–72, 362; William O'Neill, ed., *Echoes of Revolt: The Masses, 1911–1917* (Chicago: Quadrangle Books, 1966), p. 21; Albert Parry, *Garrets and Pretenders: A History of Bohemianism in America* (New York: Covici, Friede, 1930), p. 278. Technically, the term "bohemia" is often reserved for the nineteenth century; its twentieth-century scope was the product of mass culture.

44. W. David Sievers, *Freud on Broadway: A History of Psychoanalysis and the American Drama* (New York: Hermitage House, 1955), p. 53. See in particular Eugene O'Neill's *The Emperor Jones* (1920), *Desire Under the Elms* (1924), *Strange Interlude* (1928), and *Mourning Becomes Electra* (1931). See also Christine Stansell, *American Moderns: Bohemian New York and the Creation of a New Century* (New York: Metropolitan Books, 2000), p. 301.

45. The case of American Jews is worth noting. Ludwig Lewisohn, a German-born southern Jew and the founder of American psychoanalytic literary criticism, was both a critic of assimilation and a supporter of psychoanalysis. For him, analysis was an effort "on the part of the Jewish people to heal itself of the malady of the soul contracted in the assimilatory process." In calling upon Jews to "reintegrate themselves with their culture, their instincts, their very sources of being," he held that Zionists played a psychoanalytic role. Lewisohn's extraordinary career was rediscovered serendipitously by civil-rights activist Ralph Melnick. See Ralph Melnick, *The Life and Work of Ludwig Lewisohn*, 2 vols. (Detroit: Wayne State University Press, 1998). See also David Singer, "Ludwig Lewisohn and Freud: The Zionist Therapeutic," *Psychoanalytic Review* 58 (Spring 1971): 169–82.

46. W. E. B. Du Bois, *The Souls of Black Folk* (New York: Penguin, 1903), pp. 11–12.

47. Paul Garon, *Blues and the Poetic Spirit* (San Francisco: City Lights, 1975), discusses the relations among the blues, psychoanalysis, and surrealism.

48. Jean Toomer to Mae Wright, 4 August 1922, quoted in George Hutchinson, *The Harlem Renaissance in Black and White* (Cambridge, Mass.: Harvard University Press, 1995), p. 131.

49. Edward Sapir, "From a Review of Oskar Pfister, 'The Psychoanalytic Method,' " in *Selected Writings of Edward Sapir in Language, Culture and Personality*, ed. David G. Mandelbaum (Berkeley: University of California Press, 1949), p. 522. Alfred Kroeber was a practicing analyst, but his anthropological work was not psychoanalytic.

50. Zora Neale Hurston, *Moses, Man of the Mountain* (New York: Lippincott, 1939).

51. Jean Toomer, "Negro Psychology in *The Emperor Jones*," in *Jean Toomer: Selected Essays and Literary Criticism*, ed. Robert B. Jones (Knoxville: University of Tennessee Press, 1996), p. 6.

52. Horace R. Cayton, *Long Old Road* (New York: Trident Press, 1965), p. 260.

53. Richard Wright, *The Long Dream* (New York: Harper & Row, 1987), pp. 78–79, quoted in Paul Gilroy, *The Black Atlantic: Modernity and Double Consciousness* (Cambridge, Mass.: Harvard University Press, 1993), p. 186; Richard Wright, "Psychiatry Comes to Harlem," *Free World* 12 (September 1946): 49–51; James Baldwin, "Alas, Poor Richard," in *Nobody Knows My Name: More Notes of a Native Son* (New York: Dell, 1961), pp. 181–215.

54. W. E. B. Du Bois, "My Evolving Program," quoted in Claudia Tate, *Psychoanalysis and Black Novels: Desire and the Protocols of Race* (New York: Oxford University Press, 1998), p. 51.

55. In 1800 Wordsworth had asked, "What information does a poet require? Unlike the lawyer, physician or mariner," only that which he possesses "as a man . . . the sympathies of daily life." William Wordsworth, "Observations Prefixed to 'Lyrical Ballads,' " in Mark Schorer, Josephine Miles, and Gordon McKenzie, eds., *Criticism: The Foundation of Modern Literary Judgment* (New York: Harcourt, Brace, 1958), p. 36.

56. "Guiltless revelation" and the quote from Gauguin are both from Donald Kuspit, *Signs of Psyche in Modern and Postmodern Art* (New York: Cambridge University Press, 1993), pp. 3, 14.

57. Meyer Schapiro, *Modern Art, 19th and 20th Centuries* (New York: G. Braziller, 1978), p. 202. Similarly, the Russian artist Vladimir Markov: "Where concrete reality, the tangible, ends, there begins another world." See Herschel B. Chipp, ed., *Theories of Modern Art* (Berkeley: University of California Press, 1968), p. 334.

58. George Groddeck's *Der Seelensucher* may be earlier. See Jacques Le Rider, "La Psychanalyse en Allemagne," in *Histoire de la psychanalyse*, ed. Roland Jaccard (Paris: Seuil, 1982), p. 129; and Harry Goldgar, "The Square Root of Minus One: Freud and Robert Musil's 'Törless,' " *Comparative Literature* 17 (1965): 117–32.

59. Virginia Woolf's unsigned review of J. D. Beresford's *An Imperfect Mother*, titled "Freudian Fiction" and published in *Times Literary Supplement*, 25 March 1920.

60. James Joyce, *Finnegans Wake* (New York: Viking Press, 1939), pp. 378, 411.

61. Ronald Clark, *Freud: The Man and the Cause* (London: Paladin Grafton, 1982), p. 418; Judith Ryan, *The Vanishing Subject: Early Psychology and Literary Modernism* (Chicago: University of Chicago Press, 1991), pp. 207–8; Jean Finck, *Thomas Mann und die psychoanalyse* (Paris: Les Belles Lettres, 1973).

62. Roger Fry, "The Artist and Psychoanalysis," in *The Hogarth Essays*, ed. Leonard S. Woolf and Virginia S. Woolf (1928; repr., Freeport, N.Y.: Books for Library Press, 1970), pp. 279–303.

63. For a worthwhile discussion, see E. H. Gombrich, "Freud's Aesthetics," *Encounter* 26, no. 1 (January 1966): 30–40.

64. D. H. Lawrence, *Women in Love* (London: Heineman, 1954), p. 223.

65. Letter of 4 December 1921, *The Letters of D. H. Lawrence*, ed. James T. Boulton, 8 vols. (Cambridge, U.K., and New York: Cambridge University Press, 1979–2000), pp. 142, 151. "I know . . . elsewhere" is from the letter of 19 February 1924, ibid., p. 585.

66. D. H. Lawrence, "Apropos of Lady Chatterley," *Lady Chatterley's Lover* (London: Phoenix, 1960), p. 34.

67. Wyndham Lewis, "Paleface," in *Enemy* 2 (1927): 61, 65, quoted in *Freudianism and the Literary Mind*, 2d ed., ed. Frederick John Hoffman (Baton Rouge: Louisiana State University Press, 1957), p. 247; Wyndham Lewis, *The Art of Being Ruled* (New York: Harper Brothers, 1926), p. 287.

68. There were other important factors, of course. France had long been the center of the avant-garde tradition and the chief support for an exalted view of the artist. Since the late nineteenth century, it had resisted the rationalizing and Americanizing aspects of the second industrial revolution, instituting policies to preserve the family farm, the petty-bourgeois artisan, and fresh food. France never partook of the vogue for psychoanalysis, and thus there was no analytic profession with which the surrealists had to contend.

69. André Breton, *Surrealism and Painting* (New York: Harper & Row, 1972), p. 2; Richard Wolin, *Walter Benjamin: An Aesthetic of Redemption* (New York: Columbia University Press, 1982), p. 127.

70. Hans Richter, *Dada: Art and Anti-Art* (New York: Abrams, 1964), p. 57. Much scholarship has called attention to the influence of French psychiatrists on the surrealists, but they turned to Freud in search of a theory of primary-process thinking.

71. "Only on the analogical plane have I ever experienced any intellectual pleasure," wrote Breton. "For me, the only real *evidence* is a result of the spontaneous, extra-lucid, and defiant relationship suddenly sensed between two things which common sense would never bring together." Quoted in Herbert S. Gershman, *The Surrealist Revolution in France* (Ann Arbor: University of Michigan Press, 1969), p. 1.

72. Kuspit, *Signs of Psyche*, pp. 81, 52.

73. Among them: Violette Papin, a parricide; Breton's Nadja; the anarchist Germaine Barton; and Edwarda, a mystic and prostitute celebrated by Bataille. These figures look back to Charcot's famous hysteric Augustine and forward to Lacan's Aimée.

74. Quoted in John MacGregor, *The Discovery of the Art of the Insane* (Princeton, N.J.: Princeton University Press, 1989), p. 289.

75. Victor Ehrlich, *Modernism and Revolution* (Cambridge, Mass.: Harvard University Press, 1994); Elisabeth Roudinesco, *Jacques Lacan & Co.: A History of Psychoanalysis in France, 1925–1985*, trans. Jeffrey Mehlman (Chicago: University of Chicago Press, 1990), p. 32; Anna Balakian, *Surrealism: The Road to the Absolute* (New York: Dutton, 1959), p. 132.

76. Roudinesco, *Lacan & Co.*, pp. 6–7. Hysteria, they wrote, "is not a pathological phenomenon and can in every respect be considered a supreme vehicle of expression. . . . Hysteria is a more or less irreducible mental state characterized by a subversion of the relations between the subject and the ethical universe in which he believes himself a practical participant, outside of any systematic delirium. This mental state is based on the need for reciprocal seduction, which explains the hastily accepted miracles of medical suggestion (or counter-suggestion)." *Revolution surréaliste*, March 1928, quoted ibid., p. 7.

77. Freud to Stefan Zweig, 20 July 1938, quoted in Jones, vol. 3, p. 235. When psychoanalysis did finally enter France on a mass, popular basis, it did so because Jacques Lacan followed surrealist precedents in rejecting any hint of positivism, linking psychoanalysis to cultural critique, and dressing it in the attire of an esoteric avant-garde.

Chapter Seven

1. *SE*, vol. 9, p. 248.

2. Quoted in Morris Eagle, *Recent Developments in Psychoanalysis: A Critical Evaluation* (Cambridge, Mass.: Harvard University Press, 1987), pp. 81, 109. See also *SE*, vol. 22, p. 94 (1933): "What is feared, what is the object of the anxiety, is invariably the emergence of a traumatic moment, which cannot be dealt with by the normal rules of the pleasure principle."

3. *SE*, vol. 19, p. 30.

4. Richard P. Blackmur, *Anni Mirabilis, 1921–1925: Reason in the Madness of Letters* (Washington, D.C.: Library of Congress, 1956), p. 30.

5. *SE*, vol. 23, p. 122.

6. Sigmund Freud, *New Introductory Lectures on Psycho-Analysis* (New York: Norton, 1933), p. 79.

7. Elisabeth Young-Bruehl, *Anna Freud: A Biography* (New York: Summit Books, 1988), p. 162.

8. *SE*, vol. 19, pp. 48–59.

9. Ibid., p. 18.

10. Clara Thompson, later an associate of Ferenczi and Horney, has described the time as one in which there was "growing pessimism about the therapeutic effectiveness of psychoanalysis," but Thompson has displaced later discontents backward. Clara Thompson, *Psychoanalysis: Evolution and Development* (New York: Hermitage House, 1950), p. 172.

11. Pearl King and Riccardo Steiner, eds., *The Freud-Klein Controversies, 1941–45* (London and New York: Tavistock/Routledge, 1991), p. 90.

12. Karl Abraham, "A Particular Form of Neurotic Resistance Against the Psycho-analytic Method," originally published in the *Internationale Zeitschrift*, October 1919.

13. Ann Douglas, *Terrible Honesty: Mongrel Manhattan in the 1920s* (New York: Farrar, Straus and Giroux, 1995). As we saw, mind cure was especially pervasive in the United States, where it overlapped with a woman-centered, amateur therapeutic ethos in which the self-help traditions of American women and of evangelical Protestantism were mixed. Christian Scientists lobbied for a "Father-Mother God," stripped of masculine authority. "Give us this day our daily bread" became "Feed the famished affections."

14. Karl Abraham, "Psychoanalytic Notes on Coué's System of Self-Mastery," *International Journal of Psychoanalysis* 7 (1926).

15. Abram Kardiner, *My Analysis with Freud: Reminiscences* (New York: Norton, 1977), pp. 67, 17, and passim.

16. Frederick Crews, "The Unknown Freud," *New York Review of Books,* 18 November 1993, and "The Revenge of the Repressed," *New York Review of Books,* 17 November and 1 December 1994.

17. Young-Bruehl, *Anna Freud,* p. 157; Myron Sharaf, *Fury on Earth: A Biography of Wilhelm Reich* (New York: St. Martin's Press, 1983).

18. Wilhelm Reich, *Character-Analysis* (New York: Farrar, Straus and Giroux, 1972), p. xx; Sharaf, *Fury on Earth,* pp. 160–67.

19. Reich, *Character-Analysis,* pp. 31, 54, and chap. 4.

20. Freud to Reich, 14 December 1924, British Psychoanalytic Society Archives (hereafter BPS), London, CFE/F20/02.

21. As one commentator of the time remarked: "Character resistance is distinguishable phenomenologically from transference-resistance in that it appears impersonal and lacking in affective vitality . . . the analyst feels untouched." Hellmuth Kaiser, "Probleme der Technik," *Internationale Zeitschrift für Psychoanalyse* 20 (1934): 490–522, translated and republished in *The Evolution of Psychoanalytic Technique,* ed. Martin S. Bergmann and Frank R. Hartman (New York: Basic Books, 1976), p. 398. See also *Reich Speaks of Freud,* ed. Mary Higgins and Chester M. Raphael (New York: Farrar, Straus and Giroux, 1967); and Reich, *Character-Analysis,* p. 25.

22. Richard F. Sterba, "Clinical and Therapeutic Aspects of Character Resistance," *Psychoanalytic Quarterly* 22 (1953); Reich, *Character-Analysis,* p. 70.

23. A highly influential 1924 article by Abraham correlated a detailed schema for infantile development with stages of object relations: ingesting, retaining, and expelling correlated with the oral character and anal character. Karl Abraham, "A Short Study of the Development of the Libido in the Light of Mental Disorders" (1924), in Abraham, *Selected Papers on Psychoanalysis* (New York: Brunner/Mazel, 1927), pp. 418–502. Also see Abraham's "The First Pregenital Stage of the Libido" (1916) in the same volume, as well as his works on character.

24. Sachs proposed three stages of technique: (1) interpretation of symptoms; (2) interpretation of resistance; and (3) the substitution of recollection for repetition. The second stage was Reich's "character analysis." Sachs called this method "metapsychological" because each stage corresponded to a way of viewing the mind: conscious vs. unconscious, ego vs. id, and action vs. memory. See Hanns Sachs, "Metapsychological Points of View in Technique and Theory," *International Journal of Psychoanalysis* 6 (January 1925): 6.

25. Freud to Abraham, 30 March 1922, *Freud-Abraham,* p. 330.

26. Sándor Ferenczi and Otto Rank, *The Development of Psycho-Analysis* (1923; repr., New York and Washington, D.C.: Nervous and Mental Disease Publishing, 1925), pp. 3–4, 23; E. James Lieberman, *Acts of Will: The Life and Work of Otto Rank* (New York: Free Press, 1985), pp. 208 ff. For Franz Alexander, a younger Berlin ego psychologist who had fled Hungary, "the old abreaction [catharsis] theory began to emerge from the past." Franz Alexander, "The Problem of Psychoanalytic Technique," *Psychoanalytic Quarterly* 4 (1935): 588–611.

27. Sándor Ferenczi's 1919 article "Technical Difficulties in the Analysis of a Case of Hysteria (Including Observations on Larval Forms of Onanism and 'Onanistic Equivalents')," in Sándor Ferenczi, *Further Contributions to the Theory of Psychoanalysis* (London: Hogarth Press, 1950), p. 193; *SE,* vol. 11, p. 145.

28. Ferenczi and Rank, *Development,* p. 20.

29. Quoted in Ruth Leys, "Traumatic Cures: Shell Shock, Janet, and the Question of Memory," *Critical Inquiry* 20 (Summer 1994): 633–34 fn.

30. Jones, vol. 3, p. 58.

31. The analyst invariably stood for the mother. What Freud called the id was "the striving of the libido to re-establish a lost primal condition." "Identification," which Rank termed "enigmatic," was the setting up again of the old relation with the mother. Otto Rank, *The Trauma of Birth* (New York: Dover, 1993), pp. 6, 35, 90, 92.

32. Viennese analyst Siegfried Bernfeld has written that it is difficult to grasp what Freud's "death and resurrection" meant to the older generation. According to Bernfeld: "There were . . . outbursts of the id forces and reaction-formations against them. The case of Rank [who feared that Freud's death would end the whole project of analysis] may quite

suitably illustrate the outburst of the id. . . . Some of the others grew intensely anxious because of the threatened loss, and became very eager to establish a solid dam against heterodoxy, as they now felt themselves responsible for the future of psychoanalysis." Paul Roazen, *Helene Deutsch: A Psychoanalyst's Life* (Garden City, N.Y.: Anchor Press/Doubleday, 1985), p. 221; Siegfried Bernfeld, "On Psychoanalytic Training," *Psychoanalytic Quarterly* 31 (1962): 453–82.

33. Jones, vol. 3, pp. 59. Perhaps "we were wrong to stop at the oedipus complex," he added when writing to Abraham, 4 March 1924, *Freud-Abraham*, p. 352.

34. Freud's circular letter of 15 February 1924 is included in *Freud-Abraham*, pp. 344–48; Lieberman, *Acts of Will*, p. 222.

35. Jessie Taft, *Otto Rank* (New York: Julian Press, 1958), p. 107; Peter L. Rudnytsky, *The Psychoanalytic Vocation: Rank, Winnicott and the Legacy of Freud* (New Haven, Conn.: Yale University Press, 1991), p. 44.

36. *SE,* vol. 23, p. 216.

37. Ibid., vol. 12, p. 115; vol. 17, pp. 10–11.

38. Helen Swick Perry, *Psychiatrist of America: The Life of Harry Stack Sullivan* (Cambridge, Mass.: Harvard University Press, 1982), p. 228.

39. Quoted in Peter Gay, *Sigmund Freud: A Life for Our Time* (New York: Norton, 1988), p. 477.

40. Samuel Eisenstein, "Otto Rank," in *Psychoanalytic Pioneers,* ed. Franz Alexander, Samuel Eisenstein, and Martin Grotjahn (New Brunswick, N.J.: Transaction Publishers, 1995), p. 48.

41. Freud to Abraham, 4 July 1920, *Freud–Abraham*, p. 315.

42. Freud to Abraham, 15 February 1924, ibid., p. 345.

43. Jones, vol. 3, pp. 146–47; Ronald W. Clark, *Freud: The Man and the Cause* (London: Paladin Grafton, 1982), pp. 449 ff.

44. Anna Freud to Max Eitingon, 16 September 1924. Quoted in Young-Bruehl, *Anna Freud,* p. 149. Rank was replaced as managing editor of the *Internationaler Psychoanalytischer Verlag* by A. J. Storfer, a Romanian-born Viennese analyst who held the post until 1932.

45. According to Jones: "After the Innsbruck Congress [1927] we changed the structure of the Committee by converting it into a group, no longer private, of the officials of the International Association. They were Eitingon, the President; Ferenczi and myself, Vice-Presidents; Anna Freud, Secretary; and van Ophuijsen, Treasurer. Sachs, who had for years been rather a silent partner, dropped out." Jones, vol. 3, p. 135.

46. Clark, *Freud,* pp. 449–56; Taft, *Rank,* p. 103.

47. Clark, *Freud,* p. 402; Roazen, *Helene Deutsch,* p. 229.

48. Freud to Abraham, 3 October and 2 November 1919, *Freud-Abraham,* pp. 291, 293.

49. At least until after World War II, when Rádo succeeded in getting psychoanalysis accepted at Columbia University's medical school.

50. Freud to Ferenczi, 14 August 1925, *Freud-Ferenczi,* vol. 2, p. 222.

51. Henry Abelove, "Freud, Male Homosexuality, and the Americans," in Henry Abelove, Michèle Aina Barale, and David M. Halperin, eds., *The Lesbian and Gay Studies Reader* (New York: Routledge, 1993), pp. 282–83.

52. Lieberman, *Acts of Will,* p. 176.

53. Freud is quoted in Kenneth Lewes, *The Psychoanalytic Theory of Male Homosexuality* (New York: Simon and Schuster, 1988), p. 33.

54. Ferenczi to Eitingon, 1 December 1919, quoted in Gerhard Wittenberger, "The *Circular Letters (Rundbriefe)* as a Means of Communication of the 'Secret Committee' of Sigmund Freud," in *Behind the Scenes: Freud in Correspondence,* ed. Patrick Mahoney, Carol Bonomi, and Jan Stensson (Stockholm: Scandinavian University Press, 1997), p. 299.

55. Lavinia Edmunds, "His Master's Choice," *Johns Hopkins Magazine,* April 1988. In a 1923 letter Clarence Oberndorf described Frink to Jones as "Freud's new Christian son," BPS, COA/F02/30.

56. Karen Brecht et al., *Here Life Goes On in a Most Peculiar Way* (Hamburg: Kellner Verlag, n.d.).

57. See *Freud–Abraham,* pp. 306–13; Edith Kurzweil, *The Freudians: A Comparative Perspective* (New Haven, Conn.: Yale University Press, 1989), pp. 44–47; and Perry Meisel and Walter Kendrick, eds., *Bloomsbury/Freud: The Letters of James and Alix Strachey, 1924–1925* (New York: Basic Books, 1985). In 1930, either Eitingon or Otto Fenichel drew up a ten-year balance sheet documenting 1,955 consultations, including 721 analytic treatments. Elisabeth Roudinesco and Michel Plon, *Dictionnaire de la psychanalyse,* p. 30, credits Eitingon. But also see Otto Fenichel, "Statistischer Bericht Über die Therapeutische Tatigkeit 1920–1930," in his *Zehn Jahre Berliner Psychoanalytisches Institut Zeitschrift für Psychoanalyse* (1930), pp. 13–19.

58. Bertram Lewin and Helen Ross, *Psychoanalytic Education in the United States* (New York: Norton, 1960), p. 6; Adam Phillips, *D. W. Winnicott* (Cambridge, Mass.: Harvard University Press, 1989), pp. 39–40.

59. In 1934 Anna Freud replaced Helene Deutsch as director of training. *Freud–Ferenczi,* vol. 3, p. 116 fn. 2.

60. Anna Freud, *The Ego and the Mechanisms of Defense* (New York: International Universities Press, 1985), pp. 6, 13–14, 22; italics in original. The work was presented to the Vienna Psychoanalytic Society in 1935, published in German in 1936 and in English in 1946. Albert J. Solnit, *International Journal of Psychoanalysis* 64 (1983): 379. Anna Freud later described the book as a response to four major revisions of the ego theory: the active technique of Ferenczi and Rank; Rank's conception of the birth trauma; the "significance which Ferenczi ascribed to certain frustrations suffered by the infant in early phases of its mother-relationship," and "Reich, who attributed the failure of normal development of genital faculties to an early repression of aggressive attitudes." Phyllis Grosskurth, *Melanie Klein: Her World and Her Work* (Cambridge, Mass.: Harvard University Press, 1987), p. 337.

61. Bruce Fink, *The Lacanian Subject: Between Language and Jouissance* (Princeton, N.J.: Princeton University Press, 1995), p. 84.

62. As Balint summarized: The first stance of the ego is "almost entirely passive." It can be expressed in words as: "I shall be loved always, everywhere, in every way, my whole body, my whole being—without any criticism, without the slightest effort on my part." Michael Balint, "Critical Notes on the Theory of the Pregenital Organization of the Libido" (1935), reprinted in Michael Balint, *Primary Love and Psychoanalytic Technique* (New York: Liveright, 1965), pp. 46–50. Even active object love is a detour to its original passive state: "We love and gratify our partner in order to be loved and gratified by him in return."

63. Other Hungarian analysts included David Rapaport, a founder of American ego psychology, Thomas Szasz, a founder of "anti-psychiatry," and Géza Róheim, a psychoanalytic anthropologist. Roazen, *Helene Deutsch,* p. 204; Ernst Federn, *Witnessing Psychoanalysis* (London: Karnac, 1990), p. 286; André E. Haynal, *Controversies in Psychoanalytic Method: From Freud and Ferenczi to Michael Balint* (New York: New York University Press, 1989), pp. 45–48; Jean-Michel Palmier, "La psychanalyse en Hongrie," in *Histoire de la psychanalyse,* ed. Roland Jaccard (Paris: Hachette littérature générale, 1982); Joseph Gabel, *Mannheim and Hungarian Marxism* (New Brunswick, N.J.: Transaction, 1991), p. 5.

64. The term "corrective emotional experience" originated with Franz Alexander.

65. *SE,* vol. 20, p. 73.

66. Roudinesco and Plon, *Dictionnaire,* p. 238–39. For Gemelli, see Victoria De Grazia, *How Fascism Ruled Women: Italy, 1922–1945* (Berkeley: University of California Press, 1992), pp. 10–11, 218.

67. Quoted in Peter Kutter, ed., *Psychoanalysis International: A Guide to Psychoanalysis Throughout the World,* vol. 1 (Stuttgart: Fromman-Holzboog, 1992), p. 9. Esther Menaker, a trainee from the United States, found it "in-groupy" and exclusive. See Menaker, *Appointment in Vienna: An American Psychoanalyst Recalls Her Student Days in Pre-War Austria* (New York:

St. Martin's Press, 1989); for Helene Deutsch's similar views, see Lisa Appignanesi and John Forrester, *Freud's Women* (New York: Basic Books, 1993), p. 323.

68. Pierre Janet, the dominant figure in French psychiatry, told an international medical conference that psychoanalysis was the outcome of Viennese immorality. Roudinesco and Plon, *Dictionnaire*, p. 320.

69. But see the experience of Stanislaw Ignacy Witkiewicz in Daniel Gerould, *Witkacy: Stanislaw Ignacy Witkiewicz as an Imaginative Writer* (Seattle: University of Washington Press, 1981). Constantin Vlad was more successful in Romania.

70. This was Samuel Beckett's recollection. See James Knowlson, *Damned to Fame: The Life of Samuel Beckett* (New York: Simon and Schuster, 1996), p. 167.

71. Thomas F. Glick, "The Naked Science: Psychoanalysis in Spain, 1914–1948," *Comparative Studies in Society and History* 24, no. 4 (October 1982): 540; Rockwell Gray, *The Imperative of Modernity: An Intellectual Biography of José Ortega y Gasset* (Berkeley: University of California Press, 1989).

72. Raúl Páramo-Ortega, *Freud in Mexico: Zur Geschichte der Psychoanalyse in Mexiko* (Berlin: Quintessenz, 1992), stresses the connections between analysis and Marxism.

73. H. Stuart Hughes, *The Sea Change: The Migration of Social Thought, 1930–1965* (New York: Harper & Row, 1975), p. 10; Jones, vol. 3, p. 170. Earlier pioneers include Gustavo Modena and Roberto Assagioli. Marco Levi-Bianchini started a society in 1925. See Abraham to Freud, 31 October 1914, *Freud–Abraham*, pp. 199–200, on Levi-Bianchini, and see Paul Roazen's forthcoming book on Edoardo Weiss.

74. These are the words of A. B. Zalkind. Martin A. Miller, "The Reception of Psychoanalysis and the Problem of the Unconscious in Russia," *Social Research* 57, no. 4 (Winter 1990): 876–88; also see Alexander Etkind, "Russia," in Kutter, *Psychoanalysis*, vol. 2, p. 339; Alexander Etkind, *Eros of the Impossible: The History of Psychoanalysis in Russia*, trans. Noah and Maria Rubens (Boulder, Colo.: Westview Press, 1997), p. 116.

75. Martin A. Miller, *Freud and the Bolsheviks: Psychoanalysis in Imperial Russia and the Soviet Union* (New Haven, Conn.: Yale University Press, 1998), p. 92.

76. Quoted in Hans Lobner and Vladimir Levitin, "A Short Account of Freudism: Notes on the History of Psychoanalysis in the USSR," *Sigmund Freud House Bulletin* 2, no. 1 (1978): 14. In 1913 Freud had told the son of Theodor Herzl, the founder of Zionism, "Your father is one of those people who have turned dreams into reality. This is a very rare and dangerous breed. . . . I would simply call them the sharpest opponents of my scientific work." A. Falk, "Freud and Herzl," *Midstream*, January 1977, p. 19.

77. Sheldon Gardner and Gwendolen Stevens, *Red Vienna and the Golden Age of Psychology* (New York: Praeger, 1992), p. 96. The university faculty included Paul Lazersfeld, Karl and Charlotte Bühler, and Paul Schilder, as well as many figures from the earlier history of analysis: Alfred Adler, Franz Brentano, Ernst Mach, Ernst Brücke, Sigmund Exner, Theodor Meynert, Josef Breuer, and Richard von Krafft-Ebing. Postwar refugee relief had spurred interest in child development. In 1921 George Bakeman, the American Red Cross commissioner in Vienna, wrote in *Survey:* "The fight in Vienna is not only to save the lives of Vienna's children, but to save their childhood."

78. The two societies were the loosely associated Société Psychanalytique Suisse and the Groupe Psychanalytique de Genève.

79. Other members included Raymond de Saussure, son of the famous linguist, and Édouard Claparède. John Kerr, *A Most Dangerous Method: The Story of Jung, Freud, and Sabina Spielrein* (New York: Knopf, 1993); Mireille Cifali, "Entre Genève et Paris: Vienne," *Le Bloc: Notes de la psychanalyse* 2 (1982): 91–130; Jones to Freud, 17 March 1919, *Freud–Jones*, p. 337 fn. 1; Fernando Vidal, "Piaget et la psychanalyse: Premières rencontres," *Le Bloc: Notes de la psychanalyse* (1986).

80. Richard von Mises, *Probability, Statistics and Truth* (New York: Macmillan, 1938), pp. 237–38. Marie Jahoda, "The Migration of Psychoanalysis: Its Impact on American Psychology," in *The Intellectual Migration: Europe and America, 1930–1960,* ed. Donald Fleming and

Bernard Bailyn (Cambridge, Mass.: Harvard University Press, 1969), p. 427. According to David Shakow and David Rapaport, *The Influence of Freud on American Psychology* (New York: International Universities Press, 1964), p. 142: "Freud's concepts were turned into vague conceptions, barely related, and at times actually contradictory, to their original forms."

81. John Dollard et al., *Frustration and Aggression* (New Haven, Conn.: Yale University Press, 1939). Dollard's externalist model of development denied infantile aggressivity, thereby fostering the emphasis on the mother's all-powerful role.

82. Terman is quoted in George E. Gifford, Jr., *Psychoanalysis, Psychotherapy and the New England Medical Scene, 1894–1944* (New York: Science History Publications, 1978), p. 33. Hull is quoted in Jahoda, "Migration," p. 427.

83. Freud to Saul Rosenzweig, 24 February 1934, quoted in Adolf Grünbaum, *The Foundations of Psychoanalysis: A Philosophical Critique* (Berkeley: University of California Press, 1984), p. 101.

84. The first Dutch psychoanalyst was August Stärcke; he had practiced analysis in the Netherlands since 1905. See Ilse N. Bulhof, "Psychoanalysis in the Netherlands," *Comparative Studies in Society and History* 24, no. 4 (October 1982): 573; Christine Brinkgreve, "The Psychoanalytic Underground (Holland, 1940–5)," *Current Issues in Psychoanalytic Practice* 3, no. 1 (New York: Haworth Press, 1986); *Freud–Jung*, p. 522 fn. 1. Jan E. G. van Emden and Jeanne Lampl–de Groot were other leading figures. During World War I van Emden acted as intermediary between Jones and Freud.

85. Miller, *Freud and the Bolsheviks*, p. 61.

86. Roudinesco and Plon, *Dictionnaire*, p. 774. The Belgian Psychoanalytic Society was founded by Julien Varendonck.

87. Jacques Quen and Eric T. Carlson, *American Psychoanalysis: Origins and Development* (New York: Brunner/Mazel, 1978), p. 81; Jones, vol. 3, p. 112; Sandor Lorand, "Reflections on the Development of Psychoanalysis in New York from 1925," *International Journal of Psychoanalysis* 50 (1969): 591.

88. Jones, vol. 3, pp. 297–98.

89. Douglas, *Terrible Honesty*, p. 123.

90. Freud wrote Rank on 23 May 1924: "You now have nearly all my former analysands whose analyses I recall without any satisfaction." Quoted in Phyllis Grosskurth, *The Secret Ring: Freud's Inner Circle and the Politics of Psychoanalysis* (Reading, Mass.: Addison-Wesley, 1991), p. 158.

91. Freud to Abraham, 6 January 1920, *Freud–Abraham*, p. 301.

92. Jones, vol. 3, pp. 168–69.

93. Gay, *Freud*, p. 496.

94. Grosskurth, *Secret Ring*, p. 183.

95. Jones, vol. 3, pp. 168–69, 145–46, 287–301; Clarence Oberndorf, *A History of Psychoanalysis in America* (New York: Grune and Stratton, 1953), p. 176; Lewin and Ross, *Psychoanalytic Education*, p. 33. See also Jones to Freud, 5 May 1932, *Freud–Jones*, pp. xxxvi, 694–95.

96. According to the psychoanalyst Heinz Kohut, there were two groups of American analysts. The larger, but decreasingly influential, was mainly "East European Jewish, a generation or two removed from the ghetto, to whom the haven of American institutions was liberation." The other, which included such figures as William Alanson White and Harry Stack Sullivan, Kohut characterized as "of that attractive branch of Protestantism" that sought to replace dogma with "missionary work, progressive social action, and social reforming." They maintained "a close tie to psychiatry with an emphasis on interpersonal healing, helping and reform." Heinz Kohut to Anna Freud, 4 August 1964, in *The Curve of Life: The Correspondence of Heinz Kohut, 1923–1981*, ed. Heinz Kohut (Chicago: University of Chicago Press, 1994), p. 101. See also Perry, *Psychiatrist of America*, p. 223; Nathan G. Hale, Jr., "From Berggasse XIX to Central Park West: The Americanization of Psychoanalysis, 1919–1940," *Journal of the History of Behavioral Sciences* 14 (1978): 299–315; Fred Matthews,

"In Defense of Common Sense: Mental Hygiene as Ideology and Mentality in 20th Century America," *Prospects* 4 (1979): 459–516; Arcangelo R. T. D'Amore, ed., *William Alanson White: The Washington Years, 1903–1937* (Washington, D.C.: U.S. Government Printing Office, 1976); E. Fuller Torrey, *Freudian Fraud: The Malignant Effect of Freud's Theory on American Thought and Culture* (New York: HarperCollins, 1992), p. 151. White had been superintendent of St. Elizabeth's Hospital in Washington, D.C., since 1903, a translator of Adler, and cofounder of the *Psychoanalytic Review,* the first English-language journal of psychoanalysis. Sullivan, heavily influenced by White, came to St. Elizabeth's in 1922.

97. Harry Stack Sullivan, visiting Berlin, checked out Alexander's "dress and deportment" to see if he would fit in as psychoanalyst in residence at the University of Chicago. Apparently, Alexander passed the test. When he attended the first International Congress of Mental Hygiene in Washington, D.C., he was esteemed "much higher . . . than Freud." According to Helene Deutsch, he "had a magic power that made all homosexual [i.e., dependent] men in highest places his slaves. One must have been in America to understand such things." Herbert Hoover was the honorary president of the congress. Much of the money was put up by Clifford Beers, author of *The Mind That Found Itself.* See Frankwood E. Williams, *Proceedings of the First International Congress on Mental Hygiene* (New York: International Committee for Mental Hygiene, 1932); Franz Alexander, *The Western Mind in Transition: An Eyewitness Story* (New York: Random House, 1960), pp. 94–99; Roazen, *Helene Deutsch,* pp. 271 ff.; Susan Quinn, *A Mind of Her Own: The Life of Karen Horney* (New York: Summit Books, 1987), p. 249. Analytic interest in Chicago began with Lionel Blitzen, a 1921 analysand of Rank's and the first president of the Chicago society, at Northwestern University Medical School in the 1920s. See Harry Stack Sullivan, *The Fusion of Psychiatry and Social Science* (New York: Norton, 1964), p. xxviii; Oberndorf, *History,* p. xvi.

98. An analyst living in modest circumstances in Vienna, as Paul Roazen remarked, would "be welcomed as a celebrity in America." Roazen, *Helene Deutsch,* p. 271.

99. Linda Donn, *Freud and Jung: Years of Friendship, Years of Loss* (New York: Scribners, 1988), p. 111; Freud to Jones, 12 April 1921, *Freud–Jones,* pp. 418–42; Grosskurth, *Secret Ring,* p. 192. For "dollaria," see Gay, *Freud,* p. 210.

100. Ilse Grubrich-Simitis, *Back to Freud's Texts: Making Silent Documents Speak,* trans. Philip Slotkin (New Haven, Conn.: Yale University Press, 1996), pp. 176–81.

101. *SE,* vol. 21, p. 39.

102. Warwick Anderson, "The Trespass Speaks: White Masculinity and Colonial Breakdown," *American Historical Review,* December 1997, pp. 1343–1370. The quotation is from p. 1360.

103. Christiane Hartnack, "British Psychoanalysts in Colonial India," in *Psychology in Twentieth-Century Thought and Society,* ed. M. G. Ash and W. Woodward (Cambridge, U.K.: Cambridge University Press, 1987), p. 247.

104. T. C. Sinha, "Development of Psychoanalysis in India," *International Journal of Psychoanalysis,* 1966, p. 430. For China, see Lieberman, *Acts of Will,* p. 187, and Jones, vol. 3, pp. 191.

105. Sudhir Kakar, *Culture and Psyche: Psychoanalysis and India* (New York: Psyche Press, 1997), pp. 50–51.

106. Ashis Nandy, "The Savage Freud," in *The Savage Freud and Other Essays on Possible and Retrievable Selves* (Princeton, N.J.: Princeton University Press, 1995), pp. 103, 109 n.; Sinha, "Psychoanalysis in India," p. 430.

107. Kutter, *Psychoanalysis International,* vol. 2, pp. 124–131; T. Takahashi, "La Psychanalyse au Japon," in *Histoire de la psychanalyse,* ed. R. Jaccard (Paris: Hachette, 1982), pp. 417–38; Jones to Anna Freud, 12 July 1934, British Psychoanalytic Society Archives, CFA/F02/01.

108. Wang Ning, "Confronting Western Influence: Rethinking Chinese Literature of the New Period," *New Literary History* 24, no. 4 (Autumn 1993): 905–26.

109. Vera Schwarcz, *The Chinese Enlightenment: Intellectuals and the Legacy of the May Fourth Movement of 1919* (Berkeley: University of California Press, 1986), p. 104.

110. Jingyuan Zhang, *Psychoanalysis in China: Literary Transformation, 1919–1949* (Ithaca, N.Y.: East Asia Program, 1992), p. 13. Still, by 1949 only five of Freud's works had been translated

into Chinese, along with commentaries by Barbara Low and other analysts. Wilhelm Reich, however, was much translated.

111. *Tafsir el ahlam* (Al Qahirah: Dar el M'aref, 1958). Safouan also produced the first Arabic translation of Hegel's *Phenomenology of the Mind.*

112. Wulf Sachs, *Black Hamlet* (London: G. Bles, 1937); Megan Vaughan, *Curing Their Ills: Colonial Power and African Illness* (Cambridge, U.K.: Polity Press, 1991).

113. Zhang, *Psychoanalysis in China,* p. 6.

114. Freud to Andreas-Salomé, 13 March 1922, *Freud–Salomé,* p. 114; Kalpana Seshadi-Crooks, "The Primitive as Analyst: Postcolonial Feminism's Access to Psychoanalysis," *Cultural Critique,* Fall 1994.

115. Freud, *Letters,* p. 392, quoted in Roudinesco, *Dictionnaire,* p. 82; Jones, vol. 3, p. 128, quoting Freud to Ferenczi, 13 December 1926.

116. *SE,* vol. 22, p. 179.

117. Ibid., vol. 21, pp. 64–68.

118. Moshe Gresser, *Dual Allegiance: Freud as a Modern Jew* (Albany: SUNY Press, 1994), p. 175.

Chapter Eight

1. Marshall Stalley, ed., *Patrick Geddes: Spokesman for Man and the Environment* (New Brunswick, N.J.: Rutgers University Press, 1972), pp. 289–380; Frank G. Novak, Jr., ed., *Lewis Mumford and Patrick Geddes: The Correspondence* (New York: Routledge, 1995).

2. H. G. Wells quoted in Susan Kent, *Making Peace* (Princeton, N.J.: Princeton University Press, 1993), p. 42.

3. Elaine Showalter, "Introduction," *These Modern Women: Autobiographical Essays from the Twenties* (Old Westbury, N.Y.: Feminist Press, 1978), p. 22. The popularity of Margaret Sanger's writings on birth control and Marie Stopes's manual, *Married Love,* attest to this change.

4. Quoted in Mari Jo Buhle, *Feminism and Its Discontents* (Cambridge, Mass.: Harvard University Press, 1999), p. 96. Part of the reason for Ellen Key's popularity was that she linked motherhood and sexuality. Everybody who once read Charlotte Gilman has turned to Key, noted one feminist in 1924. Rheta Chile Dorr, *A Woman of Fifty* (New York: Funk and Wagnalls, 1924), p. 224.

5. Quoted in George Chauncey, *Gay New York: Gender, Urban Culture, and the Making of the Gay Male World, 1890–1940* (New York: Basic Books, 1994), p. 188.

6. Suzanne LaFollette, *Concerning Women* (New York: Albert and Charles Bond, 1926), p. 270.

7. For Salt Lake City, see John D'Emilio and Estelle B. Freedman, *Intimate Matters: A History of Sexuality in America* (New York: Harper & Row, 1988), p. 288; Vern Bullough and Bonnie Bullough, "Lesbianism in the 1920s and 1930s: A Newfound Study," *Signs* 2, no. 4 (1977): 895–904. For Pelletier, see P. Vigné d'Octon, *La vie et l'amour: Les doctrines freudiennes et la psychanalyse* (Paris: Éditions de l'Idée Libre, 1934), pp. 71–72; Joan Scott, *Only Paradoxes to Offer* (Cambridge, Mass.: Harvard University Press), pp. 140–47.

8. Quoted in Ann Douglas, *Terrible Honesty: Mongrel Manhattan in the 1920s* (New York: Farrar, Straus and Giroux, 1995), pp. 245–47.

9. Nellie Thompson, "Early Women Psychoanalysts," *International Review of Psychoanalysis* 14 (1987): 392.

10. W. R. D. Fairbairn, "Impressions of the 1929 International Congress of Psychoanalysis," in *From Instinct to Self: Selected Papers of W. R. D. Fairbairn,* ed. Elinor Fairbairn Birtles and David Scharf (Northvale, N.J.: J. Aronson, 1994), p. 457.

11. Jill Stephenson, "Women and the Professions in Germany, 1900–1945," in *German Professions: 1800–1950,* ed. Geoffrey Cocks and Konrad H. Jarausch (New York: Oxford University Press, 1990), p. 279: "By 1933, their own professional organizations had imposed a 5 percent quota on women physicians applying for certification."

12. Atina Grossman, "German Women Doctors from Berlin to New York: Maternity and Modernity in Weimar and Exile," *Feminist Studies* 19, no. 1 (Spring 1993): 67.

13. Sarah Kofman, *The Enigma of Woman: Woman in Freud's Writings*, trans. Catherine Porter (Ithaca, N.Y.: Cornell University Press, 1985), p. 194.

14. *SE*, vol. 22, pp. 116, 130–31, 135.

15. Nancy J. Chodorow, *Feminism and Psychoanalytic Theory* (New Haven, Conn.: Yale University Press, 1989), pp. 202–3; italics in original.

16. Charlotte Wolff, *Hindsight: An Autobiography* (London: Quartet, 1980), p. 66.

17. Joan Riviere, "Womanliness as a Masquerade," *International Journal of Psychoanalysis* 10 (1929): 303–4.

18. Lisa Appignanesi and John Forrester, *Freud's Women* (New York: Basic Books, 1993), p. 312; George E. Gifford, ed., *Psychoanalysis, Psychotherapy, and the New England Medical Scene, 1894–1944* (New York: Science House, 1978), pp. 360–61; Paul Roazen, *Helene Deutsch: A Psychoanalyst's Life* (Garden City, N.Y.: Anchor Press/Doubleday, 1985), pp. x, 244. For Deutsch's experience with abuse, see her essay "On the Pathological Lie" (1921), *Journal of the American Academy of Psychoanalysis* 10 (1982): 369–86. See also Helene Deutsch, *Confrontations with Myself* (New York: Norton, 1973).

19. Roazen, *Helene Deutsch*, pp. 159, 178; Deutsch's lecture "George Sand: A Woman's Destiny" was delivered in March 1928 and is reprinted with an introduction by Paul Roazen in *International Review of Psychoanalysis* 9 (1982): 445–60.

20. Phyllis Grosskurth, *Melanie Klein: Her World and Her Work* (New York: Knopf, 1986), p. 134.

21. Elisabeth Young-Bruehl, *Anna Freud: A Biography* (New York: Summit Books, 1988), p. 15.

22. *The Adolescent Diaries of Karen Horney* (New York: Basic Books, 1980), pp. 90–93, quoted in Buhle, *Feminism*, pp. 69–70.

23. Dee Garrison, "Karen Horney and Feminism," *Signs* 6 (Summer 1981): 672–91; Janet Sayers, *Mothers of Psychoanalysis: Helene Deutsch, Karen Horney, Anna Freud, Melanie Klein* (New York: Norton, 1991), pp. 85–91. Abraham to Freud, 25 February 1912, *Freud–Abraham*, p. 114.

24. Buhle, *Feminism*, p. 70.

25. Atina Grossman, "Abortion and the Economic Crisis: The 1931 Campaign Against Paragraph 218," in *When Biology Becomes Destiny: Women in Weimar and Nazi Germany*, ed. Renata Bridenthal et al. (New York: Monthly Review Press, 1984), p. 125.

26. Riviere to Jones, 25 October 1918, in Vincent Brome, *Ernest Jones: Freud's Alter Ego* (London: Caliban Books, 1982), p. 113; Jones to Freud, 21 January 1921. Both quotes are cited in Stephen Heath, "Joan Riviere and the Masquerade," in *Formations of Fantasy*, ed. Victor Burgin et al. (London and New York: Methuen, 1986), p. 45.

27. Atina Grossman, *Reforming Sex: The German Movement for Birth Control and Abortion Reform, 1920–1950* (New York: Oxford University Press, 1995).

28. Payne to Klein, 16 March 1942, British Psychoanalytic Society Archives (hereafter BPS), CKB/F01/06.

29. *SE*, vol. 18, p. 164.

30. Letters of Melanie Klein, 15 and 27 April 1941, BPS, PP/KLE.

31. Roazen, *Helene Deutsch*, p. 338; see also Marie Bonaparte, "Passivity, Masochism, and Femininity," in *Psychoanalysis and Female Sexuality*, ed. Hendrik M. Ruitenbeek (New Haven, Conn.: Yale University Press, 1966), p. 136.

32. *SE*, vol. 21, pp. 225–43.

33. Ibid., vol. 11, p. 205.

34. Karen Horney, "Inhibited Femininity" (1926–7), in Horney, *Feminine Psychology*, ed. Harold Kelman (New York: Norton, 1973), p. 74. In 1917 J. H. W. Van Ophuijsen distinguished between the masculinity complex and the female castration complex. In the former, "the feeling of having been ill-treated and the consequent reaction of bitterness" is not accompanied by guilt. Van Ophuijsen's "Contributions to the Masculinity Complex" can

be found in Ruitenbeek, *Psychoanalysis and Female Sexuality,* p. 61. It was read before the Dutch Psychoanalytic Society in 1917, although not published until 1924.

35. *SE,* vol. 19, p. 251.

36. Karl Abraham, "Manifestations of the Female Castration Complex," *International Journal of Psychoanalysis* 3 (March 1922): 1–29. The paper was first presented in 1920 at a conference in The Hague. For Louise Kaplan, the article was "an all-encompassing catalogue of men's typical complaints and nagging worries about the Female." Kaplan, *Female Perversions* (New York: Doubleday, 1991), p. 79. See also Abraham's letter of 5 May 1919 in *Freud–Abraham,* p. 287.

37. In a 1928 letter, conceding to Jones that all analytic knowledge of early female development was "unsatisfactory and uncertain," Freud suggested that female heterosexuality began in the girl's sucking relation to the mother's breast, which prefigured the vagina's receptivity. Freud to Jones, 22 February 1928, *Freud–Jones,* p. 641; Grosskurth, *Melanie Klein,* p. 181.

38. *SE,* vol. 19, pp. 142, 175. Two years earlier, three years after Abraham's essay, Freud had introduced the ideas of a "phallic stage" and a "castration complex." Still earlier, he had hypothesized three stages of sexual development: oral, anal, and genital. Each stage corresponded to a way of organizing the world: subject/object, active/passive, and masculine/feminine. The new work postulated a fourth stage as an intermediate between the anal and the genital: the phallic stage. In this stage both sexes were aware of only one genital: the male. The dichotomy characteristic of this stage, phallic/castrated, was a prelude to the knowledge—characteristic of adolescence—that there are two different genital organs.

39. *SE,* vol. 20, p. 143; vol. 22, p. 124.

40. Ibid., vol. 20, pp. 137–38.

41. Vienna had an adolescent clinic directed by August Aichhorn. Erik Erikson and Peter Blos also pioneered the analytic study of adolescence. See *SE,* vol. 19, p. 273; Denise Riley, *War in the Nursery: Theories of the Child and Mother* (London: Virago Press, 1983), p. 71; Anna Freud, *The Psychoanalytic Treatment of Children: Technical Lectures and Essays,* trans. Nancy Procter-Gregg (London: Imago Publishing, 1947), pp. x, 319–20; Edith Kurzweil, *The Freudians: A Comparative Perspective* (New Haven, Conn.: Yale University Press, 1989), p. 134. For child analysis in Budapest, see Ferenczi to Freud, 31 May 1931, *Freud–Ferenczi,* vol. 3, p. 410.

42. Helene Deutsch, "The Psychology of Woman in Relation to the Functions of Reproduction," *International Journal of Psychoanalysis* 6 (1925): 405–18 (her talk at the Salzburg congress); Karen Horney, "The Flight from Womanhood: The Masculinity Complex in Women, as Viewed by Men and Women," *International Journal of Psychoanalysis* 7 (July–October 1927): 324–39; Roazen, *Helene Deutsch,* pp. 338–43; Helene Deutsch, *Zur psychologie der weiblichen Sexualfunktionen* (Vienna: Verlag, 1925), trans. as *Psychoanalysis of the Sexual Functions of Women* (a new edition was published in London by Karnac in 1991); Helene Deutsch, "On Female Homosexuality," *Psychoanalytic Quarterly* 1 (1932): 484–510. See also Appignanesi and Forrester, *Freud's Women,* p. 307.

43. Horney, "Flight," passim.

44. Melanie Klein, "The Psychological Principles of Infant Analysis" (1926), in *Contributions to Psychoanalysis, 1921–1945* (London: Hogarth Press, 1948), pp. 140–51. Tracing learning difficulties to children's fear of *maternal* retaliation, she argued that even the very youngest evinced unconscious guilt (*Schuldbewusstsein*). Grosskurth, *Melanie Klein,* pp. 123–24; Perry Meisel and Walter Kendrick, eds., *Bloomsbury/Freud: The Letters of James and Alix Strachey, 1924–1925* (New York: Basic Books, 1985), p. 21.

45. As Ernest Jones wrote: "Men analysts [had] been led to adopt an unduly phallocentric view . . . the importance of the female organs being correspondingly underestimated." The term "phallocentric" first appeared in the *OED* in 1927. Jones is sometimes credited with coining the term.

46. Jeanette C. Gadt, "The 'New' Democratic Woman of Modernity: Georgia O'Keeffe and Melanie Klein," *American Journal of Psychoanalysis* 54, no. 2 (1994): 173–87.

47. Melanie Klein, "The Psychotherapy of the Psychoses" (1930), in Klein, *Contributions to Psychoanalysis,* pp. 251–53, 268.
48. Melanie Klein, *The Psycho-analysis of Children,* trans. Alix Strachey, rev. Strachey with H. A. Thorner (New York: Free Press, 1984), pp. 35–57.
49. *SE,* vol. 21, pp. 230–31.
50. Sudhir Kakar, *Culture and Psyche: Psychoanalysis and India* (New York: Psyche Press, 1997), p. 60. See also Ashis Nandy, "The Savage Freud," in *The Savage Freud and Other Essays on Possible and Retrievable Selves* (Princeton, N.J.: Princeton University Press, 1995), pp. 103, 109 fn.; T. C. Sinha, "The Development of Psychoanalysis in India," *International Journal of Psychoanalysis* 47 (1966): 430.
51. In one variation, the goddess Devi proclaimed that she would accept only a husband who has defeated her in battle. The demon Mahisasaura appeared to claim her, with a great, armed host; Devi came alone, naked, riding a lion. "Dismounting, Devi started dancing and cutting off the heads of millions and millions of demons with her sword to the rhythm of her movement." Mahisasaura, terrified, turned into an elephant. Devi cut off his trunk. He then became a buffalo, which Devi rode to its death. Only when Shiva appeared and lay down in front of her did she stop her frenzied dancing, stick out her tongue, and feel shame. The mother, in other words, is omnipotent, sexual, and phallic, but the father or son can subdue her by being supine.
52. The value of this intimacy, and its implications for psychoanalysis, are often forgotten in contemporary work on modernism. For example, Ann Douglas, in her *Terrible Honesty,* suggests that a sexist-modernist culture arose by attacking the powerful female guardian— the Titaness—who patrolled the Victorian cultural landscape. Thus, James Joyce hailed T. S. Eliot's *The Waste Land* as the poem that ended "the idea of poetry for ladies," Joseph Hergesheimer described U.S. literature as "strangled with a petticoat," and Georg Simmel likened the mother to "an immovable prehistoric boulder in the landscape of modernity." However, Douglas does not attempt to reconcile this interpretation of modernism with her own observations concerning how oppressive the Titaness often was to her own daughters. Just as the modernist male had to free himself from his mother's "silver cord," so did the modernist female. As guardians of their daughters' sexuality, mothers could smother their female children through "the threat of castration imminent in [their] overwhelming love." As Douglas also shows, the famous 1926 series in *The Nation* on women and modernity spoke of the "injurious strain of [the] mother's devotion," a strain powerfully conveyed in the movie *Stella Dallas,* which pictured the mother as a vampire, feeding figuratively on her daughter.
53. Horney's analysis with Abraham is discussed in Elisabeth Roudinesco and Michel Plon, *Dictionnaire de la psychanalyse* (Paris: Fayard, 1997), pp. 460–61. The quote is from Horney, "Flight," pp. 331, 338.
54. Alex Zwerdling, *Virginia Woolf and the Real World* (Berkeley: University of California Press, 1968), pp. 294–96.
55. Jacques Quen and Eric T. Carlson, *American Psychoanalysis: Origins and Development* (New York: Bruner/Mazel, 1978), p. 148. The "Culture and Personality" school of anthropology, founded by John Dollard and Edward Sapir, sought to describe a society's basic or "modal" personality, the personality structure "shared by the bulk of the society's members as a result of the early experiences which they have in common." Anthropologists' interest in Freud goes back to Franz Boas, who taught a seminar on Freud at Columbia after the Clark lectures. Elsie Clews Parsons was the first anthropologist to discuss Freud in the *American Anthropologist* (in 1916), but Edward Sapir was the main inspiration. According to Weston LaBarre, "At a time when the official anthropology journals were systematically ignoring psychoanalysis and the prevailing climate of opinion was chilly if not hostile, Sapir was giving his students as required reading the works of Abraham, Jones, Ferenczi and other classic writers." For additional reading, see Steven Marcus, "Psychoanalytic Theory and Culture," *Partisan Review* 49, no. 2 (1982): 224–37; Ralph Linton, *The Study of Man* (New

York: D. Appleton-Century Co., 1936); Thomas Hartshorne, *The Distorted Image: Changing Conceptions of the American Character Since Turner* (Cleveland: Case Western Press, 1968), pp. 119–34; Fred W. Vogt, *A History of Ethnology* (New York: Holt, Rinehart and Winston, 1975), p. 440; Edward Sapir, "The Emergence of the Concept of Personality in a Study of Cultures" (1934), in *Culture, Language, and Personality* (Berkeley: University of California Press, 1949); Géza Róheim, *The Origin and Function of Culture* (New York: Nervous and Mental Disease Monographs, 1943), pp. 83–84; B. J. Bergen and S. D. Rosenberg, "The New Neo-Freudians," *Psychiatry* 34, no. 1 (1971): 31; Paul Robinson, *The Freudian Left: Wilhelm Reich, Geza Roheim, Herbert Marcuse* (New York: Harper & Row, 1969), especially pp. 93–96; Weston LaBarre, "Geza Roheim," in Franz Alexander, *Psychoanalytic Pioneers* (New York: Basic Books, 1966).

56. Erich Fromm's 1941 list of American social scientists especially influenced by psychoanalysis includes Dollard, Lasswell, Benedict, J. Hallowell, Linton, Mead, Sapir, and Kardiner. See Fromm, *Escape from Freedom* (New York: Farrar & Rinehart, 1991), p. 13 n. The effects of the Yale school can be seen on social psychologist Otto Klineberg and anthropologist Hortense Powdermaker.

57. Karen Horney, *The Neurotic Personality of Our Time* (New York: Norton, 1937), pp. 46–47, 14, 34–36, 76–77, 86, 140, 270, 276, 280, 284–87.

58. Horney, "Inhibited Femininity," pp. 74, 89.

59. Horney, *Feminine Psychology,* p. 83 and passim. Horney relied on Robert Briffault's *The Mothers* (1927).

60. According to Horney, masochism "aims not at suffering but at relinquishment of the self." Quoted in Susan Quinn, *A Mind of Her Own: The Life of Karen Horney* (New York: Summit Books, 1987), p. 270 fn. 61.

61. Quoted in Martin Birnbach, *Neo-Freudian Social Philosophy* (Stanford, Calif.: Stanford University Press, 1961), p. 52.

62. Carl Rollyson, *Rebecca West: A Life* (London: Hodder and Stoughton, 1995), pp. 134–35.

63. Quoted in Kent, *Making Peace,* pp. 136–37.

64. Ibid., p. 134.

65. Virginia Woolf to Molly McCarthy, in *The Letters of Virginia Woolf,* ed. Nigel Nicholson (London: Hogarth Press, 1977), vol. 3, pp. 134–35.

66. Zwerdling, *Virginia Woolf and the Real World,* pp. 294–96; Virginia Woolf, *A Room of One's Own* (San Diego: Harcourt Brace Jovanovich, 1989), p. 58. *Three Guineas* was originally entitled *Men Are Like That.*

67. Some have argued that the six years of silence that followed Freud's 1925 essay reflected his conflicted relations to his own mother, Amalie. Didier Anzieu has written: "For Freud it was the father who devoured his children, like Kronos; the mother was threatening only insofar as she was desirable and prohibited; he treated fragmentation and persecutory anxiety with cocaine or tobacco, not with psychical analysis." Didier Anzieu, *Freud's Self-Analysis,* trans. Peter Graham (London: Hogarth Press and the Institute of Psycho-Analysis, 1986), p. 570. Others, including Elisabeth Roudinesco, have suggested that Freud's silence in the late twenties was related to his support for his daughter Anna's views against those of Melanie Klein. Roudinesco and Plon, *Dictionnaire,* p. 976.

68. *SE,* vol. 21, p. 226.

69. Jones to Freud, 10 January 1932, and Freud to Jones, 23 January 1932, *Freud–Jones,* pp. 689 ff.; Appignanesi and Forrester, *Freud's Women,* p. 444.

70. *SE,* vol. 21, p. 234.

71. Ibid., vol. 22, p. 120.

72. Donald L. Burnham, "Freud and Female Sexuality: A Previously Unpublished Letter," *Psychiatry* 34 (August 1971): 329.

73. *SE,* vol. 21, pp. 236–37, 243. In rejecting the idea that the little girl was already feminine, Freud was insisting on the psychological as opposed to the biological character of her sexuality. As he wrote in 1930, "It would be a solution of ideal simplicity if we could suppose

that from a particular age onwards the elementary influence of the mutual attraction between the sexes makes itself felt and impels the small woman towards men," but in fact we cannot (ibid., vol. 22, p. 119). Male sexuality was also psychological, of course, but its psychology, with its early female object and its unswerving cathexis of the penis, more closely followed lines laid down by biology. Freud's view of female sexuality, contrary to the characterizations of many of his critics, stressed its divergence from the biological path. This, as much as any other quality, had placed it at the center of psychoanalytic thought and modernist culture.

74. Ibid., vol. 21, p. 157.

75. Riviere, "Womanliness as a Masquerade." See also James Strachey, Paula Heimann, and Lois Munro, "Joan Riviere," *International Journal of Psychoanalysis* 44 (1963): 228–35.

76. *SE*, vol. 23, pp. 250–53.

Chapter Nine

1. The concepts "public" and "private" were "rediscovered" by Hannah Arendt in her 1956 *The Human Condition.* Arendt, however, used these terms in what she considered to be their ancient Greek sense. In the early seventies, under the impact of second-wave feminism, the concepts were again revised, beginning with my own *Capitalism, the Family, and Personal Life,* which originally appeared in 1971–72 in the journal *Socialist Revolution* and was published as a book in 1976. *Capitalism, the Family, and Personal Life* historicized the terms "public" and "private," applying them to the division between the family and economic life that began with industrialization.

2. Zeev Sternhell, "Fascism," in *The Blackwell Encyclopedia of Political Thought,* ed. David Miller (Oxford: Blackwell, 1987), pp. 148–50.

3. The German title of Freud's study, *Massenpsychologie,* connotes a quality of "unreflecting communion" according to Max Horkheimer and Theodor W. Adorno, *Aspects of Sociology* (1956; repr., Boston: Beacon Press, 1972), p. 72.

4. *SE*, vol. 23, p. 126.

5. Ibid., vol. 18, p. 69.

6. Hippolyte Taine, *Les origines de la France contemporaine* (Paris: Hachette, 1875–93). Freud to Minna Bernays, 3 December 1885, is quoted in Jones, vol. 1, and in Peter Gay, *Sigmund Freud: A Life for Our Time* (New York: Norton, 1988), p. 48. See also Jaap van Ginneken, "The Killing of the Father: The Background of Freud's Group Psychology," *Political Psychology* 5, no. 3 (1984): 391–414.

7. *SE*, vol. 18, p. 78.

8. Wilhelm Reich, *Reich Speaks of Freud,* ed. Mary Higgins and Chester M. Raphael (New York: Farrar, Straus and Giroux, 1967), pp. 20, 35.

9. Paul Weindling, *Health, Race, and German Politics Between National Unification and Nazism, 1870–1945* (Cambridge, U.K.: Cambridge University Press, 1989).

10. Helmut Gruber, *Red Vienna: Experiment in Working-Class Culture, 1919–1934* (New York: Oxford University Press, 1991); Otto Felix Kanitz, the party's educational theorist and a follower of Max Adler, believed that new forms of education should teach proletarian children to overcome their "social inferiority complex." Anson Rabinbach, *The Crisis of Austrian Socialism* (Chicago: University of Chicago Press, 1983), pp. 188–89.

11. Paul Robinson, *The Freudian Left: Wilhelm Reich, Geza Roheim, Herbert Marcuse* (New York: Harper & Row, 1969), p. 53.

12. Rabinbach, *Austrian Socialism,* pp. 32–33.

13. Wilhelm Reich, *People in Trouble* (New York: Farrar, Straus and Giroux, 1976).

14. Canetti was also struck by a 1922 workers' demonstration in Frankfurt protesting the assassination of Walter Rathenau by right-wing anti-Semites. He has written that his reading of

Freud marked the beginning of his independent intellectual life, although he did not complete his response to Freud, *Crowds and Power,* until 1959. Elias Canetti, *The Torch in My Ear,* trans. Joachim Neugroschel (New York: Farrar, Straus and Giroux, 1982), pp. 147–49; Thomas H. Falk, *Elias Canetti* (New York: Twayne, 1993), p. 84.

15. Elias Canetti, *Crowds and Power* (New York: Seabury, 1978), p. 29.

16. Schreber's crowd fantasies presaged those of the Nazis, according to Canetti; both drew on the German people's special crowd symbol, the army, which had arisen out of the forests of medieval Germany. Ritchie Robertson, "Between Freud and Nietzsche: Canetti's *Crowds and Power,*" in Edward Timms and Ritchie Robertson, *Psychoanalysis in Its Cultural Context* (Edinburgh: Edinburgh University Press, 1992), pp. 109–24.

17. Gruber, *Red Vienna,* pp. 158, 161–62. Atina Grossman, *Reforming Sex: The German Movement for Birth Control and Abortion Reform, 1920–1950* (New York: Oxford University Press, 1995), warns against overestimating Reich's importance.

18. *SE,* vol. 21, p. 113 fn. 1.

19. Reich's fullest exposition of his ideas on matriarchy are to be found in his 1932 "Imposition of Sexual Morality," available in *Sex-Pol: Essays, 1929–1934,* ed. Lee Baxandall (New York: Vintage, 1972), pp. 89 ff.

20. Elisabeth Roudinesco, *Histoire de la psychanalyse en France,* 2 vols. (Paris: Fayard, 1994), vol. 2, p. 45. For psychoanalysis in Russia, also see the articles in *Die Internationale Zeitschrift für Psychoanalyse* by Alexander Luria in 1923, 1924, and 1926, and by Siegfried Bernfeld in 1932.

21. Martin A. Miller, "The Origins and Development of Russian Psychoanalysis, 1909–1930," *Journal of the American Psychoanalytic Association* 14, no. 1: 132; Alexander Etkind, *Eros of the Impossible: The History of Psychoanalysis in Russia,* trans. Noah and Maria Rubens (Boulder, Colo.: Westview Press, 1997), pp. 243–34; "Leon Trotsky and Wilhelm Reich: Five Letters," *International Socialist Review,* vol. 28, no. 5 (1967).

22. Wilhelm Reich, *The Sexual Revolution: Toward a Self-Governing Character Structure,* rev. ed., trans. Theodore P. Wolfe (New York: Farrar, Straus and Giroux, 1969), pp. 123–25, 142–43, 238. Also see Wilhelm Reich, "Dialectical Materialism and Psychoanalysis" (originally published in the Moscow journal *Under the Banner of Marxism* in 1927), and *The Sexual Struggle of Youth* (1932; repr., London: Socialist Reproduction, 1972).

23. Higgins and Raphael, *Reich Speaks,* p. 114.

24. Wilhelm Reich, "Die Stellung der Psychoanalyse in der Sowjetunion," *Die psychoanalytische Bewegung,* no. 4 (1929): 359–68; Moshe Wulff, "Zur Stellung der Psychoanalyse in der Sowjetunion," *Die psychoanalytische Bewegung* no. 1 (1930): 70–75.

25. Gruber, *Red Vienna,* pp. 158, 161–62.

26. A 1929 essay by Emil Lederer argued that the two groups would join in a common cause. The most important contemporary account, Siegfried Kracauer's 1930 *White Collar Workers,* stressed the middle class's insecurity and emotional vulnerability. They suffered, Kracauer wrote, from "ideational homelessness . . . stemming from the fact that they feel unable to find refuge in the liberal system so shaken by economic crisis but are also unwilling to take shelter within Marxism." Kracauer, *The Mass Ornament: Weimar Essays* (Cambridge, Mass.: Harvard University Press, 1995), p. 123. Also see Arno Mayer, "The Lower Middle Class as Historical Problem," *Journal of Modern History* 47 (September 1975): 409–36.

27. The fascist mentality, he added, "is the mentality of the 'little man,' who is enslaved and craves authority and is at the same time rebellious." See Wilhelm Reich, *The Mass Psychology of Fascism* (New York: Farrar, Straus and Giroux, 1970), p. 47.

28. Grossman, *Reforming Sex,* pp. 120–21; Gruber, *Red Vienna,* pp. 158–59, 169–70; Roudinesco, *Histoire,* vol. 2, p. 45; Daniel Burston, *The Legacy of Erich Fromm* (Cambridge, Mass.: Harvard University Press, 1991), p. 208; David Boadella, *Wilhelm Reich: The Evolution of His Work* (Boston: Arkana, 1985), pp. 82–83.

29. According to Grossman, *Reforming Sex*, pp. 120–21, SEXPOL was the Unity Committee or League for Proletarian Sexual Reform of the German Communist Party.

30. Freud to Ferenczi, 24 January 1932, *Freud–Ferenczi*, vol. 3, p. 426; Jones, vol. 3, p. 166; Robinson, *Freudian Left*, pp. 36–37. Freud's characterization of Reich's view as "nonsense" is quoted in Michael Molnar, ed., *The Diary of Sigmund Freud: A Record of the Final Decade*, trans. Michael Molnar (New York: Scribners; Toronto: Maxwell Macmillan Canada; New York: Maxwell Macmillan International, 1992), p. 119. The text of Freud's proposed editorial comment appears in Higgins and Raphael, *Reich Speaks*, p. 155.

31. Anna Freud to Jones, 27 April 1933, CFA/F01/30; Jones to Anna Freud, 9 December 1933, CFA/F01/06; Anna Freud to Jones, 1 January 1934, CFA/F01/06, British Psychoanalytic Society Archives (hereafter BPS).

32. Karl Fallend and Bernd Nitzschke, eds., *Der "Fall" Wilhelm Reich zum Verhältnis von Psychoanalyse und Politik* (Frankfurt: Suhrkamp, 1997); Zvi Lothane, "The Deal with the Devil to 'Save' Psychoanalysis in Nazi Germany," *The Psychoanalytic Review* 88 (2001): 197–224.

33. Wilhelm Reich, *The Function of the Orgasm: Sex-Economic Problems of Biological Energy*, trans. Theodore P. Wolfe (New York: Noonday Press, 1961), p. 265; Higgins and Raphael, *Reich Speaks*, pp. 189, 255–61.

34. Quoted in Russell Jacoby, *The Repression of Psychoanalysis* (New York: Basic Books, 1983), p. 82.

35. Robinson, *Freudian Left*, p. 56.

36. Quoted in Geoffrey N. Cocks, *Psychotherapy in the Third Reich: The Göring Institute* (New York: Oxford University Press, 1985), p. 88. See also Geoffrey N. Cocks, "The Professionalization of Psychotherapy in Germany, 1928–1949," in *German Professions: 1800–1950*, ed. Geoffrey Cocks and Konrad H. Jarausch (New York: Oxford University Press, 1990), pp. 308–28.

37. Molnar, *Diary*, entry of 17 April 1933. In addition to the cited material, my account also draws on Regine Lockot, *Erinnern und Durcharbeiten: Zur Geschichte der Psychoanalyse und Psychotherapie im Nationalsozialismus* (Giessen: Psychosozial-Verlag, 2002), and Karen Brecht et al., *Here Life Goes On in a Most Peculiar Way* (Hamburg: Kellner Verlag, n.d.).

38. Harald Schultz-Hencke's 1927 *Einführung in die Psychoanalyse* stressed the role of adult life and culture in "extinguishing" infantile wishes, and in that sense represented an opposing point of view to Reich's. Reich and Schultz-Hencke were important influences on Karen Horney.

39. Jones, vol. 3, pp. 185 ff.; Cocks, *Psychotherapy*, p. 90. This, in turn, was part of a larger migration. Whereas in 1933 there were about two thousand psychiatrists in Germany, by 1939, six hundred remained. Edward Timms and Naomi Segal, eds., *Freud in Exile: Psychoanalysis and Its Vicissitudes* (New Haven, Conn.: Yale University Press, 1988), p. 54; Uwe Henrick Peters, "The Psychoanalytic Exodus: Romantic Antecedents and the Loss of German Intellectual Life," in *Freud in Exile*, pp. 65–79; Susan Quinn, *A Mind of Her Own: The Life of Karen Horney* (New York: Summit Books, 1987), p. 241. Eitingon was in Palestine during much of the critical period.

40. Anna Freud to Jones, 18 August 1934, CFA/F02/10, BPS.

41. *Psychoanalysis and Contemporary Thought* 11, no. 2 (1988): Norbert Freedman, "The Setting and the Issues," pp. 200–202; Anna Antonovsky, "Aryan Analysis in Nazi Germany," pp. 218–19; Karen Brecht, "Adaptation and Resistance: Reparation and the Return of the Repressed," p. 235; Robert S. Wallerstein, "Psychoanalysis in Nazi Germany: Historical and Psychoanalytic Lessons," p. 356. See also Edith Kurzweil, *The Freudians: A Comparative Perspective* (New Haven, Conn.: Yale University Press, 1989), p. 48.

42. The letter appears in Bernd Nitzschke, "La psychanalyse considerée comme une science <a>-politique," *Revue internationale d'histoire de la psychanalyse*, no. 5 (1992): 174.

43. Anna Freud also believed that Edith Jacobson had been "uncautious," and put the analytic movement in danger: see Mrs. Hoel to Ernest Jones, 4 January 1935, G07/BC/F01/01, BPS.

44. Jones, vol. 3, pp. 185 ff.; Cocks, *Psychotherapy*; Kurzweil, *Freudians*, p. 48; Dierk Juelich,

"Critique of Civilization and Psychoanalytic Identity," *Psychoanalysis and Contemporary Thought* 11, no. 2 (1988): 321–35. For *Gleichschaltung,* see Renate Bridenthal, Atina Grossman, and Marion Kaplan, *When Biology Became Destiny: Women in Weimar and Nazi Germany* (New York: Monthly Review Press, 1984), p. 21.

45. Quoted in Aryeh Maidenbaum and Stephen A. Martin, eds., *Lingering Shadows: Jungians, Freudians, and Anti-Semitism* (Boston: Shambhala, 1991), p. 37.

46. Jones to Anna Freud, 11 November 1935, G07/GC/F01/15, BPS.

47. Van Ophuijsen to Jones, 18 July 1933, COA/F06/56, BPS.

48. Jones, vol. 3, pp. 296–301.

49. Edith Kurzweil, "The New York Psychoanalysts Between 1933 and 1943," unpublished ms.

50. Fenichel to Jones, BPS.

51. Anna Freud to Jones, 3 November 1936, BPS.

52. Molnar, *Diary,* p. 300.

53. This was the so-called Gruppe A, between four and fourteen people. According to some reports, pictures of Hitler and Freud hung side by side.

54. Molnar, *Diary,* p. 209; Richard F. Sterba, *Reminiscences of a Viennese Psychoanalyst* (Detroit: Wayne State University Press, 1982).

55. Norbert Freedman, "Setting," p. 200; Brecht, "Adaptation," pp. 240–41; Marie Langer, *From Vienna to Managua: Journey of a Psychoanalyst* (London: Free Association Books, 1989), pp. 1, 78–80.

56. Elisabeth Roudinesco, *La Bataille de cent ans,* vol. 1 (Paris: Ramsay, 1982; Seuil, 1986), pp. 181–221, 395–411.

57. Roudinesco, *Histoire,* vol. 2, pp. 170 ff.; Elisabeth Roudinesco, "Documents concernant l'histoire de la psychanalyse en France durant l'Occupation," *Confrontations* 16 (Autumn 1986): 243–78; Alain de Mijolla, "La psychanalyse et psychanalystes en France, 1939–1945," *Revue internationale d'histoire de la psychanalyse,* no. 1 (1988): 167–222.

58. Paul Roazen, "Psychoanalytic Ethics: Edoardo Weiss, Freud, and Mussolini," *Journal of the History of Behavioral Sciences* 27 (October 1991): 370; A. M. Accerboni, "Psychoanalysis and Fascism, Two Incompatible Approaches: The Difficult Role of Edoardo Weiss," *Review of the International History of Psychoanalysis* 1 (1988): 225–40; Glauco Carloni, "Freud and Mussolini: A Minor Drama in Two Acts, One Interlude, and Five Characters," *L'Italia nella Psicoanalisis* (1989): 51–60.

59. H. Stuart Hughes, *The Sea Change, 1930–1965* (New York: Harper & Row, 1975), p. 10; Jones, vol. 3, pp. 180, 221. See Abraham to Freud, 31 October 1914, *Freud–Abraham,* p. 201, on Levi-Bianchini. Mussolini's offer of assistance, cited by Jones and Hughes, is still a matter of scholarly investigation.

60. Ferenczi had been hurt by his failure to be elected president of the IPA in the late twenties, although Freud tried to get him to take the position in 1931. Ferenczi gained a reputation as "the haven of lost cases." Michael Balint, "Sándor Ferenczi, Obit 1933," *International Journal of Psychoanalysis* 30 (1949): 30, 215–19; Michel Franz Basch, "The Self-Object Theory of Motivation and the History of Psychoanalysis," in *Kohut's Legacy,* ed. Paul Stepansky and Arnold Goldberg (Hillsdale, N.J.: Analytic Press, 1984), p. 10.

61. Molnar, *Diary,* p. 111.

62. Freud to Eitingon, 9 January 1932, quoted in Molnar, *Diary,* p. 119.

63. In his words: "The restrained coolness, the professional hypocrisy and—hidden behind it but never revealed—a dislike of the patient which, nevertheless, he felt in all his being—such a situation was not essentially different from that which in [the patient's] childhood had led to the illness." Sándor Ferenczi, "Confusion of Tongues Between Adults and the Child," in *Final Contributions to the Problems and Methods of Psychoanalysis* (London: Hogarth Press, 1955), pp. 159–60.

64. The father, like every other member, "would be subject to thoroughgoing criticism, which he would accept, not with the absurd superiority of the *pater familias.*" Sándor Ferenczi, "Über den Lehrgang des Psychoanalytikers," in *Bausteine zur Psychoanalyse, Band III:*

Arbeiten aus den Jahren 1908–1933 (Bern: Huber, 1964), pp. 468–89; André E. Haynal, *Controversies in Psychoanalytic Method: From Freud to Ferenczi to Michael Balint* (New York: New York University Press, 1989), pp. 27–28. Preparing for the Wiesbaden congress of 1932, Ferenczi read his defense of the seduction theory to Freud, who described it in a letter to Anna: "I listened thunderstruck. He has totally regressed to the etiological views I believed in and gave up thirty-five years ago. . . . No word about the technique by which he obtains this material." See Molnar, *Diary,* 2 September 1932, p. 131. At the congress Ferenczi overrode attempts to silence him. Besides the Oedipus complex, he insisted, "a deep significance must also be attached to the repressed incestuous affection of adults, which masquerades as tenderness." See Sándor Ferenczi, "The Principle of Relaxation and Neocatharsis" in *Internationale Zeitschrift* (1930), reprinted in Ferenczi, *Final Contributions.* The last part of the quotation is in italics in the original.

65. Balint to Ernest Jones, 22 January 1954, CBC/F02/11, BPS.

66. Sigmund Freud, "In Memoriam S. Ferenczi," *International Journal of Psychoanalysis* 14 (1933): 299.

67. Peter Kutter, ed., *Psychoanalysis International: A Guide to Psychoanalysis Throughout the World* (Stuttgart: Fromman-Holzboog, 1992).

68. Benjamin Harris and Adrian Brock, "Otto Fenichel and the Left Opposition in Psychoanalysis," *Journal of the History of Behavioral Sciences* 27 (April 1991): 159.

69. Jacoby, *Repression,* pp. 90, 105, 96, 132. An example of Fenichel's Marxo-Freudian thinking can be seen in his "Psychoanalysis as the Nucleus of a Future Dialectical Materialist Psychology," *American Imago* 24, no. 4 (Winter 1967): 290–311.

70. Landauer had emigrated to Holland before his arrest. Christine Brinkgreve, "The Psychoanalytic Underground (Holland, 1940–5)," *Current Issues in Psychoanalytic Practice* 3, no. 1 (New York: Haworth Press, 1986); Ernst Federn, *Witnessing Psychoanalysis: From Vienna Back to Vienna via Buchenwald and the USA* (London: Karnac, 1990). Interview with Ernst Federn in Vienna, November 1994.

71. *Freud–Jung,* pp. 260 n. 4, 411 n. 4.

72. Maurice Haber, "Belgium," in Kutter, ed., *Psychoanalysis International,* vol. 1, p. 25.

73. Frederik van Gelder, "Psychoanalysis and the Holocaust," *Institut für Sozialforschung* 6: 81. Frankl was apparently in the camps for a matter of hours.

74. William M. Johnston, *The Austrian Mind: An Intellectual and Social History, 1848–1938* (Berkeley: University of California Press, 1983), p. 381.

75. Gottfried R. Bloch, *Unfree Associations: A Psychoanalyst Recollects the Holocaust* (Los Angeles: Red Hen Press, 1999).

76. Elisabeth Roudinesco and Michel Plon, *Dictionnaire de la psychanalyse* (Paris: Fayard, 1997), p. 906.

77. Gay, *Freud,* p. 460; Ruth Jaffe, "Moshe Wulff," in Franz Alexander et al., *Psychoanalytic Pioneers* (New Brunswick, N.J.: Transaction, 1995), pp. 200–209. The earliest evidence we have of an interest in psychoanalysis among Palestine's Jewish intelligentsia is a 1910 letter from Freud to the Jewish folklorist Alter Druyanov, in which Freud denies that his dream theory was indebted to the Talmud, citing instead its resemblances to Hellenic dream theories.

78. Jones, vol. 3, p. 30.

79. Martin Shepherd, *Fritz* (New York: Dutton, 1975).

80. Wulf Sachs, *Black Anger,* quoted in Saul Dubow, introduction to Wulf Sachs, *Black Hamlet* (Baltimore: Johns Hopkins University Press, 1996), p. 27.

81. Marcia Reynders Ristaino, *Port of Last Resort: The Diaspora Communities of Shanghai* (Stanford, Calif.: Stanford University Press, 2001), p. 131; Kutter, *Psychoanalysis International,* vol. 2, p. 97.

82. Arnaldo Rascovsky, "Notes on the History of the Psychoanalytic Movement in Latin America," in *Psychoanalysis in the Americas: Original Contributions from the First Pan-American Congress for Psychoanalysis,* ed. Robert E. Litman (New York: International Universities Press, 1966); Jorge Balán, *Cuéntame tu vida: Una biografía colectiva del psicoanálisis*

argentino (Buenos Aires: Planeta Espejo de la Argentina, 1991); Mariano Ben Plotkin, "Freud, Politics, and the Portenos: The Reception of Psychoanalysis in Buenos Aires, 1910–1943," *Hispanic American Historical Review* 77, no. 1 (February 1997).

83. Marie Langer, *Vienna to Managua: Journey of a Psychoanalyst* (London: Free Association Press, 1989).

84. Quoted in E. Fuller Torrey, *Freudian Fraud: The Malignant Effect of Freud's Theory on American Thought and Culture* (New York: HarperCollins, 1992), pp. 35–37. In 1933, under the heading "Farewell to Freud," *Commonweal* said psychoanalysis had "run its course." In 1935 the *American Mercury* published an article called "The Twilight of Psychoanalysis."

85. Franz Alexander, "Psychoanalysis Comes of Age," *Psychoanalytic Quarterly* 7 (1938): 99–106.

86. K. R. Eissler, *Medical Orthodoxy and the Future of Psychoanalysis* (New York: International Universities Press, 1965), p. 232 n. 50.

87. Jones, vol. 3, p. 300; Clarence Oberndorf, *A History of Psychoanalysis in America* (New York: Grune and Stratton, 1953), pp. 180–81.

88. Elisabeth Young-Bruehl, *Anna Freud: A Biography* (New York: Summit Books, 1988), p. 262; Jones, vol. 3, p. 300; Oberndorf, *History*, p. 204; Bertram Lewin and Helen Ross, *Psychoanalytic Education in the United States* (New York: Norton, 1960), pp. 6–7; "Minimal Standards for the Training of Physicians in Psychoanalysis," *Bulletin of the American Psychoanalytic Association* 1 (1937–38): 35–37. Jones wrote to Anna Freud, 4 May 1938, of the "new American attitude of regarding their Association as separated from the International" (OFF/F01/17, BPS).

89. Freud to Jelliffe, 9 February 1939, in John C. Burnham and William McGuire, *Jelliffe, American Psychoanalyst and Physician: His Correspondence with Sigmund Freud and C. G. Jung* (Chicago: University of Chicago Press, 1983), p. 279; *SE*, vol. 21, pp. 254–55. Oberndorf, *History*, p. 172. Freud also called the United States a "gigantic mistake." Linda Donn, *Freud and Jung: Years of Friendship, Years of Loss* (New York: Scribners, 1988), p. 111; Freud to Jones, 12 April 1921, *Freud–Jones*, p. 419; Jones, vol. 2, p. 60. Brill, Freud wrote to Eitingon in 1932, "has American anti-semitism, latently gigantic, against him." Gay, *Freud*, pp. 497, 562–70. The remark concerning Brill is cited on p. 563.

90. Gay, *Freud*, p. 566; Franz Alexander, *The Western Mind in Transition: An Eyewitness Story* (New York: Random House, 1960), p. 99; Alexander, "Sandor Rádo," in Alexander et al., *Psychoanalytic Pioneers*, p. 243; Jacques M. Quen and Eric T. Carlson, *American Psychoanalysis: Origins and Development* (New York: Brunner/Mazel, 1978).

91. Quoted from H.D.'s *Tribute to Freud* in William H. Gass, *The World Within the Word* (Boston: David R. Godine, 1978), p. 214.

92. Freud to Zweig, 5 March 1939, *The Letters of Sigmund Freud and Arnold Zweig*, ed. Ernst Freud (New York: Harcourt, Brace, 1970), p. 179.

93. Rolf Wiggershaus, *The Frankfurt School: Its History, Theories, and Political Significance*, trans. Michael Robertson (Cambridge, Mass.: MIT Press, 1994), p. 113.

94. Ibid., passim; Gay, *Freud*, p. 571. Also part of the Frankfurt Institute were Ernst Schneider and the Foulkes, among the founders of group psychotherapy in England. Alexander et al., *Psychoanalytic Pioneers*, p. 340.

95. Erich Fromm, *The Working Class in Weimar Germany: A Psychological and Sociological Study* (Cambridge, Mass.: Harvard University Press, 1984); Wiggershaus, *Frankfurt School*, pp. 52–60. Gershom Scholem complained that some of his best students, such as Fromm, "had their Orthodox Judaism analyzed away." Gerschom Scholem, *From Berlin to Jerusalem: Memories of My Youth* (New York: Schocken, 1980), p. 156.

96. Erich Fromm, "The Theory of Mother Right and Its Relevance for Social Psychology," originally published in *Zeitschrift für Sozialforschung* (1934), reprinted in *The Crisis of Psychoanalysis* (New York: Holt, Rinehart, and Winston, 1970), pp. 84–109; Martin Jay, *The Dialectical Imagination: A History of the Frankfurt School and the Institute of Social Research, 1923–1950* (Boston: Little, Brown, 1973), p. 95.

97. Fromm, "The Social Psychological Significance of Matriarchal Theory," *Zeitschrift für Sozialforschung* (1934); Wiggershaus, *Frankfurt School*, pp. 151–55.

98. Siegfried Kracauer, "Girls and Krise" (1931), *Frankfurter Zeitung*, quoted in Patrice Petro, "Discourse on Sexuality," *New German Critique* 57 (1987): 137.

99. Kracauer, *Mass Ornament*, p. 24.

100. Roland Marchand, *Advertising the American Dream* (Berkeley: University of California Press, 1986), p. 146.

101. Henry M. Sayre, *The Object of Performance: The American Avant Garde Since 1970* (Chicago: University of Chicago Press, 1989), p. 10, quoting Thomas Crow.

102. Adorno to Horkheimer, 8 June 1935, quoted in Wiggershaus, *Frankfurt School*, p. 194.

103. Theodor W. Adorno, "Notizen zur neuen Anthropologie" (Frankfurt am Main: Adorno Estate, 1942), p. 6. Theodor Adorno, "Sociology and Psychology," *New Left Review*, no. 46 (November–December 1967): 67–80, and no. 47 (January–February 1968): 79–97.

104. Theodor Adorno, "Freudian Theory and Patterns of Fascist Propaganda," in *The Frankfurt School Reader*, ed. Andrew Arato and Eike Gebhardt (New York: Urizen Books, 1978), pp. 134–35; Herbert Marcuse, *Five Lectures* (Boston: Beacon Press, 1970), pp. 45, 47, 50, 61.

105. After the war ended, Adorno wrote to Horkheimer: "Our relationship to parents is beginning to undergo a sad, shadowy transformation. Through their economic impotence they have lost their awesomeness." Max Horkheimer and Theodor Adorno, *Dialectic of Enlightenment* (New York: Herder & Herder, 1972), p. 203.

106. Richard Wolin, *Walter Benjamin: An Aesthetic of Redemption* (New York: Columbia University Press, 1982), pp. 127 ff.

107. Another figure who struggled with the surrealists, as well as with psychoanalysis, was Georges Bataille. Bataille's 1933 essay "The Notion of Expenditure" attacked all forms of utilitarianism that linked to the traditional family and reproduced "the servile mode of father/son relations." Psychoanalysis, for him, merely fostered submission to the everyday rules of family life. By contrast, Bataille affirmed social activities that passed beyond production: for example, luxury, mourning, war, cults, the construction of sumptuary monuments, games, spectacles, arts, as well as perverse sexual activity (i.e., deflected from genitality and thereby reproduction). Bataille's 1933 *Psychological Structure of Fascism* rejected Freud's *Group Psychology* because it was based on the model of repression. Instead, Bataille conceived "the splitting off of the heterogeneous" as a form of exclusion resulting from the creation of boundaries that can only be transgressed violently. Freud, Bataille insisted, did not appreciate the need for transgression. Fascism was triumphing, he argued, because it understood "the transgressive, antiutilitarian and hence revolutionary quality of self-loss."

108. Freud to Andreas-Salomé, 6 January 1935, *Freud–Salomé*, pp. 205.

109. Freud to Zweig, 17 November 1937, quoted in Max Shur, *Freud, Living and Dying* (New York: International Universities Press, 1972), p. 492.

110. Freud to Bonaparte, 23 February 1938, quoted in Gay, *Freud*, p. 618.

111. *SE*, vol. 22, p. 179. In 1937 Freud responded to a letter that argued that neither Marx nor Engels denied the influence of ideas and superego factors by saying "that invalidates the main contrast between Marxism and psychoanalysis which I had believed to exist." Jones, vol. 3, p. 345.

112. *SE*, vol. 21, pp. 111–12.

113. Ibid., p. 113.

114. Richard Sterba, *Reminiscences of a Viennese Psychoanalyst* (Detroit: Wayne State University Press, 1982), p. 116.

115. Heinz Hartmann, *Ego Psychology and the Problem of Adaptation* (New York: International Universities Press, 1977), p. 65. Hartmann's book was presented as a series of lectures at the Vienna Psychoanalytic Society in 1937 and was originally published in German in 1939.

116. *SE*, vol. 22, pp. 247–48; italics in original.

117. Ibid., vol. 23, pp. 106–7.

118. Ibid., vol. 21, p. 141.

119. Ibid., vol. 23, p. 109.

120. Molnar, *Diary,* 13 October 1935, p. 191.

121. Freud to Andreas-Salomé, 6 January 1935, *Freud-Salomé,* 1966, pp. 204 ff.

122. Freud to Jones, 3 March 1936, *Freud-Jones,* p. 751. Leo Strauss and Gershom Scholem were among those who condemned Freud for this.

123. *SE,* vol. 23, p. 43.

124. Freud to Zweig, September 1934, quoted in Kurzweil, *Freudians,* p. 293.

125. *SE,* vol. 23, p. 136.

126. Evan Burr Bukey, *Hitler's Austria: Popular Sentiment in the Nazi Era, 1938–1945* (Chapel Hill: University of North Carolina Press, 2000), p. 131.

127. Young-Bruehl, *Anna Freud,* pp. 224, 226, 227.

128. George Sylvester Viereck, *Glimpses of the Great* (New York: Macaulay, 1930), p. 30; M. Johnson, "Pro-Freud and Pro-Nazi: The Paradox of George S. Viereck," *Psychoanalytic Review* 58 (1971–72): 553–62.

129. *SE,* vol. 13, p. xv.

130. Quoted in Gay, *Freud,* p. 597. For "Herodic Wall," see Sigmund Freud to Chaim Koffler, 26 February 1930, Schwadon Collection of Autographs, Jewish University and National Library, Jerusalem. After disbanding the Vienna Psychoanalytic Society, Freud invoked the memory of Rabbi Jochanan ben Zakkai, who, after Titus's destruction of the Second Temple, fled into the wilderness to begin a school of Torah studies. Cited in the introduction in Molnar, *Diary,* p. xxiv; Sander L. Gilman, *Freud, Race, and Gender* (Princeton, N.J.: Princeton University Press, 1993), p. 35.

131. *SE,* vol. 23, p. 301.

132. Except for Richard and Edith Sterba and August Aichhorn, the membership of the Vienna society had been exclusively Jewish.

Chapter Ten

1. *SE,* vol. 17, p. 245.

2. Stephen A. Marglin and Juliet B. Schor, eds., *The Golden Age of Capitalism: Reinterpreting the Postwar Experience* (New York: Oxford University Press, 1990).

3. As an example, Aneurin Bevan said in 1948, "No society can legitimately call itself civilized if a sick person is denied medical aid because of lack of means": quoted in *New York Times,* 30 January 1997.

4. Peter Stansky and William Abrahams, *London's Burning: Life, Death, and Art in the Second World War* (London: Constable, 1994), p. 84. Leonard Woolf's *After the Deluge: A Study of Communal Psychology* offers another example of the mixed influences of Marx and Freud in England in the 1930s. Woolf portrayed history as the outcome of an interaction between three worlds: the unconscious, communal psychology, and social structure. *After the Deluge* was published between 1931 and 1939 and expanded as *Principia Politica* in 1953. Leonard Woolf, *Principia Politica: A Study of Communal Psychology* (London: Hogarth Press, 1953). See also Ted Winslow, "Bloomsbury, Freud, and the Vulgar Passions," *Social Research* 57, no. 4 (Winter 1990): 782–819.

5. "It is better that a man should tyrannise over his bank balance than over his fellow citizens." Keynes quoted in Winslow, "Bloomsbury, Freud," pp. 815–16.

6. Until then, and even after, British industry remained largely under familial control. For a fuller discussion, see J. Urry, "Scientific Management and the Service Class," in *Production, Work, Territory: The Geographical Anatomy of Industrial Capitalism,* ed. Allen J. Scott and Michael Storper (Boston: Allen and Unwin, 1986), p. 58.

7. Ross McKibbin, *Classes and Cultures: England, 1918–1951* (New York: Oxford University Press, 1998), p. 87.

8. Raymond Williams, "The Bloomsbury Fraction," in *Problems in Materialism and Culture: Selected Essays* (London and New York: Verso, 1980), p. 149.

9. Paul Johnson, *Modern Times: The World from the Twenties to the Eighties* (New York: Harper & Row, 1983), p. 167.

10. John Maynard Keynes, "My Early Beliefs" (1938), quoted in Robert Skidelsky, *John Maynard Keynes* (New York: Penguin, 1983), p. 141.

11. Elizabeth Abel, *Virginia Woolf and the Fictions of Psychoanalysis* (Chicago: University of Chicago Press, 1989), pp. 25 ff.

12. Perry Meisel and Walter Kendrick, eds., *Bloomsbury/Freud: The Letters of James and Alix Strachey, 1924–1925* (New York: Basic Books, 1985), p. 45.

13. Felix Boehm claimed in 1933—inaccurately but tellingly—that the British Psychoanalytic Society had only one Jewish member, presumably Melanie Klein. Karen Brecht, *Here Life Goes On in a Most Peculiar Way* (Hamburg: Kleiner Verlag, n.d.), p. 133.

14. Charles Rycroft, *Psychoanalysis and Beyond* (Chicago: University of Chicago Press, 1985), p. 34.

15. Klein to Jones, 24 October 1926, quoted in Phyllis Grosskurth, *Melanie Klein: Her World and Her Work* (New York: Knopf, 1986), pp. 133, 161.

16. For example: "Dick's further development had come to grief because he could not bring into phantasy the sadistic relation to the mother's body." See Melanie Klein, "The Importance of Symbol Formation in the Development of the Ego" (1930), in Klein, *Contributions to Psychoanalysis, 1921–1945* (London: Hogarth Press, 1948), pp. 236–37, 246, 249.

17. For a different point of view, see Joan Riviere: "The concept of *objects* within the ego, as distinct from identifications, is hardly discussed in Freud's work." Joan Riviere, "A Contribution to the Analysis of the Negative Therapeutic Reaction," *International Journal of Psycho-Analysis* 17 (1936): 304–20, reprinted in *The Evolution of Psychoanalytic Technique,* ed. Martin Bergmann and Frank Hartman (New York: Basic Books, 1976), pp. 414–29.

18. Klein's idea that authority, guilt, and responsibility emerged in the child's early relation to its mother was at the center of her first conflict with Anna Freud. In her first published work, her 1927 lectures on child analysis, Anna Freud had argued that very young children were amenable to external influence, having not yet developed the kind of categorical morality associated with the superego. She gave the example of an eighteen-month-old girl whose anxiety about toilet training disappeared when her parents relaxed their demands. This result would not have been possible, Anna Freud claimed, had the child's anxiety come from her superego. Klein rejected this interpretation. Anna Freud had failed to see the child's superego, Klein argued, because she had worked with the positive transference, attempting to win the child over. By helping the child suppress her more frightening feelings, Anna Freud had herself assumed the role of the superego and become "the representative of the repressing faculties." Klein wrote: "If Anna Freud had submitted the instinctual impulses to a more thorough analysis, there would have been no necessity to teach the child how to control them." Melanie Klein, *Love, Guilt, and Reparation, and Other Works, 1921–1945* (New York: Free Press, 1984), pp. 143, 163; Anna Freud, *Introduction to the Technic of Child Analysis* (New York: Nervous and Mental Diseases, 1928), p. 7; Elisabeth Young-Bruehl, *Anna Freud: A Biography* (New York: Summit Books, 1988), p. 177.

19. For Klein, guilt and responsibility derive from being frustrated or satisfied in one's primary needs. Freud stated his disagreement with this view in a 1930 footnote to *Civilization and Its Discontents,* in which he criticized Ernest Jones, Susan Isaacs, and Klein, as well as Reik and Alexander, for their "idea that any kind of frustration, any thwarted instinctual satisfaction, results or may result in a heightening of the sense of guilt." According to Freud, this was true only of frustrations of the aggressive instincts. See *SE,* vol. 21, p. 138. Freud, in other words, assumed that the superego distinguished between impulses, condemning those determined by the Oedipus complex. For Klein, by contrast, aggression and guilt are components of the earliest dependent relations; these relations evolve but will never be transformed and are not subject to the ego's self-critique.

20. Melanie Klein, "Draft Statement," 1 January 1942, CKB/F01/32, British Psychoanalytic Society Archives (hereafter BPS). Klein was not the first analyst to formulate an object-relational theory. Ferenczi, Klein's first analyst and teacher, emphasized receptivity and entitlement as the first stage in the development of the ego, but this constrained his ability to develop a concept of the object, since he lacked a concept of separation. Abraham, however, influenced Klein directly. Abraham viewed instinctual processes such as oral incorporation or anal retention as prototypes for relations to objects. In our early instinct life, he argued, we hold, expel, or devour, as we do in our later object-relational life. Abraham, Klein wrote, "came near to the conception of the internal objects. His work on the oral impulses and phantasies goes beyond F's work. A. represents the link between my own work and F's." See Klein, "Draft Statement." See also Grosskurth, *Melanie Klein*, p. 109. Still, for Abraham, object relations are a function of the ego, something the ego does. For Klein, object relations constitute the ego. While there was no question that Freud had a concept of internal objects, there was a question of when and how these objects emerged. For Klein, the earliest psychic processes, such as introjection, included a psychical object. See Joan Riviere, introduction to *Developments in Psychoanalysis*, ed. Melanie Klein et al. (London: Hogarth Press, 1952), p. 13.

21. Klein, "Draft Statement."

22. Melanie Klein, "A Contribution to the Psychogenesis of Manic-Depressive States," in Klein, *Contributions*.

23. Thus, Klein wrote, "not until the object is loved as a whole can its loss be felt as a whole." Klein, *Contributions*, p. 284.

24. Klein's unpublished essay on *Citizen Kane* can be found in the Melanie Klein Papers, Section C, Wellcome Library, London.

25. D. W. Winnicott, "The Manic Defense," in *Through Pediatrics to Psychoanalysis: Collected Papers* (New York: Brunner/Mazel, 1992), p. 131. Meltzer is quoted in Adrian Stokes, *The Critical Writings* (London: Thames and Hudson, 1978), vol. 3, pp. 221, 222, 226. Richard Wollheim, ed., *The Image in Form: Selected Writings of Adrian Stokes* (Harmondsworth, U.K.: Penguin, 1972), p. 68.

26. Riviere, "Negative Therapeutic Reaction," pp. 304–20.

27. Adam Phillips, *D. W. Winnicott* (Cambridge, Mass.: Harvard University Press, 1989), pp. 39, 45. Winnicott's second analyst was Joan Riviere.

28. Grosskurth, *Melanie Klein*, p. 133.

29. See note 18 above for an explanation of the content of this dispute.

30. In general I have followed the accounts given in Young-Bruehl, *Anna Freud*, pp. 140–85; Grosskurth, *Melanie Klein*, pp. 162 ff., 209.; Jones, vol. 3, p. 197; Peter Gay, *Sigmund Freud: A Life for Our Time* (New York, Norton, 1988), 467–69; and Riccardo Steiner, "Some Thoughts About Tradition and Change Arising from an Examination of the British Psychoanalytic Society's Controversial Discussions (1943–1944)," *International Journal of Psychoanalysis* 15 (1985): 27–71. Ferenczi to Freud, 30 June 1927, *Freud–Ferenczi*, vol. 3, p. 313, gives an alternative translation for "domineering." Freud to Jones, 23 September 1927, *Freud–Jones*, p. 623: "You make the accusation that she has not been deeply enough analyzed . . . such a criticism is as dangerous as it is impermissible. Who, then, has been sufficiently well-analyzed? I can assure you that Anna has been more deeply and thoroughly analyzed than, for instance, yourself." But see Jones's reply. For "tolerance," see Freud to Jones, October 9, 1927, ibid., p. 633.

31. Freud to Eitingon, 23 November 1926, quoted in Young-Bruehl, *Anna Freud*, p. 163.

32. Young-Bruehl, *Anna Freud*, p. 258. In a letter to me, Paul Roazen has questioned Young-Bruehl's assertion.

33. Joan Riviere and others rejoined that infantile phantasy life was based on "knowledge . . . inherent in bodily impulses" and attempted to develop a theory of unconscious phantasy. See Grosskurth, *Melanie Klein*, p. 221. Wälder's "Problems in Ego Psychology"

has never been published. The other papers are available in Pearl King and Riccardo Steiner, *The Freud-Klein Controversies, 1941–45* (London: Tavistock, 1991).

34. Quoted in Grosskurth, *Melanie Klein,* p. 293.

35. Ibid., p. 299.

36. Ibid., p. 208; Winnicott to Donald Meltzer, 25 October 1966, in *The Spontaneous Gesture: Selected Letters of D. W. Winnicott,* ed. F. Robert Rodman (Cambridge, Mass.: Harvard University Press, 1987), p. 160.

37. Grosskurth, *Melanie Klein,* p. 237.

38. Quentin Bell, *Virginia Woolf: A Biography* (New York: Harcourt Brace Jovanovich, 1972), vol. 2, p. 209, quoting Virginia Woolf's diary entry of 29 January 1940; Leonard Woolf, *Downhill All the Way: An Autobiography of the Years 1919–1939* (New York: Harcourt, Brace, 1967), p. 168, describes Freud as a "half-extinct volcano."

39. In 1936, on his eightieth birthday, Freud wrote Marie Bonaparte: "I know that the attitude of the world toward me and my work is really no friendlier than twenty years ago. Nor do I any longer wish for any change in it, no 'happy end' as in the cinema." Quoted in Jones, vol. 3, p. 202. "Fame?" he had remarked to Woolf. "I was infamous rather than famous." Woolf, *Downhill,* p. 169.

40. *SE,* vol. 23, p. 300.

41. Max Schur, *Freud, Living and Dying* (New York: International Universities Press, 1972), p. 529.

42. Young-Bruehl, *Anna Freud,* p. 239.

43. Linda Donn, *Freud and Jung: Years of Friendship, Years of Loss* (New York: Scribners, 1988), p. 20; Isidoro Berenstein, "Analysis Terminable and Interminable, Fifty Years On," *International Journal of Psychoanalysis* 68, no. 21 (1987): 24.

44. According to Sylvia Payne, the situation on the eve of World War II was one of "economic fear . . . added to the difference of scientific outlook." BPS.

45. Young-Bruehl, *Anna Freud,* p. 265; Grosskurth, *Melanie Klein,* pp. 283, 287.

46. Young-Bruehl, *Anna Freud,* p. 268.

47. Anna Freud once compared her defense of classical analysis to the Spartans' valiant but unsuccessful defense of Thermopylae, asking her nephew Ernest Freud to quote Simonides' epitaph to the Americans: "Go tell the Spartans, all ye who pass by,/That here, obedient to their laws, we lie." Michael John Burlingham, *The Last Tiffany: A Biography of Dorothy Tiffany Burlingham* (New York: Atheneum, 1989), p. 312.

48. Grosskurth, *Melanie Klein,* pp. 279 ff., 301, 352; Young-Bruehl, *Anna Freud,* pp. 259–75.

49. Klein to Marjorie Brierley, PP/KLE/E7, BPS. "I don't think it's right to go on speaking of Freudian analysis," Klein insisted on another occasion.

50. Young-Bruehl, *Anna Freud,* p. 286.

51. Payne to Klein, 16 March 1942, CKB/F01/06, BPS. On the other hand, male analysts believed the society was female-dominated. In 1941 Jones wrote Klein that Glover was "the only male analyst who can appear before a non-analytical audience without arousing . . . ridicule." Jones to Klein, 6 April 1941, CKB/F01/01, BPS.

52. McKibbin, *Classes,* pp. 168–73.

53. Riviere to Klein, 3 June 1940, PP/KLE/C95, BPS.

54. Melanie Klein, "What Does Death Represent to the Individual?" Melanie Klein Papers, Section C, Wellcome Library.

55. The official position of the British society combined militant opposition to the criminalization of homosexuality with the view that homosexuality was likely to produce immature relationships.

56. Peter Homans, *The Ability to Mourn: Disillusionment and the Social Origins of Psychoanalysis* (Chicago: University of Chicago Press, 1989), pp. 114, 226 f.; Ian Suttie, *The Origins of Love and Hate* (London: Paul, 1945).

57. Stansky and Abrahams, *London's Burning,* p. 101.

58. Harold Perkin, *The Rise of Professional Society* (New York: Routledge, 1988), p. 411.

59. Stansky and Abrahams, *London's Burning,* passim.

60. Peter Hennessy, *Never Again: Britain, 1945–1951* (New York: Pantheon, 1993), p. 37.

61. Stansky and Abrahams, *London's Burning,* p. 65. Hussey was also the patron behind Graham Sutherland's Crucifixion painting.

62. Perkin, *Professional Society,* pp. 334–43.

63. Hennessy, *Never Again,* p. 123. Churchill, the refugee social theorist Franz Neumann observed, transformed an unknown into a known danger and therefore "fulfilled those functions of leadership . . . [that are] fulfilled in the life of the individual by the organization of the ego." See Neumann, *The Democratic and Authoritarian State* (New York: Free Press of Glencoe, 1957), pp. 406–7.

64. According to Rudolph Klein: "At the time of its creation it was a unique example of the collectivist provision of health care in a market society." Hennessy, *Never Again,* p. 132.

65. Philip Ziegler, *London at War* (New York: Knopf, 1995), p. 170.

66. Phillips, *D. W. Winnicott,* p. 62.

67. Burlingham, *Last Tiffany.* Parallel developments unfolded in the United States, where René Spitz formulated the diagnosis "hospitalism" to describe depression among institutionalized infants.

68. W. R. Bion, *Experience in Groups, and Other Papers* (New York: Basic Books, 1961), p. 134. Bion's reference is to Freud's theory of hysteria.

69. Ibid., pp. 141–42.

70. Edward Glover, "The Birth of Social Psychiatry," 24 August 1940, p. 239, quoted in Nikolas S. Rose, *Governing the Soul* (London: Routledge, 1990), p. 22.

71. Ben Shepherd, "A Bunch of Loony-bin Doctors," *Times Literary Supplement,* 7 June 1996.

72. Siegmund Heinz Foulkes, "Discussion of the Soviet View on the Basis of Group and Psycho-analysis," PP/SHF/F.3/15, BPS. Foulkes's original name was Fuchs, and he was an important early figure in the Frankfurt Psychoanalytic Institute.

73. Jacques Lacan, "La psychiatrie anglaise et la guerre" (1947), in *Travaux et interventions,* quoted in John Forrester, *The Seductions of Psychoanalysis* (Cambridge, U.K.: Cambridge University Press, 1990), pp. 186–87.

74. Quoted in Grosskurth, *Melanie Klein,* p. 307.

75. Phyllis Kurzweil, *The Freudians: A Comparative Perspective* (New Haven, Conn.: Yale University Press, 1989), p. 285.

76. John Bowlby, *Maternal Care and Mental Health: A Report Prepared on Behalf of the World Health Organization as a Contribution to the United Nations Programme for the Welfare of Homeless Children* (New York: Schocken Books, 1966).

77. Melanie Klein, *Envy and Gratitude* (London: Tavistock, 1957), p. 180. The nursing couple was "transformed into a haven of asexual, good enough maternal care and preoccupation." Lisa Appignanesi and John Forrester, *Freud's Women* (New York: Basic Books, 1992), p. 4.

78. Jacques Lacan, *The Seminar of Jacques Lacan,* ed. Jacques-Alain Miller (New York: Norton, 1988).

79. Denise Riley, *The War in the Nursery: Theories of the Child and Mother* (London: Virago Press, 1983), p. 88, discusses Winnicott's BBC broadcasts.

80. William Graebner, "The Unstable World of Benjamin Spock: Social Engineering in a Democratic Culture," *Journal of American History* 67, no. 3 (December 1980): 612–29.

81. He's apt to ask, where is her "wee wee"? Spock cautioned mothers about their Oedipal-age sons. *New York Times,* 5 March 1992; Benjamin Spock, *The Common Sense Book of Baby and Child Care* (New York: Duell, Sloan and Pearce, 1946), pp. 299, 301, 303. On Spock's role as an analyst, see Lynn Z. Bloom, *Doctor Spock: Biography of a Conservative Radical* (Indianapolis: Bobbs-Merrill, 1972), p. 84; Michael Shulman, "The Humanization of the American Child: Benjamin Spock as a Popularizer of Psychoanalytic Thought," *Journal of the History of Behavioral Sciences* 9 (1973): 258–65; William G. Bach, "The Influence of Psychoanalytic Thought on Benjamin Spock's *Baby and Child Care,*" *Journal of the History of Behavioral Sciences* 10 (1974): 91–94.

82. D. W. Winnicott, "The Meaning of the Word 'Democracy,' " in *Home Is Where We Start From,* ed. Clare Winnicott, Ray Shepherd, and Madeleine Davis (New York: Norton, 1986).

83. D. W. Winnicott, *Playing and Reality* (London: Tavistock Publications, 1971).

84. Michael Balint, "The Unobtrusive Analyst," in *The British School of Analysis: The Independent Tradition,* ed. Gregorio Kohon (New Haven, Conn.: Yale University Press, 1988), p. 276.

85. "The failure to understand the distinction between clinging and being held has led to a practice," he wrote of all forms of psychoanalysis, "based prominently on the study of ambivalent relations to part objects, and embodying a great amount of unsatisfiable anger and rage on the one hand, and profound guilt feelings and abject contrition on the other." Michael Balint, *Thrills and Regressions* (New York: International Universities Press, 1959), pp. 32–39, 55, 79, 84, 98, 103–5.

86. Donald W. Winnicott, *The Maturational Processes and the Facilitating Environment: Studies in the Theory of Emotional Development* (New York: International Universities Press, 1965), p. 9.

87. Quoted in Judith Hughes, *Reshaping the Psychoanalytic Domain: The Work of Melanie Klein, W. R. D. Fairbairn, and D. W. Winnicott* (Berkeley: University of California Press, 1989), p. 177.

88. Christopher Bollas, "The Transformational Object," in Kohon, *British School,* p. 97.

89. Jones to Klein, 6 April 1941, CKB/F01/01, BPS.

90. Anna Freud to J. C. Hill, 21 October 1974, cited in Young-Bruehl, *Anna Freud,* pp. 332, 457. Those familiar with the analytic tradition will not find a statement such as André Green's ridiculous: "So much has been lost in the zealous quest for the first year . . . of life. I have a patient for whom to understand her anal phase is to understand her life." André Green, *The Work of the Negative,* trans. Andrew Weller (London and New York: Free Association Books, 1999), p. 31.

Chapter Eleven

1. Erich Heller, "Observations on Psychoanalysis and Modern Literature," in *Literature and Psychoanalysis,* ed. Edith Kurzweil and William Phillips (New York: Columbia University Press, 1983), pp. 72–73; Lionel Abel, *The Intellectual Follies: A Memoir of the Literary Venture in New York and Paris* (New York: Norton, 1984), p. 222, writes: "The way of life of Americans in the fifties was, by and large, a psychoanalytic one."

2. Lewis A. Coser, *Refugee Scholars in America: Their Impact and Their Experiences* (New Haven, Conn.: Yale University Press, 1984), p. 20; Hans Gerth and C. Wright Mills, *From Max Weber: Essays in Sociology* (New York: Oxford University Press, 1946), p. 345.

3. Fred Matthews, "The Utopia of Human Relations: The Conflict-Free Family in American Social Thought, 1930–1960," *Journal of the History of the Behavioral Sciences* 24 (October 1988): 348; Harold Lasswell, *Propaganda Technique in World War I* (1927; repr., Cambridge, Mass.: MIT Press, 1971), pp. 4–5.

4. H. Stuart Hughes, *The Sea Change* (New York: Harper & Row, 1975), pp. 201–3; Marie Jahoda, "The Migration of Psychoanalysis," in *The Intellectual Migration: Europe and America, 1930–1960,* ed. Donald Fleming and Bernard Bailyn (Cambridge, Mass.: Harvard University Press, 1985), pp. 201–17; Ruth S. Eissler and K. R. Eissler, "Heinz Hartmann: A Biographical Sketch," in *Psychoanalysis—A General Psychology: Essays in Honor of Heinz Hartmann,* ed. Rudolph M. Loewenstein et al. (New York: International Universities Press, 1966), pp. 3–15.

5. Quoted in Daniel Yankelovich and William Barrett, *Ego and Instinct* (New York: Random House, 1970), p. 97. Heinz Hartmann, *Ego Psychology and the Problem of Adaptation* (New York: International Universities Press, 1958), pp. 8, 24–26, 56–59, 65, 69, 94. According to Roy Schafer, a leading ego psychologist of the next generation, Hartmann had once written, "psychoanalysis was in new theoretical terrain." See Roy Schafer, *A New Language for*

Psychoanalysis (New Haven, Conn.: Yale University Press, 1976), pp. 64–65. George Klein stated that the framework of psychoanalytic ego psychology is as much Hartmann's achievement as Freud's. Hartmann hoped that his account would open up "the no-man's land between sociology and psychoanalysis," while also situating psychoanalysis in regard to other academic disciplines.

6. Talcott Parsons, "Propaganda and Social Control" (1942), in *Essays in Sociological Theory, Pure and Applied,* 2d ed. (Glencoe, Ill.: Free Press, 1954), pp. 89–103. Similarly, in his famous "long telegram" initiating the post–World War II containment policy, George Kennan urged that the United States adopt the attitude of a doctor who patiently studies an "unruly and unreasonable individual," i.e., the Soviet Union. Parsons apparently also underwent an analysis with Grete Bibring.

7. This figure includes both those rejected at induction and psychiatric dismissals. Medical Department, United States Army, *Neuropsychiatry in World War II,* vol. 1, ed. Robert S. Anderson, *Zone of the Interior* (Washington, D.C.: Office of the Surgeon General, Dept. of the Army, 1966). See the articles by Albert Glass and Norman Brill and the appendix by Bernard D. Karpinos and Albert Glass; introduction by Adolf Meyer and articles by Edward Strecker and Harry Stack Sullivan in "Mental Hygiene in the Emergency," *Mental Hygiene* 25, no. 1 (January 1941).

8. John G. Howells, ed., *World History of Psychiatry* (New York: Brunner/Mazel, 1975), p. 464; William Claire Menninger, *Psychiatry in a Troubled World: Yesterday's War and Today's Challenge* (New York: Macmillan, 1948), p. 452.

9. Paul Starr, *The Social Transformation of American Medicine* (New York: Basic Books, 1982), p. 344. These numbers are minimums. Richard A. Gabriel, *No More Heroes: Madness and Psychiatry in War* (New York: Hill and Wang, 1987), p. 117, says 1.6 million men (18.5 percent) were rejected.

10. Ellen Herman, *The Romance of American Psychology: Political Culture in the Age of Experts, 1940–1970* (Berkeley: University of California Press, 1995), p. 266.

11. James W. Callicut and Pedro J. Lecca, *Social Work and Mental Health* (New York: Free Press, 1983); Smith College School of Social Work, *Ego-Oriented Casework* (Family Service Association of America, 1962). Often Otto Rank's thought was the major influence on social work.

12. Gerald Grob, *From Asylum to Community: Mental Health Policy in Modern America* (Princeton, N.J.: Princeton University Press, 1991), p. 3.

13. Starr, *Social Transformation,* p. 344; Nathan G. Hale, *The Rise and Crisis of Psychoanalysis in America* (New York: Oxford University Press, 1995), p. 246; Herman, *Romance,* pp. 242–43; Morris Janowitz, *The Last Half-Century: Societal Change and Politics in America* (Chicago: University of Chicago Press, 1978), p. 429. Still, the fastest-growing professional association in the United States in this period was the American Psychological Association—the clinical psychologists—spurred on by the expansion of the Veterans Administration's psychological services.

14. E. Fuller Torrey, *Freudian Fraud: The Malignant Effect of Freud's Theory on American Thought and Culture* (New York: HarperCollins, 1992), p. 165; Hale, *Rise and Crisis,* pp. 211–12; Thomas Stephen Szasz, *Law, Liberty, and Psychiatry: An Inquiry into the Social Uses of Mental Health Practices* (New York: Macmillan, 1963).

15. Torrey, *Freudian Fraud,* p. 165; Szasz, *Law, Liberty, and Psychiatry.*

16. Samuel Klausner, *Psychiatry and Religion* (New York: Free Press of Glencoe, 1964).

17. Janowitz, *Half-Century,* pp. 417–29.

18. Ibid.

19. Nikolas Rose, *Governing the Soul: The Shaping of the Private Self* (New York: Routledge, 1990), pp. 257–58.

20. Other psychiatric films of the period include Jacques Tourneur's *Cat People* (1942), Otto Preminger's *Whirlpool* (1949), Nunnally Johnson's *The Three Faces of Eve* (1957), Edmund Goulding's *Nightmare Alley* (1947), Curtis Bernhardt's *High Wall* (1947), William Dieterle's

The Accused (1949), Robert Siodmak's *The Spiral Staircase* (1945), Curtis Bernhardt's *Possessed* (1947), and Mitchell Leisen's *Lady in the Dark* (1944), the latter a musical written by Moss Hart and dedicated to his analyst.

21. Michel Foucault, *Discipline and Punish* (New York: Vintage Books, 1979), p. 203.

22. For homosexuals in the military in World War II: John Costello, *Virtue Under Fire* (Boston: Little, Brown, 1985), and Alan Berube, *Coming Out Under Fire* (New York: Free Press, 1990), pp. 150, 131. From 1947 to 1955, twenty-one states and the District of Columbia enacted sex-psychopath laws. Such terms as "child molester," "homosexual," "sex offender," "sex psychopath," "sex degenerate," and "deviate" became interchangeable. Berube, *Coming Out*, pp. 158, 259.

23. Bruno Bettelheim, "Individual and Mass Behavior in Extreme Situations," *Journal of Abnormal and Social Psychology* 38 (1943): 417–52.

24. Terence Des Pres, *The Survivor: An Anatomy of Life in the Death Camps* (New York: Oxford University Press, 1976), makes the most important criticisms of Bettelheim's account of the camp. Bettelheim's well-known review of Lina Wertmuller's *Seven Beauties* also gives a very different account. Finally, Richard Pollak's *The Creation of Dr. B: A Biography of Bruno Bettelheim* (New York: Simon and Schuster, 1997), makes a strong case against Bettelheim's integrity in general.

25. Bettelheim considered Reich the most important analytic thinker and sometimes used the camp example to criticize Freud for not sufficiently appreciating the influence of the environment over the personality. "Psychoanalytic therapy . . . is basically no more than a powerfully conditioning social situation . . . a very special environment with its unique consequences." Bruno Bettelheim, *The Informed Heart: Autonomy in a Mass Age* (Glencoe, Ill.: Free Press, 1960), pp. 11, 22, 36 fn. If Freud had allowed himself to leave Vienna, Bettelheim argued, he would have been more aware of this. Karen Horney, too, attributed her awareness of the role of culture to her emigration.

26. Friedan wrote: "The women who 'adjust' as housewives, who grow up wanting to be 'just a housewife,' are in as much danger as the millions who walked to their own death in the concentration camps—and the millions more who refused to believe that the the the concentration camps existed. . . . [Isn't the] house in reality a comfortable concentration camp?" Within it women "have become dependent, passive, childlike." Quoted in Wilfred M. McClay, *The Masterless: Self and Society in Modern America* (Chapel Hill: University of North Carolina Press, 1994), p. 232.

27. Paul A. Carter, *Another Part of the Fifties* (New York: Columbia University Press, 1983), p. 160.

28. Quoted in Herman, *Romance*, p. 179.

29. Holden Caulfield's obsession with "phonies" and "bullshit detection" in Salinger's 1951 *Catcher in the Rye* was a popular expression of the new mood.

30. Quoted in William Graebner, *The Age of Doubt: American Thought and Culture in the 1940s* (Boston: Twayne, 1991), p. 20.

31. The emergence of mass consumption must be seen in relation to the New Deal. In 1935 a recent immigrant, Mrs. Olga Ferk, wrote President Roosevelt complaining that she had been mistreated at her relief station, was only $19 behind in her government HOLC mortgage payments, not three months as accused, and that her son's Civilian Conservation Corps check was always late in arriving. "How long is this rotten condition going to last?" she demanded. "I am at the end of the rope. The rich get richer and the poor can go to -H- that is what it looks like to me. . . . Let's have some results." Mrs. Ferk's assumption that the national government owed her family relief, a mortgage, employment, and broad support for its social class was unprecedented in American life. The basis for her assumption lay in America's powerful ethnic communities, in the industrial-union drives that organized American working-class life in the 1930s, and in the political coalition that had brought together ethnics, blacks, white southerners, women, and liberal intellectuals. Lizabeth Cohen, *Making a New Deal: Industrial Workers in Chicago, 1919–1939* (New York: Cambridge University Press, 1990), p. 252.

32. Quoted in Christopher Lasch, *Haven in a Heartless World: The Family Besieged* (New York: Basic Books, 1977), p. 108; another discussion of maturity can be found in Robert Lindner, *Must You Conform?* (New York: Rinehart, 1956), pp. 183 ff. The 1950s concern with adolescence was also permeated by a "maturity" language. Fred Hechinger's *Teen-Age Tyranny* held that "American civilization . . . is in danger of becoming a teen-age society, with permanently teen-age standards of thought, culture and goals." Quoted in Luisa Passerini, "Youth as a Metaphor for Social Change: Fascist Italy and America in the 1950s," in *A History of Young People in the West,* ed. Giovanni Levi and Jean-Claude Schmitt (Cambridge, Mass.: Harvard University Press, 1997), p. 322.

33. Philip Rieff, *The Feeling Intellect: Selected Writings* (Chicago: University of Chicago Press, 1990), p. 8. Rieff praised Freud for revealing that "the secret of all secrets is not to attach oneself too passionately to any one particular meaning or object," an extraordinary characterization of the founder of psychoanalysis. See Philip Rieff, *The Triumph of the Therapeutic: Uses of Faith After Freud* (New York: Harper & Row, 1966), p. 59.

34. In fact, the number of women working continued to increase. However, the culture stressed domesticity.

35. William Menninger, "Public Relations," chap. 7 in *Zone of the Interior,* vol. 1 of *Neuropsychiatry in World War II.* The debate was leaked to the press, leading to censorship of any statement on psychiatry. Another psychiatrist, Edward Strecker, described how "moms" undermined their soldier sons by writing them plaintive letters begging them to return. Black inductees were frequently described as crying at train stations because they couldn't bear to leave their mothers, evidence of the pathology of the black family. See Edward A. Strecker, *Their Mothers' Sons: The Psychiatrist Examines an American Problem* (Philadelphia: Lippincott, 1946), pp. 28–29.

36. Rebecca Plant, "Combat Exhaustion, Masculinity, and Democracy: Psychiatrists and Their Subjects During World War II," unpublished paper; Ladislas Farago, *Patton: Ordeal and Triumph* (New York: Ivan Oblensky, 1964), pp. 318–42.

37. Graebner, *Age of Doubt,* p. 15. Probably the richest of the films centered on men's acceptance of vulnerability is *The Best Years of Our Lives* (1946).

38. Coser, *Refugee Scholars,* pp. 42–54. See Ives Hendrick, "Professional Standards of the American Psychoanalytic Association," *Journal of the American Psychoanalytic Association* 3 (October 1955): 561–99, and *The Birth of an Institute* (Freeport, Me.: Bond Wheelwright Co., 1961); Bertram Lewin and Helen Ross, *Psychoanalytic Education in the United States* (New York: Norton, 1960).

39. These include the Commonwealth, Josiah Macy, Jr., and Rosenwald Foundations. Clarence Oberndorf, *A History of Psychoanalysis in America* (New York: Grune and Stratton, 1953), p. 190; Jones, vol. 3, p. 291; Sandor Lorand, "Reflections on the Development of Psychoanalysis in New York from 1925," *International Journal of Psychoanalysis,* no. 50 (1969): 590.

40. In 1933 the American Psychiatric Association set up a special section on psychoanalysis. See Matthew Gitelson, "On the Identity Crisis in American Psychoanalysis," *Journal of the American Psychoanalytic Association* 12 (1964): 468–69, 473.

41. Psychiatric case conferences were "psychoanalytically oriented"; out of a group of ten medical interns, writes Matthew Gitelson, "three about whom I knew were being formally analyzed, while the rest of us were, of course, 'analyzing' each other." In his examination in psychiatry he was asked "to account psychoanalytically for the disappearance of a lifelong stammer." Gitelson, "Identity Crisis," p. 468; Coser, *Refugee Scholars;* Edward Timms and Naomi Segal, eds., *Freud in Exile: Psychoanalysis and Its Vicissitudes* (New Haven, Conn.: Yale University Press, 1988), p. 30; Susan Quinn, *A Mind of Her Own: The Life of Karen Horney* (New York: Summit Books, 1987), p. 296; Report from the Boston Institute, 1937, printed in *Psychoanalytic Quarterly* 8 (1939): 406–7, warned of the danger of "dilution." An announcement of three fellowships at the Boston Psychoanalytic Institute in 1938 generated 75 inquiries. The number of candidates at the New York Institute rose from 70 in 1937 to

110 four years later, leading to calls for the raising of standards. With these developments came analytic textbooks, examinations, and licensing.

42. Edith Kurzweil, *The Freudians: A Comparative Perspective* (New Haven, Conn.: Yale University Press, 1989), pp. 39–44.

43. Coser, *Refugee Scholars,* p. 48; Jahoda, "Migration"; Geoffrey Cocks, *Psychotherapy in the Third Reich: The Göring Institute* (New York: Oxford University Press, 1985); Lewin and Ross, *Psychoanalytic Education,* p. 15. Not all émigrés remained analysts. Fritz Perls, treated by Reich, began the South African Institute of Psychoanalysis in 1935. The inventor of "Gestalt therapy," Perls joined Fromm and Sullivan in the William Alanson White Institute in New York in 1946. See Martin Shepherd, *Fritz* (New York: Dutton, 1975). Several key institutes, including Topeka, founded in 1938, San Francisco (1942), and Los Angeles (1946), were the direct product of the emigration.

44. Robert Wälder wrote to Richard Sterba: "How can I teach here where one cannot use a single classical quotation?" See Frederic Wyatt, "The Severance of Psychoanalysis from Its Cultural Matrix," in Timms and Segal, *Freud in Exile,* pp. 148–55.

45. Wyatt, "Severance," pp. 148, 151. Martin Grotjahn, one of the few émigrés who was unambiguously enthusiastic about American medicine's pragmatic orientation, described his joy at applying "psychodynamic reconstruction to the American dream of patient-directed therapy," as opposed to the "research" orientation of the European analyst. See Grotjahn, "On the Americanization of Martin Grotjahn," in *The Home of the Learned Man: A Symposium on the Immigrant Scholar in America,* ed. John Kosa (New Haven, Conn.: College and University Press, 1968), pp. 51–54.

46. Young-Bruehl, *Anna Freud,* p. 243.

47. Karl Menninger to Franz Alexander, 13 April 1938, in *The Selected Correspondence of Karl Menninger, 1919–1945,* ed. Howard J. Faulkner and Virginia D. Pruitt (New Haven, Conn.: Yale University Press, 1988), p. 265. According to a 1971 study, 62.1% of all U.S. analysts gave "Jewish" for their "cultural affinity." Another 18.6% gave none. The other figures were Protestant, 16.7%, and Catholic, 2.6%. Psychiatrists were 50.5% Jewish, psychologists 49.8%. The same studies listed analysts as liberal or strongly liberal in their politics. See William E. Henry, John H. Sims, and S. Lee Spray, *The Fifth Profession* (San Francisco: Jossey Bass, 1971), pp. 11, 74. William Menninger, Karl's younger brother, became president of the American Psychoanalytic Association in 1946. An "avid assimilationist," he felt himself drawn not to the "analyst per se" but to the "analytically oriented psychiatrist," and even more to "the general practitioner." He sought to expand the APA to include physicians who were not analyzed; however, they got only nonvoting affiliate status. In response, Ives Hendrick argued that analysis was already threatened with stagnation due to its rapid growth in membership. See Hale, *Rise and Crisis,* p. 213.

48. Samuel Klausner, *Psychiatry and Religion* (New York: Free Press of Glencoe, 1964), p. 226.

49. *Freud–Ferenczi,* vol. 1, p. 130, n. 1; see also p. 311, n. 3.

50. Edith Kurzweil, *Freudians and Feminists* (Boulder, Colo.: Westview Press, 1995), pp. 39–40; Oberndorf, *History,* p. 207; Robert Coles, "Karen Horney's Flight from Orthodoxy," in *Women and Analysis,* ed. Jean Strouse (New York: Grossman, 1974), pp. 171–86.

51. Quoted in Karen Brecht et al., *Here Life Goes On in a Most Peculiar Way* (Hamburg: Kellner Verlag, n.d.), p. 73.

52. Oberndorf, *History,* 1953, p. 247; Hendrick, *Professional Standards,* pp. 562, 589; Kurt Eissler, *Medical Orthodoxy and the Future of Psychoanalysis* (New York: International Universities Press, 1965), pp. 91–93.

53. Had not Freud changed his ideas in relation to "the accumulation of new facts"? Franz Alexander, *Fundamentals of Psychoanalysis* (New York: Norton, 1948), pp. 5–6.

54. Franz Alexander and Sheldon Selesnick, "Freud–Bleuler Correspondence," *Archives of General Psychiatry* 12 (1965): 1–9.

55. Coser, *Refugee Scholars,* passim.

56. Hale, *Rise and Crisis,* pp. 211–12; James Gilbert, *Another Chance: Postwar America, 1945–1968* (Philadelphia: Temple University Press, 1981), p. 28.

57. The American Psychoanalytic Association increased its membership more than fivefold between 1940 and 1960. From three institutes in 1933, analysis grew to twenty-nine societies and twenty institutes in 1960. By 1978, about one out of every seven psychiatrists—4,500 of the total—described themselves as practicing analysis. See Coser, *Refugee Scholars;* Lewin and Ross, *Psychoanalytic Education,* pp. 10, 53, 245; Kurzweil, *Freudians,* pp. 54, 208. R. P. Knight gives the following chart:

Year	Number of APA Members
1932	92
1938	157
1940	192
1942	230
1944–45	247
1946	273

From Knight, "The Present Status of Organized Psychoanalysis in the United States," *Journal of the American Psychoanalytic Association* 1, nos. 1–4 (1953): 207, table 1. In 1958 there were 888 students, 100 graduates, 222 supervising analysts. By the 1960s the membership of the American Psychoanalytic Association was 1,302. In 1945 there were 69 training analysts in the United States. Torrey, *Freudian Fraud,* p. 93.

58. Paul A. Robinson, *The Freudian Left: Wilhelm Reich, Geza Roheim, Herbert Marcuse* (New York: Harper & Row, 1969), p. 56. Kurt Eissler, reflecting on the fate of psychoanalysis in the 1950s, was "inescapably reminded of those tales of the last century in which the ne'er-do-well scion is shipped to this country, where, so the fable went, he becomes a millionaire." Eissler, *Medical Orthodoxy,* pp. 92–93.

59. Alfred Kazin, "The Freudian Revolution Analyzed," *New York Times Magazine,* 6 May 1956, p. 22.

60. It is also the case that in this period especially, the commitments to science, medicine, and professionalization retained an ethical character. As David Hollinger has argued, Hitler's claim to create a "Nazi science" had reminded many of the links between science and individual freedom, links that go back at least to the seventeenth century. Appearing when anti-Semitism had been discredited, the postwar explosion of psychoanalysis was part of the broad entrance of Jews into the university, medicine, and law that Hollinger has termed "deChristianization." Here, too, charisma and rationalization were intermixed. David A. Hollinger, *Science, Jews, and Secular Culture: Studies in Mid-Twentieth-Century American Intellectual History* (Princeton, N.J.: Princeton University Press, 1996), p. 81.

61. Alan A. Stone, "Where Will Psychoanalysis Survive?" *Harvard Magazine,* January–February 1997, p. 35.

62. Another tragic consequence was the blurring of the distinctions between organic and psychological conditions, for example, in the treatment of autism and schizophrenia.

63. Frederick Crews, "The Unknown Freud," *New York Review of Books,* 18 November 1993, p. 60. By way of contrast, at a time before psychoanalysis was absorbed into the welfare state, Helene Deutsch referred to it as a "phantom method" and even a "swindle," Ferenczi reluctantly conceded that "originally Freud really did believe in analysis," and Freud regularly warned of the difficulties and limits of analysis, arguing that its greater value lay in research and not in treatment. *The Clinical Diary of Sándor Ferenczi,* 1 May 1932; Lisa Appignanesi and John Forrester, *Freud's Women* (New York: Basic Books, 1992), p. 324. For Freud, the most famous example is "Analysis, Terminable and Interminable."

64. Mortimer Ostow in *The Hartmann Era,* ed. Martin S. Bergmann (New York: Other Press, 2000), pp. 232–33.

65. In 1967 the IPA acceded to a request by Portuguese analysts to approve candidates who, though personally unqualified, were well connected to the ruling dictator. Lucia Villela, "Cale-se, the Chalice of Silence: The Return of the Oppressed in Brazil," unpublished paper; Gerard Haddad, "Judaism in the Life and Work of Jacques Lacan: A Preliminary Study," *Yale French Studies,* no. 85 (1994): 214–15; Helena Besserman Vianna, *Politique de la psychanalyse face à la dictature et à la torture: n'en parlez à personne* (Paris: L'Harmattan, 1997), and the discussion of this book by Robert Wallerstein in the *Journal of the American Psychoanalytic Association* 47 (1999): 965–73.

66. Arthur Miller, *Timebends: A Life* (New York: Grove Press, 1987), pp. 320–21.

67. One Beverly Hills psychoanalyst eased the pangs of conscience of eight witnesses before the HUAC, all of them cooperative. The moral angle was simple: "Hell, they've all been named already." David Caute, *The Great Fear: The Anti-Communist Purge Under Truman and Eisenhower* (New York: Simon and Schuster, 1977), pp. 505–6. For the relationship of analysts to the cold war, see "Come Over, Red Rover," in Robert Lindner, *The Fifty-Minute Hour: A Collection of True Psychoanalytic Tales* (New York: Holt, Rinehart and Winston, 1954).

68. At the same time, when Hayden said he could admit to having been in the party but refuse to name names, his analyst said, "Of course, you can. Why don't you?" Sterling Hayden, *Wanderer* (New York: Knopf, 1964), pp. 371, 377, 387. Victor S. Navasky, *Naming Names* (New York: Penguin, 1981), pp. 133–43, identifies Hayden's analyst as Phil Cohen.

69. Steve Heims, *The Cybernetic Group* (Cambridge, Mass.: MIT Press, 1991), p. 170.

70. Horney is quoted in Edith Kurzweil, "Psychoanalytic Science: From Oedipus to Culture," *Psychoanalytic Review* 79 (Fall 1992); Harry Stack Sullivan, "Remobilization for Enduring Peace and Social Progress," *Psychiatry* 10 (1947): 239; Lasch, *Haven in a Heartless World,* p. 97; Stansfield Sargent and Marian W. Smith, eds., *Culture and Personality* (New York: Wenner-Gren Foundation for Anthropological Research, 1949), pp. 203–4. "Our culture is sick, mentally disordered and in need of treatment," said Lawrence Frank, "Society as the Patient," *American Journal of Sociology* 42 (November 1936): 335.

71. J. Victor Koschmann, *Revolution and Subjectivity in Postwar Japan* (Chicago: University of Chicago Press, 1996), p. 174; Kurzweil, *Freudians,* pp. 136, 211, 232; Helmut Thomä, "Some Remarks on Psychoanalysis in Germany, Past and Present," *International Journal of Psychoanalysis* 50 (1969): 683–92; Edith Kurzweil, "The Freudians Meet in Germany," *Partisan Review* 52, no. 4 (1985). For Balint's role, see Wyatt, "Severance," p. 151. The occupation authorities also encouraged analysis in Austria, but there was little interest, just as there was little honesty concerning the Austrian role in the war. Only in the 1970s, when Freud became a tourist icon, his bust on the fifty-shilling note, did this change.

72. Michael Balint, "On the Psychoanalytic Training System," *International Journal of Psychoanalysis* 29 (1948): 167.

73. Stone, "Where Will Psychoanalysis Survive?" p. 35; Kris to Anna Freud, 13 March 1950, quoted in Elisabeth Young-Bruehl, *Anna Freud: A Biography* (New York: Summit Books, 1988), pp. 345–58.

74. The training analysis aimed at a "firmly established identification with an idealized figure" (though it often produced, in reaction formation, as Heinz Kohut noted, "rebelliousness against this identification"). See Kohut, "Creativeness, Charisma, and Group Psychology: Reflections on the Self-Analysis of Freud," in *The Search for the Self: Selected Writings of Heinz Kohut,* ed. Paul H. Ornstein (New York: International Universities Press, 1978–1991), pp. 793 ff.

75. Quoted in Young-Bruehl, *Anna Freud,* p. 271.

76. S. Lustman, "The Scientific Leadership of Anna Freud," *Journal of the American Psychoanalytic Association* 15 (1967): 822.

77. Even Erik Erikson's revisionist *Young Man Luther* (1950) was a work of remembrance. Freud and Luther both had "a grim willingness to do the dirty work of their respective ages." Erik Erikson, *Young Man Luther: A Study in Psychoanalysis and History* (New York: Norton, 1958), pp. 9–10.

78. Heinz Hartmann, Ernst Kris, and Rudolph Loewenstein, "Comments on the Formation of Psychic Structure," *Psychoanalytic Study of the Child* 2 (1946): 16.

79. Young-Bruehl, *Anna Freud*, p. 313. Jones also used the biography to settle old scores, for example, with Rank and Ferenczi.

80. Jones, vol. 1, p. 56.

81. Peter Homans, *The Ability to Mourn: Disillusionment and the Social Origins of Psychoanalysis* (Chicago: University of Chicago Press, 1989), pp. 17, 68.

82. Malcolm Pines, "The Question of Revising the Standard Edition," in Timms and Segal, *Freud in Exile*, pp. 177, 194. Jones: "If I can produce a Collected Edition of your works in my lifetime and leave the Journal on a soundly organized basis, I shall feel that my life has been worth living though I hope to do more for Psa. even than that." Jones to Freud, 10 April 1922, *Freud-Jones*, p. 473.

83. Perry Meisel and Walter Kendrick, eds., *Bloomsbury/Freud: The Letters of James and Alix Strachey, 1924–1925* (New York: Basic Books, 1985), p. 317.

84. Riccardo Steiner, " 'Die Weltmachtung des Britischen Reichs': Notes on the Term 'Standard' in the First Translations of Freud," in Timms and Segal, *Freud in Exile*, pp. 188–90.

85. Quoted in Meisel and Kendrick, *Bloomsbury/Freud*, pp. x–xi. Winnicott commented that "what Strachey has done is to take Freud's writings and place them in literature where intellectual honesty reigns supreme." D. W. Winnicott, *Psycho-analytic Explorations*, ed. Clare Winnicott, Ray Shepherd, and Madeleine Davis (Cambridge, Mass.: Harvard University Press, 1989), p. 509.

86. Thus: "Eine große Halle—viele Gaste, die wir empfangen.—Unter ihnen Irma, die ich sofort beiseite nehme, um gleichsam ihren Brief zu beantworten, ihr Vorwufe zu machen, daß sie die Losung' noch nicht akzeptiert. Ich sage ihr . . ." *Gessamelte Werke*, pp. ii–iii, III, which is best translated: "A large hall—we are receiving many guests—Irma is among them. Right away I take her aside in order to answer her letter and scold her because she doesn't accept my 'solution.' I say to her . . ." became: "A large hall—numerous guests, whom we are receiving. Among them was Irma. I at once took her on one side, as though to answer her letter and to reproach her for not having accepted my 'solution' yet. I said to her . . ." *SE*, vol. 4, p. 107; Darius Ornston, "Freud's Conception Is Different from Strachey's," *Journal of the American Psychoanalytic Association* 33, supp. (1985): 382, 403–4; Timms and Segal, *Freud in Exile*, pp. 204, 208, 212–13, 216. The copyright to the *Standard Edition* expired in September 1989, with the result that its contents can be retranslated into English. In April 1989 the Institute of Psychoanalysis in London held a three-day conference on the question of whether Freud should be retranslated. The most useful scholarly versions in German are the *Studienausgaben* published by S. Fischer, but they are not complete. A complete Swedish edition is also under way.

87. Josef Hayim Yerushalmi, *Freud's Moses: Judaism Terminable and Interminable* (New Haven, Conn.: Yale University Press, 1991), p. 39. The English translation of the 4 September 1883 letter is in *LSF*, p. 54.

88. Maria Torok, "Unpublished by Freud to Fliess: Restoring an Oscillation," *Critical Inquiry* 12, no. 2 (Winter 1986).

89. Robert S. Wallerstein, "Reflections," in *The Identity of the Psychoanalyst*, ed. Edward D. Joseph and Daniel Widlocher (New York: International Universities Press, 1983), pp. 265–76; Nancy Chodorow, "Beyond Drive Theory: Object Relations and the Limits of Radical Individualism," *Theory and Society* 14, no. 3 (May 1985): 271.

90. In the 1930s, 30 percent of the analysts in the world were women, but this percentage declined drastically after the war. Lewin and Ross, *Freud in Exile*, pp. 53, 245; Kurzweil, *Freudians*, pp. 45, 208; Appignanesi and Forrester, *Freud's Women*, p. 6.

91. In 1942 Philip Wylie's *Generation of Vipers* sold 180,000 copies and generated 60,000 letters to the author by arguing that "Momism" had emasculated American masculinity. See Truman Keefer, *Philip Wylie* (Boston: Twayne, 1977).

92. For "matriarchal," see Edward Glover, "An Examination of the Klein System of Child Psychology," *Psychoanalytic Study of the Child* 1 (1945). This was also Jones's "favorite hypothesis." Jones, 28 January 1944, quoted in Phyllis Grosskurth, *Melanie Klein: Her World and Her Work* (Cambridge, Mass.: Harvard University Press, 1987), p. 343.

93. Young-Bruehl, *Anna Freud,* pp. 428–29; Betty Friedan, *The Feminine Mystique* (New York: Norton, 1963), p. 111; Erik Erikson, "Womanhood and the Inner Space," *Daedalus,* Spring 1964. For the history of the clitoral/vaginal orgasm debate, see Daniel Brown, "Female Orgasm and Sexual Inadequacy," in *Human Sexual Response,* ed. Edward and Ruth Brecher (Boston: Little, Brown, 1966), pp. 125–75.

94. Kurzweil, *Feminists,* pp. 40, 51–52.

95. Ferdinand Lundberg and Marynia F. Farnham, *Modern Woman, The Lost Sex* (New York: Universal Library, 1947), p. 142. Dorothy Parker's 1947 response is worth noting: "There is something curiously flattering in being described by the adjective 'lost.' . . . I find myself digging my toe into the sand and simpering, 'Oh Dr. Farnham and Mr. Lundberg, come on now—you say that to every sex!' " Quoted in Mari Jo Buhle, *Feminism and Its Discontents: A Century of Struggle with Psychoanalysis* (Cambridge, Mass.: Harvard University Press, 1998), p. 128.

96. They "essayed a difficult task in a field where there are few valid signposts and little scientific psychological information. It is unfortunate that this book adds only confusion." Frances S. Arkin, *Psychoanalytic Quarterly* 6 (1947): 573.

97. Roy Schafer, "Problems in Freud's Psychology of Women," *Journal of the American Psychoanalytic Association* 22 (July 1974): 459–85.

98. Winifred Breines, *Young, White, and Miserable: Growing Up Female in the Fifties* (Boston: Beacon Press, 1992).

99. Diana Trilling, *The Beginning of the Journey: The Marriage of Diana and Lionel Trilling* (New York: Harcourt Brace, 1993), p. 240.

100. Calvin Trillin, *Remembering Denny* (New York: Farrar, Straus and Giroux, 1993).

101. Dan Wakefield, *New York in the Fifties* (Boston: Houghton Mifflin, 1992), p. 152.

102. Elisabeth Roudinesco and Michel Plon, *Dictionnaire de la psychanalyse* (Paris: Fayard, 1997), pp. 454–55.

103. Stephen Farber and Marc Green, *Hollywood on the Couch: A Candid Look at the Overheated Love Affair Between Psychiatrists and Moviemakers* (New York: Morrow, 1993), pp. 58–61.

104. James Merrill, *A Different Person: A Memoir* (New York: Knopf, 1993), p. 229. Detre's family died in Auschwitz. He later emigrated to the United States.

105. Patricia Bosworth, *Montgomery Clift* (New York: Harcourt Brace, 1978), pp. 203–6, 215–16, 230–33. For the odyssey of a gay psychoanalyst from the late fifties on, see Richard A. Isay, *Becoming Gay* (New York: Pantheon, 1996).

106. Robert Lindner, "Homosexuality and the Contemporary Scene," in *The Problem of Homosexuality in Modern Society,* ed. Hendrik M. Ruitenbeek (New York: Dutton, 1963), p. 58.

107. Sándor Rádo, "A Critical Examination of the Concept of Bisexuality," *Psychosomatic Medicine* 2, no. 4 (October 1940); Ronald Bayer, *Homosexuality and American Psychiatry: The Politics of Diagnosis* (New York: Basic Books, 1981), pp. 28, 30; C. W. Socarides, "The Psychoanalytic Theory of Homosexuality, with Special Reference to Therapy," in *Sexual Deviation,* ed. I. Rosen (New York: Oxford University Press, 1979), p. 246.

108. Young-Bruehl, *Anna Freud,* pp. 428–29. For Jones's view that Freud was " 'over-reconciled' to bisexuality," see Jones to James Strachey, 11 January 1954, CSD/F01/09, British Psychoanalytic Society Archives.

109. Kenneth Lewes, *The Psychoanalytic Theory of Male Homosexuality* (New York: Simon and Schuster, 1988), pp. 74, 93.

110. Edmund Bergler, "Homosexuality and the Kinsey Report," in *The Homosexuals as Seen by Themselves and Thirty Authorities,* ed. Aron Krich (New York: Citadel Press, 1954). Ruitenbeek, *Problem of Homosexuality,* contains many analytic statements but says, on p. xii: "The omission of any essay by Edmund Bergler is quite deliberate." Lewes, *Male Homosexuality,* p. 153; Bayer, *Homosexuality and American Psychiatry,* pp. 36, 78; Lionel Trilling, *The Liberal Imagination: Essays on Literature and Society* (Garden City, N.Y.: Doubleday, 1957), pp. 216–17; Socarides, "Theory of Homosexuality," p. 78. Other researchers on homosexuality include Cleland Ford, Frank Beach, and Evelyn Hooker.

111. Bayer, *Homosexuality and American Psychiatry,* p. 36.

112. Berube, *Coming Out,* pp. 158, 259. Significantly, the psychiatric diagnosis built on the standardized nomenclature developed in the military.

113. Lewes, *Male Homosexuality,* p. 137.

114. For "creative era," see Kurzweil, *Freudians,* p. 209; for "my father," see Jeffrey Masson, *Final Analysis: The Making and Unmaking of a Psychoanalyst* (Reading, Mass.: Addison-Wesley, 1990), p. 167.

115. Other centers of anti-rationalizing thought and action in the 1950s include *Politics* magazine, Black Mountain College, Brandeis University, and the San Francisco jazz and poetry scene.

116. Richard King, *The Party of Eros* (Chapel Hill: University of North Carolina Press, 1972); James Gilbert, *Writers and Partisans* (New York: Wiley, 1968). The term "New York intellectuals" is generally used to refer to those who published in *Partisan Review.* Of great importance too was Dwight Macdonald, the editor of *Politics* magazine, who argued that the problem of modernity was alienation, not economics, an idea bolstered by Erich Fromm's 1951 translation of Marx's *Economic and Philosophic Manuscripts.* Dwight Macdonald, "The Root Is Man: Part II," *Politics,* July 1946.

117. Hannah Arendt wrote in *The Human Condition* (1956), p. 71: "A life spent entirely in public, in the presence of others, becomes, as we would say, shallow. While it retains its visibility, it loses the quality of rising into sight from some darker ground which must remain hidden if it is not to lose its depth in a very real, non-subjective sense."

118. Quoted in Hugh Wilford, *The New York Intellectuals: From Vanguard to Institution* (Manchester, U.K., and New York: Manchester University Press, 1995), p. 66.

119. Ellison and Baldwin both published frequently in *Partisan Review.*

120. Milton Klonsky, "Greenwich Village: Decline and Fall," *Commentary,* November 1948, quoted in King, *Party of Eros,* p. 44.

121. Miller, *Timebends,* pp. 320–21.

122. Paul Goodman, "The Political Meaning of Some Recent Revisions of Freud," *Politics* 2 (July 1945). C. Wright Mills criticized Goodman's "gonad theory of revolution" but drew on other currents of psychoanalysis for his own critique of rationalization. See C. Wright Mills and P. J. Salter, "The Barricades and the Bedroom," *Politics,* October 1945.

123. Lionel Trilling, *Beyond Culture: Essays on Literature and Learning* (New York: Viking Press, 1965), pp. 104, 118.

124. Lionel Trilling, "Art and Neurosis," in *Liberal Imagination,* p. 156.

125. Lionel Trilling, "Freud and Literature," in *Liberal Imagination,* pp. 32–33. Trilling also praised *The Kinsey Report* for "the long way it goes toward establishing the *community* of sexuality." But the report established this community, Trilling continued, on *quantitative* and thereby alienated grounds. "While all cultures create sexual fears, ours was unique in strictly isolating the individual in the fears that society has devised. The report now reassures us by statistical science that the solitude is imaginary." Not only science, but the simplest, most materialistic science: a "science of statistics and not ideas. The way for the Report was prepared by Freud, but Freud, in all the years of his activity, never had the currency or authority that the Report has achieved in a matter of weeks." Trilling, "The Kinsey Report," in *Liberal Imagination,* pp. 216–28.

126. Philip Rieff, *Freud: The Mind of the Moralist,* 3d ed. (Chicago: University of Chicago Press, 1979), especially pp. 329–57.

127. Norman Podhoretz, *Breaking Ranks: A Political Memoir* (New York: Harper & Row, 1979), pp. 40, 47–49.

Chapter Twelve

1. Thomas Frank, *The Conquest of Cool: Business Culture, Counterculture, and the Rise of Hip Consumerism* (Chicago: University of Chicago Press, 1997), p. 23.

2. Nancy Fraser, "From Redistribution to Recognition? Dilemmas of Justice in a 'Post-Socialist' Age," *New Left Review* 212 (July–August 1995): 68–93.

3. For the idea that the 1970s constitute a fin de siècle era, see Natasha Zaretsky, "The End of the American Century? National Decline and Family Decline in the 1970s" (Ph.D. dissertation, Brown University, 2003).

4. David Riesman with Nathan Glazer and Reuel Denney, *The Lonely Crowd: A Study of the Changing American Character* (New Haven, Conn.: Yale University Press, 1961), p. 139.

5. Aimé Césaire, *Discours sur le colonialisme* (Paris: Présence Africaine, 1955).

6. Dominique Octave Mannoni, *Prospero and Caliban,* 2d ed. (New York: Praeger, 1964), pp. 8, 46–47, 63.

7. Erikson also argued that identity was a special problem in the United States due to its disparate cultural composition, and he wrote of the difficulty in sustaining ego ideals in a land "characterized by expanding identifications and by great fears of losing hard-won identities." Erik Erikson, "The Problem of Ego Identity," *Journal of the American Psychoanalytic Association* 4 (January 1956): 56–21; William Graebner, "The Unstable World of Benjamin Spock: Social Engineering in a Democratic Culture, 1917–1950," *Journal of American History* 67, no. 3 (December 1980): 617.

8. Heinz Hartmann, Ernst Kris, and Rudolph Loewenstein, "Comments on the Formation of Psychic Structure," *Psychoanalytic Study of the Child* 2 (1946): 16.

9. Edith Jacobson, *The Self and the Object World* (New York: International Universities Press, 1964).

10. Joseph Sandler and B. Rosenblatt, "The Concept of the Representational World," *Psychoanalytic Study of the Child* 17 (1962): 128–45.

11. Depression, for example, was no longer seen as a matter of "oral frustration" but rather of lowered self-esteem.

12. George S. Klein, *Psychoanalytic Theory: An Exploration of Essentials* (New York: International Universities Press, 1976); Merton M. Gill and Philip S. Holzman, eds., *Psychology vs. Metapsychology: Psychoanalytic Essays in Memory of George S. Klein* (New York: International Universities Press, 1976).

13. Henry Lowenfeld and Yela Lowenfeld, "Our Permissive Society and the Superego," *Psychoanalytic Quarterly* 39 (1970): 590–607.

14. Lawrence S. Kubie, "Pitfalls of Community Psychiatry," *Archives of General Psychiatry* 18 (1968): 257–66.

15. Leo Rangell, "Psychoanalysis—A Current Look," *Journal of the American Psychoanalytic Association* 15 (1967): 425. In general, APA presidential addresses of the sixties were models of denial.

16. Oral History Collection, Columbia University.

17. G. K. Hofling and R. Meyers, "Recent Discoveries in Psychoanalysis," *Archives of General Psychiatry* 26 (1972): 518–23. The study is discussed in Edith Kurzweil, *The Freudians: A Comparative Perspective* (New Haven, Conn.: Yale University Press, 1989), p. 209.

18. Kurt Eissler, *Medical Orthodoxy and the Future of Psychoanalysis* (New York: International Universities Press, 1965), pp. 94–95, 232.

19. Stephen Farber and Marc Green, *Hollywood on the Couch* (New York: Morrow, 1993), pp. 14–17, 63, 157.

20. Erica Jong, *Fear of Flying: A Novel* (New York: Holt, Rinehart and Winston, 1973), pp. 4–5.

21. Marshall Brickman, "The Analytic Napkin," in *The Best of Modern Humor*, ed. Mordecai Richler (New York: Knopf, 1983), pp. 448–52. Mel Brooks thanked his analyst for breaking him of his habit of vomiting between parked cars. Farber and Green, *Hollywood on the Couch*, p. 147.

22. "To end a training analysis on the high-minded note of a shared admiration for Freud," Kohut observed, "is . . . not only a socially acceptable step of great respectability, it can also be a moving experience for the candidate, which soothes his pain at the parting." Heinz Kohut, "Thoughts on Narcissism and Narcissistic Rage," in *The Search for the Self* (New York: International Universities Press, 1978), vol. 2, p. 803. The quote in the text appears in vol. 1, pp. 162–63, 479, 481. See also Heinz Kohut, *The Analysis of the Self* (New York: International Universities Press, 1971), pp. 64, 46. For another argument that narcissism had been denigrated in the psychoanalytic tradition, see Bela Grunberger, *Narcissism: Psychoanalytic Essays* (New York: International Universities Press, 1979).

23. Kernberg contrasted the warm and expansive narcissism of the child to the cold, hostile narcissism of the pathological adult; whereas the child sought love and beauty, the adult needed to be the sole possessor of these goods. Otto Kernberg, *Borderline Conditions and Pathological Narcissism* (New York: J. Aronson, 1975). Jacobson, *Ego and the Object World*, pp. 20, 35–36, 46, 94; Rubin Blanck and Gertrude Blanck, *Beyond Ego Psychology: Developmental Object Relations Theory* (New York: Columbia University Press, 1986), pp. 10, 12; René Spitz, *A Genetic Field Theory of Ego Formation: Its Implications for Pathology* (New York: International Universities Press, 1959), pp. 96–97.

24. "The immature couple, in contrast, loses its opposition to the group—indeed it returns to the group." Otto Kernberg, "The Couple and the Group," in Kernberg, *Love Relations: Normality and Pathology* (New Haven, Conn.: Yale University Press, 1995), pp. 176–88.

25. See also the concept of restoration in Mary Wright, *The Last Stand of Chinese Conservatism: The Tung-chih Restoration, 1862–1874* (Stanford, Calif.: Stanford University Press, 1957).

26. Meredith Tax, *Woman and Her Mind: The Story of Daily Life* (Cambridge, Mass.: Bread and Roses, 1970).

27. See, for example, Angelo Quattrocchi and Tom Nairn, *The Beginning of the End: France, May, 1968* (London: Panther Books, 1968), pp. 163–64.

28. *SE*, vol. 21, pp. 64–72.

29. Herbert Marcuse, *Eros and Civilization: A Philosophical Inquiry into Freud* (Boston: Beacon Press, 1974). Against Kant, Marcuse extolled the philosopher Friedrich Schiller, who sought to show that reason was reconciled with sensuality in art and play.

30. Norman O. Brown, *Life Against Death: The Psychoanalytical Meaning of History*, 2d ed. (Middletown, Conn.: Wesleyan University Press, 1985), pp. 118, 123, 128–29, 132, 142. Also see Herbert Marcuse, "Love Mystified: A Critique of Norman O. Brown," *Commentary* 43, no. 2 (February 1967): 71–75.

31. Quoted in Mikkel Borch-Jacobsen, *Lacan: The Absolute Master*, trans. Douglas Brick (Stanford, Calif.: Stanford University Press, 1991), pp. 40–41.

32. Elisabeth Roudinesco, *La Bataille de cent ans*, vol. 1 (Paris: Ramsay, 1982; Seuil, 1986), pp. 181–221, 395–411.

33. Bruce Fink, *The Lacanian Subject: Between Language and Jouissance* (Princeton, N.J.: Princeton University Press, 1995), p. 84.

34. Jacques Lacan, *The Seminar of Jacques Lacan*, ed. Jacques-Alain Miller (New York: Norton, 1988), vol. 2, p. 37.

35. The "Rome Discourse" can be found in Jacques Lacan, *Écrits: A Selection* (New York: Norton, 1977).

36. Kristin Ross, *Fast Cars, Clean Bodies: Decolonization and the Reordering of French Culture* (Cambridge, Mass.: MIT Press, 1995).

37. Daniel Lagache, the French analyst, remarked: "He embodied the analyst's bad conscience. But . . . a good conscience in a psychoanalyst is no less dangerous." Roudinesco, *Bataille*,

vol. 2, pp. 225, 231, 346. For a complementary, firsthand account, see Didier Anzieu, *A Skin for Thought* (London: Karnac, 1990), pp. 27–28.

38. Lacan's associates in the fifties included Wladimir Granoff, Serge Leclaire, Didier Anzieu, Jean-Bertrand Pontalis, Jean Laplanche, and Moustapha Safouan, the Arabic translator of *The Interpretation of Dreams* and *The Phenomenology of the Mind*.

39. Lacan's new students included François Roustang, Michel de Certeau, Catherine Backès-Clément, Cornélius Castoriadis, Félix Guattari, and Luce Irigaray. Roudinesco, *Bataille*, vol. 2, p. 321; John Forrester, *The Seductions of Psychoanalysis* (Cambridge, U.K.: Cambridge University Press, 1990). The starting membership of the École Freudienne de Paris was 134.

40. In addition, Lacan influenced then-ongoing efforts to rethink Marxism. In particular, he influenced Althusser's restatement of the Marxist theory of ideology, in which Althusser rejected the formulation "Men represent their real conditions of existence to themselves in an imaginary form," which preserved orthodox Marxism's base/superstructure distinction, in favor of the Lacanian alternative, "Ideology represents the imaginary relationship of individuals to their real conditions of existence." Ideology, in other words, was not an illusory representation of reality; rather, it was a practical but unconscious relation to it.

41. Quoted in Lawrence D. Kritzman, *Michel Foucault: Politics, Philosophy, Culture,* from *Le Magazine Littéraire,* no. 121 (February 1977).

42. Roudinesco, *Bataille,* vol. 2, p. 640.

43. When Didier Anzieu asked Lacan why he did not give more credit to his surrealist antecedents, Lacan responded that, without repudiating the surrealists, "it is rather under the aegis of Monsieur de Tocqueville that I would situate my [contribution]." Ibid., vol. 2, p. 268.

44. In Philip Roth's 1974 novel *My Life as a Man,* Peter Tarnapol, a twenty-nine-year-old Jewish novelist, accidentally discovers that his analyst has disguised him in a case study as a successful Italian-American poet in his forties. Tarnapol complained: between a man in his forties and one in his twenties, between a Jewish-American and an Italian-American, between a poet and a novelist, there are "fundamental distinctions." Roth, *My Life as a Man* (London: Jonathan Cape, 1974), pp. 239–40.

45. For Goffman's little-understood role, see Howard Brick, *Age of Contradiction: American Thought and Culture in the 1960s* (New York: Twayne, 1998).

46. R. D. Laing, *Sanity, Madness and the Family* (New York: Basic Books, 1964, 1971), p. 12.

47. *Madness and Civilization* was published in English in 1963 in a series that also included R. D. Laing and David Cooper's Sartrean *Reason and Violence* and Thomas Szasz's *The Myth of Mental Illness.* David Cooper, inventor of the term "antipsychiatry," wrote the introduction.

48. Lynn Z. Bloom, *Doctor Spock: Biography of a Conservative Radical* (Indianapolis: Bobbs-Merrill, 1972), pp. 72, 83–84.

49. Betty Friedan, *The Feminine Mystique* (New York: Norton, 1963), p. 112.

50. Kate Millett, *Sexual Politics* (Garden City, N.Y.: Doubleday, 1970); Freud's view, Millett continued on p. 189, was that "a female's discovery of her sex is, in and of itself, a catastrophe of such vast proportions that it haunts a woman all through life."

51. Gayle Rubin, "The Traffic in Women," in *Toward an Anthropology of Women,* ed. Rayna R. Reiter (New York: Monthly Review Press, 1975), p. 185. For a different but compelling view of the relations of analysis and feminism, see Mari Jo Buhle, *Feminism and Its Discontents: A Century of Struggle with Psychoanalysis* (Cambridge, Mass.: Harvard University Press, 1998).

52. Shulamith Firestone, *The Dialectic of Sex: The Case for Feminist Revolution* (New York: Morrow, 1970), pp. 49, 51. Likewise, what Freud had called a neurosis was now explained in terms of social restraints. For Charles Bernheimer, "Victorian women developed defensive strategies whereby they disavowed the intense anger and aggressive impulses for which the culture gave no outlet. Thus were generated the conversion reactions." See Charles Bernheimer and Claire Kahane, *In Dora's Case: Freud—Hysteria—Feminism* (New York: Colum-

bia University Press, 1985), pp. 5–6; Maria Ramas, "Freud's Dora, Dora's Hysteria," *Feminist Studies* 6 (1980): 472–510.

53. Hélène Cixous and Cathérine Clement, *The Newly Born Woman,* trans. Betsy Wing (Minneapolis: University of Minnesota Press, 1986), pp. 153–54.

54. Jong, *Fear,* pp. 20–22. Nor was the preference for the active role restricted to women. Even Woody Allen's middle-aged, bookish alter ego, Kugelmass, caught the new externalizing element as he whined to his analyst, "I need to meet a new woman. . . . I need to have an affair. I may not look the part, but I'm a man who needs romance." When his analyst replied, "The worst thing you could do is act out. You must simply express your feelings here, and together we'll analyze them. . . . After all, I'm an analyst, not a magician," Kugelmass answered, "Perhaps what I need is a magician," and (like Dora) walked out. Woody Allen, "The Kugelmass Episode," in Richler, *Modern Humor,* pp. 409–10.

55. Juliet Mitchell, *Psychoanalysis and Feminism: Freud, Reich, Laing, and Women* (New York: Vintage, 1974), p. xv.

56. Wardell Baxter Pomeroy, *Dr. Kinsey and the Institute for Sex Research* (New York: Harper & Row, 1972), p. 68. Questioning "whether the terms 'normal' and 'abnormal' belong in a scientific vocabulary," Kinsey was not sure that analysts could be considered part of the scientific community. See Alfred E. Kinsey, Wardell B. Pomeroy, and Clyde Martin, *Sexual Behavior in the Human Male* (Philadelphia: W. B. Saunders, 1948), pp. 199–200, 637, 639, quoted in Jonathan Ned Katz, "The Invention of Heterosexuality," *Socialist Review* 90, no. 1 (1990): 21.

57. Ronald Bayer, *Homosexuality and American Psychiatry: The Politics of Diagnosis* (New York: Basic Books, 1981), p. 105.

58. Ibid., pp. 55, 95, 103–4.

59. Dennis Altman's writings exemplified this shift. Altman began as a Marcusean who described "perversions" as incipient rebellions, but in the early seventies he urged a shift in the use of the term "homosexual" from an adjective—implying a neutral person who had a particular sexuality—to a noun, which implied that homosexuality was constitutive of identity. In the late sixties, historians of homosexuality began to draw a related distinction between homosexual behavior, which had always existed, and homosexual identity, which emerged in the second half of the nineteenth century. See John D'Emilio, *Sexual Politics, Sexual Communities: The Making of a Homosexual Minority in the United States, 1940–1970* (Chicago: University of Chicago Press, 1983). For Foucault, prior to the nineteenth century, sodomy was "a category of forbidden acts," their perpetrator "the juridical subject of them." But during the nineteenth century, the "homosexual became a personage, a past, a case history, and a childhood, in addition to being a type of life, a life form." Michel Foucault, *The History of Sexuality,* trans. Robert Hurley (New York: Vintage, 1980), vol. 1, pp. 42–43. See also John D'Emilio, "Capitalism and Gay Identity," in *Powers of Desire: The Politics of Sexuality,* ed. Ann Snitow, Christine Stansell, and Sharon Thompson (New York: Monthly Review Press, 1983), pp. 100–113. Furthermore, identity, not sexuality, was at the center of the homosexual community. Lesbians, wrote one theorist, are "women who love women, who choose women to nurture and to create a living environment in which to work creatively and independently. . . . Lesbians cannot be defined simply as women who practice certain physical rites together." Shane Phelan, *Identity Politics: Lesbian Feminism and the Limits of Community* (Philadelphia: Temple University Press, 1989), pp. 73–74.

60. Theodor Reik, *From Thirty Years with Freud* (London: Hogarth Press, 1942), p. 28.

Epilogue

1. For Freud, as for so many of his contemporaries, Lamarck's theory of acquired characteristics supplied the link between biology and history.

2. Daniel N. Stern, *The Interpersonal World of the Infant* (New York: Basic Books, 1985); J. Lichtenberg, *Psychoanalysis and Infant Research* (Hillsdale, N.J.: Analytic Press, 1983).

3. As one analyst noted, psychiatry was "once again on the march in search of a scientific foundation." Quoted in Matthew Gitelson, "On the Identity Crisis in American Psychoanalysis," *Journal of the American Psychoanalytic Association* 12 (1964): 462–63. For the defense of nineteenth-century psychiatry, see ibid. For *DSM*, see Tanya M. Luhrmann, *Of Two Minds: An Anthropologist Looks at American Psychiatry* (New York: Vintage, 2000).

4. Steven E. Hyman and Eric J. Nestler, *The Molecular Foundations of Psychiatry* (Washington, D.C.: American Psychiatric Press, 1993).

5. Luhrmann, *Of Two Minds*, pp. 173, 176.

6. Beginning from the controversial Popperian premise that the mark of a scientific theory is its falsifiability, Grünbaum concluded that drugs and behavioral techniques were scientific because they had predictable, testable consequences, whereas analytic interventions were not. (To be precise, Grünbaum argued that analytic interventions were falsifiable, and that when tested they proved that analysis was false.) In defining science in terms of falsifiable experiments, however, Grünbaum pushed aside the idea that a science requires a conceptual object, a body of interrelated concepts, which was what psychoanalysis achieved when it posited a nonconscious psychic reality describable through developmental, structural, quantitative, and evolutionary coordinates.

7. Edith Kurzweil, *The Freudians: A Comparative Perspective* (New Haven, Conn.: Yale University Press, 1989), p. 252.

8. Luhrmann, *Of Two Minds*, p. 181.

9. Harold Bloom, "Freud, the Greatest Modern Writer," *New York Times*, 23 March 1986.

10. Leo Bersani, *The Freudian Body: Psychoanalysis and Art* (New York: Columbia University Press, 1986), p. 12.

11. Kristeva's views soon changed.

12. Jacques Derrida, "Cogito and the History of Madness," in *Writing and Difference* (Chicago: University of Chicago Press, 1978). In a personal conversation in New York in 2001, Derrida confirmed to me that he also thought of himself as a figure in the history of psychoanalysis rather than simply in the history of philosophy, and that it was not merely his writings on psychoanalysis that he had in mind but his entire body of thought. Derrida has written important critiques of the reified language of psychoanalysis. Nevertheless, he told me that when he writes, he feels "the unconscious is present."

13. *New York Times*, 22 October 1979, p. A20.

14. Robert Wallerstein, "One Psychoanalysis or Many," *International Journal of the Psychoanalytic Association* 69 (1988): 17 n.

15. Mary Douglas, *The Active Voice* (London: Routledge & Kegan Paul, 1982), p. 14.

16. By contrast, Philip Roth responded to descriptions of Freud as a "kind of charlatan or . . . worse" by exclaiming, "This great tragic poet, our Sophocles!" *The New Yorker*, 8 May 2000.

17. It is not only the Jewish identity of psychoanalysis that needed normalization; it is also its relation to Christianity. In 2003 Julia Kristeva lectured at the New School about psychoanalysis and women. When she was attacked from the floor for introducing such Christian concepts as "incarnation," she responded by saying that she was proud that one of her parents was Jewish and the other Christian, and that she wanted to affirm both traditions in her work as a psychoanalyst.

18. Rafael Moses, "Address of Welcome, Jerusalem Congress," *International Journal of Psychoanalysis* 59, no. 3 (1978): 3.

19. Paul Schwaber, "Title of Honor: The Psychoanalytic Congress in Jerusalem," *Midstream*, March 1978.

20. Robert Wallerstein, "Psychoanalysis in Nazi Germany: Historical and Psychoanalytic Lessons," *Psychoanalytic Quarterly* 11 (1986): 351–70. In the December 1983 issue of *Psyche*, an article by Helmut Dahmer told the story. Edith Kurzweil, "The Freudians Meet in Germany," *Partisan Review* 52, no. 4 (1985); Susan Quinn, *A Mind of Her Own: The Life of Karen Horney* (New York: Summit Books, 1987), p. 241; Elisabeth Roudinesco, *Histoire de*

la psychanalyse en France, 2 vols. (Paris: Fayard, 1994), vol. 2, p. 615. In the United States Freud remained a hero to many Jews. When Robert Lowell accused his student Philip Levine of stealing Freudian insights from Auden, Levine responded: "I'm Jewish. I steal Freud directly from Freud. He was one of ours." *New York Times Book Review,* 26 February 1993.

21. Masud Khan, *The Long Wait and Other Psychoanalytic Narratives* (New York: Summit Books, 1988). A more complete picture of Masud Khan reached me only after this book was complete. He was apparently a psychotic. The fact that he was allowed to continue to practice is another of the great crimes in the history of analysis. This was, above all, Winnicott's doing, although the entire British society was complicit. For a convincing account, see Wynne Godley, "Saving Masud Khan," *London Review of Books,* February 2001.

22. W. R. Bion, "Attacks on Linking," *International Journal of Psychoanalysis* 40 (1959).

23. Interviews with Werner Bohleber, Helmuth Dahmer, and Lutz Rosenkutter, 1997. Critical theory also played a role in the rediscovery of German psychoanalysis. Largely through Adorno and Horkheimer's initiative, Freud's hundredth birthday was celebrated in 1956 in Frankfurt at an international conference, "Freud in der Gegenwart." Jürgen Habermas described the conference as "the first opportunity for young German academics to hear . . . that Sigmund Freud was the founding father of a living scientific and intellectual tradition." Habermas, "Psychic Thermidor and the Rebirth of Rebellious Subjectivity," in *Habermas and Modernity,* ed. Richard J. Bernstein (New York: Polity Press, 1985), p. 68.

24. Nancy Caro Hollander, *Love in a Time of Hate: Liberation Psychology in Latin America* (New Brunswick, N.J.: Rutgers University Press, 1997), pp. 12–15.

25. Mariano Ben Plotkin, "Freud, Politics, and the Porteños: The Reception of Psychoanalysis in Buenos Aires, 1910–43," *Hispanic American Historical Review* 77, no. 1: 45; Isaac Tylim, "Psychoanalysis in Argentina: A Couch with a View," *Psychoanalytic Dialogues* 6, no. 5 (1996): 713–27.

26. Aleksandr Mikihalevich, "Russia: The Revenge of Subjectivity," *UNESCO Courier,* March 1993, p. 36; Arnold Rothstein, *The Moscow Lectures on Psychoanalysis* (New York: International Universities Press, 1991); Martin A. Miller, *Freud and the Bolsheviks: Psychoanalysis in Imperial Russia and the Soviet Union* (New Haven, Conn.: Yale University Press, 1998), offers a full account.

Index

Page numbers beginning with 345 refer to notes.
Page numbers in *italics* refer to illustrations.

A NOTE ON THE TYPE

This book was set in Adobe Garamond. Designed for the Adobe Corporation by Robert Slimbach, the fonts are based on types first cut by Claude Garamond (c. 1480–1561). Garamond was a pupil of Geoffroy Tory and is believed to have followed the Venetian models, although he introduced a number of important differences, and it is to him that we owe the letter we now know as "old style." He gave to his letters a certain elegance and feeling of movement that won their creator an immediate reputation and the patronage of Francis I of France.

Composed by North Market Street Graphics,
Lancaster, Pennsylvania
Printed and bound by Berryville Graphics,
Berryville, Virginia
Designed by Anthea Lingeman